Collected Readings on
Community Development in
Singapore

Other Related Titles from World Scientific

Critical Issues in Asset Building in Singapore's Development
edited by S. Vasoo and Bilveer Singh
ISBN: 978-981-3239-75-3

Community Development Arenas in Singapore
edited by S. Vasoo, Bilveer Singh and Xian Jie Chan
ISBN: 978-981-120-411-1

How Working Together Matters: Adversity, Aspiration, Action
edited by David Chan
foreword by Lee Hsien Loong
ISBN: 978-981-3278-40-0

50 Years of Social Issues in Singapore
edited by David Chan
foreword by Tharman Shanmugaratnam
ISBN: 978-981-4696-91-3 (box-set)
ISBN: 978-981-4632-60-7
ISBN: 978-981-4632-61-4 (pbk)

Social Futures of Singapore Society
edited by David Chan
ISBN: 978-981-3222-22-9

Collected Readings on Community Development in Singapore

Editor

S Vasoo

National University of Singapore, Singapore

NEW JERSEY · LONDON · SINGAPORE · BEIJING · SHANGHAI · HONG KONG · TAIPEI · CHENNAI · TOKYO

Published by

World Scientific Publishing Co. Pte. Ltd.
5 Toh Tuck Link, Singapore 596224
USA office: 27 Warren Street, Suite 401-402, Hackensack, NJ 07601
UK office: 57 Shelton Street, Covent Garden, London WC2H 9HE

Library of Congress Cataloging-in-Publication Data
Names: Vasoo, S., author.
Title: Collected readings on community development in Singapore / S. Vasoo.
Description: New Jersey : World Scientific, [2019] | Articles chiefly by S. Vasoo,
    some with various co-authors. | Includes bibliographical references.
Identifiers: LCCN 2019009257 | ISBN 9789811203824 (hardcover)
Subjects: LCSH: Community development--Singapore. | Social problems--Singapore.
Classification: LCC HN700.67.Z9 C678 2019 | DDC 306.095957--dc23
LC record available at https://lccn.loc.gov/2019009257

British Library Cataloguing-in-Publication Data
A catalogue record for this book is available from the British Library.

Copyright © 2019 by World Scientific Publishing Co. Pte. Ltd.

All rights reserved. This book, or parts thereof, may not be reproduced in any form or by any means, electronic or mechanical, including photocopying, recording or any information storage and retrieval system now known or to be invented, without written permission from the publisher.

For photocopying of material in this volume, please pay a copying fee through the Copyright Clearance Center, Inc., 222 Rosewood Drive, Danvers, MA 01923, USA. In this case permission to photocopy is not required from the publisher.

For any available supplementary material, please visit
https://www.worldscientific.com/worldscibooks/10.1142/11369#t=suppl

Desk Editor: Jiang Yulin

Typeset by Stallion Press
Email: enquiries@stallionpress.com

Printed in Singapore

Contents

Acknowledgement ix
Introduction: Community development issues and interventions xi

Part 1   Working with Urban Children and Youth   **1**

Chapter 1   Issues and challenges in urban youth work   3
               S. Vasoo

Chapter 2   Directions in youth research and preventive services in Singapore   13
               A. E. Y. Lee and S. Vasoo

Part 2   Ageing Issues, Eldercare and Service Delivery   **31**

Chapter 3   Community programmes and services for long-term care of the elderly in Singapore: Challenges for policy-makers   33
               Kalyani K. Mehta and S. Vasoo

Chapter 4   Organization and delivery of long-term care in Singapore: Present issues and future challenges   55
               Kalyani K. Mehta and S. Vasoo

Chapter 5   Ageing population in Singapore: A case study   75
               Paul Cheung and S. Vasoo

Chapter 6   Singapore's ageing population: Social challenges and responses   119
               S. Vasoo, Tee-Liang Ngiam and Paul Cheung

Part 3	**Examining Family Issues and Services**	**145**
Chapter 7	Promoting family values: Some issues and challenges *Tee Liang Ngiam and S. Vasoo*	147
Chapter 8	Transmitting family values in a cultural context: The Singapore experience *Tee Liang Ngiam and S. Vasoo*	161
Chapter 9	The impact of social policies on the family in Singapore *Rosaleen Ow and S. Vasoo*	179
Part 4	**Advocating for Inclusiveness for the Disabled**	**197**
Chapter 10	Employment opportunities for the disabled in Singapore: Some issues and challenges *S. Vasoo*	199
Part 5	**Community Development Issues and Volunteerism**	**209**
Chapter 11	Reviewing the direction of community development in Singapore *S. Vasoo*	211
Chapter 12	Community development in Singapore: New directions and challenges *S. Vasoo*	231
Chapter 13	New directions of community development in Singapore *S. Vasoo*	253
Chapter 14	Community organisation — An attempt in the local setting *S. Vasoo*	271
Chapter 15	Neighborhoods and precincts: Government-initiated organizations are catalysts for political participation and self-help *S. Vasoo*	279

Chapter 16	Residents' organisations in the new towns of Hong Kong and Singapore: Some issues and future developments *S. Vasoo*	299
Chapter 17	Contributions to charitable organizations in a developing country: The case of Singapore *Chung Ming Wong, Vincent C. H. Chua and S. Vasoo*	315
Chapter 18	Non-governmental organizations in Singapore and nation building: Some emerging trends and issues *S. Vasoo and Mohd Maliki Osman*	341
Chapter 19	Studying neighbourhood leaders' participation in residents' organizations in Hong Kong and Singapore: Some theoretical perspectives *S. Vasoo*	365
Chapter 20	Grass-root mobilisation and citizen participation: Issues and challenges *S. Vasoo*	383
Chapter 21	Promoting voluntary efforts in meeting community needs in Singapore: Some challenges *S. Vasoo*	395
Chapter 22	Neighbourhood leaders' participation: Conclusions and implications *S. Vasoo*	409
Part 6	**Examining Social Issues and Social Development**	**435**
Chapter 23	The development of new towns in Hong Kong and Singapore: Some social consequences *S. Vasoo*	437
Chapter 24	Some emerging social issues in Singapore *S. Vasoo*	459

Chapter 25	Social policy based on assets: The impact of Singapore's Central Provident Fund *Michael Sherraden, Sudha Nair, S. Vasoo, Tee Liang Ngiam and Margaret S. Sherraden*	485
Chapter 26	Singapore: Social development, housing and the Central Provident Fund *S. Vasoo and James Lee*	515
Chapter 27	Implementing socioeconomic measures to tackle economic uncertainties in Singapore *S. Vasoo and Kwong-leung Tang*	533
Chapter 28	Achieving social development and care through the Central Provident Fund and housing in Singapore *S. Vasoo and James Lee*	559
Chapter 29	Singapore: Social investment, the state and social security *James Lee and S. Vasoo*	581
Chapter 30	Investments for social sector to tackle some key social issues *S. Vasoo*	601

Part 7 Social Work Training and Practice — **617**

Chapter 31	Some challenges for social work education *S. Vasoo*	619
Chapter 32	The social work profession in response to challeging times: The case of Singapore *S. Vasoo*	627
Chapter 33	Straddling teaching and field practice: Facing the challenges — Associate Professorial Fellow S Vasoo, 1987–2001	635

Part 8 Conclusion — **653**

Chapter 34	The future of community development: Issues and challenges *S. Vasoo*	655

Acknowledgement

I am particularly indebted to a number of personalities for nudging me to collate all my writings I have published in various publications known and unknown to the academic world. In particular and without prejudice, I appreciate the reminders and nudges given by my former Head of Department of Social Work, Prof Ann Elizabeth Wee, Dr Ngiam Tee Liang and Dr Rosaleen Ow who both succeeded myself as Heads of Department and lastly Associate Professor Esther Goh, who took over the Headship. Nudges are necessary in social work life as one can be waylaid into doing and doing things without timely reflections on knowing the outcomes of all the social and community development interventions. I also remembered the inspirations and tutelage on community development by my late Professor Peter Hodge, former Head of the Department of Social Work and Administration, University of Hong Kong where I took my postgraduate studies and the academic support from Emeritus Professor Nelson Chow W. S., also from the Department of Social Work and Administration, University of Hong Kong.

Also not to forget, my appreciation for the ardent support and encouragement for my academic work in the Faculty of Arts and Social Sciences by former Dean, Emeritus Professor Edwin Thumboo. He has also helped to enhance both the Social Work and Psychology programmes whilst I was heading these areas.

I must acknowledge the impressive efforts of all my co-writers and editors who have inspired me over the years to produce articles, which now appear as reprints in this book volume. Their contributions have added diversity of ideas to this publication and offer a good platform for sharing out thoughts for younger generation of people involved in promoting community betterment and community problem-solving. Many of those who have co-written some of the articles are or have been my academic colleagues and associates from the National University of Singapore, Singapore University of Social Sciences, Hong Kong Polytechnic University and University of Washington in St. Louis-George Warren Brown School of Social Work. They are namely, Professor Paul Cheung, Professor Kalyani K. Mehta, Professor James Lee, Dr Mohamad Maliki bin Osman, Associate Professorial Fellow Ngiam Tee Liang, Professor Margaret Sherraden, Professor Michael Sherraden, Dr Sudha Nair, Professor Tan Ngoh Tiong, the late Professor Tang Kwong Leung, Dr Vincent C. H. Chua and Associate Professor Wong Chung Ming. These co-writers are academic luminaries in their own making and I was fortunate to be able to cajole them to contribute their thoughts which I must say are not simple as they seem but have good sense for humanity and human betterment. Without their contributions, this publication will not be that socially colourful.

I have been inspired in my social and community development work by many both staff and volunteers who supported by giving ideas in promoting innovative social service delivery programmes in my work in the then Singapore Council of Social Service (SCSS), now the National Council of Social Service (NCSS) between early 1970s to 2000. Namely, the former SCSS President, the late mentor, Dr Ee Peng Liang, the former Executive Director of SCSS, Mrs S. C. Tang, Dr Tan Bee Wan, former Executive Director of NCSS and the staff then, had contributed in different and inspiring ways for my service to the social service agencies.

I am also very indebted to Ms Yong Hui Hua for assisting me untiringly to go through the different years of collating the publications and this enabled me to produce the package of relevant collected readings which I hope will be useful to students, researchers, social and community workers and those who volunteer in the community to encourage community self-help.

Finally, I must also declare my eternal gratitude that my many years of commitment to community betterment and academic work would not have been possible without the affectionate and hearty endearing endorsements from my spouse, Jane and my three children, Sheila, Sharon and Shawn and all those associated with me in my long march in community work.

Introduction: Community development issues and interventions

This volume of **Collected Readings on Community Development in Singapore** consists articles written by myself and jointly with other academic colleagues over the last 48 years when I was a social work practitioner in the field of community development and later as a social work teacher. I am still actively engaged in volunteering in community work in the housing heartland of Singapore and advising a number of social service and grassroots organisations.

Since I first started as a young social worker in Singapore Children's Society in Toa Payoh New Town, there have been significant changes in the delivery of social services given the limited financial and manpower resources. The community development efforts were centred more on self-help rather than the focus on the delivery of services or programmes. The focus of the delivery of community services has been based on community-centric approaches but has in some ways gravitated towards being programme-centric because of efficiency in meeting the demand than simply helping people to become more capable to solve their problems. Such an emphasis should be reviewed and more steps be taken to ensure that it includes a preventive dimension, besides a remedial one. A remedial approach to community problem-solving can be insular and it may not necessarily attack the source of social problems. In short, a preventive and developmental approach in community problem-solving is critical and community development in social work arena must emphasise this.

The community development landscape has changed significantly especially with the rapid relocation of people into a number of housing estates in New Towns. This social transformation in housing has ushered many new urban communities, the consequences of which required the establishment of new social networks for relationship building. Social and community organisations, which are either governmental or voluntary, have been formed to help community building and support for residents needing social services (Chan, 2018, pp. 75–98).

Community development in Singapore should brace itself in facing challenging times ahead. These challenges are precipitated by changing demographic profiles and emerging disruptive social issues such as the loss of employment through competitive wages, sudden market disruptions from new aggregative technologies, widening social class gaps and inflow of economic migrants which to some extent remain unpredictable. At the same time, the expectations and demands of various people are changing. Since independence in 1965, Singapore has undergone significant economic and social transformation. The social and economic landscape of the island city-state has changed progressively. Better housing, security, health, education, environment and employment opportunities have been achieved because of good leadership led by responsible and honest people in government. This has been a precursor and the backbone for economic and social progress, which Singapore has been able to make. This will change if we do not have good governance in various social institutions (Vasoo, 2018, pp. 21–36).

Social workers in community development practice have to be aware of the trends in social changes confronting Singapore. In order that social workers can continue to play an effective role, it is important for them to become more aware of internal and external factors, which affect the efficiency and effectiveness of social service and community organisations in which they are involved. The identifications of a number of factors such as manpower, facilities, funding resources, leadership and other related organisational issues, and the manner in which these areas are managed, will determine whether the social work will make meaningful contributions.

The book carries a number of selected readings under various sections covering different areas of community development work and community issues, which have been and could be addressed by community development interventions. The collected readings are organised around seven themes, which more or less reflect some of the main social and community issues that can and are being addressed by community development efforts. These themes cover at least some of the past and current contemporary issues facing the Singapore community particularly the public housing heartland. Community and social workers can find some resonance to the work and challenges they are facing in community problem-solving and meeting needs of people in the various neighbourhoods.

The first section on, **Working with Urban Children and Youth** reviews various issues and challenges faced by youth workers and youth organisations in the urban Asian setting in the light of the changing social landscape. Some of the views are also reflected in other articles on youth work and be relevant for work with urban children. It is recommended that there is a need for more future research and preventive services to meet new emerging needs and problems of the youth. With more analytical work, much insights could be gained to better improve service delivery by youth agencies.

The following section on **Ageing Issues, Eldercare and Service Delivery** written together with my colleagues, starts off with an article taking a case study approach to review ageing issues facing Singapore and the policies and measures introduced to moderate the impact of the population ageing. Some of the ideas in this article are also reflected in other topics related to ageing. The next write-up explores the social challenges of Singapore's population ageing issues and recommends more efforts and resources to be directed for the development of community care and support services for the elderly. Subsequent two articles provides an overview of the long-term care services available for the elderly followed by a discussion of the policy issues put forward by the Inter-Ministerial Committee (IMC) on Ageing Population. They also explore Singapore's population ageing issues and recommend more efforts and resources for the development of community care as well as support services for the elderly.

The next section is on **Examining Family Issues and Services.** It carries three papers jointly produced with my colleagues. These papers reflect some of the earlier views on family values and the move by the Singapore government in adopting the promotion of family values in response to the rapid social and environmental changes affecting the family institution. They consolidate some earlier comments and analyses of Singapore's evolving experience in trying to balance economic growth with social well-being. In particular, the well-being of the family, emphasising the promotion of core family values as an aspect to keep the family institution alive is highlighted. More efforts that are educational can be undertaken to promote family values. The last paper of this section discusses the various social policies, which have been carefully devised to strengthen the social fabric of family life in Singapore, encouraging self-help and mutual support among family members, their kin groups and the community. The implications of these policies are touched.

The coming section on **Advocating for Inclusiveness for the Disabled** is an important and often neglected area namely about employment opportunities for the disabled persons.

Those interested in community development work can refer to the section **Community Development Issues and Volunteerism** and reflect on how they can be improved by seeking innovative approaches to tackle community issues and meeting community needs. One of the many key aspects presented in this volume covers the reviews of the trends in community development over the last few decades in Singapore. The discussions examine the approaches in community development in the local context and propose some realistic ways that can be carried out by community and social workers in community development. The need for manpower to cover and work with people in the different neighbourhoods of the public housing estates and neighbourhood low-rise estates cannot be under estimated and it will be prudent for all social- and community-based agencies to plan and recruit volunteers from the resident population in the area. The participation of volunteers living in the neighbourhoods together with people in need of services will help to facilitate community problem-solving which is the basic tenet in community development. The discussions in this section cover a number of key domains in community development and volunteerism in the community. Volunteerism issues, which have been touched in previous writings, are being revisited in this section. A number of articles examine some of the factors affecting participation in voluntary social and welfare organisations in Singapore and discuss on the strategies taken by the voluntary social and welfare services to ensure viability to deliver services.

A few key areas are presented about involving volunteers in community services. Community development efforts cannot be effectively carried out without the mobilisation of volunteer manpower as they form a major backbone for implementing many community programmes for the young and old living in diverse neighbourhoods. The community has much indigenous resources, which can be tapped for community building and enhancing social well-being (Chan, 2015, pp. 15–28).

There are a number of articles that review the direction of community development in Singapore from the early 1950s to early 1980s, with the government playing an interventionist role through setting up of various grassroots organisations and the voluntary sector playing a supplementary role. Some of the crucial factors in shaping community development directions in Singapore and its challenges for future directions have been explored. The writers have made attempts to showcase how social workers in Singapore using community organisation techniques to resolve problems that confront many people in the community including the low-income families which have been articulated in publications by others (Ng, 2018, pp. 113–136).

An interesting coverage, which is relevant to community development, is people's inclination to donate to charities in the community. Sustainable financial resources is essentially critical for the operations of charitable and community programmes. This coverage is presented in the form of a case study of charitable giving in Singapore. The data have been collated from individual charitable organisations over the period 1980 to 1989. The analyses in this article appearing in Chapter 17 of this volume on giving to charities show the charitable causes which are commonly supported by individuals.

This section also consolidates earlier ideas on the participatory behaviour of people in social service agencies. The prevailing theoretical frameworks for studying the neighbourhood leaders' participative behaviour in residents' organisations are also touched. Further discussions on some of the consequential factors of grassroot mobilisation and citizen participation, particularly in the Asian region are deliberated and some approaches to strengthen participation are proposed.

An insight into neighbourhood leaders' motivation to take leadership is reviewed in a monograph on *Neighbourhood Leaders' Participation in Community Development* (1994). Neighbourhood leaders and their participative behaviour, particularly the neighbourhood leaders' satisfaction in their participation in community development, frequency of involvement in the work of residents' organisations, and their inclination to continue their association with the residents' organisations are discussed. The views were based on findings of a concluding chapter on Neighbourhood Leaders' Participation in Neighbourhood Organisations in Singapore in the 1990s. The conclusions and implications of the neighbourhood leaders' participative behaviours are still relevant and they are still expressed in the various community organisations today.

This section on **Examining Social Issues and Social Development** covers a number of writings which discuss the changes in Singapore's social landscape and some of the more pertinent social issues and problems such as the impact of population ageing, re-employment of retirees, increasing financial burdens of health care systems and potential erosion of human values. The comments made in the papers cover a collection of views and analyses undertaken in the earlier years of Singapore's development.

Those interested in community development work can reflect on how they can be improved by seeking innovative approaches to tackle community issues and meeting community needs. One of the many key aspects raised in this and other sections covers the reviews of the trends in community development over the last few decades in Singapore. A number of the recurrent discussions examine the approaches in community development in the local context and propose some realistic ways that can be carried out by social workers in community development.

Discussions in this section also reiterate the importance of involving volunteers in community services. Community development efforts cannot be effectively carried out without the mobilisation of volunteer manpower as they form a major backbone for implementing many community programmes for the young and old living in diverse neighbourhoods. The community has much indigenous resources, which can be tapped for community building and enhancing social well-being. Volunteers have varied talents and they can be encouraged to contribute meaningfully to uplift individuals and community groups who require social support and assistance to improve their vulnerable social situation in life in such aspects as poor literacy, ill health, financial burden, failures and social stresses in their life course and disruptions in employability. Volunteerism plays an important role in helping to meet social needs in communities, which require mutual support.

In respect to current debates and increased attention on ageing of the Singapore population, some views on how community development efforts can be deployed to deal with various social consequences of population ageing have been proposed.

Readers are to note that economic and political factors are not dealt with in this section as well in this volume. These issues are covered in a separate publication by the author and Professor Bilveer Singh in a recent book (Vasoo and Singh, 2018). Both economic and political factors are recognised to be important but the lack of attention to the development of human and social capital can make communities to be regressive because there will be a lack of decent and people-centred leadership to contribute in helping to drive societal progress. The social and community divide can worsen if we do not have social and community institutions to devise and open up more social thoroughfares for people with different social and economic backgrounds to pursue at their best and to also encourage them to have the mind-set to care and share (Chan, 2018, pp. 115–137).

This final section **Social Work Training and Practice** examines the need for training, preparation of social and community workers to be competent in the community development work in different arenas. This is critical because the community needs and issues are changing dramatically especially with the rise of social, economic and political disruptions. In the light of these changing community scenarios, some points are raised on the need for social and community workers to acquire more social and analytical skills so that they will be able to predict and socially diagnose the social ills and development issues that can have an impact on community well-being. Therefore, it is necessary to review and strengthen the social work educational curriculum on the management of social service delivery, policy analyses, social analytics and community development and group work. Much of the points are also touched on subsequent discussions on social work education.

Points on the challenges of the social work profession in Singapore have been highlighted. The professional social work intervention should be less casework or client-centred in perspective and pay close attention to the social and environmental changes affecting the client system. In short, the intervention should be not be programme-centred but more people-centric in the environmental system. Such an emphasis was proposed in the recollections of the author's experiences in straddling between academic teaching and doing social work and as one of the past Heads of the Social Work Department at the National University of Singapore (NUS). Vasoo also touched on the social service projects which he had pioneered, some challenges of social work education, and social issues facing Singapore in the near future. Some of the comments presented were drawn from his earlier writings and working experience in the social work arena (Vasoo, 2012, pp. 25–35).

Conclusion

Community development intervention can only be effective provided that there are adequate resources such as good human and financial capital; drive for mutual concern, care and help; community-centric leadership and not self-centred motivation; proactive policies which are people-centred; and conscious efforts to implement supportive measures to uplift those who fall behind for reasons outside their control. Community development will be meaningless if it is not based on the central drive to get the people living in the community to appreciate one another, develop a social network of supportive individuals and social groups to weather any social setbacks and to enable people to be caring for one another irrespective of their stations in lives.

References

1. David Chan (2018) (ed.). How Working Together Matters, World Scientific Publishing. Singapore. pp 75–98.
2. S. Vasoo (2018). Investment for the Social Sector to Tackle Key Social Issues, in Critical Issues in Asset Building in Singapore's Development. S. Vasoo and Bilveer Singh (eds.). World Scientific Publishing. Singapore. pp 21–36.

3. David Chan (2015). People Matters, World Scientific Publishing. Singapore. Pp. 15–28.
4. Irene Ng (2018). Asset Building Challenges with Low Income Families, in Critical Issues in Asset Building in Singapore's Development. S. Vasoo and Bilveer Singh (eds.). World Scientific Publishing. Singapore. pp 112–136.
5. S. Vasoo and Bilveer Singh (2018) (eds.). Critical Issues in Asset Building in Singapore's Development. World Scientific Publishing. Singapore.
6. David Chan (2018) (ed). How Working Together Matters. World Scientific Publishing. Singapore. pp. 115–137.
7. S. Vasoo (2012). Straddling Teaching and Field Practice: Facing the Challenges. In Ebb and Flow: 60 Years of Social Work Education in Singapore. NUS Department of Social Work. pp 25–35.

Part 1

Working with Urban Children and Youth

Chapter 1

Issues and challenges in urban youth work*

S. Vasoo[†]

Urban youth work in Asia faces tremendous challenges in trying to meet the needs of youths and enable them to cope more effectively with issues related to modernization. Some of the more common issues such as rural to urban migration, youth unemployment and underemployment, drug abuse and juvenile delinquency, sexual exploitation and erosion of moral values have to be addressed quickly and realistic long-term solutions found.

Youth workers and youth organizations have to examine their organizational mission and discover more effective and efficient ways to deliver youth services. More importantly, youth organizations in urban settings have to move away from mainly a centre-based approach in

---

*From Vasoo, S. (1995). Issues and challenges in urban youth work. *Asia Pacific Journal of Social Work*, 5(1), 16–24. Copyright © Department of Social Work, National University of Singapore, Singapore, reprinted by permission of Taylor & Francis Ltd, http://www.tandfonline.com on behalf of Department of Social Work, National University of Singapore, Singapore.

This article reviews various issues and challenges faced by youth workers and youth organisations in the urban Asian setting in the light of the changing social landscape. Some of the views are also reflected in other articles on youth work and also relevant for work with urban children.

[†]S. Vasoo is Head, Department of Social Work and Psychology, National University of Singapore.

service delivery to a more outreach emphasis. In doing so, urban youth work will be more dynamic and responsive to meet the needs of youths.

Introduction

Youth workers and youth organizations in urban settings in the Asian region are facing increasing challenges to prepare youths for varying social and economic opportunities and reduce social problems facing youths. Besides these two major pressing concerns, both youth workers and their organizations are also pressured to review and improve the service delivery of their respective organizations so that the youth programmes continue to remain relevant and dynamic.

It has become more evident today that youth problems have become more transparent and complex. Youth unemployment or underemployment still remains a major problem. Drug abuse and juvenile delinquency problems have become acute in some cities and urban centres. AIDS affliction is on the increase among the young and if not managed effectively, it could become an epidemic.

Malnutrition, ill health and illiteracy are still a serious problem in Asia (UNICEF, 1993; Phillips, 1990). Juvenile prostitution and sexual exploitation of youths have not abated. Efforts to tackle all these social problems by various youth agencies and governments have been difficult and trying (Sewell & Kelly, 1991).

About 45 per cent of the population in the Asian region comprises young persons below the age of 35 years (World Bank, 1988). Many of them leave their homes in the rural sectors for urban settings and cities. This migratory phenomenon has become obvious in the last three decades because of the downturn in the rural economy and the attractions of better social and economic opportunities in the cities and urban centres (United Nations, 1984; Appleyard, 1989; Cox, 1990). The rural to urban flow of youths could not be stamped out as the cities are seen as capable of fulfilling their hopes and aspirations in alleviating them from their rural poverty trap. Such a large exodus of the young not only contributes to the worsening of the already vulnerable social and economic conditions in the cities and urban centres, but also depresses the rural economy further.

Some major issues and potential solutions

In highly urbanized societies in Asia, many youths are trying their best to come to grips with the strains and pressures of social change and development. Some have been able to adjust and cope with the demands of various social institutions whether they be economic, educational, family or community institutions. Others who are less endowed fall by the wayside and become more susceptible to various social consequences leading to diswelfare. It is therefore important to discuss the broader social issues affecting youths generally and the social landscape in urban youth work. Some of these issues have had impact and will continue to have influence on future directions of urban youth work in the Asian region.

1. *Opening up parochial orientation*

It appears that the main emphasis in urban youth work is to serve youths who are enrolled in the membership of youth organizations. Youths who are members of various youth groups become a focus of primary concern whilst others who are vulnerable to social problems such as drug abuse, delinquency and interpersonal conflicts, do not get as much support and attention as they should.

We are also witnessing that a large number of youths are unattached to any social or youth groups. These unattached youths idle away their time and participate in leisure activities which are antisocial. Two of the commonest activities they indulge in are drug abuse and juvenile crime. They are a very high risk group for social problems because they remain divorced from the ambit of youth organizations. Many youth organizations have not attempted to reach out to these youths nor assessed how they could plan constructive social and recreational activities for these unattached youths.

There are a few youth groups that have implemented a more comprehensive programme to meet the needs of unattached youths. In order that urban youth work could be more effective and strengthened, there is an urgency to implement more preventive programmes directed at unattached youths. This thrust in urban youth work will help youth groups to respond to a sector of young people who would otherwise be left out in the planning of youth programmes. Some innovative programmes such as outreach service, drop-in youth centres, family life education programmes, delinquency prevention programmes and environmental improvement programmes could be launched.

2. *Reducing youth unemployment and underemployment*

Social and economic development in the Asian region has begun to pick up in the recent decade. This is due to the liberalization of trade practices, government stability and more open-door policies adopted by various governments. Countries which have implemented free trade policies and market principle approaches in governance have experienced significant economic development (World Bank, 1988, 1993). However, despite the economic transformation in the Asian region, youth unemployment is still high. It ranges between 5% and 30% of the youth population. This is a serious problem which has to be addressed and it is precipitated by a few factors.

Firstly, the nature of development is uneven and manifest particularly between urban and rural areas, regions and economic sectors. There is underutilization of human potential for productive work. Inequalities have increased between the impoverished majority and the privileged minorities in a number of countries in the Asian region (Rigg, 1991; Cox, 1990).

Secondly, rural to urban migration of youths is phenomenal. Many of the rural youths are ill prepared for their new environment and there is a lack of educational opportunities for their self-development. The rural economy has stagnated and failed to absorb the surplus youth manpower for work. There is over-centralization of industries in the urban centres as the rural areas do not have good basic infrastructures and agrarian reforms which make them accessible and attractive (Myrdal, 1968).

Thirdly, education in Asia has not been gearing up quickly enough to prepare youths for the productive sectors of the economy. In spite of post-war interest in technical and vocational education, the majority of secondary schools in Asia have retained general academic and literary emphasis. Most of the resources are still directed to this area (Myrdal, 1968) and there are only some signs but not strong signals to place more emphasis on industrial skills training.

Several plans have to be actively pursued by youth policy-makers, youth workers and those involved in the management of youth organizations. Several pronged actions to prepare for the employability of youths in the rural and urban sectors have to be implemented. These include actions to

(a) ensure that adequate capital and financial resources are deployed to meet the basic needs of youths;
(b) initiate projects of self-reliance amongst both rural and urban youths who have creative capability and could be encouraged to take up projects which contribute to economic growth;
(c) restructure educational training of youths to prepare them for industrial and technological fields and to reduce the growth of the "educated unemployed". In order to maintain a concerted effort to implement successful skills training for the youths, it is necessary to establish an Industrial and Technical Education Board which will be charged with the responsibility of carrying out the task; and
(d) set up more local and neighbourhood youth organizations to mobilize youths who are unemployed to be trained and retrained for suitable employment in the urban and rural development projects. Guidance and job placements could also be undertaken by the youth organizations concerned.

3. *Dealing with the erosion of moral values*

Our youths are more exposed to various positive and negative information as a result of the 'open sky' policy adopted by various governments. Under such a policy, there is always the danger that negative and hedonistic values would be propagated. It is becoming more obvious that the young people in Asian societies are facing more value conflicts. With the weakening of social institutions such as the school, family and community, the problems of moral degradation have become more evident. Personal and social misbehaviours such as dishonesty, promiscuity, delinquency, prostitution and other criminal offences are more tolerated and are on the increase.

One area of grave concern is the increase in sexual promiscuity of youths and this has led to the spread of AIDS and venereal diseases amongst young people. In particular, the scourge of AIDS will be so widespread that it will become a national threat to the health of the young in many countries in the Asian region. It is therefore timely for youth workers and organizations to take immediate steps and long-term plans to educate the young about sex and AIDS.

The social health of any society varies inversely with the state of prevailing moral values. The stronger the moral values of its people, the less likely will be the social breakdowns. Values education, which begins at home and is incorporated in the school curriculum, can become a social antigen or future panacea to neutralize the effects of decadent values that erode the sense of social responsibility of the young.

In the developing countries of the region, a lot of resources have been invested on the education of youths. This is based on the assumption that social and economic betterments could be achieved. However, such betterments are slow to realize (Eng, 1983). It is sad to witness that more societies are becoming divisive, violent, corruptible and inhumane. All these consequences do affect education, which is influenced by the prevailing social and political ethos. Throughout the history of human civilization, it has been repeated that without an open and honest socio-political ethos, the roles of education and other social institutions are undermined as social and moral transmitters (Gopinathan, 1980).

For young people to thrive, youth workers and organizations must help to promote in their societies a socio-political ethos based on respect, honesty and integrity, tolerance, non-communalism, non-corruptibility, adherence to law and order, equal opportunity based on meritocracy and mutual support. The right place to begin this is through values education in the homes and schools. Values education, if carefully planned and encouraged by youth workers and youth organizations in concert with the homes and schools, can prevent the young from becoming self-centred and uncaring (Vasoo, 1990).

More young people could be nurtured by youth organizations to be "others oriented" and to promote public good. With more of such young people, they can help to strengthen the leadership of our social and public institutions, which will then become effective bastions in dealing with the erosion of moral values.

4. *Strengthening partnership between managements and youth workers*
Good partnership between the managements of youth organizations and professional youth workers will make their organizations more dynamic and innovative. Besides this requirement, they must have a shared institutional mission. It is therefore pertinent for managements and professional

youth workers to identify factors which affect the efficiency and effectiveness in the delivery of their youth programmes. In short, we have to deal with organizational appraisal, which seems to be a much neglected area in the management of youth organizations. This is because those involved in youth organizations tend to be impressed by the number of programmes delivered and to be influenced by the voluntary nature of their participation.

In order for youth organizations to be relevant and effective, those who manage them must address these key questions:

- Are our youth programmes meeting the changing needs of our young?
- What are the outcomes of our programmes?
- What steps are being taken to ensure the good quality of our youth programmes?

Only when management personnel and professional youth workers conscientiously find answers to the pertinent questions indicated, will they be able to make their organizations viable and progressive.

It is noticeable that some of the people who lead youth organizations are busy with their own commitments. When their participation is poor, it can lead to weak bonding with their organizations. As a result, they will not be able to get appropriate feedback for organizational growth. Professional youth workers could become disillusioned by the lack of direction and they resign when the leadership puts further obstacles in their work. Hence, both youth leaders and professional youth workers must mutually respect that they each have useful contributions to make. An effective partnership is an essential driving force for their organizations.

5. Renewing the greying youth leadership

Many youth organizations are affected by family life cycle events and demographic transitions. In the last few decades, some of the youth organizations are witnessing the greying of their leadership. This situation will become more serious in the next two decades. There is a danger of gerontocratization of youth organizations. When this condition takes place, these organizations will lose their capacity to promote the aspirations of the young and be less attractive for their participation.

The greying of leadership may lead to organizational lethargy (Vasoo, 1992) and punctuated response to the changing needs of youths. Such a situation can stifle leadership succession as younger echelon leaders may not have the opportunities to exercise their leadership qualities. Also, the greying of leadership without renewal can lead to organizational decline, which, if not treated, can cause the demise of the organizations. Therefore, the leadership must continue to attract youths with impeccable character and "others oriented" inclinations into leadership positions. This will enable the youth organizations to be effective and developmental. However, youth workers and youth organizations should not ignore the contributions of older leaders whose wealth of experience is useful. They can be retained as resource persons or advisors to respective youth organizations. Transfer of leadership from the older to the younger must be planned and carried out smoothly.

Based on cursory surveys of youth organizations in the region, the renewal of youth leadership is still slower than desirable. The pace of renewal has to be stepped up so that youth organizations can continue to be responding relevantly to the needs of youths.

Conclusion

The social landscape of the youths in the Asian region has undergone significant transformation because of a number of factors such as demographic transition, relocation and rehousing, downturn in the rural economy, rural to urban migration, social and economic changes, modernization and erosion of moral values (ESCAP, 1989).

Urban youth workers and youth organizations should take cognizance of these factors so that they respond more effectively by delivering realistic and cost effective programmes to meet the impacts of social changes confronting youths.

More importantly, urban youth work can be dynamic provided both the managements of youth organizations and the professional youth workers work in close partnership to make their organizations more accessible and developmental in their service provisions. The reaching-out approach should be adopted and traditional centre-based work should be de-emphasized.

To add further mileage and fresh thrust in urban youth work, continuing efforts must be made to bring renewal to the greying leadership of youth organizations.

References

Appleyard, R.T. (1988). International migration in Asia and the Pacific. In Appleyard, R.T. (ed.), *International Migration Today*. Belmont, California: Wadsworth Publishing Company.

Cox, D. (1990). Patterns of migration in the Asia South Pacific Region. In Sewell, S. & Kelley, A. (eds.), *Social Problems in the Asia Pacific Region*. Brisbane: Boolarong Publications, pp. 154–173.

Economic Commission for Asia and the Pacific (ESCAP) (1989). *Compendium of Social Development Indicators in the ESCAP Region*. Bangkok: ESCAP.

Eng, S.P. (1983). Education and development: Era of hope and disillusionment. *Singapore Journal of Education, 15*(1), 14–19.

Gopinathan, S. (1980). Moral education in a plural society: A Singapore case study. *International Review of Education, 25*, 171–185.

Myrdal, G. (1968). *Asian Drama: An Inquiry into the Poverty of Nations*. London: Penguin Press.

Phillips, D. (1990). *Health Care in the Third World*. England: Longman.

Rigg, J. (1991). *Southeast Asia: A Region in Transition*. London: Allen and Unwin.

Sewell, S. & Kelley, A. (eds.) (1991). *Social Problems in the Asia Pacific Region*. Brisbane: Boolarong Publications.

United Nations (1984). *International Migration: Policies and Programmes, A World Survey*. New York.

United Nations Children's Fund (1993). *The State of the World's Children 1993*. New York: Oxford University Press.

Vasoo, S. (1990). *Enhancing Citizen Participation in Voluntary Organizations: Some Issues and Challenges*. Hong Kong: Department of Social Work and Administration, University of Hong Kong.

Vasoo, S. (1992). Promoting voluntary efforts in meeting community needs in Singapore: Some challenges. *Asia Pacific Journal of Social Work, 2*(2), 25–37.

World Bank (1988). *World Development Report*. New York: Oxford University Press.

World Bank (1993). *The East Asian Miracle: Economic Growth and Public Policy*. New York: Oxford University Press.

Chapter 2

Directions in youth research and preventive services in Singapore*

A. E. Y. Lee[†] and S. Vasoo[‡]

Only a little more than two years remain before the next millennium arrives. There is no doubt that rapid social and economic transformation that has taken place in Asia and Singapore will continue to gather momentum in the new millennium. These changes will have significant implications on Asian and Singaporean youths of today, who will be the primary resource and principal stakeholders in tomorrow's society. It is timely that research on youth becomes a focus of attention, where systematic and in-depth studies may enable youth workers and policy planners to become aware of the effects of the changing environment on our youth, and the implications for preventive services for them.

---

*Reprinted with permission by the publisher from Lee, A. E. Y., & Vasoo, S. (1997). Directions in youth research and preventive services in Singapore. *Journal of Youth Study*, *1*(1), 83–92. (Hong Kong)

This paper proposes the need for proactive research and recommends the direction for future research and preventive services to meet new emerging needs and problems of the youth. As analytical work is lacking, much insights could be gained to improve service delivery by youth agencies.

[†]Lecturer at the Dept. of Social Work and Psychology, National University of Singapore
[‡]Head of the Dept. of Social Work and Psychology, National University of Singapore

Indeed, in Singapore, human resources have been recognised as the primary national asset. Much is expected of Singapore's youth. They have the responsibility of upholding the prosperity of Singapore amidst a shrinking youth population and a rapidly expanding ageing population. For these reasons, the government of Singapore has targeted youth development as a priority in the national agenda and has set aside more resources for the educational development of children and youths.

It is hoped that as Singaporean youths respond to various competing social values, they will acquire the cultural balance and mental acumen to be versatile, civic-minded, and have the social antigen to resist and counter hedonistic values that inadvertently will invade the social fabric of our society.

The participation of youths in our youth services and organizations will be subjected to more and more challenges than before because of changing expectations and demands for expertise and programs. Unless youth groups and organizations can make their programs more interesting and innovative, they will not be able to attract and sustain our youth. It has been identified that youth organizations that offer mundane and routine programs can become moribund in due course.

The effectiveness of our youth groups and organizations in their activities must count on good leadership that will be responsive to the changes of the external environment. Their ability to organize themselves to meet new emerging needs and problems of the youth, particularly on issues related to their human and skills development, will dictate whether they will be viable organizations and relevant to our young. One problem with some of our youth groups and organizations is that they have not developed adequate measures to monitor changes in the external environment. Hence, their service delivery is remedial rather than preventive. This paper will suggest some research and service directions to address these issues.

Brief background of youths in Singapore

The focus on youth in Singapore is particularly urgent when we consider the patterns of recent demographic changes and predictions of future societal problems. Singapore is currently facing rapid population aging. According to the United Nations Bureau of Census, Singapore ranks second in the rate of population aging among developing countries (UN, 1987). A major contribution to the high rate of aging is the shrinking youth population. At 6.55 in 1947, total fertility rates in Singapore began dropping below replacement levels from 2.11 in 1976 to 1.42 in 1986 (Saw, 1990, p. 15). As a result, fertility policies in Singapore took on a pro-natal direction aimed at increasing births. Despite aggressive pro-natal policies and numerous incentives for families who can afford to have more children, total fertility rates continued to stay below replacement rates.

Currently, 22.81% of Singapore's population are youths aged 15 to 19 (Year book of Statistics, 1996). Most youths who are in secondary schooling age are currently enrolled in schools. All males must go through National Service from two years to two and a half years upon completion of secondary school education or upon the age of 18. Most youths who have completed schooling are gainfully employed. The three major ethnic groups of Chinese, Malay, and Indian youths live relatively harmoniously together in multi-racial Singapore (See Table 1).

Early youth research in Singapore

Having gained independence in 1965, Singapore is a young nation with a relatively short history. Youths in early Singapore had to struggle with nation building and contend with limited resources amidst a rapidly changing social and economic environment. It is not surprising that youth research during the 1960s and early 1970s focused on the relationship between youths and nation building (Chen, 1976, 1977). Concerned about the effects of a possible population explosion, rapid urbanization and modernization, youth research in the late 1970's and 1980's concentrated on the values and attitudes of Singapore youth toward sexuality, family, life, and work (Ratnam, 1979; Saw & Wong, 1981; Tai, 1979; Ong, 1980).

Early research on teenage sexuality were mainly initiated by the Family Planning Association in Singapore, an organization created by the government in the early 1950's to address concerns about family planning (Ratnam, 1979; Saw & Wong, 1981). In particular, researchers were

Table 1. Singapore youth resident population by age, ethnicity and sex

Ethnicity & Sex	Thousands						
	Total	0–4	5–9	10–14	15–19	20–24	25–29
Total	3,044.3	244.0	241.5	209.0	203.1	232.3	259.0
Male	1,531.1	125.9	124.9	108.6	104.6	116.3	127.8
Female	1,513.2	118.1	116.6	100.4	98.5	116.0	131.2
Chinese	2,352.7	170.9	170.7	150.9	158.2	184.7	200.8
Male	1,176.1	88.4	88.6	78.6	81.4	92.3	98.9
Female	1,176.6	82.5	82.1	72.3	76.8	92.4	101.9
Malays	430.9	47.2	46.8	39.1	29.3	30.8	36.3
Male	219.0	24.3	24.0	20.2	15.2	15.8	18.3
Female	211.9	22.9	22.8	18.9	14.1	15.0	18.0
Indians	222.1	20.1	19.6	16.2	13.7	14.8	19.2
Male	117.9	10.3	10.0	8.4	7.0	7.3	9.7
Female	104.2	9.8	9.6	7.8	6.7	7.5	9.5
Others	38.6	5.8	4.4	2.8	1.9	2.0	2.7
Male	18.1	2.9	2.3	1.4	1.0	0.9	0.9
Female	20.5	2.9	2.1	1.4	0.9	1.1	1.8

Year book of Statistics, 1996

concerned about teenage sexuality and the rising number of teenage abortions. Results from the studies showed that teenage abortions increased dramatically in the later 1970's following the liberalization of abortion laws in 1974 (Saw, 1979).

In the areas of family, life and work, Tai and Ong surveyed a random sample of 1,135 youths between the ages of 15 and 24 to examine their values systems and attitudes in these areas (Tai, 1979; Ong, 1980). They found that two thirds of the youths were generally satisfied with life and were optimistic about the future. Our youths were forward looking, independent and tolerant toward other ethnic groups. Most of them were conservative in the area of sexual practices and more than half would accept divorce as a reasonable solution for an unhappy marriage. After marriage, the majority of youths preferred not to live with parents. When asked to choose the most important symbols of success in life, Singaporean youths chose, in order of importance, education, money and occupation.

The importance of education was found again in the results of a survey by Youth for Christ given to 1000 secondary one to four students (Lim, 1985). The questionnaire asked about student's relationships with family members, their peers, views about school and work, and satisfaction in life. Calling them the youths-in-transition, Lim highlighted that Singaporean secondary school students tended to place high priority in education, felt that parents were very important, and were not overly influenced by peers although they liked to hang out with their peers.

Recent youths studies in Singapore

The phenomena of youths hanging out began to receive close attention as more youth groups began to gather around prominent shopping centers. Besides spending a lot of time around shopping centers, incidents of fighting and other conflicts among various youth groups became frequent. A survey of 2000 youths in various shopping centers by Youth Challenge revealed about half of the youths interviewed were students with slightly less than a third of them unemployed (Teen Challenge, 1986). Most of them expressed restlessness and poor family relationships to be the main reasons for hanging out.

To address the issues, the Singapore Council of Social Service conducted a survey among five groups of 217 youths who hang out at certain popular shopping areas to examine their needs and characteristics (Singapore Council of Social Service, 1989). The study disclosed that members of these youth groups were predominantly students who were more susceptible to influence by friends than by parents. A majority of youths surveyed were not attached to any community organizations other than school organizations. The unattached youths in the various groups came from different ethnic and family backgrounds. Although they have different scholastic achievements and were not uniform in vulnerability to at-risk behaviors such as crime and sexual promiscuity, they all appeared to have some threads of commonality such as boredom, poor family relationships and an expressed desire for peer interactions.

In order to gain a deeper understanding of Singapore youth, an Advisory Council on Youth was formed in February 1988 to identify the needs, interests and aspirations of our youths. In addition, the Council reviewed the impact of youth related policies and recommended new programmes to enable Singapore youths to maximise their developmental potential. The Council comprised of cabinet ministers, members of parliament, academicians, journalists, teachers, students, community leaders, professionals and representatives of youth groups. The Council's deliberations were based on data from 450 questionnaires, dialogue and discussion sessions, and consultation with key community leaders and related government officials and its report was published the following year.

In general, the Council found that Singapore youths were generally well adjusted with only a minority associated with crime, delinquency and substance abuse (Advisory Council on Youth, 1989). The majority of youths placed high priority on education, career and personal upgrading in skills and qualifications. The pursuit of academic and career excellence, however, was achieved at the cost of neglect in sports, arts and cultural development, as well as activities related to nation building and community service. As a direct result of the recommendations by the Council, the National Youth Coordinating Committee, a non-executive coordinating body, was upgraded to a National Youth Council to undertake policy making, policy implementation and administration of youth related matters in the areas of sports, social development and culture. The National Youth Achievement Awards scheme was also launched to reward youths with exceptional achievements in social, economic, cultural and educational fields.

Youth problems in Singapore continued to be a concern of policy makers as they receive attention in the media from time to time. In 1993, Prime Minister Goh Chok Tong observed that youth crimes, juvenile delinquency and drug addiction among youths had been rising and he commissioned an Inter-Ministry Committee to study the problems of dysfunctional families, juvenile delinquency and drug abuse. The Committee published their findings in the Report of the Inter-Ministry Committee on Dysfunctional Families, Juvenile Delinquency and Drug Abuse in 1995.

Juvenile delinquency

The inter-ministry report noted that the types of crimes committed by Singapore youths were not of the serious nature, and that figures of arrests were small compared to other countries (Report of the Inter-Ministry Committee on Dysfunctional Families, Juvenile Delinquency and Drug Abuse, 1995). Nevertheless, the number of youth arrests had been on the increase in the last decade, doubling from 691 in 1980 to 1,205 in 1990. The numbers increased by another three-quarters to 2,102 in 1994. Among the crimes committed were shoplifting, theft, vandalism, violence and secret society involvement. Numerous students were also given warnings by police against gang involvement. In general, the Committee found that the typical young offender was a 14 to 15 years old male whose family income was below SG$1,500. Despite the male dominance among youth offenders, young female offenders were a source of special concern as the number of crimes committed by girls increased fivefold from 77 in 1984 to 395 in 1994.

Among the reasons for the rise in youth crimes, the Committee mentioned that busy parents, weak parent-child relationships, pressure from school, and negative peer influence were the main factors. The relationships among these factors were later explored in a more recent study, which predicted that susceptibility to antisocial peer pressure was related to family/parental, peer, and personal factors. (Sim, 1997). Data were taken from 577 students in Secondary One to Four. The results supported to a certain extent the Committee's proposition and showed that youths in closely knitted and responsive families had lower levels of susceptibility to antisocial peer pressure, in part because they were more likely to regard peers as less important to them than parents. Furthermore, youths with higher self-esteem or who spent less time with peers were less susceptible to antisocial peer pressure.

Drug addiction

Various tough approaches have been implemented to deal with drug addiction and trafficking in Singapore. Nevertheless, the problems have not been reduced significantly as there was an increase in the number of inmates in Drug Rehabilitation Centres (DRC) from 3,726 in 1985 to 8,856 in 1994. The Inter-Ministry Committee found that, on average, new addicts admitted to DRCs each year between 1989 and 1994 were 25 percent higher than the previous five years. In particular, recidivism rates rose from 57 percent in 1985 to 81.2 percent in 1994. This translates to about eight persons out of every ten returning to drug addiction within two years after going through rehabilitation. These figures raise special concern as more than a third of both new and relapsed drug addicts were aged below 30. The committee suggested that stress, boredom, depression, low self-esteem, rebelliousness, antisocial peer pressure and thrill seeking were some of the common factors contributing to first time and repeated drug addiction. When these factors occurred within the context of poor family supervision, poor grades and poor family relations, young people were likely to turn to drugs as a form of escape.

Need for proactive research

In recent years, youth research in Singapore has two demonstrable characteristics: Firstly, major studies on youth have largely been responses to initiatives from government policy makers who had identified the problem areas and called for study in those areas. Few large scale studies were conducted without government first identifying the problems of national interests, such as youth delinquency and substance abuse. Secondly, studies were mostly conducted by government institutions or government funded organizations. Only a few studies were undertaken by private bodies or non-government organizations, such as those by Youth Challenge and Youth For Christ. This was probably because most private organizations their financial resources in service delivery rather than in conducting research.

In many respects, government initiated studies encompass partly what the goal of research should be, a response to finding solutions for certain undesirable social trends and national needs. Nevertheless, there is a need for youth research to move beyond reactionary research derived from government initiatives to proactive, independent and intervention research. While research activities initiated by government are vital and significant, they tend to suggest urgency and cover specific issues which have policy implications. As a result, studies are often under serious restrictive time constraints and do not extend to broader areas beyond specific objectives.

Proactive research, on the other hand, primarily functions to discover potential and anticipated problem areas even before these issues are recognized to pose possible harm. Research conducted independent of government initiatives, though not necessarily without government funding and support, are free to explore matters that are not necessarily high on the national agenda but are of concern to the community, and in the long run may serve to complement current research topics of national interests. Examples may include research initiatives from youth organizations that aim to fill in gaps in knowledge, or examine social trends and issues in their budding stage. This kind of research may also focus on life transitions, family life and enhancement of the quality of life in addition to solving problems. For example, research on marriage and adolescent sexuality would provide insights into future family patterns and relationships. Intervention research, additionally, allows youth practitioners and policy makers to evaluate the effectiveness of programs, and to refine and sustain intervention efforts.

Agencies which lack the financial or personnel resources to conduct research independently may undertake a pooling of resources with other agencies. They can also tap on community/grassroots organizations, which may have limited expertise in research but are willing to contribute through other means.

Youth practitioners may also be encouraged to participate in more research. As youth practitioners have direct contact with youth daily, they may be more sensitive to the issues germane to youth work and may more readily identify areas that call for in-depth investigation. This suggests a need to equip interested youth practitioners with skills in designing, conducting, and reporting research. Currently, however, training in social research skills, except what is provided in the University, is not readily available. Besides research funding, more avenues for training in social research must be encouraged and made accessible.

Directions for future research

One area for future youth research in Singapore is to build on existing knowledge of Singaporean youths, juvenile delinquency and substance abuse. Since some background and base rate data have been collected, and since certain factors have been identified to associate closely with youth problems, the next logical step will be to examine the nature of relationships among salient variables such as family, stress, peers and self-esteem on outcomes. In this regard, there is a need for theory-driven research, as opposed to doing more exploratory research. While exploratory research may function to provide descriptive data on scarcely studied social phenomena, theory-driven research will allow the researcher to test hypotheses and revise theories for intervention and practice, as well as help practitioners to understand how some factors affect social problems and how these factors may be mediated.

Secondly, the review on youth literature has revealed scarce attention on youths with disabilities. With high value placed on human resources, the development of each child to reach his or her fullest potential must receive increasing attention. In this respect, children and youths with various physical or developmental disabilities must not be ignored. There are currently few research on the availability, appropriateness and accessibility of social and educational services for children and youths with special needs. Indeed, the call for systematic assessment and diagnosis of children with developmental disabilities and support for their families has already been sounded and deserve immediate attention (Ow, 1994).

In a similar vein, research attention must be placed on marginal youths as well. Unlike larger countries, where there are larger youth populations and less pressure for early achievement, greater flexibility and alternative models for youth development can be obtained. The youths of Singapore, however, are under high pressure to succeed in school and at work. The issue is not so much on those who can make it, but those on the margin who, for some reasons, have difficulty following the rigorous exam and achievement oriented in Singapore model. These youths who cannot cope with the current system may, however, thrive under different conditions and should not be allowed to fall by the wayside. Alternative routes must be provided to enable them to develop their full potential according to their own pace.

Thirdly, program evaluation and outcome research will have to form the base for the continuation of current programs and services. Since more resources are deployed by various institutions to enhance the lives of our youths, there is a need to conduct outcome research and to evaluate whether current programs are meeting objectives cost effectively. There is a tendency for youth organizations to perpetuate existing programs as long as a minimum level of demand for these programs is present. Demand for a program, however, does not necessarily mean that the program is successful in meeting its goals. Programs that have been successful in the past may also suffer inertia and resistance to change despite a need for program innovation and adaptation to changing circumstances. Evaluation and outcome research will therefore help youth organizations in Singapore refine their programs and ensure effectiveness and relevance. At the higher level, outcome research can enable policy makers to decide how resources can be allocated more effectively to areas that produce the best results in solving youth problems.

Fourthly, more research attention must be placed on intergenerational relationships between youth and their families. Surveys on attitudes of youth throughout the 1980's have revealed that even though young teenagers admire their parents, they generally do not want to live with their parents after marriage. Recent studies further showed deteriorating family relationships especially among troubled youths. In the light of these findings, plus the forthcoming burden of an aged society, families may expect to experience increased intergenerational tension in the near future. Research in intergenerational relationships in the areas of interpersonal relationships, conflict resolution and mediation, change in family roles, parenting issues and care-taking of the aged, may help ease the transition of families in current times to the next millennium.

Finally, cross-cultural and regional studies on the aspirations and problems of youth could be encouraged. Although many countries in Asia and South-East Asia have our own unique history, language and geographical size, we share sufficient commonalities such as a value system of filial piety, rapid economic and industrial growth. We are also likely to share similar challenges and problems with our youths. Cross cultural research will add richness to the understanding of youths living in our neighboring countries and perhaps enable us to achieve a new dimension of understanding for our own youths in Singapore. Singapore youth organizations are well positioned to initiate these studies together with other youth groups in the region.

Directions in youth services in Singapore

In the light of rising youth problems in the 1990s, several researchers have called for greater attention to research and program planning for preventive work (Vasoo, 1995; Tan, 1995). Preventive youth work requires youth agencies to increase their knowledge about youths, evaluate the effectiveness of current preventive programs and design creative new programs. Several approaches have been suggested to enable youth agencies to provide preventive services (Vasoo, 1995). One approach is to identify and focus on youths who are not members of any social or youth groups. In contrast to youths who are members of youth organizations, unattached youth have more discretionary time and are more susceptible to negative peer pressure. Youth organizations that do not traditionally reach out to unattached youth are encouraged to actively initiate research and programs that can engage and help unattached youths. A second approach is to ensure that capital and financial resources are deployed adequately to meet the basic needs of youths, and to reduce youth unemployment and underemployment. This approach requires careful study of the allocation and usage of national resources at the policy level. Thirdly, there is a need to examine the effects of eroding moral values on youths in view that traditional Asian value systems are being challenged by modern values and lifestyles. The implications of changing values on youths, especially in the areas of sexual behaviors, interpersonal behaviors and family relations, must be examined to ensure relevance in program and policy planning. A fourth approach is to understand and strengthen the relationship between the management and youth workers within youth organizations. This is to help create more dynamic organizations with heightened communication and mutual understanding between the ground workers and the top decision makers. Finally, there is a need to beware the effects of a graying leadership within youth organizations. As youth leaders age the possibility of burn-out and stagnation may seep in and result in the eventual moribund of programs.

These approaches to preventive youth work are useful guidelines for current youth organizations in planning for youth services in general, and more specifically preventive services for unattached youths.

Preventive services for unattached youth

Youth services in Singapore have to be systematically reviewed in the context of the changing needs of our youths. Earlier reviews of youth research have suggested that an important area of need that youth services must address is the area of needs among unattached youths and suitable preventive services for them.

The term unattached youths is used to identify groups of youth people who do not utilise normal youth service provisions within their communities. They are youths who are detached from youth organisations and prefer to gather in small loose groups. Membership in these groups tends to be fluid because of diverse interests and background amongst the members. What holds the group together is normally nothing more than peer affiliation.

Peer affiliation, however, is not to be underestimated as anti-social attitudes and behaviours are easily transmitted through these peer influences. In our work with unattached youth groups, it is found that at least one or two members in each of these groups have criminal records or have violated the law. Young members are often the most susceptible to undesirable influences.

Generally, most youth groups and clubs in Singapore currently direct their efforts to serve youths who are either known or enrolled in their membership. Unattached youths who are more vulnerable to social problems, however, do not receive as much service support and attention as they should. Youths who are enrolled as members of various groups therefore become a focus of primary concern whilst others who are most vulnerable to social problems such as drug abuse, delinquency and personal conflicts, do not receive as much service support and attention as they should.

Few youth organisations have embarked on a more comprehensive program to meet the needs of youths in their neighbourhood. It is important, therefore, for youth groups to undertake more preventive programs directed at unattached youths. In developing programs to cater for the unattached youths, youth organisations should become less parochial in their orientation on catering to the needs of the young living in their respective neighbourhoods. Some pertinent suggestions will be highlighted in this discussion.

Reviewing program objectives and needs of youths

Presently, the objectives of youth organisations in Singapore are primarily confined to the promotion of social and recreational activities. It is necessary to examine whether these objectives are sufficient for twenty-first century youths, and whether social and recreational activities will meet the needs of unattached youths. In order to evaluate the relevance of current programs, youth organisations need to have a deeper understanding the profiles and needs of the youths in the neighbourhood.

Some relevant information that may be useful to youth groups may include: the number of school drop-outs in the neighbourhood, the localities with most unattached youths, the social-economic profile of youth in the neighbourhood, the number of youths with social problems in the neighbourhood, the types of problems youths would like to participate in, and the areas of interests among the youths in the neighbourhood. Having these information will help youth organisations to better locate their target group for intervention and plan for relevant programs.

Initiating a service for unattached youths

When initiating a service for unattached youths, it is necessary to consider several pertinent factors to ensure success. The pertinent factors include deciding the locality where the service can be initiated, quality of staff, the methods of intervention and the types of programs.

Identification of a locality is important since new towns and communities are constantly being established in Singapore. Established youth organisations tend to be situated in older towns and neighbourhoods and may not be known among youths in newer communities. Youths who are relocated in new towns tend to experience a period of disorganisation and disorientation. To minimise the stress that may accompany adaptation to the new environment, it is essential to provide guidance and development services for these youths.

Secondly, it is important to identify the type and quality of staff required to work with unattached youths. In most existing youth organisations, staff are more experienced in working with normal youths. This experience may be insufficient for work with unattached youths as unattached youth work may require different approaches and skills. Special training may be provided to enable staff to work effectively. In addition, it may be useful to engage groups of volunteers to assist staff, provided they are trained and supervised carefully.

The methods for intervention among unattached youths require the ability for youth workers to establish trust and rapport. These skills are vital since unattached youths tend to be suspicious of the motives of the worker. Continued presence of the same worker is important as a change of staff will disrupt the relationship building process. Workers may have to establish trust with just a few youths initially. Once the relationships with a few are established, other youths in the group may be attracted to the worker.

Programs for unattached youths must be innovative and be able to sustain interest. While the main objectives of the programs are to provide for their developmental and social needs, the form of the programs may include a wide range of activities and methods, such as sports, camps, hobbies, computer classes etc. The types of programs may take the following forms:

1. Out-reach services
   Youth volunteers and leaders can be trained to locate and befriend unattached youths at their hang-out localities. The purpose is to provide friendship initially, with guidance and counselling later on. Eventually, through out-reach services, the unattached youths can be known and mobilised to participate in useful activities.
2. Drop-in youth centres
   Drop-in centre for youth can be designed to attract unattached youths who hang-out at various neighbourhood localities and do not have suitable healthy outlets for recreation and group activities. The idea is to provide a healthy alternative for youths to hang-out. Youth workers and leaders manning these centres can provide unattached youths information on career development and vocational guidance while providing programs that develop their interests.
3. Neighbourhood improvement programs
   Potential youth leaders can be recruited to work with youths in their respective neighbourhoods to be involved in environmental improvement programs. Examples include tree planting, cleanliness, etc. The

involvement of youths in these activities will help inculcate a strong sense of attachment to the neighbourhood.
4. Family life education programs
   Family life education can help youths understand the dynamics that occur within the family and provide them with skills to deal with family problems that may occur. These programs may include classes that help youths communicate better with their parents, manage conflicts within families, and enable youths to understand family role changes that occur.
5. Crime and delinquency prevention program
   Unattached youths in the neighbourhood can be organised to help in the prevention of crime and delinquency. In addition, educational and recreational programs such as camps can be organised for vulnerable youths.

Some challenges to preventive services

Since solutions to youth problems are very often dependent on how problems are defined, care must be exercised in defining the issues and identifying the phenomena that requires prevention or intervention. Tan suggested that the challenges to preventive youth work include 1) understanding the problem and defining the target for intervention, 2) obtaining base rates for intervention, and 3) evaluation of the success of intervention (Tan, 1995). These three tasks require careful consideration and study to prevent imposing preventive treatments on misidentified targets. For instance, for some problems, the target for intervention may not be the youths themselves but the structural environment such as family, education system, and the justice institutions. Additionally, the need to establish base rates of certain problems is important since without a base rate, there is no way to know if an intervention actually works. Building in an evaluation component to any intervention will require a clear idea of what outcomes need to be measured and which objectives are being met.

Conclusion

Youths in Singapore are recognized as a vital asset to the development and prosperity of Singapore. There is a need for more research in youth development as this will assist youth workers and policy planners to better understand the needs and aspirations of our youths. Since youth research in Singapore tend to be exploratory and descriptive in nature, the next step in youth research will be to move into hypotheses testing to explain current youth phenomena and to predict future trends. In addition, future directions of youth research must move beyond reactionary research to proactive research, preferably conducted by youth practitioners themselves. There is also a need for intervention and evaluation research to assess the effectiveness of youth programs.

This paper has highlighted some of the early and recent studies on Singapore youth. Two high level government committees, one formed in 1989 and the other in 1995 have provided considerable impetus to research in youth matters in recent years. The studies found that Singapore youths are generally well-adjusted. The studies have also shown that there is still a segment of youth that require special attention among researchers and practitioners. They are the unattached youths in Singapore.

To address the issues raised by unattached youths in Singapore, several areas for preventive work have been raised. These include the need for youth agencies to provide innovative and attractive programs, such as outreach programs and drop-in centers targeted specifically at unattached youths rather than normal youths.

Youth services should not be remedial in their orientation but be geared towards the implementation of preventive programs which will enable our youths to be productive and effective citizens of the future.

References

Advisory Council on Youth (1989). *Report of the Advisory Council on Youth.* Singapore: Singapore National Printers.

Chen, Peter S. J. (1976). Youth in Singapore's development process. *New Directions*, 3(1), 30–32.

Chen, Peter S. J. (1977). The characteristics of Singapore's youth and the future of our country. *Prospect*, 9, 1(84), 7–9.

Inter-Ministry Committee on Dysfunctional Families, Youth Delinquency and Drug Abuse (1995). *Report of the Inter-Ministry Committee on Dysfunctional Families, Youth Delinquency and Drug Abuse.* Singapore: Singapore National Printers.

Leong, Choon Cheong (1978). *Youth in the Army*. Singapore: Federal Publications.

Lim, John (1985). *Learning to Think About Singapore Youths in Transition*. Singapore: Youth for Christ.

Ong, Teck Hong (1979). *Survey on Youth Attitudes in Singapore: Report II*. (Research Project Series No. 11). Singapore: Institute of Humanities and Social Sciences, College of Graduate Studies, Nanyang University.

Ow, Rosaleen (1994). Families with intellectually disabled children. *Asia Pacific Journal of Social Work*, 4, 1, 46–61.

Ratnam, S. S. (1979). *Adolescent Sexuality*. Singapore: Family Planning Association of Singapore.

Saw, Swee-Hock (1990). *Changes in the Fertility Policy of Singapore*. Singapore: Institute of Policy Studies, Times Academic Press.

Sim, Tick Ngee (1997). A Model of Susceptibility to Antisocial Peer Pressure for Adolescents: Integrating Process, Person, Context, and Time. Unpublished doctoral dissertation, University of Wisconsin-Madison.

Singapore Council of Social Service (1990). Survey of Youths who "Hang Out" at Marina Square/Bay and Orchard Road Area. Unpublished manuscript.

Tai, Ching Ling (1980). *Survey on Youth Attitudes in Singapore: Report I*. (Research Project Series No. 13). Singapore: Institute of Humanities and Social Sciences, College of Graduate Studies, Nanyang University.

Tan, Ngoh-Tiong (1995). The challenge to preventive youth work. *Asia Pacific Journal of Social Work*, 5, 2, 68–74.

United Nations Department of International Economic and Social Affairs (1987). *Global Estimates and Projections of Population by Sex and Age*. New York: United Nations.

Vasoo, S. (1995). Issues and challenges in urban youth work. *Asia Pacific Journal of Social Work*, 5, 1, 16–24.

Youth Challenge (1985). Report of Findings From Youth Survey at Shopping Complexes. Unpublished manuscript.

Part 2

Ageing Issues, Eldercare and Service Delivery

Chapter 3

Community programmes and services for long-term care of the elderly in Singapore: Challenges for policy-makers*

Kalyani K. Mehta and S. Vasoo[†]

Introduction

Health policy-makers are often confronted by the future burden of increasing public expenditure and cost in the care of the elderly who require long-term continual care. Hence, there will be increasing social and political pressure to review present service delivery systems in the care of the elderly and implement more innovative policies to promote community-based,

---

*From Mehta, K. K., & Vasoo, S. (2000). Community programmes and services for long-term care of the elderly in Singapore: Challenges for policy-makers. *Asian Journal of Political Science*, 8(1), 125–140. Reprinted by permission of the publisher (Taylor & Francis Ltd, http://www.tandfonline.com).

The article examines the need to review long-term care services for the elderly. It is important to promote ageing in place rather than deploying more resources for institutionalised services. More community-based support services can ensure a cost effective approach. Challenges of such community-based long-term care services for the elderly are proposed.

[†]Kalyani K. Mehta, Ph.D., and S. Vasoo, Ph.D., are Assistant Professor and Associate Professor respectively in the Department of Social Work and Psychology, National University of Singapore.

non-institutionalised services for the families to care for their elderly as long as it is possible. Cost-effective measures in service provision have to be organised. Policy-makers in ageing societies cannot escape these issues as the elderly will form a sizeable proportion of voters and politics of accommodation will come to play in meeting the needs of such a large interest group. Therefore, a tripartite partnership of the state, community and family in the delivery of community-based services will be more useful and acceptable. Such a development can be a strategy to meet the needs of the elderly but, it is not a panacea to solving the problems of their long-term care.

In Singapore, this significant demographic transition will have serious implications on the provision of social services for the elderly. It is estimated that about 5% of the elderly population will require long-term institutional care. However, this provision will not be an effective solution in the longer term as the number of elderly requiring care and assistance in their daily living will be increasing and the building of more nursing homes and related facilities will not be a realistic solution to cope with the demands which cannot be curtailed. It is, therefore, important for policy-makers and service providers to think of other innovative services to help the elderly to remain healthy as long as possible, and remain socially integrated into the family and community.

The dilemma that many policy-makers face is the pressing demand for setting up more and more institutional care programmes, and how such a demand could be mediated and met in the most cost-effective way. Inevitably, one cannot avoid the debate of finding more cost-effective ways to deliver programmes to address the long-term care of the elderly. The cost issues will be the main concern to policy-makers. The cost is very likely to be prohibitive and will create serious strains on the government and the voluntary sectors. Both manpower and facilities would be required and this means that public expenses will have to be incurred, and the public would have to bear the burden through higher taxation to maintain the services. Continual care in the form of institutional provisions such as community hospitals, nursing homes, homes for the elderly and hospice centres are going to be costly to run and could be impersonal. At the same time, more elderly persons would be relocated from their community to be placed in these institutions. There will also be a social cost to the elderly persons. In the provision of long-term services for the elderly we must examine how more preventive and community-based programmes can be organised and delivered to them. Such an emphasis will make care programmes accessible and enable the elderly to remain within their community. It will also encourage the community to be mobilised to participate in promoting long-term care programmes. This approach will make the programmes more cost effective and help the elderly to be independent.

The sweeping demographic situation in most countries around the world forces nations to look at these issues urgently. A case in point is Singapore, the fastest ageing nation in the Asia-Pacific region, after Japan. At least one in four persons in Singapore will be 60 years and above in the year 2030.[1] Life expectancy at birth today is 75 years for males and nearly 80 years for females — this is expected to rise further in future. A significant point to note is that other countries have taken about 85–150 years to double the percentage of older persons in the total population. For example, Sweden took 85 years to increase its aged population from 7% to 14%, while it will take Singapore only 18 years to do so.[2] The speed of this critical demographic transition will have serious implications not only for health and social services but also for other sectors of society as well. Table 1 summarises the demographic projections till 2030.

A key concern in Singapore is "that the sheer rise in the numbers and proportion of older persons could potentially put stress on families and eldercare services".[3] As in other Asian countries, the family has been providing the major proportion of care and support for elderly family members. Although there is no strong data to show that families are shirking their filial responsibilities in Singapore, several social and demographic changes mitigate against the continuity of family care as the primary form of eldercare in Singapore. These factors include, among others, the shift towards dual

---

[1] See *Report of the Inter-ministerial Committee on the Ageing Population* (Singapore: Ministry of Community Development, 1999).
[2] See *Population Ageing in Asia and the Pacific* (New York: Economic and Social Commission for Asia and the Pacific, 1996), p. 9.
[3] *Report of the Inter-ministerial Committee on the Ageing Population*, p. 33. This concern has surfaced in earlier reports too, such as *Report of the Advisory Council on the Aged* (Singapore: Singapore National Printers, 1989), p. 40.

Table 1. Number and proportion of elderly population in Singapore

	1999	2000	2020	2030
No. of elderly, aged 65+ (in thousands)	235	312	529	796
Proportion of elderly, aged 65+*	7.3	8.4	13.1	18.9
Median age (Yrs.)	33.4	36.9	39.3	41.2
Dependency Ratio (D.R.)	42.0	38.7	44.9	56.4
D.R. (young) 0–14 years	31.7	27.1	25.9	26.9
D.R. (old) 65+ years	10.4	11.6	19.0	29.5

*As percentage of total population

Source: *Report of the Inter-ministerial Committee on Ageing Population* (Singapore: Ministry of Community Development, 1999), p. 29.

income nuclear families, increase in young Singaporeans working and living abroad, more single elderly, and changing social values.

The present paradigm of eldercare in Singapore is a partnership between the government, the community and the family.[4] In tandem with the "Many Helping Hands" policy of the Ministry of Community Development, the community and the government are expected to lend a hand to ageing families in order to reduce the stress of care giving for older members. It has been the stand of the government all along that the "family setting is still the best approach — it provides the elderly with the warmth and companionship of family members and a level of emotional support which cannot be found elsewhere".[5] The government encourages and provides financial as well as other forms of support to voluntary welfare organisations (VWOs) in their efforts to offer quality long-term care in the community. The services and programmes will be discussed in later sections of this article. Suffice it to mention at this juncture that with the

---

[4] K. Mehta, "Paradigms of Elder Care in Singapore," in W. Liu and H. Kendig (eds.) *Who Should Give Care to the Elderly? An East-West Social Value Divide* (Singapore: Singapore University Press, 2000), pp. 249–268.

[5] Opening speech given by the then Minister of Health, Mr. Yeo Cheow Tong at the Conference on "Choices in Financing Health Care and Old Age Security," in Singapore on November 8, 1997.

rise in percentages of older Singaporeans, non-family partners will be required to play a bigger role in the next few decades.

Given the differentials in ageing patterns, it would be a fallacy to presume that all older persons require continual care. However, those in the "old old" and "very old" categories are generally more likely to need constant supervision and socio-emotional as well as instrumental support. In other words, those above 75 years are potential target groups. Statistics show that the 75+ age group is likely to increase even faster than the 60–75 years age group.[6] This group is at risk for care and attention. More family resources will have to be drawn to attend to their social and physical requirements and some families would face stress to provide care to the sick and disabled. Other vulnerable categories include aged couples living alone (which has increased from 9% in 1990 to 15% in 1997); those suffering from senile dementia; elderly prone to chronic illnesses such as arthritis, asthma; and single, poor elderly who are living alone. A seamless system of service delivery is being planned in order to assist these categories of Singaporeans. Such a system would be effective provided there is systematic proper planning and a sensitised approach towards the needs of older persons, good economic sense and an understanding of ethnic values and preferences.

In older housing estates, the ageing process has become more apparent. There are increasing numbers of older senior citizens living in these estates and it is urgent that community groups and organisations begin to plan the establishment of more community-based programmes such as day care, meals programmes, home-help service and domiciliary nursing care and a crisis-response service. In taking a proactive approach to initiate a network of services in older housing estates, we will be able to provide support for families with vulnerable aged and prevent disruptions to the social and economic lives of the families.

The development of ageing policies

It is estimated that about 15 years ago the Singapore government began to recognise the impact an ageing population would have on its society. In

---

[6]Refer to Paul Cheung "Population Ageing in Singapore", *Asia Pacific Journal of Social Work,* Vol. 3, No. 2 (1993), pp. 77–89.

tandem with its approach and philosophy of foresight and visionary planning, in 1984 an Inter-ministerial Population Committee was set up. In 1988, the National Advisory Council on the Aged was formed to undertake a comprehensive review of the status of ageing in Singapore. One of the key recommendations proposed by the Advisory Council was that a National Council on Ageing be set up with the character and authority of a statutory board to effectively plan and co-ordinate policies and programmes for older persons. Other proposals included raising the retirement age from 55 to 60 as continued employment provides a sense of worth, dignity and financial independence to older persons; adjusting the seniority-based wage system so that more older people will be employed; expanding and strengthening public education programmes on older persons and ageing so that the right attitudes towards older persons could be inculcated; making land available for voluntary organisations to set up homes for older persons; lengthening the term leases for homes; studying the feasibility of providing health and medical services for frail older persons living in their own homes; and increasing the dependency tax rebate for families who look after older persons.

To meet further challenges of population ageing, the 1990s saw the development of two milestone policies which were implemented to deal with anticipated problems related to the social and health care of older persons. Various community groups and the Parliamentary Select Committee introduced a very significant legislation called the Maintenance of Parents Act in 1994, after many deliberations. There was public endorsement for the policy to impose a legal obligation on children to maintain their parents. Such a social policy, which is unique in Asia, deals with prevention and the problems related to the neglect of elderly parents. In 1996, the amendments to the Women's Charter provided channels for elderly parents to exercise legal action if they were victims of physical, mental or psychological abuse. In most urban societies, family breakdown will become a critical social problem and this will have consequences on care and support for the elderly. Another enlightened policy covering medical care for the terminally ill was put in place in 1996. More specifically, under the Advanced Medical Directive Act, persons who have been medically certified to be brain dead can now under their earlier directives be relieved of medical life support. Such a progressive and futuristic policy would reduce unnecessary suffering to both the terminally ill older persons and their families.

A national policy on ageing in Singapore has taken shape after a number of successive policy reviews. Two characteristics in the policy formulation process have been noted. First, the various committees have the benefit of representation from various sectors. This has the advantage of receiving diverse inputs and making implementable decisions. Historically, cross-sectored representation has worked well in the local context and it is a standard feature in the Singapore government's problem-solving approach. Second, the committees were given much publicity. Public awareness of the issues was heightened especially when controversial recommendations were made. The enhanced discussion on policy changes by the public sees an increasing emphasis on the social care of older persons in Singapore. Public inputs thus become an important consideration in the committees' deliberations.

The most recent Inter-ministerial Committee on the Ageing Population formed in 1998 has revisited many of the earlier recommendations of various committees on ageing matters and is expected to propose a more co-ordinated and comprehensive plan to deal with challenging issues of Singapore's ageing population in the 21st century.

In terms of funding policies for elderly services (as well as services for the general population) the state applies the "co-payment" principle as far as possible. The individual consumer/his family is expected to pay a portion of the charges while the government subsidises the rest. This applies to the Medisave scheme, which is a compulsory medical savings scheme under the rubric of the Central Provident Fund, the Singapore-style social security system. An individual may use his Medisave for his own or his parent's hospitalisation expenses (including expenses incurred at a hospice).

A sliding scale of charges is imposed based on household income at community-based services such as home nursing, day care and rehabilitation services. Recipients of public assistance, a financial scheme targeted towards the destitute/frail/disabled elderly and disbursed by the Ministry of Community Development, are entitled to free medical service at the government polyclinics. All Singaporeans above age 60 are entitled to a subsidy of 50% of the fees charged at polyclinics.

A new strategy, which is being considered for implementation, is a special insurance scheme that provides coverage against severe disability, especially in old age. The rationale behind this type of scheme is that in the productive years, one should be able to put aside some savings for old age disability.

The rest of this article discusses the system of community-based long-term care delivery for the elderly Singaporean population, case management, and lastly the major issues and challenges. It may interest the reader to note that less than 2% of Singaporean elderly live in institutions. Community-based long-term care provides supportive services to the family and can help the elderly to be cared for within their homes or through day-care facilities in the neighbourhood. The services can be organised by voluntary organisations and co-operatives, which are provided with financial grants by the government on the basis of programme funding and donations from the families and the community. These voluntary organisations will mobilise residents to volunteer their services. In the community it is possible to enlist the help of women and retirees to man the services together with a pool of paid healthcare workers. Such a service delivery approach can encourage citizen participation and promote a sense of community bonding and ownership. However, it must be stated that the delivery of community-based services for long-term care faces some difficulties. It is not easy to sustain the efforts of the volunteers, as they may not be interested to commit themselves to serve the elderly for a long period. Staff turnover in voluntary organisations can be high as their terms and conditions of services are not attractive and market-driven. Government grants are at times inadequate to meet cost increases in the care of the elderly and the use of these grants can sometimes be inflexible. The management of voluntary organisations may change their mission and this will mean that services could be curtailed. In spite of the aforementioned limitations, community-based organisations with the full support of volunteers, community leaders and government can be effective avenues to deliver personalised services to the elderly who require long term care.

Community-based long-term care delivery

"At the heart of the social policy regarding elderly people lies the question of the relationship between the informal and formal worlds of care."[7] Community care has received attention in the United Kingdom since the 1981 White Paper *Growing Older,* and reinforced by the Audit Commission Report in 1986 called *Making Community Care a Reality.*[8] "Community-based long-term care is a relatively recent phenomenon in the United States.... The new dimension of this approach is the *community-based* aspect which attempts to maintain frail elders at home. This differentiates it from the traditional approach which utilises nursing homes to provide long-term care for the elderly."[9] In their conceptualisation of community-based long-term care, the term "kinstitution", which was coined by Schatzman, is found to be apt. "A kinstitution is a hybrid, symbiotic relationship consisting of familial and formal organisational structures that serve to meet the needs of a particular individual or group."[10]

From this brief introduction, it clear that the trend towards community-based long-term care is not only feasible especially in an ageing society, but also perhaps the preferred choice of the elderly themselves.

Who are the providers of community-based long-term (or continual) care? Clearly, the service providers may be located in the formal or informal sector, or both. The interweaving of both sources of care to suit the needs of individual clients/families is its forte.

In order to avoid problems of duplication, fragmentation and frustration from the consumers, the strategy of case management has been adopted in some countries. In some discussions, arguments in favour of community-based long-term care (in comparison to institutionalisation) have added cost-effectiveness. This would vary from nation to nation, community to community, depending on the cost of labour and availability of the type of skilled expertise needed. There is immense intangible benefit in involving the community, in the form of friends, neighbours,

---

[7] See D. Gordon and S. Donald, *Community Social Work, Older People and Informal Care: A Romantic Illusion?* (Aldershot: Avebury, 1993), p. 1.
[8] Refer to M. Richards, *Community Care for Older People: Rights, Remedies and Finances* (Bristol: Jordans, 1996), pp. 14–15.
[9] A. Pelham and W. Clark, (eds.) *Managing Home Care for the Elderly* (New York: Springer Publishing, 1986), p. 1.
[10] The concept of "kinstitution" was coined by Schatzman and cited in *ibid.,* p. 6.

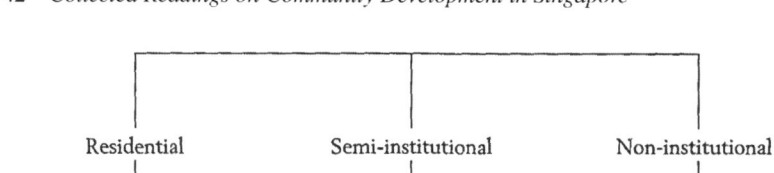

```
                    ┌──────────────────────┼──────────────────────┐
                Residential          Semi-institutional      Non-institutional
                    ↓                      ↓                      ↓
```
1) Nursing Homes   1) Day Care Centres   1) Doorstep services
   (private and VWOs)   & Rehabilitation Centres 2) Befriending/Counselling
2) Hospices   2) Social Centres
3) Community Hospitals   3) Day Activity Centres   3) Socio-recreational
4) Sheltered Homes

Figure 1. Continual care services and programmes in Singapore

schools, religious and ethnic institutions. The spin-off could be a spirit of caring and sharing as a process of community development, which is in itself immeasurable. If it leads to intergenerational cohesion, the whole society stands to gain in the long run.

Figure 1 provides a descriptive summary of the range of long-term services, which are currently being provided in Singapore, mainly by voluntary welfare organisations. The private sector plays a role in the delivery of nursing home facilities. The Ministry of Community Development (MCD) and Ministry of Health support the efforts of VWOs and act as a mechanism of quality management. The homes have to abide by the guidelines stipulated by the ministries. These guidelines are reviewed from time to time. If a particular home does not practise any of these requirements, it may be forced to terminate its operations. There is a set of guidelines for non-residential community-based services for the elderly, which are strongly recommended but not mandatory.[11] In addition to the two ministries, a third statutory body, the National Council of Social Service, plays a co-ordinating role among non-government welfare organisations and helps to represent their views to the government. Since the focus of this article is on community-based services, the ensuing discussion will focus on the semi-institutional and non-institutional services.

---

[11] *Because We Care: Guidelines for Community-based Services for Elderly* (Singapore: Ministry of Community Development, 1998).

Semi-institutional services and programmes

In 1998, there were 20 Day Care and Rehabilitation Centres. They are distributed across the island and are operated by a variety of government and non-government organisations. Six of them are Senior Citizens' Health Care Centres that offer both social and health care programmes especially for newly-discharged patients from hospitals. They play a crucial role in the smooth transition of the elderly from acute care to home care. Family caregivers are given informal training at these centres. Other centres are operated by secular and religious organisations e.g., Wan Qing Lodge and Adventist Church. There are some Day Centres that are located within the premises of residential homes, thus providing a dual function for the latter as well as a source of income generation. Research has shown that day care centres help to relieve the stress of family caregivers, in the form of respite care, and ensure the safety of the elderly especially if the rest of the family members are not at home during the day. It has been projected that there will be an increasing need for more day care centres for the elderly in future. An interesting experiment is being carried out in the form of 3-in-1 Centres wherein day care for three age groups is co-located within one vicinity i.e. young children, school-going children and elderly. Intergenerational programmes such as celebration of festivals, teaching of handicrafts and community singing inculcate a greater sense of affiliation between the generations.

In addition to the above, there are three day care centres which specialise in the care of the elderly suffering from senile dementia. There are 11 Social Day centres that cater mainly to the relational and social needs of elderly citizens. They are neighbourhood hubs characterised by informality and greater self-management by the senior citizens. These centres are mostly located within Family Service centres, and require minimal funds and manpower. Volunteers, including robust elderly, provide the main backbone of the programme.

Day activity centres (DACs) are different from the above services in that they meet the needs of low-income elderly, who live alone in government flats. The National Survey of Senior Citizens[12] showed that about

---

[12] *National Survey of Senior Citizens in Singapore 1995* (Singapore: Singapore National Press, 1996), p. 15.

8.3% of non-institutionalised elderly aged 55 and above lived alone or with spouse only. Among these, approximately 10,000 belong to the low-income category — a visible group needing community support and companionship. The DACs are linked to a joint project between the MCD and the Housing Development Board (HDB), which is the statutory board in charge of the public housing programme. Under the government upgrading scheme for HDB flats, the low income, one-room rental flats have been upgraded at no cost to the tenants. Installation of elderly-friendly facilities such as non-slip tiles in the bathroom, handle bars and pedestal toilets, and an alarm system which alerts neighbours and the DAC nearby of an emergency, comprise the main features of this Congregate Housing project which has been expanded to more than 13 blocks. A reputable voluntary welfare organisation has been selected by the MCD to run the DAC, which is manned by a lean staff and volunteers. The DAC represents to these poor and lonely elderly a refuge for social interaction and a shoulder to depend on in times of crisis. In sum, the day care and rehabilitation centres offer comprehensive services for the senior citizens living with their family members while the DACs offer social and emergency services for the poor elderly living alone.

Non-institutional services

In the realm of home-care services, or door-step programmes, there is a wide range of services for vulnerable/frail older people. These include home help such as meal delivery, household chores, escort to polyclinics and hospitals; home nursing and home medical care; and lastly, befriending services. The organisations concerned sometimes draw geographical boundaries due to limited resources, both financial and manpower.

There are community-based services that are located in the VWO, as opposed to the door-step concept. These include hotline (telephone) counselling, casework and counselling (face-to-face), carer support groups and weekly lunches prepared by volunteers. There are two key organisations, namely the Singapore Action Group of Elders (SAGE) and the Tsao Foundation that specialise in the delivery of gerontological and geriatric services. SAGE not only provides direct services such as hotline and counselling, but also has a Centre for the Study of Ageing Research, which is of paramount importance in charting the changing profiles and needs of successive cohorts of elderly in a fast-changing society such as Singapore. Given that Singapore is a multi-racial society, not only changing profiles but also ethnic permutations need to be tracked for the systematic planning of services, both health and social. The Tsao Foundation, in contrast, focuses on the delivery of medical services to low-income elderly. It also runs an acupuncture clinic. Voluntary bodies provide free Chinese medical treatment e.g., the Realm of Tranquility renders free medical treatment at its mobile clinic, which is staffed by volunteer doctors.

Lastly, socio-recreational community-based programmes form an integral part of the repertoire of elderly services. While the "old old" tend to be frail and vulnerable due to ageing processes, the "young old" are usually active and desire to remain productive members of society. The Retired and Senior Volunteer Programme (RSVP) provides an avenue for professional and educated retired senior citizens. For the major proportion of the elderly, Senior Citizens' Clubs (SCCs), which are scattered throughout the island and totalled 384 in 1998, have been established by the People's Association. Programmes organised by the SCCs include tours to Malaysia, dancing, singing, exercise classes such as tai chi and qigong. These clubs are located by and large in the community centres, which are multi-purpose secular centres catering to the general Singaporean population, regardless of age, ethnicity or religion. The SCCs play a very active part in the celebrations for Senior Citizens Week, held in November every year. Competitions are held in various activities between the clubs throughout the year, e.g. gate ball and karaoke. SAGE has an ongoing programme of lifelong learning in Chinese calligraphy and other local handicrafts. There are other organisations conducting training for the middle-aged and elderly in computer skills, training for family caregivers by the Tsao Foundation and enrichment skills by the Soka Association. However, it is the view of the authors that more needs to be done in this area in view of the fact that future cohorts of Singaporean elderly will be better educated and will possess greater savings.

The Inter-ministerial Committee has offered some suggestions for consideration by policy-makers. The first is the idea of Golden Manpower

Centres (GMCs) at Community Development Councils. "GMCs will work with the Ministry of Manpower's Career Centres and provide information, training and job placement of older workers, particularly the lower educated ones. The GMCs will source for jobs as well as voluntary work in the community."[13] It is hoped that the GMCs will rectify the present relatively low rate of labour force participation of older workers. In 1997, the labour force participation for the age group 55–64 years was 52%, 64%, 67% and 43% in Hong Kong, Korea, Japan and Singapore respectively.[14] In addition, it is hoped that the volunteer participation rate for senior citizens can be increased.

The second suggestion that is significant is for the establishment of Multi-Service Centres across the island. These are conceptualised as centralised locations for the integration of health, social and other community-based services. If implemented, they would contribute towards integrating the array of services available but are not easily accessible for our elderly and their families.

In conclusion to this section, it can be said that the recent exercise of the six workgroups of the Inter-ministerial Committee on the Ageing Population has been fruitful in galvanising feedback from various sectors of the population, and has initiated the crafting of a national strategy for dealing with the challenges of an ageing society in the coming decades. The Inter-ministerial Committee is a standing committee that will oversee the implementation of the resulting recommendations. It will also serve as a coordinating body between the relevant ministries, thus enhancing a system of integrated service delivery.

Case management

The National Council of Social Service has launched a two-year pilot project in May 1998 as an experiment in the case management approach through the Tsao Foundation and SAGE. By definition, "Case Management is a new service which involves the assessment of an elderly person's

---

[13] *Report of the Inter-ministerial Committee on the Ageing Population*, p. 55.
[14] Statistics from the International Labour Organisation Yearbook of Statistics 1998 cited in *ibid.*, p. 54.

health, psychological and social needs and maximisation of services to attain optimal and most cost-effective care of the elderly and their caregivers to prevent unnecessary institutionalisation."[15] This strategy of service delivery is being examined in order to mitigate the problems of an uneven distribution of services and fragmentation in service delivery. The aim is to develop viable models of case management to suit the Singapore context.

As awareness levels of services are relatively low (as evident from the 1995 National Survey of Senior Citizens) coupled with the fact that services are often dispersed and fragmented, the case management concept is attractive in Singapore's context. However, case management service is costly and there is clearly a need to target this service only for those who need it most i.e. the poorly-educated senior citizens without families or the frail senior citizens with multiple needs and problems.

In terms of eligibility criteria, frail elderly, 60 years and older, regardless of gender or ethnicity, who require three or more community-based services are eligible. However, the gross household income must not exceed S$2,000 per month. The SAGE project restricts applicants to the central geographical region and Tsao Foundation's project draws its parameters around the western region. At present, the expenses of the pilot project are borne by the National Council of Social Service including the salaries of the staff.

An interview with the social worker in charge of the case management service at SAGE revealed that they offer more than 15 different types of services. The initial holistic assessment is very thorough, covering demographic, family, medical, financial and psychosocial dimensions. Most of their referrals at present come from a government hospital in the central region. Other sources include family service centres and voluntary welfare organisations. The staff includes two professionals and one administrative support officer. They are using the brokerage model, whereby no direct service is rendered but the case manager taps the community-based services and co-ordinates them for the client's benefit. Presently, they have 76 ongoing cases. During this two-year period the service is provided free of charge. She cited problems such as shortage and lack of training of

---

[15] See Singapore Action Group of Elders Counselling Centre pamphlet on Case Management Service, 1998.

volunteers, pressure of time when services have to be arranged prior to a client's hospital discharge, monitoring of quality and efficiency of services, and lastly difficulties in meeting dietary preferences (especially in minority groups). Much time is spent building rapport with family members (where relevant) since a family-oriented approach is applied.

While the case management team at SAGE consists of social workers, the team at the Tsao Foundation consists of a psychologist and a retired nurse. The latter are also linked to a home medical team under the Hua Mei Mobile Clinic, which facilitates the provision of immediate medical care and guidance where necessary. The SAGE team relies on doctors from the hospital of referral as well as nurses from the Home Nursing Foundation for the medical data. At the end of the pilot project, the National Council of Social Science would conduct an evaluation to determine the feasibility of continuation and selection of the appropriate model.

Like Hong Kong, Singapore's relatively small geographical area reduces travelling time in the provision of services. To conclude this section, it may be asked whether community-based long-term care is a cost-effective alternative in meeting the needs of older people?

The jury is still out on this question. Secondly, in the past the argument had been put forward that increasing the community care support might reduce the caregiving efforts of immediate and extended family members. This does not appear to be the case, as was seen in the Kent Community Care scheme. "The community care scheme did not appear to have any negative effects on the availability of informal care networks; indeed it appeared that care-givers were if anything less likely to reduce their support when the scheme was involved."[16]

Issues and challenges

This section discusses six major issues and challenges facing policy-makers and service providers regarding continual or long-term care for older persons in Singapore.

---

[16] See D. Challies and B. Davies, *Case Management in Community Care: An evaluated experiment in the home care of the elderly* (Aldershot: Gower Publishing, 1986), p. 165.

1. Cost issues

The cost issues will be the main concern to policy-makers. The cost is very likely to be prohibitive and will create serious strains on the government and the voluntary sectors. Both manpower and facilities would be required and these means that public expenses will have to be incurred and the public would have to bear the burdens of higher taxation to maintain the services. Continual care in the form of institutional provisions such as community hospitals, nursing homes, homes for elderly and hospice centres are going be costly to run and could be impersonal. At the same time, more elderly persons would be relocated from their community to be placed in these institutions. The dramatic change of environment, both physical and social, would take a heavy toll on the older individual.

The dilemma many policy-makers face is the pressing demand for setting up more and more institutional care programmes. How can this demand be mediated and met in the most cost-effective way? A balance between institutional and community-based long-term care services has to be achieved based upon projections of future needs (both health care and social) of the elderly (See Table 2).

Table 2. Projected need for elderly health services, year 2000 to year 2030

Types of Services	Planning Ratio	1997	2000	2010	2020	2030
Day Rehabilitation and Day Care Places*	3.5 places per 1,000 elderly	761 (701)	821 [820]	1,100	1,900	2,800
Home Medical Care Service	5 elderly needing 1 visit per month per 1,000 elderly	1,087 (750)	1,173 [825]	1,600	2,700	4,000
Home Nursing Service	15 elderly needing 2 visits per month per 1,000 elderly	6,522 (5,000)	7,035 [5,500]	9,400	15,900	24,000
Home Help Service	4 elderly needing daily visits	870 (255)	938 [300]	1,250	2,120	3,200

Note: ( ) = Availability in 1997
[ ] = Estimated availability in year 2000
*Including places for dementia patients

Source: *Report of the Inter-ministerial Committee on Health-Care for the Elderly* (Singapore: Ministry of Health, 1999).

Overall, the cost is likely to be exorbitant and will create serious strains on the government and voluntary sectors. Continual care in the form of institutional provisions such as community hospitals, nursing homes, sheltered homes and hospice centres would place a burden on the government that in turn would lead to higher taxation on the public. At the same time, elderly persons would be relocated from their communities, leading to problems of re-orientation. The path that Singapore intends to take is to examine how more preventive and community-based programmes can be organised and delivered effectively in an integrated manner. Such an emphasis will make care services accessible and enable ageing-in-place for the elderly with concomitant community mobilisation. It is believed that such a strategy will make the programmes more cost-effective and help the elderly and their families to remain independent.

2. *Manpower issues*

Singapore, in general, has a shortage of trained nurses, occupational therapists and physiotherapists. A large proportion of staff aides at residential institutions consist of foreign workers. This leads to language barriers and communication breakdown. Homes and day care centres have to train these staff in the area of dialects, attitudes and skills in working with older people, in particular the frail and terminally ill. An area which is likely to demand more attention in future, is the training of family caregivers and volunteers to increase their effectiveness.

3. *Implementation of recommendations of the Inter-ministerial Committee Report*

The numerous suggestions that have been raised in the Inter-ministerial Committee Report would have to be systematically examined and, if feasible, implemented without delay. Issues of funding, manpower recruitment and training, facilities, management and equitable geographical distribution for e.g. Multi-Service Centres[17] and effective monitoring in the initial period are but some of the challenges ahead. The urgent need

---

[17] See *Report of the Inter-ministerial Committee on Health Care for the Elderly* (Singapore: Ministry of Health, 1999), p. 9.

for a strong co-ordinating body that would oversee the smooth delivery of integrated services has been reiterated by many sectors. The Inter-ministerial Committee Standing Committee may need to consider if it is feasible for it to effectively execute this role. An alternative would be the setting up of a unit with full-time staff (under the auspices of the MCD) to ensure that the various plans proposed are executed with minimum gaps and wastage of resources. One advantage is that Singapore has a stable economic and political climate, a powerful factor in ensuring continuity of strategies and programmes.

4. *Need for more innovative elderly services suited to the local context*

As part of the community-based long-term care effort, the promotion of community care co-operatives has been seriously discussed. The National Trade Union Congress (NTUC) has embarked on its first Eldercare Co-operative. As conceived, these co-operatives would provide a range of services at affordable rates, including home help, meal service, transport and escort service, employment placement and day care. Members of the co-operatives would be eligible for rebates if they wish to use the services. This whole service approach will be community based and will have the participation of families who need the support, as well as interested residents. There will be ownership of such set-ups and they are likely to flourish. The setting up of community care co-operatives will change the mindset that institutional care is a sound solution to long-term care of the elderly. Community care co-operatives will bring more dignity to the care of the aged and will involve the community in solving the problem of our elderly.

Community mobilisation of retirees, housewives, and even students looking for part-time employment could provide the much-needed manpower. For transport, voluntary organisations and residents could form a transport pool to meet the needs of the elderly who require transport and companionship for the purpose of follow-up medical treatment. A well-managed database could match needs of residents in the vicinity with organisations and suppliers of skills or equipment. Similarly, day care and employment placements could be arranged. The co-operatives can be viable; as volunteers and some paid staff will manage them on a not-for-profit principle. The notion of the common ownership of the co-operative by the residents and for the residents will be the key to the success of such co-operatives.

Other innovative ideas, which have to be expanded, are telephone contact, community kitchens manned by ethnic self-help community organisations, and carer support groups as well as elderly self-help groups. As for home care and help and meal services, these could be provided for by mobilising housewives who are looking for part-time employment. They could be trained to acquire simple nursing aid and bedside nursing skills. They can also help to run the community kitchens. Under the supervision of a community nurse, the housewives could look after the elderly who require home help and care within the neighborhood. Such an arrangement will prevent the need for institutional care.

In the area of employment placement, the community care co-operatives can maintain a data base to match those requiring employment to those employers needing workers. At the same time, elderly who have various households in need of handyman service. The co-operatives can levy an administrative charge for the matching service provided.

5. *Leadership and management issues*

Leaders and managers with vision and creativity need to be nurtured. Community-based programmes require problem-solving in creative and cost-effective ways. This will be a major challenge to voluntary welfare bodies, because demands are in most arenas higher than the resource supply. The spirit of voluntarism in Singapore is relatively low as compared to many western countries. Less than 10% of our population is involved in voluntary activities. It will be necessary to recruit more volunteers to man the community-based programmes. The healthy young-old would be a potential target group to involve, bearing in mind their ability to empathise with problems of old age.

6. *Need for more research and data on future needs of elderly cohorts*

Both quantitative and qualitative data are needed to assist the planning for appropriate services and programmes for the future decades. Thus far, the emphasis has been on the health and financial needs. However, social care has also to be factored in order that a comprehensive plan is put in place for the future. This challenge is indeed daunting because social needs are more difficult to project. The complexity arises from the fact that social care is shared between formal and informal carers. Nevertheless, with more sophisticated computer technologies and estimates based on community studies, such projections should be possible.

Conclusion

In sum, this article has examined the need for policy-makers to review a more cost-effective approach in the delivery of services and suggest the feasibility of developing community-based services and programmes for the long-term care of the elderly in Singapore. Policy-makers in the field of health care will face increasing pressure to address the high cost for the long-term care of the elderly. There will be various competing demands between the young and the elderly and policy-makers have to mediate and find realistic solutions to cater to these groups. Policies promoting community-based services constitute an approach to deal with families requiring long-term care for their elderly.

This article has also highlighted the role played by the Inter-ministerial Committee on the Ageing Population to seek multi-sectoral feedback and suggestions for policy development and implementation. The National Council of Social Service is piloting the case management service, following which the model suited for Singapore will be decided upon. Since the ageing challenge affects almost every sector of the society, the government has decided on a holistic response involving several ministries, voluntary welfare organisations, the private sector and ageing families as well.

Since Singapore is not a welfare state, the public is urged to look upon ageing as a personal responsibility, albeit shared with their immediate families. The Asian cultural ethos of communal reciprocity as a public good is harnessed as a way of positive response to the societal challenge of an ageing society. Singapore is adopting a tripartite approach, which involves the government, the community mainly through the voluntary sector, and the family to meet the needs of the long term care of the elderly. This reinforces common ownership for meeting the needs of the elderly.

Chapter 4

Organization and delivery of long-term care in Singapore: Present issues and future challenges*

Kalyani K. Mehta[†] and S. Vasoo[‡]

---

*From Mehta, K. K., & Vasoo, S. (2001). Organization and delivery of long-term care in Singapore: Present issues and future challenges. *Journal of Aging & Social Policy*, *13*(2/3), 185–201. Reprinted by permission of the publisher (Taylor & Francis Ltd, http://www.tandfonline.com).

The article provides an overview of the long-term care services available for the elderly followed by a discussion of the policy issues put forward by the Inter-Ministerial Committee (IMC) on Ageing Population.

[†]Dr. Kalyani K. Mehta is Associate Professor, Department of Social Work and Psychology, National University of Singapore. She has done research on elderly services and policies for the past 10 years, has published articles in international and regional journals, and presented conference papers in the United States, China, Australia, and South East Asia. As a member of the National Committee on the Aged as well as a consultant to the United Nations Economic and Social Commission for Asia and the Pacific (ESCAP), Dr. Mehta has recommended policies and services for the improved quality of life of older persons. Her edited volume, *Untapped Resources: Women in Aging Societies Across Asia* (1997), added greatly to the literature on the status and roles of older women in aging societies. Her research interests include family caregiving, religion and aging, widowhood, remarriage, and cross-cultural patterns of aging.

Summary

This paper focuses on the Singaporean model of long-term care for older people. With only about 2% of the older population living in institutions, the mainstay of long-term care is community care. The reader is provided an overview of the Singaporean services, including case management, followed by a discussion of the current issues and future challenges. In keeping with the prospect of a rapidly aging population profile, the Singapore government plays a leading role in framing policy and planning for future needs of this sector of the population. [Article copies available for a fee from The Haworth Document Delivery Service: 1-800-HAWORTH. E-mail address: <getinfo@haworthpressinc.com> Website: <http://www.HaworthPress.com> © 2001 by The Haworth Press, Inc. All rights reserved.]

Keywords: Aging policy, long-term care, Singapore

The need for care

The demographic revolution of population aging that was well advanced in most developed countries by the end of the 20th century is evident in Asia, too. After Japan, Singapore is the fastest aging nation in the Asia Pacific region, and in recognition of the significance of this development,

---

[‡] Dr. S. Vasoo is Associate Professor, Department of Social Work and Psychology, National University of Singapore. He is actively involved as an advisor to many social and community organizations, including NGOs of senior citizens. He is a member of the Inter-Ministerial Committee on Ageing and has chaired its Committee on Social Integration of the Elderly. He studies voluntary action of the elderly.

Both authors can be contacted at the National University of Singapore, 10 Kent Ridge Crescent, Singapore 119260 (Dr. Kalyani Mehta's E-mail: swkkkm@nus.edu.sg; Dr. S. Vasoo's E-mail: swkvasoo@nus.edu.sg).

[Haworth co-indexing entry note]: "Organization and Delivery of Long-Term Care in Singapore: Present Issues and Future Challenges." Mehta, Kalyani K., and S. Vasoo. Co-published simultaneously in *Journal of Aging & Social Policy* (The Haworth Press, Inc.) Vol. 13, No. 2/3, 2001, pp. 185–201; and: *Long-Term Care in the 21st Century: Perspectives from Around the Asia-Pacific Rim* (ed: Iris Chi, Kalyani K. Mehta, and Anna L. Howe) The Haworth Press, Inc., 2001, pp. 185–201. Single or multiple copies of this article are available for a fee from The Haworth Document Delivery Service [1-800-HAWORTH, 9:00 a.m.–5:00 p.m. (EST). E-mail address: getinfo@haworthpressinc.com].

an Inter-Ministerial Committee (IMC) on Health Care and another on the Aging Population were convened by the Singapore Government in 1997 and 1998, respectively. The IMCs released two reports on their deliberations in 1999, and these reports both review the need for care and preview the challenges that are likely to be forthcoming in the early years of the 21st century.

As an island state with a total resident population of just over 3.5 million in 2000, the impact of the demographic processes of population aging is highly visible in Singapore. Life expectancy at birth is already high, at 75 years for males and nearly 80 years for females, and these figures are expected to rise further. The demographic data given in Table 1 show that the proportion of the population aged 65 and over will almost double from 7.3% in 1999 to 13.1% in 2020, and by 2030, close to one in every five Singaporeans will be aged 65 and over. Within this rapidly aging demographic profile, the increase of those in late life, above 75 years, is even more conspicuous.

The doubling of the proportion aged 65 and over in Singapore will occur in a far shorter time, less than 25 years, compared to up to 150 years in the already older countries of western Europe, and around 80 years in the developed Pacific Rim countries of North America, Australia, and New Zealand, which are now reaching the 14% mark (ESCAP, 1996). The speed of this demographic transition has major implications not only for health and social services but for other sectors of society as well, and the planning of long-term care for the elderly population requires consideration of both the development of formal services and the changing roles of families in informal care.

Table 1. Characteristics of aged population, Singapore, 1999–2030

Characteristic	1999	2000	2020	2030
Aged 65+ (,000)	235	312	529	796
Proportion of total population aged 65 and over	7.3	8.4	13.1	18.9
Median Age (Yrs)	33.4	36.9	39.3	41.2
Dependency Ratio Total	42.0	38.7	44.9	56.4
Young (0–14 years)	31.7	27.1	25.9	26.9
Old (65+ years)	10.4	11.6	19.0	29.5

Source: Singapore Department of Statistics, cited in the Inter-Ministerial Report, 1999: 29.

Changing family structures and roles

The IMC has noted that one key concern is that the sheer rise in the numbers and proportion of older persons could potentially put stress on families and eldercare services (IMC Report, 1999b). As in other Asian countries, the family in Singapore has been providing the major part of care and support for elderly family members (Knodel & Debavalya, 1997). Although there are no strong data to show that families are shirking their filial responsibilities, several social and demographic changes mitigate against the continuity of family care as the primary form of eldercare in Singapore.

These trends take on added importance in the context of the present paradigm of eldercare in Singapore, which is a partnership among the government, the community, and the family (Mehta, 2000). In tandem with the "Many Helping Hands" policy of the Ministry of Community Development, the community and the government are expected to lend a hand to aging families in order to reduce the stress of caregiving for older members. Reiterating the government's long-standing position at the opening of a conference on choices in financing health care and old age security, convened under the auspices of the World Bank in Singapore in 1997, the Minister for Health noted that "the family setting is still the best approach; it provides the elderly with the warmth and companionship of family members and a level of emotional support which cannot be found elsewhere" (Prescott, 1998).

In line with this partnership approach, the government encourages voluntary welfare organizations (VWOs) in their efforts to offer quality long-term care in the community through provision of financial and other forms of support. These services and programs are discussed in detail below, but it is becoming apparent to many in government, in VWOs, and in the community at large that with rising numbers of older Singaporeans, non-family partners will be required to play bigger roles over the next few decades.

Declining mortality and low fertility rates mean that the aged are being recognized as a more integral part of Singaporean society. As in Japan, the Singapore government recognizes that a large proportion of citizens is fast approaching the age of retirement, and acknowledges the implications of aging for policy-making and government expenditures. There is a concern to maintain the health and vitality of the elderly as their life spans increase, so that the older population does not become an unduly heavy financial and social burden on the society. Perhaps even more so than in Japan, the Singapore government sees a viable family structure that is able to provide love, care, and support for its elderly members as crucial, and indeed the ideal, if the formal support system for the elderly is to be kept to a minimum.

At the same time, and notwithstanding a continuing Confucian value system, the traditional caregivers of the family, and more specifically female relatives, are coming under increasing pressures from modernization and urbanization. These changes include a shift to dual-income nuclear families, living apart from older generations, increasing levels of education and high rates of participation in the formal workforce for women, more young Singaporeans working and living abroad, more single elderly among the generation for whom family formation was interrupted by World War II, and changing social values. Two demographic indicators point to the extent of these intergenerational changes.

First, age-specific sex ratios provide an indicator of need for health care services arising from the interaction of advancing age, gender differences in chronic diseases, and social support from spouses. In the 1990 census, men constituted 47% of the aged population, but the sex ratio dropped from 97 males per 100 females at age 60 to 69 years, to 80 in the 70–79 age group, and only 60 at 80 years and above. Since women generally outlive men and mortality rates are falling faster among females than males, the net result is a growing sex imbalance, especially with increasing age (Shantakumar 1994,1995). The health problems of the elderly consequently reflect the conditions and needs of a larger proportion of older women, and as women generally use health services more often than men, differential demand will be increasingly pronounced in future. The lower sex ratio with increasing age does not of itself necessarily lead to a higher demand for social services, as family structure and marital status come into play. Again in the 1990 census, 29% of the aged population were widowed, but the figure was 54% for aged women compared to about 19% for aged men.

Second, the ratio of the elderly to the working-age population, the old age dependency ratio, is projected to increase from around 10 currently to 30 by 2030. The need for more old people to be supported by a proportionately smaller working population has major implications for labor supply and financial security, and for the provision of social services, especially health care, as alternatives or adjuncts to family care (Teo, 1994). Population movements due to changes in living arrangements and employment patterns can exacerbate the need for external assistance (Ministry of Health, 1984).

Vulnerable groups

Given the differentials in aging patterns, not all older persons require continual care. However, those in the "old old" and "very old" categories are generally more likely to need constant supervision, social and emotional support as well as instrumental help. Focusing on these categories as the potential target groups for care services, population projections show that the 75-and-over age group will increase even faster than the 60–75 years age group (Cheung, 1993). This older group is at risk of needing care and attention, and as more family resources will have to be drawn into attending to the social and physical requirements of very old relatives, some families are likely to face considerable stress in providing care to the sick and disabled.

Another vulnerable category are aged couples living on their own, who have increased from 9% of households with persons aged 60 years and above in 1990 to 15% in 1997. Poor older people living alone are also identified as being at risk, and the aging process has become especially apparent in housing estates that were constructed in the 1960s. There are increasing numbers of older senior citizens living in these estates, and it is urgent that community groups and organizations begin to plan the establishment of more community-based programs such as day care, meals programs, home-help service and domiciliary nursing care, and crisis-response services. In taking a proactive approach to initiate a network of services in older housing estates, it will be possible to provide support for families with vulnerable aged relatives and minimize disruptions to the social and economic lives of the families.

Services provided by the social welfare system

Those involved in developing community-based services in Singapore can draw on several decades of experience in the United Kingdom and in the United States and other countries that have sought to expand community care as an alternative to institutional care (Challis & Davies, 1986; Gordon & Donald, 1993). As well as recognising that the trend towards community-based long-term care is not only feasible but also the preferred choice of the elderly themselves, as in other countries, Singapore is starting from a very different position. With only some 2% of its elderly living in institutions at present, Singapore is well-placed to embark on the development of community care as the mainstay of long-term care rather than as an alternative to the kind of large, long-established, and costly institutional care sectors that most other countries are seeking to counter.

The paradigm of elder care in Singapore has been evolving for some time now and as with other areas of health and social services, a distinctive Singapore model has emerged. Three main features of this model are the interweaving of informal and formal care to suit the needs of individual clients and their families; the support of a diversity of VWOs to provide a range of services and develop innovative projects in service delivery, including case management; and the attention given to improving health and well-being among vulnerable groups with a view to reducing future needs for long-term care services. The range of services now available is summarized in Table 2, which shows the different levels of care provided by sub-systems of home-based, community-based, and residential services. The following account focuses on community care, detailing the non-institutional services delivered to the home and semi-institutional services based in the community.

Table 2. Long-term care services and programs in Singapore

Community Care		Institutional Care
Home-Based (Non-Institutional)	**Community-Based (Semi-Institutional)**	**Residential Services**
1. Socio-recreational	1. Day activity centres	1. Sheltered homes
2. Befriending/counselling	2. Social Centres	2. Hospices
3. "Doorstep" services delivered in the home	3. Day Care Centres and Rehabilitation Centres	3. Nursing Homes (private & VWOs)
		4. Community Hospitals

Who are the providers of community-based long-term care?

The main providers are voluntary welfare organisations (VWOs), with the private sector playing a role only in the delivery of nursing home care. As of January 2000, there were 24 private sector nursing homes compared to VWO provision of 23 nursing homes, three hospices, and one residential facility for dementia patients. In addition, there were four community hospitals and two hospitals for the chronically sick.

The Ministry of Community Development and Sports and the Ministry of Health support the efforts of VWOs and administer mechanisms for quality management. As well as mandatory guidelines for nursing homes, the Ministry of Community Development and Sports has issued a set of guidelines for community-based services for the elderly. The guidelines are strongly recommended but not mandatory (Ministry of Community Development, 1998). A third statutory body, the National Council of Social Service, plays a coordinating role among non-government welfare organizations and helps in representing their views to the government.

Day care and home modification services

In 1998, there were 20 day care and rehabilitation centers distributed across the island and operated by a variety of government and non-government organizations. Six are Senior Citizens' Health Care Centres that offer both social and health care programs especially for patients newly discharged from acute hospitals. These services play a crucial role in the smooth transition of elderly from acute care to home care. Family caregivers are given informal training at these centers. Three day care centers specialize in the care of elderly suffering from dementia.

Other day centers are operated by secular and religious organizations, for example, the Wan Qing Lodge and the Adventist Church. Some day centers are located within the premises of residential homes, thus providing a dual function for the latter as well as a source of income generation. Day care centers have been found to help relieve the stress of family caregivers by providing respite care and ensuring the safety of the elderly, especially if other family members are not at home during the day (Kua, 1987).

In planning to meet the projected increase in need for day care centers, there has been some experimentation in different forms of provision. One such experiment takes the form of 3-in-1 centers, where day care for three age groups is located within one vicinity. Bringing young children, school-age children, and elderly together in intergenerational programs such as the celebration of festivals, teaching of handicrafts, and community singing inculcates a greater sense of affiliation between the generations.

There are 11 social day centers that cater mainly to the relational and social needs of elderly citizens. These centers are neighborhood hubs characterized by informality and self-management by the senior citizens. Most are located within Family Service Centres and require minimal funds and manpower because volunteers, including robust young elderly, are the backbone of these programs.

Day activity centers are different again in that they meet the needs of low-income elderly who live alone in government flats. This vulnerable group has been identified as needing community support and companionship, and the day activity centers are linked to a joint project between the Ministry of Community Development and the Housing Development Board (HDB), the statutory body in charge of the government-housing program. A reputable voluntary welfare organization is selected by the Ministry to run the day activity centers with a lean staff and a large volunteer input. The day activity center provides an opportunity for social interaction for these poor and lonely elderly and a contact to depend on in times of crisis. Together, the day care and rehabilitation centers offer comprehensive services for the senior citizens living with their family members, while the day activity centers offer social and emergency services for the poor elderly living alone.

A further function of the HDB is the upgrading of the low-rent, one-room flats at no cost to tenants. Installation of elderly-friendly amenities, such as non-slip tiles in the bathroom, handle bars, and pedestal toilets, and an alarm system that alerts neighbors and the day activity center nearby of an emergency, are the main features of this Congregate Housing project that in the last seven years has been expanded to 25 blocks, each housing approximately 150 elder tenants.

Home care services

Care services delivered in the home, or "door-step" programs as they are known in Singapore, provide a wide range of services for vulnerable and frail older people, including home help and household chores, meal delivery, escort to polyclinics and hospitals, home nursing and home medical care, and befriending services. The organizations concerned usually draw geographical boundaries for their services due to limited resources, both financial and manpower.

Other community-based services are located in the VWO rather than being delivered to the home. These include telephone hotlines for counseling, face-to-face casework and counseling, caregiver support groups, and weekly lunches prepared by volunteers. There are two key organizations, the Singapore Action Group of Elders (SAGE) and the Tsao Foundation, that specialize in the delivery of aged care services. The former not only provides direct services but also has a Centre for the Study of Ageing (CENSA) because research is seen to be of paramount importance in charting changing profiles and needs of successive cohorts of elderly in Singapore's fast-changing society. The Tsao Foundation, in contrast, focuses on the delivery of medical services to low-income elderly and the training of informal caregivers; it also runs an Acupuncture clinic. Other voluntary bodies provide free Chinese medical treatment, in one case via a mobile clinic staffed by volunteer doctors.

Socio-recreational services

Socio-recreational community-based programs form an integral part of the repertoire of elderly services and are directed to the "young old" who are usually active and desire to remain productive members of society. The Retired and Senior Volunteer Program (RSVP) provides an avenue for professional and educated retired senior citizens. For the wider majority, there are almost 400 Senior Citizens' Clubs (SCC) established by the People's Association scattered across the island. Most SCCs are located in Community Centres, which are multi-purpose, secular centers catering to the general Singaporean population, regardless of age, ethnicity, or religion. Programs organized by the SCCs include tours to Malaysia, dancing, singing, exercise classes such as Tai Chi and Qigong, and competitions between clubs. The SCCs play a very active part in the celebrations for Senior Citizens' Week held in November every year.

Some of the social programs have an emphasis on education. For example, SAGE offers a program of lifelong learning that includes Chinese calligraphy and traditional crafts, and other organizations conduct training in computer skills, training for family caregivers, and enrichment skills. As future cohorts of Singaporean elderly will be better educated and will have greater savings, there is likely to be a greater demand for these programs.

Case management

The introduction of case management in Singapore illustrates the way in which a distinctive Singaporean approach has been developed from the experience of other countries. Besides using case management to address the problems of duplication, fragmentation, and frustration for consumers as reported by Austin (1986) and Schneider et al. (2000) and to achieve added cost-effectiveness in comparison to institutionalization as argued by Greene et al. (1998), Singapore has embraced case management as a means to gaining wider benefits of community development (Atchley, 2000).

The National Council of Social Service (NCSS) launched a two-year pilot project in case management in May 1998 through the Tsao Foundation and SAGE. In this project, case management was defined as a new service that involves the assessment of an elderly person's health and psychological and social needs, and maximization of services to attain optimal and most cost-effective care of the elderly and their caregivers to prevent unnecessary institutionalization (SAGE, 1998). This strategy of service delivery is being examined to mitigate the problems of uneven distribution and fragmentation in service delivery, and aims to develop viable models of case management to suit the Singapore context.

Since public awareness of services is relatively low, as evident from the 1995 National Survey of Senior Citizens (Ministry of Health, 1996), and services are often dispersed and fragmented, the case management concept is attractive in Singapore's context. It is, however, a costly service, and the IMC has noted that case management needs to be closely targeted to those who need it most, namely the poorly-educated senior citizens without families or the frail senior citizens with multiple needs and problems (Ministry of Community Development, 1999b).

Eligibility criteria for the pilot project were frail elderly, 60 years and older, regardless of gender or ethnicity, who required three or more community-based services, and whose gross household income did not exceed S$2000 per month. The SAGE project covers applicants in the Central geographical region and the Tsao Foundation project covers the Western region. At present, the National Council of Social Service funded the project, including the salaries of the staff, but in time it may be expanded to higher income groups on a paid basis.

The SAGE Case Management Service offers more than 15 different types of services to a caseload of 76 clients, as of January 2000. The initial holistic assessment is very thorough, covering demographic, family, medical, financial, and psychosocial dimensions. Most referrals to date have come from a government hospital in the Central region, and other sources include family service centers and VWOs. The staff includes two professionals and one administrative support officer. A brokerage model is used, whereby no direct service is rendered but the case manager taps the community-based services and coordinates them for the client's benefit. During the two-year pilot period, the service has been provided free of charge to users.

The problems identified in this pilot project have been a shortage and lack of training of volunteers, pressure of time when services must be arranged prior to a client's discharge from hospital, monitoring of quality and efficiency of services, and lastly, difficulties in meeting ethnic preferences of diet of the clients, especially minority groups. Much time is spent building rapport with family members where they are involved since a family-oriented approach is applied.

While the case-management team at SAGE consists of social workers, the Tsao Foundation team consists of a psychologist and a retired nurse. This team is linked to a home medical team at the Tsao Foundation's Hua Mei Clinic, facilitating provision of immediate medical care and guidance where necessary. The SAGE team relies on doctors from the hospital of referral as well as nurses from the Home Nursing Foundation for medical support. At the end of the pilot project, the NCSS conducted an evaluation to determine the feasibility of continuation of the project. Positive outcomes were identified, thus leading to the expansion of the Case Management Service to three organizations altogether.

Current issues–future challenges

In the Singapore context, the mechanism of IMCs has proved to be highly effective. The Committee consists of high-level representatives from the ministries concerned, as well as other relevant statutory boards and selected voluntary welfare organizations. At the initial stage, the IMC is assigned the task of collating data as well as feedback from the public with regard to the matter at hand. At the later stage, when the report of the IMC is released, the status of the Committee can change into a standing Committee. The standing IMC is a national-level, policymaking and decision-taking tool established by the state to integrate policies and services in a particular sector or for a particular population. The IMC on Ageing Population currently oversees the implementation of the recommendations of the Report. Needed resources, such as funding and staff, are also channeled to the respective sector to ensure that the process is smooth and efficient. In multidisciplinary areas such as aging, where several ministries are involved, such a strategy is highly apt and effective. With the state's backing, the recommendations tend to be translated into reality with minimum barriers.

Through 1999, six working groups convened by the Inter-Ministerial Committee on the Aging Population provided the means for assessing the present status of Singapore's long-term care services and identifying the issues that will have to be addressed to meet future needs. The working groups have been effective in generating feedback from various sectors of the population, and the IMC has initiated the crafting of a national strategy to deal with the challenges of an aging society in the coming decades. The scope of the IMC illustrates that long-term care is viewed in the wider context of aging in Singapore.

As a standing committee of the government, the IMC oversees the implementation of the resulting recommendations. It also serves as a coordinating body between the relevant Ministries, thus enhancing the prospects for a system of integrated service delivery. In its 1999 report, the IMC put forward proposals for two major service innovations and made six other suggestions for consideration by policymakers. It was clear from the outset that the IMC would be a standing committee, tasked to "Steer and guide the comprehensive, holistic and coordinated development of policies and programs for the elderly; review such policies and programs periodically..." (*Straits Times*, 15/11/98).

Service innovations

The first proposal for service innovation was the establishment of Multi-Service Centres across the island. These centers are conceptualized as centralized locations for the integration of health, social, and other community-based services. When implemented, they would contribute to boosting the array of services that are available but not easily accessible for the elderly and their families. The Multi-Service Centres would be at the core of the Five-Year Strategic Plan for an aging population. The government has announced its intention to allocate $(Singapore)30 million towards setting up three centers to be ready by 2005.

The second proposal is for Golden Manpower Centres (GMCs), which would work with the Ministry of Manpower Career Centres and provide information, training, job placement, and access to voluntary work for older workers and retired people, particularly those with less education. Low-income elderly tend to form the majority of older workers who are least likely to find jobs due to their low levels of education and lack of skills. If these GMCs can provide training as well as job placement, poverty and health deterioration could be prevented. Retirement age in Singapore is currently 62, but the labor participation rate of those between the ages 55–62 years is relatively low. In 1997, the labor force participation rate for older persons 55–64 years was only 43%, while in Japan it was 67%, and the GMCs are seen as having a role in keeping more older workers in the workforce.

Policy issues

The first of the five policy issues identified by the IMC is how to contain the cost pressures associated with demands for setting up more and more institutional care programs. The pressures are largely coming from

Table 3. Projected need for elderly health services, 2000 to 2030

Types of Services	Planning Ratio Per 1000 Aged 65 and Over	Projection number of places needed				
		1997	2000	2010	2020	2030
Day Rehabilitation and Day Care Places*	3.5 places per 1,000	761 (701)	821 [820]	1,100	1,900	2,800
Home Medical Care	5 elderly needing 1 visit per month per 1,000	1,087 (750)	1,173 [825]	1,600	2,700	4,000
Home Nursing	15 elderly needing 2 visits per month per 1,000	6,522 (5,000)	7,035 [5,500]	9,400	15,900	24,000
Home Help	4 per 1000 needing daily visits	870 (255)	938 [300]	1,250	2,120	3,200
Acute Geriatric Beds	1 per 1000 elderly	217 (188)	235 [226]	310	530	800
Geriatric Specialist	1 per 10,000 elderly	22 (15)	25 [21]	30	55	80
Community Hospital Beds*	3.5 per 1000 elderly	761 (426)	820 [426]	1090	1855	2800
Chronic sick Beds*	1.5 per 1000 elderly	326 (218)	352 [218]	480	800	1200
Nursing Home Beds incl. for dementia patients*	28 beds per 1000	6087 (4703)	6566 [5635]	8800	14,900	22,400

Notes: ( ) availability in 1997
[ ] estimated availability in year 2000
*Estimated availability will improve by the year 2003: Community Hospital Beds to 940, Chronic Sick Hospital Beds to 400 and Nursing Home Beds to 7300
Source: Report of the Inter-Ministerial Committee on Health-Care for Elderly, 1999

families seeking alternative care arrangements, as well as from hospitals wanting to discharge patients who no longer require acute care. In seeking a balance between institutional and community-based services, projections of future needs have been made by the IMC, as set out in Table 3. It is evident that community services are already lagging behind the planning ratios, especially in home nursing and home help. Substantial additional resources are needed to reach the targets set for community care services in the future, but these resources are still fewer than those required for institutional care even within the target levels. Unless strictly controlled, expansion of institutional services will place an even greater burden on the government, which in turn would lead to higher taxation on the public, and at the same time, undermine the development of community care.

The path that Singapore intends to take is to examine how more preventive and community-based programs can be organized and delivered effectively in an integrated manner. This approach is consistent with the overall national policy of encouraging active and successful aging. The community emphasis will make services accessible and enable aging-in-place for the elderly, with concomitant community mobilization. It is believed that such a strategy will make the programs more cost-effective and help the elderly and their families to remain independent.

The second policy issue concerns manpower for long-term care. The combination of a well-educated, highly skilled labor force and a high demand for labor in Singapore means that, along with many areas of economic activity, long-term care faces a shortage of trained nurses, occupational therapists, and physiotherapists. A large proportion of staff aides in residential care institutions already consists of foreign workers, giving rise to cultural and communication problems. Residential care facilities and day care centers must train these staff members in the areas of dialects, attitudes, and skills in working with older people, in particular the frail and terminally ill. Another area that is likely to demand more attention in future is the training of family caregivers and volunteers to increase their effectiveness.

Third, in canvassing the need for more innovative elderly services suited to the local context to further the development of community-based long-term care, the promotion of community care cooperatives has been seriously discussed. The National Trade Union Congress (NTUC) has embarked on its first Eldercare Cooperative. As conceived, these cooperatives would provide a range of services at affordable rates, including home help, meal service, transport and escort service, employment placement, and day care. Members of the cooperatives would be eligible for rebates if they choose to use the services. Community mobilization of retirees, housewives, and even students looking for part-time employment could provide the much-needed manpower. For transport, voluntary organizations and residents could form a transport pool to meet the needs of elderly who require transport and companionship for the purpose of follow-up medical treatment. A well-managed database could match needs of residents in the vicinity with organizations and suppliers of skills or equipment. The cooperatives can be viable because volunteers and some paid staff will manage them on a not-for-profit basis. The notion of the common ownership of the cooperative *by* the members and *for* the members will be the key to the success of such cooperatives. Other innovative ideas have been proposed to expand services such as telephone contact, community kitchens manned by ethnic self-help community organizations, and caregiver support groups, as well as elderly self-help groups.

The growth of service provision through involving community organizations is highly consistent with the government policy of encouraging affordable and accessible community-based services. A further important corollary of this approach is that services provided by community organizations do not carry the stigma that is often attached to usage of "voluntary welfare" services. The emphasis on self-help organizations is also aimed at reducing the burden of expensive health and personal care of older relatives for their families, and these innovative programs are meant to provide more options for Singaporeans in addition to the ones that already exist.

The fourth policy issue concerns the need to nurture leaders and managers with vision and creativity. Problem solving in creative and cost-effective ways will be a major challenge to voluntary welfare bodies because demand for managerial staff exceeds the supply in many areas. Further, the spirit of voluntarism in Singapore is relatively low compared to many western countries. With less than 10% of the population involved in voluntary activities, it will be necessary to recruit more volunteers for community-based programs. One step toward this goal was the setting up of a National Volunteer Centre in 1998 to coordinate and promote the spirit of voluntarism. The healthy young old, those aged 55–65 years, are a potential target group to involve, bearing in mind their ability to empathize with problems of old age.

The fifth area for policy attention is the need for more research and data on the future needs of elderly cohorts. Both quantitative and qualitative data are needed to assist the process of planning of appropriate services and programs for future decades. Thus far, the emphasis has been on health and financial needs. However, social care must be factored in if a comprehensive plan is to be put in place for the future. This task is more challenging because social needs are more difficult to project.

Conclusion

The future of long-term care in Singapore will be shaped by the extent to which the recommendations of the IMC are implemented.

The announcement made by the Minister for Community Development and Sports at the opening of the Regional Gerontological Conference in January 2001, in which he outlined the Five-Year Masterplan of Elder Care Services, reflects the endorsement of a number of recommendations of the IMCs on Health Care and Ageing Population. In particular, the initiatives regarding Multi-Service Centres, community support for caregivers, and revamping of the funding formula for VWOs were emphasized.

The suggestions put forward in the IMC Reports first must be systematically examined by the government through its various ministries and, if feasible, implemented over the next five years as far as possible. The Singapore government has taken a different route from other countries, where policy challenges of preparing for an aging population are assigned to specific administrative bodies established for that purpose. Since Singapore is such a small country, geographically as well as population-wise, this path seems to be appropriate for its use, phased in over a specified time frame. The administrative functions of the IMC on Ageing Population are executed by the Elderly Development Division, which is located in the Ministry of Community Development and Sports.

Singapore has the advantage of a stable economic and political climate, a powerful factor in ensuring continuity of strategies and programs not only for economic development but also for social and health services.

Since the aging challenge affects almost every sector of Singaporean society, the government has decided on a holistic response involving several ministries, voluntary welfare organizations, the private sector, and even aging families. While Singapore is not a welfare state, the government takes a leading role in framing social policy. Thus, not only does the government promote the attitude that the public should look upon aging as a personal responsibility, shared with their immediate families; it also seeks to provide a social infrastructure in which these responsibilities can be realized. In so doing, the Asian cultural ethos of communal reciprocity as a public good is harnessed as a way of positive response to the societal challenge of an aging society.

References

Atchley, R. (2000). *Social Forces and Aging: An Introduction to Gerontology* (9th Ed.) Wadsworth: Singapore.

Austin, C. (1986). Case management in long-term care. In *C. Meyer's Social Work and Aging* (2nd Ed.). National Association of Social Workers. Silver Spring: MD.

Challis, D., & Davies, B. (1986). *Case Management in Community Care: An Evaluated Experiment in the Home Care of the Elderly.* Gower Publishing: Aldershot, UK.

Cheung, P.L. (1993). Population ageing in Singapore. *Asia Pacific Journal of Social Work*, 3(2): 77–89.

Economic and Social Commission for Asia and the Pacific (1996). *Population Ageing in Asia and the Pacific.* ESCAP, Bangkok, with Japanese Organisation for International Cooperation in Family Planning, Inc., Tokyo. United Nations: New York.

Gordon, D., & and Donald, S. (1993). *Community Social Work, Older People and Informal Care: A Romantic Illusion?* Avebury: Aldershot, UK.

Greene, V.L., Ondrich, J., & Laditka, S. (1998). Can home care services achieve cost savings in long-term care for older people? *Journal of Gerontology*, 53B(4): 228–328.

Knodel, J., & Debavalya, N. (1997). Living arrangements and support among the elderly in South-East Asia: An introduction. *Asia-Pacific Population Journal*, 12(4): 5–16.

Kua, E.H. (1987). Psychological distress for families caring for frail elderly. *Singapore Medical Journal*, 3: 42–44.

Mehta, K. (2000). Caring for the elderly in Singapore. In W. Liu & H. Kendig (Eds.). *Who Should Give Care to the Elderly? An East-West Social Value Divide*. Singapore University Press: Singapore.

Ministry of Community Development (1998). *Because We Care: Guidelines for Community-Based Services for Elderly*. Ministry of Community Development: Singapore.

Ministry of Community Development (1999b). *Report of the Inter-Ministerial Committee on the Ageing Population*. Ministry of Community Development: Singapore.

Ministry of Health (1984). *Report of the Committee on the Problems of the Aged*. Ministry of Health: Singapore.

Ministry of Health (1999a). *Report of the Inter-Ministerial Committee on Health Care for the Elderly*. Ministry of Health: Singapore.

Ministry of Health, Ministry of Community Development, Department of Statistics and National Council of Social Services (1996). *National Survey of Senior Citizens in Singapore*. National Press: Singapore.

Pelham, A., & Clark, W. (Eds.) (1986). *Managing Home Care for the Elderly*. Springer Publishing: New York.

Prescott, N. (Ed.) (1998). *Proceedings of a Conference on Choices in Financing Health Care and Old Age Security*. World Bank Discussion Paper No. 2. World Bank. Washington, DC: USA.

Richards, M. (1996). *Community Care for Older People: Rights, Remedies and Finances*. Jordans: Bristol, UK.

Schneider, R., Kropf, N., & Kisor, A. (2000). *Gerontological Social Work: Knowledge, Service Settings, and Special Populations*. Brooks/Cole: Australia.

Shantakumar, G. (1994). *The Aged Population of Singapore*. Census of Population 1990, Monograph No. 1, Singapore.

Shantakumar, G. (1995). Aging and social policy in Singapore. *Ageing International*, 22(2): 49–54.

Siegel, J.S., & Hoover, S.L. (1982). Demographic aspects of health of the elderly to the year 2000 and beyond. *World Health Statistics Quarterly*, 35(3/4): 140–141.

Singapore Action Group of Elders (SAGE) (1998). *Case Management Service*. SAGE: Singapore.

Straits Times (1998). *Committee's 21 Members Named*. Singapore, November 15.

Teo, P. (1994). The national policy on elderly people in Singapore. *Ageing and Society*, 14: 405–427.

World Health Organization (1995). *World Health Report, 1995. Bridging the Gaps*. WHO: Geneva.

Chapter 5

Ageing population in Singapore: A case study*

Paul Cheung and S. Vasoo[†]

Background

Founded in 1819 as a British trading station, Singapore has since been transformed into a modern, industrialized city-state and a major economic centre in Asia. Nation building and economic modernization efforts began in earnest after full independence was achieved in 1965. Taking full advantage of her strategic location and human resources, Singapore's economy expanded rapidly. By 1989, Singapore's GNP per capita of $17910[1] was the third highest in Asia, after Japan and Brunei. In slightly over two decades after independence, a firm economic base has now been established with manufacturing, services and commerce as the major economic sectors (You and Lim, 1984). With a land area of only about 623 km^2 and a population of 2.6 million, Singapore's economic future inevitably lies in the further improvement and utilization of her human resources.

---

*Reprinted with permission by the publisher from Vasoo, S., & Cheung, P. P. L. (1992). Ageing Population in Singapore: A Case Study. In D. R. Phillips (Ed.), *Ageing in East and South-East Asia* (pp. 77–104). London: Edward Arnold.

This paper takes a case study approach to review ageing issues facing Singapore and the policies and measures introduced to moderate the impact of the population ageing. Some of the ideas in this article are also reflected in other topics related to ageing.

[†]Department of Social Work and Social Psychology, National University of Singapore

[1]*Singapore dollars are used throughout this chapter.*

In the early years of nationhood, the need to achieve the nation's economic and social aspirations was translated into a number of major social policies. The public housing policy, for example, resulted in 87 per cent of Singapore's population residing in government-built high-rise apartments. With increasing affluence, Singaporeans are aspiring to wider choice and better housing. The educational policy led to the development of a comprehensive and technologically-oriented educational system providing equal opportunities for all. In the case of population planning, the impact of the National Family Planning and Population Programme on population growth is well known: in a single generation, the fertility rate of Singapore dropped well below the replacement level.

Introduction

A major challenge which will confront Singapore in the future has been identified by the government as the ageing of its population, expressed as the expected dramatic increase in the number of elderly persons and in the relative proportion of the elderly to other age groups. While the aged population in Singapore is relatively small (8.6 per cent) compared to most developed countries (11.4 per cent) (Binstock, Chow and Schulz, 1982), demographers in Singapore have predicted a sizeable increase in the age group of those aged 65 and over in the next 50 years. It is anticipated that this trend, shared by many other newly industrializing countries, will result in a broad-based transformation of the society, requiring adjustments and adaptations at all levels. This would significantly alter the dependency ratio between the young and the old.

Two implications have received particular emphasis. Firstly, concern is expressed as to whether ageing of the population will increase the dependency ratio on the state for welfare and financial assistance. A related question is whether the traditional caring institutions will remain intact given the rapid social changes that Singapore is experiencing. Secondly, concern is also expressed about the economic implications of population ageing and its potential impact on the economy's future development.

Increasing awareness of the issues related to the elderly in Singapore emerged as early as the 1970s. At least seven studies (Chen, 1982b) were conducted on the elderly during that time. In the 1980s, the number of studies increased significantly. Even before the beginning of 1985, at least ten were known of, one of which, Social Policy and the Elderly' (1981), was conducted by the Singapore Council of Social Service. In addition, the appointment of two high-level committees in 1982 and 1988 to review the problems arising from population ageing further reflected this concern. There was also an awareness that the rapidity of the ageing process and its consequences were related to, if not an outcome of, the policies implemented in the past. The two committees, chaired by cabinet ministers and comprised of representatives from various sectors, were therefore given the task of reviewing the policy options and recommending policy changes. These two committees, as well as other initiatives, marked the beginning of Singapore's effort to plan for an ageing society.

The report of the Committee on Problems of the Aged (1984), commonly known as the Howe Report, further opened the gate for public attention and debate on issues facing the elderly.

This paper is a case study of the ageing of Singapore and the policies and measures introduced to moderate the impact of the ageing process.

Definition of elderly population: Demographic profile

Different countries have different cut-off points for defining the chronological age of the elderly population, and these depend on the average life expectancy of the population. In Singapore, where the average life expectancy at birth is over 72 years, it is appropriate to consider the elderly population as comprising those who are 60 years and above. Although there is presently no official retirement age, there appears to be an implicit recognition that the retirement age should be raised from the previous level of 55 years to 60 years.

Population projections prepared by the Singapore government's Population Planning Unit have shown that the age profile of Singapore will undergo a significant transformation by early next century (Cheung, 1988a). The key feature of this transformation will be the dramatic increase in the number and proportion of older persons in the population.

Ageing population

Since independence, Singapore has benefited from a youthful and vibrant population. In 1957, 43 per cent of the population were below 15 years of age, and the elderly population aged 60 years and over constituted less than 4 per cent. In 1989, the age profile reflected a more mature population, with the young constituting only 23.1 per cent and the elderly 8.5 per cent of the population. With the bulk of the population of working age, dependency ratios have been on the decline (Cheung, 1988b). Over the same period, the median age of the population has risen steadily from 18.8 years in 1957, to 19.7 in 1970 and to 28.8 in 1988. Projections show that the median age is likely to rise to about 33 years in the year 2000 and to 38 years in 2030 (Chen and Cheung, 1988).

Shift in the age structure — the changing age profile

In a growing population, the increase in the number of elderly persons may not alter the age profile significantly. In a slow-growth population, the increase in the absolute numbers is associated with a corresponding increase in the proportion of the elderly. The relative proportion of the elderly population is therefore a function of the comparative sizes of successive cohorts.

The decline in the population growth rate between 1957 and 1980 that was due to the success of the family planning programme, education, rapid industrialization and increased female labour participation, has affected the age structure of the Singapore population. The effects of the declining population growth rate have resulted in:

- a drop in the young population (0 to 14 years) from 43 per cent to 23.1 per cent,
- an increase in the adult population (15 to 59 years) from 53 per cent to 68.5 per cent,
- an increase in the elderly population (60 and above) from 4 per cent to 8.5 per cent.

Based on the trends of the past 30 years, demographers have predicted a further decline in the proportion of the young population to 17 per cent

Table 1. Demographic indicators, 1960 to 1989

	Number of Live Births	CBR	TFR	Rate of Natural Increase
1960	61775	37.5	5.76	3.5
1965	55725	29.5	4.66	2.5
1970	45934	22.1	3.07	1.7
1975	39948	17.8	2.07	1.4
1980	41217	17.1	1.73	1.2
1985	42848	16.6	1.62	1.1
1987	43616	16.7	1.64	1.2
1988	52957	20.0	1.97	1.5
1989 (estimated)	47735	17.8	1.78	1.3

Note: CBR (Crude Birth Rate)
TFR (Total Fertility Rate)

in the next 50 years. By then, the adult population is expected to be reduced by 58 per cent while the population of aged persons will increase to 25 per cent.

The decline in Singapore's birth cohort sizes is shown in Table 1, along with major fertility indicators. The speed of the decline is clearly shown. The Total Fertility Rate (TFR) fell rapidly from 5.76 in 1960 to 3.07 in 1970, a drop of more than 2.5 children per woman over a 10-year period. Since 1975, Singapore's fertility has fallen below replacement level and a historic low was reached in 1986 when the TFR fell to 1.44. The number of births also declined from about 62 000 in the 1960s to about 42 000 in the 1980s. Table 1 also shows the rebound in the number of births in 1987, 1988 and 1989, after the announcement of the New Population Policy.

Based on a long-run average TFR of 1.8, projections prepared by the Population Planning Unit have shown that the proportion of persons aged 60 and over will increase from 7 per cent in 1980 to about 26 per cent in 2030. With one out of four Singaporeans aged 60 and over, Singapore by 2030 will be a truly 'mature' society.

The need to maintain a balanced age structure was one of the main objectives of Singapore's New Population Policy, announced in 1987 with the slogan 'have three or more if you can afford it' (Cheung, 1989). The policy offers a number of incentives to encourage parents to attain a family size of three or more children. The stated goal of the policy is to return the TFR to replacement level. Over time, by raising fertility gradually, the policy hopes to stabilize the population structure with a more even distribution across the age groups. If this is achieved, the proportion of the elderly will stabilize at about 20 per cent. Before this occurs, however, the proportion of the elderly is likely to rise beyond the 25 per cent level.

Is it possible to bring the targeted 20 per cent even lower to bring about a rejuvenation of the population structure? This is possible in the long run if a higher than replacement population growth rate is adopted by the government as a policy objective and is eventually achieved. In view of Singapore's limited land and water resources, there is an absolute upper limit on the carrying capacity of the island. Sustained high population growth may bring about a younger age structure, but the adverse effects of over-population may be serious. Moreover, in modern Singapore, small family size has been internalized by many parents during the 'antinatalist era'. This norm may not be easy to overcome. Thus, it appears that a population structure with 20 per cent to 25 per cent of the population being elderly may have to be accepted as inevitable for Singapore. The socio-economic impact of this change in age profile will be fully felt within the next 40 years.

Size of the elderly population

Attention to overall population structure as presented, however, tends to mask the social implication of growth in actual numbers. If one were to compare the actual number of elderly persons over time, the rate of growth of the elderly would have increased even more drastically! The increase in the number of elderly persons in Singapore is and has been rapid. In 1970, there were about 118 300 persons aged 60 and above. The number increased by 47 per cent to 173 600 in 1980. In 1984, there were about 193 900 persons aged 60 and over which, by 1989, had increased by 18 per cent to 229 700. By the turn of the century, the number will rise to about 332 000 and to 835 000 by 2030 (Table 2). The number of elderly persons will therefore increase by about 300 per cent from the present level to the year 2030.

Table 2. Actual and projected elderly population in Singapore, 1980 to 2030

Age Group	1980 No	1980 Percentage	1990 No	1990 Percentage	2000 No	2000 Percentage	2030 No	2030 Percentage
Total population	2413.9	100.0	2716.0	100.0	2995.0	100.0	3214.0	100.0
60 to 64	59.7	2.5	81.8	3.0	111.7	3.7	196.3	6.1
65 to 69	49.3	2.0	58.0	2.1	81.7	2.7	213.0	6.6
70 to 74	33.3	1.4	43.4	1.6	60.0	2.0	183.3	5.7
75 to 79	18.6	0.8	30.1	1.1	35.6	1.2	118.1	3.7
80 and above	12.7	0.5	25.7	0.9	43.4	1.4	124.7	3.9
All 60 years and above	173.6	7.2	238.9	8.8	332.4	11.1	835.3	26.0

Notes: Projections based on 'medium' fertility assumptions
Numbers in thousands

The rapid increase in the number of elderly persons is due to two factors. The first arises from the ageing of the postwar baby-boom cohorts. At present, these cohorts are in the 20 to 39 age range. By 2030, they will be in the age range of 70 and above. With the passage of the baby-boom cohorts in the next century, the number of elderly persons will subsequently decline because of the smaller cohorts born since the 1960s. The second contributing factor is the increase in the life expectancy of the population, resulting in more persons surviving to older ages. Life expectancy at birth has been increasing steadily over time. In 1957, the life expectancy of an average Singaporean was only 64 years. In 1989, it was 74 years. Life expectancy at the age of 60 has also increased: in 1989, it was 17 years for men and 20 years for women.

The change in the population structure in Singapore will result in a gradual shift from the burden of child dependency to old dependency. With a fall in the birth rate, the age distribution is affected in such a way as to lower the overall economic dependency ratio. There will be a shift in the composition of the dependent population as elderly dependents make up a larger proportion and youth a declining proportion. Demographers have established through this ratio that there will be fewer adults to support the increasing number of the elderly. In 1957, the old dependency ratio was 0.07. In 1980, however, it had increased to 0.11 and, with the forecast growth of the aged persons from 7 per cent in 1980 to about 26 per cent in 2030, the old dependency ratio will increase to 0.46.

The composition of Singapore's elderly population

Singapore's development over the past few decades will not only have a lasting impact on the numerical dimensions of the elderly population. Their socioeconomic characteristics are also changing, mirroring the social transformations that have occurred (Chen and Cheung, 1988).

Literacy

The average educational attainment of the elderly is expected to increase as the younger, better-educated cohorts move into old age. In 1980, 71 per cent of the elderly men and 93 per cent of the elderly women had no formal education. By 2030, these proportions will be reduced to about 18 per cent for men and 35 per cent for women. The elderly with secondary and higher education will increase from about 4 per cent in 1980 to about 20 per cent in 2030. The gain in educational advancement among elderly women will be particularly noticeable, reflecting the educational advancement of women over the last 20 years.

Economic status

In 1970, the male labour-force participation rate for the age cohort of 60 to 64 was 56 per cent. It then declined to 53 per cent in 1980 and to 48 per cent in 1989. A similar trend may be observed for those aged 65 and over. The participation rates for elderly women have been much lower than for elderly males (Table 3). The relatively small percentage of elderly people in the workforce suggests that there is a lot more room for elderly people to work or to continue working. Increasing affluence in Singapore and the rising demand for leisure could have reduced the elderly's commitment to work. Lack of appropriate employment opportunities and some employers' discriminatory hiring practices have also hindered greater participation. The steady decline is likely to continue if obstacles to continued employment are not removed. On the part of

Table 3. Labour-force participation rate of older persons by sex and age, 1970 to 1988

		1970	1975	1980	1988
Male					
	55 to 59	73.9	73.6	70.7	65.1
	60 to 64	55.6	54.2	52.5	47.3
	65+	31.7	31.7	28.6	21.2
Female					
	55 to 59	16.2	14.2	14.5	17.4
	60 to 64	13.4	14.0	11.3	11.9
	65+	6.5	6.4	6.4	4.7

the government, appropriate incentives have to be given to both employers and potential elderly employees to induce them to remain in the workforce.

In terms of age, there are significantly more younger elderly workers than older elderly workers. The distribution for both males and females within each age group is quite similar. A majority (84 per cent) of the working elderly are employed in sales, service and production lines (National Survey on Senior Citizens, 1983). The large percentage of working elderly in these three areas suggests that there is either no mandatory retirement age or that there is a high demand for workers for these jobs. Only a small percentage (5 per cent) are engaged as salaried professionals, managers and administrative workers.

Country of origin

Due to Singapore's demographic history, 75 per cent of the elderly population in 1980 were foreign-born. This proportion is expected to decline gradually to about 20 per cent by 2030. The increase in the number of indigenous elderly people also implies greater generational depth and a firmer grounding for families ties in Singapore.

Demographic characteristics

It is common knowledge that women tend to outlive men and, in Singapore, the difference in life expectancy is about 5 years. In 1989, there were about 122 200 women and 107 500 men aged 60 and older, giving a sex ratio of 0.88. In the future, older women will continue to outnumber men, especially in the oldest age group. There are also sex differences in the incidence of widowhood among the elderly. In 1980, 80 per cent of the elderly men were married and only 14 per cent were widowed. The pattern was reversed for elderly women, with 37 per cent married and 57 per cent widowed. This pattern is likely to persist into the future as men continue to marry women younger than themselves and women continue to outlive men.

Economic and social life

The economic and social well-being of elderly people is of interest and concern. As the population structure changes, it will inevitably bring with it changes in their economic and social life. Some major features are now considered.

Retirement

Like most other people, elderly people want to be independent. In the National Survey on Senior Citizens, most elderly people indicated that they favoured the idea of extending the retirement age. In fact, 85 per cent of the respondents indicated that they had no intention of retiring. Of those not working, only a small percentage (16.3 per cent) indicated that they stopped work because of reaching retirement age. Most of these elderly people indicated domestic reasons and ill-health as the main reasons for not continuing to work. These findings certainly demonstrate that the elderly are keen to be financially and socially independent rather than a burden on the community. Extension of the retirement age is thus a wise move, allowing the elderly to work as long as possible to ensure a sense of financial independence. This would then provide them with the means to live an economically viable life and to remain active in the community. Although a delayed retirement is desirable in view of the increased life expectancy, it could affect firms that want to employ younger and more educated workers. At the same time, it might limit job openings and delay promotions for young and middle-aged workers.

Consequently, some friction between the young and old workers should be expected.

An interesting question to ask is: will inducing the elderly to work or continue working deprive the young of valuable jobs in the tight labour market in Singapore? The Howe Report (1983) asserted that the young would not be deprived of valuable jobs for three reasons:

- the small family size of Singaporeans will reduce the number of younger entrants into the labour force,
- young people are expected to join the labour force at a later age because of extended educational opportunities and National Service,
- foreign unskilled workers will be gradually phased out.

The National Survey on Senior Citizens indicates that financial problems and boredom are foreseen by elderly people as the most pressing issues during retirement.

Interestingly, retirees or those not working do not appear to be eager to re-enter the labour force. The National Survey on Senior Citizens found that relatively few of the elderly people surveyed wanted to return to the labour force. This phenomenon is also compounded by a reluctance of most firms to re-employ retired workers. In order to provide an incentive for firms to be more ready to employ older workers, it may be necessary to either waive or reduce Central Provident Fund (CPF) contributions for both the older workers and the employers. The suggestion that there should be a reduction of wages with increasing age may also help to encourage employers to employ or retain elderly workers.

Social security

Personal income is the most basic form of social security for elderly people and, in Singapore, personal income is negatively correlated with age (National Survey on Senior Citizens, 1983). This happens because the tendency to stop work grows with age. A higher proportion of elderly females than males is without any personal income. This difference is accounted for by the difference in the labour-force participation between the male and female elderly.

Household income is an important source of social security for the economic life of Singapore's elderly people. The National Survey on Senior Citizens (1983) revealed that 13 per cent of those surveyed had a household income of less than $500 per month. This percentage is quite close to the national percentage of low-income households in Singapore. This group of elderly people is, however, more vulnerable than others to risk and social problems. An interesting finding is that more elderly people who are not working but who are looking for work come from the lower-income household group. This suggests that they are eager to maintain financial adequacy.

The National Survey on Senior Citizens (1983) reveals that the majority of elderly people (84 per cent) do receive financial and material support from their immediate family members and other relatives. These forms of support are significantly more pronounced for those who do not have a source of income than for those who have. Similarly, more than 80 per cent of elderly people receive support in kind. These findings indicate that elderly persons in Singapore generally have a source of financial security in their families or relatives. The findings also imply that there is still a sense of filial piety and family obligation among many Singaporeans towards their aged parents. Few elderly people receive contributions in cash or in kind from non-relatives or from voluntary organizations. However, among those who might need such support, it is not surprising that many do not seek support because of the possible social embarrassment brought both on themselves and their family members.

Only a small percentage (7.2 per cent) of the elderly surveyed have Central Provident Fund (CPF) as a form of social security (National Survey on Senior Citizens, 1983) although the 1984 Labour Force Survey indicated that 25 per cent of elderly people are CPF members. Males outnumbered females in having CPF as a reserve fund. This is because many females have never worked and therefore have never been CPF members. The reserves in the CPF for elderly people are however generally low because of the low rate of contributions during their working years. Nevertheless, it is envisaged that with the current CPF rates of 40 per cent and higher wages, the CPF is likely to become a critical source of reserve funds in the future, especially for those who are currently below 45 years old. Those above this age are unlikely to benefit much as most of their

CPF funds would be tied up with repayments of housing loans leaving very little for old age.

While the CPF scheme may ensure a sense of financial security for those who are about to retire, there are still groups of workers who are not covered by the CPF scheme. These groups include the self-employed, employees who are casual or family labourers, and employees who work outside permanent employment relationships. A social insurance scheme for these workers should be seriously considered to ensure their financial independence in retirement.

Another form of social security for elderly people is the pension given upon retirement. Major developments in the course of the CPF's evolution, however, have drastically reduced the number of people with pensions. While pensions act as an important source of income for retired persons, mostly government civil servants, there is some suggestion that adjustment to the amount paid should be made commensurate with rising inflation and cost of living.

The social support system of elderly people

The family has been a potent source of support for both young and old through the ages. To what extent is it still playing a supportive role for the elderly in Singapore today? The National Survey on Senior Citizens found that a high percentage of elderly people is confident that they can depend on their family members when they fall ill (88 per cent) or when they need to confide in them (78 per cent). Although there are no past data to make accurate comparisons, it is our contention that there may actually be a slight drop in family support for the elderly. This drop could be attributed to the rapid industrialization and modernization, the assimilation of Western educational-system values and philosophy, and the government's resettlement programme which encourages the formation of nuclear families. In order to allow the family to be a continuing source of support for elderly people the government should continue its policy of giving priority public housing to young couples who apply for flats on a joint basis with their parents (see also Chapter 4). At the same time, efforts should be made to help young couples obtain flats that are close to the homes of their parents.

Of those elderly people living separately from their children, about 60 per cent are visited by their children at least once a week. The survey also reveals that elderly people who live alone or with non-relatives receive far fewer visits. In accord with Asian culture the eldest son was likely to be the most frequent contact or visitor for elderly parents, although on the whole daughters tend to visit elderly parents more often than sons do. Interestingly, children who contact their elderly parents most frequently are not likely to be the ones providing the most financial support in cash or in kind.

Overall, the findings generally suggest that most of the elderly who have immediate family members would have little problem in getting help and assistance in times of need. Many elderly people have maintained meaningful interaction and contact with their children. This provides the basis for their confidence in securing help from their children in times of need.

Spending habits

'Modest' would be the word to describe the spending habits of elderly people in Singapore. The National Survey on Senior Citizens found that 80 per cent of the elderly spend less than $500 (US$250) per month, with 37 per cent spending less than $100 per month. Because of their higher rate of labour-force participation, males tend to spend more than females. An interesting question relating to the spending habits of the elderly is: whether their income is adequate to cover their monthly expenses? According to the National Survey of Senior Citizens, 93 per cent of elderly people reported that they have sufficient income to cover monthly expenses. Only 7 per cent have to draw on their savings and CPF or rely on other means to meet their monthly expenditure.

An adequate standard of living among the elderly — at least until recently can be attributed to rapid economic growth during the past two decades. The period of economic growth following the independence of Singapore, despite spells of instability, facilitated the foundation of economic support for most elderly people. However, when the economy hits a downturn, it might be expected that a higher proportion of elderly people would find it difficult to meet their monthly expenditure.

Health status of elderly people

In order to achieve and maintain a viable economic and social life, it is important that the elderly maintain a good and healthy life. In the following section we discuss the health status of elderly people in Singapore.

Perception of health status

Perceptions of health are critical to how elderly people feel about life and to how they behave. The National Survey on Senior Citizens reveals that more than two-thirds of the elderly people surveyed perceived themselves to possess good health. People who perceive themselves to have good health tend to be happier, more satisfied, more involved in social activities, less anxious and less lonely (Verbrugge, 1983). Although the causal relationships among these factors are still unclear, it is not unrealistic to expect life to be much more pleasant for those elderly people who feel healthy than for those who feel unhealthy.

It is very likely that the elderly people in the National Survey on Senior Citizens compared themselves to their own contemporaries, including friends who had died. Hence their health assessments are more positive than if they were to compare their health with that of younger adults or with their own health during younger days. If residents in institutions were included in the survey, the findings of poor health amongst the elderly would no doubt increase. This is because those in institutional care have generally poorer health than those outside it. The study also establishes that the elderly's perception of poor health increases with age. Differences between the sexes in the perception of their health status, however, were not analysed.

Mortality

Standardized death rates of elderly people in Singapore dropped by 30 per cent between 1957 and 1982, suggesting an improvement in the health of the elderly. Between 1974 and 1989 mortality rates for elderly males were higher than for females (Department of Statistics, 1989). This is true for all age categories of 59 years and above. Although large sex differences in health and mortality persist, the reasons for such differences are not fully understood. Various authors have attributed the differences to genetic factors, risks acquired during life, and from attitudinal effects of illness perception and curative behaviour. None the less, it is a fact that men's health risks are higher than women's. Life expectancy figures also reflect a higher risk for elderly males. For example, men who were 60 in 1980 could expect to live for another 9 years compared to 14 years for women. Between 1957 and 1980, the increase in life expectancy was higher for females than for males (Ministry of Health, 1982).

The main causes of death for elderly people in Singapore have not changed much. The trends over the years show heart disease, malignant neoplasms and cerebrovascular disease to be the major causes of death. Death due to senility, which was once the most common reason, has declined significantly as a result of better death certification from qualified personnel. Slight differences exist between the sexes; for example, while there are more males dying of heart disease and tuberculosis, more females die of cerebrovascular disease (Ministry of Health, 1982).

Morbidity

An analysis of hospitalization rates reveals that there is an increasingly high proportion of total admission for the elderly, rising from 12 per cent in 1977 to 14.2 per cent in 1988. The increase in hospitalization rates seems to suggest that the health of elderly people is getting poorer. However, it should be pointed out that this need not necessarily be so. Indeed, it may suggest that elderly people are either more health conscious or that there are more ailments being reported as a result of more and better medical services. There are also suggestions that some doctors may induce admission of their clients even when it is not absolutely necessary.

In the National Survey on Senior Citizens, the hospitalization rate among elderly people was found to increase with age — 6.6 per cent, 9.9 per cent and 11.6 per cent for the 55 to 64, 65 to 74, and above 74 age groups respectively. Longitudinal records from government hospitals further reveal that the number of admissions among the various age groups of the elderly increased significantly by 168 per cent in 1982 (Ministry of Health, 1982). The above data clearly points to the vulnerability of the people in the oldest age group who are more susceptible to illness and poor health.

According to the National Survey of Senior Citizens, the most common reasons for admission of elderly people to hospital are diseases of the respiratory system followed by heart disease. This finding closely corresponds to the statistics on major causes of death, although the ranking order is slightly different due to possible differences in classification.

Mental health

With regard to mental health, the National Survey on Senior Citizens shows that 3.7 per cent of elderly respondents exhibited some degree of maladjustment. More elderly females are found to be less well adjusted than males. Only a small minority (0.2 per cent males and 0.5 per cent females) are reported to need urgent psychiatric treatment. As with other health indicators, mental well-being is found to deteriorate slightly with age. Analysis of the mental health of elderly people by ethnic group reveals that Indians have a higher mental health risk while Malays appear to be the best adjusted.

Sensory and dental status

In terms of vision and hearing, the results indicate a deterioration of vision and hearing ability with age. However, it should be noted that a higher proportion of elderly people indicate that they can 'hear well' (95 per cent) than say they can 'see well' (68 per cent). This certainly suggests a need to prevent further deterioration of the eyesight of the elderly. Although differences between sexes were not analysed in the study, research elsewhere has established that elderly women may have more vision problems than men (Verbrugge, 1983).

The National Survey on Senior Citizens also establishes that many elderly people do not have good dental health. About two-thirds of the elderly are found to be without any teeth or with fewer than 14 teeth.

Again, the status of dental health deteriorates with advancing age. Elderly people of Indian origin are found to have better dental health than other ethnic groups.

Personal care

An important indicator of health status is the ability of elderly people to attend to their own personal needs. In Singapore, a majority of elderly people are able to attend to their personal needs independently; only about 1–2 per cent of elderly people were found to need help in feeding, bathing and dressing. The ability of elderly people to attend to their daily needs, however, declines with advancing age (National Survey on Senior Citizens, 1984).

Mobility

According to the National Survey a very high percentage of the elderly people in the community (95 per cent) are completely mobile. Only 4.2 per cent require some form of assistance from time to time. A very small percentage (0.6 per cent) are bedridden; this percentage increases with age from 0.2 per cent among those below 75 years to 2.1 per cent for those in the 75 and above age group. In a survey on Homes for the Elderly in Singapore (1985), it was found that 37 per cent of the elderly in the homes are either semi-ambulant or non-ambulant.

One can conclude from the above discussion that the health status of the elderly in Singapore is generally good. This gives a sound basis for the encouragement of policies for care in the community.

The national infrastructure for population ageing

The national infrastructure for dealing with population ageing will be considered in two aspects: policy formulation and programme implementation. Three general features of the infrastructure deserve special mention at the outset. First, population ageing and its implications have been accorded high political emphasis. The ruling political party, the People's

Action Party, has explicitly mentioned population ageing as an important issue in its agenda for national discussion. As a result, efforts in policy formulation and programme implementation have benefited from such political patronage. Second, Singapore is a relatively small place and an extensive network of government and non-government organizations are already in place. Thus, it is possible to exploit what is already in existence to create a support infrastructure for the aged. Third, the growing affluence of Singapore makes it possible for the government and society in general to divert resources to programmes and services for elderly people, leading to a rapid expansion of the formal support network.

Policy formulation

In the 1970s, concern for the welfare of the immigrant aged led to the establishment of a number of services catering for the special needs of this group. Such services were formulated by the then Ministry of Social Affairs in conjunction with the Singapore Council of Social Service. Although they attracted much attention, planning efforts were essentially sectoral and services were treated as an extension of the existing social welfare schemes. In the 1980s, the concern broadened as the implications of population ageing were recognized. The fact that the problems and needs of the aged will not disappear with the passage of the group of immigrants, often destitute in old age, led to serious reviews of the issue. In June 1982, the appointment of a high-level 13-member committee marked the beginning of the government's efforts to understand the implications of population ageing and to implement appropriate measures.

The Committee on the Problems of the Aged was chaired by the then Minister for Health. In its deliberations, the Committee took the problems of old age beyond the realm of humanitarian and social welfare concerns. It took note of the long-term impact of population ageing, and its ramifications. As a result, the Committee stressed the potential contributions of the elderly to society and the importance of incorporating them in socio-economic development, while concurrently acknowledging and meeting their special needs. They were thus moving away from looking at elderly people solely as a 'problem'. To assist in its deliberations, the

Committee commissioned the National Survey on Senior Citizens in 1983, providing updated information from an earlier study conducted in 1976 (Chen, 1982a). The survey report was released in 1983. The National Survey on Senior Citizens was conducted jointly by the then Ministry of Social Affairs, and the Ministry of Health for the Committee on the Problems of the Aged in 1983. The Survey was based on 5 538 persons aged 55 years and above and who were living in private households.

The report of the Committee was finalized and released in March 1984. Several controversial policy recommendations such as raising the proportion of aged people eligible for provident fund withdrawal, and legislation on filial piety led to much public outcry and discussion. However, the bulk of the Committee's recommendations were accepted. The major ones included the change in provident fund contribution rates for older persons to generate employment for older workers; legislation on minimum standards for homes for the aged; increased aged dependents' relief under the Income Tax Act and measures to foster family and inter-generational cohesion.

To implement the report's recommendations, several committees were established with members drawn from relevant ministries, statutory boards, institutions of higher learning and non-government agencies. The Coordination Committee to implement the Report on the Problems of the Aged was set up in August 1985 under the Ministry of Community Development (formerly the Ministry of Social Affairs) to evaluate and oversee the implementation of the report's recommendations. The Committee to Co-ordinate the Development Programmes and Activities was formed in January 1986 by the Ministry of Community Development to promote, direct and supervise the implementation of the report's recommendations with respect to health and recreational needs, social services, and institutional care by government and non-government agencies. The Committee on Public Awareness on Ageing to spearhead a public education and awareness programme was set up by the Ministries of Community Development, Communication and Information to educate the public with a view to projecting a more wholesome image of senior citizens. The Public Awareness Programme on Ageing was launched in November 1987 and a tripartite Task Force on the Employment of the Elderly was established by the Ministry of Labour. The task force comprised employers, and government and union representatives and studied the need to provide counselling for and retraining of older workers.

Recognizing that population ageing is also a demographic matter, in 1984 the government established an Inter-Ministerial Population Committee (IMPC) to undertake a comprehensive review of Singapore's population trends and to make recommendations on policy measures to arrest the declining fertility rate and to bring about the desired population size and composition. Chaired by the Permanent Secretary of the Ministry of Health and reporting to the First Deputy Prime Minister, the members of the IMPC comprised Permanent Secretaries of relevant government ministries. Following the IMPC's recommendations, Singapore's population policy was revised in 1987. The Committee, assisted by the Population Planning Unit, continues to monitor population trends in Singapore.

In June 1988, the Advisory Council on the Aged, headed by the Minister for Home Affairs, was formed to undertake a comprehensive review of the status of ageing in Singapore. Its terms of reference include, amongst other things, the review of programmes and services now available to aged people; the examination of premises, assumptions and policy recommendations contained in the 1984 Report on the Problems of the Aged; to suggest ways to enable the aged to work beyond the age of 55; and finally to examine how families can be helped to look after their aged dependants.

The Advisory Council appointed four committees to look into the specific issues of concern. The four committees were: a Committee on Community-Based Programmes for the Aged; a Committee on Attitudes Towards the Aged; a Committee on Residential Care Programmes for the Aged, and a Committee on Employment for the Aged. The members of the Advisory Council and the committees included experts from government ministries, statutory boards and voluntary organizations concerned with the provision and planning of services for elderly people.

In September 1988, the reports of the four committees were reviewed by the Council and subsequently submitted for the consideration of the government. One of the key recommendations proposed by the Council was that a National Council on Ageing should be set up, with the character and authority of a statutory board to effectively plan and co-ordinate policies and programmes for elderly people. Other proposals included raising the retirement age from 55 to 60, as continued employment provides a sense of worth, dignity and financial independence for elderly people; adjusting the seniority-based wage system so that more elderly people will be employed; expanding and strengthening public education programmes on the aged and ageing so that the 'right' attitudes towards the aged could be inculcated; making land available for voluntary organizations to set up homes for the aged; lengthening the leases for homes; studying the feasibility of providing health and medical services for frail elderly people living in their own homes; and increasing the dependency tax rebate for families who look after aged people.

A national policy on ageing in Singapore is therefore taking shape after these successive policy reviews. Two characteristics are worth noting in the policy formulation process. First, these committees have the benefit of representation from various sectors. This has the advantage of receiving diverse inputs and making implementable decisions. Historically, cross-sectoral representation has worked well in the local context and it is a standard feature of the Singapore government's problem-solving approach. Secondly, the committees were given much publicity. Public awareness of the issues was heightened, especially when controversial recommendations were made. Enhanced public discussion on policy changes places increasing emphasis on social care for elderly people in Singapore. Public input thus became an important consideration in the committees' deliberations.

Programme implementation

The programmes and activities for elderly people are co-ordinated through three principal organizations: the Ministry of Community Development, the Ministry of Health and the Singapore Council of Social Service. The two ministries, in addition to the provision of direct services, provide overall guidance in planning for welfare and health services respectively. The Singapore Council of Social Service plays a co-ordinating role among non-government organizations and helps in representing their views to the government. A total of 26 voluntary and religious organizations affiliated to the Singapore Council of Social Service are currently providing services to elderly people. In addition, other ministries or statutory bodies may also be responsible for certain schemes concerning the elderly, such as the Housing and Development Board. Taken together, the services offered by the government and non-government organizations are comprehensive (Vasoo and Tan, 1985). Basically, provision of social services for elderly people can be categorized into formal and informal care. Formal services for elderly people in Singapore include community-based services and residential care. Informal services are support given by the family or friends of the elderly people. The provision of social services for elderly people is particularly important in view of the rising number of old people in the community, the smaller size of the family and the greater number of women entering the labour force. The routine of the family can be greatly disrupted when an elderly member becomes weak and requires regular attention. In addition, the large number of elderly people (11 044) who live in one-person households (Census of Population, Release No. 6, Household and Houses, 1980) suggest the vulnerability of this group in times of need and sickness.

Family support services

Traditionally, and to a large extent today, elderly people have been informally cared for by their immediate family or kin members. However, with industrialization and modernization, the capacity to look after elderly people has been reduced. This reduced capacity stems in part from the resettlement programme, in which large extended families living either in the same household or nearby kampongs have been separated and relocated to units in different housing estates. Associated with this is the tendency of young couples to form nuclear families. The breakup of the extended family, together with the tendency to form nuclear families, inevitably leads to a shrinkage in family size which reduces the capacity to support elderly people. The reduced capacity of the family to care for its elderly members is further affected by the increase in number of married women now entering the labour force, particularly the more educated women. Their increased participation in the workforce to improve family income or for self fulfilment has meant a reduction in a traditional source of support for many elderly people during the larger part of the day. With the influence of individualistic and 'Western' values and the general acceptance of these values by the younger generation, the scope for care of some elderly people is expected to be further eroded (see also Chapters 4 and 5 for a discussion of this issue).

Neighbours and friends have also been known to be important sources of informal care for certain elderly people. However, this source of care givers seems to be diminishing as Singapore modernizes and as people are resettled into new housing estates. Not only have some elderly people been separated from old and familiar neighbours, they may also have an uphill task making new friends in the new environment.

Community-based services

Ambulant old people constitute the majority of the elderly population in Singapore, so community-based services play an important role in enabling them to function adequately in their own homes and communities. This overriding principle has been adopted in both the 1982 and 1988 reviews of services for the elderly. In response to the probable inability of the family to provide for elderly people, and the need for community care for them, various community-based services are gradually springing up to help elderly people remain independent in the community. Currently the types of community based services available include:

- *Home nursing services*, in which frail and infirm elderly people are provided with basic nursing care within their own homes. Many of the requests for nursing care arise from recently discharged hospital patients and as referrals from outpatient clinics or general practitioners.
- *Befriending service*. As the name suggests the befriending service involves mobilizing volunteers to befriend elderly people in their own homes as well as in institutional homes. Some of these volunteers, however, go further and assist elderly people with household chores and cleaning. There are presently 41 constituencies with a befriender's service managed by the Ministry of Community Development in conjunction with grassroots organizations. In addition to government initiatives, a number of voluntary welfare organizations are also involved in befriending elderly people.

- *Senior citizens' or retirees' clubs.* In order to meet the needs of the increasing number of elderly people both now and in the future, the People's Association, Residents' Committee, Citizens' Consultative Committee and voluntary organizations have recently established about 166 senior citizens' clubs with a membership of 47 600 elderly people. Most of the activities organized by these clubs are social, educational and recreational in character. The People's Association also provides employment services to retirees who wish to be re-employed through its retirees' club.
- *Day-care centres.* Establishing a day-care centre is one important way to help elderly people remain independent in the community. At present, there are four such centres which provide physiotherapy and/or basic nursing treatment. These centres are instrumental in maintaining and improving the mobility functions of certain elderly people. There are two other day-care centres which are oriented towards social and recreational activities.
- *Meal services.* There are about three voluntary agencies providing meal services to elderly people. In this service, meals at low prices are either provided for elderly people from low-income families in the premises of an agency or delivered to their residence.

With the exception of the home nursing service, most of the other community-based services have yet to be fully developed. For example, the significant increase in the number of senior citizens' clubs has resulted in some teething problems for the clubs in attracting members as well as organizing appropriate programmes for them. As with the senior citizens' clubs, the befriender's service run by the government has a short history. The provision of low-priced meals in the agencies' premises appears to be quite successful as it is patronized by many elderly people. The meal delivery scheme, however, is still trying to establish its clientele and resolve manpower problems. Nonetheless, it is envisaged that with the expected rise in the number of elderly people in the future, the meal delivery scheme may become an important service. This scheme could perhaps best be undertaken by Homes for the Elderly which have the infrastructure to provide and deliver meals to isolated elderly people living in neighbouring housing estates.

As for the day-care centres, there are currently very few with therapeutic functions; it is not generally convenient for elderly people who live far away from these centres to utilize their services. However, as there is a general agreement among policy makers and academics that elderly people should remain as long as possible in the community, more therapeutic day-care centres should be set up in public housing estates. This is necessary to make the service more accessible to the elderly people who are mainly housed in these estates. A plan by the Home Nursing Foundation to establish ten community health centres in public housing estates to provide direct therapeutic, rehabilitative, medical and educational programmes is certainly a positive step to support the independence of old people.

While existing services should be developed further, other forms of services for elderly people should also be explored and possibly introduced in Singapore to provide a broad-based service. Several of these services which merit consideration include:

- A telephone contact service which could be set up to get in touch with old people who are living very much on their own. This service would help to ensure that these elderly people are safe while they are on their own.
- Home-help service to assist with household and domestic chores. Volunteers or paid staff could help those elderly people who need such a service.
- A neighbourhood mobilization scheme in which neighbours who are not working could be approached to lend a helping hand with those elderly people who require assistance during the larger part of the day when their children are at work.
- Pre-retirement courses, which although they have been conducted by the People's Association and by certain companies, are mostly carried out on an ad hoc basis or are based on the interest of a few companies. There is no single body to co-ordinate pre-retirement courses to benefit a broader spectrum of people who are approaching retirement age.
- Health Centres, which once set up would screen the health of elderly people, educate them on health matters and identify risk factors so that early prevention against ill-health can be taken.

- Support for family care-givers because as family members are expected to play an important role in providing care for sick and disabled elderly people it would be useful to initiate a self-help group for them. This self-help group could be a source of encouragement in giving support and advice to families who are faced for the first time with having to care for sick or disabled elderly people.

Residential care

In addition to the community-based services, formal services for elderly people are also provided by various Homes for the Elderly. Admission into a long-term institutional care facility is generally discouraged unless the elderly person, for reasons of physical and/or mental infirmities, cannot be cared for at home. At present, homes for the aged cater primarily for the destitute aged. As of 31 December 1989, there were 70 institutions providing a total of 5 040 beds. Three government-run homes provided a total of 1 525 beds for the destitute aged. The non-government homes, of which 43 were voluntary and 24 were commercial homes, had a capacity of 3 515 beds. There were 1 390 residents in the government homes and 2 788 in non-government homes at the end of 1989.

The aged home was initially established to house destitute elderly migrants in need of assistance and to provide help with meals, housekeeping and other self-maintenance functions. The home normally accommodates more than 80 elderly people in large dormitories and they are usually situated in isolated areas far away from the activities of community life. To meet the changing needs of the elderly population, aged homes managed by voluntary welfare organizations have gradually been opened to a small number of ambulant elderly people who for various reasons are not staying with their own family members.

A close relative of the aged home is the nursing home. In addition to incorporating the general functions of the aged home, nursing homes provide various levels of medical and nursing care to their residents who have health problems. Unlike the aged homes, nursing homes have special provision for admitting semi-ambulant and non-ambulant elderly.

Sheltered care in the form of community homes provides elderly people with the basic necessities of life such as shelter and a sense of security. Unlike the institutional home, the community home provides a certain amount of freedom for elderly people to look after themselves. The home is intentionally located in a public housing estate to allow elderly people in these homes to mingle with the residents in the community. Another form of sheltered care is the temple home which is generally situated away from the mainstream of society. In contrast to community homes, in which residents are encouraged to be involved in the activities of the community, the activities of the residents in temple homes are mainly confined within the home itself. Commercial homes are distinguished from the other types of home by their profit-making motive. The size of commercial homes varies from as few as 20 to over 100 bedspaces. Most commercial homes provide nursing care for their elderly residents.

In a study of 45 homes for the elderly in Singapore (Singapore Council of Social Service, 1985), it was found that 70 per cent of residents were 70 years and above, and 37 per cent were semi-ambulant or non-ambulant. As most of the homes admit mainly ambulant clients, the findings certainly suggest the need for the homes as a whole to prepare for changes so as to meet an expected increase in the number of infirm and sick elderly. Without such preparation, many elderly residents will have to be transferred to other homes with nursing care facilities when they become ill and less mobile. To encourage the transfer of infirm elderly people to other homes with medical facilities and care is probably an unwise option as it may dislocate the social and psychological bearing of such elderly people.

The Council's study also revealed that there was a waiting list of some 287 for the homes. Of these, 58 per cent were waiting to be admitted to homes which provided some form of nursing care. This finding clearly suggests that the demand for care of infirm and weak elderly people will be high. However the demand for care of healthy elderly people is small and insignificant. In view of the expected lack of demand for care of the healthy elderly, aged homes should perhaps consider changing their admission policies to include the semi-ambulant and non-ambulant elderly people as well as incorporating nursing programmes. Alternatively, the aged homes should plan for a change in direction of services, perhaps providing supportive services such as day care and community-based programmes to meet the needs of elderly people in the community. In developing such supportive services, the aged homes would also provide a link between the home and elderly people in the community.

One pertinent question is: will the homes for the elderly be able to cope with the demand for bedspaces? The answer is 'yes'. By looking at the current vacancies (774) and the number of bedspaces planned for the next 5 years (467), it appears probable that demand will be met. Any additional plans to build new homes in the next 5 years should therefore be carefully considered. By building more new homes, unnecessary bedspaces will be generated as a result of an excess supply (Singapore Council of Social Service, 1985). There is therefore also a need to monitor the number of bedspaces and vacancies and the waiting lists in the homes to prevent a situation whereby supply exceeds demand.

One interesting observation about the homes for the elderly is that most of the homes which are managed by voluntary organizations mainly admit the poorer section of the community, while commercial homes mostly admit from the middle and higher income groups. The lower-middle income group hence becomes sandwiched as not rich enough to afford entry into commercial homes nor poor enough to qualify for homes operated by voluntary organizations. Homes should perhaps review their services and provide some openings to serve the often neglected lower-middle income group.

In addition, hardly any homes provide short-term convalescent services to those elderly people who are either recuperating from illness or recovering from disability. Such a service is needed for those elderly people who have working children who, for various reasons, are not able to look after their ailing parents. It is our contention that a short-term convalescent service will be not only of help to ailing elderly people recovering from their illnesses, but it will also cushion the stress that may arise if the working children were to look after elderly people at the critical stage of recuperation.

To ensure that there is a good standard of care in the increasing number of homes for the elderly, the Singapore Council of Social Service and the government have drawn up guidelines on minimum standards of care for these homes (see also Chapter 4). This move is a positive step in

Financial support services

A public assistance scheme under the Ministry of Community Development provides monthly allowances ranging from $140 for single-person households to $400 for four-person households. At present, about 2 833 persons aged 60 and above are receiving direct financial assistance. In addition, voluntary organizations also render assistance in cash and in kind to financially distressed elderly people. Churches, temples, charitable foundations and various community-service groups provide ad hoc aid such as Hong Bao and food to needy elderly people during the festive seasons. However, the various financial schemes lack co-ordination to ensure efficient and effective distribution of financial resources.

Old-age financial security for Singaporeans is provided principally through the CPF scheme, whereby monthly contributions are made by both employees and employers. At present, the rate of contribution is 17.5 per cent for employers and 22.5 per cent for employees. The scheme is run by a statutory board and guaranteed by the government. Contributors can also draw on the fund for approved purposes, such as the purchase of property, payment of medical expenses and other investment ventures. The principal sum plus interest can be withdrawn at the age of 55, except for a sum of $30 000 which can only be withdrawn after the age of 60. This is to provide an added protection for financial well-being in old age against the squandering of savings. Part of the CPF is channelled into a Medisave account which can only be drawn on for medical expenses. At present, the cap for the Medisave account is set at $15 000.

Family support and social support

In Singapore, with only 2 per cent of elderly people living in institutions, the family's role in ensuring the well-being of the elderly is of paramount importance. In a rapidly changing society such as Singapore, the family is also subjected to numerous competing demands that might affect its capability and willingness in the provision of care. In this section of the chapter, the present and future trends in living arrangements and family support are reviewed and assessed (Chen and Cheung, 1988).

Living arrangements

The National Survey on Senior Citizens (1983) showed that about 5 per cent of non-institutionalized elderly people lived alone, with the remainder living in households mainly with immediate relatives. The finding was reaffirmed in a 1986 survey noting that elderly people tended to live with immediate family members. This Survey on the Aged Living in the Community was conducted by the Ministry of Health in 1986. The survey was based on 1 013 persons aged 60 and over who were living in private households. The same survey also showed that the elderly enjoyed reasonably good accommodation with 98 per cent living in satisfactory living conditions in terms of sleeping arrangements, accessibility to facilities and cleanliness. It was also found that home ownership was high and two-thirds of elderly people lived in households with a monthly income exceeding $1 000.

Questions were asked in both surveys about preferred living arrangements. It was found that there was a distinct and overwhelming preference among elderly people to live with their children, in particular their married children. The choice of co-residence appears to be culturally influenced: the Chinese and Indians preferred to live with their married sons, while the Malays preferred to live with their married daughters. The surveys also found an overwhelming reluctance amongst elderly people to stay in old folks' homes, as was expected.

Family support

Findings from a number of studies have shown that most elderly people with immediate relatives (spouse, children and grandchildren) would have few problems in obtaining support in times of need (Chen, 1982a; Cheung, 1988c). They were also found to be engaged in meaningful interactions with the children they lived with and maintained frequent contacts with

Table 4. Care providers for the elderly when ill or needing care, by sex, age and marital status

Care Provider	Sex		Age Group			Marital Status		Total
	Male	Female	60 to 69	70 to 79	80 and Above	Widowed	Married	
Self	11.0	15.1	14.0	12.9	8.3	15.7	10.1	13.2
Spouse	47.9	9.2	32.5	22.8	6.4	0.2	47.9	27.3
Son/daughter-in-law	16.9	38.8	23.6	33.9	43.9	43.9	18.6	28.6
Daughter/son-in-law	8.3	19.6	13.2	15.8	15.9	21.6	9.0	14.3
Grandchildren	0.5	3.4	0.4	2.2	14.0	4.4	0.5	2.1
Others	2.3	3.2	2.9	2.4	3.8	2.7	1.7	2.7
No need	13.1	10.7	13.5	10.0	7.6	11.5	12.1	11.8

Source: Survey on the Aged Living in the Community (1986).

children who were living apart. The respondents were also confident that they could rely on their family for help when they were ill or when they had other problems. Table 4 shows the profile of care givers who tended to the elderly who were ill or who needed care. The prominence of family members as the care givers is clearly shown.

This pattern is really not surprising as the family has always been the primary care giver for its aged members. No evidence has been found in Singapore to suggest that the family, as an institution, is shirking its responsibilities. However, several changes could restrict the effectiveness of the familiy as the primary source of care in the future. First, the increasing involvement of married women in the labour force could reduce the availability of care givers within the family. In 1980, the labour-force participation rate of married women in the 30 to 40 age group was 33 per cent. This increased to 46 per cent in 1988 and, with the shrinking of family size, there are thus likely to be fewer people to share in the responsibility of care. In the 1960s, a woman tended to have about 6 children in her life time. This had fallen to about 4 children in the 1970s and to about 2.5 in the 1980s. There is also concern that the younger generation may not be as filial towards their ageing parents. The decline in family size, coupled with increasing external commitments and possible value changes of the family members, could erode the capability of the family to cope with the care of an aged, and particularly a sick, relative. These changes suggest that the formal support system may have an increasingly important role to play in the future.

To encourage the family to care for its elderly members to the fullest possible extent, the Singapore government has introduced measures which include intergenerational co-residence, income tax relief, a moral education programme, community-based services and legislation.

In the intergenerational co-residence scheme, married children and their parents are allowed to apply for adjoining Housing and Development Board flats. Their applications will also be given priority in allocation. As a financial incentive, a person who is caring for an elderly dependant may be given $3 500 income tax relief from Year of Assessment 1991 provided that the latter is not earning more than $1 500 a year. Moreover, children can claim tax relief of up to $6 000 a year for the equivalent sum of money they have contributed to their parents' CPF account.

Using the moral education programme, the government has initiated changes in the school curriculum to strengthen traditional family values and inculcate filial piety and respect for elderly people. An annual senior citizens' week is being organized to promote the contributions and status of elderly people. A family-life education programme has also been implemented to promote harmonious family living. In support terms, in order to help reduce the burden of care on the family, services such as home visiting, day care and respite care are being offered. The government has also launched various initiatives to promote as much community involvement in these services as possible. Two objectives are emphasized. First, elderly people should be kept fit and healthy, capable of full participation in the mainstream of community life. Second, aged sick people are to be provided with supportive services which will enable them to live with their families for as long as possible.

The Committee on the Problems of the Aged recommended that laws be passed to impose on children the obligation to care for their elderly parents. No legislation has yet been instituted and the Advisory Council on the Aged has subsequently advised against it. However, the government is prepared, if necessary, to institute legal protection for the welfare of elderly people if families appear, in the future, to be abrogating their responsibilities.

Are these measures likely to be effective in fostering greater family support? These measures reflect to a large extent a cultural emphasis on the importance of the family and they are therefore consistent with general sentiments. However, these are essentially passive measures designed to maintain rather than to foster family ties. The moral education programme is therefore special as it takes a proactive role to inculcate specific filial attitudes. Whether such intervention can help to stem the influence of 'Westernization' remains to be seen. However, education of this nature may help prepare the young to accept the challenge of caring for their aged parents.

Community participation and involvement

A major planning principle put forward by the Committee on the Problems of the Aged is the recognition of the potential contribution of elderly people to society and to their own welfare. This principle came through clearly in the committee's report and was again endorsed by the Advisory Council on the Aged. If in the future Singapore is to have a quarter of its population aged 60 and over, it is clear that this vast human resource must be tapped if Singapore is to maintain its economic prosperity. Harnessing the contributions of the elderly population is, however, easier said than done. Age-old prejudices often cast elderly people in a poor light and the emphasis is mainly placed on their problems rather than their potential contributions. The developmental emphasis of the government's approach is therefore encouraging. Recognizing that contribution is possible only through participation, the two national planning committees have given prominent attention to three aspects of participation: health maintenance, community activities and gainful employment. Each of these will be discussed in turn.

Health maintenance

Health is often the critical factor in a person's adjustment in old age. While old age is not necessarily a time of ill health and disability, a variety of chronic illnesses do occur more frequently among elderly rather than younger people. In Singapore, the large majority of elderly people enjoy reasonably good health and lead independent lives. However, they are also disproportionately large consumers of medical care. In 1986, elderly people accounted for 18 per cent of all admissions into government hospitals, while forming only 8 per cent of the population. In absolute numbers, the admission statistics showed an impressive rise of 79 per cent from 23 000 in 1977 to 40 000 in 1986. It is projected that, by the end of the century, their admissions will increase to at least 30 per cent of total admissions. To reduce the level of morbidity among elderly people, the role of primary health care has been emphasized. Three aspects, namely health education, health screening and self-help groups, have been promoted thus far.

It is felt that an elderly person must take the first step towards good health through a healthy life style and a balanced diet. In this regard, the Training and Health Education Department of the Ministry of Health has conducted regular health education classes for elderly people. These are often conducted in public housing estates and public libraries to ensure easy accessibility. The Singapore Sports Council has also assisted in planning physical education for elderly people and the Council has so far trained a number of trainers to conduct exercises for this group. These are held at venues of easy access.

Secondly, health screening is provided for elderly people through a network of screening centres. Early detection often ensures speedy recovery. Currently, there are 38 regular health screening centres located across the island. In addition, there is a network of general practitioners providing outpatient care and general medical advice.

Thirdly, encouragement is given to the formation of self-help or support groups constituted, either by type of ailment or by locality. Such groups are commonly found in day-care centres, especially those with rehabilitative activities. In the future, the establishment of community hospitals, which are intermediate-level care facilities with community involvement, will further help foster the formation of these groups. The first community hospital to be built in a public housing estate is expected to be completed by 1991.

Community activities

Participation in community activities is arguably an indication of an elderly person's integration into society, beyond the confines of the family.

Greater involvement in the community, especially in age-integrated activities, also signifies a respectable status being accorded to elderly people. Conversely, social isolation of elderly people may reflect a poor image of the elderly as a group among the younger generation.

Community participation of elderly people can be grouped into two types: age segregated or age integrated. The former is far more visible in Singapore. With the encouragement of the government, the proliferation of senior citizens' clubs has been rapid. These clubs offer recreational programmes, health screening, keep-fit activities and opportunities for community services. As the name implies, these clubs are open only to senior citizens. At present, there are 166 such clubs with a membership of about 47 600, run mostly by government or paragovernment organizations. Among the few non-government-run clubs, the Singapore Action Group of Elders (SAGE) is the largest, with a membership of about 1 500.

Such age-segregated clubs meet certain needs of the elderly population. They provide a contact point for meeting and making friends and a forum for the exchange of opinions and experiences. Unfortunately, they also segregate elderly people from the other age groups. The establishment of a network of senior citizens' clubs may therefore heighten awareness of the elderly as a distinct social group. Thus far, these clubs are not linked to form a larger organizational base. The National Council of Ageing, proposed by the Advisory Council on the Aged, could conceivably provide the linkage to these clubs, effectively organizing them into a potentially potent self-interest group.

To what extent are elderly people involved in age-integrated activities? This is difficult to assess, as empirical evidence is scarce. In a 1987 survey (The Transition of the Support Systems for the Aged in Singapore, 1987) on the support systems of elderly people, sponsored by the United Nations University, it was found that the most common avenue of participation was through religious activities. Apart from these, the study found that the higher the educational attainment, the greater the involvement in formal organizations. By and large, however, such involvements were not extensive, suggesting very strongly that avenues have to be developed for elderly people to be more involved in age-integrated activities. Reasons cited for non-involvement included being too busy with household chores, lack of interest, and lack of opportunities.

The potential for elderly people to participate in community services in Singapore has yet to be realized. This group clearly possesses varied experience and talents that could be tapped by the community for specific projects. At present, elderly persons are involved largely in ad hoc community activities. More people could be encouraged to join in community services such as child care, home nursing, crime prevention, befriending, teaching and home help. The Volunteers Development Programme of the Singapore Council of Social Service is currently exploring the recruitment of elderly volunteers.

Economic participation

The government has emphasized that elderly people should be encouraged to work for as long as possible in order to maintain mental alertness and financial independence. Moreover, in labour-short Singapore, the elderly constitute an important source of labour supply. However, as noted earlier, there has been a gradual decline in their labour-force participation rates over the past 5 years. The Advisory Council on the Aged, in its deliberations, was aware of the urgent need to promote greater economic participation of elderly people and arrived at four broad recommendations: raising the retirement age; changing the wage system; increasing employment opportunities; and training and retraining.

The Council was of the view that the customary retirement age of 55 should be raised to 60. This increase should be done through negotiations between employers and employees, taking into consideration the special needs and circumstances of each economy or job. However, the government has since indicated that such negotiations may be too slow to bring about changes in retirement age. In spite of the government's urging, only 65 per cent of unionized companies and 25 per cent of non-unionized companies in the private sector had changed their retirement age in 1990. The employers were apparently concerned with the unsuitable nature of the work, the high cost and lower productivity of employing older workers. In a survey on retirement policy conducted by the Labour Relations Department of the Ministry of Labour in 1988, it was found that 47 per cent of the companies with a retirement age below 60 reported that it was impractical to revise their retirement age. The survey was based on 711 unionized companies and 36 unions; among them, 56 per cent gave the reason of unsuitable work and about a third each indicated high cost, lower productivity and less feasibility in employment as reasons. The Ministry of Labour, therefore, announced in March 1989 that the retirement age will be raised to 60 by 1992. The 3-year period of grace is to allow companies to make necessary adjustments.

The Council also noted that wages in Singapore are largely based on seniority. Consequently, the wage bill for an older worker is far greater than for a new entrant, even if they are employed in the same job. As an inducement to encourage employers to retain older workers, the government has reduced the rate of provident fund contributions for older workers. To further facilitate the expansion of employment opportunities, the Council advocated fundamental adjustments in the wage system, taking into account considerations such as the salary being tied to the worth of a job, salary scales being shortened, costly fringe benefits tied to seniority being reduced and staff being rewarded through one-off bonuses rather than through basic wage increments. To increase the employment opportunities, the council urged employers to allow greater options such as part-time work, flexi-time work, working at home or working on alternate days. The Ministry of Labour's Employment Service Department will provide special assistance to older workers in job placements.

The Council recognized that one obstacle in continued employment for older workers is that their skills might be inadequate or outdated. It urged the Skill Development Fund, a statutory body financing skill training, to develop special schemes for older workers and to provide special subsidies to employers to retrain their older workers. It is foreseeable that, in the future, training programmes for older workers will be developed by various local training institutes.

Will these measures taken together halt the decline of the labour-force participation rate of elderly people? The answer to this question is contingent on a number of factors. First, it is clearly essential that these measures are fully implemented. While the government can take steps to encourage the employment of older workers, employers themselves must see the advantages of hiring them. Reluctance on the part of the employers will not help generate work opportunities. Secondly, the attitudes of the older workers may be changing such that leisure is increasingly, valued over continued employment. If this is the case, then Singapore may follow the example of many developed countries in which the participation rates of older workers drop steadily, regardless of employment opportunities.

Regional and international co-operation

As a member state of the United Nations, Singapore has benefited from the regional and international seminars and workshops on ageing organized by ESCAP, CSDHA and UNO. Links with the Ageing Units of the CSDHA and the Institute of the Ageing in Malta have also been established. Singapore is also one of the participating countries in a cross-national research project on support systems for elderly people co-ordinated by the United Nations University.

As noted in Chapter 2, from 1984 to 1988, a major collaborative ageing project at the regional level was launched as a component project of the phase III ASEAN population programme. The project, 'Socio-economic Consequences of the Ageing of the Population', was funded by the Australian government under the ASEAN Australian Economic Co-operation Programme and co-ordinated by Singapore. The major activities undertaken in Singapore during the project years included the conduct of three surveys on the elderly living under different environmental settings, an update on population projections, and a review of the current services available for aged people. The three surveys conducted by the Ministry of Health were the Survey on the Aged Living in the Community (1986), the Survey on the Health Care Needs of the Elderly Sick Living in Their Own Homes (1986) and the Survey on the Aged and Aged Sick Living in Institutions (1986). A national seminar was also convened to disseminate the project's findings to the public, policy makers and planners.

Certain other cross-national research activities are referred to in Chapter 2. Such activities in Singapore include participation in workshops conducted by the National Academy of Sciences of the United States and other professional bodies, and involvement in the major four-country comparative study on social change and ageing, launched in 1989 and funded by the National Institute of Ageing of the United States and co-ordinated by the University of Michigan. A number of international seminars have also been held in Singapore. These include the Seminar on

Research on Ageing in Asia and the Pacific in 1987, and the Workshop on the Transition of Support Systems for the Elderly in 1988.

The Singapore Council of Social Service has regular exchanges with major international voluntary organizations on issues related to ageing. These organizations include the International Council of Social Welfare, Help Age International and Age Concern. It is also affiliated to the International Federation of Ageing. Similarly, the Home Nursing Foundation and other social service agencies maintain contact with their counterparts in other countries.

Conclusion

This study has briefly described Singapore's experience in planning for an ageing society. As a country, Singapore has taken clear steps in meeting the challenges arising from the dramatic increase in the number and proportion of elderly people in the population. Given the current set of demographic characteristics of elderly people, specific areas of their economic and social life have been examined. The staggering fact that there will be an increase in Singapore's elderly population from 4 per cent in 1957 to 25 per cent in 2030 implies that there will be a shift in the pattern of consumption of goods and services among the population. This might well have serious implications for businesses and entrepreneurs.

The emerging national policy on ageing unequivocally emphasizes both humanitarian and developmental concerns. In considering humanitarian concerns, the needs of elderly people are to be met largely by the family with support from the state. The family, however, is expected to remain as the cornerstone of the support network for elderly people. Generally, the elderly are well supported. This shows that the sense of filial piety and family obligation among adults is still strong in Singapore. The government has an important role to play in encouraging and fostering strong ties among intergenerational families through its implementation of appropriate social policies. With respect to developmental implications, elderly people themselves are encouraged to be as fully involved and participative in the community as possible. Economic participation will be assisted through a variety of initiatives. Participation in community and health activities, already widespread, is vigorously promoted. In addition there is scope for the expansion of current services to meet the needs of those elderly people who are isolated from the mainstream of societal life, who require short-term convalescence, who are at high risk of episodes of severe illness and who are often enduring chronic illness and disabilities.

A large number of elderly people are currently left untapped by employers; only 22 per cent of elderly people are in the labour force. If this trend continues, there is a likelihood that issues relating to employment will become contentious. In particular, there will be a need to examine ways of inducing employers to employ and retain older workers. The finding that elderly people in Singapore want to be independent also points to the importance of addressing the future employment needs of the elderly as a group. One issue which will be critical in maintaining the independence of elderly people is the contribution made to the CPF. With the changes in the CPF, there is a need to review how it will affect the future social security of elderly people.

In terms of health status, this chapter shows that elderly people in Singapore are generally in good health. However, in anticipation of a drastic increase in the number of elderly people in the future, one would expect an increased need for preventive and curative medical programmes. This would also mean that there would be an expected increase in the future health expenditure.

What Singapore has done should greatly prepare her to face the uncertainties of an ageing society. What remains uncertain however, is whether elderly people themselves will take their future into their own hands and remain as productive and participative as possible. With at least one-fifth of her population projected to be aged 60 and above by the next century, Singapore's future is inexorably tied to the character and predisposition of her elderly population.

References

Binstock, R.H., Chow, W.S. and Schulz, J.H. (1982). *International Perspectives on Ageing: Population and Policy Challenges*. New York: United Nations Fund for Population Activities.

Chen, A.J. and Cheung, P. (1988). *The Elderly in Singapore.* Phase III ASEAN Population Project, Socioeconomic Consequences of the Ageing of the Population, Singapore Country Report.

Chen, P.S.J. (1982a). *The Elderly in Singapore.* Unpublished survey report, Ministry of Health.

Chen, P.S.J. (1982b). *Survey of Sociological Study in Singapore Society.* A project sponsored by the Faculty of Arts and Social Sciences, National University of Singapore.

Cheung, P. (1988a). *Household and Population Projections, 1990 to 2030.* Singapore: Ministry of Health, Population Planning Unit.

Cheung, P. (1988b). *Population Trends: The Ageing of Singapore.* Singapore: Ministry of Health, Population Planning Unit.

Cheung, P. (1988c). *The Transition of the Social Support Systems for the Aged in Singapore: Emerging Patterns and Policy Options.* Report presented at the Second International Workshop on the Social Support Systems in Transition, Singapore.

Cheung, P. (1989). Beyond Demographic Transition: Industrialization and Population Change in Singapore. *Asia–Pacific Population Journal*, 4, 35-38.

Department of Statistics, Singapore (1980). *Census of Population 1980: Administrative Report.*

Department of Statistics, Singapore (1980). *Census of Population Release No 6. Household and Houses, 1980.*

Department of Statistics, Singapore (1989). *Yearbook of Statistics.*

Ministry of Communications and Information (1990). *Singapore 1990*, Singapore.

Ministry of Community Development, Singapore (1989). *Annual Report.*

Ministry of Health, Singapore (1982). *R and E Monitor and Morbidity among Elderly in Singapore.*

Ministry of Health, Singapore (1984). *Report of the Committee on the Problems of the Aged.*

Ministry of Labour (1984a). *Report on the Labour Force Survey of Singapore*, Research and Statistics Department, Ministry of Labour, Singapore.

Ministry of Labour (1984b). *Singapore Yearbook of Labour Statistics*, Research and Statistics Department, Ministry of Labour, Singapore.

Ministry of Social Affairs, Singapore (1983). *Report on the National Survey on Senior Citizens.*

National University of Singapore (1987). *The Transition of the Support Systems for the Aged in Singapore: Emerging patterns and policy options.*

Research and Statistics Department (1984). *Report on the Labour Force Survey of Singapore.* Ministry of Labour, Singapore.

Research and Statistics Department (1984). *Singapore Yearbook of Labour Statistics*. Ministry of Labour: Singapore.

Singapore Council of Social Service (1984). *Social Policy and the Elderly in Singapore*, Report of the Study Group on the Elderly, Singapore.

Singapore Council of Social Service (1985). *A Survey on Homes for the Elderly in Singapore*.

Vasoo, S. and Tan, B.H. (1985). *The Status of Ageing in Singapore*. Unpublished manuscript, Singapore Council of Social Service.

Verbrugge, L.M. (1983). Women and men: mortality and health of older people. In *Ageing in Society: Selected reviews of recent research*, M.W. Riley, B.B. Hess and K. Bond (Eds). Lawrence Erlbaum Associates, New Jersey.

You, P.S. and Lim, C.Y. (Eds.) (1984). *Singapore: Twenty-Five Years of Development*. Nan Yang Xing Zhou Lianhe Zaobao: Singapore.

Chapter 6

Singapore's ageing population: Social challenges and responses*

S. Vasoo, Tee-Liang Ngiam and Paul Cheung

Introduction

One of the most challenging social phenomena of the future is population ageing in Singapore, one of the fastest ageing countries in the Asia-Pacific region. In Singapore, where the average life expectancy at birth is about 77 years, the elderly population is considered to comprise those who are 60 years and above (Department of Statistics 1997). The population-ageing trend has been conspicuous. In 1970, there were about 116,100 persons aged 60 and above. The number increased by over 50 per cent to 170,400 in 1980. By the turn of the century, the number will rise to about 329,900, some 11 per cent of the population. It has been estimated that 25 per cent of Singaporeans will be above 60 years by 2030 (Cheung and Vasoo 1989; Shantakumar 1994). Recently, the official retirement age has been raised from the previous 55 years old to 60

---

*Reprinted with permission by the publisher from Vasoo, S., Ngiam T.-L., & Cheung, P. P. L. (2000). Singapore's Ageing Population: Social Challenges and Responses. In D. R. Phillips (Ed.), *Ageing in Asia-Pacific Region* (pp. 174–193). London: Routledge.

The paper explores the social challenges of Singapore's population ageing issues and recommends more efforts and resources to be directed at the development of community care and support services for the elderly.

years and 62 years; it is intended to further increase this to 67 years in the near future (Shantakumar 1999).[1]

The annual growth rate of the ageing population for the next thirty years will be around 3 per cent and the elderly population will grow between 11 per cent and 26 per cent from 1990 to 2030 (Shantakumar 1994; ESCAP 1996). Such a sharp increase will have crucial implications for social policies and support services for older persons. More importantly, as in a number of other countries in the region (see Chapter 2), the number of 'old-old' persons 75 years and above will see a steep increase (Phillips and Bartlett 1995; Yap and Tan 1998) and this group is at high risk for care and attention. More family resources will have to be drawn to attend to their social and physical requirements and some families will face stress and difficulties in providing care for sick and disabled older persons. Senior citizens' organizations and community groups will be able to play a more effective role if they can now actively begin examining the potential future needs and problems facing senior citizens and organizing programmes that attract participation of senior citizens living in various neighbourhoods. They will have to review their objectives, organizational structures and management capabilities so that their programmes are able to reach out efficiently and effectively to as many senior citizens as possible.

The accelerated ageing has been identified as a major challenge that will confront Singapore in the future. This trend, shared by other newly industrializing countries, is anticipated to result in a broad-based transformation of the society, requiring adjustments and adaptations at all levels. It will significantly alter the dependency ratio between the young and the elderly.

Social issues in ageing in Singapore

In older housing estates, the ageing process has become yet more transparent. There are increasing numbers of older senior citizens living in these estates and it is urgent for community groups and organizations to begin to plan the establishment of more community-based programmes

---

[1] More demographic details of Singapore's population may be found in Shantakumar (1994) and Cheung (1988a and 1988b).

such as day care, meals programmes, home-help service and domiciliary nursing care and crisis response services. In taking a proactive approach to initiate a network of services in older housing estates, Singapore hopes to be able to provide support for families with vulnerable older members and prevent disruptions to the social and economic lives of families.

One major concern facing older persons is the maintenance of good health and it is therefore important to promote healthy living to avoid the misery of poor health in old age. The prolongation of life as a result of improved medical technology can otherwise raise various moral and philosophical issues about sustenance of life and dying. Older persons and their families will increasingly have to be better prepared to deal with this life reality and dilemma. For older persons to reduce the risk of disabling conditions, it is important to enhance their physical and mental capacities and strengthen their support networks.

Preparation for retirement is also an important issue, in which the community can take steps to help and encourage older persons. The more positive efforts the elderly take in maintaining healthy lifestyles, the less dependent they are likely to be and need care and attention. In this again the community can take action to motivate more older persons to be involved in local self-help groups. Through these self-help groups and mutual support groups, elderly people with different needs and problems could be assisted. The strong can help the less strong.

In 1997, it was estimated that 48.1 per cent or almost one out of every two persons between the age of 55 and 59 years was economically inactive, and among those between 60 years and 64 years, the percentage was even higher at 67.6 per cent (Department of Statistics 1997). The labour-force participation rate of these two age groups is indeed low and there is an urgency to encourage more older workers to be retained in the workforce. Employers therefore have to be encouraged to appreciate that retirees and potential retirees have a wealth of accumulated experience which could be tapped by their companies. Singapore recognizes that it is sad to see such a pool of talent wasted. Indeed, as the number of people in the retirement age group is on the increase and likely to affect even more people in the future, it is timely for both the public and private sectors to devote more resources and programmes to the retraining and placement of retirees. However, at present, there is a lack of specialized services to cater for the specific job placement needs of retirees.

There are a number of significant social adjustments that retirees have to make and they have to be tackled in the light of the resources and support available to them by their families, peers and the community. There is also generally a reduction of personal income faced by retirees and they need to plan how to use limited funds most effectively. Many retirees therefore need to have access to reliable advice on investments and savings, to avoid risky investments and ventures. More reliable investment advice should be made available through trade unions and bona fide companies. Lee (1998) has reviewed the changing incidence of poverty among older people and social security policy and responses in Singapore.

In the years ahead, Singapore, a modern city-state, can expect a continuing acceleration of social and technological change. As a result, retirees will inevitably be confronted with complex problems that require them to become more conscious of the need to engage with the challenges of technological demands of the modern environment. Indeed, in future, retirees might well have to become computer literate in order to operate certain modern transactions. Retraining policies are therefore expected to be promoted in line with the higher retirement age and re-employment opportunities (Shantakumar 1999). In addition, a key aspect of retired life is how to use more leisure time. All retirees have to find meaningful ways of spending their leisure time and, indeed, many retirees face leisure problems and have difficulties in coping with the increased time available, and need to view leisure activities as opportunities for self-development. They tend to believe that only work provides them with meaning. The retirees require organizations that can help them to engage in various social and economic activities that enhance or sustain their social well-being. The work of a retirees club should be strengthened by providing more comprehensive programmes to deal with social and recreational needs, employment, retirement planning, volunteer service and personal guidance.

Some impacts of an ageing population

Two social implications have received particular emphasis. First, concern has been expressed as to whether the ageing of the population will

Table 1. Actual and projected working-age persons per older person and index of ageing of the population in Singapore, 1980–2030

Year	Working-Age Persons Elderly Persons	Index of Aging (Per Hundred)
1980	13.7	17.3
1990	11.6	26.8
1997 (June)	10.0	30.9
2000	9.8	31.8
2010	8.7	40.8
2020	3.3	69.7
2030	8.5	103.9

Notes: 1 Working age persons per elderly person = residents aged 15–64 years divided by residents aged 65 years and above.
2 Index of ageing = residents aged 65 years and above divided by residents aged under 15 years.

Source: Inter-Ministerial Committee on Health Care for the Elderly (1999).

increase the dependency ratio on the state for welfare and financial assistance. A related question is whether the traditional caring institutions will remain intact given the rapid social changes that Singapore is experiencing. Second, concern has also been expressed over the social and economic implications of population ageing and its potential impact on the economy's future development. Recent data suggest that there are about ten people of working age per older person today but that this will fall to only 3.5 persons economically active per elderly person. An index of ageing, at 30.9 in 1997, will more than treble to 103.9 by 2030 (Table 1).

Increasing awareness of issues surrounding older persons in Singapore was generated as early as the 1970s. Several studies were conducted at that time and, in the 1990s, the number of studies has increased significantly. Even by 1985, there were at least ten known studies, one of which was 'Social Policy and the Elderly' (1981) conducted by the then Singapore Council of Social Service (1981). In addition, the appointment of five high-level committees since 1982 to review the various issues and problems arising from population ageing reflected this concern.[2] There was also an

---

[2] These committees, which were formed to look into issues related to ageing, included: The Committee on the Problems of the Aged (1984), Advisory Council on the Aged (1988),

awareness that the rapidity of the ageing process and its consequences are related to, if not an outcome of, the policies implemented in the past. The five committees, chaired by cabinet ministers and comprising representatives from various sectors, were given the task of reviewing the policy options and recommending policy changes. The work of these committees, as well as other initiatives, marked Singapore's continuing efforts to plan for an ageing society. The Report of the Committee on Problems of the Aged (1984), commonly known as the Howe Report, opened the door to greater public attention and debate on the issues facing older persons.

The national efforts to approach population ageing may be discussed broadly under policy responses and delivery of programmes. Three factors deserve special mention at the outset. First, population ageing and its implications have been placed high on the political agenda. The ruling political party, The People's Action Party (PAP) has explicitly identified population ageing as an important issue in its agenda for national discussion and action. Second, Singapore is spatially relatively small and an extensive network of government and non-government organizations are already in place. Therefore, it is possible to exploit what is already in existence in the creation of a support infrastructure for older persons. Third, the growing affluence of Singapore makes it possible for government and society to deploy resources to the programmes and services for older persons, leading to a rapid expansion of the formal support network.

Policy responses

In the 1970s, the concern for the welfare of immigrant older persons led to the establishment of a number of services catering to their special needs. Such services were formulated by the then Ministry of Social Affairs in conjunction with the then Singapore Council of Social Service. Although this attracted some attention, planning efforts were essentially sectoral and services were treated as an extension of the

---

National Advisory Council on the Family and The Aged (1989), Inter-Ministerial Committee on Health Care for the Elderly (1997) and the Inter-Ministerial Committee on Ageing Population (1998).

existing social welfare schemes. In the 1980s, concern broadened as the implications of population ageing were made known. The fact that the problems of older persons will not disappear along with the passage of the group of immigrant, destitute aged led to serious reviews of the issue. In June 1982, the appointment of a high-level thirteen-member committee marked the beginning of the government's efforts to understand the wider implications of population ageing and to implement appropriate policy measures.

The Committee on the Problems of the Aged was chaired by the then Minister for Health, Mr Howe Yoon Cheong. In its deliberations, the Committee took the problems of older persons beyond the realm of humanitarian and social welfare concerns and noted the long-term impact and ramifications of population ageing. As a result, the Committee stressed the potential contributions of the elderly to the society and the importance of incorporating them in socioeconomic development, while concurrently acknowledging and meeting their special needs. To assist in its deliberations, the Committee commissioned the National Survey on Senior Citizens in 1983,[3] providing updated information from an earlier study conducted in 1976.[4]

The Howe Report was finalized and released in March 1984. Several of its policy recommendations were controversial, such as raising the eligible age for provident fund withdrawal and legislation on filial piety and, indeed, led to much public outcry and discussion. However, the bulk of the Howe Report's recommendations were accepted, among which the major ones included change in provident fund contribution rates for older persons to generate employment for older workers, legislation on minimum standards for aged homes, increased elderly dependants' relief under the Income Tax Act and measures to foster family and intergenerational cohesion.

---

[3] The National Survey on Senior Citizens was conducted jointly by the then Ministry of Social Affairs and the Ministry of Health for the Committee on the Problems of the Aged. The Survey was based on 5,538 persons aged 55 years and above and who were living in private households (Ministry of Social Affairs, Singapore, 1983).

[4] *The Elderly in Singapore*: report of a survey sponsored by the Ministry of Health in 1976 (Chen, P., 1982, Ministry of Health).

To implement the Howe Report's recommendations, several committees were established with members drawn from relevant ministries, statutory boards, the education sector and non-government agencies. A Co-ordination Committee was set up in August 1985 under the Ministry of Community Development (formerly the Ministry of Social Affairs) to implement the Howe Report, as well as to evaluate and oversee the implementation of its recommendations. In January 1986, the Committee to Co-ordinate the Development of Programmes and Activities was formed in the Ministry of Community Development to promote, direct and supervize the implementation of the Howe Report's recommendations with respect to health and recreational needs, social services and institutional care by government and non-government agencies. A Committee on Public Awareness on Ageing was also established to spearhead a public education and awareness programme in the Ministries of Community Development and Communication and Information to project a more wholesome image of senior citizens (a programme was launched in November 1987). That year also saw the establishment of a tripartite Task Force on the Employment of the Elderly in the Ministry of Labour. The task force comprised employers, government and union representatives to study the need to provide counselling and retraining of older workers.

Recognizing that population ageing is also a demographic issue, the government established in 1984 an Inter-Ministerial Population Committee (IMPC) to undertake a comprehensive review of Singapore's population trends and to make recommendations on policy measures to arrest the declining fertility rate and to bring about the desired population size and composition. Chaired by the Permanent Secretary of the Ministry of Health and reporting to the First Deputy Prime Minister, the members of the IMPC comprised of Permanent Secretaries of relevant government ministries. Following the IMPC's recommendations, Singapore's population policy was revised in 1987. The Committee, assisted by the Population Planning Unit, monitored Singapore population's trends. In June 1988, the National Advisory Council on the Aged, headed by the Minister for Home Affairs, was formed to undertake a comprehensive review of the status of ageing in Singapore. Its term of reference included the review of programmes and services available to older persons, to examine the premises, assumptions and policy recommendations contained in the 1984 Report on the Problems of the Aged, to suggest ways to enable older persons to work beyond age 55 and, finally, to examine how families could be helped to look after their elderly dependants.

The National Advisory Council appointed four committees to look into the specific issues of concern: committees on community-based programmes for the aged, attitudes towards the aged, residential care programmes for the aged and employment for the aged. The composition of the members of the Advisory Council and the committees included experts from government ministries, statutory boards and voluntary organizations concerned with the provision and planning of services for the elderly. In September 1988, reports of the four committees were reviewed by the Advisory Council and subsequently submitted for government consideration. One key recommendation proposed was the establishment of a National Council on Ageing with the character and authority of a statutory board to plan and coordinate policies and programmes for older persons. Other proposals included raising the retirement age from 55 to 60, adjusting the seniority-based wage system so that more older people would be employed, expanding and strengthening public education programmes on older persons and ageing so that appropriate attitudes towards older persons could be inculcated, making land available for voluntary organizations to set up homes for older persons, lengthening the term leases for homes, studying the feasibility of providing health and medical services for frail older persons living in their own homes and increasing the dependency tax rebate for families who look after older persons.

To meet further challenges of population ageing, the 1990s saw the development of two milestone policies implemented to deal with anticipated problems related to the social and health care of older persons. Very significant legislation, the Maintenance of Parents Act, was introduced in 1994 after much deliberation by community groups and the Parliamentary Select Committee. There was public endorsement for the policy to impose a legal obligation on children to maintain their parents. Such a social policy, almost unique in Asia, deals with prevention and problems of neglect of elderly parents. In most urban societies, it appears likely that family breakdowns will increase and these have consequences on care and support for the elderly. Another enlightened policy covering medical care of terminally ill persons was put in place. More specifically, under the

Advanced Medical Directive Act, persons who have been medically certified to be brain dead can now under their earlier directives be taken off medical life support. Such a progressive and futuristic policy will perhaps reduce unnecessary suffering to both terminally ill older persons and their families.

A national policy on ageing in Singapore has taken shape after a number of successive policy reviews. Two characteristics in the policy formulation process should be noted. First, the various committees have had the benefit of representation from various sectors, providing diverse inputs and making implementable decisions. Historically, cross-sectoral representation has worked well in the local context and it is the standard feature in Singapore's government problem-solving approach. Second, the committees were given much publicity raising awareness of the issues especially when controversial recommendations were made. The enhanced discussion on policy changes by the public sees an increasing emphasis on the social care of older persons in Singapore. Public inputs thus become an important consideration in the committees' deliberations.

In anticipation of the serious social and economic challenges which will be posed by an acute ageing population in the next two decades, the government and policy-makers established the Inter-Ministerial Committee (IMC) on Ageing Population in October 1998. The IMC comprises ministers, members of parliament, senior civil servants and representatives of non-governmental organizations dealing with older persons. The IMC's tasks were to identify the challenges of a rapidly ageing population, recommend policy directions and suggest coordinated national efforts to tackle the various issues confronting Singapore's increasing elderly population. The IMC canvasses views and recommendations from a wide range of sources including community groups and those who have direct contacts with older persons. In this connection, the IMC set up workgroups to report in late 1999, on employment and employability, housing and land-use policies, financial security, social integration of the elderly, healthcare and cohesion and conflict in an ageing society (Ministry of Community Development 1999). Such a coverage of areas enables the IMC to propose comprehensive recommendations which will hopefully prepare Singapore to successfully and gracefully handle some of the challenges of its senior citizens in the future.

Programmes and services

The programme plans and services for older persons are coordinated through three principal organizations: the Ministry of Community Development, the Ministry of Health and the National Council of Social Service. The two ministries, in addition to providing some direct services, provide overall guidance in planning for welfare and health services respectively. The National Council of Social Service plays a coordinating role among nongovernment welfare organizations and helps in representing their views to the government. Some sixty-seven voluntary and religious organizations affiliated to the Singapore National Council of Social Service (1997) were providing services to older persons in 1997. In addition, other ministries or statutory bodies may also be responsible for certain schemes concerning older persons, such as the Housing and Development Board (HDB) which has been providing special housing for older persons. The services offered by government and NGOs are quite comprehensive and fall under the categories of formal and informal care. Formal services for older persons in Singapore include community-based services, residential and health care. Informal services are those given by the families or friends of older persons.

Presently, community-based services available in Singapore cover such aspects as the home nursing services, befriending service, senior citizens' or retirees' club activities, day care centres, and a free or cheap meal service. While existing community-based services should be developed further, other forms of services for older persons such as telephone contact service, home-help service, neighbourhood mobilization scheme, health centres and support for family caregivers should also be explored and possibly introduced to provide a wider coverage of community-based services.

Residential care in Singapore includes aged homes, nursing homes, community homes and commercial homes. Support services for older persons are particularly important in view of their rising number in the community, smaller size of the family and more women entering the labour-force. In addition, the number of single older persons (8,905) who live in one-person households (Shantakumar 1994) is expected to increase in the near future and they can be vulnerable in times of need and sickness. In Singapore, with only 2 per cent of elderly people living in institutions, the family's role in ensuring the well-being of older persons is of paramount importance. In a rapidly changing society, the family is also subjected to numerous competing demands that might affect its capability in the provision of care.

Family structure and care

In terms of household structure, the National Survey of Senior Citizens (1996) showed that about 8.3 per cent of non-institutionalized older persons lived alone or with their spouse; the remainder lived in households with immediate relatives or others. The 1996 rinding also confirmed an earlier survey that the elderly tended to live with immediate family members and the survey also showed that older people enjoyed reasonably good public-flat accommodation. It was observed that 93.3 per cent of the older people were staying in satisfactory living conditions in terms of sleeping arrangements, accessibility to facilities and cleanliness. It was also found that home ownership was high and 79.1 per cent of older persons were living in households with a monthly income exceeding $1,000. In terms of preferred living arrangements, there was a distinct and overwhelming preference among older persons to live with their children, in particular, their married children. The choice of co-residence appears to be culturally influenced: Chinese and Indian respondents preferred to live with their married sons while Malays preferred their married daughters. The surveys also found an overwhelming reluctance among older persons to stay in old folks' homes, as might be expected.

The findings from a number of studies have shown that most of the older persons with immediate relatives would have few problems in obtaining support in times of need (Chen and Cheung 1988; Cheung 1988c; Ministry of Health *et al.* 1996). Older persons were also often found to be engaged in meaningful interactions with the children with whom they lived and maintained frequent contacts with children who were living apart. The respondents were also confident that they could rely on their family for help when they were ill or when they had other problems. So far, no evidence has been found to suggest that the family, as an institution, is shirking its responsibilities. However, several familial changes could restrict the effectiveness of the family as the primary source in the future. First, the increasing involvement of married women in the labour-force could reduce the availability of caregivers within the family. In 1997, the labour-force participation rate among married women was about 78 per cent. This has increased since 1987 and with the shrinking of family size, there is also likely to be fewer persons to share out the responsibility of care. There is also concern that the younger generation may not be as filial towards their ageing parents. The decline in family size, coupled with increasing external commitments and value changes of the family members could erode the coping capability of the family in the care for aged sick relatives. These changes suggest that formal support system may have an important role to play in the future. Therefore, to encourage the family to care for its elderly members to the fullest extent possible, the government has introduced measures which include the intergenerational co-residence scheme, income tax relief, moral education programme and community-based services. In the intergenerational co-residence scheme, married children and their parents are allowed to apply for adjoining HDB flats and their applications are given priority. For a person who is caring for an elderly dependant, $4,500 income tax relief is given, provided that the relative is not earning more than $1,500 a year. Moreover, children can claim tax relief of up to $6,000 a year for the equivalent sum of money they have contributed to their parents' Central Provident Fund (CPF) account.

In addition to the family support and community-based services, financial support services are also available. The Public Assistance Scheme under the Ministry of Community Development provides monthly allowances ranging from $200 for single-person households to $570 for four-person households and above. Some 1,960 persons aged 60 and above receive direct financial assistance (Department of Statistics 1997). In addition, voluntary organizations also render assistance in cash and kind to the financially distressed. Churches, temples, charitable foundations and various community service groups also provide *ad hoc* aid such as *Hong Bao* ('money in red packets') and food for needy older persons during the festive seasons. However, the various financial schemes lack coordination to ensure efficient and effective distribution of financial resources. Old-age financial security for Singaporeans is provided principally through the CPF scheme, whereby both employees and employers make monthly contributions. In 1999, the contribution was 20 per cent each by employees and employers. The scheme is run by a statutory board and guaranteed by the government. Contributors can also draw on the fund for approved purposes, such as the purchase of property, payment of medical expenses and other investment ventures. The principal sum plus interest can be withdrawn at age 55, except for a minimum sum of $40,000 which can only be withdrawn after the age of 60. This is to provide an added protection for financial well-being in old age and to protect against any squandering of savings. Part of the CPF is channelled into a Medisave account, which can only be drawn for medical expenses, with the cap for this account set at $20,000.

To help reduce the burden of care on the family, services such as home visiting, day care and respite care are being offered. The government has also launched various initiatives to promote as much community involvement in provision of these services as possible. Two objectives are emphasized. First, to keep older persons fit and healthy, and capable of full participation in the mainstream of community life. Second, the elderly sick persons are to be provided supportive services which will enable them to live with their families for as long as possible.

Are these measures likely to be effective in fostering greater family support? They reflect to a large extent the cultural emphasis on the importance of the family and are therefore consistent with general sentiments. However, these are essentially passive measures designed to maintain rather than to foster families ties. The moral education programme is therefore special as it takes a proactive role to inculcate specific filial attitudes, although whether such intervention can help to stem the influence of Westernization remains to be seen. However, education of this nature may help prepare the young to accept the challenge of caring for their aged parents.

Community participation and involvement

A major planning principle put forward by the various committees dealing with issues related to the problem ageing in Singapore is the recognition of the potential contribution of older persons to society and to their own welfare. This principle came through clearly in the main reports and has been endorsed fully because older persons of the future will be resourceful. If Singapore were to have a quarter of its population aged 60 and over, it is clear that this vast reservoir of human resources must be tapped if its economic prosperity is to be maintained. Harnessing the contributions of older persons is, however, easier said than done. Age-old prejudices often cast older persons in a poor light and emphasis is mainly placed on their problems rather than their potential contributions. The developmental emphasis of the government's approach is therefore encouraging. Recognizing that contribution is possible only through participation, much prominent attention is given to three aspects of participation, covering health maintenance, community activities and gainful employment.

Health is often the critical factor in a person's adjustment in old age. While old age is not necessarily a time of ill health and disability, a variety of chronic illnesses do occur more frequently among older persons than among the younger population. In Singapore, the large majority of older persons enjoy reasonable good health and lead independent lives, but older persons are also disproportionately large consumers of medical care. It is observed that about 7 per cent of older persons in the population are reported to have been hospitalized, which accounts for a significant proportion of hospital admissions. In 1997, the projected admission of older persons based on a rate per 1000 resident population was 101.2 for those aged between 55 and 59 years old and 136.1 for those between 60 and 64 years old. The need for hospital care for older persons is likely to be more acute in the years ahead, as the population ages yet more. To reduce the level of morbidity among older persons, the role of primary health care has been emphasized and three aspects (health education, health screening and self-help groups) have been promoted actively.

Participation in community activities may be taken as an indication of the integration of older persons into society, beyond the confines of the family. Greater involvement in the community, especially in age-integrated activities, signifies a respectable status accorded to older persons. Conversely, social isolation of older persons may reflect a poor image of elderly people in the eyes of the younger generation. Community participation of older persons can be grouped into two types: age-segregated and age-integrated. The rapid proliferation of Senior Citizens' Clubs, encouraged by the government, is one example of the former and these clubs offer recreational programmes, health screening, keep-fit activities and opportunities for community services by older persons. There are over 240 such clubs with a total membership of more than 60,000 persons, run at community centres by the People's Association. Among the few non-government run clubs, the Singapore Action Group of Elders (SAGE) is the largest and such age-segregated clubs meet certain needs of older persons. They provide a contact point for meeting and making friends and a forum for exchange of opinions and experiences. However, they do, perhaps unfortunately, also segregate older persons from other age groups. The establishment of a network of Senior Citizens' Clubs may heighten the awareness of older persons as a distinct social group that can become articulate and resourceful, but, so far, these clubs are not linked to form a larger organizational base. The new Singapore chapter of the Retired and Senior Volunteer Programme (RSVP) could conceivably provide the linkage to these clubs, effectively organizing them into a potentially potent self-interest group.

On the other hand, to what extent are older persons in Singapore involved in age-integrated activities? This is difficult to assess, as empirical evidence is scarce. In a study on the support systems of older persons, sponsored by the United Nations University,[5] it was found that the most common avenue of participation is through religious activities. Apart from these, the study found that the higher the educational attainment, the greater the involvement in formal organizations. By and large, however, such involvement was not extensive, suggesting very strongly that avenues have to be developed for older persons to become more involved in age-integrated activities. Reasons for non-involvement included being too busy with household chores, lack of interest and lack of opportunities. It should be stressed that the potential for older persons to participate in community services has yet to be realized. More highly educated older persons possess varied experience and talents that could be tapped by the community for specific projects. At present, older persons are involved in *ad hoc* community activities and more could be encouraged to join in

---

[5] 'Research Project on the Transition of the Support Systems for the Aged in Singapore: Emerging Patterns and Policy Options', National University of Singapore, research sponsored by United Nations University, Japan, 1987.

community services such as child-care, home nursing, crime prevention, befriending, teaching and home-help. The Volunteer Action and Development Centre of the National Council of Social Service and the Lions Befrienders Club are exploring various avenues for the involvement of elderly volunteers.

It has been the emphasis of the government that older persons should be encouraged to work for as long as possible in order to maintain mental alertness and financial independence. In addition, Singapore has experienced labour shortages and older persons constitute an important source of labour supply. However, as noted earlier, there has been a gradual decline in their labour-force participation rates in the past five years.

Challenges of an increasing population of retirees

Re-employment of retirees

In view of the future shortage of manpower and slow growth of Singapore's population, the question of retirement from work is receiving growing attention and there will be increasing demands from trade unions and older workers to extend the retirement age beyond 62 years. However, despite the persuasions from both trade unions and government that the retirement age should be extended, the response from employers, particularly in the private sector, has been lukewarm and slow. Many employers are apparently concerned with the unsuitable nature of work, the high cost and possible lower productivity of employing elderly workers. If this situation continues into the next decade, there will be a need to take a more concerted action to popularize the extension of the retirement age.

The National Wage Council (NWC) has noted that wages in Singapore are largely based on seniority. Consequently, the wage costs for employing an older worker are generally greater than for a new entrant, even if they are employed in the same job. As an inducement to encourage employers to retain elderly workers, the government has reduced the rate of provident fund contributions for elderly workers. To further facilitate the expansion of employment opportunities, the NWC advocated fundamental adjustments in the wage system. This takes into account considerations such as tying the salary to the worth of a job, shortening salary scales, reducing costly fringe benefits tied to seniority, and rewarding staff through one-off bonuses rather than through basic wage increments. To increase employment opportunities, the NWC has urged employers to allow greater options such as part-time work, flexi-time work, working at home or working on alternate days. The Ministry of Manpower's Employment Service Department could set up a special section to assist older workers in job placements.

The NWC has recognized that one obstacle in continued employment for older workers can be inadequate or outdated skills. It urged the Skills Development Fund, a statutory body financing skills training, to develop special schemes for older workers and to provide special subsidies to employers in retraining their elderly workers. It may be foreseen that, in the future, various local training institutes will develop training programmes for elderly workers.

Will these measures taken together halt the decline in the older persons labour-force participation rate? The answer to this question is contingent on a number of factors. First, it is clearly essential that various measures to encourage employment of elderly workers are fully implemented. While the government can take steps to encourage the employment of elderly workers, employers themselves must also see the advantage of hiring them and reluctance on the part of the employers will not help to generate work opportunities. Second, the attitudes of older workers may be changing, such that leisure is increasingly valued over continued employment. If this is the case, then Singapore may follow the example of many developed countries in which the participation rates of elderly workers has dropped steadily regardless of employment opportunities. It is also important to note that the retention of retirees may affect job openings for the young and the potential problems of re-employing older persons and the resulting frustrations of younger persons deserve serious consideration.

Health care provision

Increasing demand for health care is probably inevitable due to advances in medical technology, longer life-expectancy, population ageing, increasing affluence and education and hence expectations of the people. In 1957, for example, life-expectancy at birth was only 63 years, whereas in the late 1990s it was 77.1 years (Shantakumar 1994; Department of Statistics

1997). Indeed, improvements in life-expectancy among older persons, particularly among older males, have been much greater than among the general population.

In recent years, the issue of rising costs of health care in Singapore has been a subject of considerable public debate. This has been generated in part by the government's move to restructure and corporatize public hospitals and the general concern among consumers of the increasing costs in health care. The total expenditure on health care in Singapore is about 2.8 per cent of the GDP (Ministry of Health 1997/8) and the level of health care expenditure is still low compared to many Western countries. Over the ten years from 1988, government recurrent expenditure on health care increased by two-fold from $506 million in 1988 to $1240 million in 1997 (Ministry of Health 1997/98). In the future, health care expenditure is predicted to increase steeply, especially with an ageing population and, as Singaporeans become more affluent and better educated, the demand for better health care services will expand. The important issue is that the increasing expectation for health care must be balanced with affordability (Toh and Low 1992, 205–24).

More concerted efforts by the government are anticipated to implement various cost containment measures. These include curtailing the increasing demand for health care, promotion of primary health care, regulating the supply of health services, reduction of subsidies for those who can afford care, the establishment of community hospitals, cost controls on high-tech medicine and the efficient use of health care professionals. Summaries of projected demands for health and long-term care over the next three decades may be seen in the report on health care needs of older people (Inter-Ministerial Committee on Health Care for the Elderly 1999).

What most people really want is good health and not good health care. As the major provider of health services to the population, the government could also lead in setting realistic standards of health care by regulating the amount of cost that the public is willing to pay and can afford to share. This could help in dampening or slowing down the demand for better health care and services so that it would not be incompatible with the country's economic growth. Moreover, the government could also help to contain the increasing cost of health care by improving productivity in the public health services and encouraging competition among health care providers in both the public and private sectors. On the other hand, the provision of efficient preventive health care and frontline preventive services through the primary health care services will play an increasingly important part in keeping the population healthy and curtailing the demand for health care. Comprehensive immunisation programmes have helped to prevent many serious infectious diseases and, likewise, early detection and treatment of serious conditions might reduce the need for costly hospitalization. To help with this, the government could continue to ensure that the primary health care services are easily available to the population. Careful consideration has to be taken to ensure that there are sufficient subsidized classes of hospital beds (in Singapore, B2 and C class) for those in low income groups or the group will find health care less accessible and might lead to delays in seeking treatment, which can further add to costs. On health financing, the PAP government's policy is that the Medisave Scheme (which aims to build an individual's financial resources) should be used so that people who fall sick have the means to pay for their health care, especially in old age. As this depends on an individual's personal savings, incentives have already been provided for people to stay well and use their Medisave account wisely.

Service responses at the grassroots level

Senior citizens' organizations can arguably play a more effective role at the grassroots level if they begin to examine the needs and problems facing older persons and organize programmes which attract the participation of older persons living in various neighbourhoods. In addition, they must review their objectives, organizational structures and management capabilities so that their programmes reach out efficiently and effectively to as many older persons as possible. In order that senior citizens' organizations can continue to be efficient and effective, those who are currently involved in the management of these organizations should focus their attention on pertinent areas.

Reviewing objectives

The present objectives of senior citizens' organizations are primarily confined to the promotion of recreational activities. It is therefore necessary to re-examine these objectives to see if they are relevant in the context of the future changes in the needs of older persons living in the various localities concerned. In view of the changing expectations and profiles of older persons, it will be realistic to broaden the objectives of senior citizens' organizations. In doing so, the organizations must be prepared to undergo growth and change.

In reviewing the objectives of senior citizens' organizations, the following questions might be addressed: are the organizations' objectives meeting the changing needs of older persons living in the locality? What other relevant programmes or activities do they wish to promote in the next five years? Only when leaders and those involved in the management of senior citizens' organizations begin to seriously consider answers to the above questions can they discover ways to strengthen and/or improve the programmes of the organizations. It is also important to consider other objectives in addition to the promotion of recreational activities. Other objectives could include promotion of health care, community service, personal social services, handicraft activities, mutual benefit schemes, cooperatives and home care, and a number of others.

Knowing the profiles of senior citizens

In planning and developing specific programmes for older persons, it is crucial to know the profiles of the older population living in the various constituencies. However, it appears that only very few of those in the management or leadership of senior citizens' organizations have a good appreciation of the socioeconomic profiles of older persons in their areas. Such information can enable the people managing senior citizens' organizations to shape and develop programmes appropriate and relevant to the locality.

Enlarging the leadership base

The leadership base of most senior citizens' organizations is rather narrow and the burden of leadership generally rests on a few committed volunteers. They can become overloaded by the various responsibilities and, in the end, may become burnt-out. Symptoms of burn-out leadership are indicated in various ways, such as low satisfaction from achievements, lack of drive in discharging the mission of the organization, estrangement and finally backsliding of organizational performance. In order to avert the burning out of the few committed leaders of some organizations, a change in leadership style and management may be necessary. Coopting more people into the various task forces to carry out ongoing programmes can help and these task forces will pave the way for a more equitable distribution of responsibilities, which would otherwise be undertaken by the committed few. Indeed, a number of task forces, when formed, will enlarge the leadership base and increase the participation of interested older persons as well as younger adults.

Strengthening management

Similarly, for senior citizens' organizations to remain effective, those who manage them must periodically carry out exercises to identify difficulties and challenges. It is only through such exercises that they will be able to single-out specific areas which affect their organizations and make decisions to address them. Functions such as mapping out new programmes, setting directions for the organizations for a period of time and dealing with interpersonal issues must form an essential responsibility of key leaders in the organizations.

Social programmes for older persons

One of the most important issues that arises as a result of an ageing population is the provision of programmes for older persons. Traditionally, and to a large extent still today, older persons have been informally cared for by their immediate family or kin members. However, with the actual or potential breakdown of the extended family system discussed earlier, the capacity to look after older persons may well be affected. The decline of extended families and the tendency to form nuclear families inevitably leads to shrinkage in family size, which with the other social and economic changes noted above reduces the capacity to support older persons.

Neighbours and friends have been identified as an important source of informal care to older persons. However, this source of caregivers seems to be diminishing as people are resettled in the new urban centres. Not only have older persons been separated from long-standing and familiar neighbours, but they also have the task of making new friends in their new environment.

In response to the inability of some families to provide intensive care for disabled elderly members, various community-based services are gradually developing to help them remain independent in the community. These include various types of community-based services such as the home nursing service, befriending service, senior citizens' and retirees' clubs, financial assistance, and day care centres. However, with the exception of the home nursing service, most other community-based programmes have yet to be fully developed. Like the senior citizens' organizations, the befrienders' service was formerly run by the government but is now run by a voluntary service organization. There are as yet only a few day care centres and it is not convenient for older persons who live far away from these centres to utilize their services. In view of the general policy that older persons should remain as long as possible in the community, more day care centres should be set up in a number of urban centres. This is necessary to make the service more accessible to older persons who are less mobile.

While existing services should be developed further, other forms of programmes for older persons should also be explored and possibly introduced to broaden the base of services. Several new programmes such as a meal delivery service, telephone contacts and support for family caregivers could be developed at the grassroots level. Meal delivery, for example, could be undertaken by homes for the elderly which have the infrastructure to provide and deliver meals to feeble or solitary older persons who live in neighbouring housing estates. A telephone contact service could also be set up to get in touch with older persons who are living very much on their own, to ensure their well-being. As family members are expected to play an important role in providing care to sick and disabled older persons, it would be useful to initiate a self-help group of family caregivers for older persons. This self-help group could be a source of encouragement in giving support and advice to families who are faced for the first time with the responsibility of having to care for sick and disabled older relatives.

In addition to the community-based services, formal services for older persons are also provided by various homes for older persons. The government, voluntary and commercial homes serve a total of more than 5,200 older persons which is a small proportion of the older population but one that is likely to increase as more elderly infirm people require nursing care. With the future increase in the number of private and commercial homes, it will become increasingly necessary for the government to monitor their standards and quality, to safeguard the interests of residents and families. For more voluntary initiatives to develop, the government will also have to be rather more generous in the provision of matching grants.

Conclusion

The future demands for services for older persons in Singapore are likely to become increasingly acute. It is therefore timely for voluntary organizations and the government to review and monitor more closely future trends in service demand and provision. A more imaginative spectrum of services is also envisaged. In working together, Singapore will be better prepared to deal more effectively with its ageing challenges in the years ahead. More efforts and resources should be directed at the development of community care and support programmes for mobile older persons needing some care and attention. Such a service strategy has not yet been fully explored. In addition, more neighbourhood support services will be needed to strengthen the family's capacity to look after older persons for as long as possible. If this is achieved, the social and economic burdens of care for older persons could be reduced. The government should review its funding to increase voluntary and community efforts to implement community care and multi-service centres in all housing estates and neighbourhoods of Singapore.

References

Chen, A.J. and Cheung, P. (1988) *The Elderly in Singapore*, Phase III ASEAN Population Project, Socio-economic Consequences of the Ageing of the Population, Singapore Country Report.

Cheung, P. (1988a) *Household and Population Projections, 1990 to 2030*, Singapore: Ministry of Health, Population Planning Unit.

—— (1988b) *Population Trends: The Ageing of Singapore*, Singapore: Ministry of Health, Population Planning Unit.

—— (1988c) *The Transition of the Social Support Systems for the Aged in Singapore: Emerging Patterns and Policy Options*, Singapore: Report presented at the Second International Workshop on the Social Support Systems in Transition.

Cheung, P. and Vasoo, S. (1989) 'Country study on the elderly: Singapore', paper commissioned by the Economic and Social Commission for Asia and the Pacific.

Department of Statistics (1997) *Yearbook of Statistics*, Singapore.

Economic and Social Commission for Asia and Pacific (ESCAP) (1996) *Population Ageing in Asia and the Pacific*, New York: United Nations.

Inter-Ministerial Committee on Health Care for the Elderly (1999) *Report of the Inter-Ministerial Committee on Health Care for the Elderly*, Singapore.

Lee, K.M.W. (1998) 'Income protection and the elderly: An examination of social security policy in Singapore', *Journal of Cross-Cultural Gerontology* 13, 4:291–307.

Ministry of Community Development (1999) *Report of the Inter-Ministerial Committee on the Ageing Population*, Singapore.

Ministry of Health (1997/8) *Annual Report*, Singapore.

—— (1984) *Report of the Committee on the Problems of the Aged*, Singapore.

Ministry of Health *et al.* (1996) *The National Survey of Senior Citizens in Singapore 1995*, Ministry of Health, Ministry of Community Development, Ministry of Labour, Department of Statistics and the National Council of Social Services. Singapore: Singapore Stamford Press.

Ministry of Social Affairs (1983) *Report on the National Survey on Senior Citizens*, Singapore.

National Council of Social Service (1997) *Annual Report*, Singapore.

Phillips, D.R. and Bartlett, H. (1995) 'Ageing trends — Singapore', *Journal of Cross Cultural Gerontology* 10, 4:349–56.

Shantakumar, G. (1994) *The Aged Population of Singapore*, Singapore: Singapore National Printers.

—— (1999) 'Ageing in the city-state context: Perspectives from Singapore', *Ageing International*, Summer, 46–60.

Singapore Council of Social Service (1981) *Social Policy and the Elderly in Singapore*, Report by the Study Group on the Elderly.

Toh, M.H. and Low, L. (1992) 'Health policies in the 1980s', in L. Low and M.H. Toh (eds) *Public Policies in Singapore*, Singapore: Times Academic Press.

Yap, M.T. and Tan, P. (1998) 'The age of the aged', in A. Mahizhnan and T.Y. Lee, (eds) *Singapore: Re-engineering Success*, Oxford University Press: Singapore, pp. 82–91.

Part 3

Examining Family Issues and Services

Chapter 7

Promoting family values: Some issues and challenges*

Tee Liang Ngiam[†] and S. Vasoo[‡]

There is much renewed interest in the state of the Singapore family lately. Among the efforts to preserve and strengthen the family is the promotion of shared family values. The paper traces the factors behind the move and analyses its development. Some observations and suggestions are also provided in the paper on issues and challenges of value change in family life.

Next year, Singapore will be classified by OECD[1] as a developed country (The Straits Times 6/5/95, p. 1). This is considered by many to be a remarkable achievement in the relatively short space of its history since becoming an independent nation, as it was ranked a developing country at the time of its independence in 1965. In keeping with its new status,

---

*Reprinted from paper presented at the Fifth Malaysia–Singapore Forum, 11–14 December 1995, organised by the Faculty of Arts and Social Sciences, National University of Singapore.

This paper reflects some of the earlier views on family values and the move by the Singapore government in adopting the promotion of family values in response to the rapid social and environmental changes affecting the family institution.

[†] Senior Lecturer, Department of Social Work and Psychology, National University of Singapore.

[‡] Head, Department of Social Work and Psychology, National University of Singapore.

[1] Organisation for Economic Cooperation and Development.

Singapore's Prime Minister, Mr Goh Chok Tong has expressed the need for Singapore to be developed not only in the economic sense:

> "I would like to see a balanced development of Singaporeans so that we are not just seized with material possessions. There should be a balance to Singaporeans and in Singapore society, with more emphasis on social matters, developing the family or the individual's interests whether it is in sports or reading, so that the person is more rounded and is not just an economic animal. Values like decency and society are very important" (The Straits Times 14/11/95, p. 17).

The Prime Minister's reference to "developing the family" is not a sudden new feature in the thinking of the government.[2] For many years now, it has been concerned with the well-being of the family. However, its new economic status will no doubt compel the government and the country to give added impetus to the search for appropriate and effective policy measures to ensure that the stability of the family unit is not undermined by the negative consequences of economic affluence and materialism. Like many countries, Singapore is also facing a number of family and domestic issues, for example, divorce, family violence, single parent households, parenting inadequacies, and the burden of caring for the dependent elderly.

Development and the family

Why is there this worry? Basically, it is because the socio-economic development and modernisation of any society will impact significantly on the family as a key institution. Singapore society is no exception. Economic development and growth have become national imperatives for Singapore's continued advancement to become and remain a developed country. In the process, rapid social changes are taking place and will

---

[2] For an elaboration of the Singapore Government's approach to the matter, please see Ngiam, Tee Liang, "Family and Nation Building in Singapore: Family Well-being Without State Welfarism". Paper presented at the Fourth Malaysia–Singapore Forum, 8–11 December 1994, organised by the Faculty of Arts and Social Sciences, University of Malaya, Malaysia.

continue to do so. Among other things, these rapid social changes affect the family institution in many ways.

At the same time, long-term national economic success is not possible nor desirable without the family playing a relevant role in the process. This is so because the family institution is a major partner in the social and cultural transformation of a country. And economic modernisation is interdependent with social and cultural modernisation, too. In other words, the generation of economic wealth and prosperity for Singapore is dependent on the state of family well-being of her population.

Some factors affecting the family

A number of significant social factors will have impact and influence on the dynamics of the family and family life in Singapore. Some of these social factors have already been commonly identified and they centre around a number of core areas such as the declining birth rate or fertility, increasing participation of women in the labour force, continuing breakdown in extended family composition, delayed marriages, and increasing number of persons in singlehood and divorces. All these social factors have important bearings on current and future programmes in working with families. Consequently, they will also have implications for the delivery of services by family service organisations. In the last two decades, the desire to strengthen family service organisations has increasingly attracted the attention of policy makers. Such an interest could be precipitated by a few major reasons.

Firstly, the massive relocation of people into urban centres like new towns has created some social consequences which if left unattended, could have repercussions not only for the well-being of families but also the government concerned. Social consequences such as the breakdown of traditional helping networks, the lack of effective communication channels between family policy makers and the families, the feeling of alienation and anomie among family members, and the increasing pressure from families for better services, have in some ways prompted policy makers of family service and welfare organisations to deploy resources to strengthen family functions.

Secondly, traditional institutions such as clan and lineage associations, guilds and mutual benefit societies, which in the past played an important mediatory role between families and the government bureaucracies, have lost their effectiveness and relative creditability. This is because a number of their functions have not kept abreast with the changing needs of families. They have become inadequate and inappropriate in representing the wider cross-sectional interests of families and have become less effective channels to communicate with family policy makers.

Thirdly, the socio-ecological environment is changing rapidly and becoming less predictable as a result of social and group conflicts. All these unforeseen and unplanned events have serious ramifications for family life. In addition to these scenarios, the Singapore government is also encountering rising expectations and demands from her population for better social service provisions. As a consequence, it is facing an increasing financial burden for which it will have to find alternative strategies to meet its social obligations. Hence, the move towards privatisation and restructuring of social service provisions is felt to be a feasible alternative. This has prompted the government to encourage citizens to establish more voluntary organisations to deal with social problems and emerging community needs through citizens' initiatives, as well as contributions by consumers of services in other ways.

Emphasis on a strong family unit

Not surprising then, the government has recently taken a number of measures to underline its approach towards strengthening the family. One is the revamp in the emphasis of the role and functions of the Ministry of Community Development (MCD). At a press briefing announcing the changes, Acting Mnister for Community Development Mr Abdullah Tarmugi said that his ministry will do more to strengthen families by helping them to stay well instead of concentrating, as in the past, on mending broken families (The Straits Times 1/4/95, p. 1). This means MCD will be proactive and not reactive in its approach. The rationale for it is explained in a press report:

> "Strong families are the best means not only of preventing social problems from cropping up but also of helping to solve the problems after they begin," it[3] said in a statement.

---

[3] Ministry of Community Development.

It said that Singapore should not go the way of other more permissive societies "where free love and self-indulgence have resulted in high divorce rates, single parenthood and children born out of wedlock".

'With broken homes come violence, juvenile delinquency and drug addiction,' it added.

It said that that there was no evidence so far to suggest that the family unit here was significantly weakened.

But with more nuclear families, more working women, and more absent fathers as men went abroad to work, "the family as we know it today will undergo tremendous pressures and change for the worse in the years to come". (The Straits Times 1/4/95, p. 1)

Why the need for family values?

Among the pro-active steps MCD has adopted is the promotion of family values. Values "are broad ideas regarding what is desirable, correct, and good that most members of a society share" (Vander Zanden 1993:36). The Ministry considers the prevalence of family values to be an effective means to strengthen family ties and support. They are often germane in dealing with the underlying dynamics of family and individual problems. They also form part of a set of shared values deemed vital by the Government for the country's own well-being, too. This is clearly expressed in the White Paper on Shared Values for Singaporeans (Government of Singapore 1991 and Quah 1990). One of the Shared Values is the "Family as the basic unit of society". The others are "Nation before community and society above self"; "Regard and community support for the individual"; "Consensus instead of contention"; and "Racial and religious harmony".

To elaborate on the shared value of the family as a basic unit of society, the Ministry of Community Development decided in September 1993 to embark on a project to produce a "simple document" on family values which can act as a "gentle reminder" to Singaporeans about the values. In addition, MCD hoped that people would practice the values in their daily lives. It felt that the effective practice of family values can, in many instances, help prevent the onset of family problems, as well as bring about their timely resolution were the conflicts to occur. At the same time, the ministry recognised that family values by themselves cannot guarantee the absence of family problems nor be a panacea for them, but they can help mitigate the stresses and burdens of having them.

Producing a family values document

The project entailed an invitation by the former Minister for Health and Community Development, Mr Yeo Cheow Tong, to the Committee on the Family[4] to formulate a family values document. Right at the outset, the stance of MCD was to involve public participation in formulating the values, and not leave it to its officers to do so. This was a deliberate move on the part of the ministry to let Singaporeans have a say in selecting common family values they can identify with. In this way, the values selected will not be considered as coming from the government in a top-down fashion. Consequently, there will be minimal risk of the public rejecting the chosen values because they think that the government is trying to impose the values on them. Hence the invitation to the Committee to produce the document.

The Committee formed a working group comprising its members and co-opted individuals from the public to assist in preparing a draft document in English with translations into Malay, Mandarin and Tamil. The working group started its work by reviewing background materials prepared by MCD's staff. It also publicised, through the mass media and letters to community, civic, religious and voluntary welfare organisations, its invitation to the public to submit written views and suggestions on what are the kinds of values which could go into the document.

When the Committee on the Family first took up the challenge to collate a simple document on family values, it did so with no idea of how it would turn out.[5] Initially the committee was cautious and a bit apprehensive. While convinced of the need for the document, it was uncertain of the extent of public interest and support for the document. It

---

[4] The Committee is part of the National Advisory Council on Family and the Aged, an advisory body of representatives from government ministries, community groups and members of the public, with a secretariat provided by the Ministry of Community Development.

[5] Much of the description of the process by which the values were collated and the document formulated as mentioned here is taken from a speech given by T L Ngiam as Chairman of the Singapore Family Values Promotion Committee at the Exhibition-cum-Launch of the Book on Singapore Family Values (13 August 1994, Marina Square Shopping Mall).

was also unsure whether it could put together concisely Singaporeans' views on family values. Members were aware that each family is different. Families come in many diverse forms. On top of that, Singaporeans live in a multi-racial, multi-cultural and multi-religious society. Some individual members also heard comments from sceptics that the whole exercise was a waste of time, that the document would end up gathering dust on the shelf. The sceptics said that Singaporeans are usually too busy for things like that, or are usually reticent when it comes to submitting views on abstract issues like family values.

Fortunately, the committee was glad that Singaporeans had risen to the occasion and proved the doubters and sceptics wrong. Apart from phone calls and verbal suggestions from the public, 84 written contributions were received from all quarters. The committee was pleasantly surprised not just by the quantity, but also the quality of the contributions. Many informal groups in schools, polytechnics, the grassroots organizations, unions, clan associations, religious, civic and voluntary groups actually met and brainstormed their ideas before forwarding them to the committee.

Instead of worrying about the lack of contributions, the committee faced the opposite problem — how to synthesise the many contributions, all well-thought through and carefully worded. It took the MCD secretariat involved in the working group many long hours to sieve through painstakingly the many contributions. The contributions focussed mainly on values and relationships. The working group decided to put the main points of each contribution into a matrix — values on one side and relationships on the other.

With the help of this matrix, the task of distilling the common family values held by Singaporeans become much easier. The matrix helped the group to see that despite the multi-lingual character of the contributions and the diverse backgrounds of the contributors, they had much in common. The group managed to identify five commonly recurring themes, viz. Love, Care and Concern, Mutual Respect, Filial Piety, Commitment and Responsibility. These five values formed the basis of the first draft completed in February 1994. The draft was then publicised to the public again through the press and TV, as well as given to the contributors who submitted their ideas for the draft, inviting their comments.

In addition to receiving written comments, more than 290 persons attended the three bilingual public forums held to gather feedback on the first draft. Arising from the feedback, the five values were slightly modified to be: Love, Care and Concern, Mutual Respect, Filial Responsibility, Commitment and Communication. Again, while the participants in these sessions came from a wide spectrum of backgrounds, there was a surprising degree of consensus. For example, the need for effective communication came through time and again. Strictly speaking, communication is not usually considered a value in the traditional sense of the word. Still, the working group accommodated the strong desire of the participants to see communication being highlighted as a core family value. Another feedback was to change the value, "Filial Piety" to "Filial Responsibility" as the former term could be construed to have religious significance, as it is often associated with ancestor worship by the Chinese.

In May 1994 the working group completed revising the final text for the five family values. The final document was printed and launched by the Acting Minister for Community Development, Mr Abdullah Tarmugi in August 1994. It is a useful reference book explaining the principles of the five family values and how they are woven into family relationships. The contents of the book are applicable to everyone, be he or she a child, a single person, a spouse, a parent, a parent-in-law, a brother or sister, an aunt or uncle, or a grandparent. In other words, each and everyone can lay claim to the Singapore Family Values:

> "They are considered to be the core values which are acceptable to the different cultural and religious groups in the country. If they so wish, these groups can build upon the core family values with additional values which are applicable to their own community" (Ngiam 1994:20).

Promoting family values

With the formulation of the document on the Singapore Family Values completed, an obvious question will be, "What will be done to promote the values among Singaporeans?" Towards this end, in June 1994, the Prime Minister announced the creation of the S$1 million Singapore Family Values Promotion Fund. It will be used over the next five years to help finance projects which will actively promote the five family values (The Straits Times 20/6/94, p. 1). The Fund is available to organisations and individuals to tap on a cost-sharing basis, and is managed by the Ministry of Community Development.

A Singapore Family Values Promotion Fund Committee was appointed by the Ministry to advise it in selecting suitable projects to support either with funds or ideas or both. It is also to co-ordinate efforts to encourage public and organisational involvement in promoting and transmitting the values in various ways (The Straits Times 20/7/94. p. 27). Again reflecting its public participation objective, MCD selected the members of the Committee from various sources — the government ministries, the academia, the media, and the voluntary welfare and grassroots sectors.

So far, a number of projects have been supported by the Committee. This ranged from television commercials to plays to workshops to publications to poster and periodical advertisements. The majority of the projects were undertaken by human service organisations such as voluntary welfare organisations, schools, self-help organisations, ministries, National Trades Union Congress (NTUC) and commercial bodies. The projects can be divided into two main types — those that raise awareness on a general level about the values and those which are face-to-face in nature. For example, a TV commercial, because it is very expensive to produce and air, can only, due to its short duration of exposure to viewers at any one time, raise awareness of the values in the viewers' minds.

The commercials cannot go in-depth to explain the details of the values and how to practice them with the necessary knowledge and skills involved. Hence, mass exposure-types of projects have to be supplemented and complemented by face-to-face types of events and activities, for example, experiential or skills-based training workshops which have a greater learning impact.

Promoting services to support the family

In this regard, the competence of social service organisations, such as family service agencies and related bodies, to directly and indirectly support the efforts to promote family values are critically determined by the context in which the organisations' overall service effectiveness occurs. Hence, any examination of programmes and activities dealing with family values must also take into account the capacity and capability of voluntary welfare, grassroots, religious and other family-oriented organisations to undertake family services as well. This is because often messages on family values can be more appropriately disseminated when they are embedded into the contents of activities and events of these programmes and services, and not as a stand-alone cognitive attempt.

It is envisaged that in the near future, HDB[6] community or neighbourhood centres will see more growth in support services for the family. These places are where most Singaporeans are residing. At the same time, with the growing number of the elderly among families and the increasing participation of married women in the labour force, a lot more families are likely to be dependent on support services of either its kin-group or neighbourhood, or both, if any member of the family needs long term care and attention. The capacity of the family to function effectively varies directly with its ability to mobilise help to meet the care and attention needs of its members. It is in these areas that family service organisations can pioneer programmes which will strengthen the family. Some examples of such programmes are child care services requiring parental participation, marriage counselling and guidance, and family life education programmes.

In planning and implementing more comprehensive family service programmes, it is necessary to re-examine the objectives of family service organisations to see if they are relevant to the demographic profiles of the specific urban centres or neighbourhoods. In the light of changing needs and expectations of the users and potential users of family services, it would be realistic to broaden the objectives of family service agencies. To achieve this, those who manage family service agencies must address the following questions: Are the agencies effectively meeting the needs of the

---

[6] Housing and Development Board, the national public housing authority in Singapore.

users or potential users living in the locality? What relevant programmes or activities can be promoted to reach families in need? Only when those who manage family service organisations begin to seriously consider these questions will they discover ways to strengthen and improve the programmes of their agencies.

Increasingly, more family service organisations are taking various initiatives to improve and/or expand their services. It would be useful for these agencies to come together to discuss ways in which they could co-operate in the delivery of their services to meet the needs of a wider cross-section of families in need. In this way the limited resources and expertise available in each of the agencies could be mobilised to provide more comprehensive and effective services to families. Family service programmes are cost-intensive and can be made more cost-effective, through joint efforts and co-operation among agencies. Consequently, their services and facilities could become more accessible to families in need.

For family service programmes to be effective, they must have the essential professional staff with expertise in such areas as family counselling and casework, group work, marital therapy, marriage mediation, and family life education, to name a few. It is envisaged that the current number of personnel in the family service field will come under tremendous strain if the pool of humanpower is not expanded to cater to future service demands dealing with family concerns.

In order to enhance the participation of personnel, both staff and volunteers, in family service organisations, agencies must firstly make participation attractive; and secondly, encourage personnel to be more imaginative and creative in their work. The participation of personnel in family service organisations will be subjected to more and more challenges than ever before because of competing demands for their time as well as resources. Unless family service agencies can make the planning, management and delivery of their programmes to be interesting and growing experiences for their personnel, they will be unlikely to attract and sustain these people. It has been found that social service organisations which offer mundane and routine service programmes cannot sustain the interest of their personnel to remain employed in the organisation for long.

The growth and effectiveness of family service organisations is not only dependent on good leadership in the agency structure but also on the leaders' responsiveness to changes in the external environment. Sensitivity to emerging types of family needs and problems and the identification of these for quick response, will make family service organisations relevant to the context in which they operate. The problem with some organisations is that they do not develop adequate measures to monitor changes affecting families. It is not sufficient to have the desired personnel to implement family service programmes. Importantly, these personnel must be constantly motivated to upgrade their skills and knowledge in working effectively with families.

In recognising that there is a growing need for a forum to encourage the sharing of experiences and expertise among family service personnel such as social workers, family counsellors, psychologists and other related professionals and academicians interested in family issues, it would be useful for a Family Studies Group to be formed. This Group can encourage a proliferation of research as well as the development of more effective strategies in working with the family. Through the establishment of such a Group both academic and professional excellence can be promoted among those involved in working with or researching on families.

It is hoped that the Families Study Group can organise seminars and workshops for academicians and professionals to share their experiences in working with the family; encourage the publication of local materials related to the family and family services; promote interdisciplinary research on family issues and well-being; and improve professional skills in working with families. One major area for the Group to focus on can be issues related to the communication, transmission and internalisation of family values in a multi-racial and multicultural Singapore society.

Family service organisations have to be more dynamic. How can they achieve this? Should they be allowed to take their own course and do nothing about it? Family service organisations can be vibrant provided their management, staff and significant stakeholders all make periodical reviews of the organisation's mission, goals and objectives. The review would not only enable the organisations to discover ways to strengthen their family service programmes but also to attract more family service personnel to be involved. Through the delegation of responsibilities to them, more ideas can be generated and meaningful activities could be implemented.

The challenge before social service organisations is to review their mission for more effective programmes. As they take steps to do this, they will be preparing themselves to be the base for effective involvement of personnel, both staff and volunteers, in the provision of relevant family service programmes in the future.

Conclusion

Promoting family values is recognised to be a challenging and long-term endeavour. Results cannot be seen overnight but will take many years of appropriate and sustained efforts. It requires the political will and commitment of the government and its people to remain steadfast to its belief in the worth and sanctity of the family. In this regard, the Singapore government has stated its stand very clearly. As mentioned by Senior Minister Mr Lee Kuan Yew, Singapore must insist on, and maintain, certain standards and values if it is to preserve the strength of its society and do better (The Straits Times 8/6/95, p.1).

Hence, it is very likely that the government will continue to support efforts at promoting family values in a sensitive and partnership manner. It will be up to organisations, the community, families and individuals themselves to join forces with the government in preserving and strengthening the family fabric of Singapore society.

References

Committee on the Family National Advisory Council on Family and the Aged. *Singapore Family Values*. Singapore: Ministry of Community Development, 1994.

Government of Singapore. *Shared Values*. Cmd. 1 of 1991 (White Paper). Singapore: Singapore National Printers for Government of Singapore, 1991.

Ngiam, Tee Liang. *"Family and Nation Building in Singapore: Family Well-being Without State Welfarism."* Paper presented at the Fourth Malaysia-Singapore

Forum, 8–11 December 1994, organised by the Faculty of Arts and Social Sciences, University of Malaya, Malaysia (mimeo).

Quah, Jon S. T. (ed). *In Search of Singapore's National Values*. Singapore: Times Academic Press for The Institute of Policy Studies, 1990.

The Straits Times (various issues).

Vander Zanden, James W. *Sociology: The Core* (3rd edn.). New York: McGraw-Hill, 1993.

Chapter 8

Transmitting family values in a cultural context: The Singapore experience*

Tee Liang Ngiam[†] and S. Vasoo[‡]

As Singapore continues its economic impetus to be a developed country by the turn of the century, concerns are raised about the concomitant aspects of its social development. Among the concerns is the state of the family. Will it be able to meet the challenges ahead and remain strong and cohesive in the face of countervailing forces which threaten to weaken the institution of the family? One strategy to preserve and strenghten the family is the promotion of shared family values within an

---

*Reprinted from a paper presented at a seminar "Cultures in ASEAN and the 21st Century Seminar", organised by the Centre for the Arts and the ASEAN Committee on Culture and Information (COCI), 26–29 August 1996.

This paper consolidates some earlier comments and analyses of Singapore's evolving experience in trying to balance economic growth with social well-being. In particular, the well-being of the family, highlighting the promotion of core family values as an aspect to keep the family institution alive is highlighted. More educational efforts can be undertaken to promote family values.

[†]Deputy Director, Centre for Advanced Studies, Faculty of Arts and Social Sciences and Senior Lecturer, Department of Social Work and Psychology, National University of Singapore.

[‡]Head, Department of Social Work and Psychology, National University of Singapore.

Asian context. The paper will examine the nature and scope of the strategy as well as analyse its development as a cultural catalyst. It will include observations and suggestions on issues and challenges of value change in family life amidst the impact of modernity in Singapore society.

ASEAN countries are now enjoying rapid economic development and growth. To further boost economic growth, remain economically competitive and to have comparative advantage, ASEAN Heads of Government decided on 28 January 1992 to form the ASEAN Free Trade Area (AFTA). The aim is to promote closer economic collaboration and eventual economic integration (ASEAN Secretariat, p. 95). AFTA will bring about the gradual reduction and eventual elimination of barriers to the free movement of goods and services across the region. The coming into being of AFTA will have a number of implications which go beyond its economic sphere. According to the ASEAN Secretariat's publication, *From Strength to Strength — ASEAN Functional Cooperation: Retrospect and Prospect*, some of the implications concern the well-being of individuals and their families. The implications are worth quoting at some length to indicate the type of scenario ASEAN countries will be exposed to (ASEAN Secretariat, pp. 95–96):

> "The accelerated tempo of technological adoption and upgrading as a result of AFTA will place new demands on the labour force of member countries. More specifically, it will require the continuous upgrading of workers' skills in order to closely match them with the changing quantitative as well as qualitive requirements of the labour market. This will require the retraining of workers, which will, in turn, entail additional investments in infrastructure for on-the-job and job-related training.
>
> [....]
>
> At least in the short term, changing comparative advantage will result in the phasing out of less efficient firms and the decline of some sectors and industries that will not be able to withstand the onslaught of increased competition. Workers in the adversely affected firms/sectors will be thrown out of work as a result; there may be a decline in their standards of living and in their relative share in the economy's output as

a result. But as the entire economy develops, new employment opportunities will emerge and, in the medium and long terms, the standard of living will improve.

What may befall some workers, especially the unskilled, may also happen to other vulnerable groups in society: the elderly, children and women. Starting from a position of disadvantage, and ill-prepared to cope with the quickened pace of development, these groups may fall even farther behind, unless some social safeguards and safety nets are installed to protect them and enhance their role and participation in their rapidly changing societies.

[....]

As a result of the more porous national borders ushered by AFTA, traffic in drugs and narcotics may increase. If this happens, there will be additonal resources required in the form of increased effort and expenditure for law enforcement, for the policing of borders and entry points, for treatment and rehabilitation, and for research on drugs and narcotics control.

There is another possibility, also related to AFTA, on the drug problem. The intense pressures generated by increased trade and rapid industrialization may make people more vulnerable to narcotics and drugs."

In quoting some of the implications, there is no intention of casting doubt over regional economic integration, nor to suggest its abandonment. From an economic perspective, AFTA is an imperative for ASEAN countries' continued prosperity. Being so, the implications form an extra canvas to the backdrop for social development action by individual countries and the region as a whole. As the ASEAN Secretariat's publication points out, the way for ASEAN to overcome the problems is for regional co-operation to "emphasize projects and activities aimed at mitigating the adverse social impact of rapid industrialization in the region in the wake of AFTA" (ASEAN Secretariat, p. 98).

Even without the emergence of AFTA, there are certain industrialisation and economic modernisation forces at work which can bring about heavy social costs to a country ill-prepared to counteract them. In fact, the formation of AFTA affords ASEAN countries individually and collectively an unique opportunity to examine the means and ends of socio-economic development and to maintain the appropriate balance between human and social development and economic progress. In other words, for economic modernisation to succeed and for the majority of people in ASEAN to benefit from it, human and social development must not be neglected.

It is in this context that the paper examines Singapore's evolving experience in balancing economic growth with social well-being, particularly the well-being of the family, for the nation's long-term survival. It will highlight one vital aspect of the government's thrust to keep the family institution alive and well, and that is the promotion of core family values as a cultural imprint for Singaporeans.

Although OECD[1] has not classified Singapore as a developed country, but as a "more advanced developing country" (The Straits Times 17/1/96, p. 1), the promotion of the island-state into the latter category is considered by many to be a remarkable achievement in the relatively short space of its history as an independent and sovereign nation. It was ranked a developing country at the time of its independence in 1965. In keeping with its new status, Singapore's Prime Minister, Mr Goh Chok Tong, at a Marine Parade Lunar New Year and Hari Raya Get-Together on 10 March 1966, has expressed the need for Singapore to be developed not only in the economic sense:

> "We will upgrade all areas, not just the material aspects but also the non-material and spiritual aspects which make life fulfilling — like arts, culture, sports, good social manners, the environment, family values and community ties. It will take some years before we are there, but we will make it. If we team up — the people and the Government — we can make Singapore the most attractive place to live, study, work, play and bring up our families" (National Day Parade 1996, p. 5).

The Prime Minister's reference to "family values" and making the country "most attractive" for bringing up the family is not a sudden new feature in the thinking of the government[2]. For many years now, it has

---

[1] Organisation for Economic Cooperation and Development.

[2] For an elaboration of the Singapore Government's approach to the matter, please see Ngiam, Tee Liang, "Family and Nation Building in Singapore; Family Well-being Without State Welfarism". Paper presented at the Fourth Malaysia–Singapore Forum,

been concerned with the well-being of the family. However, its new economic status will no doubt compel the government and the country to give added impetus to the search for appropriate and effective policy measures to ensure that the stability of the family unit is not undermined by the negative consequences of economic affluence and materialism. Like many countries, Singapore is also facing a number of family and social problems, for example, divorce, family violence, single parent households, parenting inadequacies, and the burden of caring for the dependent elderly.

Impact of development

Why is there this concern? Basically, it is because the socio-economic development and modernisation of any society will impact significantly on the family as a key institution. Singapore society is no exception. Economic development and growth have become national imperatives for Singapore's drive to become a developed country. In the process, rapid social changes are taking place and will continue to do so. Among other things, these rapid social changes affect the family institution in many ways.

At the same time, long-term national economic success is not possible nor desirable without the family playing a relevant role in the process. This is so because the family institution is a major partner in the social and cultural transformation of a country. And economic modernisation is interdependent with social and cultural modernisation, too. In other words, the generation of economic wealth and prosperity for Singapore is dependent on the state of family well-being of her population.

A number of significant social factors will have impact and influence on the dynamics of the family and family life in Singapore. Some of these social factors have already been commonly identified and they centre around a number of core areas such as the declining birth rate or fertility, increasing participation of women in the labour force, continuing breakdown in extended family composition, delayed marriages, and increasing number of persons in singlehood and divorces.

8–11 December 1994, organised by the Faculty of Arts and Social Sciences, University of Malaya, Malaysia.

All these social factors have important bearings on current and future programmes in working with families. Consequently, they will also have implications for the delivery of services by family service organisations. In the last two decades, the desire to strengthen family service organisations has increasingly attracted the attention of policy makers. Such an interest could be precipitated by a few major reasons.

Firstly, the massive relocation of people into urban settings like new towns has created some social consequences which if left unattended, could have repercussions not only for the well-being of families but also the government concerned. Social consequences such as the breakdown of traditional helping networks, the lack of effective communication channels between family policy makers and the families, the feeling of alienation and anomie among family members, and the increasing pressure from families for better services, have in some ways prompted policy makers of family service and welfare organisations to deploy resources to strengthen family functions.

Secondly, traditional institutions such as clan and lineage associations, guilds and mutual benefit societies, which in the past played an important mediatory role between families and the government bureaucracies, have lost their effectiveness and relative creditability. This is because a number of their functions have not kept abreast with the changing needs of families. They have become inadequate and inappropriate in representing the wider cross-sectional interests of families and have become less effective channels to communicate with family policy makers.

Thirdly, the socio-ecological environment is changing rapidly and becoming less predictable as a result of social and group conflicts. All these unforeseen and unplanned events have serious ramifications for family life. In addition to these scenarios, the Singapore government is also encountering rising expectations and demands from her population for better social service provisions. As a consequence, it is facing an increasing financial burden for which it will have to find alternative strategies to meet its social obligations. Hence, the move towards divestment and restructuring of social service provisions is felt to be a feasible alternative. This has prompted the government to encourage citizens to establish more voluntary organisations to deal with social problems and emerging community needs through citizens' initiatives, as well as contributions by consumers of services in other ways.

Emphasis on a strong family unit

Not surprising then, the government has recently taken a number of measures to underpin its approach towards strengthening the family. One is the revamp in the emphasis of the role and functions of the Ministry of Community Development (MCD). At a press briefing announcing the changes, the then Acting Minister for Community Development Mr Abdullah Tarmugi said that his ministry will do more to strengthen families by helping them to stay well instead of concentrating, as in the past, on mending broken families (The Straits Times 1/4/95, p. 1). This means MCD will be proactive and not reactive in its approach. The rationale for it is explained in a press report:

> "Strong families are the best means not only of preventing social problems from cropping up but also of helping to solve the problems after they begin," it[3] said in a statement.
>
> It said that Singapore should not go the way of other more permissive societies "where free love and self-indulgence have resulted in high divorce rates, single parenthood and children born out of wedlock".
>
> 'With broken homes come violence, juvenile delinquency and drug addiction,' it added.
>
> It said that that there was no evidence so far to suggest that the family unit here was significantly weakened.
>
> But with more nuclear families, more working women, and more absent fathers as men went abroad to work, "the family as we know it today will undergo tremendous pressures and change for the worse in the years to come". (The Straits Times 1/4/95, p. 1)

Nature and scope of the family values strategy

Among the pro-active steps MCD has adopted is the promotion of family values which accord with the cultural backgrounds of Singapore and are considered relevant for the times. Culture is considered to consist of

> "the *values* the members of a given group hold, the *norms* they follow, and the material goods they create. Values are abstract ideals, while norms are

---

[3] Ministry of Community Development.

definite principles or rules which people are expected to observe. Norms represent the 'dos' and 'don'ts' of social life" (Giddens, p.31).

Values are therefore the "broad ideas regarding what is desirable, correct, and good that most members of a society share" (Vander Zanden 1993:36). The Ministry considers the prevalence of family values to be an effective means to strengthen family ties and support. They are often germane in dealing with the underlying dynamics of family and individual problems. They also form part of a set of shared values deemed vital by the Government for the country's own well-being, too. This is clearly expressed in the White Paper on Shared Values for Singaporeans (Government of Singapore 1991 and Quah 1990). One of the Shared Values is the "Family as the basic unit of society". The others are "Nation before community and society above self"; "Regard and community support for the individual"; "Consensus instead of contention"; and "Racial and religious harmony".

To elaborate on the shared value of the family as a basic unit of society, the Ministry of Community Development decided in September 1993 to embark on a project to produce a "simple document" on family values which can act as a "gentle reminder" to Singaporeans about the values. In addition, MCD hoped that people would practice the values in their daily lives. It felt that the effective practice of family values can, in many instances, help prevent the onset of family problems, as well as bring about their timely resolution were the conflicts to occur. At the same time, the ministry recognised that family values by themselves cannot guarantee the absence of family problems nor be a panacea for them, but they can help mitigate the stresses and burdens of having them.

Producing a family values document

The project entailed an invitation by the former Minister for Health and Community Development, Mr Yeo Cheow Tong, to the Committee on the Family to formulate a family values document. The Committee is part of the National Advisory Council on Family and the Aged, an advisory body of representatives from government ministries, community groups and members of the public, with a secretariat provided by the Ministry of

Community Development. Right at the outset, the stance of MCD was to involve public participation in formulating the values, and not leave it to civil servants to do so. This was a deliberate move on the part of the Ministry to let Singaporeans have a say in selecting common family values they can identify with. In this way, the values selected will not be considered as coming from the government in a top-down fashion. Consequently, there will be minimal risk of the public rejecting the chosen values because they think that the government is trying to impose the values on them. Hence the invitation to the Committee to produce the document.

The Committee formed a working group comprising its members and co-opted individuals from the public to assist in preparing a draft document in English with translations into Malay, Mandarin and Tamil, all four being Singapore's official languages. The working group started its work by reviewing background materials prepared by MCD's staff. It also publicised, through the mass media and letters to community, civic, religious and voluntary welfare organisations, its invitation to the public to submit written views and suggestions on what are the kinds of values which could go into the document.

When the Committee on the Family first took up the challenge to collate a simple document on family values, it did so with no idea of how it would turn out.[4] Initially the committee was cautious and a bit apprehensive. While convinced of the need for the document, it was uncertain of the extent of public interest and support for the document. It was also unsure whether it could put together concisely Singaporeans' views on family values. Members were aware that each family is different. Families come in many diverse forms. On top of that, Singaporeans live in a multi-racial, multi-cultural and multi-religious society. They have similar as well as different views on what constitute "family values". Some individual committee members also heard comments from sceptics that the

---

[4] Much of the description of the process by which the values were collated and the document formulated as mentioned here is taken from a speech given by Dr Ngiam Tee Liang as Chairman of the Singapore Family Values Promotion Committee at the Exhibition-cum-Launch of the Book on Singapore Family Values (13 August 1994, Marina Square Shopping Mall).

whole exercise was a waste of time, that the document would end up gathering dust on the shelf. The sceptics said that Singaporeans are usually too busy for things like that, or are usually reticent when it comes to submitting views on abstract issues like family values. Worse, some even heard that it was a government ploy to shun its responsibility to help individuals in trouble by passing the buck to the family.

Fortunately, the committee was glad that Singaporeans had risen to the occasion and proved the doubters and sceptics wrong. Apart from phone calls and verbal suggestions from the public, 84 written contributions were received from all quarters. The committee was pleasantly surprised not just by the quantity, but also the quality of the contributions. Many informal groups in schools, polytechnics, the grassroots organizations, unions, clan associations, religious, civic and voluntary groups actually met and brainstormed their ideas before forwarding them to the committee.

Instead of worrying about the lack of contributions, the committee faced the opposite problem — how to synthesise the many contributions, all well-thought through and carefully worded. It took the MCD secretariat involved in the working group many long hours to sieve through painstakingly the many contributions. The contributions focussed mainly on values and relationships. The working group decided to put the main points of each contribution into a matrix — values on one side and relationships on the other.

With the help of this matrix, the task of distilling the common family values held by Singaporeans become much easier. The matrix helped the group to see that despite the multi-lingual and multi-cultural character of the contributions and the diverse backgrounds of the contributors, they had much in common. The group managed to identify five commonly recurring themes, viz. Love, Care and Concern, Mutual Respect, Filial Piety, Commitment and Responsibility. These five values formed the basis of the first draft completed in February 1994. The draft was then publicised to the public again through the press and TV, as well as given to the contributors who submitted their ideas for the draft, inviting their comments.

In addition to receiving written comments, more than 290 persons attended the three bilingual public forums held to gather feedback on the first draft. Arising from the feedback, the five values were slightly modified to be: (1) Love, Care and Concern, (2) Mutual Respect, (3) Filial Responsibility, (4) Commitment and (5) Communication. Again, while the participants in these sessions came from a wide spectrum of backgrounds, there was a surprising degree of consensus. For example, the need for effective communication came through time and again. Strictly speaking, communication is not usually considered a value in the traditional sense of the word. Still, the working group accommodated the strong desire of the participants to see communication being highlighted as a core family value. Another feedback was to change the value, "Filial Piety" to "Filial Responsibility" as the former term could be construed to have religious significance, as it is often associated with ancestor worship by the Chinese.

In May 1994 the working group completed revising the final text for the five family values. The final document was printed and launched by the then Acting Minister for Community Development, Mr Abdullah Tarmugi in August 1994. It is a useful reference book explaining the principles of the five family values and how they are woven into family relationships. The contents of the book are applicable to everyone, be he or she a child, a single person, a spouse, a parent, a parent-in-law, a brother or sister, an aunt or uncle, or a grandparent. In other words, each and eveiyone can lay claim to the Singapore Family Values:

> "They are considered to be the core values which are acceptable to the different cultural and religious groups in the country. If they so wish, these groups can build upon the core family values with additional values which are applicable to their own community" (Ngiam 1994:20).

Promoting family values

With the formulation of the document on the Singapore Family Values completed, an obvious question will be, "What will be done to promote the values among Singaporeans?" Towards this end, in June 1994, the Prime Minister announced the creation of the S$1 million Singapore Family Values Promotion Fund to be used over five years to help finance projects which will actively promote the five family values (The Straits

Times 20/6/94, p. 1). The Fund is available to organisations and individuals to tap on a cost-sharing basis, and is managed by the Ministry of Community Development.

A Singapore Family Values Promotion Fund Committee was appointed by the Ministry to advise it in selecting suitable projects to support either with funds or ideas or both. It is also to co-ordinate efforts to encourage public and organisational involvement in promoting and transmitting the values in various ways (The Straits Times 20/7/94. p. 27). Again reflecting its public participation objective, MCD selected the members of the Committee from various sources — the government Ministries, the academia, the media, and the voluntary welfare and grassroots sectors.

So far, a number of projects have been supported by the Committee. These ranged from television commercials, plays, skills-based workshops, essay competitions, story writinng and telling competitions, children's story books, articles in popular periodicals and organisational newsletters, to advertisements in cinemas, magazines and on taxis, buses and bus shelters. The majority of the projects were undertaken by human service and other organisations such as voluntary welfare organisations, schools, self-help organisations, government Ministries, the National Trades Union Congress (NTUC), theatre groups, religious bodies and commercial establishments.

The projects can be divided into two main types — those that raise awareness on a general level about the values and those which are face-to-face in nature. For example, a TV commercial, because it is very expensive to produce and air, can only, due to its short duration of exposure to viewers at any one time, raise awareness of the values in the viewers' minds. The commercials cannot go in-depth to explain the details of the values and how to practice them with the necessary knowledge and skills involved. Hence, mass exposure-types of projects have to be supplemented and complemented by face-to-face types of events and activities, for example, experiential or skills-based training workshops which have a greater learning impact.

Promoting services to support the family

In this regard, the competence of social service organisations, such as family service agencies and related bodies, to directly and indirectly support the efforts to promote family values are critically determined by the context in which the organisations' overall service effectiveness occurs. Hence, any examination of programmes and activities dealing with family values must also take into account the capacity and capability of voluntary welfare, grassroots, religious and other family-oriented organisations to undertake family services as well. This is because often messages on family values can be more appropriately disseminated when they are embedded into the contents of activities and events of these programmes and services, and not as a stand-alone cognitive attempt.

It is envisaged that in the near future, HDB[5] community or neighbourhood centres will see more growth in support services for the family. These places are where most Singaporeans are residing. At the same time, with the growing number of the elderly among families and the increasing participation of married women in the labour force, a lot more families are likely to be dependent on support services of either its kin-group or neighbourhood, or both, if any member of the family needs long term care and attention. The capacity of the family to function effectively varies directly with its ability to mobilise help to meet the care and attention needs of its members. It is in these areas that family service organisations can pioneer programmes which will strengthen the family. Some examples of such programmes are child care services requiring parental participation, marriage counselling and guidance, and family life education programmes.

In planning and implementing more comprehensive family service programmes, it is necessary to re-examine the objectives of family service organisations to see if they are relevant to the demographic profiles of the specific urban centres or neighbourhoods. In the light of changing needs and expectations of the users and potential users of family services, it would be realistic to broaden the objectives of family service agencies. To achieve this, those who manage family service agencies must address the following questions: Are the agencies effectively meeting the needs of the users or potential users living in the locality? What relevant programmes or activities can be promoted to reach families in need? Only when those who manage family service organisations begin to seriously consider

---

[5] Housing and Development Board, the national public housing authority in Singapore.

these questions will they discover ways to strengthen and improve the programmes of their agencies.

Increasingly, more family service organisations are taking various initiatives to improve and/or expand their services. It would be useful for these agencies to come together to discuss ways in which they could co-operate in the delivery of their services to meet the needs of a wider cross-section of families in need. In this way the limited resources and expertise available in each of the agencies could be mobilised to provide more comprehensive and effective services to families. Family service programmes are cost-intensive and can be made more cost-effective, through joint efforts and co-operation among agencies. Consequently, their services and facilities could become more accessible to families in need.

For family service programmes to be effective, they must have the essential professional staff with expertise in such areas as family counselling and casework, group work, marital therapy, marriage mediation, and family life education, to name a few. It is envisaged that the current number of personnel in the family service field will come under tremendous strain if the pool of humanpower is not expanded to cater to future service demands dealing with family concerns.

In order to enhance the participation of personnel, both staff and volunteers, in family service organisations, must firstly make participation attractive; and secondly, encourage personnel to be more imaginative and creative in their work. The participation of personnel in family service organisations will be subjected to more and more challenges than ever before because of competing demands for their time as well as resources. Unless family service agencies can make the planning, management and delivery of their programmes to be interesting and growing experiences for their personnel, they will be unlikely to attract and sustain these people. It has been found that social service organisations which offer mundane and routine service programmes cannot sustain the interest of their personnel to remain employed in the organisation for long.

The growth and effectiveness of family service organisations is not only dependent on good leadership in the agency structure but also on the leaders' responsiveness to changes in the external environment. Sensitivity to emerging types of family needs and problems and the identification of these for quick response, will make family service organisations relevant to the context in which they operate. The problem with some organisations is that they do not develop adequate measures to monitor changes affecting families. It is not sufficient to have the desired personnel to implement family service programmes. Importantly, these personnel must be constantly motivated to upgrade their skills and knowledge in working effectively with families.

In recognising that there is a growing need for a forum to encourage the sharing of experiences and expertise among family service personnel such as social workers, family counsellors, psychologists and other related professionals and academics interested in family issues, it would be useful for a family studies group to be formed. This group can encourage a proliferation of research as well as the development of more effective strategies in working with the family. Through the establishment of such a group both academic and professional excellence can be promoted among those involved in working with or researching on families.

It is hoped that the proposed families study group can organise seminars and workshops for academics and professionals to share their experiences in working with the family, encourage the publication of local materials related to the family and family services; promote interdisciplinary research on family issues and well-being; and improve professional skills in working with families. One major area for the group to focus on can be issues related to the communication, transmission and internalisation of family values in a multi-racial and multi-cultural Singapore society.

Family service organisations have to be more dynamic. How can they achieve this? Should they be allowed to take their own course and do nothing about it? Family service organisations can be vibrant provided their management, staff and significant stakeholders all make periodical reviews of the organisation's mission, goals and objectives. The review would not only enable the organisations to discover ways to strengthen their family service programmes but also to attract more family service personnel to be involved. Through the delegation of responsibilities to them, more ideas can be generated and meaningful activities could be implemented.

The challenge before social service organisations is to review their mission for more effective programmes. As they take steps to do this, they will be preparing themselves to be the base for effective involvement of personnel, both staff and volunteers, in the provision of relevant family service programmes in the future.

Family values as a cultural catalyst

From the nature and scope of activities undertaken in promoting family values so far, the intention is to utilise as many different ways of transmitting the core set of family values as much as possible. It will also enable the Singapore Family Values Promotion Committee to gain valuable experience in knowing what would be effective transmission channels to reach families. In public education efforts there is usually the danger that the message is only heard by the "converted", that is, those who are already receptive to the message and are motivated to participate in public education activities. It is much more difficult to educate the "unconverted", those whom the message is especially targetted at, but are often "hard to reach" for various reasons.

As such, the Committee tries to incorporate various cultural forms, concrete as well as symbolic, into its promotional activities in order to maximise the impact of its efforts. At the same time, it is hoped that the increased level of publicity and activities generated will raise public awareness about the family values. In turn this will lead to some degree of consciousness, internalisation and in time to come, regular practice. In doing so, public learning about family values through cultural means will be enhanced with long term impact. This can be so if we bear in mind that culture

> "refers to the ways of life of the members of a society, or of groups within a society. It includes how they dress, their marriage customs and family life, their patterns of work, religious ceremonies and leisure pursuits. It also covers the goods they create and which become meaningful for them — bows and arrows, ploughs, factories and machines, computers, books, dwellings" (Giddens, p.31).

Conclusion

Promoting family values is recognised to be a challenging and long-term endeavour. Results cannot be seen overnight but will take many years of appropriate and sustained efforts. It requires the political will and commitment of the government and its people to remain steadfast to its belief in the worth and sanctity of the family. In this regard, the Singapore government has stated its stand very clearly. As mentioned by Senior Minister Mr Lee Kuan Yew, Singapore must insist on, and maintain, certain standards and values if it is to preserve the strength of its society and do better (The Straits Times 8/6/95, p.l).

Hence, it is very likely that the government will continue to support efforts at promoting family values in a sensitive and partnership manner. It will be up to organisations, the community, families and individuals themselves to join forces with the government in preserving and strengthening the family fabric of Singapore society

(Parts of the paper have been extracted and adapted from Ngiam, Tee Liang and Vasoo, S., "Promoting Family Values: Some Issues and Challenges", paper presented at the Fifth Malaysia–Singapore Forum, 11–14 December 1995, organised by the Faculty of Arts and Social Sciences, National University of Singapore.)

References

ASEAN Secretariat. *From Strength to Strength—ASEAN Functional Cooperation: Retrospect and Prospect.* Jakarta: The Secretariat, 1993.

Committee on the Family, National Advisory Council on Family and the Aged. *Singapore Family Values.* Singapore: Ministry of Community Development, 1994.

Giddens, Anthony. *Sociology.* (2nd edn.) Cambridge, UK: Polity Press, 1993.

Government of Singapore. *Shared Values.* Cmd. 1 of 1991 (White Paper). Singapore: Singapore National Printers for Government of Singapore, 1991.

National Day Parade 1996. Singapore: Souvenir Programme Sub-committee, NDP '96 Executive Committee, 1996.

Ngiam, Tee Liang. "*Family and Nation Building in Singapore: Family Well-being Without State Welfarism.*" Paper presented at the Fourth Malaysia–Singapore Forum, 8–11 December 1994, organised by the Faculty of Arts and Social Sciences, University of Malaya, Malaysia (mimeo).

Quah, Jon S. T. (ed). *In Search of Singapore's National Values.* Singapore: Times Academic Press for The Institute of Policy Studies, 1990.

The Straits Times (various issues).

Vander Zanden, James W. *Sociology: The Core.* (3rd edn.) New York: McGraw-Hill, 1993.

Chapter 9

The impact of social policies on the family in Singapore*

Rosaleen Ow[†] and S. Vasoo[‡]

State welfarism, as practiced in most developed western societies, is not a model adopted in Singapore. In contrast, social policies for families in the city state are aimed at strengthening the family's resource capacity in coping with the demands of rapid social and demographic changes, the effects of globalization and the influences of the new economy through a tripartite system of shared social care involving the state, the family and the employer. This paper discusses how various social policies related to financial security, housing, healthcare, eldercare, care and protection of children and the institution of marriage and

---

*Reprinted with permission by the publisher from Ow, R., & Vasoo, S. (2002). The impact of social policies on the family in Singapore. *Hong Kong Journal of Youth Studies*, 5(1), 106–118.

This paper discusses the various social policies which have been carefully devised to strengthen the social fabric of family life in Singapore, encouraging self-help and mutual support among family members, their kin groups and the community. The implications of these policies are touched.

[†]Assistant Professor, Department of Social Work and Psychology, National University of Singapore.

[‡]Associate Professor, Department of Social Work and Psychology, National University of Singapore.

procreation, are interwoven to promote self-help among family members, kin groups and the community with the state acting as a final safety net only for the most vulnerable who have limited means of support. It also emphasizes the need for social policy makers to be proactive in anticipating social needs arising from demographic and socio-economic trends currently observed. The social policies with a social development emphasis are reviewed.

Introduction

In Singapore, social policy makers are very conscious to ensure that a family's resource capacity is strengthened to deal with various competing demands and that they have the social antigen to protect its members where needed. In short, social policies are carefully devised so as not to erode the family from being a viable social institution with a strong foundation, especially in the light of the sweeping social changes and the move towards the new economy of tomorrow. Almost all the social policies, which have a direct or an indirect bearing to the family that have been implemented, do not promote dependency on the state. The Singapore family is expected to be self-supporting and the kinship group is encouraged to provide assistance when needed. The Singapore Government avoids state welfarism, which is commonly practiced in most western developed countries (Lee, KY, 2000) where various measures adopted have been reported to be economically unsustainable as national expenditure outstrips income. Many of these governments find it politically difficult to roll back social security benefits to the people, as these are explosive issues that often become political tools to ensure the survival of existing or succeeding governments (Vasoo and Lee, 2001).

According to the 2000 Census, Singapore has a multicultural population of about 3.6 million, excluding foreigners, living in a land area of approximately 641 square kilometers. Given its land scarcity and vulnerability as a small nation state, social policies are also aimed at building a harmonious, caring and cohesive society. The rapid socio-economic changes due to globalization, together with a changing demographic profile, pose a number of challenges to the stability and well being of families and their role as building blocks of society. Indeed, the ageing of

Singapore's population will one day be acute. There will be fewer younger family members in households and this will definitely stretch families' abilities to provide adequate care and attention to elderly family members. Some families will need more support from the community when they cannot mobilize assistance from amongst their kin groups and the burdens of care are likely to increase (Vasoo, *et al.*, 2000). Therefore, social policies to deal with an ageing population will also have to be put in place so as to deal with the challenges facing the family with elderly members (IMC Report 2000).

Social policies are directed at meeting the challenges posed to the family on matters arising in the social sphere, such as domestic violence, single parent families and single-hood, low fertility rate and the maintenance of parents; as well as in the economic sphere, such as financial security, healthcare and dual income. There are many challenges to the family and these have been identified in the latest publication of APFAM (Asia Pacific Forum on Families) on the strategic plan for families in the region. Singapore is no exception and in its country profile, one of the features in the changing family structure was highlighted as the increase of nuclear households (APFAM, 2001:18). For example, families with 3 or more generations living together in the same household decreased from 13.7% in 1990 to 12.6% in 1995 (Ang, 1999:2; Census 2000). The trend of single persons and young couples establishing their own households have implications on family structures and relationships, as well as on the care of the very young and elderly. A declining fertility rate due to an increase in people choosing to be single, or generally marrying at a later age, are other factors that have an impact on family structures. Since 1977, the total fertility rate has fallen below the replacement level, with 1,818 births per 1,000 females in 1980 to 1,465 births per 1,000 females in 1998. Recent changes in family policies have boosted the figure to 1,586 births per 1,000 females in 2000 (Department of Statistics Singapore, 2001). This, together with an increasing ageing population estimated to be 26% of the total population by the year 2030 (APFAM, 2001:18), would have serious implications on maintaining a consolidated family structure. In addition to these demographic factors, other threats to the consolidation of the family include registered divorces and the concurrent rise in the number of single parent families. Divorces registered under the Women's

Charter increased by 85% from 1,912 in 1987 to 3,546 in 1996. There were similar trends in the number of family disputes reported and Protection Orders issued by the Family Court (Ang, 1999:4).

Globalization and the move towards the new economy will see a rise in the number of dual income families. This can also lead to stress and strains on parenting, including the transmission of family values and the development of strong family relationships. In the face of these challenges to the family, the state's involvement in providing leadership and impetus to address these concerns are reflected in major social policies directed at strengthening the family's capacity to fulfill its role as provider and nurturer to its members and by its own solidarity, to contribute to the sense of well being and harmony in society. In this article a number of pertinent social policy areas dealing with the family's financial security, housing, healthcare, care and maintenance of elderly parents, protection and care of children, family violence and marriage and family procreation will be reviewed.

Family financial security policy

Almost every family is covered by the Central Provident Fund (CPF), which is a financial security scheme (CPF, 1998). Family members above the age of 18 and working are by law required to contribute to the CPF. Each working member who is either employed in the private or public sector, along with their employers each have to contribute 20% based on the individual's basic monthly salary, making a total contribution of 40% of the monthly income to the Fund. Employers who fail to contribute are penalized heavily. Such a legalized contributory savings scheme provides financial security for family members in their old age because of the substantial savings made throughout their working careers.

The establishment of the CPF as a compulsory saving institution was initiated in 1955 during the colonial period and this incurred very low financial risks to the colonial government. As it was manageable, the CPF scheme was subsequently revised through incremental social policy changes under the People's Action Party (PAP) Government. Working family members have been allowed to use their CPF savings for housing, investments in trustee stocks and annuity and endowment schemes. Such varied, but secure investment portfolios, do ensure a reasonable financial return to the individual CPF account holder. However, economic downturns and global economic setbacks, for example those arising from the terrorist attack in the United States on 11 September 2001, do affect the returns on CPF savings no matter how prudent one is on the investments. Based on these unpredictable events, a family's financial security can also be vulnerable if the long-term employability of family members is disrupted through economic restructuring and recession. However, there are major packages to help the economy ride over the downturn. These also include long term measures to upgrade the skills of family members which may be relevant to the globalize economic markets (Lee, HL: 12 October 2001) and to make them more employable in the future.

The financial requirements under the CPF scheme for each working family member to set aside a minimum sum after their retirement age at the age of 60, enabled them to have some financial security without having to be entirely financially dependent on their children (IMC Report 2000). The minimum sum is now set at S$80,000. Although it has been agreed that the said amount may not be sufficient in some cases, it is anticipated that the elderly family members can also sell their assets, for example, their purchased flats and downgrade to smaller flats, if more funds are required to meet their future financial commitments.

Family and housing policy

Singapore's housing program only began in 1960 and now her public home ownership scheme is well known internationally. It is an effective social development tool for the integration of the family into the community. Public housing consists mainly of flats built and sold by the State to some 86% of its people. These flats range from the simple 2 to 3 room variety, to the more luxurious 4 to 5 room style. Thus, public housing caters for both the working class, as well as the more affluent middle class. The private housing market takes care of only about 10% of the population, usually in the upper income group. Families are encouraged to upgrade to bigger flats, as a chain factor in motivating others to move up the economic ladder.

Housing in Singapore has moved from the mere provision of simple shelter to asset accumulation for the future, unlike most other countries that do not make provision for an ownership stake for families in public housing schemes. In line with the Singapore's social development objectives, public housing is seen as an asset accumulation for Singaporean families at an affordable cost. Individuals may use their CPF savings to become homeowners. This is in contrast with western countries, where most public housing is meant for marginalized and less well off families. Sherraden *et al.* (1995) have also pointed out that provision of housing has greatly enhanced the dignity of the Singapore family and made them more socially integrated (Vasoo and Lee, 2001). It must also be noted that the housing of families in Singapore is linked with economic development as well as social development objectives, wherein households become socially integrated with other Singaporeans of various social and ethnic backgrounds.

The housing program in Singapore is, therefore, designed for the integration of all Singaporeans, but lower income families are given special attention to help them purchase low cost apartments to ensure that as far as possible, all families may stay together under one roof. Since 1985, the tenants of public housing with household incomes of less than S$800.00 were provided with various financial concessions to enable them to purchase their own homes. Families with household incomes of less than S$2000.00 per month were able to buy public housing apartments also at a subsidized rate, but with a 100 per cent mortgage loan and a waiver on credit assessments. If the buyer is an existing tenant of the Housing and Development Board, a 30 per cent discount on the tenant's paid rent is also provided up to a sum of S$15,000.00.

In addition, Singapore, as an Asian society, recognizes the need for families to maintain and fulfill their roles and responsibilities to the extended family. To facilitate the consolidation of the extended family unit, other special housing schemes include the Multi-Tier Family Housing Scheme whereby a family comprising parents/grandparents and married child/grandchildren staying together in the same household will be given priority allocation for public housing apartments. Another scheme aimed at facilitating regular contact among extended family members is the housing grant of S$40,000.00 for families who are first time purchasers of a resale flat in the same town or within 2 kilometers of their parents/married child's flat (Online: http:// www.hdb.gov.sg 30 Aug 2001).

Family and health care policies

In Singapore, both the government and the private sector provide health care services for family members. Currently, the public sector provides 80% of hospital care and 20% of primary health care. The financing policy for health care is based on individual responsibility, familial commitment, coupled with state subsidies to keep basic health care affordable.

These are three specific health care policy measures which have been implemented under the health reform plans to meet the medical needs of the family. Not only are they easy to manage, but are also simple to administer. At the same time, new administrative structure or bureaucracy has been established to implement exisiting policy measures namely, the Medisave, Medishield and Medifund.

1. *Medisave scheme*

Medisave (MOH, 2000) is an innovative scheme to meet medical and hospitalization expenses. This scheme was implemented in 1984 under the CPF. Currently, the total monthly CPF contribution is 40%, which is comprised of a 20% contribution by employees based on their monthly gross wages, equally matched by 20% from the employers (Lim, 1997: 279).

Medisave covers all workers, including the self-employed, who earn more than S$2,400 a year (MOH, Annual Report, 1998), thereby also including low-income earners. Such wide coverage ensures that most individuals are encouraged to save and set aside some funds for their medical needs, especially in their old age. The administration of Medisave has not posed any difficulties, as it is managed under the purview of CPF and the contributions are deducted at source from workers' wages. The employees contribute between 6% and 8% of their monthly wages to their Medisave accounts. Those who are below 35 years of age contribute 6% of their salary, or up to a maximum contribution of S$360 per month. Those between 35 and 44 years old contribute 7% of their salary, and or up to a maximum of S$420 per month. Older employees who are 45 years and above, have to make an 8% contribution of their monthly salary or up to S$480 per month, subscribing to the view that as medical needs increase with age, older employees should increase their contributions, and thus ensuring that they do not become dependent on the state to pay for their entire hospitalization charges. The copayment system does empower employees to decide on the class of ward should they be hospitalized.

The unique feature about Medisave is that it allows for inter-generation transfers. Besides usage by individual account holders, it can also be used to cover hospitalization expenses and other medical treatments of family members, including relatives who have either no, or low, Medisave funds. Such an extended coverage of Medisave for the kin group helps strengthen mutual support and familial bonds. The Medisave may support even distant relatives if it is established that they have no means to pay for a portion of their hospitalization costs.

There are more than 2.71 million Medisave accounts and the total Medisave balance stands at a healthy S$22.7 billion, which can be used to meet an individual's future medical expenses. According to current figures, the total Medisave withdrawal was about S$391 million in the year 2000. It is also estimated that the ratio of contributions to withdrawals is positive. (MOH Report 2001). This low utilization rate is due to the relatively young adult Singapore population with a median age of 33.4 years (IMC, Report, 1999: 29). With such a population profile, there is currently less of a public or familial burden on health care.

The Medisave policy measure encourages the individual to exercise responsibility for his immediate and future health care needs. Individuals have to be cautious about splurging on their funds, as they have to pay their medical expenses at the point of consumption. Unlike other social security policies for health care, which are based on common pooling funds, the Medisave fund is different in the sense that it is a personal health care savings system and can only be accessed by the specific contributor. The cumulative public burden for health care is not passed from one generation to another under the Medisave scheme. Instead, when each generation looks after its own health care needs, then succeeding generations of a smaller population base of younger adults will not have the heavy financial burden of the family members (Lim. 1997: 281).

2. Medishield scheme

There is no doubt that individuals who are affected by chronic or catastrophic illness can be burdened financially in meeting their medical treatment expenses. A more comprehensive insurance coverage is therefore necessary and thus the Medishield scheme was implemented in 1990. Medishield is designed to be a low cost insurance scheme, which is affordable even to low income wage earners. It also complements the Medisave scheme. The yearly premium for Medishield scheme is based on the contributor's age. For those below 30 years of age, the premium is S$12 per year. For those between 31 and 75 year old, payments can range from S$18 to S$240 per year.

3. Medifund scheme

For families that find it difficult to meet the medical costs of a particular member can tap into the Medifund Scheme. This fund is a safety net for those people, who despite all sources cannot meet their medical expenses. In the year 2000, Medifund assistance was extended to 91,000 applicants at the cost of S$12.7milion (MOH Report 2001).

4. Eldershield scheme

To help those families with elderly members, a further a new low-cost insurance plan, Eldershield, will be launched in the second quarter of year 2002 for citizens and permanent residents between the ages of 40–60 years with an opting-out feature. The insurance would provide older people who might become disabled a sum of S$300 per month for a maximum of 5 years. Unlike the Medishield, whose coverage ends at 75 years and with premiums that rise with age, Eldershield members stop paying premiums at 65 years old, but can still make claims if they become disabled later, as coverage is for life. The government expects to spend over S$400 million under the scheme, which will enhance a family's ability to provide care for disabled old people in the community, as the money from the insurance can be used in any way that the recipient wishes.

Policy for the care and maintenance of elderly parents

Singapore has one of the fastest ageing populations in the Asia Pacific region after Japan. As a result, families will soon face the burden of care for elderly parents. There is an anticipation that, as a result, the number of cases of neglect will increase. One significant policy to prevent this, and for ensuring that the social care of elderly parents, particularly amongst those less able to do so, was the introduction of the Maintenance of Parents Act in 1994. The unique act allows parents to file a petition at the Parents Maintenance Tribunal, which consists of community leaders along with a judge to hear the cases. The Tribunal has the legal powers to impose a maintenance order on children for the support of their neglected elderly parents.

It is estimated at least one in four persons will be 60 years old, or above, in the year 2030 (IMC Report, 1999). This significant demographic transition will have serious implications to the provision of care for the elderly who will occupy most of the hospital beds and with a low turnover. It is estimated that about 5% of the elderly population will require long-term geriatric care. However, this provision will not be an effective solution in the long term as the building of more geriatric facilities will not be a realistic solution to cope with the demands. In view of the fact that some of the elderly may be terminally ill or in a vegetative state, a futuristic social policy to deal with this dilemma was put in place.

The Advanced Medical Directive Act will enable medical doctors, only with the consent of elderly persons made earlier in their lifetime, and with the support of family members, to discontinue the life support systems to such persons who are certified brain dead.

It is also important for policy makers and service providers to think of other innovative services to help the elderly remain healthy as long as possible and be socially integrated in the family and community. The cost issues are the main concern and institutional provisions, such as community hospitals, nursing homes and hospice centers are not only expensive to run, but are also impersonal. The relocation of an elderly person from his own community into residential care can also be considered a social cost.

Emphasis must also be paid to the provision of health related services for the elderly, particularly in the areas of preventive health care and community based programs. Such an emphasis will make programs accessible and enable the elderly to remain within their community, while also mobilizing the community to participate in the promotion of long term care programs. This approach will make the programs more cost effective and help the elderly to be independent. An innovative community care co-operative could be established to meet the long-term care and health needs of the elderly. Social workers can help to promote community care co-operatives in various neighborhoods and it could be a good long-term solution to cater for frail or sick elderly. The co-operatives with the involvement of the concerned elderly, including those who have retired, can provide a range of services such as home care, transportation, and health screening and health education, wellness programs and day care service. These services can be charged affordable rates and members of the co-operatives will be granted rebates for use of the services.

Policies for the care and protection of the family and children

With rising income levels among the general population, problems presented to social workers have changed over the years, from those related to financial and practical needs to difficulties associated with interpersonal relationships, behavioral problems, marital and intergenerational conflicts. In addition, the rise of dual income families has also increased the needs related to childcare and parenting that require supportive social policies. Between 1990 and 2000, the participation of women in the labor force increased from 48.8% (504,300) to 50.2% (634,800) (Department of Statistics, 2000). With more mothers engaged in the labor force, alternative arrangements for the care of young and school going children, before and after school hours, has become more important.

Since the family is the primary institution for the care of the young, the government through the Ministry of Community Development and Sports (MCDS), works together with other voluntary organizations to promote responsible and effective parenting by organizing family life seminars, talks and workshops. The Family Life Program receives financial support as well as help in sourcing and training facilitators from the Ministry of Community Development and Sports.

Although homecare is recognized as the best form of care for young children, in a situation where parents are unable to provide the regular care, center-based care is the major substitute. In order to ensure that childcare centers are widely available and that they subscribe to acceptable standards, the government has put in place various schemes that include financial support for childcare, the need for childcare registration and a recognized teacher-training course for childcare personnel. For example, the Government Child Care subsidy is available to working and non-working mothers and single fathers so that childcare remains affordable to families where the mother is not always available. The rate of subsidy is based on the employment status of the mother/single father and also on whether it is a full-day or half-day program. Some very low-income families are not able to afford center-based childcare in spite of the government subsidy in which case, an additional financial scheme called the Center-Based Financial Assistance Scheme for Child Care (CFAC), administered by the National Council of Social Service, is available.

Apart from public utility services such as described above, there are also a number of case services for the protection and care of children in special circumstances. The state is actively involved in providing help to that small segment of families where there are children and youths at risk for child abuse, juvenile delinquency or referred to as beyond parental control. Every family's dream is to bring up children who are socially responsible and can make a positive contribution to the family unit and to society. However, in situations where the family is unable to fulfill its role in preventing the children from falling into delinquent behavior, the state provides community rehabilitation programs such as probation and community service orders and institutional rehabilitation that act as temporary substitutes for training and correction. Probation is a community-based program that provides the Courts with an alternative sentencing option. Under the supervision and personal care of a Probation Officer, the juvenile is allowed to stay in the community and more importantly, the family is given another opportunity to stay and work together to resolve family problems in the nurturing and socialization process.

In recent years, public awareness of child abuse has increased, partly due to the attention given to cases made public through the Family Court. The Children and Young Person Act Chapter 38 (CYPA) is the legal instrument for the protection and intervention by relevant authorities if a child (below the age of 14) or young person (from 14 to below 16 years of age) is abused or neglected. Child abuse covers physical abuse, neglect, sexual abuse and emotional/psychological abuse. It also covers any act committed by a parent or guardian, which would endanger or impair the child, or any act judged by community values and authorized professionals to be inappropriate. Although the reporting of suspected child abuse by the public is not mandatory, there is a network in place, in which the police, medical professionals and social workers work together with the relevant social service and legal authorities to ensure that appropriate investigation and intervention are conducted to prevent further harm to the child. Professional assistance is also available to the abused child and the family.

****

Parenting is not a role that suits everyone and families often express the need to seek help for their children or themselves to improve family relationships and to resolve difficulties in role fulfillment. In a survey of about 200 families, the Committee on Destitute Families (1989) found that a combination of family dysfunction, irregular employment of heads of households, breadwinners committed for drug or criminal offences, and divorce and broken homes was responsible for family destitution. In order to facilitate family problem-solving skills and prevent family discord, the state's pro-family policy supports a wide range of activities such as seminars and workshops, as well as the establishment of family service centers in the major housing estates. These centers are funded by a tripartite relationship between the state, the private sector and the National Council of Social Service. The state provides 90% of the capital expenditure with the rest from private donations. The National Council of Social Service funds part of the operation costs for specific programs. To date there are 27 family service centers providing a one-stop social service center within easy reach of families in the community. The objectives of these centers are to provide preventive, remedial and developmental programs that will help families cope with their responsibilities and prevent family breakdown (Vasoo and Osman, 2000).

Family domestic violence and social policy

Singapore is one of the earliest countries to implement the Women's Charter, which offered a wide range of legal protection for women and welfare for the family. Following reported increases in wife abuse, the Charter was amended to cover psychological and physical abuses. So far, there has been very little formal data on battered women and their families in Singapore, but the increasing applications for personal protection orders (restraining orders against the perpetrators) from 27 in 1986 to 150 in 1990 (Subordinate Court Register, Singapore, 1991) indicate a growing trend. Family service centers and non-governmental organizations, such as the Singapore Council of Women's Organizations, the Society Against Family Violence and the Association of Women for Action and Research, provide hotlines, public education and legal advice for women in crisis. However, the service growth of the non-profit sector is highly dependent on policies related to mandatory counseling for the perpetrators. This requirement also enforces the rehabilitation of abusing spouses. The success of such a rehabilitation scheme depends on intensive work with the abusing spouses who, without the amendments to the Women's Charter, could not be legally dealt with. The Women's Charter was incrementally revised to provide more bite to bring legal recourse to helpless and abused wives. It also tries to gain financial protection for mothers and children who are not maintained by their husbands or fathers. Women who previously did not get any financial support after a divorce, now have the legal right to get at least half of the matrimonial asset. This is a milestone change towards the protection of the female spouse who often ends up a loser when the marriage is dissolved. The amended Women's Charter now provides a new lease of support for financially vulnerable wives and children who are now better protected than they were a decade ago.

Marriage and family procreation policy

Singapore's population growth has slowed down in the last two decades. The growth rate is below replacement and has shrunk from 2.5 in 1970 to 1.2 in 2000. This dramatic shrinkage by half in the last 30 years will have serious ramifications for domestic demands for goods and services, aged dependency, productivity, quality of manpower, income generation and defense. The lower growth rate is the result of low fertility rate of families and the increase in the number of single persons (Census, 2000). Such a low level of population growth has also been partly influenced by very successful family planning and population policies implemented by the Singapore government. Furthermore, the increasing number of dual career families over the last decade has also changed the perception of spouses on the need for more children. Most working parents have to face the competing demands between the need for additional children or continuity in their respective careers (MCDS, 2001). Hence, despite the government persuasion for the family to have more children, it has not been enough for those who can afford it. This is further compounded by the delay in marriage age of young people, which has increased from 25 years to 29 years (Census, 2000).

In recognition that there is a need for rejuvenation of Singapore's population and to arrest the downward trend in population growth, the government has introduced a number of measures. First, all working mothers who give birth to the first and up to three children will be given a baby bonus of S$20,000. Mothers are also given child tax incentives up to three children. All working mothers with up to two children will also be granted a childcare subsidy up to S$150 per month. The impact of all these monetary incentives to reduce the financial burden in childcare and to promote procreation has yet to shore up Singapore's population. The prospects seem positive and if they work, more social policies to induce population growth can be expected in the near future. The social and economic consequences of a poor population growth will be serious, as have been identified earlier.

Other than monetary incentives to encourage population growth, attempts have also been set-up to enable unmarried singles to have opportunities to meet and socialize with each other. The Social Development Unit and Social Development Section, which are government bodies, have been established to promote social activities and matchmaking programs for unmarried singles in Singapore (MCDS, 2001). It is felt that perhaps more voluntary and community organizations will be able to undertake such programs to facilitate marriage amongst younger single persons.

Concluding remarks

There has been a systematic implementation of social policies, all of which have a direct bearing on the family in Singapore. In the last two decades, it has been observed that more steps have been taken by the government to formulate and enact policies, which strengthen the social fabric of family life in Singapore. In essence, most of the social policies help to promote self-help and mutual support among family members, their kin groups and the community. Welfarist approaches to deal with a family's needs are avoided and the promotion of a tripartite system in caring for one another is adopted. In such a tripartite system, the family, state and employer are encouraged to share the costs for social care. This is indeed an effective model to enhance mutual help among different key players in society and it will encourage the buffet syndrome in the use of social services where there are high subsidy to maintain the delivery of the services in the health and welfare arenas.

The social policies discussed above have been aimed at addressing specific family requirements arising from the need for financial security, low income, healthcare, low fertility, ageing, domestic violence, procreation and the care and protection of children. The 21st Century will be a time when personal choices about family life will impact on the well being of society. The need to raise awareness among Singaporeans that their life choices could have serious repercussions on family relationships needs to be addressed. As a result, the government has set up the Public Education Committee on Family with the objective of working with civic groups and the community to develop programs that will modify attitudes and mindsets and to create awareness of the importance of an early start to marriage and parenthood; mutual support of spouses in domestic responsibilities and parenting; preparation for different stages of the family life cycle and the transmission of core values to the young (online: http://www.mcds.gov.sg/HTML/ families/pec/pechome.html, http://www.mcds.gov.sg/HTML/families/pec/pechome.html, 8 Mar 2001).

References

Ang, B.L. (1999). *Key social challenges facing Singapore*. Paper presented at the first joint MCD-NCSS-NUS-SASW research symposium, 15 November 1999, Marriott Hotel Singapore.

APFAM (2001). *A strategic plan for families in the asia pacific region.* A joint project of APFAM, APFAM member countries and the center for health research, University of Indonesia.

Central Provident Fund Board (1998). *The CPF story.* Singapore.

Lee, H.L. (2001). *Tackling the economic downturn.* Proceedings of Parliament of Singapore on 12 October 2001.

Lee, K.Y. (2000). *From third world to first — the Singapore story: 1965–2000* (pp. 116–130). Singapore.

Lim, J. (1997). Health care reform in Singapore: The medisave scheme. In T.M, Tan and S.B. Chew (Eds.). *Affordable health care* (pp. 277–285). Singapore: Prentice Hall.

Ministry of Community Development (2001). *Family forum interim recommendations of the public education committee on family.*

Ministry of Health (2001). *Annual report 2001.* Singapore.

Report of Inter-ministerial Committee (IMC) on ageing 1999. Singapore.

Report of the committee on destitute families. Ministry of Community Development, December 1988.

Republic of Singapore (1991). *Subordinate court register.* Singapore: Subordinate Court.

Singapore Department of Statistics. *Census 2000 report.* Singapore.

Sherraden, M., Nadir, S., Vasoo, S. and Guam, T.L. (1995). Social policy based on assets: The impact of Singapore's central provident fund. *Asian Journal Political Science, 3*(2), 112–133.

Vasoo, S. and Lee, J. (2001a). Singapore: Social development, housing and the central provident fund. *International Journal of Social Welfare, 10*(4), 276–283.

Vasoo, S. and Lee, J. (2001b). Translating economic and socio-political objectives for development: The case of central provident fund on public housing in Singapore. *International Journal of Social Welfare, 9*(1).

Vasoo, S., Ngiam, T.L. and Cheung, P.P.L. (2000). Singapore's ageing population: Some emerging trends and issues. In D.R. Phillips (Ed.), *Ageing in Asia-Pacific Region* (pp. 174–193). London: Routledge.

Vasoo, S. and Osman, M.M. (2000). Non-governmental organizations in Singapore and nation building: Some emerging trends and issues. *Social Development, 22*, 54–63.

Part 4

Advocating for Inclusiveness for the Disabled

Chapter 10

Employment opportunities for the disabled in Singapore: Some issues and challenges*

S. Vasoo[†]

Employment opportunities for the disabled in Singapore have improved in the last two decades. Despite good prospects for their employment, there are a number of factors which affect their employability. The paper explores some of these issues and suggests some ways which will enhance the employability of the disabled in Singapore.

Introduction

The employment opportunities for the disabled in Singapore have increased in the last two decades because of strong economic development (Bizlink, 1995). Various types of jobs requiring different skills have emerged and

---

*From Vasoo, S. (1997). Employment opportunities for the disabled in Singapore: Some issues and challenges. *Asia and Pacific Journal on Disability*, *1*(1), 17–23. (Hong Kong). Reprinted by permission of *Asia and Pacific Journal on Disability*.

This paper examines the various challenges and problems affecting the employability of the disabled persons in Singapore despite improved employment opportunities. It is advocated that some inclusive solutions to tackle these issues have to be looked into.

[†]Head, Department of Social Work and Psychology, National University of Singapore.

such a situation poses challenges to the disabled persons as they need to be adequately prepared and trained for open employment.

More lower and higher end jobs are now available as a result of the tight labour market. At the same time, with the low unemployment rate of about two percent in Singapore (Yearbook of Statistics, 1995) as compared to ten percent (The Economist, 1996) in many developed countries, the competition for jobs between the disabled and the able-bodied is less stiff. Employers are more prepared to consider a trained disabled for employment as he is unlikely to job-hop.

Since the Ministry of Community Development's (MCD) macrosurvey in 1985, there has been no study on problems and the needs of the disabled. Centralised record on employment patterns of the disabled have not been compiled yet. There is some scattered information on the employment situation of the disabled compiled by agencies dealing with them. However, to tackle the problems of employment of the disabled more effectively, it will be necessary for the Ministry of Community Development and the National Council of Social Service to work together to collate information of the problems and the needs of the disabled. A comprehensive information on their needs and problems will be useful for more effective plans to be implemented to assist them to develop their potentials.

Based on the 1985 MCD data and recent informed opinions from voluntary service agencies, it is assessed that unemployment rate continues to be high among the visually, intellectually and neuro-muscular disabled. Most of them are between 21 and 35 years old. These groups of disabled will continue to dominate and there is a good potential for promoting their employability (Bizlink, 1995).

Since the establishment of Bizlink Centre in 1986, a more concerted effort has emerged to assess and place disabled for employment. In the past 8 years (1988–1995), the Bizlink Centre has helped to place 1903 disabled persons into various gainful occupations from professional and technical positions to production work. About 76 percent of the disabled have found employmnet in the service and production fields and 21 percent in the clerical field (Bizlink, 1995a). The employment profiles of the disabled will change when they acquire better educational and skilled training. Therefore, archaic and outmoded training and preparation of the disabled by various concerned agencies should be discontinued as it will make them less employable, particularly in the changing Singapore job market.

Despite the improved prospects for employment of the disabled, the number of disabled who have been placed in jobs has not grown significantly. Bizlink Centre placed an average of about 225 disabled annually onto jobs excluding the attrition resulting from job mismatch (Bizlink, 1995a).

The less than attractive rate of employment of the disabled is affected by a number of factors such as negative community attitude, transportation problems, environmental barriers, ineffective service delivery, lack of skills and inadequate facilities. These factors are examined subsequently in some details.

Negative community attitude

Generally many people including potential employers are still prejudiced against the disabled who are often stereotyped as incapable and have no abilities to manage work. Such an orthodox perception is still prevalent. Perhaps worse than this attitude is the indifference. Disabled are seen as an economic liability and have no potential. The community tries to evaluate the disabled in terms of the capabilities of the normal population (Report of the Committee on Employment, 1988).

Another common phenomenon is social stigmatization. Many disabled who are stigmatized are seen as not normal. People exercise a lot of discrimination and rationalize a number of ways for not giving appropriate treatment to the disabled.

It must be pointed out that not all members of the community have adverse attitude towards the disabled. There are people who are sympathetic and take pity of their needs. It is noteworthy that a large number of benevolent organisations have been set-up by these people to help meet the needs of the disabled. Pity which is patronising can prevent the disabled from being independent. Some parents and managements of organisations are so protective that they fail to encourage their disabled to learn to work independently.

Minority status

The disabled can be affected by the minority status. They usually form a minority of the Singapore population and hence are likely to be assigned a minority status. As a consequence, they may inadvertently be marginalised by the non-disabled to helpless roles. Transfer of resources from the more able can be less forthcoming unless their social conscience is prodded. In the Singapore context, it is still fortunate that there are people who are willing to come forward to contributing either effort and/or funds to support organisations assisting the disabled.

Transportation problems

The transportation problem is one of the major issues facing the disabled. Without a customised transportation system, many disabled who will otherwise be able to join workforce will be confined to their homes. Although some attempts have been made to deal with the transportation needs of the disabled, the problem has remained complex but not insolvable (Report of the Committee on Employment, 1988).

Here in Singapore, due to the limited land area and dense population, effective solutions have yet to be found to solve the increasing traffic congestions and problems. Therefore, given this situation, the transportation problem of the disabled is unlikely to be given priority attention. It is likely that the National Council of Social Service will be assigned the task to find various arrangements to tackle the issue. For a long term solution, it cannot be avoided that some subsidies will be necessary for operating a customized transportation scheme for the disabled who can be economically productive. For without such a scheme, some disabled will find it difficult to join the workforce and hence become more financially dependent.

Physical barriers

Besides human barriers, the disabled do continue to face problems of access to public facilities and buildings. Generally work places have not been fully accessible and therefore a deterrence to employment of the disabled. However, it is encouraging to note that more enlightened employers have taken active steps to make their workplaces barrier-free.

A barrier-free and user friendly environment will facilitate the mobility of the disabled and remove barrier to their employability. Almost 90 percent of our population live in high-rise housing estates. As our population is aging faster than many developing countries and the incidence of disability among the aged population would increase, it is essential to make our estates more user friendly. Accessibility code should be implemented more vigorously (Report of the Committee on Employment, 1988).

Non-proactive management

Some of the agencies serving the disabled have not made progressive changes in the delivery of their services. Their rehabilitation and training programmes have not kept in tandem with the changes of the job market. Most of the skills and training programmes including the tools used are antiquated. Hence, without relevant training to meet the job requirements in the market, the disabled become less employable.

Some managements of agencies serving the disabled are not as proactive as they should be and they adopt "laissez faire" approach in their service delivery The managements are not responsive to market demands for relevant vocational skills and preparation. The facilities and resources of the agencies are under-utilized and a dwindling number of disabled are engaged on vocational activities which are outdated and non-viable. It is urgent for managements of agencies serving the disabled to take more pragmatic decisions to network and share out premises for either training or setting of sheltered workshops to cater for various disabled groups.

Inadequate vocational skills and educational level

Generally, the disabled who are trainable lacked the vocational skills for work in the manufacturing and commercial sectors. The vocational training programmes for the disabled are not relevant to the job requirements in the industries hence it is more difficult to place the disabled on the jobs.

The lack of a systematic vocational skills training package in most agencies dealing with the disabled reflects the lack of professional expertise available to provide inputs. Therefore, some existing training settings function as holding units to keep the disabled occupied in mundane activities such as basket weaving, polishing, folding cartons and cutting wires. A complete review of the vocational training programme should be undertaken (Report of the Committee on Employment, 1985).

It is noted that many of the disabled have primary education and below. This being the case, their educational standards must first be improved prior to vocational skills training.

Some realistic solutions

In enhancing the employability of the disabled, one must prepare them to have marketable skills. To digress from this objective, will lessen their work opportunities. First and foremost fact is that the disabled must be adequately trained with a vocational skill and then placed in suitable employment. Other realistic solutions to make them employable should also be pursued.

Public education

A comprehensive public relation exercise to publicize successful disabled in various occupations could be undertaken. These successful human interest portrayals will increase public awareness of the potentials of the disabled. When more people become enlightened about the potentials of the disabled, the employment opportunities of the disabled could improve.

Public education should steer clear from dwelling in pity and sympathy for the disabled. The positive aspects of their human potentials must be emphasized.

Changing employer attitude

Employers who have hired disabled and those who have prospects to employ the disabled should be identified and formed into a task force to promote employment of the disabled. It is through the publicity of successful cases of disabled that more positive attitude among employers could be developed. Agencies dealing with disabled should reach out to more potential employers who can be enlisted to become friends of the organisations.

The government has employed some disabled persons. She can take the lead to employing more of them in information and counter services. Through government endorsement in employing the disabled, private sectors will also become more open to employ them.

Perhaps more tax incentives can be given to employers who are disabled friendly. This can change the attitude of employers and can be more effective than legislating the employment of the disabled.

Reducing physical barriers

Physical barriers in work settings in which the employers are interested in employing the disabled have to be reduced and better incentives to modify buildings should be considered. The present relief of up to a maximum of $100,000 accorded to owners of buildings is a small sum and should be increased. Besides, the relief should cover the purchase of special equipment to assist the disabled to be productive.

Where possible the housing estate environment should be further modified for easy commutation of the disabled to work places.

Customised transportation

In order to meet point to point transportation to work for the disabled, it is necessary to expand the present customised transport service. The fleet of vehicles managed by Handicaps Welfare Association and Society for Aid to Paralysed could be centralized to meet economy of scale. The fleet of vehicles could be increased with the support of additional grants from the Transport Authority to operate the transport system more efficiently. To make it viable, the fleet of vehicles should be allowed to pick up passengers when they are not used by the disabled.

Proactive management

The service delivery system of some agencies must be reviewed to make it more cost effective. Agencies serving a small declining number of the disabled should join force with needy disabled agencies to serve a bigger pool of other disabled. Better use of space and facilities for vocational training could result with the pooling of agencies and their resources. Where possible, control by interested parties and groups in the management of agencies should be prevented. This will reduce parochial interest in the management and better strategies for the employability of the disabled could be implemented without delay.

Co-operative workshops and enterprises

The prospects for setting up co-operative workshops and enterprises to take on contract work such as packaging, horticultural, environmental, cleansing and building maintenance have not been fully explored. Viable co-operative enterprises through share ownership by the disabled and his family members, interested individuals, trade unions, and business could be established. These certainly generate more gainful employment for the disabled.

Conclusion

The efforts to promote the employment of the disabled are fragmented. A number of salient issues which hamper their employability are interrelated and they must be all tackled concertedly. Most importantly the disabled must be trained to have marketable skills. There must be barrier free work places, available customised transportation systems, positive employer attitude and a proactive management in agencies serving the disabled.

References

Bizlink (1995). *Report on Bizlink Centre*. Singapore.
Bizlink (1995a). *Overview of Services of Bizlink Centre*. Singapore.

Report of the *Committee on Employment, Accessibility and Transportation for Disabled People* (1998). Singapore.
The Economist (1996). Vol 338 No 7954. p 118. London.
Yearbook of Statistics (1995). No. 10. Singapore: Department of Statistics.

Part 5

Community Development Issues and Volunteerism

Chapter 11

Reviewing the direction of community development in Singapore*

S. Vasoo[†]

Introduction

Community development in Singapore[1] has undergone significant changes since 1959, and these changes have come about as a result of the conscious efforts of the Government to build a more cohesive community comprising people of various ethnic origins such as Chinese, Malays and Indians. Because of the diverse linguistic and cultural backgrounds of these people, the Government has always felt that it would be vital to set

---

*From Vasoo, S. (1984). Reviewing the direction of community development in Singapore. *Community Development Journal*, 19(1), 7–19. Reprinted by permission of Oxford University Press.

This paper attempts to review the direction of community development in Singapore from the early 1950s to early 1980s, with the government playing an interventionist role through setting up of various grassroots organisations and the voluntary sector playing a supplementary role.

[†]The author is grateful to Professor Peter Hodge, Professor and Head, Department of Social Work, University of Hong Kong, for his comments on the earlier draft of this article.

[1] Singapore is a small city-state of about 616 sq. kilometres in size and is situated at the tip of the Malayan Peninsular. It was under the British colonial administration for 140 years since it was founded in 1819. Its population comprises 76% Chinese, 15% Malay, 7% Indians and 2% others.

clear policy directions that will help to enhance social and economic integration of the population (which now stands at 2.5 million). Its efforts in promoting nation-building are becoming evident in the many and varied programmes it has implemented in the social and economic fields.

In the social field, the Government has initiated many grassroots organisations such as Community Centres (CCs), Citizens' Consultative Committees (CCCs) and Residents' Committees (RCs). These organisations promote community development, which is aimed at the mobilisation of mass support, the provision of opportunities for political participation, and the promotion of more community cohesiveness and mutual help among people living in the urban neighbourhoods of Singapore.[2] Besides the Government's initiatives in promoting community development, the voluntary sector also plays a supplementary role through a number of social service's agencies. This role is limited in comparison with the Government's, and its attempts have been concentrated on the pioneering of community development projects which help to facilitate the growth of community self-help groups, particularly in public housing estates of various New Towns.[3]

This article will attempt to review the direction of community development in Singapore since the British colonial administration period (i.e. specifically from 1950 to 1958) and up until recently (i.e. 1981). Some issues with regard to community development approaches attempted by community workers employed by the Government and the voluntary sector will also be examined.

The beginnings of community development

The beginnings of community development in Singapore can be traced back to the early 1950s when the Social Welfare Department was charged

---

[2] In the context of this paper, community development is defined rather broadly. It includes government and voluntary sector efforts to encourage citizen participation in social, recreational and cultural activities and the promotion of social and community integration by stimulating people to come together to work for the common good of all.

[3] New Towns are large residential complexes built by the Singapore Housing and Development Board (HDB) to provide accommodation for about 150,000 — 250,000 people. For further details, see *Housing and Development Board, Annual Reports 1965–80*, Singapore.

with the responsibility of initiating community development. The then colonial administration saw the relevance in this aspect of work because:

> "there was already a high degree of development in Singapore and there existed a highly integrated society with definite racial, social and political and cooperative groups?"[4]

At the same time, the pattern and nature of community development was felt to be somewhat different and complex in undeveloped areas of Singapore. The colonial administrators saw that in order to assist the co-ordination of this work, it was necessary to establish a Standing Committee for Community Development.[5] This Committee was set up in 1951 and the Secretary of Social Welfare was one of the members together with others nominated from amongst various civic and community groups. The function of this Committee was primarily advisory, and involved in the co-ordination of various civic organisations. As noted succinctly in the Social Welfare Department Report, 1952:

> "Its main work will be to foster in all areas of Singapore the growth of responsible bodies which can take their full part in initiation, planning and carrying out of the many aspects of betterment work that are now developing"[6]

Birth of community centres

The interest in promoting community development or what is sometimes termed "community work", by the colonial administrators, led the Department of Social Welfare to usher in the birth of a number of community centres, of which a few grew out of the feeding and children's centres.[7] The success of such centres enabled the Social Welfare Department

---

[4] *Social Welfare Department Annual Report 1952*, Singapore, p. 33.
[5] Ibid. pp. 33–34.
[6] Ibid. p. 33.
[7] These feeding and children's centres were established by the Social Welfare Department in the early 1950s to provide food supplements for children who were from low-income families. Some of these centres also offered literacy classes for children not in school.

to take more concrete steps to deploy funds to build the so-called "model" type community centres (CCs). The first two of these opened in 1953 in Serangoon and Siglap constituencies.[8] Subsequently a number of other centres were established in both the suburban and rural areas.

Between 1953–1956, more than a dozen CCs were established. These centres provided a place for local residents to meet their social and recreational needs and more specifically to disseminate colonial government policies and information. Also, the centres' hidden function, which was not made obvious then, was to identify local opinions that were relevant to the colonial administrators in reshaping policies which were not well received by the people.

On the whole, one could rightly conclude that during the 1950s, community centres were not seriously promoting community development but were established with an intention to gauge the extent of anti-colonial sentiments amongst the local population. If any activities were undertaken, they were mainly centred around the promotion of indoor recreational programmes. The community centres during that period adopted a 'boys' club mentality' and hence acted as a sanctuary for a small group of youngsters to socialise. Their functions remained parochial and it was not until 1959 that their entire management was overhauled. This sweeping change came about because of the need to build up rapport between the common people and the newly elected political leaders from the People's Action Party (PAP).

Community centres reorganised with a new perspective

It was only after Singapore attained internal self-government in 1959 that the work of community centres was reshaped and decisions regarding the introduction of community development techniques were centralised. As a result of this, more concrete actions were undertaken by Government, one of which was the establishment in July 1960 of the People's

---

[8] Siglap and Serangoon constituencies are two suburban areas where the first community centres were established.

Association (PA), a statutory body, to co-ordinate the work of community centres. The PA is managed by a board of management comprising both elected and appointed members, including representatives of social organisations which are corporate members of PA, top civil servants, and leading politicians holding important portfolios. All policy matters pertaining to PA are deliberated by the Board and those policies which are endorsed are implemented by senior administrators of PA down to the community centres' management committees (CCMCs). These are supported by a large pool of operational staff, namely the organising and assistant organising secretaries.[9]

The CCMCs are made up of members who are nominated from among the informal grass-roots leaders in the community. This being the case, it provides the Government with an additional channel to communicate with the ordinary citizens. Almost all the CCMCs have members who are of different ethnic origins and such an ethnic diversity in the membership of the CCMCs is closely maintained by the Government through its policies of selection on the assumption that a heterogenous ethnic composition in the CCMCs would enable the authorities to better achieve its racial integration and community building policies.

The CCMCs have two major functions; the first being the management of the routine activities of the CCs and the second the raising of funds to meet their operational costs. These two traditional responsibilities receive the most attention of the CCMCs and have become their raison d'etre. Although it is necessary for the CCMCs to concentrate efforts in these two areas, there are other equally important management functions which should not be neglected. The most pressing of these seem to be: reviewing the CCs' programmes to see if they are meeting the changing needs of residents living in the neighbourhood; encouraging the growth of self-help groups among children, youths or adults; and setting up more volunteer groups to initiate services in the neighbourhoods that are not within the precincts of the CCs. In order for the CCMCs to steer

---

[9] The People's Association employs two categories of staff (the organising secretaries and the assistant organising secretaries) to manage CCs. Most of them have either formal or some in-service training in community work organised by the National Youth Leadership Training Institute.

away from their concentration on these traditional management functions, it will be necessary for them to encourage residents with organisational and management skills to be involved in their leadership. With the involvement of this kind of expertise, the leadership of the CCMCs will be further strengthened. There will be less likelihood for the CCMCs' leadership to become fossilized and they can still remain as viable as they were in the 1960s.

The need to involve more residents with professional backgrounds, who generally abstain from the activities of the CCs because of their scepticism about being associated with party politics, is crucial. Through their participation, new ideas and suggestions could be solicited to enable the CCs to be more innovative. So far, the participation of this category of people is not very encouraging although there are signs that more of them are beginning to be interested. They need to be cajoled and encouraged to be involved and perhaps by creating more challenging voluntary management tasks which are currently absent in the CCs, the talents of these professionals could be tapped. It is indeed vital to attract more professionals into the CCs as they have the expertise to contribute to the social betterment of the various neighbourhoods in Singapore.

The growth of the number of CCs during the 1960s and 1970s precipitated the need for more staff to manage them. Concomittantly, training of large numbers of personnel became urgent and as a result, the National Youth Leadership Training Institute was formed to provide community work and leadership training to organising and assistant organising secretaries. These two categories of personnel work with the CCMCs, some well-known local leaders and residents to organise various community development programmes for people living in the neighbourhoods. They are responsible for implementing the many activities of the CCs. In theory, one of the major roles of the organising secretaries besides their administrative and organising duties, is to provide direction to the CCMCs in implementing the types of programmes which would be most feasible for residents. But in actual practice, this role has not been fully realised. In most instances, the CCMCs consciously or unconsciously relegate the organising and assistant organising secretaries to play the role of a 'messenger' and they do not encourage them to be more active in planning and implementing programmes of the CCs.[10] If this skewed relationship continues, it may have unintended consequences for the future viability of the CCs. The remedy to the potential turn-over of the personnel is not simple, as it has to deal with the re-orientation of the management philosophy of the CCMCs. For a start, there should be more attempts to adopt a shared leadership between the CCMCs and the staff of the CCs.

The 1960s and 1970s saw a definite growth of the People's Association style of community development which could be distinguished from the style adopted by community workers trained in social work and employed by the voluntary sector.[11] The People's Association type of community development is rather centralised and 'community centre-based' in its approach. The programmes are organised at the CC level for the people who are interested in them. Some direct efforts are undertaken to decentralize programmes into the neighbourhoods of the CCs, but the reaching-out concept does not form an integral part of the strategies that can make a community development impact in community. However, it must be stated that the People's Association through its various CCs still carry out a prominent role in local attempts to develop community participation in meeting neighbourhood needs.

The People's Association has set up many CCs in various parliamentary constituencies[12] in Singapore. Up until the end of the 1970s, more than 165 CCs were built and towards the late 1970s, many larger centres with more sophisticated facilities were established. The purpose behind such a move is to cater to a population which has seemingly become more demanding for better indoor recreational facilities. Also, in the light of the growing number of demanding young adults in the urban population, the policy-makers as well as the top level administrators of the community centre machinery, are beginning to realise how important it is for the CCs

---

[10] Seah Chee Meow. *Community Centres in Singapore: Their Political Involvement.* Singapore: Singapore University Press. 1973. p. 54.

[11] Voluntary sector covers those social and welfare agencies established through private initiative of citizens, and civic or religious groups. There are about 80 voluntary agencies providing direct social and welfare programmes to various beneficiaries in Singapore.

[12] There are at the moment 75 parliamentary constituencies in Singapore. Each constituency has about 40,000 — 60,000 people and is represented by a Member of Parliament who is elected by popular mandate.

to be more adept in catering to the needs and aspirations of the young for community participation. However, although the participation of the young is viewed to be important, the response to recruit them into the CCMC leadership has been noticeably slow.

Further enlargement of the base for community development

The Government, besides establishing community centres in different parts of Singapore, has also taken steps to initiate parallel organisations to penetrate further into the grass-roots. This move is the most recent development in the community development scene in Singapore and the underlying reason for such a massive effort by the Government to stimulate participation of people in community affairs is perhaps to enlarge the base for community development. At the same time, it appears that the Government, through such a concerted effort, would like to close the gap between the governing elites and the governed, prevent the bureaucracy at the local level from being inflexible, promote better understanding and acceptance of important policy issues, and identify and recruit people with organisational skills to revitalize government-supported grass-roots organisations in a constituency.

The Government's increased interest in grass-roots organisations came about when it recognised that the rapid relocation of people into public high rise estates (a result of its housing programmes) has not promoted cohesive communities and community identity.[13] This is due, as Goh states, to the fact that;

> "many of these estates are new and their residents have moved in only recently from other parts of Singapore. They have to grow new roots in

---

[13] For more details on the social implications of public housing programmes, see Yeh, Stephen H.K., *Public Housing in Singapore*, Singapore: Singapore University Press, 1975; Hassan, Riaz, *Families in Flats*, Singapore University Press, 1977; Chen, Peter S. J. and Tai, C. H., *Social Ecology of Singapore*, Singapore: Federal Publication, 1977; and Wee, Ann. E., *Some Implications of Rehousing Programmes in Singapore*, in D. J. Dwyer (ed.), *The City as a Centre of Change in Asia*, Hong Kong: Hong Kong University Press, 1972.

a new environment, know neighbours, make new friends. If they are left alone, new housing estates will take a long time before they become a friendly, throbbing community bustling with life and activities. Maybe never."[14]

Public housing estates have become a notable feature of the landscape of Singapore, constructed by the Housing and Development Board (HDB), and the Government's plan to provide decent homes to many Singaporean families earning below $3500 has been successful. About 65% of the population are already housed in the public housing scheme and the success of such a scheme:

"should be judged not only by the number of housing units we construct, or the percentage of our population housed in HDB flats, but by the spirit of camaraderie that exists between residents of these housing estates. These housing estates must have a character, a soul, and their residents, a strong sense of group commitment."[15]

In a move to hasten the process of community bonding, the Government established the Citizens' Consultative Committees (CCCs) in 1965 and subsequently in 1978, the Residents' Committees (RCs) to further complement the work of the CCCs and to reach out to most residents. These two elaborately organised grass-roots organisations are formed with an intention to promote community development within the neighbourhoods.

The CCCs have acted as intermediary organisations whose membership comprises residents with some local standing in community affairs or with connections with a number of voluntary organisations such as clan association, merchants' organisation and trade union. Most of the CCCs are constituency-based and the number of members in each CCC varies from constituency to constituency. The CCCs, like the CCMCs, have members with different ethnic origins and these members are nominated by the Government upon the recommendation of the Members of

---

[14] Goh Chok Tong, *Eunos Crescent RC Seminar Souvenir Programme*, Singapore, September, 1980, p. 13.

[15] Ibid, p. 13.

Parliament of the various constituencies in Singapore. The members' tenure of office in the CCCs is one year and it is renewed yearly depending on their interests and performance.

Besides the CCCs' mediatory role, they run a number of programmes on a constituency-wide basis. Campaigns which are of importance to the Government and which have an educational value to the ordinary citizens, are undertaken. Campaigns such as anti-crime, tree-planting, physical fitness, health, family planning and courtesy, are scheduled during different times of the year and the CCCs assist in organising them in their respective constituencies. The effects of these campaigns have been significant and have created positive social attitudes in the area. Other than the launching of various campaigns, the CCCs also make recommendations to the Government to improve the facilities in the neighbourhoods. As members of the CCCs are drawn from the informal leaders within and outside the constituencies, some of them have, with the support of local resident, acquired the role of mediators between them and the Government.

The community development roles of these intermediary leaders were more significant in the 1960s and 1970s because they were dealing with the 'bread and butter issues' prevalent at that time, faced by ordinary citizens ignorant about how to seek redress to their problems. In the 1980s, the leadership roles of the CCCs will be subjected to close scrutiny by a more demanding younger generation who are well educated and resourceful, particularly in their abilities to solve the more complex problems of the urban high rise environment of Singapore. Whether the CCCs will continue to play an important role remains to be seen.

The Residents' Committees (RCs) are the most recent grass-roots organisations which have been introduced by the Government in various public housing estates of Singapore's New Towns. The Government's inducement is necessary because in most urban settings and particularly the high rise public housing environment, it has been found that unless Government facilitates the formation of neighbourhood-level residents' organisations, such organisations are unlikely to develop from within. Even if they do, it will take a long time for them to gain a foothold in the community where residents are no longer able to find common affiliations to come together readily.[16] RCs which are enthusiastically promoted by Government on a massive scale, are the most down-to-earth residents' organisations set up in the neighbourhoods of various housing estates. A number of underlying reasons could account for the Government's enthusiasm to establish RCs. Firstly, the HDB is beginning to give more attention to its social management role as it recognises that the prevention of physical deterioration of public housing and the solutions to some social problems faced by residents can best be tackled by encouraging the residents to be involved in solving problems.[17] Secondly, CCs and CCCs are limited in their effectiveness to gauge the opinions of residents and mobilise them to participate in community programmes. Therefore, a more sensitive infra-structure is required to assess and respond to the changing needs of residents living in the public housing estates. Thirdly, as more residents with better educational levels are living in the public housing estates, they would be expected to be more articulate and motivated to partake in the decision-making processes affecting their neighbourhoods and the wider community.

The RCs, unlike the CCs and the CCCs, are confined to public housing estates and interested residents are encouraged by the Residents' Committees Group Secretariat under the Prime Minister's Office, to take up leadership in the RCs. So far more than 230 RCs have been formed in 69 Parliamentary Constituencies and there are plans to form more in other constituencies.

The objectives of the RCs are primarily to promote neighbourliness among residents; provide a more effective channel of communication between the residents and the various government authorities or departments; ensure better maintenance of the physical conditions in the housing estates; enhance better social order and security; and encourage mutual assistance among residents. The stated objectives are broad and all-embracing; and in essence they are aimed at the promotion of community development at the neighbourhood level.[18] However, the

---

[16] Taub. R. P., et al., Urban Voluntary Associations. Locality Based and Externally Induced, *American Journal of Sociology*, Vol. 83, No. 2, 1977, pp. 425–442.

[17] *Straits Times* (Singapore), 2 February 1979.

[18] These objectives are a summarized version of those which are listed in the model rules and regulations governing the work of RCs prepared by the RC Central Secretariat.

realisation of these objectives depends heavily on the socio-political orientation of the people who are nominated into the leadership of the RCs. Probably, people with high deference values which includes such characteristics as high civic consciousness, high neighbourhood activism, less self-centredness, and high devotion to community service, in the leadership of the RCs are more likely to help the RCs' objectives to be realised. At this juncture, no in-depth analyses of the leadership profiles of the RCs' members have been undertaken and it would be too premature to forecast the type of leaders who would be suitable for these organisations.

Generally, the RCs do not vary very much in their organised activities. They mediate between the relevant government authorities and the residents on matters concerning the physical environment and undertake various national campaigns such as crime prevention, tree-planting, and courtesy. Besides these, they recommend improvements to the estates and organise family-oriented programmes; for example, picnics, excursions, family-life education, and social get-togethers. At the moment, it appears that the community development strategies adopted by the RCs are more service-delivery focused but there seems to be great potential for more resident-focused work which will encourage a higher degree of citizen participation. With greater emphasis on resident-focused work, the RCs can eventually help to facilitate the growth of small self-help or interest groups among residents to deal with problems which may arise as a result of urban high-rise living.

Community development by the voluntary sector

Only after 1969, did there appear to be evidence of some interest in the voluntary sector to contribute directly to the growth of community development in Singapore. From this point, community workers were employed[19] to carry out community development projects, including several in the New Towns. In the pioneering years, this group of community workers, together with some concerned Christians and church

---

[19] Community workers include those trained in social work and those untrained but provided with in-service training in community work skills.

groups took an active role in promoting projects in a few selected urban public housing estates namely, Jurong, Bukit Ho Swee and Toa Payoh.[20]

The first three community development projects, the Jurong Industrial Mission Project (JIMP), the Bukit Ho Swee Community Service Project and the Toa Payoh Community Development Project were established in 1969.[21] The objectives of these Projects were more or less similar and were firstly, to interest local residents to solve problems relevant to their neighbourhoods, secondly, to develop leadership and skills among residents to deal with their needs, and thirdly, to encourage residents to form self-help groups in meeting their social, cultural and recreational needs.

The Bukit Ho Swee Project was initiated by a few community workers in concert with the Franciscan Sisters of Mary, a religious order which has developed a number of educational institutions and health centres in the voluntary welfare field.

Since the inception of the Project, many children and young persons have been encouraged to be involved in the various activities, such as the children's clubs which organise outings, outdoor camps, tuition, excursions and concerts, and the youth clubs which concentrate on vocational guidance, literacy education, excursions, outdoor camps, leadership training, and voluntary service work. So far, all the programmes undertaken tend to focus on the personal needs of small groups of children or young persons and the programmes provided are supposedly to assist them in their socialisation and personal growth. A tentative assessment suggests that the Project has not achieved its community development objectives, as the groups involved are still dependent on the community workers of the Project to plan programmes for them.

The Toa Payoh Community Development Project came into existence as a result of the work of some priests attached to the Methodist and Roman Catholic churches in Toa Payoh New Town and community workers, providing services for the less privileged sector in the New Town. The main service so far has been remedial education for school children

---

[20] These are three of the many urban housing estates set up in the 1960s by the HDB.

[21] The brief illustrations of the three Projects are based on the author's own follow-up of developments since their inception. There have been no official publications of the Projects concerned.

because it was found at the beginnings of the Project that many of the families in the low-income group were concerned about the educational under-achievement of their children. Parents of the children who were in need of remedial education programmes were organised as a group by the community workers to assist in the recruitment of voluntary trained teachers living in the community. As a result of this exercise, an action group comprising both the parents and the voluntary teachers was formed to manage the remedial education programme which has become the life of the Project. Since 1973, no new area of growth in community development has been recorded by the Project because the remedial education programme appeared to have consumed most of its available resources, both in terms of finance and manpower. To date, the remedial education programme is still the prime concern of the Project.

JIMP was started by a group of concerned Christians and community workers with the support of the Jurong Christian Church in 1969. The prime motivation of those associated with JIMP at that time was to promote urban industrial mission work aimed at assisting young workers and residents to integrate better in the Jurong industrial setting which had been designed as one of the largest industrial zones of Singapore. JIMP, in its earlier stages of development, (between 1969–73), concentrated on organising residents living in the working class neighbourhood of Jurong to request better services from the various government departments, especially those dealing with education, health, environment and management of estates. In 1974, JIMP shifted its emphasis from working with residents in the working class neighbourhood to young workers employed in some of the factories operating in Jurong. This change of focus was accidental, because at that time there happened to be more demands from the young workers on the Project to advise them in their negotiations with employers for improvements in working conditions. Aside from the change in JIMP's client group, it adopted in totality the Alinsky model[22] for solving the problems faced both by the residents living in the working class neighbourhood

---

[22] The Alinsky model prescribes a conflict approach in problem-solving based on the view that the disadvantaged or the deprived sectors of the community, if organised, can have the power to influence the resource-holders to meet their needs. For a further understanding of this model, the reader is referred to the work, Saul D. Alinsky, *Rules for Radicals: A Practical Primer for Realistic Radicals*, New York, Random House, 1971.

and the young workers. The adoption of this model of intervention in JIMP's work led to its failure to take roots in the Jurong community.

In the early years since the inception of the three Projects, each developed its own ways to entrench itself in the community. The community workers attached to these Projects devised differing strategies and these had subsequent consequences on the life-span of the Projects.

JIMP, which concentrated on confrontational strategies in community problem solving, ceased to exist when it failed to gain the co-operation of various power groups within the community, and because of the lack of funds to support its work. In the case of the Bukit Ho Swee Community Service Project and the Toa Payoh Community Development Projects, they managed to find their roots in the respective localities. The community workers in these two Projects used collaborative strategies in community problem solving, and in doing so, they were able to bring different groups in the community, consisting of organised resident groups as well as community power groups (e.g. the CCC and CCMCs) to meet needs and problems within their localities.

Since the initiation of the three early Community Development Projects, community workers, who were subsequently employed in a number of other voluntary agencies, began to make more serious attempts to promote community development through their agencies in the public housing estates which had been established rapidly by the HDB. The increase in the number of housing estates and the realisation that some people needed to be supported in their adjustments to life in the high-rise environment, have contributed directly or indirectly to an increase in interest among local community workers to influence voluntary agencies to embark on community development projects. The result of this influence is seen by an additional number of agencies participating in community development, including the Singapore Children's Society, the Ang Mo Kio Social Service Centre and the Salvation Army — Kallang Bahru Centre.

Community development approaches

The major approach towards community development both by Government and voluntary sector seems to concentrate on the provision of services to consumers whether they be clients or citizens living in the locality where the agencies operate. It has become apparent that very little effort has been directed towards the encouragement of citizen or consumer participation which can in the long run motivate the beneficiaries of the services to undertake self-help projects in meeting their needs. In essence, it can be stated that the emphasis in community development by the respective sectors is 'service delivery focus' rather than 'resident focus'.[23] It may be interesting to examine some of the underlying reasons leading to this situation.

Firstly, community workers and the local leaders involved in community development are uncertain about the approaches most applicable to the local context. They all have attempted to try the following approaches[24]:

a. Locality Development approach.
   This approach presupposes that 'community change may be pursued optimally through broad participation of a wide spectrum of people at the local community level in goal determination and action.'
b. Social Planning approach
   This encompasses a 'technical process of problem-solving with regard to substantive social problems such as delinquency, housing and mental health. The emphasis of this approach is planned change through research and rational planning.'
c. Social action approach
   This is based on a presupposition of 'a disadvantaged segment of the population that needs to be organised, perhaps in alliance with others, in order to make demands on the larger community for increased resources or treatment in accordance with social justice and democracy.'

All the above approaches have been applied with minimal consideration as to their applicability to the field context. More often than not, an

---

[23] Briscoe, Catherine, *Community Work in Social Service Departments*, in Henderson, Paul, and Thomas. D. N. (eds.) *Readings in Community Work*, London: Allen and Unwin, 1981, pp. 171–175.

[24] Rothman, Jack. *Three Models of Community Organisation Practice*, in Cox. Rolhman and Tropman (eds.). *Strategies of Community Organisation*, Itasca: F. E. Peacock, 1974, pp. 22–38.

approach is applied haphazardly without being given sufficient time to assess its consequences on the community. The haphazard application of the various approaches postulated by community development theorists has led to a situation whereby community workers and local leaders are unable to say for certain which approach can work and under what specific circumstances.

Secondly, many community workers are engaged by voluntary agencies which have been established to provide services to specific client groups such as children, youth, aged and families. As a result of this, the service orientation of these agencies is directed towards clients who are identified to have social problems and in need of assistance from the agencies. This being the case, the services of the agencies become remedial in nature and this in turn influences the community workers to carry out a remedial function which is confined to the provision of services and implementation of programmes for clients who are referred by other agencies or refer themselves. The services of the voluntary agencies delivered in this way do not in the long run make any relevant impact on the wider community where the agencies operate.

Thirdly, most efforts in local community development by the voluntary and government sectors seem to concentrate on 'service delivery focus'. This is because the staff find it easier either to exercise control on the types of programmes their organisations offer to the community or curtail programmes which are not attractive to the potential consumers. Besides this, the attitudes prevalent amongst the providers and controllers of the resources, particularly those in the voluntary sector, also influence the way the service is provided.

On the whole, community workers are more biased towards adopting 'service delivery focus' in community development. This is because it is much easier to expand and/or extend the programmes of their agencies to meet the needs of the consumers than to organise self-help groups to initiate programmes on their own. In any case, the extension and expansion of agency programmes are seen by community workers as useful ways to cope with the demands of the consumers who are often less able to articulate their needs or participate in problem-solving.

Fourthly, most community workers as well as local leaders tend to perceive that community development is effective when more programmes are promoted in the community. Although programmes are essential in enhancing community development, these are unfortunately developed for their own sake and serve as ends rather than as means to encourage participation of local people. This perspective is overzealously guarded by community workers and local leaders and as such, they measure the success of their work by the number of programmes implemented and not by assessing the extent to which people involved in the programmes are capable of initiating actions on their own to meet community needs. The latter is the end objective of community development but it is often not vigorously pursued by community workers and local leaders because they are muddled about means and ends in programme implementation.[25]

Finally, the lack of discussion and exchanges of information on progress of community development among community workers as well as local leaders contributes to a stalemate situation and a strong desire in community workers to maintain that 'service delivery focus' is the most practical approach in community development even though this may not be necessarily the case. A confusion about the precise nature of 'community development' has also inhibited the development of practice.

The essence of community development

The term 'community development' is so often misunderstood by those who preach it and wrongly applied by those who practice it. This is so because the term is itself elusive and open to many subjective interpretations by those involved directly or indirectly in community development whether they be community workers, politicians, social and welfare agency administrators, local leaders or concerned citizens. Frequently, the term is visualised by those involved as an activity directed towards organising services or programmes for people living in a specific community

---

[25] The origins of this approach are obscure but Peter Hodge used the term 'dustbin' when discussing in the British context the muddle in the use of 'community work' as a method and 'community' as a prefix for a wide variety of supposedly community development approaches. Hodge, Peter, *The Future of Community Development*, in Robson, William A. and Crick, Bernard, *The Future of the Social Services*, London: Pelican Books, 1970, p. 67.

and not as a planned process to encourage people living in a specific community themselves to initiate services or programmes to meet their felt needs. The latter is the actual reflection of the term 'community development' and should connote:

> 'the process by which the efforts of the people themselves are united with those of governmental authorities to improve the economic, social and cultural conditions of communities, to integrate these communities into the life of the nation and to enable them to contribute fully to national progress'[26]

Community development should be primarily concerned with two essential elements which should be emphasised strongly. It entails the encouragement of:

> 'the participation by people themselves in efforts to improve their level of living with as much reliance as possible on their own initiative, and the provision of technical and other services in ways which encourage initiative, self-help and mutual help and make these more effective.'[27]

In short, community development should in the long run encourage people to become more self-reliant in social and economic pursuits and be more participative in improving their communities.

Conclusion

Community development in Singapore appears to have been influenced by various social and political factors during the period under review. In the colonial administration period, community development programmes were undertaken with extreme caution and were more inclined to a non-interventionist stance. This stance was adopted because it was presumed that a more concerted effort to promote community development

---

[26] *Report of the United Nations Seminar on Community Development and Social Welfare in Urban Areas, Geneva*, United Nations, 1959, p. 5.
[27] Ibid, p. 5.

would have unintended consequences for the colonial administration, the main concern of which was that it would kindle the fire of anti-colonialism which was surfacing during that time.

After attainment of internal self-rule and then independence, the Government saw an urgent necessity to play an interventionist role in promoting community development through various government-sponsored grass-roots organisations such as the CCs, CCCs and RCs. More resources in terms of staff, finance and facilities have been and are being channelled to these networks to operationalise community development programmes in the various neighbourhoods. In fact, government interest to induce the growth of grass-root organisations has been very significant over the last 20 years and this emphasis reflects a need to provide an organised channel for citizen involvement in community affairs. The issue which rises from such an interventionist role by the Government is whether these grass-root organisations, induced and supported by governmental efforts, will provide the culture for the development of indigenous leadership.

The voluntary sector's role in community development has remained supplementary and it is unlikely to grow significantly. It should therefore concentrate on an educational role, pioneering community projects which could be used in demonstrating to those involved in community development the use of appropriate effective local approaches. Meanwhile, the continued and widespread use of the 'service delivery focus' approach may in the long run stifle citizen initiatives in community development and consequently, citizens may be socialised to assume less responsibilities in neighbourhood affairs. Therefore, it is crucial for community development agencies, both public and voluntary, to encourage local citizens to be involved in promoting activities which are relevant to their own interests.

S. Vasoo teaches in the Department of Social Work, National University of Singapore.

Chapter 12

Community development in Singapore: New directions and challenges*

S. Vasoo[†]

Introduction

Community development is defined as planned changes undertaken through the efforts of the government, corporate sector and non-governmental organisations (NGOs) or voluntary welfare organisations (VWOs) to promote community better and community problem solving.[1] The community

---

*From Vasoo, S. (2001). Community development in Singapore: New directions and challenges. *Asian Journal of Political Science*, 9(1), 4–17. Reprinted by permission of the publisher (Taylor & Francis Ltd, http://www.tandfonline.com).

This paper reiterates some of the earlier points raised on some of the crucial factors in shaping community development directions in Singapore and their challenges for future directions. It reinforces some views made in the previous publications.

[†]S Vasoo is Associate Professor of the Department of Social Work & Psychology, National University of Singapore.

[1]This definition captures broadly the essence of community development, the outcome of which is to promote self-help. For other readings on community development see the following: Allan B. Edwards, *Community and Community Development* (The Hague: Mouton, 1976); David Korten, "Community Based Resource Management," in David Korten (ed.), *Community Management: Asian Experiences and Perspectives* (Kumarian Press, 1987), pp. 1–12 ; David J. Obrien, "The Public Goods Dilemma and the Apathy of the Poor," in Paul Henderson and David Thomas (eds.), *Readings in Community Work*

development scenario in Singapore has undergone major changes in the last four decades since the changeover from colonial administration to self-government in 1959. These changes as compared to those during the period towards the end of colonial rule were influenced by socio-economic and ecological factors. The need for active involvement of people in community problem solving and the promotion of self-help among various community groups also added to it.

During the colonial period, community development was neglected as administrators were not serious about promoting citizen participation. They adopted a reactive approach in organising community groups to deal with problems of public health and sanitation matters. Clan and ethnic groups were encouraged to function separately to manage their own affairs. Thus, the main focus of the colonial administration was directed at segmenting and segregating the community and social groups so that it could prevent ethnic competition and problems. At the same time, these groups were prevented from posing threats to the social harmony and security of the community. Colonial administration adopted a divide and rule strategy in its early efforts to promote community development in Singapore.[2]

A number of key social and economic factors together with the changing ecological variables could account for influencing the directions in community development. The development of public housing and new towns and the increase in governmental support for neighbourhood organisations (e.g. the Residents' Committees, Town Councils and Community Development Councils), the demographic changes, the increase in labour force participation, and involvement of non-governmental voluntary organisations, have contributed to visible changes in the current community development scene in Singapore. Such a remarkable increase in the participation in various groups

---

(London: Allen and Unwin, 1981), pp. 115–9; Hebert J. Rubin and Irene Rubin, *Community Organising and Development* (Columbus: Merrill), pp. 156–88; James Midgley, *Social Development: The Development Perspective in Social Welfare* (Thousand Oaks: Sage, pp. 12–36; Michael J. Austin and Jane L. Lowe (eds.), *Controversial Issues in Communities and Organisations* (Boston: Allen and Bacon, 1994); Murray Ross, *Community Organisation* (London: Harper Row, 1969); S. Vasoo, "Reviewing the Direction of Community Development in Singapore," *Community Development Journal*, Vol. 19, No.1 (1984), pp. 7–19.

[2] Vasoo, "Reviewing the Direction", pp. 7–19.

has shaped the democratisation of Singapore's various neighbourhoods. The social landscape of community participation has seen many key players who are contributing toward community building.

This article will discuss some of the crucial factors which have played an important role in shaping the community development directions in Singapore. Researchers in community development studies should include important analyses of these factors because they are critical domains which have helped in shaping the contemporary community development directions.[3] This article also examines the issues challenging future directions in community development.

Factors influencing community development

There are a number of factors which have influenced community development in Singapore. These factors have, in different combinations, affected its directions. It is essential to identify and discuss some of these significant factors. No investigator interested in Singapore's community development can afford to ignore a review of such factors which are highlighted in the following section.

Colonial administration and community development

It cannot be denied that Singapore's early beginnings in community development framework in the 1950s was initiated by the colonial administration which managed the Social Welfare Department. A Standing Committee for Community Development was established to promote co-ordination and co-operation among various civic,[4] clan and lineage organisations. Many of these groups were allowed to flourish as the colonial administration could not fully comprehend and appreciate the cultural intricacies of the mutual help administered by these traditional organisations. At best the function of the Standing Committee was primarily advisory, and

---

[3] Chan Soo Sen, "Building Community for Good Times and Bad," in Arun Mahizhnan and Lee Tsao Yuan (eds.), *Singapore Re-engineering Success* (Singapore: Oxford University Press, 1998), pp. 92–7.
[4] See *Annual Report of the Singapore Social Welfare Department*, (Singapore: Government Printing Office, 1952).

involved the co-ordination of various civic organisations with little interference in their work except when they became politicised and engaged in anti-colonial struggle. These organisations would then be deregistered or their social activities curbed.

The colonial administrators took steps to promote community development by setting up a few community centres which were originally started out as feeding and children's centres to combat nutritional problems facing children at that time.[5] Encouraged by the success of these centres to provide information to deal with public health problems of children, the Service Welfare Department deployed more resources to build a model type of community centre (CC). Two of these were first introduced in 1953 in the Serangoon and Siglap areas, and three years later, more than a dozen were set up to provide a focus point for people to come together for social and recreational activities. These activities were piecemeal, and they discouraged the active participation of citizens in managing local issues. The primary emphasis of these early type of community centres was to provide information on policies of the colonial government and to obtain feedback about any pressing displeasures against government so that remedial action could be taken on policies which were not popular. It was also used as a base to stamp out any pressure group movement against the colonial administration. On the whole, community development efforts at the neighbourhood level was not proactive but rather reactive in the sense that the approach was parochial and sectarian. The agenda was to keep various community groups apart and divided. It was not directed at community building. However, credit must be given to the colonial administrators for having laid a good administrative framework based on meritocracy in the appointment of civil servants to promote future community development efforts. Such a system which was absolved of nepotic practices became a fundamental hallmark of future community development endeavours. This fortunate situation did not happen in many developed and developing societies as they were riddled by corrupt and nepotic community leaders who were more self-centred rather than people-centred.

---

[5] *Ibid.*

Impact of relocation into new towns and rehousing

Community development trends have also been influenced by the relocation and rehousing of people into New Towns. It is estimated that about 88% of Singapore's population of 4.01 million people live in owner-occupied public housing in various New Towns,[6] which are large satellite self-contained towns. The relocation and rehousing of people into public housing estates is a spectacular social provision undertaken by the People Action Party (PAP) government to give home ownership to most Singaporeans. This decent high-rise living environment has made significant transformation to the social landscape in the various neighbourhoods. It has also brought about some social implications such as the lack of neighbourliness and mutual support, latchkey children, stress in families with high household density, impersonal and social isolation and the lack of ownership of public space and environment. A few consequences may occur. First, the residents' social and personal needs are more often met by groups and social network outside their community. Second, younger residents particularly of older housing estates, tend to move out of their parents' flat when they set up their own households. This weakens the family support networks. Third, there is a rising expectation among better educated residents for more effective urban service delivery and when their expectations are not met, they can become critical. Finally, the lack of attachment to their neighbourhoods can make residents uncaring of their environment and less committed to participate in building better community ties.

Demographic transition

The demographic transition is very marked in older neighbourhoods where population graying is more conspicuous. Population aging will be

---

[6] See *Statistics on Demographic Characteristics: A Quick Count* (Singapore: Department of Statistics, 2000); *Annual Report of the Singapore Housing and Development Board*, 1999/2000 (Singapore: HDB, 2000); Phang Sock Yong, "Housing Policy Changes in Singapore," in Linda Low and Toh Mun Heng (eds.), *Public Policies in Singapore* (Singapore: Times Academic Press), 1992, pp. 114–26.

a very significant phenomena in Singapore by 2030.[7] The median age in 1990 was 29 years and in 2000, was 34 years. The Singapore population is facing acute population aging. It is one of the fastest graying societies in Asia where the aged population 65 years and above has increased significantly the last decade from 8.6% in 1990 to 10.2% in 2000.[8] Such a dramatic demographic transition do impose service demands on both the family and community to provide care and support services for the elderly. Smaller families are likely to face increasing burden and stress in providing care for their aged sick. They will have to depend on the neighbourhood to organise different types of community services such as day care, home help, meal support and community nursing for their frail elderly members.[9]

However, one cannot look at the negative aspects of population aging alone. There are positive contributions to community development by the elderly population. With surplus manpower as a result of retirement, many social service agencies can tap the wide ranging talents and expertise of retirees for community development activities. This big pool of elderly manpower resource was not fully harnessed for many community development programmes such as environmental protection, education, health care, personal services, crime prevention, child care and neighbourhood improvements. Social and service organisations must take proactive steps to recruit and plan programmes to engage the elderly population to contribute their expertise to mainstream activities in the community.

Obsolescence of traditional organisations

Many traditional organisations such as guilds, mutual aid societies, dialect groups, clan associations and lineage groups have in the past provided protection and support for their members. They played an important

---

[7] See *Report of the Inter-Ministerial Committee on Aging* (Singapore: Ministry of Community Development and Sports, 2000).

[8] See *Statistics on Demographic Characteristics: A Quick Count* (Singapore: Department of Statistics, 2000).

[9] S. Vasoo, *Neighbourhood Leaders Participation in Community Development* (Singapore: Academic Press, 1994).

part in mediating between residents and the government bureaucracy but now have not been able to maintain their efficacy. This is because their institutional missions have not evolved over time to meet the rising aspirations of the younger residents who are skeptical about the ability of the leadership of traditional organisations to represent and meet their demands. Many of the traditional organisations have archaic management which are unacceptable to the younger people who believe in the transparency of these organisations which have lost their legitimacy to lead in community development activities. It is now obvious that some of these traditional organisations are becoming moribund because of the lack of renewal of younger and more authentic leaders into their management. In recognition of this depressing situation, both local and outside efforts have been mobilised to usher residents' organisations, namely Residents' Committees[10] (RCs) to facilitate local residents to participate in community development.[11]

Contextual changes

Singapore's ecological environment has been transformed and reshaped by various urban renewal. The Urban Renewal Authority (URA) has painstakingly worked out a Master Plan to ensure that both people and environment are well managed and balanced.

The old housing estates have older residents and less resourceful people. Many of the older neighbourhoods become less socially active because their leadership is depleted through social mobility and upgrading of the more capable and successful residents. This ecological shift of the more successful residents into private and better public housing neighbourhoods can reduce the problem solving capacities of these older neighbourhoods. In order to revitalise these older neighbourhoods and prevent them from being socially depressed, swift actions should be implemented to rebuild bigger housing units in these neighbourhoods. The rebuilding of

---

[10] *Ibid.*

[11] S. Vasoo, "Enhancing Citizen Participation in Voluntary Organisations: Some Issues and Challenges," A public lecture delivered and documented by the Department of Social Work and Social Administration, University of Hong Kong, 1990.

the older communities would attract more younger residents there and consequently social and community rejuvenation will take place.

With the setting up of many New Town communities, there will be a larger pool of professionals and resourceful residents whose talents and expertise could be utilised for community betterment. It is envisaged that in participation voluntary activities will be locally or community based. This will help to strengthen the social support networks of residents provided more social, recreational and community organisations are encouraged to blossom and given the essential support for their operations.

Changing composition of labour force participation and time constraint

The growth of the industrial sector in the last two decades particularly in the electronic industries has attracted an increasing female labour force. Between 1990 and 2000, the female labour force participation increased from 48.8% (504,300) to 50.2% (634,800).[12] Such a noticeable proportion of females in the workforce which account for half of the employable female population will affect the participation of family members in community development activities. With more mothers engaged in the labour force, fathers have to share familial responsibilities and become more housebound. These changes which are more evident in younger families, do limit the participation of fathers in community activities. Apparently in older generation households, there are more spouses involved in voluntary activities. This is because the labour force participation of mothers in these households is low.[13] There are also less young dependent children in these households who require care and attention.

With better improvements in working conditions, family members are envisaged to have more discretionary time or leisure period. However, they often face competing demands for their involvement from many sources including social and community organisations. As discretionary

---

[12] See *Statistics on Economic Characteristics of Singapore Resident Population* (Singapore: Department of Statistics, 2000).

[13] Stella Quah, *Study on the Singapore Family* (Singapore: Ministry of Community Development and Sports, 2000).

time is limited, individuals and family members will only participate in those community activities which are beneficial directly or indirectly.[14] Therefore, those who promote community development activities in various neighbourhoods must ensure that people who are involved do have a growing experience and satisfaction in their participation. It must be borne in mind that any social activity big or small, significant or less significant, does incur social or economic cost and unless it evokes a hearty warm glow or some tangible benefits, people will not participate in community development.[15]

Influence of NGOs

The NGOs have contributed a major role in community development and this is because the state ideology emphasises the many helping hands concept. State welfarism policies based on high government subsidy and expenditure implemented in many advanced economies have not been adopted here as these are believed to erode work ethics and the promotion of self-help.[16] Therefore the principle of co-payment by consumers of social

---

[14] David H. Smith, "Determinants of Individual's Discretionary Use of Time," in David H. Smith *et al.* (eds.), *Participation in Social and Political Activities* (London: Jossey-Bass, 1980), pp. 34–75; Benjamin Gidron, "Social of Satisfaction among Service Volunteers," *Journal of Voluntary Action Research*, Vol. 12 (1973), pp. 21–35; Ramadhar Singh, Ong Teck Hong and S. Vasoo, "Volunteer Participation in Social and Welfare Organisations," an unpublished report prepared for the Singapore Ministry of Community Development and Sports, 1997; T. D. Kemper, "Alturism and Voluntary Action," in Smith *et al.* (eds.), *Social Participation in Social and Political Activities*, pp. 306–38.

[15] Vasoo, "Enhancing Citizen Participation".

[16] For further insights into Singapore's policies in not adopting the western models of state welfarism, the following readings are recommended: Lee Kuan Yew, *From Third World to First — The Singapore Story: 1965–2000* (Singapore: Times Media, 2000), pp. 116–30; Goh Chok Tong, *Prime Minister's National Day Rally Speech*, 1997 (Singapore: Ministry of Information and the Arts, 1997), pp. 26–7; Lee Hsien Loong, "Singapore of the Future," in Mahizhnan and Lee (eds.), *Singapore Re-engineering Success*, pp. 2–9; Phua Kai Hong, "Social Welfare and Healthcare," in Gillian Koh and Ooi Giok Ling (eds.), *State-Society Relations in Singapore* (Singapore: Oxford University Press, 2000), pp. 147–55; Linda Low and Ngiam Tee Liang, "An Underclass among the Overclass," in Linda Low (ed.), *Singapore Towards a Developed Status* (Singapore: Oxford University Press, 1999), pp. 226–49;

services is adhered to closely. Such an emphasis can prevent increasing welfare burden now experienced in other communities. Also in keeping with this ethos, social and community problems are seen by policy makers to be resolved more effectively on a tripartite basis which includes the government, non-government organisations and the private corporate sectors.[17] Such an emphasis is believed to prevent dependency of the NGOs on the government to solve social ills.[18]

In the last decade, many NGOs have been formed and they have moved into old and new Town communities to deliver community sources.[19] This has been precipitated by a few underlying reasons. Firstly, with improvements to the social and economic conditions and quality of life, Singaporeans want to be involved in various social and community organisations to influence decisions which may affect their lives directly or indirectly. This is a trend when societies modernise. Secondly, urban and high-rise housing environments do have unintended consequences such as alienation and anomie, interpersonal abrasion, latchkey children, vandalism and physical and social barriers. All these social and personal abrasions nurture the formation of NGOs serving different client and community groups. In many Singapore New Towns, NGOs serving children, families, youths and the aged have been established. Lastly, the changes in government subvention policy for NGOs on a dollar to dollar basis for approved social and community service projects and the allocation of funds by the National Council of Social Service (NCSS) through its fundraising aim, the Community Chest of Singapore has boosted the viability and morale of NGOs. Besides government subvention, the funding through the Community Chest to the NGOs increased from $4 million in 1984 to $35 million in 1998.[20]

This quantum leap in allocation of funds for the voluntary charitable sector has enabled some small NGOs a renewed lease of life and social

---

Singapore the Next Lap (Singapore: Government of Singapore, 1991); Yap Mui Teng (ed.), *Social Services: The Next Lap* (Singapore: Academic Press, 1991)

[17] See *Singapore the Next Lap*.

[18] See S. Vasoo and Mohd. Maliki Osman, "Non Governmental Organisations and Nation Building in Singapore: Some Emerging Trends and Issues," unpublished paper, 1994.

[19] See National Council of Social Service, *Annual Report 1994*, Singapore: NCSS, 1994.

[20] See National Council of Social Service, *Annual Report 1998*, Singapore: NCSS, 1998.

purpose and encouraged new NGOs to pioneer community development services in the New Town communities and older housing estates. It must be acknowledged that the centralised funding support for NGOs has rationalised the allocation of charitable donations and reduced overheated competitions in fund-raising amongst the NGOs. However, the challenge facing the Community Chest of Singapore is its ability to control the insatiable demand by the member NGOs for more funding. Some cost control and cost effective measures have to be instituted to ensure that the services provided by the NGOs are indeed helpful and productive.

Formation of organisations for community development

Community development was given fresh attention after Singapore attained self-government in 1959 under the auspice of the PAP Government. There was a need to reach out to people with different racial, religious and linguistic backgrounds. The People's Association (PA) was instituted in 1960 to co-ordinate the work of community centres,[21] which have continued to be managed by the Community Centre Management Committees (CCMCs). These CCMCs comprise informal grassroots leaders appointed from among professionals, businessmen, socially active residents and volunteers. A good social and ethnic balance is maintained so that such a heterogeneous ethnic and varied social composition can help to enhance racial integration and community bonding. As the CCMCs' reach to residents is confined to the community centres, a different strategy to reach out to residents and engage them in community development activities is needed. Effective ways to communicate and obtain feedback from residents have to be developed and as such a parallel organisation, namely the Citizens' Consultative Committee[22] (CCC) was launched in 1965 to compensate the limitations of the CCMCs to cover a wider social ground.

---

[21] Seah Chee Meow, *Community Centres in Singapore: Their Political Involvement* (Singapore: Singapore University Press, 1973).

[22] Chan Heng Chee, *The Dynamics of One Party Dominance* (Singapore: Singapore University Press, 1976).

Both the CCMC and the CCC have since their inception in the 60s, evolved their own style in delivering community services. Their focus seems to be a programme-centred approach in community development and the community centre is used as a rallying point for residents. This approach has its limitations as it retards the initiative of the residents to take full ownership in community problem solving. In recognition of this constraint and the need to reach out to more residents, the policy makers devised a few other neighbourhood organisations to penetrate various public housing estates. This strategy gave an impetus to new direction in community development. The formation of the Residents' Committees (RCs),[23] Town Councils[24] and Community Development Councils[25] unleashed new potentials to mobilise residents to form a wider community base to extend further the frontiers of community development. These newly instituted community organisations have made reasonable impact on the development and betterment of various urban neighbourhoods in the housing estates. It is therefore timely to examine the strategies adopted by these aforementioned organisations in the promotion of community development since their inception and postulate some of the challenges facing them in the new millennium.[26]

Neigbourhood level community development

The next noticeable change in the community development scene in Singapore was the establishment of the Residents' Committees (RCs) two decades ago. These neighbourhood level organisations have developed extensive social networks through which residents living in different zones or locality are encouraged to participate in social, recreational, educational and environmental improvement programmes.[27] Since the 1980s, the increase of RCs has been phenomenal and between 1989 and 2000, the

---

[23] See Vasoo, *Neighbourhood Leaders Participation in Community Development*.

[24] See Ooi Giok Ling, *Town Councils in Singapore: Self-Determination for Public Housing Estates* (Singapore: Academic Press, 1990).

[25] See Chan Soo Sen, "Bonding Community for Good Times and Bad," Mahizhnan and Lee (eds.), *Singapore Re-engineering Success*, pp. 92–7.

[26] *Ibid.*, p.96.

[27] Vasoo, *Neighbourhood Leaders Participation in Community Development*.

number of RCs increased from 378 to 509.[28] These neighbourhood level organisations recruited 11,499 residents to serve on the Committees. Such a pool of local leaders are engaged in neighbourhood betterment activities and they require an elaborate People's Association administrative structure to support them. Some of Singapore's resources in terms of funding, staff and premises, have been committed to enhance the work of RCs in community development, which have helped to make the social landscape of Singapore more cohesive and better integrated. A few pertinent reasons account for the close attention and support given by the Government.

First, to combat the side effects of urban life, namely anomie and social isolation, the RCs provide a conduit for social interaction and support networks. Second, better educated and younger residents could be enlisted to deal with more complex community needs and aspirations, than bread and butter issues faced in the 1960s. The RCs are newly designed neighbourhood level organisations which allow more elbow rooms for younger neighbourhood leaders to exercise their leadership in helping to solve social problems and mediate between government bureaucracies and residents in maintaining cost effective and efficient delivery of urban services. Third, the desire by policy makers is to minimise the impact of various policy decisions on the social and economic lives of residents who form the majority of the public housing heartland by obtaining authentic feedback and explanation of policy changes.

The RCs have made their presence felt in their neighbourhoods. However, like other organisations, they face problems of declining resources and increase competition for funds to sustain their work. The RCs leadership base is small and hence, the more active the RC becomes, the more burdensome it will be on a few leaders who are active. Their physical facilities are limited and as such, they face constraints to organise ongoing activities. Although funding from Government is limited, this does not deter the RCs from organising activities which can be self-financing. Fees for activities are on the whole, affordable.

The RCs have implemented many community activities since their inauguration and residents have benefited directly or indirectly from their involvement. However, no in-depth evaluations have been carried

---

[28] See *Yearbook of Statistics 2000* (Singapore: Singapore National Printer, 2000).

out on the outcomes of the programmes. It is therefore, useful for some evaluations to be conducted so that better community development strategies can be adopted.

Development of town councils

Following the realisation that estate management responsibilities could be decentralised from the Housing and Development Board (HDB), a pilot Town Council project was started. The project was successful and demonstrated that red tapes could be attained when estate management functions were delegated to the charge of the elected Members of Parliament (MPs) and appointed Town Councillors.

In 1988, Town Councils were formed to look after the physical maintenance of public housing estates which included repairs, cleaning and redecoration of the external facades of the estates. The elected Parliamentarians together with his nominated Town Councillors looked after their respective wards. This devolution of estate management functions to Town Councils have made the MPs and his Town Councillors accountable to the fate of their housing estates and residents could play a part in its management and maintenance.[29]

The setting up of Town Councils have helped to consolidate the functions of RCs as they now have more control in the physical maintenance of their neighbourhood housing estates. There are new Town Councils of which five are managed by the governing party and two by the opposition parties. Their establishment have added a new dimension in community development.

Residents and their elected Parliamentarians have proven to influence the future environmental maintenance and improvements of their neighbourhoods. Good leadership and support of residents will be important variables to high standard of estate maintenance and asset enhancement.

Each Town Council manages a budget between S$20 to S$50 million. The Town Councillors and their Parliamentarians will decide jointly how the funds will be utilised in the management of their estates. Cost effectiveness of delivery of services will be an issue which has to be addressed. Any

---

[29] See Ooi, *Town Councils in Singapore*.

misdirection or misuse of funds can have disastrous consequences to community development.

Community bonding through Community Development Councils

The concern about the eventualities of social class stratification and the danger of disaffection for the disadvantaged sector of the community was raised by policy makers.[30] It was observed that many developed countries are experiencing problems of social cohesion and community bonding because their governments have usurped the social responsibilities of caring for the disadvantaged, leaving behind a diminished role for community leaders and able members of their society.[31] Such a social dilemma should be avoided in Singapore. More importantly, various avenues should be identified to encourage residents particularly the more able to help the less able in their communities. Hence, a number of Community Development Councils (CDCs) have been formed recently in 1997 to promote community care and social cohesion.[32] The Councils would co-ordinate the efforts of the various grassroots organisations namely the CCCs, CCMCs, RCs and NGOs, in community problem solving and implement programmes to enhance social and family well-being. In short, the CDCs deal with the social management of the neighbourhoods and strengthen the social support networks amongst residents and families. Various social and community service programmes are devised for the implementation by the CDCs on their own and NGOs with the support of the CDCs.

It is too early at this juncture to assess the work of the CDCs as it has only been implemented about a year ago. However, the development of CDCs do give a new lease of social energy for community development and

---

[30] Refer to Lee, *From Third World to First*, pp. 128–9; see also Lee, "Singapore of the Future," pp. 5–6; Goh Chok Tong, *Prime Minister's National Day Rally Speech 2000* (Singapore: Ministry of Information and the Arts, 2000).
[31] Refer to Goh Chok Tong, *Prime Minister's National Day Rally Speech 1996* (Singapore: Ministry of Information and the Arts, 1996), pp. 10–3.
[32] See Goh, *Prime Minister's National Day Rally Speech 2000*, pp. 45–6; Chan, "Bonding Community for Good Times and Bad", pp. 92–7.

have a few implications. Firstly, a macro-level social betterment plan could be developed and key players could be invited to collaborate and co-operate in implementing community projects. Both long term and short term projects could be undertaken and the CDC is assessed to have a much bigger impact.[33] Secondly, inter-organisational exchanges and complementation of resources and expertise could be realised through the lead by the CDCs. Competition for resources and limited facilities could be minimised.

Thirdly, residents and local leaders will have ownership of the problems and will become more motivated to tackle social problems and prevent others from arising.

Fourthly, it is tempting for CDCs to carry all the social burdens. Therefore, they must avoid taking over the roles of various community groups and NGOs and dilute the participation of these players. It is important for CDCs to play a facilitating and co-ordinating role. In summary, it must not become a super CC by replicating the activities of CCs.

Challenges in community development

There are a number of challenges confronting community development in Singapore. It is appropriate to discuss a few key issues which policy makers and those promoting community development should address.

The challenges for community organisations are to attract and retain more younger professionals to participate in community development activities. With the graying of the organisational leadership, there is an urgency to quicken the pace for renewal of leadership. This will ensure that the leadership will continue to be vibrant and relevant to meet the needs and aspirations of the succeeding younger generation of residents. It is also observed that a significant number of grassroots leaders of community organisations in the mature housing estates are above 50 years old. These organisations face difficulties in recruiting younger residents to take up leadership.[34] Whilst the mature estates are being rebuilt, it is very important to ensure the leadership of community organisations are able to reflect the changing aspirations of both the older and the younger

---

[33] Chan, "Bonding Community for Good Times and Bad," p. 96.
[34] See Vasoo, *Neighbourhood Leaders Participation*.

families so that the social and community activities organised will remain meaningful and relevant.

With the move towards information technology, community development could face both negative and positive consequences. Positively, more people will be kept well informed of the developments and social issues facing the respective neighbourhoods. They can contact and network with people immediately. Problems could be attended to quickly and time could be saved. On the negative side, people could become impersonal and more homebound, social interactions could be reduced and social bonding could be threatened. Human values could be eroded because minds could be corrupted by exposure to negative values. Therefore, community values education should be carried out so that more residents particularly the young could be socially immunised to become more responsible and caring.

Community organisations should create more opportunities for residents to participate in decision making. The danger lies in making participants passive recipients of services and not take control of solving the problems they face. The leadership in community organisations can enlarge the base of participation by the residents. This can be done through the setting up of various interest groups or task forces to work on various social issues facing the neighbourhoods. With the involvements of residents in tackling their estate management issues like prevention of crime, improvements to recreational facilities, pollution control, and environmental enhancement, they are likely to become more conscious of their social responsibility and become less dependent on the local bureaucracies to take charge of local municipal matters which require the participation of residents. In short, it will be necessary for residents to take charge in finding more effective ways to deal with local matters with the support of the Town Councils and Community Development Councils. This will truly be promoting community development as local residents will learn and find more realistic solutions to solve their specific needs and problems and become accountable for their decisions.

It is anticipated that the widening income gap will become more apparent,[35] and this is due to the economic restructuring process taking

---

[35] See Goh, *Prime Minister's National Day Rally Speech 2000*, pp. 22–5.

place in Singapore as well as the digital revolution which is sweeping across most developing and developed nations. Singaporeans with better skills and knowledge are likely to move ahead while those with low skills and not information technology literate will lag behind. Consequently, social stratification based on social classes may surface more prominently in future if excessive free market competition is not mediated or tempered with and opportunities for upgrading of skills and educational training in the field of information technology are not accessible to the lower income families. The less better off and the less able will be left behind and this can cause social friction. When this happens, social conflicts could emerge and it could be worse when this is capitalised by political fanatics. Our social cohesion could be disrupted.[36] The Community Development Councils could play a major role in implementing community based programmes which are directed at encouraging the participation of the more able to help the socially disadvantaged groups in our community. Community programmes such as social and educational assistance, computer training, children's development and child care services, youth vocational guidance and counselling programmes, family-life and development activities, and continuing learning programmes could be carried out. In this way the Community Development Councils will help to reduce the social abrasions as a result of social and economic restructuring in Singapore.

Community development should pay more attention to the promotion of social programmes which are directed at strengthening racial harmony and interaction. As Singapore is a multi-racial society comprising of Chinese (77.7%), Malays (14.1%), Indians (7.9%) and others (1.4%),[37] it is crucial that various efforts both in social policies and community activities, are undertaken to generate better racial understanding and concern amongst the diverse ethnic groups. Wherever necessary, community groups and organisations should have multi-racial involvement of residents and leaders in social and recreation activities, grassroots organisations, civic and social organisations, Town Councils and Community. In adopting this principle, we can enrich and strengthen the social

---

[36] See Lee, *From Third World to First*, pp. 143–57.
[37] See *Statistics on Demographic Characteristics*.

landscape of Singapore and prevent ethnic divisions and problems which have fractured many societies in the last decade.[38]

As can be seen, some of the older housing estates will see a steep increase in the number of families who will need to provide care of aged sick parents. At the same time many of these families will have mostly working children who will not be able to provide close care and attention. They will be faced with the burden of care and without social support and community care services, their social and economic lives will be seriously affected. Therefore there will be mounting local pressure to set up more community-based programmes to cater to the needs of families who have frail aged family members. The number of such families is expected to increase from 12,000 to 18,000 in the next decade.[39] In light of this situation, more community groups and voluntary welfare organisations together with the involvement of residents, will be required to deliver community care services such as home-help, meals service, day care, integrated housing and community nursing. Here as a community development effort, the Community Development Council, the Ministry of Health and NGOs providing health-related services can jointly work together to form community care co-operatives which will be able to provide affordable community care services which will be more convenient and accessible to the families with frail elderly needing care and attention.[40]

With the devolution of the social services to the local neighbourhoods by the Ministry of Community Development and Ministry of Health, one would expect that more NGOs will be solicited to initiate various social and healthcare programmes to cater to the needs of families. There will be more NGOs competing to deliver these programmes. Hence the neighbourhood arena will see an increase in the growth of social, health and community care programmes. However it is not sufficient for the NGOs,

---

[38] Raj Vasil, *Governing Singapore* (St Leonards: Allen and Unwin, 2000), pp. 84–118. The chapter on "Managing National Development" addresses the dangers of a multi-racial society and how these have been managed in Singapore. Ethnic conflicts have become more common in recent years. There have been many reports of ethnic cleansing in a number of places such as Bosnia, Albania, Serbia, Kosovo, Rwanda, Fiji, Sri Lanka, and Borneo. As seen, most societies have broken up because of ethnic conflicts.

[39] Refer to the *Report of the Inter-Ministerial Committee on Aging*.

[40] *Ibid.*

in partnership with the private sector and various government departments, to just deliver needed programmes but to also encourage the participation of residents to be involved in the management and decision making of the delivery of the various programmes. In doing so, there will be promotion of self-help amongst residents and they will learn to be less dependent on the service providers to do everything. The prospects of Community Development Councils playing a key mediating and catalyst role will be very good and essentially relevant community needs will be addressed more efficiently and effectively.[41]

Finally, for effective community development to be carried out, we must attract more people-centred community leaders who must be given all the social support for them to carry out their responsibilities. By nature, people-centered community leaders are active and they should not be overburdened by increasing task assignments so much so that they become burn-out. Continuing leadership training in management skills should be made available as this can make them more versatile.

Conclusion

The tripartite working partnership of the Government, community groups and corporate sector can prevent the adoption of a welfarist model of community development where residents expect and demand a high subsidy based provision of social, health and community care services in the neighbourhood. In essence community development should not promote dependency and in Singapore the emphasis has been on encouraging mutual help, which has not led to dependency and helplessness. In fact, it has led to shared social responsibilities in community problem solving through mutual help among key actors. The matching Government grant for community groups and NGOs has made them respond quickly to deal with emerging social problems in the various public housing neighbourhoods.

The progress in community development is due to conscious planned change and tripartite partnership which entails the involvement of the

---

[41] Read case studies presented at the *Symposium 2001 of Community Development Councils* (Singapore: People's Association, 31 March 2001).

Government, NGOs and the corporate business sector in what is termed as the many helping hands.[42] Without this principle, the community could become divided. To strengthen community development further, more efforts and attention must be given to involve a succeeding generation of younger leaders who can bring organisational renewal to tackle future social issues and problems arising from demographic changes and economic restructuring of the Singapore society affected by globalisation and the internet revolution.

---

[42] See *Singapore the Next Lap*.

Chapter 13

New directions of community development in Singapore*

S. Vasoo

Introduction

The community development scenario in Singapore has undergone significant changes in the last five decades since the transfer from colonial administration to self-government in 1959. These changes, as compared to those during the period under colonial rule, have been influenced by socio-economic and ecological factors (Vasoo, 1984; Vasoo & Osman, 2000). Added to these has been the desire for policy makers to facilitate the involvement of people in community problem solving and the promotion of self-help among various community groups.

During the colonial period, community development was given 'lassiez fare' treatment. The colonial administrators were not serious about the promotion of citizen participation. They adopted a rather remedial

---

*Reprinted with permission by the publisher from Vasoo, S. (2002). New Directions of Community Development in Singapore. In N. T. Tan & K. Mehta (Eds.), *Extending Frontiers: Social Issues and Social Work in Singapore* (pp. 20–36). Singapore: Eastern Universities Press.

In this article, some major assertions which have been made earlier have been resurfaced and in particular have brought up the major factors in shaping community development directions in Singapore. Also discussions on the new directions and challenges for future community development are reaffirmed.

approach in organizing community groups to deal with problems of public health and sanitation matters. Clan and ethnic groups were encouraged to function separately to manage their own affairs. In summary, the main focus of the colonial administration was directed at segmenting and segregating the community and social groups in order to prevent ethnic competition and problems.

At the same time, these groups were prevented from posing threats to social harmony and security of the community. Colonial administration adopted a divide and rule strategy in its early efforts to promote community development in Singapore (Vasoo, 1984).

A number of key social and economic factors together with the changing ecology could account for influencing the directions in community development. The development of public housing and new towns and the increase in governmental support for neighborhood organizations (e.g. the residents' organizations, town councils and community development councils), the demographic changes, the increase in labor force participation, and involvement of non-governmental voluntary organizations, have contributed to visible changes in the community development scene in Singapore. Such a remarkable increase of participation of various groups does shape the democratization of Singapore's various neighborhoods. The social landscape of community participation has seen many key players who are contributing toward community building.

This chapter will examine and discuss some of the crucial factors which have played an important role in shaping the community development directions in Singapore. Any researcher in community development studies cannot exclude such an important analysis of these factors because they are critical domains which have helped in shaping the contemporary community development directions. The paper will also discuss these new directions and examine the issues challenging future community development.

Factors influencing community development

There are a number of factors which have influenced community development in the context of Singapore. These factors have in different combinations affected its directions. It is therefore essential to identify and discuss some of these significant factors. Investigators interested in Singapore's community development can ill afford to ignore a review of such factors which are highlighted in this section.

Colonial administration and community development

It cannot be denied that Singapore's early beginnings of a community development framework in the 1950s were initiated by the colonial administration who managed the Social Welfare Department. A Standing Committee for Community Development (Social Welfare Department, 1952) was established to promote co-ordination and co-operation of various civic, clan and lineage organizations. Many of these groups were allowed to flourish as the colonial administrators could not fully comprehend and appreciate the cultural intricacies of the mutual help administered by these traditional outfits. At best, the function of the Standing Committee was primarily advisory and involved the co-ordination of various civic organizations with little interference in their work except when they became politicized and engaged in anti colonial struggles. These organizations would then be deregistered or their social activities curbed.

The colonial administrators took steps to promote community development by setting up a few community centres which originally started out as feeding and childrens' centres to combat nutritional problems facing children at that time (Social Welfare Department, 1952). Encouraged by the success of these centres to provide information to deal with public health problems of children, the Service Welfare Department deployed further resources to build model types of community centres (CCs). Two of these were first started in 1953 in the Serangoon and Siglap areas and three years thereafter more than a dozen were set up to provide a focal point for people to come together for social and recreational activities. These activities were piecemeal and discouraged the active participation of citizens in managing local issues. The primary emphasis of these early type of community centres was to provide information on policies of the colonial government and to obtain feedback about any pressing displeasures against the government so that remedial action could be taken on policies which were not popular. It was also used as a base to stamp-out any pressure group movement against the colonial administration. On the whole, a community development effort at the neighborhood level was not proactive but rather reactive in the sense that the approach was parochial and sectarian. The agenda was to keep various community groups apart and divided. It was not directed at community building. However, credit must be given to the colonial administrators for having laid a good administrative framework based on meritocracy in the appointment of civil servants to promote future community development efforts. Such a system that was free of nepotism became a fundamental hallmark of future community development endeavors. This fortunate situation did not happen in many developed and developing societies as they were saddled by corrupt community leaders who were not people centered.

Impact of relocation into new towns and re-housing

Community development trends have also been influenced by the relocation and rehousing of people into New Towns. It is estimated that about 86% of Singapore's population of 3.8 million people live in owner occupied public housing in various New Towns, which are large satellite self-contained towns. (Department of Statistics, 2000, Housing and Development Board Report 1999, 2000; Pang 1992). The relocation and re-housing of people into public housing estates is a spectacular social provision undertaken by the People's Action Party (PAP) government to give home ownership to most Singaporeans. This decent high-rise living environment has made a significant transformation to the social landscape in the various neighborhoods. It has also brought about some social implications such as the lack of neighborliness and mutual support, latch key children, stress in families with high household density, impersonal and social isolation and the lack of ownership of public space and environment. A few consequences may occur. First, residents' social and personal needs are more often met by groups and social networks outside their community. Second, younger residents particularly of older housing estates tend to move out of their parents' flats when they set up their own households. This weakens the family support networks. Third, there are rising expectations among better educated residents for more effective urban service delivery and when demands fail to meet their expectations, they can become critical. Finally, the lack of attachment to their neighborhoods can make residents uncaring of their environment and less committed to participate in building better community ties.

Demographic transition

The demographic transition is very marked in older neighborhoods where population graying is more conspicuous. Population aging will be a very challenging phenomenon in Singapore by 2030. The median age in 1989 was 28.3 years and in 2001 was about 34.4 years and the Singapore population is facing acute population aging. It is one of the fastest graying Asian societies where the aged population 65 years and above has almost doubled from 71000 to about 105000 in the last two decades (Department of Statistics, 2000; Vasoo & Osman, 2000). Such a dramatic demographic transition does impose service demands on both the family and community to provide care and support services for the elderly. Smaller families are likely to face increasing burden and stress in providing care for their aged sick elderly. They will have to depend on the neighborhood to organize different types of community services such as daycare, home-help, meal support and community nursing for their frail elderly members.

However, one cannot look at the negative aspects of population ageing alone. There are positive contributions to community development by the elderly population. With surplus manpower as a result of retirement, many social service agencies can tap the wide ranging talents and expertise of retirees for community development activities. This big pool of elderly manpower resources has not been fully harnessed for many community development programs such as environmental protection, education, health care, personal services, crime prevention, child care and neighborhood improvements. Social and service organizations must take proactive steps to recruit and plan programs to engage the elderly population to contribute their expertise to mainstream activities in the community.

Inertia of traditional organizations

Many traditional organizations such as guilds, mutual aid societies, dialect groups, clan associations and lineage groups have in the past provided protection and support for their members. They played an important part in mediating between residents and the government bureaucracy but now have not been able to maintain their efficacy. This is because their institutional missions have not evolved over time to meet the rising aspirations of younger residents who are skeptical about the ability of the leadership of traditional organizations to represent and meet their demands. Many of the traditional organizations have archaic management which is unacceptable to the younger people who believe in the transparency of these organizations which are seen to have lost their legitimacy to lead in community development activities. It is obvious that some of these traditional organizations are becoming moribund because of the lack of renewal of younger and more authentic leaders into their management. In recognition of this depressing situation, both local and outside efforts have been mobilized to usher residents organizations, namely Residents' Committees (RCs), to facilitate local residents to participate in community development (Vasoo, 1994).

Socio-ecological changes

Singapore's ecological environment has been transformed and reshaped by various urban renewal schemes. The Urban Renewal Authority (URA) has painstakingly worked out a Master Plan to ensure that both people and environment are well managed and balanced.

The old housing estates have older residents and less resourceful people. Many of the older neighborhoods become less socially active because their leadership is depleted through social mobility and upgrading of the more capable and successful residents. This ecological shift of the more successful residents into private and better public housing neighborhoods can reduce the problem-solving capacities of these older neighborhoods. In order to revitalize these older neighborhoods and prevent them from being socially depressed, swift actions should be implemented to rebuild bigger housing units in these neighborhoods. The rebuilding of the older communities would attract younger residents to live there and consequently social and community rejuvenation will take place.

With the setting up of many New Town communities, there will be a larger pool of professionals and resourceful residents whose talents and expertise could be utilized for community betterment. It is envisaged that in participation voluntary activities will be locality or community based. This will help to strengthen the social support networks of residents provided more social, recreational and community organizations are encouraged to blossom and given the essential support for their operations.

Effects of labor force participation and time constraint

The growth of the industrial sector in the last two decades particularly in electronic industries has resulted in an increase in the female labor force. Between 1989 and 2000, the female labor force participation increased from 48.4% to about 52.7% (Department of Statistics, 2000). Such a noticeable proportion of females in the workforce which accounts for half of the employable female population must affect the participation of family members in community development activities. With more mothers engaged in the labor force, fathers have to share familial responsibilities and become more housebound. These changes, which are more evident in younger families, do limit the participation of fathers in community activities. Apparently in older generation households, there are more spouses involved in voluntary activities. This is because the labor force participation rate of mothers in these households is low (Quah, 1994). There are also less young dependent children in these households who require care and attention.

With improvements in working conditions family members are envisaged to have more discretionary time or leisure periods, but they often face competing demands for their involvement from many sources, including social and community organizations. As discretionary time is limited, individuals and family members will only participate in community activities which are beneficial directly or indirectly (Kemper, 1980; Smith 1980; Gridon, 1983; Singh, Ong, & Vasoo, 1997). Therefore, those who promote community development activities in various neighborhoods must ensure that people who are involved do have a growing experience and satisfaction in their participation. It must be borne in mind that any social activity big or small, significant or less significant, does incur social or economic cost and unless it evokes a warm hearty glow or some tangible benefits, people will not participate in community development (Vasoo, 1990).

Influence of non-governmental organizations

The Non-Governmental Organizations (NGOs) have contributed a major role in community development and this is because the state ideology emphasizes the many helping hands concept. State welfarism policies adopted in many advanced economies are not adopted here as these would erode work with ethics and the promotion of self-help. At the same time the increasing welfare burden now experienced in other communities could be avoided. In keeping with the ethos that social and community problems can be resolved more effectively on a tripartite basis, the government, non-government organizations and the private corporate sectors are jointly involved in this shared responsibility. Such an emphasis is believed to prevent dependency of the NGOs on the government to solve social ills (Vasoo & Osman, 2000).

In the last decade, many NGOs have been formed (Vasoo & Osman, 2000) and they have moved into old and New Town communities to deliver community services. This has been precipitated by a few underlying developments. Firstly, with improvements to the social and economic conditions and quality of life, Singaporeans want to be involved in various social and community organizations to influence decisions which may affect their lives directly or indirectly. This is a trend when societies are modernized. Secondly, urban and high-rise housing environments do have unintended consequences such as alienation and anomie, interpersonal abrasion, latchkey children, vandalism and physical and social barriers. All these social and personal abrasions nurture the formation of NGOs serving different client and community groups. In many Singapore New Towns, NGOs serving children, families, youths and aged have been established. Lastly, the changes in government subvention policy for NGOs on a dollar for dollar basis for approved social and community service projects and the allocation of funds by the National Council of Social Service (NCSS) through its funds raising arm, the Community Chest of Singapore, have boosted the viability and morale of NGOs.

Besides government subvention, the funding through the Community Chest to NGOs increased from S$4 million in 1984 to about S$40 million (NCSS, 2000).

This quantum leap in allocation of funds for the voluntary charitable sector has enabled some small NGOs to have a renewed lease of life and social purpose and encouraged new NGOs to pioneer community development services in the New Town communities and older housing estates. It must be acknowledged that the centralized funding support for NGOs have rationalized the allocation of charitable donations and reduced overheated competitions in fund raising amongst NGOs. However, the challenge facing the Community Chest of Singapore is its ability to control the insatiable demand by member NGOs for more funding. Some cost control and cost effective measures have to be instituted to ensure that the services provided by the NGOs are indeed helpful and productive.

New directions in community development

Community development was given fresh attention after Singapore attained self-government in 1959 under the auspices of the PAP Government. There was a need to reach out to people with different racial, religious and linguistic backgrounds. The People's Association (PA) was instituted in 1960 to co-ordinate the work of community centres which have continued to be managed by the Community Centre Management Committees (CCMCs). These CCMCs comprise informal grassroots leaders appointed from among professionals, businessmen, socially active residents and volunteers. A good social and ethnic balance is maintained so that such a heterogeneous ethnic and varied social composition can help to enhance racial integration and community bonding.

The CCMC's primary responsibilities are to promote social, recreational and educational activities and to raise funds to self support their operations. There are currently 103 CCMCs with a participation of 2776 committee members (Department of Statistics, 2000). Such a varied representation of volunteers with diverse social and economic backgrounds, together with the administrative support of PA staff, constitute community centres which strive to attract residents living around its locality to participate in social and recreational programs. Although the community centre serves a useful socializing and educational role, its focus is primarily program oriented and many activities are community centre based. To strengthen its service delivery and community development role, the managements of community centres must adopt a more developmental role by reaching out to residents living in various neighborhoods and supporting them to form self-help groups such as befrienders, recreational groups and hobby groups. This move will make the community centres more relevant and vibrant.

The relocation and rehousing of the majority of Singapore's population (86%) necessitated a different strategy to reach out to residents and engage them in community building activities. Effective ways to communicate and obtain feedback from residents have to be developed and as such a parallel organization, namely Citizens' Consultative Committee (CCC) was launched in 1965 to compensate the limitations of the CCMCs to cover a wider social ground. The CCCs comprise residents with good local standing, professionals, businessmen, and trade union activists. To make it more representational, minority ethnic groups have been appointed to be members of the CCCs. The main thrust of this set-up is to play a mediatory role between the government and the residents. The CCCs have been perceived to have strong influence over locality development affairs, forming channels to convey public sentiments on policy issues and organizers of various national campaigns such as anti-crime, healthy life styles, tree-planting, anti-drug education and values education.

Generally, the educational role of the CCC remains active but its developmental role in promoting more active self-help groups is rather lukewarm. This is because the leadership is task oriented and the completion of programs is viewed as the end rather than as a means to promote self-help. Participants in CCCs programs can be encouraged to be in planning and implementation of the community programs.

Both the CCMC and the CCC have, since their inception in the 60s, evolved their own style in delivering community services. Their focus seems to be a program centred approach in community development and the community centre is used as a rallying point for residents. This approach has its limitations as it retards the initiative of residents to take full ownership in community problem-solving. In recognition of this constraint and the need to reach out to more residents, the policy makers devised a few institutions to penetrate various public housing neighborhoods. This strategy gave an impetus to new directions in community development. The formation of Residents Committees (RCs), Town Councils and Community Development Councils unleashed new potential to mobilize residents to form a wider community base to extend further the frontiers of community development. These newly instituted community organizations have made reasonable impact on the development and betterment of various urban neighborhoods in the housing estates. It is therefore timely to examine and discuss the strategies adopted by these aforementioned organizations in the promotion of community development since their inception and postulate some of the challenges facing them in the new millennium.

Neighborhood level community development

The next noticeable change in the community development scene in Singapore was the establishment of Residents' Committees (RCs) two decades ago. These neighborhood level organizations have developed extensive social networks through which residents living in different zones or localities are encouraged to participate in social, recreational, educational and environmental improvement programs (Vasoo, 1994). Since the 1980s, the increase of RCs has been phenomenal and between 1987 and 2000, the number of RCs increased from 378 to 509. These neighborhood level organizations recruited 11,499 residents to serve on the Committees (Department of Statistics, 2000). Such a pool of local leaders are engaged in neighborhood betterment activities and they require an elaborate People's Association's administrative structure to support them. Some of Singapore's resources in terms of funding, staff and premises, have been committed to enhance the work of RCs in community development which have helped to make the social landscape of Singapore more cohesive and better integrated. A few pertinent reasons account for the close attention and support given by the Government.

First, to combat the side-effects of urban life, namely anomie and social isolation, the RCs provide a conduit for social interaction and support networks. Second, better educated and younger residents could be enlisted to deal with more complex community needs and aspirations, than bread and butter issues faced in the 1960s. The RCs are newly designed neighborhood level organizations which allow more elbow room for younger neighborhood leaders to exercise their leadership in helping to solve social problems and mediate between government bureaucracies and residents in maintaining cost effective and efficient delivery of urban services. Third, the desire by policy makers is to minimize the impact of various policy decisions on the social and economic lives of residents who form the majority of the public housing heartland by obtaining authentic feedback and explanation of policy changes.

The RCs have made their presence felt in their neighborhoods. However, like other organizations, they face problems of declining resources and increased competition for funds to sustain their work. The RC's leadership base is small and hence, the more active the RC becomes, the more burdensome it will be on a few leaders who are active. Their physical facilities are limited and as such, they face constraints to organize on-going activities. Although funding from Government is limited, this does not deter the RCs from organizing activities which can be self-financing. Fees for activities are, on the whole, affordable.

The RCs have implemented many community activities since their inauguration and residents have benefited directly or indirectly from their involvement. However, no in-depth evaluations have been carried out on the outcomes of the programs. It would therefore be useful for some evaluations to be conducted so that better community development strategies could be adopted.

Development of Town Councils

Following the realization that estate management responsibilities could be decentralized from the Housing Development Board (HDB), a pilot Town Council project was started. The project was successful and demonstrated that red tapes could be attained when estate management functions were delegated to the charge of the elected Members of Parliament (MPs) and appointed Town Councilors.

In 1988, Town Councils were formed to look after the physical maintenance of public housing estates which included repairs, cleaning and redecoration of the external facades of the estates. The elected Parliamentarians together with their nominated Town Councilors looked after their respective wards. This devolution of estate management functions to Town Councils has made the MPs and their Town Councilors accountable for the fate of their housing estates and residents can play a part in their management and maintenance (Ooi, 1990).

The setting up of Town Councils has helped to consolidate the functions of RCs as they now have more control in the physical maintenance of their neighborhood housing estates. There are new Town Councils of which five are managed by the governing party and two by opposition parties. Their establishment has added a new dimension in community development.

Residents and their elected Parliamentarians have proven that they have influence on the future environmental maintenance and improvement of their neighborhoods. Good leadership and support of residents will be important variables for high standards of estate maintenance and asset enhancement.

Each Town Council manages a budget of between S$20 to S$40 million. The Town Councilors and their Parliamentarians decide jointly how the funds will be utilized in the management of their estates. Cost effectiveness of delivery of services will be an issue which has to be addressed. Any misdirection or misuse of funds could have disastrous consequences to community development.

Community bonding through Community Development Councils

The concern about the eventualities of social class stratification and the danger of disaffection for the disadvantaged sector of the community was raised by policy makers.

It was observed that many developed countries are experiencing problems of social cohesion and community bonding because their governments have usurped the social responsibilities of caring for the disadvantaged, leaving behind a diminished role for community leaders and able members of our society (Goh, 1996). Such a social dilemma should be avoided in Singapore. More importantly, various avenues should be identified to encourage residents, particularly the more able, to help the less able in their communities. Hence, a number of Community Development Councils (CDCs) have been formed recently under the charge of a Mayor each of whose major others is to promote community care and social cohesion. The Councils will co-ordinate the efforts of the various grassroots organizations namely the CCCs, CCMCs, RCs and NGOs, in community problem-solving and implementing programs to enhance social and family well-being. In short, the CDCs deal with the social management of the neighborhoods and strengthen the social support networks amongst residents and families. Various social and community service programs are devised for implementation by the CDCs on their own and NGOs with the support of the CDCs.

It is too early at this juncture to assess the work of the CDCs as they have only been implemented about four years ago. However, the development of CDCs does give a new lease of social energy for community development and has a few implications. In the main, a macro-level social betterment plan could be developed and key players could be invited to collaborate and co-operate in implementing community projects. Both long-term and short-term projects could be undertaken.

Secondly, inter-organizational exchanges and complementation of resources and expertise could be realized through the lead by the CDCs. Competition for resources and limited facilities could be minimized.

Thirdly, residents and local leaders will have to be encouraged to take ownership of the problems so that they will become more motivated to tackle social problems and prevent others from arising.

Fourthly, it is tempting for CDCs to carry all the social burdens. Therefore, they must avoid taking over the roles of various community groups and NGOs and diluting the participation of these players. In summary, it must not become a super CC by replicating the activities of CCs. And there is a danger for CDCs to move into that direction. It is important for the respective Mayors to ensure that the CDCs work more closely with the grassroots organizations in various neighborhoods to initiate community problem-solving activities which will meet the social needs of the old and young. In this way the CDCs will play a facilitating and reaching out role in community development.

Challenges in community development

There are a number of challenges confronting community development in Singapore. It is appropriate to discuss a few key issues which policy makers and those promoting community development should address.

The challenges for community organizations are to attract and retain more younger professionals to participate in community development activities. With the graying of the organizational leadership, there is an urgency to quicken the pace for renewal of leadership. This will ensure that community organizations will continue to be vibrant and relevant to meet the needs and aspirations of the succeeding younger generation of residents.

With the move towards information technology, community development could face both negative and positive consequences. Positively, more people will be kept well informed of the developments and social issues facing the respective neighborhoods. They can contact and network with people immediately. Problems could be attended to quickly and time could be saved. On the negative side, people could become impersonal and more homebound, social interactions could be reduced and social bonding could be threatened. Human values could be eroded because minds could be corrupted by exposure to negative values. Therefore, community values education should be carried out so that more residents, particularly the young, could be socially immunized to become more responsible and caring.

Community organizations should create more opportunities for residents to participate in decision making. The danger will be to make participants passive recipients of services who do not take control of solving the problems they face. The leadership in community organizations can enlarge the base of participation by residents. This can be done through the setting up of interest groups or task forces to work on various social issues facing the neighborhoods.

Social stratification based on social classes may surface more prominently in future if excessive free market competition is not mediated or tempered. The less well off and the less able will be left behind and this can cause social friction and, even worse, is that racial discrimination can be assigned to this social dilemma. When this happens, racial and communal problems could emerge. When this is capitalized by fanatics, our community harmony could be disrupted. Community development efforts must be directed at encouraging the participation of all racial and socially disadvantaged groups in our community life and social activity. This will in the longer run enable our community to maintain social and racial harmony.

Finally, for effective community development to be carried out, we must attract more people-centered community leaders who must be given all the social support for them to carry out their responsibilities. By nature, people-centered community leaders are active and they should not be overburdened by increasing task assignments so much so that they suffer burn-out. Continuing leadership training in management skills should be made available as this can make them more versatile.

Implications for social work practice

Social work practice has generally adopted the remedial approach and this makes the intervention less effective as the genesis of the problem is not tackled at its source. More often than not the practice adopts a medical model approach to problem-solving and such an emphasis requires a lot of time and resources which are not available in developing countries. Fortunately, social work practice has not completely abandoned the community development approach and a number of social workers have continued to mobilize citizens to participate in community problem-solving. This has enabled many participants to become more self-reliant and less dependent on the state to meet their personal needs. This type of social work practice does in the longer term prevent the development of a crutch mentality in people. The community development approach does inoculate people against welfare dependency (Mehta & Vasoo, 2001) and encourages people living in various neighborhoods in Singapore to participate in mobilizing and generating resources to promote activities which increase social and economic well-being, such as crime prevention, estate management, community bonding, volunteerism at individual and corporate levels, preventive health, and co-operatives covering insurance, transport, food, and child-care. In order that social work practice can make notable contributions we must pay more attention to the education and training of social workers to acquire community work or community development skills so that more of them could contribute their professional expertise to Town Councils, Community Development Councils and neighborhood community organizations (Mehta & Vasoo, 2001).

Conclusion

The tripartite working partnership of the Government, community groups and corporate sector has prevented a welfarist model of community development from being adopted. In essence, community development in Singapore has been concentrating on the mutual help model which has not led to dependency and helplessness. In fact, it has led to shared social responsibilities in community problem-solving and promoted mutual help among key actors.

The matching government grant for community organizations has reinforced their capacity to respond quickly to deal with emerging social problems in the various public housing neighborhoods.

The progress in community development is due to conscious planned change and tripartite partnership. Without this principle, the community could become divided. Community development can be further strengthened through the engagement of a succeeding generation of younger leaders who can bring organizational renewal to treat future social issues and problems. Social work practice must increasingly take on a preventive and development role. It must further strengthen its community development approach and also be proactive in finding a place in the work world to help in the promotion of worker productivity and well being. In short it must move into the realm of social health and wealth creation by helping in the development of human capital. Social work must have social entrepreneurial drive and remake itself in order to contribute to social and human capital development.

References

Department of Statistics (2000). *Year Book of Statistics*, Singapore.
Goh, C. T. (1996). *Prime Minister's National Day Rally, 1996*, Singapore, Ministry of Information and the Arts.

Gridon, B. (1973). Sources of Satisfaction Among Service Volunteers, *Journal of Voluntary Action Research*, 12, 21–35.

Housing and Development Board (1999). *Annual Report*. Singapore.

Housing and Development Board (2000). *Annual Report*. Singapore.

Kemper, T. D. (1980). Altruism and Voluntary Action. In D. H. Smith *et al.* (eds), *Participation in Social and Political Activities*, 306–338. London: Jossey Bass.

Mehta, K. K. & Vasoo, S. (2001). Social Security and the Social Development Perspective. *Asia Pacific Journal of Social Work*, 11(1): 1–5.

Mehta, K. K. & Vasoo, S. (2002). The Development of Human Capital. *Asia Pacific Journal of Social Work*, 12(1): 1–5.

National Council of Social Service (2000). *Annual Report*. Singapore.

Ooi, G. L. (1990). *Town Councils in Singapore: Self-Determination for Public Housing Estates*. Institute of Policy Studies, Singapore: Times Academic Press.

Pang, S. Y. (1992). Housing Policy Changes in Singapore. In L. Low and Toh. M. H. (Eds.), *Public Policies in Singapore*, 114–126. Singapore: Academic Press.

Quah, S. (1994). *Family in Singapore*. Singapore: Academic Press.

Singh, R., Ong, T. H., & Vasoo, S. (1997). *Volunteer Participation in Social & Welfare Organizations*, Unpublished Report, Singapore.

Smith, D. H. (1980). Determinants of Individuals' Discretionary Use of Time. In D. H. Smith *et al.* (Eds.), *Participation in Social and Political Activities*, 34–75. London, Jossey-Bass.

Social Welfare Department (1952). *Annual Report*. Singapore.

Vasoo, S. (1990). *Enhancing Citizen Participation in Voluntary Organizations; Some Issues and Challenges*, Department of Social Work and Social Administration, University of Hong Kong.

Vasoo, S. (1984). Reviewing the Direction of Community Development in Singapore, *Community Development Journal*, 19, 7–19.

Vasoo, S. (1994). *Neighborhood Leaders' Participation in Community Development*. Singapore. Academic Press.

Vasoo, S. & Osman, M. M. (2000). Non Governmental Organizations in Singapore and Nation Building: Some Emerging Trends and Issues. *Social Development Issues*, 22, 54–63.

Chapter 14

Community organisation — An attempt in the local setting*

S. Vasoo[†]

Social workers in Singapore have now become more conscious of the use of community organisation as a method to meet and ameliorate social problems affecting large sectors of people in the community. Community organisation is no new gimmick in social work, but for various reasons it is only quite recently that it has been used in any systematic way in Singapore. The term itself seemed to imply a programme of vast magnitude. But this method of approach is in essence just working with groups of people, enabling them to build stronger community bonds: not just as an end in itself but so that they can organise themselves to resolve common problems.

Some definitions of community organisation

What is meant by community organisation? A number of definitions were offered over the years but nothing seemed comprehensive. The terms community organisation and community development have also been

---

*Reprinted from *Social Perspective* journal which is now out of circulation.

This paper examines the historical development of community organisation efforts in Singapore. Attempts have been made to showcase how social workers in Singapore using Community Organisation techniques can resolve problems that confront many people in the community.

[†]Social Worker, Singapore Children's Society, Toa Payoh Branch.

used sometimes interchangeably to talk about the same phenomenon. In short, community organisation can be defined as the process of bringing and maintaining a progressively more effective adjustment between community resources and community needs within a geographical area. Its goals are consistent with social work goals in that the principal focus is upon the needs of people and provision of means to meet such needs.

Community organisation enables people to co-operate and identify social needs and to meet them from their own efforts as far as possible; also to improve material and social conditions by co-operation with outside efforts when that is found to be necessary.

To put it in a nutshell, community organisation is promoting effective citizen participation in decision making. In theory, this proposition appears attractive. How can social workers achieve this in practice in our local setting? The initial prescription is to acquaint ourselves with the people whom we intend to work with so that they will find security in relating their social problems or "social issues" to us.

Knowing people in the community

Knowing people in the community is one primary step to the organisational process. When we work in a rural district, a housing estate or a community centre, it is necessary to acquaint ourselves with members who live in the area. By constant knowledge of our presence, they will be more open to express their views of the community. Many suspicions that are commonly expected wear away as acceptance is gained, and we become identified as "enablers" who help to bring about changes to their social conditions.

One best way to understand people and to persuade them is to listen to them. Perhaps few of us are good listeners, particularly, if we regard ourselves as experts, accustomed to tell others rather than let them tell us.

We are sometimes seen as authority figures. This will make our position more confusing if not clarified. Passive attitudes can encourage our local people to express their ideas and to convince themselves of the desirability of doing what they themselves have suggested.

Knowing the community is one aspect, but everyone who works with people in a professional capacity must be able to assemble comprehensive and reliable data about those with whom he works and about their background and environment. To assist our effort at understanding other people, and in turn our capacity to help, information must be recorded. The community social worker, like his colleagues who work in other settings, too, needs to assemble reliable data about his area of concern, to build up an objective profile of the community. This can be obtained from relevant socio-economic studies, and partly from his own observations.

Assessing needs of the community

Our community needs are diverse and the social worker has to accept some priorities in these. Needs can be tested out with the groups which have been organised and they will work out solutions to needs that are immediate, realizable and specific. These are sometimes called "felt needs"; best discovered by free discussions in a meeting of all the inhabitants. Priorities may well be decided in the same manner. The social worker may advise, but decisions made without co-operation of the citizens have probably less permanent results.

Joint social action

People will act when they are clear about their capacity to play roles in the programmes for community action. The job of the social worker is to get them to move, to be active, to participate, to gain confidence in their own abilities and to harness that power necessary to tackle effectively the prevailing social problems in the area.

It is necessary under such circumstances to have low powered salesmanship and never to oversell issues. Having found a specific issue (problem), interested persons are called to meetings in community centres or a place near their residence. At these meetings the group discusses openly how it could work towards solving the issue. The social worker assists by providing alternative suggestions acceptable to the persons involved so that they become clear about their objectives.

The next stage is to work with them at their own pace so that means are worked out to fulfil their needs. Various actions are taken at subsequent meetings to arrive at their ultimate goal. It is important to make them feel that it is their effort that brought success. Very often one successful experience results in a chain reaction by which further needs are met by self-help, resulting in a more self-reliant community.

A case study — Workers in conflict

It is proposed to include in this paper an illustration of some community organisation techniques used in the case of two groups of workers to resolve their conflicts.

The case entailed some serious problems of two rival groups of bachelor workers living in Block A, from Texco[1] and Pancho[1] factories. The conflicts between them had been going on for nearly six months and relationships became so tense that at one stage violence seemed almost inevitable. Intervention was rather coincidental and the social worker had to organise the two conflicting groups to solve their differences.

Presenting Problem. The families and six other groups of young workers living in Block A complained that workers from Texco and Pancho factories were making a lot of noise throughout the night. It appeared that these two groups were challenging each other by banging doors loudly, shouting abusively and turning their amplifiers at top volume. As the result of this, most of the families and six other groups of workers could not sleep well during the night.

Interviews with Families and Other Groups of Factory Workers. They confirmed that problems existed between the Texco and Pancho workers, and suspected that the deterioration of relationship was due to misunderstanding over some girls who were working in Texco and living at the same block. The Pancho workers were accused of disturbing these girls.

Assessment of the Problem. The conflict appeared to be limited to the Texco and Pancho workers. Other groups had remained non-involved, but, at the same time were unwilling to play mediatory roles for fear of being branded as "intruders". The members of the conflicting groups were

---

[1] The names are fictional, though the details are factual.

all in the late-adolescent age range, which perhaps explains why they became easily provoked by incidents which seemed trivial and rather vague at this stage. Moreover each group seemed to live in social isolation, with few if any ties with other neighbours: this factor almost certainly added weight to the existing problem between the two groups.

Plan of Action.

(a) To contact Texco workers and explore why they were at conflict.
(b) To inquire what they thought would be their alternatives to reach an understanding with some Pancho workers.

Interviews with Texco Workers. Two interviews were held with a group of 18 young men and women Texco workers. All of them were English educated and were earning between $4/- and $5/- per day. It was gathered from 2 Texco girls that they had once been approached by 3 Pancho boys for dates but had not responded. Following this, whenever they came back from work abusive language was hurled at them. The Texco boys were rather protective of their coworkers and they became involved in the conflict. The Texco workers were a cohesive group with a leader, Mr. Kim[2] to look up to when they had problems. The group leader agreed that they could have been noisy when they returned from second shift duty, and agreed that it could be interpreted by the Pancho workers as purposeful. In the midst of the interviews, it came to light that Texco canteen was also open to the other group of workers whose factory had no such facilities. Mr. Kim described an incident when a few Pancho workers were insulted by some non-resident Texco workers for using the canteen carelessly. This he thought could have also added to their present conflicts. Mr. Kim was eager to see the differences settled amicably and he was afraid that it would lead to further repercussions which would be bad for both groups sharing the same Block.

Assessment of the Problem. The problem appeared to show that it might be due to misunderstandings which involved group sentiments. The Texco girls had been rather defensive when they were first approached by

---

[2]The name is fictional.

the Pancho boys. The approach made towards the girls could have been misinterpreted by the Texco group as "disturbing" even though it might have been a genuine interest towards promotion of friendship. The incidents at the canteen could have further aggravated the problems and developed tensions between them.

The positive aspect was that Mr. Kim was prepared to pave the way for his group to meet and get to know the Pancho workers so that differences could be thrashed out.

Plan of Action.

(a) The next step was to study more about the Pancho workers' views.
(b) To seek clarifications and not appear to favour any one leader at the expense of the other rival leader.
(c) To make both groups of workers understand that their conflicts would destroy prospects of harmonious relationship and living within their Block, besides other disadvantages for both groups.
(d) Through explanations and further interviews it was hoped that an educational process could take place between them.

Interviews with Pancho Workers. All the 24 Pancho workers were boys younger than the Texco group. Their salary scale was $5/- to $6/- per day and they claimed to be "extravagant". This group of workers included some 6 Chinese educated boys who remained much to themselves. The leader of the Pancho group, Mr. Soon was very outspoken. He claimed that the Texco girls looked down on them and often passed comments about their looks. He said that his colleagues had been called by various names e.g. "monkey face", therefore they were dissatisfied. In return the Pancho group retaliated by teasing the girls. He also brought out the canteen incident where his friends were insulted by the Texco group during break-hours. The Pancho group agreed that tuning of amplifiers, and shouting late at night were measures of retaliation against the other group. By doing so, they thought one party would have to give up in the long run.

Mr. Soon, a dynamic young leader, was prepared to work with his colleagues and assured that he would be ready to sit with the Texco group if this could be arranged. He was optimistic that a meeting would help to bring about a better understanding into their problem.

Assessment of the Problem. It has now become quite clear that misconceptions of intentions among members of the two groups had led to conflicts. As tensions mounted, the groups drifted apart more. This was further aggravated by the fact that neither the members of Texco group nor Pancho group knew each other well enough to make any steps to improve their strained relationship.

Plan of Action.

(a) Since both Texco and Pancho groups were motivated to such a degree that they were ready to meet, a date for a meeting would be decided upon by both interested group leaders.
(b) Social worker is to remain neutral and be seen to remain neutral in all arguments during that meeting.
(c) Social worker is to encourage the members present at the meeting to arrive at some solutions.

The "Summit Meeting". A summit meeting was arranged between the Texco and Pancho factory workers at the Jurong Civic Centre. Both groups came in time to participate in the process of solving their differences. It could be observed, the two groups were lined opposite each other, ready to confront each other. The social worker was quite anxious at first, at what looked like "battle array." Fortunately, events went smoothly as planned. In the meeting it could be observed that there was a heated exchange of words between both factions. The social worker had to come into the various arguments to pacify the parties so that they could be clear about each other's good intentions to reach some solution.

The Pancho workers admitted that they "disturbed" the Texco girls because they were upset for being called names. At the same time the Texco workers said that they had to retaliate by banging their doors during the night. After the two groups poured out their deep seated differences, they became more friendly. Finally both leaders agreed that they should be more informal when they are at their flats. They could call on one another to clarify any future differences. The Pancho leader, Mr. Soon, added that he now had a better picture after talking things over. He spoke of ex-roommates who had encouraged the conflict.

---

[3] The name is fictional.

The groups left the meeting appearing to be satisfied. The members of the two groups began to communicate after the meeting.

Assessment of the Problem. The problem between the two groups became very obvious at the final stage of the "summit meeting". Two factors seemed to have been mainly responsible:

(a) A misunderstanding over their approaches towards members of the other group. No doubt intentions were good, but were misconstrued by both parties.
(b) Deep seated emotionally charged events which made both groups unable to reach out to each other to solve their problems.

Plan of Action — Follow-up. The case was followed up. It was reported by the workers at respective floors in the Block that there was less noise and the situation was by then much improved. It was gathered that members of Texco and Pancho had a get-together party on the eve of Chinese New Year. Since the groups have been organised to meet their problems, the case was terminated.

Conclusions

Community organisation is an approach in social work to tackle social problems that confront many people in the community. Some social workers prefer to call this approach, "Social Inter-Group Process", "Social Engineering" or "Social Welfare Planning". Whatever the terminology is, it calls for:

(a) determining social needs,
(b) arrangement for conscientious and careful planning to meet the needs of the community,
(c) organising people in the community to achieve this goal.

The social worker has the task of contributing his professional knowledge, skill and experience towards the development of this area of work in our local setting.

Chapter 15

Neighborhoods and precincts: Government-initiated organizations are catalysts for political participation and self-help*

S. Vasoo

Introduction

In view of the diverse linguistic and cultural backgrounds of the people of Singapore, the Government has always felt that it would be of vital importance to set clear policy directions to help enhance the social and economic integration of the population which now stands at 2.5 million. Its efforts in promoting nation building are becoming evident in the many and varied social and economic programs it has implemented.

In the social field, the Government has initiated many grassroots organizations such as Community Centers (CCs), Citizens' Consultative Committees (CCCs) and Residents' Committees (RCs). These have been designed to promote community development which is aimed at the mobilization of mass support, the provision of opportunities for political

---

*Reprinted from *Solidarity* journal which is now out of circulation.

This paper attempts to review the growth of community development in Singapore from the early 1950s to early 1980s. Some issues with regard to community development approaches are also examined.

participation, and the promotion of more community cohesiveness and mutual help among people living in the urban neighborhoods of Singapore. Those Government initiatives, moreover, are supported by the voluntary sector which plays a supplementary role through a number of social service agencies. Though limited when compared to that of the Government's, the voluntary sector's efforts have been concentrated on pioneering community development projects which help to facilitate the growth of community self-help groups particularly in the public housing estates of various New Towns.

What will be attempted here will be a review of the growth of community development in Singapore since the British colonial administration period (specifically from 1950 to 1958) and up until recently (1981). Some issues with regard to community development approaches as attempted by community workers employed in the Government and the voluntary sectors will also be examined.

The beginnings of community development

The beginnings of community development in Singapore can be traced to the early 1950s when the Social Welfare Department was at that time made responsible for initiating community development. The then colonial administration saw the relevance in initiating this because:

> there was already a high degree of development in Singapore and there existed a highly integrated society with definite racial, social and political and co-operative groups.

At the same time, the pattern and nature of community development was felt to be somewhat different and complex in the undeveloped areas of Singapore. The colonial administrators also saw that in order to better coordinate this effort, it was necessary to establish a Standing Committee for Community Development. This Committee was set up in 1951 with the Secretary of Social Welfare designated one of its members. The others were nominated from among various civic and community groups. The function of this Committee was primarily advisory and involved the coordination of various civic organizations. As noted succinctly in the Social Welfare Department Report, 1952:

> Its main work will be to foster in all areas of Singapore the growth of responsible bodies which can take their full part in initiation, planning and carrying out of the many aspects of betterment of work that are now developing.

Birth of community centers

The interest in promoting community development by the colonial administrators, sometimes termed "community work", led the Department of Social Welfare to usher in the birth of a number of community centers, of which a few grew out of the feeding and children's centers. The success of such centers enabled the Social Welfare Department to take more concrete steps to deploy some funds to build the so called "model" type community centers (CCs), the first two of which were opened in 1953 in Serangoon and Siglap constituencies. Subsequently a number of other centers were established in both the sub-urban and rural areas.

Between 1953–1956, more than a dozen CCs were established. These centers provided a place for local residents to meet their social and recreational needs and more specifically for the colonial government to disseminate policies and information. Also, the centers' hidden function, which was not made obvious then, was to identify local opinions relevant to the reshaping of policies which were not well received by the people.

On the whole, one could rightly conclude that during the 1950s, community centers were not seriously promoting community development but were established with the intention of gauging the extent of anti-colonial sentiments of the local population. If at all any activities were undertaken, they were mainly centered around the promotion of indoor recreational programs. The community centers during that period adopted a "boys' club mentality" and hence acted as a sanctuary for a small group of youngsters to socialize. Their functions remained parochial and it was not until 1959 when their entire management was overhauled. This sweeping change came about because of the need to build up rapport between the common people and the newly elected political leaders from the People's Action Party (PAP).

Community centers reorganized with a new perspective

It was only after Singapore attained internal self-government in 1959 that the work of community centers was reshaped and the decisions regarding community development directions of community centers were centralized. As a result of this, more concrete actions were undertaken by Government, one of which was the establishment of the People's Association (PA) in July, 1960, a statutory body, to coordinate the work of community centers.

The PA is managed by a board of management comprising both elected and appointed members, who are representatives of social organizations which are corporate members of PA; top civil servants; and leading politicians holding important portfolios. All policy matters pertaining to PA are deliberated upon by the Board and those policies which are endorsed are implemented by senior administrators of PA down to the community centers' management committees. (CCMCs) which are supported by a large pool of operational staff, namely the organizing and assistant organizing secretaries.

The CCMCs are made up of members who are nominated from among the informal grassroot leaders in the community. This being the case, it provides the Government an additional channel to communicate with the ordinary citizens, through their informal leaders. Almost all the CCMCs have members who are of different ethnic origins and such an ethnic diversity in the membership of the CCMCs is closely maintained by the Government through its policies of selection because it is felt that a heterogenous ethnic composition in the CCMCs would better achieve racial integration and community building policies.

In analyzing the functions of the CCMCs, one could categorize them into two major areas; the first being the management of the routine activities of the CCs and the second the raising of funds to meet the operational costs in maintaining the CCs. These two traditional responsibilities receive the most attention of the CCMCs and have become the *raison d'etre* of the CCMCs. Although it is necessary for the CCMCs to concentrate efforts in the two areas highlighted, there are other equally important management functions that need their attention. The most pressing of these seems to be: reviewing the CCs' programs to see if they are meeting the changing needs of residents living in the neighborhood; encouraging the growth of self-help groups among children, youth or adults; and setting up more volunteer groups to initiate services in the neighborhoods that are not within the precincts of the CCs. To allow the CCMCs to steer away from their concentration on traditional management functions they have found it necessary to encourage residents with organizational and management skills to be involved in their leadership. With the involvement of this kind of expertise, the leadership of the CCMCs are not only further strengthened, there is also less likelihood for the CCMCs' leadership to become fossilized. Thus, they can possibly be as viable as they were in the 60s.

The need to involve more residents with professional backgrounds, who generally abstain from the activities of the CCs because of their skepticism about being associated with party politics, is crucial. Through their participation, new ideas and suggestions could be solicited to enable the CCs to be more innovative. So far, the participation of this category of people is hardly encouraging although there are signs that more of them are beginning to be interested. Oftentimes, they need to be cajoled and encouraged in order to be involved. By creating more challenging voluntary management tasks currently absent in the CCs, the talents of these professionals could be tapped. It is indeed vital to attract more professionals into the CCs as they have expertise to contribute to the social betterment of the various neighborhoods in Singapore.

The growth of the number of CCs during the '60s and '70s precipitated the need for more staff to manage them. Concomitantly, training of large numbers of personnel became urgent and as a result, the National Youth Leadership Training Institute was formed to provide community work and leadership training for organizing and assistant organizing secretaric. These two categories of personnel work with the CCMCs and with some well known local leaders and residents in the organization of various community development programs for people living in the neighborhoods. They are responsible for implementing the many activities of the CCs.

In theory, one of the major roles of the organizing secretaries besides their administrative and organizing duties, is to provide direction to the CCMCs in implementing the types of programs which would be most feasible for residents. In actual practice, however, this role has not been fully realized. In most instances, the CCMCs consciously or unconsciously relegate the organizing and assistant organizing secretaries to play the role of a 'messenger' and they do not encourage them to be more active in planning and implementing the programs of the CCs.

If this askewed relationship continues, it may have unintended consequences on the future viability of the CCs. The remedy to the potential turnover of personnel is not simple, as it has to deal with the reorientation of the management philosophy of the CCMCs. For a start, it is felt that there should be more attempts to adopt a shared leadership between the CCMCs and the staff of the CCs.

The 1960s and 1970s saw a definite growth of the People's Association style of community development which could be distinguished from the style adopted by community workers trained in social work and employed by the voluntary sector. The PA type of community development is rather centralized and 'community center based' in its approach. The programs are organized at the CC level for the people who are interested in them. Only some direct efforts are undertaken to decentralize programs into the neighborhoods of the CCs. The reaching out concept does not form an integral part of the strategies that can make community development impact in the community. However, it must be stated that the People's Association through its various CCs still carrry out a prominent role in local attempts to develop community participation in meeting neighborhood needs.

The People's Association has set up many CCs in various parliamentary constituencies in Singapore. Up until the end of the 1970s, more than 165 CCs were built and sometime towards the late 1970s, many larger centers with more sophisticated facilities were established. The purpose behind such a move has been to cater to a population which has seemingly become more demanding for better indoor recreational facilities. Also, in the light of the growing number of young adults in the urban population, the policy makers as well as the top level administrators of the community center machinery, are beginning to realize how important it is for the CCs to be more adept in catering to the needs and aspirations of the young for community participation. Although the participation of the young is viewed as important, the response to recruit them into the CCMC leadership has been noticeably slow.

Further enlargement of the base for community development

The Government, besides establishing community centers situated in different places in Singapore, has also taken steps to initiate other parallel organizations to penetrate further into the grassroots. This move is the most recent development in the community development scene in Singapore and the underlying reason for such a massive effort to stimulate the participation of people in community affairs is, perhaps, to enlarge the base for community development. At the same time, it appears that the Government through such a concerted effort would like to achieve the following: close the gap between the governing elites and the governed; prevent the bureaucracy at the local level from being arthritic; promote better understanding and acceptance of important policy issues; and identify people with organizational skills in order to recruit their services in the revitalization of government supported grassroots organizations.

The Government's increased interest in promoting more grassroots organizations came about when it recognized that the rapid relocation of people into public high rise estates as a result of its housing programs did not necessarily promote cohesive communities and community identity. According to Goh Chok Tong, this has been mainly due to the fact that:

> many of these estates are new and their residents have moved in only recently from other parts of Singapore. They have to grow new roots in a new environment, know neighbors, make new friends. If they are left alone, new housing estates will take a long time before they become a friendly, throbbing community bustling with life and activities. May be never.

Public housing constructed by the Housing and Development Board (HDB) have become a notable feature of the landscape of Singapore, and the Government's plan to provide decent homes to many Singaporean families earning below Singapore $3500 per annum has been successful. About 65% of the population have already benefited from the public housing scheme. The success of such a scheme, however, cannot be judged simply by the sheer numbers of people housed. As Goh reiterates:

> the success of our public housing should be judged not only by the number of housing units we construct, or the percentage of our population housed in HDB flats, but by the spirit of camaraderie that exists between residents of these housing estates. These housing estates must have a character, a soul, and their residents, a strong sense of group commitments.

In a move to hasten the process of community bonding, the Government established the Citizens' Consultative Committees (CCCs) in 1965 and subsequently in 1978, the Residents' Committees (RCs) to further complement the work of the CCCs and to reach out to most residents. These two elaborately organized grassroots organizations were intended to promote community development in the various neighborhoods of Singapore.

The CCCs have acted as intermediary organizations. Their membership is comprised of residents who have acquired some local standing either in community affairs or who have connections with a number of voluntary organizations such as clan associations, merchants' organizations and trade unions. Most of the CCCs are constituency-based and the number of members in each CCC vary from constituency to constituency. The CCCs, like the CCMCs, have members with different ethnic origins and these members are nominated by the Government upon the recommendation of the Members of Parliament of the various constituencies in Singapore. The members' tenure of office in the CCCs is one year and it is renewed yearly depending on their interest and performance.

Besides playing the role of mediator, the CCCs run a number of programs on a constituency-wide basis. Campaigns which are of importance to the Government and which have an educational value to the ordinary citizens are undertaken. Campaigns such as anti-crime, tree-planting, physical fitness, health, family planning and courtesy, are scheduled during different times of the year and the CCCs assist in organizing them in their respective constituencies. The effects of these campaigns have been significant and have created positive social attitudes in the Singaporean. Other than the launching of various campaigns, the CCCs also make recommendations to the Government to improve the facilities in their neighborhoods. As members of the CCCs are drawn from the informal leaders within and outside the constituencies, some of them have gained the confidence of some people in the process of their mediating between them and the Government.

The community development roles of the intermediary leaders were decidedly more significant in the '60s and '70s because they were dealing with the 'bread and butter issues' prevalent at that time. These were issues faced by ordinary citizens who were generally ignorant about how to seek redress for their problems. In the '80s, it is be expected that the leadership roles of the CCCs will be subjected to close scrutiny by a more demanding younger generation who are well educated and resourceful, particularly in their abilities to solve more complex problems involving the urban high rise environment of Singapore. Whether the CCCs will continue to play an important role remains to be seen.

The Residents' Committees (RCs) are the most recent grassroots organizations which have been introduced and formed by the Government in various public housing estates of the New Towns in Singapore. The Government's inducement is necessary because in most urban settings and in particular the high rise public housing environment, it has been found that unless Government helps to facilitate the formation of neighborhood level residents' organizations, such organizations are unlikely to develop from within. For even if they do, it will take a long time for them to gain a foothold in the community where residents are no longer able to find common affiliations that will allow them to come together readily. The urban milieu of the high rise stagnates the growth process of endogenous organizations.

RCs which are enthusiastically promoted by Government on a massive scale, are the most down-to-earth resident's organizations set up in the neighborhoods of various housing estates. A number of underlying reasons could account for the enthusiasm of the Government. Firstly, the

HDB is beginning to give more attention to its social management role as it begins to recognize the fact that the prevention of the physical deterioration of the public housing environment and the solutions to some social problems faced by residents can best be tackled by encouraging the residents themselves to be involved in solving these problems. Secondly, CCs and CCCs have limited capacities to gauge the opinions of residents and mobilize them to participate in community programs. Therefore, a more sensitive infrastructure is required to assess and respond to the changing needs of residents living in these public housing estates. Thirdly, as more residents with better educational levels begin to live in the public housing estates, they would be expected to be more articulate and motivated to partake in the decision making processes affecting both their neighborhoods and the wider community.

The RCs, unlike the CCs and the CCCs, are confined to public housing estates and interested residents are encouraged by the Residents' Committees Group Secretariat under the Prime Minister's Office, to take up leadership in the RCs. So far more than 230 RCs have been formed in 69 Parliamentary Constituencies and there are plans to form more RCs in other constituencies.

The objectives of the RCs are primarily to promote neighborliness among residents; provide a more effective channel of communication between the residents and the various government authorities or departments; ensure better maintenance of the physical conditions in the housing estates; enhance better social order and security; and encourage mutual assistance among residents. The stated objectives are broad and all-embracing; and in essence they are aimed at the promotion of community development at the neighborhood levels in the various housing estates. However, the realization of these objectives depends heavily on the types of socio-political orientation of the people who are nominated into the leadership of the RCs. In the leadership of the RCs, people with high deference values, including such characteristics as high civic consciousness, high neighborhood activism, less self-centeredness, and high devotion to community service, are thought to be more likely to help bring about the realization of the RCs' objectives. At this juncture, no in-depth analyses of the leadership profiles of the RCs' members have been undertaken and it would be too premature to forecast the type of leaders who would be suitable for these organizations.

Generally, the RCs do not vary very much in their organized activities. They mediate between the relevant government authorities and the residents on matters concerning the physical environment and undertake various national campaigns such as crime prevention, tree-planting, and courtesy. Besides these, they recommend improvements to the estates and organize family oriented programs such as picnics, excursions, family life education, and social get togethers. At the moment, it appears that the community development strategies adopted by the RCs are more service-delivery focused but there seems to be great potential for more resident-focused work which will encourage a higher degree of citizen participation. With greater emphasis on resident-focused work, the RCs can eventually help facilitate the growth of small self-help or interest groups among residents to deal with problems which may arise as a result of urban high-rise living.

Community development by the voluntary sector

Only after 1969 did there appear to be evidence of some interest in the voluntary sector as to the matter of their contributing directly to the growth of community development in Singapore. Community development has, since then, gained the support of the voluntary sector which has employed community workers to carry out community development projects. As a result of this move, a number of community development projects were initiated in the New Towns. In the pioneering years, this group of community workers together with some concerned Christians and church groups took an active role in promoting projects in a few selected urban public housing estates namely, Jurong, Bukit Ho Swee and Toa Payoh.

The first three community development projects, the Jurong Industrial Mission Project (JIMP), the Bukit Ho Swee Community Service Project and the Toa Payo Community Development Project were established in 1969. The objectives of these projects were more or less similar: firstly, to interest residents to solve problems relevant to their neighborhoods; secondly, to develop leadership and skills among residents in order to better deal with their own needs; and thirdly, to encourage residents to form self-help groups designed to meet their social, cultural and recreational needs.

The Bukit Ho Swee Project was initiated by a few community workers in concert with the Franciscan Sisters of Mary, a religious order which has developed a number of educational institutions and health centers in the voluntary welfare field. Since the inception of this project, many children and young persons have been encouraged to come forward and to be involved in the various activities. Among these are the children's clubs which organize outings, out-door camps, excursions and concerts; and the youth clubs which concentrate on vocational guidance, literacy education, excursions, outdoor camps, leadership training, and voluntary service work. So far, all the programs undertaken tend to focus on the personal needs of small groups of either children or young persons and the programs provided are supposedly geared to assist them in their socialization and personal growth. In assessing whether this project has achieved its community development objectives, one could tentatively conclude that it has not and this is based on the observation that the groups involved are still dependent on the community workers of the project to plan programs for them.

The Toa Payoh Community Development Project came into existence as a result of the recognition by some priests attached to the Methodist and Roman Catholic churches in Toa Payoh New Town and community workers, to provide services for the less privileged sector in the New Town. The main service delivered to this sector so far has been remedial education for school children because it was discovered earlier on that many of the families in the low-income group were concerned about the educational underachievement of their children. Parents of the children who were in need of remedial education programs were organized as a group by the community workers to assist in the recruitment of voluntary trained teachers living in the Toa Payoh community. As a result, an action group comprising both the parents and the voluntary teachers was formed to manage the remedial education program which has since become the main activity of the project. Since 1973, no new area of growth in community development has been recorded by the project because the remedial education program appears to have consumed most of its available resources, both in terms of finance and manpower. To date, the remedial education programme is still the prime concern of the Project.

In the case of the Jurong Industrial Mission Project, it was started by a group of concerned Christians and community workers with the support of the Jurong Christian Church also in 1969. The prime motivation of those associated with the JIMP at that time was to promote urban industrial mission work aimed at assisting young workers and residents to integrate better in the Jurong industrial setting which happened to be designed as one of the largest industrial zones of Singapore. The JIMP in its earlier stages of development (1969–1973) concentrated on organizing residents living in the working class neighborhood of Jurong in their efforts to secure better services from the various government departments, especially those dealing with education, health, environment and management of estates. In 1974, the JIMP shifted its emphasis from working with residents in the working class neighborhood to young workers employed in some of the factories operating in Jurong. This change of focus was accidental, because at that time there happened to be more demands from the young workers who wanted the project staff to advise them in their negotiations with their employers for improvements in their working conditions. Aside from the change in the JIMP's client group, it adopted in totality the Alinsky model for solving the problems faced by the groups the project organized whether they be residents living in the working class neighborhood or young workers. The adoption of this model of intervention in the JIMP's work led to its failure to establish roots in the Jurong community.

In the early years following the inception of these three projects, they each developed their own ways of entrenching themselves in the community concerned. The community workers attached to these three project devised various strategies to operationalize the objectives of the respective projects. The strategies adopted by the community workers had subsequent consequences on the life-span of the projects mentioned.

The Jurong Industrial Mission Project which concentrated on confrontative strategies in community problem-solving, ceased to exist when it failed to gain the cooperation of various power groups within the community. Also, in view of the lack of funds to support its work, the JIMP had to be discontinued. In the case of the Bukit Ho Swee Community

Service Project and the Toa Payoh Community Development Project, they managed to find their roots in their respective localities. The community workers in these two projects used collaborative strategies in community problem-solving. In using these strategies, they were able to bring together different groups in the community, consisting of organized resident groups as well as community power groups (e.g. the CCC and CCMCs) to meet needs and problems within the localities of Bukit Ho Swee and Toa Payoh.

Since the initiation of these three early projects, community workers, who were subsequently employed in a number of other voluntary agencies, began to make more serious attempts to promote community development through their agencies in the public housing estates. The increase in the number of housing estates and the realization that some people need to be supported in their adjustment to life in a high-rise environment, contributed directly or indirectly to an increase in interest among local community workers to influence voluntary agencies to embark on community development projects. The result of this influence was an increase in the number of agencies participating in community development. Just to name a few, the Singapore Children's Society, the Ang Mo Kio Social Service Centre and the Salvation Army — Kallang Bahru Centre.

Community development approaches

The trend in the practice of community development in the government and voluntary sectors seems to be primarily concentrated on the provision of services to consumers whether they be clients or citizens living in the locality where the agencies operate. It has become apparent that very little effort has been directed towards the encouragement of citizen or consumer participation which can, in the long run, motivate the beneficiaries of the services to undertake self-help projects in meeting their needs. In essence, it can be stated that the emphasis in community development by the respective sectors is 'service delivery focus' rather than 'resident focus'. It is perhaps interesting to examine some of the underlying reasons leading to this situation and the following reasons appear to be pertinent:

Firstly, community workers and the local leaders involved in community development are unclear and uncertain about the approaches most applicable to their local context. They all have attempted to try out the following approaches:

Locality Development approach
This approach presupposes that 'community change may be pursued optimally through broad participation of a wide spectrum of people at the local community level in goal determination and action.'

Social Planning approach
This encompasses a 'technical process of problem solving with regard to substantive social problems such as delinquency, housing and mental health. The emphasis of this approach is planned changes through research and rational planning.'

Social Action approach
This is based on a presupposition of 'a disadvantaged segment of the population that needs to be organised, perhaps in alliance with others, in order to make demands on the larger community for increased resources or treatment in accordance with social justice and democracy.'

All the above approaches have been applied with minimal consideration of the implications for the applicability of such approaches to their field context. More often than not, the approaches were applied haphazardly without being given a sufficient time frame to assess its consequences on the community. The haphazard application of the various approaches postulated by community development theorists then often led to a situation whereby community workers and local leaders were unable to say for certain which approach could work and under what specific circumstances.

Secondly, many of the community workers were engaged by voluntary agencies established to provide services to specific client groups such as children, youth, aged and families. As a result of this, the service orientation of these agencies was directed towards clients who were identified as having social problems and who were in need of assistance from the agencies. This being the case, the services of the agencies became remedial in nature and this in turn influenced community workers to carry out remedial functions confined to the provision of services and the implementation of programs for clients either referred by other agencies or in the process of seeking assistance from the agencies on their own. As a result, the services of the voluntary agencies did not, in the long run, make any relevant impact on the wider community.

Thirdly, most efforts in local community development by the voluntary and government sectors seemed to concentrate on 'service delivery focus'. This was because the staff found it easier either to exercise control on the types of programs their organizations offered to the community or else curtailed programs which were not attractive to the potential consumers. Besides this factor, the benevolent attitudes prevalent amongst the providers and controllers of the resources, particularly those in the voluntary sector, also influenced the way the service was provided.

On the whole, community workers are still more biased in favor of adopting the 'service delivery focus' in community development. This is because it is much easier to expand and/or extend the programs of their agencies to meet the needs of the consumers rather than to organize self-help groups to initiate programs on their own. In any case, the extension and expansion of programs of the agencies are seen by the community workers as useful ways to cope with the demands of the consumers who are often less able to articulate their needs or to participate in problem solving.

Fourthly, most community workers as well as local leaders tended to perceive that community development was effective when more programs were promoted in the community. Although programs are essential in enhancing community development, these are unfortunately developed for their own sake and serve as ends rather than as means to encourage the participation of people living in a locality. This perspective is overzealously guarded by community workers and local leaders and as such, they tend to measure the success of their work by the number of programs implemented and not by assessing the extent to which people involved in the programs are capable of initiating actions on their own to meet the needs in the community. The latter is the end objective of community development but it is often not vigorously pursued by community workers and local leaders because they are muddled about the means and ends in program implementation.

Finally, the lack of discussion and exchange of information on the progress of community development among community workers as well as local leaders has contributed to the development of a statement situation and a strong desire in community workers to maintain that the 'service delivery focus' is the most practical approach in community development even though this may not necessarily be the case

As discussed, a number of reasons have been highlighted to account for this parochial orientation with regard to community development in Singapore and the confusion in the understanding of the means and ends of community development programs among our community workers and local leaders. In analyzing this situation further, it has come to light that those involved in community development are somewhat muddled about the essence of 'community development' and because of this, they have not been able to practice community development in the way it should be intended.

The essence of community development

The term 'community development' is so often misunderstood by those who preach it and wrongly applied by those who practise it. This is so because the term is itself elusive and open to many subjective rather than objective interpretations by those involved directly or indirectly in community development whether they be community workers, politicians, social and welfare agency administrators, local leaders or concerned citizens. Frequently, the term is visualized by those involved as an activity directed towards organizing services or programs for people living in a specific community and not as a planned process to encourage people living in a specific community to initiate services or programs by themselves in order to meet their felt needs. The latter is the actual reflection of the term 'community development' and in fact it should connote:

> the process by which the efforts of the people themselves are united with those of governmental authorities to improve the economic, social and cultural conditions of communities, to integrate these communities into

the life of the nation and to enable them to contribute fully to national progress.

Community development in essence should be primarily concerned with two essential elements which should be given as much emphasis as possible. It entails the encouragement of:

the participation by people themselves in efforts to improve their level of living with as much reliance as possible on their own initiative, and the provision of technical and other services in ways which encourage initiative, self-help and mutual help and make these more effective.

In short, community development should, in the long run, encourage people to become more self-reliant in social and economic pursuits and be more participative in improving their communities.

Conclusion

The scenario of community development in the context of Singapore appears to be punctuated by various social and political flavors of the period under review.

During the colonial administration period, community development programs were undertaken with extreme caution and were more inclined to take a non-interventionist stance. This stance was adopted because it was presumed that a more concerted effort to promote community development would have unintended consequences to the colonial administration, the main concern of which was that it would kindle the fire of anticolonialism which was surfacing during that time.

After attainment of internal self-rule and then independence, the Government saw an urgent necessity to play an interventionist role in promoting community development through various government-sponsored grassroots organizations such as the CCs, CCCs and RCs. More resources in terms of staff, finance and facilities have been and are being channelled to these networks to operationalize community development programs in the various neighborhoods of Singapore. In fact, government interest to induce the growth of grassroots organizations has been very significant over the last 20 years and this emphasis is motivated by a need to provide an organized channel for citizen involvement in community affairs. The issue which confronts such an interventionist role by the government is whether these grassroots organizations, induced and supported by governmental efforts, will provide the culture for the development of indigenous leadership.

The voluntary sector's role in community development had remained supplementary and it is unlikely to grow significantly. It should therefore concentrate on pioneering community projects which could be used in demonstrating to those involved in community development the use of appropriate local approaches which are found to be effective. Thus, it may be projected that the voluntary sector has an educational role in the domain of community development in Singapore.

The community development approach as it is practiced in both the governmental and voluntary sectors, seems to have more of a 'service delivery focus'. The continued use of this local approach may, in the long run, stifle citizen initiatives in community development and consequently, citizens may be conditioned to assume fewer responsibilities in neighborhood affairs which require their involvement and support. Therefore, it is necessary and crucial for community development agencies, both public and voluntary, to encourage local citizens to be involved in promoting activities which are relevant to their interests and, where possible, such opportunities should themselves be created.

NIGHT WALK MARINE PARADE

Midnight having stars
we walk mindful not to step on lovers
or uncover their limb appointed cars;
ourselves not in love, not (yet) lovers.

This sea wall we come to is old
as whatever secrets the sand whispers to its tide
coming in, troughing bright and dark
in the unsleeping seaboard lights

and we, sitting, are as old,

needing to worry of the oldest things:
that should we shed ourselves, we moult our skin
to scales and twine our tongues in hissing.
But there is a bird that sings
without being named, and it sings the morning;
And the canal runs and for once brings,
like a river, no sulphur. Here is hope and choices.
Here grass is soft, and the trees full of voices.

Simon Tay

Chapter 16

Residents' organisations in the new towns of Hong Kong and Singapore: Some issues and future developments*

S. Vasoo[†]

In most urban new towns it is observed that residents' organisations, which is a form of locality organisation, do not blossom on their own. More often than not, they have to be ushered into existence by either external agents or governmental efforts. They provide opportunities for the participation of local citizens in social and community development and also offer channels for citizens to provide feedback on government policies as well as take actions to deal with local problems. Both Hong Kong and Singapore governments have deployed much resources in the establishment of residents' organisations in their respective New Towns.

---

*From Vasoo, S. (1987). Residents' organisations in the new towns of Hong Kong and Singapore: Some issues and future developments. *Asian Journal of Public Administration*, 9(2), 143–153. Reprinted by permission of *Asian Journal of Public Administration*.

This paper discusses the development of residents' organisations in Hong Kong and Singapore, focussing on the structure, organisation and leadership characteristics in these organisations. Similarities and differences between the two countries are highlighted.

[†]S. Vasoo is a Lecturer teaching in the Department of Social Work, National University of Singapore.

This article will examine briefly the growth, development and organisation of residents' organisations in Hong Kong and Singapore generally and more specifically in Tsuen Wan and Toa Payoh New Towns in the respective country settings. Attempts will be made to assess the participative behaviours of the neighbourhood leaders in the residents' organisations as well as the future development of these organisations in Hong Kong and Singapore. It is predicted that residents' organisations are likely to become weakened in their contribution in Hong Kong but whereas in Singapore their work will be strenghtened further.

Introduction

In the last two decades, a significant interest has developed among researchers to understand fully the dynamics of neighbourhood leaders' participation in community development,[1] particularly of citizens who are either elected or co-opted into the leadership of various residents' organisations.[2] Such an interest has been generated by the fact that governments in both developed and developing nations have recognised the importance of mobilising neighbourhood leaders for the betterment of the neighbourhood.[3] Moreover, governments have realised that without the participation of neighbourhood leaders in local affairs, they would be less sensitive and effective in responding to the needs of the ordinary citizens.[4] Also, by mobilising neighbourhood leaders, it is envisaged that the gaps between the governing and the governed could be bridged. This is seen as

---

[1] In the context of this article, the term neighbourhood leaders' is defined to cover Chairmen, Secretaries and Treasurers of various residents organisations. They are principal office-bearers. 'Participation' here refers to the action component of the neighbourhood leaders. It's sometimes used interchangeably with the term 'involvement'. Community development refers to action undertaken by neighbourhood leaders to promote activities directed at the betterment of the neighbourhood.

[2] This term refers to government sponsored organisations established to promote community development. In the context of this article it covers Mutual Aid Committees (MACs) in Hong Kong and Residents' Committees (RCs) in Singapore.

[3] The term neighbourhood is defined to include a block of public housing flats or a few blocks in a specific zone or area.

[4] United Nations: *Popular Participation in Decision Making for Development*, New York, 1975.

essentially vital for governments to keep in touch with the pulse and the aspirations of the people so that policies and social programmes of the government would be popularly supported.

In recent years, it is becoming more obvious that many urban communities lack the inducements for the growth of residents' organisations. This is because urban neighbourhoods are more complex than what they appear to be, and as such, residents' organisations are found not to have entrenched themselves so easily in locality.[5]

Most often, residents' organisations have to be induced into existence by governments or external agents to maintain dialogues and contacts with local residents. This need to maintain links with local residents is increasingly emphasised by most governments today.

It is now becoming evident, in many developing countries like Hong Kong and Singapore, that governments are making vigorous attempts to encourage the setting up of new forms of intermediaries in the urban neighbourhoods. This is because the respective governments feel that they cannot rely on traditional structures or leadership as these have become ossified and less creditable in the eyes of the residents, namely the young.[6]

In the case of Hong Kong and Singapore, new forms of intermediaries are initiated by the respective governments. Much governmental resource has been deployed to encourage the formation of residents' organisations to facilitate neighbourhood leaders' participation in community development. Residents' organisations, namely, the Mutual Aid Committees (MACs) and residents Committees (RCs) have became a backbone for neighbourhood leaders to participate in community development in the various new towns of Hong Kong and Singapore.[7]

---

[5] Taub, R.P. *et al.*, Urban Voluntary Associations, Locality Based and Externally Induced, *American Journal of Sociology*, Vol. 83(2) 1977, pp. 425–442.

[6] Esman, M.J. Development Administration and Constituency Organisation, *Public Administration Review*, Vol. 38(2), 1978, pp. 166–172.

[7] The discussions are drawn from author's study of *Residents' Organisations in the New Towns of Hong Kong and Singapore: A Study of Social Factors Influencing Neighbourhood Leaders' Participation in Community Development*, Ph.D. Thesis, University of Hong Kong, 1985. New Towns are self-contained public housing estates which have a population of more than 150,000 people. They have been developed by the governments of Hong Kong and Singapore to solve housing needs of the growing population in the respective

This article will deal briefly with the development of residents' organisations in Hong Kong and Singapore, its structure and organisation and the leadership characteristics in these organisations. Also implications of government sponsorship, factors influencing the participation of the neighbourhood leaders, areas of further research and the future of residents' organisations in Hong Kong and Singapore will be touched. Where possible, the differences and similarities on the growth, development and organisation of residents' organisations and the participative behaviours of their leadership in the respective settings will be highlighted. At the same time, the presentation would not be complete without suggesting the more important implications of the neighbourhood leaders' participation in community development.

The discussions are based on the author's research on neighbourhood leaders in residents' organisations in Tsuen Wan in Hong Kong and Toa Payoh New Town in Singapore respectively.

Development of residents' organisations

It has been observed that a number of common factors have accounted for the development of residents' organisations in Hong Kong and Singapore. First, the massive re-location of people particularly into public housing estates in the new towns of the two country settings created some social consequences which if left unattended, would have repurcussions not only to the welfare of residents but also the governments concerned. Social consequences such as the breakdown of traditional helping networks, the loss of effective communication channels between those who govern and the people, the feeling of alienation and anomie among residents, the increasing pressure from residents for better urban services by local governmental bureaucracies, disgruntlements arising from residents whose needs are unmet as a result of relocation and the like, have provoked the respective governments to direct significant resources to encourage the formation of residents' organisations. These intermediate organisations are established to provide solutions to deal with the effects of resettlement and high-rise living in public housing estates.

---

countries. The two new towns concerned here are Tsuen Wan and Toa Payoh New Towns in Hong Kong and Singapore respectively.

Second, about 50% of the residents in the new towns of Hong Kong and Singapore, and in particular, those in Tsuen Wan and Toa Payoh, are below 25 years old. In time to come it is envisaged that they would form a rather articulate group who would be demanding for more participatory democracy in the affairs of their neighbourhoods.

It would be a gross underjudgement of the respective governments not to devise appropriate channels for them to participate in neighbourhood affairs. Hence, residents' organisations were crystalized as basic grassroots structures to mobilize the young who are socially active in the neighbourhoods of the new towns in Hong Kong and Singapore. However, it is not sufficient to merely have intentions to provide the young the channels for participation. Such intentions must be translated into concrete actions to encourage them to be involved. More programmes to attract the young could be implemented and young residents should be given more opportunities for participation in the neighbourhood leadership.

Third, traditional institutions which in the past played an important mediatory role between the residents and the government have lost their effectiveness.[8,9] This is because their functons have not evolved to keep abreast with the changing needs of residents. They have become impotent in representing broader cross-sectional interests of residents and have hence lost their grounds to be effective channels to communicate with the government bureaucracies in the respective settings. Their lethargy has precipitated the interests of both Hong Kong and Singapore governments to encourage alternative organisational forms such as the residents' organisations. Like other traditional institutions in Hong Kong and Singapore, the residents' organisations in the two places, will also face the danger of becoming inactive. This can be precipitated if more low resident orientation (LRO) neighbourhood leaders[10] dominate the leadership and the respective governments do not give active support to residents' organisations.

---

[8] Seah, C.M. Grassroots Leaders Political Participation, *25th Anniversary Publication, Petir*, People's Action Party, 1979, pp. 276–281.

[9] Lau, S.K. The Government Intermediate Organisations and Grassroots Politics in Hong Kong, *Asian Survey*, Vol. 21(8), 1981, pp. 865–884.

[10] The term 'low resident orientation' (LRO) is defined as low level of concern for promoting self-help of residents as well as representing residents on matters which affect their welfare in a neighbourhood.

Government sponsorship and its implications

Both Hong Kong and Singapore governments adopted an interventionist approach to establish residents' organisations as channels for participation in community development. Their efforts results in the formation of an elaborate network of residents' organisations in the neighbourhoods of various new towns. As a consequence there was plenty of room to fill the void in neighbourhood leadership. Neighbourhood leaders were co-opted by the respective governments to encourage citizens' participation. Critics have argued that such a co-optive process has given rise to doubts among residents in Hong Kong and Singapore about the authenticity of these neighbourhood leaders' intentions.[11-14] Where neighbourhood leaders have been preselected or nominated by the authorities, such skepticism does arise and this attitude can be further reinforced if the respective governments do not provide avenues for direct dialogue with residents and other bona-fide groups on various matters of concern. The availability of these alternative channels will make citizens' participation more representative and thereby reduce skepticism among residents of the governments' intentions.

Government sponsorship of residents' organisations may produce some counter-effects to community development if the neighbourhood leaders rely heavily on government administrative bureaucrats to chart programme directions for their residents' organisations. They can become insular by undertaking, mainly programmes which are standarised and acceptable to government. In the long run, residents' organisations and their leadership may suffer from alienation. It would be important for the

---

[11] Jones, J.F. et al. *Neighbourhood Associations in A New Town: The Mutual Aid Committee in Shatin*, The Social Research Centre, Chinese University og Hong Kong, 1978, pp. 72–78.

[12] Loy, Jackson, D.E. *The Residents' Committees in Singapore: A Exploratory Study*, An Academic Exercise, Department of Sociology, University of Singapore, 1979.

[13] Leung, C.B. Community Participation: From Kaifong Association, Mutual Aid to District Board in Cheung, Joseph, Y.S. (ed.), *Hong Kong in the 1980's*, Hong Kong, Summerson Eastern Publishers, 1982, pp. 152–170.

[14] Yuen, Kathy. *Report of Survey on Residents' Opinions About Community Participation and the Residents' Committees*, 1983, pp. 12–13.

neighbourhood leaders to have the independence to redefine the objectives of their organisations and work in concert with various governmental structures to improve the delivery of urban services.

The continued reliance of the residents' organisations in Hong Kong and Singapore on a small leadership base can contribute to organisation-inertia. This condition would stem from a lack of initiative of these leaders to create opportunities for residents to participate in decision making. There is an apparent danger that the leadership may become omnipotent if it assumed that it knows best the problems faced by residents.

In the case of Hong Kong, the government sponsorship of residents' organisations has led to further segmentation among neighbourhood groups and therefore dilution of the efforts for community development. The potential for conflict and competition for resources is thereby created. In Singapore's context, a structured framework has evolved for further political education of residents. It also acts as a conduit through which anti-government or communist inspired activities can be contained. This strategy has been adopted by the government since independence.

In both Hong Kong and Singapore, residents' organisations are conceived as administrative statelites through which citizens and their leaders can be mobilised to participate in improving the urban service delivery systems. It is a devise by the two governments to encourage local residents to take an active interest as volunteers to tackle various problems confronting the urban setting. These problems such as environmental deterioration, anomie, crime and psychological stress, will not be effectively solved by the administrative machinery of the governments alone unless the support and co-operation of neighbourhood leaders and residents are harnessed.

Organisation and structure of residents' organisations

On the whole, the organisation and structure of residents' organisations in the Hong Kong and Singapore settings are similar. They are estabished with the initial assistance of the government bureaucrats, namely the Liaison Officer (LOs) and Temporary Community Organisers (TCOs) in the District Office, in the case of Hong Kong, and the LOs and the Assistant Liaison Officers (ALOs) in the Residents' Committees Group Secretariat, in Singapore. All these organisations are centrally co-ordinated by a Steering Committee which is located in the Home Affairs Department (HAD) in Hong Kong and the Ministry of Community Development (MCD) in Singapore. As a result of this centralization, all policies decided by the Steering Committee on the operations of the residents' organisations have a uniform impact. Such a centralised co-ordinating system has its pros and cons. It provides uniformity in the deployment of government resources and the immediacy to take corrective actions when they deviate from their objectives. On the other hand, the organisational variations in terms of their activities specific to the neighbourhood needs may be sacrificed for the sake of maintaining similarity in the structure and activities. It is indeed useful to ensure that flexibility is given to the residents' organisations to design organisation structures which are relevant to their operational context. Innovative organisation structure can encourage more residents' participation.

One particular difference which stands out clearly between the organisation of residents' organisation in Hong Kong and Singapore is the extent of flexibility allowed for them to co-operate in carrying out joint activities. The Hong Kong government in contrast with Singapore, adheres very stringently to a separatist policy which stifles the initiatives of the neighbourhood leadership to co-operate at the inter-organisational level in dealing with issues affecting residents widely. Unless inter-organisation and co-operation among the leadership of various residents' organisations is promoted, the maximum leadership resources available will remain untapped. Consequently, wider issues facing residents may not be effectively resolved.

Characteristics of the neighbourhood leaders

Generally, the neighbourhood leadership in the residents' organisation in the two new towns of Hong Kong and Singapore has a higher percentage involvement of people with professional and technical background than other occupational status.

The dominance by members of this group is as expected because they seem to have high political efficacy — a characteristic that has been substantiated by other studies.[15,16] Their presence strenghtens the leadership of the residents' organisation as their expertise could be tapped.

What appears more significant in the two new towns settings is that there is an under-representation of neighbourhood leaders with lower socio-economic status (SES) although the majority of their working population is engaged in production and service related occupations. This situation is more acute in Toa Payoh New Town. The low representation of people with lower SES in residents' organisation could be attributed to the lack of tangible rewards which are important to meet their needs.[17]

The under representation of people with lower SES in the neighbourhood leadership can hamper the work of the residents' organisations. This is particularly so when the current leadership is unable to reflect and respond to the needs of residents in the lower income group in the various neighbourhoods. This danger of a more bias organisational outlook reflecting interests of elites can be averted by the respective governments. This can be achieved by encouraging a good mix of people and high SES to be involved in the residents' organisations.

A majority of the neighbourhood leaders in the residents' organisations in Toa Payoh as compared to those in Tsuen Wan, has high resident orientation (HRO).[18] This difference can be attributed to the utilitarianistic familialism prevalent among the people in the Hong Kong setting.[19] However despite this difference, it is interesting to observe that there is a correlation between HRO neighbourhood leaders and their past membership in school clubs in both the new towns. Their past association with school clubs seemed to produce a socializing effect on their resident orientation which is viewed to play a role in influencing their participative behaviour.

---

[15] Jones, *et al.*, op.cit., p. 78.

[16] Yuen, op.cit., pp. 12–13.

[17] O'Brien, D.J. *Neighbourhood Organisations and Interest Group Process*, Princeton, New Jersey, Princeton University Press, 1975.

[18] The term 'high resident orientation' (HRO) is defined as high level of concern for promoting self-help of residents as well as representing residents on matters which affect their welfare in a neighbourhood.

[19] Lau, S.K. op.cit., p. 872.

In Tsuen Wan a majority of the neighbourhood leaders are young as compared to Toa Payoh which has more middle aged neighbourhood leaders. Both these categories of neighbourhood leaders in the two new town settings have HRO and are better educated. The level of education does influence the resident orientation, perhaps not so directly on young neighbourhood leaders in Tsuen Wan as contrasted to Toa Payoh. Better education can make the neighbourhood leader critical about prevailing organisational conditions which may hamper their performance in their residents' organisations.

The system of selection of neighbourhood leaders into residents' organisations as practised in the Tsuen Wan and Toa Payoh context, is based on the notion of free will and interests to volunteer. In such an open system, neighbourhood leaders with either low or high resident orientation are attracted to be involved. It is sometimes difficult to predict how they would perform in their residents' organisations. However, despite this dilemma, it cannot be denied that steps can be undertaken to encourage more people with HRO to take up leadership position in the residents' organisations. When more neighbourhood leaders with this characteristics are attracted to be involved in the residents' organisations, they could help them to be viable. This is because HRO neighbourhood leaders are motivated to represent problems of residents.

Neighbourhood leaders in community development

The neighbourhood leaders in Tsuen Wan are less actively involved in carrying out various activities to promote community betterment than their counterparts in Toa Payoh. This state of involvement of neighbourhood leaders in Tsuen Wan is more pervasive among those who are young and with HRO. Whereas, in Toa Payoh, it is confined more to those with LRO.

Given the situation in Tsuen Wan, the neighbourhood leaders would maintain a status-guo in participation in community development. This is partially due to the fact that the objectives of their residents' organisations are inflexible and circumscriptive. Frustrations will be felt more by the HRO neighbourhood leaders as their concern for promoting the welfare of residents is not realized through their participation.

In contrast, Toa Payoh's neighbourhood leaders, especially those with HRO would form the driving force behind any activities for community betterment. This is partly because the objectives of their residents' organisations are sufficiently flexible to encourage innovations to improve the welfare of residents in the neighbourhoods. As a result, less frustrations are encountered by them in their participation.

Both Tsuen Wan and Toa Payoh's HRO neighbourhood leaders, unlike their LRO counterparts, are motivated by 'people oriented' desires. These neighbourhood leaders who have such traits require high social support conditions to sustain their participation.

Social factors influencing the neighbourhood leaders' participation in community development

It seems that Tsuen Wan's and Toa Payoh's neighbourhood leaders' participation in community development varies directly with the level of social support. Therefore, it is necessary to ensure that high social support conditions[20] are all the time present in the residents' organisations. This is important for the sustainence of the neighbourhood leaders' performance. High social support acts as an incentive or a motivator and it provides the impetus for them to discharge their responsiblities satisfactorily. Elsewhere in other research[21,22] job satisfaction has been also found to be significantly related to the presence of satisfiers.

The two social support elements, namely officials' and committee members' support are the more important of the four support elements identified. They appear to account for activating the participation of the neighbourhood leaders. This is because non-profit organisations like

---

[20] This term social support conditions refers to four primary elements. It includes the degree of co-operation among committee members (committee members' support), the degree of participation by residents (residents' support), the degree of assistance in the form of administrative help and guidance given by government officials (government officials' support) and the financial adequacy of the residents' organisations (financial support).

[21] Herzberg, F. *Work and Nature of Man*, Cleveland, Ohio, World Publishing Co., 1966.

[22] Gidron, B. Sources of Satisfaction Among Service Volunteers, *Journal of Voluntary Action Research*, Vol. 12, 1983, pp. 21–35.

residents' organisations have no tangible incentives to offer their neighbourhood leaders except for these two social support elements which play a significant part in dictating their performance.

Different social support conditions have a differential effect on the neighbourhood leaders with varying degrees of residents' orientation in the respective new towns. HRO neighbourhood leaders in Tsuen Wan and Toa Payoh are more positively responsive to high social support conditions. This is because the HRO neighbourhood leaders by the very nature of their concern to better the welfare of residents in their respective neighbourhoods, expect high social support conditions in order that they can carry out their work effectively. High social support conditions are therefore relevant and have motivating effect on the HRO neighbourhood leaders in the new towns concerned. To develop further from these findings, it can be surmised that irrespective of the two new town settings, HRO and high social condition are universal factors enhancing satisfaction, frequency of participation and continuity in the work of residents' organisations.

It is also interesting to note that low social support conditions have different effects on the participative behaviour of HRO and LRO neighbourhood leaders in Tsuen Wan and Toa Payoh. The HRO neighbourhood leaders in Tsuen Wan unlike their HRO counterparts in Toa Payoh, are more dissatisfied. This dissatisfaction could be accounted by the extremely low social support conditions which have deleterious effects on their motivation to perform their roles. Moreover, the HRO neighbourhood leaders in Tsuen Wan who are younger tend to have a lower threshold of tolerance for low social support conditions.

In the case of Toa Payoh, the LRO neighbourhood leaders are more dissatisfied than their HRO counterparts. This situation is contributed by the pressure asserted by the HRO neighbourhood leaders on the LRO neighbourhood leaders who have generally been found not to be performing as expected. As a consequence, the LRO neighbourhood leaders become dissatisfied. The pressure asserted by the HRO neighbourhood leaders in Toa Payoh in the form of ridicule, private or public sanction and criticism, is not practiced by Tsuen Wan's HRO neighbourhood leaders who have perhaps become demoralised by prolonged lack of social support.

Implications for specific areas

Finally, the discussion will be incomplete if it overlooked two specific areas;

(a) future research on neighbourhood leaders in residents' organisations; and
(b) the future of the neighbourhood leaders' participation in community development.

Future research on neighbourhood leaders in residents' organisations

The scope for future research on neighbourhood leaders in residents' organisations in Hong Kong and Singapore is wide as there are a number of areas which remain unexplored at this stage.

Future research can concentrate on the discretionary time at the disposal of the neighbourhood leaders and examine how this affects their participative behaviour in residents' organisations. This area of research is yet to be developed.

There are no studies at the moment on how the family life cycles of the neighbourhood leaders affect their participation in residents' organisations. An attempt to look into this aspect can provide further insights into the oriental family life cycle activities and their effects on the neighbourhood leaders' participative behaviour.

Finally, longitudinal studies on neighbourhood leaders' participation in residents' organisations can be attempted and such studies can provide further knowledge of participative behaviour over a given period.

The future of the neighbourhood leaders' participation in community development

It is predicted that the future of the neighbourhood leaders participation in community development in Tsuen Wan will remain inactive or decline. This is because the low social support conditions prevalent in the residents' organisation have generally affected the motivation of both HRO and LRO neighbourhood leaders in their work. This condition will deter the HRO neighbourhood leaders in their continued participation, and as an end result, will leave behind a leadership comprising of LRO neighbourhood leaders who will not be active in their participation in community development. It appears that unless the government through the Tsuen Wan District Office is willing to give more administrative and financial assistance and select more HRO residents to be involved, neighbourhood leaders' participation in community development cannot be revitalised. This can be true of the entire residents' organisation movement in Hong Kong.

However, if there is any hope for revitalization of the residents' organisations, it could come about indirectly as a result of the influence by implementation of the District Administration Scheme and democratic reforms in Hong Kong.[23,24] This scheme would provide opportunities for HRO neighbourhood leaders to activate their residents' organisations and use them as an organisational base in seeking popular representation into the District Boards.

It is envisaged that the future of neighbourhood leaders' participation in community development in Toa Payoh, will continue to be active, if not strengthened. This is because of the high social support conditions under which the neighbourhood leadership is operating. Besides this, the residents' organisations comprise of more HRO neighbourhood leaders who will remain a dominating force in the leadership. Such a leadership, comprising mainly of committed HRO neighbourhood leaders will by direct or indirect group pressure wean out the LRO neighbourhood who are unmotivated. In the long run, more HRO neighbourhood leaders can be expected to be retained in the residents' organisation and with the given

---

[23] For other administrative changes especially in the New Territories, please refer to Scott, Ian, Administrative Growth and Change in the New Territories, in Leung, C.K., Cushman, J.W. and Wang, Gungwu (eds), *Hong Kong: Dilemmas of Growth*, Canberra, Australian National University, 1980, pp. 95–114.

[24] Since 1982, several administrative reforms have been implemented in Hong Kong. The District Boards have been set-up. Following these, elections among functional groups into the Legislative Council were recently implemented in 1985. All these changes had not affected the organisation structure and work of residents' organisations in Hong Kong.

high social support conditions, the neighbourhood leadership will continue to be effective.

In Hong Kong and Singapore, neighbourhood leaders tend to generally rely on guidance from liaison officers. Such a dependency, can in the long run negate 'self-help' and hinder initiatives to organise residents to be involved in dealing with neighbourhood issues. In order to enhance participation in community development, the primary objective of liaison officers should be directed at the encouragement of neighbourhood leaders themselves to improve their neighbourhoods on their own efforts but with essential co-operation of various governmental authorities.

Conclusion

Organisational activism in residents' organisations can be adversely affected, especially when HRO neighbourhood leaders perceive that they do not have high social support. They by nature being more inclined to be active, are often left to carry the burdens of their organisations. As a consequence, they become burn-out leaders[25] portraying various symptoms such as low satisfaction from achievements, lack of drive in discharging the mission of their organisations, feelings estranged and back-sliding in performance. To prevent HRO neighbourhood leaders from being burn-out, it is essential that there be a more equitable distribution of organisational responsibilities.

More urgently, residents' organisations in Hong Kong and Singapore must have a majority of HRO neighbourhood leaders in its leadership so that they can counter the effects of demotivation by LRO neighbourhood leaders. Together with this, flexible organisational objectives and administrative support by the respective governments for the neighbourhood leaders, it is anticipated that the future work of residents' organisations could be strengthened.

---

[25] Burn-out leadership is a common phenomenon in voluntary organisations. Burn-out is defined as a process of wearing out or becoming exhausted through excessive demands in energy and resources.

Chapter 17

Contributions to charitable organizations in a developing country: The case of Singapore*

Chung Ming Wong, Vincent C. H. Chua and S. Vasoo[†]

Introduction

Many studies have been conducted to examine the determinants of charitable giving by individuals. Underlying such studies are various theories and models attempting to explain altruistic behavior. According to one type of such models, altruistic behavior may be due to the interdependence of individual utility functions. If an individual values not only his/her own consumption but also that of his/her neighbor, it would be perfectly rational for him/her to make charitable contributions. An individual may also give because of social pressure, because he/she expects that help may be reciprocated, or because he derives direct benefits from such contributions. Clotfelter (1985) noted that, for the purpose of prediction, in

---

*Reprinted with permission by the publisher from Wong, C. M., Chua, V. C. H., & Vasoo, S. (1998). Contributions to charitable organizations in a developing country: The case of Singapore. *International Journal of Social Economics*, 25(1), 25–42.

This article is a case study of charitable giving in Singapore. The data have been collated from individual charitable organisations over the period 1980 to 1989. The analyses on giving to charities show the causes which are commonly supported by individuals.

[†]Department of Economics and Statistics, National University of Singapore, Singapore.

most of these cases the individuals may simply be assumed to value their own consumption and charitable contributions as two goods, and to maximize utility subject to a tax-defined budget constraint. Within such a framework, the deductibility of charitable contribution from taxable income has an income effect and a substitution effect. First, deductibility of contributions raises disposable income, which tends to encourage giving as long as the latter is a normal good. Second, deductibility lowers the price of giving. This is because if the marginal tax rate facing the individual is t, the price of giving a dollar, in terms of foregone personal consumption or saving when deductibility is allowed, is only $1 - t$. The magnitudes of these two effects would, of course, depend crucially on the values of income and tax price elasticities.

Based on this reasoning, most studies have typically tried to explain — in a multiple regression framework — the level of charitable contributions by variables such as income, the tax price of giving, and individual or family characteristics. Some of the results have been summarized in Clotfelter (1985), Jencks (1987) and Weisbrod (1988).[1] Most of these studies found charitable giving to be elastic with respect to the tax price, but income elasticities are usually below unity. While their estimates of income and price elasticities differ, there seems to be agreement that both income and the tax price of giving do affect the level of charitable donations.

It has also been recognized (e.g., Clotfelter, 1985) that if giving is motivated by interdependence of utility functions, an increase in government expenditure on social services or grants to charitable organizations would lead to a reduction of private philanthropic contributions. Warr (1982) and Roberts (1984) have presented models in which under certain assumptions, a dollar-for-dollar crowding-out may occur. While this prediction is rather extreme, Abrams and Schmitz (1978; 1984) have found evidence of partial crowding-out in the USA Jones (1983) and Steinberg

---

[1] Studies on the determinants of charitable giving by individuals are too numerous to be cited here in full. For studies conducted in the USA, see — for example — Boskin and Feldstein (1977), Clotfelter (1980), Feldstein (1975), Feldstein and Clotfelter (1976) and Feldstein and Taylor (1977). Recently, there have been an increasing number of studies being conducted for other developed countries such as Canada (Glenday et al., 1986; Kitchen and Dalton, 1990; Kitchen, 1992) and the UK (Jones and Posnett, 1991).

(1985) found similar evidence for the UK, and Weinblatt (1992) for Israel. Crowding-out is, however, not inevitable. Weisbrod (1988), for example, noted that government spending may in fact encourage private donations if donors see this as a signal that particular activities or programs are deserving of private support. Similarly, government grants to charitable organizations could serve as an indicator of governmental confidence in them, and thus encourage private donations.

While most of the studies have analyzed charitable contributions from the donor's point of view and tended to disregard the characteristics of recipient organizations, a number of recent studies — notably by Weisbrod and Dominguez (1986) for the USA and Posnett and Sandler (1989) for the UK — looked instead at the determinants of allocation of gifts by donors among charitable organizations. These authors viewed non-profit firms as supplying public and mixed goods. As in the case of private goods, the demand for output of non-profit firms depends on conventional market variables such as advertising, price and quality. Since donors typically know little about the marginal effect of their contributions on charitable output, fundraising activities play the same role as that of advertising in the case of private goods markets in providing information to potential donors. They also argued that donors are interested in contributing not a dollar's worth of money, but rather a dollar of charitable output. This depends crucially on the efficiency of the organization in converting charitable donations into final services rather than into administration and fundraising costs. As demonstrated by Posnett and Sandler (1989), the price to the donor of increasing output of a particular charity by one dollar is $1/[1 - (f + a)]$, where f and a are the proportions of total expenditure devoted to fundraising and administration.[2] If donations to the charity are tax-deductible, the price is $(1 - t)/[1 - (f + a)]$.

Within such a framework, fundraising activities by the charity have two effects. Fundraising helps to provide information about the

---

[2] The idea that donors may dislike, and therefore give less to charities that spend a high proportion of their receipts on fundraising activities was first suggested by Rose-Ackerman (1982). In contrast, Steinberg (1985) argued that average fundraising shares influence the price of charitable services only in a very complicated way, and contain little helpful information on how to rationally allocate donations between charities.

organization to donors and tends to increase donations. At the same time, more fundraising increases f and therefore the price of giving, and this tends to offset the first effect. In these studies, the authors found donations to be responsive to price, fundraising and other variables including the organization's reputation (reflected for example by its age since founding). Posnett and Sandler also tried to test for crowding-out but did not find such effect.

Most of the studies on charitable giving have been for the USA and other developed countries. To date, we are not aware of any study being conducted for a developing country. This article is intended to fill this gap by looking at the case of Singapore, a relatively high income newly-industrializing country. Our study is based on data from individual charitable organizations over the period 1980 to 1989. As in Weisbrod and Dominguez (1986) and Posnett and Sandler (1989), we look at the determinants of allocation of donations by donors among charitable organizations. But as will be seen in the next section, there are special institutional and other characteristics in the Singapore case that need to be taken into account in the choice and definitions of variables in the regressions. Our results indicate, as in the other studies, that donations are sensitive to the price of giving and other variables such as the age and size of the organization. In addition, we find some evidence of crowding-out in the Singapore case.

Charitable organizations and private donations in Singapore

Singapore has achieved very impressive economic growth in the last three decades as a result of rapid export expansion, inflow of foreign direct investment and other favorable factors. Unemployment and extreme poverty generally do not exist to any great extent, although income inequality — which had declined during the early phase of export-oriented industrialization — has shown some signs of increase in recent years. Nevertheless, less-privileged groups — for example, the disabled and the destitute who lack the means to satisfy their basic needs — do exist in Singapore. In general, the government does not believe in a welfare state or massive transfers to the poor. Rather, community organizations and voluntary bodies are encouraged to play a major role in the care of the needy (Lim *et al.*, 1988, Ch. 14). The government has recently increased its efforts to raise private donations to the charitable cause. In Singapore, as in many developed countries, the tax-deductibility of charitable contributions has been an important government policy affecting private giving. The Institution of Public Character (IPC) status is granted by the Inland Revenue Department to non-profit organizations providing social, educational, sports and even cultural services. Organizations with the IPC status can issue tax-exempt receipts to donors, who can then claim deduction in their annual income tax assessments. However, not all organizations providing direct welfare services qualify for IPC status. In 1988–1990, of all the member organizations of the Singapore Council of Social Service (SCSS), only slightly more than half had IPC status, though their shares in the total donations received were substantially greater.[3]

The Community Chest of Singapore (CCS) was set up by the SCSS in 1983, and since then has played an important role in helping the less fortunate in Singapore. The Community Chest does not provide direct social services, but specializes in raising funds for some 50 charities who are its members. Donations to the Community Chest are tax-deductible, though not all CCS member organizations have IPC status. An individual who wishes to make a donation to a CCS member may either give to it directly, or alternatively donate to the Community Chest and earmark the sum for that particular agency. Funds which have not been earmarked are allocated by the Community Chest to its members according to various criteria, including need and the financial situation of the agencies. Member organizations of the Community Chest are generally not allowed to have independent fundraising activities, except for special fundraising events. Much of the contribution to Community Chest is through the SHARE (social help and assistance raised by employees) program, under which a working person can voluntarily contribute to charity with a monthly pledge of a sum which is deducted from his salary. Most of the donations to the Community Chest are from individuals. Up to 1989, corporate donations

---

[3] For a description of the various types of social services provided by charitable organizations in Singapore, see for example Yap (1991).

had been maintained at a relatively low 5 to 6 percent of the total (Yap, 1991, p. 11).

The importance of the Community Chest in Singapore raises certain issues for our study. The member organizations of the Community Chest receive donations not only directly from individuals (and corporations) but also indirectly through the chest. Thus, for such organizations, it is necessary for us to analyze not only direct donations but also total donations (which include allocations from the chest). Another problem is in the definition of fundraising expenditure for the member organizations, since as mentioned earlier such organizations are usually not allowed to raise funds independently. For this reason, fundraising expenditure is not included as an explanatory variable in the regressions, or in the definition of the price of giving to a charitable organization. Instead, we derive in the next section an implicit price of giving which depends on whether the organization has IPC status so that donations to it are tax-deductible, and (if it is a member charity) the proportion of its donations received indirectly through the Community Chest. The efficiency of the organization in converting donations into charitable output could still, however, be reflected indirectly through its other characteristics, such as its age and size (and therefore reputation), the presence of governmental support, and so on.[4]

Membership in the Community Chest can also affect the total donations to an organization and its efficiency in providing charitable output, though the effects are difficult to estimate. Rose-Ackerman (1982), for example, argued that competition among charities for donations may push fundraising shares to very high levels. Thus a united charity (like the United Way) can help to economize on fundraising costs by reducing competition between the member charities, and donors may give more because the donations are now more efficiently spent. Rose-Ackerman also suggested that donors may have poor information about charities and therefore delegate the difficult allocation task to someone else.[5] But while

---

[4] For the case of Singapore, the fundraising shares of charities are seldom mentioned or publicized and therefore their omission in the definition of the price of giving may not present a serious problem. By contrast, tax-deductibility of donations is often highlighted in fundraising campaigns.

[5] See Steinberg (1987) for a discussion of these arguments.

the price of giving tends to be pushed down by the saving in solicitation costs, it tends to be pushed up by the united charity's "tie-in sales". The donors can decide only on the amounts donated but not how they are to be allocated among charities. If donors care only for particular charities, the price of giving to these charities may increase. Fisher (1977) noted that even when the donors can earmark their donations for particular charities, their actions can be offset by the united charity in the distribution of the unallocated money. When donors perceive that they cannot affect the final distribution of their gifts, they may lower their donations to the combined charity.[6]

In the case of Singapore, it appears that charities could increase the total donations received by being Community Chest members. The Community Chest's access to the payroll deduction system through the SHARE Program greatly increases the convenience (and thus lowers the price) in giving. Also, the SHARE Program has the support of many firms and employers in Singapore who encourage a high participation rate among their employees. In this situation, employees may make contributions out of true philanthropy, but in addition may expect to gain goodwill and other direct results.[7] Lastly, since the Community Chest monitors the needs and performance of its members, donors may be convinced that their donations are used more efficiently in the provision of charitable services, and thus increase their giving. While we are not able to test the above hypotheses directly, we shall attempt to draw implications from our study regarding how the level and determinants of giving may differ for the member and non-member charities.

Empirical specification

We adopt the same basic model as Weisbrod and Dominguez (1986) and Posnett and Sandler (1989). The demand for donations to charities in

---

[6] Bilodeau (1992) noted that if the united charity recognizes that total contributions may fall, its optimal policy would involve trading off a less desirable mix of services for higher contributions. It may want to guarantee donors that earmarked contributions will not be offset completely.

[7] Keating et al. (1981) found such motives to be present in their analysis of donations to the United Way.

Singapore is assumed to depend on price, alternative revenue sources, and characteristics such as age and size of the organization. The equation to be estimated is:

$$\ln TD \text{ (or } \ln DD) = b_0 + b_1 D_1 + b_2 D_2 + b_3 D_3 + b_4 D_4 + b_5 M + b_6 \ln P + b_7 \ln N + b_8 A + b_9 \ln E + b_{10} y + b_{11} g + b_{12} T + u$$

where bs are the coefficients to be estimated and u is the error term. The dependent variables in the regressions are the natural logarithms of total donations (TD) or direct donations (DD) received in the current year.[8] Direct donations refer to donations received by the charity directly from individuals and corporations, and also include income from sales of donated goods and from special fundraising activities. For charitable organizations which are not members of the Community Chest, direct donations and total donations are the same. For the member charities, total donations also include allocation of funds to them by the Community Chest (F). Thus TD = DD + F. We now examine the explanatory variables.

Price of donations (P)

The price to the donor of increasing output of a particular charity depends, among other things, on whether donations are tax-deductible, and on that charity's efficiency in converting donations into charitable output (as shown by the proportions of total expenditure devoted to fundraising and administration). But as explained earlier, given the dominant role of the Community Chest of Singapore in the charitable sector, fundraising for the member charities has a rather ambiguous meaning. Instead, we derive a measure of price of giving to a charity that depends mainly on whether donations are tax-deductible, and on the proportion of its donations received indirectly through the Community Chest.

In Singapore, donations to organizations with IPC (Institution of Public Character) status are tax-deductible. Contributions to the Community Chest are also tax-deductible, regardless whether the donations are not

---

[8] Throughout this article, all values are expressed in Singapore dollars. One US dollar was approximately equal to two Singapore dollars over the period under study.

earmarked, earmarked for an IPC member organization or earmarked for a non-IPC (nondeductible) organization. In all the cases just mentioned, the price of giving is $1 - t$ where t is the marginal tax rate. But our data are not classified according to donors' income brackets, and thus we have to replace t by t_a, the average tax rate on income. The latter is computed by dividing the total income tax assessed in a given year by total assessable income.[9] This is admittedly a rather crude measure, but since we have time series data for the organizations, the effect of taxes on the price of giving is still captured to some extent as t_a changes over time.

In the regressions for total donations (TD), the price of donation is $1 - t_a$. This is because whether the individual gives directly to the organization or indirectly through the Community Chest, the contribution is tax-deductible. For non-IPC organizations, this price is calculated as a weighted average of the prices of giving through the Community Chest (tax-deductible and thus price = $1 - t_a$) and of giving directly to the organization (nondeductible and thus price = 1). The formula is $P = (F/TD)(1 - t_a) + (DD/TD)1$. Note that the weights are the shares of allocations to the organization through the Community Chest (F) and direct donations to the organization (DD) in total donations (TD).[10]

---

[9] The total income tax assessed and total assessable income include those of individuals (e.g., employees, self-proprietors, and partners) as well as corporations.

[10] It may be noted that P is the actual implicit price of giving and different individuals may perceive this price differently. It may be asked, for example, why some people should give to the Community Chest instead of directly to member organizations which already have IPC status. Since in fact many people give to the Community Chest without earmarking their donations to any particular charity, it may be that some individuals are truly indifferent about where their contributions go and are just interested in giving to a general cause. They may believe in the superior information and judgement of the Community Chest in allocating funds to the worthy organizations. Alternatively, they may believe that even if they earmark their donations or give directly to the member organizations, the Community Chest can offset their contributions so that the final outcome is not affected. A second question which may be raised is why should some people give directly to non-IPC organizations which are members of the Community Chest at a higher price rather than indirectly through the Chest (which is tax-deductible). One possible explanation is that these individuals have a strong liking for the specific purposes and characteristics of these organizations and believe that the Community Chest would not offset their contributions completely by allocating less funds to them.

For regressions with direct donations (DD) as the dependent variable, it is more straightforward. The price of giving to organizations with IPC status is $1 - t_a$, and to those without IPC status is 1.

Dummy variables for organization type (M, D_1, D_2, D_3, D_4)

Since members of the Community Chest have to operate under certain rules, their ability to raise donations and to convert them into charitable services may differ from that of non-members. Due to the Community Chest's advantage in fundraising, member organizations are likely to receive greater total donations although they generally cannot engage in independent fundraising. Also, the Community Chest's surveillance over the activities of its members may also help to increase donors' confidence in their efficiency. On the other hand, donations may be lower if donors are unhappy about the package of charitable services provided by the Chest. Thus we use the dummy variable M (set equal to 1 if the organization is a member of the Community Chest and 0 otherwise) to test for difference between member and non-member charities in their ability to raise donations.[11]

Similarly, since charitable organizations providing different types of services may differ in size and other characteristics, their ability to raise funds may also differ. Thus we introduce another set of 0–1 dummy variables denoting the type of service provided by the organization. In defining these dummy variables, the organizations providing services for children and youth are used as the base. The dummy variables are: D_1 for organizations providing services for the aged, D_2 for those providing health services, D_3 for those caring for the disabled, and D_4 for those providing family services.

Variables of government crowding-out (E, g)

As discussed earlier, an increase in government spending on social services may result in a reduction in private charitable donations. Generally,

---

[11] Other than the Community Chest of Singapore, the only other important fundraising body is the Children Charities Association, of which seven charities were members in the period under study. For simplicity we treat them analytically in the same way as Community Chest members.

this crowding-out is more likely, the greater is the substitutability between government output and the goods purchased by charitable giving. It is recognized (e.g., Driessen, 1985; Schiff, 1990) that government and charitable goods may also be complements. For example, increased public spending in the social welfare context may help to advertise particular concerns and attract greater non-profit provision. In that case, private donations may increase at the same time.

Government grants and subsidies to non-profit organizations generally have effects quite different from those of direct provision of social services by the government. Untied government grants are more or less perfect substitutes for private donations and tend to cause more crowding-out than government provision of social services.[12] But in practice grants often come with strings attached. Rose-Ackerman (1986) has analyzed various situations in which government grants may either increase or reduce private giving. A large government grant may enable a charity to increase significantly the number of clients served and reap economies of scale. The resulting improvement in efficiency in producing charitable output tends to encourage donations. Government grants to charities may require them to move toward a given ideology or alter the nature of their outputs, and if donors agree with the government's ideology giving would again increase. (Of course, if donors disagree with the government's ideology they may divert their giving to other charities.) Lastly, in accepting grants from the government, charities also accept its monitoring of their activities. If donors lack information about the charities, they may interpret government support as a "seal of approval" of their quality and increase their giving.[13]

Empirical studies have suggested that different types of government spending can affect charitable contributions differently. Schiff (1985; 1990) found that in the USA, while cash transfers to the poor cause crowding-out, other types of welfare spending, including government support of the charitable sector tend to encourage donations. In view of this,

---

[12] Rose-Ackerman (1987) also argued that untied government grants can enable charities to lower their fundraising activities and reduce dependence on solicitation of donors who do not share the charity managers' ideologies and preferences. An implication of this result is that cuts in public support may induce charities to pay closer attention to donors' wishes.

[13] See Schiff (1990) and Rose-Ackerman (1986; 1987) for detailed discussions of these issues.

we use two variables to test for crowding-out. The first (E) is government recurrent expenditure on health and social and community services including family services and welfare services. The second is government grants and subsidies to the charity (g). Since government subvention is often on a per beneficiary basis, we express g in per capita terms.

Number of staff employed by the organization (N)

Weinblatt (1992) argued that economies of scale may exist in charitable contributions. Large non-profit organizations may find it easier to raise donations because they are perceived to be more trustworthy than smaller ones. Also, the larger organizations may be perceived to be more efficiently and tightly administered and subject to more rigorous public control, so that the probability of misuse of funds is lower. Weinblatt used total expenditure of non-profit organizations in a given sector (e.g., health, education) to measure the effect of an organization's volume of activity in a given field on the private donations it receives. He recognized, however, that there could be a causality problem between total expenditure and donations received by the organization. In our study, the use of total expenditure as the explanatory variable is clearly inappropriate, since at the individual organization level it must be strongly related to the amount of donations received. Thus instead we use the number of staff employed by the charity as a measurement of its size. Also, it may be argued that for any given type of charitable activity, organizations employing more staff are able to serve more beneficiaries, and thus tend to receive more donations.

Age of organization (A)

Hansmann (1987) has noted the informational asymmetries between non-profit organizations and donors. These institutions are in a better position than donors in judging the quality and quantity of outputs. Since donors do not receive the outputs they help provide, they typically rely on the organizations for information. As in Weisbrod and Dominguez (1986) and Posnett and Sandler (1989), we use the age since founding of the charity (A) as a proxy for its reputation and quality of output. For example, donors may be more willing to give to the older charities which have built up a stock of goodwill or trust over the years, and are believed to be more reliable and better managed.

Other income (y)

This refers to income of the charity from sources other than donations and government subsidies. It includes program fees, membership fees, interest and investment income, and gains from sales of assets. It may be argued that income earned through sales and other activities, just like government grants and subsidies, can have a crowding-out effect on private donations. But the coefficient for this variable may also be positive. Cornes and Sandler (1984) and Posnett and Sandler (1986), for example, argued that charities often produce outputs with both private and public characteristics. The income from the sale of a private good may be used by the charity to finance its general operation, including the provision of its public output. In that situation, income from other sources actually augments the charity's ability to attract donations. It may also be argued that other income acts in a way like age in providing information to potential donors about the reputation of the organization. Just like government grants and subsidies (which are often given on a per beneficiary basis), this variable is expressed in per capita terms because of the lack of data for beneficiaries.[14]

Time trend (T)

A time trend has been included to take into account various factors affecting donations which may have changed over time. Other variables have also been tried in the regressions but their explanatory powers were found to be rather low.

Data set and estimation

The data set on individual charitable organizations in Singapore is the outcome of a research project funded by the National University of

---

[14] In our notation, variables in per capita terms are shown by lower case letters. They are government grants and subsidies to the charity (g) and other income (y).

Singapore. Research assistants were sent to the various charitable organizations to examine and extract data from their audited accounts. In general we have been able to obtain data for the period 1980 to 1989 from 67 charitable organizations under the Singapore Council of Social Service. Practically all charitable organizations under the Council were included in the sample. Data on direct and total donations and government grants and subsidies to the organizations, and other income are all obtained in this manner. The number of observations sometimes varies slightly among organizations because some organizations were formed after 1989, and for a few organizations data for one or two years are missing because the accounts could not be located for various reasons. The data on the number of staff employed by the organizations are obtained from the Directory of Social Services of the SCSS. Data on government expenditures on health and social and community services are obtained from the *Yearbook of Statistics Singapore*. Data on total income tax assessed and assessable income are obtained from various issues of *Inland Revenue Department Annual Report*. All monetary values have been converted to 1989 prices using the consumer price index.

Overall the data set is of good quality and covers practically all charitable organizations of any importance in Singapore. It is the first of its kind being compiled for Singapore, and to the best of our knowledge, for any developing country. It would be interesting to see how our results compare with those of similar studies in the developed countries.

Since we have time series data for the individual organizations over the period 1980–1989, we combine the data and adopt a pooling methodology in estimating the total donations and direct donations functions. For the full sample there are a total of 472 observations. We also run separate regressions for the member organizations of the Community Chest (178 observations) and non-members (294 observations) in order to see if there is any difference in giving behavior. The estimates of parameters from ordinary least squares (OLS) regressions are shown in Table 1 (total donations) and Table 2 (direct donations). Note that since for non-members direct donations are the same as total donations, the results for these organizations are not shown in Table 2 for direct donations.[15]

---

[15] Two observations have zero direct donations and are therefore dropped in estimating the direct donations functions with lnDD as the dependent variable (Table 2).

Table 1. Coefficient estimates of total donations function (dependent variable lnTD): Ordinary least squares (OLS) and weighted least squares (WLS) results

	Full Sample		Members of Community Chest of Singapore		Non-Members	
	OLS (1)	WLS (2)	OLS (3)	WLS (4)	OLS (5)	WLS (6)
Const.	−2.906		5.769		−3.344	
	(2.249)		(3.620)		(2.764)	
b_0/s_j		−3.203		4.210		−3.200
		(2.130)		(3.500)		(2.597)
D_1	0.043	0.053	−0.054	−0.063	0.076	0.098
	(0.152)	(0.147)	(0.275)	(0.279)	(0.186)	(0.191)
D_2	0.544*	0.552*	0.793*	0.798*	0.394*	0.394*
	(0.137)	(0.127)	(0.201)	(0.193)	(0.176)	(0.157)
D_3	0.688*	0.696*	0.170	0.190	0.898*	0.900*
	(0.154)	(0.129)	(0.225)	(0.194)	(0.190)	(0.157)
D_4	0.157	0.181	0.578*	0.598*	−0.239	−0.248
	(0.139)	(0.157)	(0.195)	(0.203)	(0.176)	(0.200)
M	0.493*	0.383*				
	(0.102)	(0.096)				
lnP	−1.993*	−1.866*	−4.991*	−4.383*	−1.006	−0.857
	(0.597)	(0.569)	(1.167)	(1.138)	(0.671)	(0.636)
lnN	0.429*	0.453*	0.202*	0.215*	0.483*	0.507*
	(0.045)	(0.041)	(0.073)	(0.070)	(0.059)	(0.055)
A	0.009*	0.009*	0.002	0.003	0.011*	0.010*
	(0.002)	(0.002)	(0.004)	(0.003)	(0.003)	(0.003)
lnE	−0.271	−0.217	−1.645*	−1.367*	−0.227	−0.251
	(0.428)	(0.406)	(0.675)	(0.654)	(0.530)	(0.499)
y	−0.248	−0.315	3.683*	3.651*	−0.481*	−0.485*
	(1.149)	(1.113)	(1.144)	(1.215)	(0.155)	(0.111)
g	−0.525	−0.597	1.900	1.890	−2.546	−3.650*
	(1.229)	(1.077)	(1.326)	(1.255)	(2.017)	(1.653)
T	−0.04	−0.008	−0.097*	−0.089*	0.029	0.023
	(0.020)	(0.019)	(0.028)	(0.027)	(0.025)	(0.024)
No. obs	472.000	472.000	178.000	178.000	294.000	294.000
F	24.425	249.134	10.936	115.479	22.760	189.243
R^2	0.390	0.876	0.420	0.893	0.470	0.890
Adj. R^2	0.374	0.872	0.382	0.885	0.450	0.885
Breusch-Pagan	46.783	17.956	24.964	18.612	36.155	3.399

Notes: Standard errors are in parentheses

*Significant at 0.05 level or better

Table 2. Coefficient estimates of direct donation functions (dependent variable lnDD): Ordinary least squares (OLS) and weighted least squares (WLS) results

	Full Sample		Members of Community Chest of Singapore	
	OLS (1)	WLS (2)	OLS (3)	WLS (4)
Const.	−2.197		10.591*	
	(2.656)		(4.958)	
b_0/s_j		−2.127		6.234
		(2.429)		(4.394)
D_1	0.337	0.360*	0.715	0.822*
	(0.182)	(0.170)	(0.400)	(0.413)
D_2	0.674*	0.695*	1.127*	1.252*
	(0.164)	(0.150)	(0.293)	(0.271)
D_3	0.807*	0.842*	0.318	0.431
	(0.184)	(0.152)	(0.329)	(0.274)
D_4	0.164	0.177	0.569*	0.612
	(0.166)	(0.199)	(0.285)	(0.320)
M	−0.339*	−0.396*		
	(0.120)	(0.109)		
lnP	−2.789*	−2.513*	−6.987*	−5.493*
	(0.664)	(0.618)	(1.230)	(1.130)
lnN	0.439*	0.441*	0.128	0.105
	(0.053)	(0.046)	(0.106)	(0.086)
A	0.013*	0.015*	0.010*	0.014*
	(0.003)	(0.003)	(0.005)	(0.005)
lnE	−0.415	−0.429	−2.632*	−1.860*
	(0.505)	(0.463)	(0.914)	(0.815)
y	−0.298	−0.372*	6.449*	6.278*
	(0.177)	(0.125)	(1.666)	(1.779)
g	−0.921	−0.967	0.504	0.256
	(1.467)	(1.207)	(1.923)	(1.513)
T	−0.048*	−0.046*	−0.214*	−0.186
	(0.024)	(0.021)	(0.041)	(0.036)
No. obs.	470.000	470.000	176.000	176.000
F	23.062	240.909	15.165	21.903
R^2	0.377	0.873	0.504	0.899
Adj. R^2	0.361	0.869	0.471	0.892
Breusch-Pagan	86.514	38.185	24.777	18.260

Notes: Standard errors are in parentheses

*Significant at 0.05 level or better

The fits of the OLS regressions are generally good but the Breusch-Pagan statistics indicate the presence of heteroscedasticity. We have tried to correct for this by the method of weighted least squares (WLS). We first divide the organizations into five groups according to the types of social services provided and then compute for each group s_j ($j = 1, 2, \ldots 5$), the standard error of the regression for that group under OLS.[16] Dividing through the original equation by s_j, we obtain the following equation based on the transformed data:

$$\ln TD/s_j \text{ (or } \ln DD/s_j) = b_0/s_j + b_1(D_1/s_j) + b_2(D_2/s_j) + b_3(D_3/s_j) + b_4(D_4/s_j)$$
$$+ b_5(M/s_j) + b_6(\ln P/s_j) + b_7(\ln N/s_j) + b8(A/s_j)$$
$$+ b_9(\ln E/s_j) + b_{10}(y/s_j) + b_{11}(g/s_j) + b_{12}(T/s_j)$$

which is then estimated without a constant term. The coefficient estimates under WLS are also shown in the same tables. Our discussion will be based mainly on the WLS estimates, but in general they do not change the qualitative nature of the results.

Empirical results and implications

From the regression results, it is immediately seen that both the types of services provided by the charitable organizations and membership in the Community Chest have significant effects on donations. The coefficients for the dummy variables D_2 and D_3 are positive and highly significant for both the total donations and direct donations functions. For direct donations, the coefficient for D_1 (services for the aged) is also positive and significant. The magnitudes of the coefficients indicate that organizations providing health services and services for the disabled tend to receive more donations than those providing other services. These results are due largely to the different types of activities these charities specialize in, and will not be discussed further.

---

[16] The classification of organizations according to the types of services has been provided by the Singapore Council of Social Service. The types of services are: services for the aged, health services, services for the disabled, family services, and services for children and youth. Note that we have earlier used the same classification in the definition of dummy variables.

More interesting, however, are the coefficients for M, the dummy variable for membership in the Community Chest. This coefficient is positive and significant for total donations, but negative and significant for direct donations. These results are to be expected since total donations also include allocations of funds to the organization by the Community Chest. Direct donations tend to be lower for member organizations of the Community Chest because they are not usually allowed to solicit funds on their own. But because of the advantage of the Community Chest in fundraising — due, for example, to the economizing of fundraising costs by a united fund drive and its access to the payroll deduction system through the SHARE Program — the total volume of funds raised, and thus total donations received by member organizations tend to be higher. While some donors may be concerned with the possible loss of sovereignty over the allocation of their gifts, others may believe in the superior judgement of the Chest in its allocation of funds to the various charities. Our results are consistent with the hypothesis of the greater efficiency of the Community Chest in fundraising.

The price of donations is one of main variables of interest in our study. Despite the rather imperfect nature of our price measure, its coefficients in the full sample regressions are highly significant for both the total donations and direct donations functions. In both cases the elasticities are quite high — in the neighborhood of -2 for total donations and -2.5 for direct donations. For member organizations of the Community Chest, the elasticities are even higher — about -4.4 for total donations and -5.5 for direct donations. Thus in general donors are very sensitive to the price of donations in allocating their contributions among charities.

But for non-member organizations, the price elasticity of donations is much lower (around -1) and the coefficients are not significant. One possible explanation is that charities may be viewed as providing differentiated outputs. Since non-member organizations do not have the benefit of the Chest's fund drives, the very fact that some people give directly to them suggests that they may know these organizations well and have a strong liking for their purposes and characteristics. In such cases, donations are likely to less sensitive to price changes. On the other hand, one would expect the reputation or stock of goodwill accumulated by these organizations to be important. This explanation is supported by our results, since (as will be seen later) the age since founding of the organization is not a significant variable in explaining total donations to member organizations of the Community Chest, but is highly significant in explaining donations to non-members.

In general, our results indicate donations to be quite elastic to price, especially for member organizations of the Community Chest. Thus lowering the price of giving can be a effective means to increase private donations. This result is encouraging since the government is withdrawing from providing direct welfare services, thus putting pressure on charitable organizations and fundraising bodies like the Community Chest to increase funding. The price of giving may be reduced, for example, through tax incentives to potential donors. Also, the literature suggests that the price that donors really care about may be the price of providing actual charitable output, and this price can be lowered through greater efficiency in fundraising and in the provision of social services.

The coefficients for staff size ($\ln N$) are found to be positive and highly significant for total donations for the full sample as well as for members and non-members of the Community Chest individually. (For direct donations, the coefficient remains positive but is not significant for member organizations.) A larger staff size, for example, may enable an organization to serve more clients or beneficiaries and thus reap economies of scale, and the resulting increase in efficiency may attract more donations. Alternatively, as Weinblatt (1992) has suggested, donors may give more to larger organizations because the latter are believed to be more reliable and better managed. Still another possible implication, which is especially encouraging, is that when individuals perceive the need for funds by charitable organizations to increase their staff size in order to meet the rising demand for social services, they would readily respond by increasing their donations.

The age of the organization since founding (A) is found to have a positive and significant impact on donations for the full sample and for non-members of the Community Chest. For member organizations, its coefficient is significant for direct donations but not for total donations. This lends support to the view that donors do care about the quality of charitable output they help provide, and in the absence of good information may look upon the age of the organization as an indicator of its reliability and quality of output. The stock of goodwill accumulated (for which age may serve as a proxy) is especially important for non-member organizations. For member organizations, the Community Chest's monitoring of their activities may help to some extent in assuring donors of their efficiency, but age (which reflects the reputation of the organization) is still significant in affecting direct donations. Age is not significant in affecting total donations, because the latter also include allocations of funds from the Community Chest, which are often determined by the financial situation and needs of the organizations.

We next examine the implications of our results on the crowding-out hypothesis. The coefficients for government expenditures on health and social services ($\ln E$) are negative throughout for both the total donations and direct donations functions, but are significant only in the regressions for members of the Community Chest. Thus government spending tends to have a significant effect in crowding out private contributions to member charities but not those to non-member charities. One explanation for this result relies again on the view that charities are producing differentiated outputs. In joining the Community Chest, the activities of the member charities are subject to its monitoring. Therefore, the fact that many organizations are members suggests that they have a more or less common ideology and purpose and their outputs tend to be relatively homogeneous for any given line of activity.[17] In such a situation, it is likely that government spending is a closer substitute for charitable outputs produced by member charities than those produced by non-member charities. For example, some non-member charities may produce outputs with characteristics not emphasized by the others, but which some donors may prefer. In this case, crowding-out is less likely. As for government grants and subsidies (g), they appear to crowd out private donations only for non-member charities. It may be argued that non-member charities which receive government grants and subsidies tend to produce outputs which are closer substitutes for government output and thus crowding-out occurs. The same argument should apply to member charities but the effects may have been obscured by the allocation of funds from the Chest.

---

[17] Rose-Ackerman (1982) argued that united charities realize their fundraising advantages by providing an ideologically homogeneous package of charities. Ideological differences among member organizations in a united charity are unlikely to be great, or otherwise people will give directly to member charities (and to non-member charities) whose output characteristics they prefer.

It may be noted that while there is some evidence of crowding-out in our study, the implied magnitudes are rather small. As noted by Weinblatt (1992), partial crowding-out suggests that individuals and the government consider themselves as jointly responsible for providing social services.

Income from other sources (y) has a significant negative effect on direct donations but not on total donations. Moreover, it has a significant positive effect on donations to members of Community Chest but a significant negative effect on donations to non-members. As discussed earlier, the sign of this coefficient may be negative or positive: higher income from other sources may cause a charity to depend less on donations, but may also increase its ability to attract donations. What causes the difference in results for member and non-member charities is, however, not immediately clear. Lastly, the trend term (T), which is used to pick up the effects of unidentified factors affecting donations that have changed over time, has negative and significant coefficients for direct donations, and also for total donations in the case of Community Chest members.

The results obtained in our study are plausible and are fairly consistent with those of earlier studies. Thus in the case of Singapore, donations to charitable organizations appear to be influenced by the same set of factors as in the case of the developed countries.

Summary and conclusions

In this study, we have conducted regression analysis based on cross-section and time series data to examine the factors determining the demand for donations to charitable organizations in Singapore, a rapid-growing newly-industrializing country. The results indicate that, as in the case of the USA and other developed nations, donations to charitable organizations in Singapore are sensitive to the price of giving and characteristics of the organizations such as their size and age. There also appears to be evidence that government expenditures on social services, and to a lesser extent government grants and subsidies, have some crowding-out effect on private donations.

In the case of Singapore, the government has decided to rely on community organizations and voluntary bodies to play the major role in caring for the needy. The Community Chest of Singapore has played an important role in the charitable sector in raising funds for its member organizations. It is often believed that a united charity like the Community Chest can help to economize on fundraising costs by reducing competition among the member charities, and may also possess other advantages in fundraising — such as access to the payroll deduction system through the SHARE Program. The Chest's monitoring of the activities of its members may also help to increase donors' confidence in their efficiency. All these favorable factors tend to raise the total volume of donations to the combined charity. The results of this paper are consistent with these hypotheses.

In Singapore, the tax-deductibility of charitable contributions has been an important policy instrument to encourage private giving. The results of this study indicate that donors are very responsive to the price of giving in allocating their gifts among charitable organizations. Thus lowering the price of giving — for example through tax incentives to potential donors — can be a very effective means to raise private donations. The price of giving can also be lowered by granting tax-deductibility of contributions to more charitable organizations, and by increasing the convenience in giving — for example, through further popularization of the SHARE Program. Also, the literature suggests that the price that donors really care about is the price of providing actual charitable output, and this price can be reduced through greater efficiency in fundraising and in the provision of social services.

The findings of high price elasticity of donations and of partial crowding-out effect of government expenditure on private donations have important policy implications, in view of the fact that the government is withdrawing from the direct provision of welfare services, and has recently increased its efforts to encourage private donations to the charitable cause. The evidence of partial crowding-out suggests that in Singapore, individuals and the government consider themselves as jointly responsible for the provision of social services. Since donors are quite responsive to tax and other incentives, it would be quite feasible for the government to use these measures to encourage private donations and rely on charitable organizations to play a larger role in the provision of social services. The evidence suggests that when the public perceive the greater need for funds by these organizations to meet the rising demand for social services, they would readily respond by increasing their donations.

References

Abrams, B.A. and Schmitz, M.D. (1978), "The 'crowding-out' effect of governmental transfers on private charitable contributions", *Public Choice*, Vol. 33 No. 1, pp. 29–39.

Abrams, B.A. and Schmitz, M.D. (1984), "The crowding-out effect of governmental transfers on private charitable contributions: cross-section evidence", *National Tax Journal*, Vol. 37 No. 4, pp. 563–8.

Bilodeau, M. (1992), "Voluntary contributions to united charities", *Journal of Public Economics*, Vol. 48 No. 1, June, pp. 119–33.

Boskin, M.J. and Feldstein, M. (1977), "Effects of the charitable deduction on contributions by low income and middle income households: evidence from the national survey of philanthropy", *Review of Economics and Statistics*, Vol. 59 No. 3, August, pp. 351–4.

Clotfelter, C.T. (1980), "Tax incentives and charitable giving: evidence from a panel of taxpayers", *Journal of Public Economics*, Vol. 13 No. 3, pp. 319–40.

Clotfelter, C.T. (1985), *Federal Tax Policy and Charitable Giving*, The University of Chicago Press, Chicago, IL, and London.

Cornes, R. and Sandler, T. (1984), "Easy riders, joint production and public goods", *The Economic Journal*, Vol. 94 No. 375, September, pp. 580–98.

Driessen, P.A. (1985), "Comment on 'the crowding-out' effect of governmental transfers on private charitable contributions", *National Tax Journal*, Vol. 38 No. 4, December, pp. 571–3.

Feldstein, M. (1975), "The income tax and charitable contributions: part I — aggregate and distributional effects", *National Tax Journal*, Vol. 28 No. 1, March, pp. 81–100.

Feldstein, M. and Clotfelter, C. (1976), "Tax incentives and charitable contributions in the United States", *Journal of Public Economics*, Vol. 5 No. 1–2, January–February, pp. 1–26.

Feldstein, M. and Taylor, A. (1997), "The income tax and charitable contributions", *Econometrica*, Vol. 44 No. 6, November, pp. 1201–22.

Fisher, F.M. (1977), "On donor sovereignty and united charities", *American Economic Review*, Vol. 67 No. 4, September, pp. 632–8.

Glenday, G., Gupta, A.K. and Pawlak, H. (1986), "Tax incentives for personal charitable contributions", *Review of Economics and Statistics*, Vol. 68 No. 4, November, pp. 688–93.

Hansmann, H. (1987), "Economic theories of nonprofit organization" in Powell, W.W. (Ed.), *The Nonprofit Sector: A Research Handbook*, Yale University Press, New Haven and London, pp. 27–42.

Jencks, C. (1987), "Who gives to what?", in Powell, W.W. (Ed.), *The Nonprofit Sector: A Research Handbook*, Yale University Press, New Haven and London, pp. 321–39.

Jones, A. and Posnett, J. (1991), "Charitable donations by UK households: evidence from the family expenditure survey", *Applied Economics*, Vol. 23 No. 2, February, pp. 343–51.

Jones, P.R. (1983), "Aid to charities", *International Journal of Social Economics*, Vol. 10 No. 2, pp. 3–11.

Keating, B., Pitts, R. and Appel, D. (1981), "United way contributions: Coercion, charity or economic self-interest?", *Southern Economic Journal*, Vol. 47 No. 3, January, pp. 816–23.

Kitchen, H. (1992), "Determinants of charitable donations in Canada: a comparison over time", *Applied Economics*, Vol. 24 No. 7, July, pp. 709–13.

Kitchen, H. and Dalton, R. (1990), "Determinants of charitable donations by families in Canada: a regional analysis", *Applied Economics*, Vol. 22 No. 3, March, pp. 285–99.

Lim, C.Y. et al. (1988), *Policy Options for the Singapore Economy*, McGraw-Hill Book Company, Singapore.

Posnett, J. and Sandler, T. (1986), "Joint supply and the finance of charitable activity", *Public Finance Quarterly*, Vol. 14 No. 2, April, pp. 209–22.

Posnett, J. and Sandler, T. (1989), "Demand for charity donations in private non-profit markets: the case of the UK", *Journal of Public Economics*, Vol. 40 No. 2, November, pp. 187–220.

Roberts, R.D. (1984), "A positive model of private charity and public transfers", *Journal of Political Economy*, Vol. 92 No. 1, February, pp. 136–48.

Rose-Ackerman, S. (1982), "Charitable giving and 'excessive' fundraising", *Quarterly Journal of Economics*, Vol. 97 No. 2, May, pp. 193–212.

Rose-Ackerman, S. (1986), "Do government grants to charity reduce private donations?", in Rose-Ackerman, S. (Ed.), *The Economics of Nonprofit Institutions: Studies in Structure and Policy*, Oxford University Press, New York, NY, pp. 312–29.

Rose-Ackerman, S. (1987), "Ideals versus dollars: donors, charity managers, and government grants", *Quarterly Journal of Economics*, Vol. 95 No. 4, August, pp. 810–23.

Schiff, J. (1985), "Does government spending crowd out charitable contributions?", *National Tax Journal*, Vol. 38 No. 4, pp. 535–46.

Schiff, J. (1990), *Charitable Giving and Government Policy*, Greenwood Press, Inc., Westport, Ct.

Steinberg, R. (1985), "Empirical relations between government spending and charitable donations", *Journal of Voluntary Action Research*, Vol. 14 Nos. 2–3, April–September, pp. 54–64.

Steinberg, R. (1986), "Should donors care about fundraising?", in Rose-Ackerman, S. (Ed.), *The Economics of Nonprofit Institutions: Studies in Structure and Policy*, Oxford University Press, New York, NY, pp. 347–64.

Steinberg, R. (1987), "Nonprofit organizations and the market", in Powell, W.W. (Ed.), *The Nonprofit Sector: A Research Handbook*, Yale University Press, New Haven, CT and London, pp. 118–38.

Warr, P.G. (1982), "Pareto optimal redistribution and private charity", *Journal of Public Economics*, Vol. 19 No. 1, October, pp. 131–8.

Weinblatt, J. (1992), "Do government transfers crowd out private transfers to non-profit organizations? The Israeli experience", *International Journal of Social Economics*, Vol. 19 No. 2, pp. 60–66.

Weisbrod, B.A. (1988), *The Nonprofit Economy*. Harvard University Press, Cambridge, MA.

Weisbrod, B.A. and Dominguez, N.D. (1986), "Demand for collective goods in private non-profit markets: can fundraising expenditures help overcome free-rider behavior?", *Journal of Public Economics*, Vol. 30 No. 1, June, pp. 83–95.

Yap, M.T. (Ed.) (1991), *Social Services: The Next Lap*, Times Academic Press, Singapore.

This article has been cited by:

1. Abd Halim Mohd Noor, Nurul Amyra Mat Isa, Hamidah Muhd Irpan, Hasan Bahrom, Arifin Md Salleh, Abdul Rahim Ridzuan. Does Performance and Transparency Matter to Individual Donors' Giving in Malaysia? 3–12. [Crossref]
2. Qianhua Ling, Daniel Gordon Neely. 2013. Charitable ratings and financial reporting quality: Evidence from the human service sector. *Journal of Public Budgeting, Accounting & Financial Management* **25**:1, 69–90. [Abstract] [PDF]
3. René Bekkers, Pamala Wiepking. 2011. A Literature Review of Empirical Studies of Philanthropy. *Nonprofit and Voluntary Sector Quarterly* **40**:5, 924–973. [Crossref]
4. Teresa P. Gordon, Cathryn L. Knock, Daniel G. Neely. 2009. The role of rating agencies in the market for charitable contributions: An empirical test. *Journal of Accounting and Public Policy* **28**:6, 469–484. [Crossref]

5. M.B. Gutiérrez Villar, R.A. Araque Padilla, M.J. Montero Simó. 2009. LA CAPTACIÓN DE RECURSOS PRIVADOS ENTRE LAS ONGD ESPAÑOLAS: UNA APROXIMACIÓN PROBABILÍSTICA. *Investigaciones Europeas de Dirección y Economía de la Empresa* **15**:3, 15–31. [Crossref]
6. Rodoula Tsiotsou. 2007. An empirically based typology of intercollegiate athletic donors: High and low motivation scenarios. *Journal of Targeting, Measurement and Analysis for Marketing* **15**:2, 79–92. [Crossref]
7. Erik Schokkaert. Chapter 2 The Empirical Analysis of Transfer Motives 127–181. [Crossref]
8. Marc Bilodeau, Richard Steinberg. Chapter 19 Donative nonprofit organizations 1271–1333. [Crossref]
9. J. Mark Schuster. Chapter 36 Tax Incentives in Cultural Policy 1253–1298. [Crossref]
10. Richard Steinberg, Burton A. Weisbrod. 2005. Nonprofits with distributional objectives: price discrimination and corner solutions. *Journal of Public Economics* **89**:11–12, 2205–2230. [Crossref]
11. Vincent C.H. Chua, Chung Ming Wong. 2003. The Role of United Charities in Fundraising: The Case of Singapore. *Annals of Public and Cooperative Economics* **74**:3, 433–464. [Crossref]
12. Katharina J. Srnka, Reinhard Grohs, Ingeborg Eckler. 2003. Increasing Fundraising Efficiency by Segmenting Donors. *Australasian Marketing Journal (AMJ)* **11**:1, 70–86. [Crossref]
13. David T. Owyong. 2000. Measuring the trickle-down effect: a case study on Singapore. *Applied Economics Letters* **7**:8, 535–539. [Crossref]
14. Vincent C.H. Chua, Chung Ming Wong. 1999. Tax incentives, individual characteristics and charitable giving in Singapore. *International Journal of Social Economics* **26**:12, 1492–1505. [Abstract] [Full Text] [PDF]

Chapter 18

Non-governmental organizations in Singapore and nation building: Some emerging trends and issues*

S. Vasoo and Mohd Maliki Osman[†]

This paper traces the development and role of the non-governmental organisations in nation building in Singapore. The authors argue that Singapore's social, economic and political environments influence the nature and functions of these organisations. From the colonial administration to self government and independence, the voluntary welfare sector have developed and established a tripartite relationship with the government and the relationship with the government and the private sector to provide an effective social service delivery system vis-à-vis a rapid nation building process. The future challenges and issues faced by these organisations in Singapore are also discussed.

---

*From Vasoo, S., & Osman, M. M. (2000). Non-governmental organizations in Singapore and nation building: Some emerging trends and issues. *Social Development Issues*, 22(2 & 3), 54–63. (United States). Copyright ©2000 by the International Consortium for Social Development (ICSD). Reprinted by permission of ICSD.

This paper traces the growth and development of Singapore's voluntary welfare sector, discussing some of the emerging trends and issues as well as the various challenges and problems confronting the sector.

[†]Department of Social Work and Psychology, National University of Singapore, 10 Kent Ridge Crescent, Singapore 119260

Introduction

Non-governmental organisations (NGOs) particularly those in the voluntary welfare sector play a significant role in the provision and delivery of social and welfare programmes for the disadvantaged groups and individuals in Singapore. This paper will discuss some of the emerging trends and issues affecting the voluntary welfare sector and its contribution to nation building. More specifically, the paper will trace the growth and development of Singapore's voluntary welfare sector which is a powerful base for mobilising people for voluntary work and to fund charitable causes. Also the various challenges and problems confronting the Singapore's voluntary welfare sector will be examined.

The rise of the voluntary welfare organisations

In the last six decades more formal voluntary welfare organisations have been established in Singapore (NCSS, 1998/99). A number of factors can account for such a conspicuous rise. Firstly, the increasing levels of socio-economic development in Singapore as well as the search for economic opportunities do contribute to more participation of people in various social and civic organisations. It has been observed that participation in social and political activities varies directly with social and economic progress (Weiner & Huntington, 1987; Randall, 1998). With increasing affluence and improved working conditions, more Singaporeans have increased leisure time. About half the working population have at least 14 hours of leisure per week and hence some of them channel their interests to voluntary activities. With the move towards the implementation of a five-day work week in some of the firms in the government and commercial sectors, one would expect the increase in volunteer participation. (Singh, Ong, Vasoo, 1997; Vasoo, 1998).

Secondly, the massive success in the resettlement and rehousing of Singaporeans in public housing estates is an international achievement and an important social landmark in solving the housing problem. About 87% of the population of 3.5 million people have been housed in the Housing and Development Board (HDB) flats (HDB, 1998/99). The relocation of people into new towns has brought about a total social transformation of living arrangements and social interaction patterns of people (Wong & Yeh, 1985; Pang, 1992; HDB, 1995) and has generated some social consequences. Besides improved physical and social environment, the feeling of alienation and anomie among residents, the breakdown of traditional helping networks, the weakening of family support system and the acceleration in nuclear family formation have become somewhat obvious in the urban housing estates. Concomitantly it has been observed (Taub, 1988) that in most modernised and urbanised communities, the growth of indigenous organisations would be slow and more often external agents or government would have to be engaged in sponsoring the establishment of intermediaries or formal social and welfare organisations to deal with various community issues and problems (Vasoo, 1994).

Thirdly, the budget of voluntary welfare organisations funded by the National Council of Social Service (NCSS) through the Community Chest of Singapore has increased steeply from $4 million in 1984 to $36.2 million in 1998 (NCSS Annual Report, 1984, 1998/99). In the last few years, competition for fund raising has become stiffer as many voluntary welfare organisations have been formed. Given the modest government subventions for voluntary welfare organisations, most organisations have to establish effective fund raising machinery to raise their funding requirements. Smaller voluntary welfare organisations face serious threats to survive because they are unable to compete to raise their charity dollar. As a consequence, they join the Chest to have better leverage to secure their funding requirements. Such a unified fund raising effort and its allocation policies do have impact on the development of social welfare service directions (NCSS Reports, 1983 to 1999).

Fourthly, an important national ethos on encouraging many helping hands to solve the problems of Singapore's disadvantaged groups does reinforce the tripartite nature of community problem solving which requires the involvement of the government, voluntary welfare groups and the private corporate sectors. Such an emphasis promotes community self-help and thereby prevents Singapore from moving into state welfarism which will in the long run cause dependency of voluntary welfare sector on the government for solving social and community ills. The voluntary welfare sector therefore works in partnership with both the governmental and corporate sectors to enhance community well being. This is a new development in community problemsolving as the underlying principle is to galvanize three key players to deal with various community concerns to forge an ownership to the problem. Normally, in many societies, the government is seen to be responsible for the ills of society and have to face the brunt. However, the ills of society cannot be solved by one key player alone and requires the partnership of the voluntary, corporate and government sectors and such an approach or model is being adopted in the Singapore context. This approach has helped to strengthen and facilitate the development of voluntary efforts and organizations.

While the above four factors could be seen to facilitate the formation of new voluntary welfare organisations, one factor has also been identified as affecting their ability to continue their existence. In the ensuing decades, many of the voluntary welfare organisations will be confronted very seriously with the greying of its leadership. Such a phenomenon does have ramifications for the dynamism and organisational responsiveness to deal with complex social issues, problems and demands. These organisations will become gerontocratic and could lead to organisational lethargy and parochialism. In order that they can contribute effectively to nation building, active plans for leadership and organisational renewal would have to be implemented. Although it cannot be ignored that older volunteer leaders do provide organisational wisdom, the viability and survival of organisations depend on the preparedness of the older leaders to induct and train the young to takeover the leadership in an orderly manner. With smooth transition of leadership, more younger and able professionals could be attracted to participate in voluntary activities.

The voluntary welfare sector: Growth and development

Singapore's clan and benevolent associations which formed a large bulk of the voluntary welfare sector in the eighteenth century, have been playing a very significant role in the delivery of social and welfare services to various client groups such as the disabled, aged poor and sick, children at risk, delinquents, the depressed and the disturbed and distressed families. The roles of these indigenous organisations have been influenced by social, political and economic changes between the period of colonial administration and independence of the city-state (Wee, 1983).

In fact, early immigrant leaders who saw the need to provide care and protection for migrant workers from China, India and Southeast Asian countries formed these indigenous non-governmental organisations in the eighteenth century. These organisations based on clan and lineage ties surfaced because of the *laissez faire* attitudes of the colonial administrators in the provision of services to assist the immigrants (Purcell, 1980; Cheng, 1990). Various ethnic communities established their own mutual help and support organisations which gave supportive services, namely financial assistance, accommodation, repatriation, job placements and advice (Wong, 1998). They also mediated with officials in event when the immigrants faced difficulties with the colonial bureaucracies. However, the colonial administrators were cautious in lending their support to make the indigenous organisations credible, as these officials were concerned that they would become political pressure group and anti-colonial movements (Cheng, 1990). The lack of endorsement and assistance by the colonial policy makers and administrators led to the gradual demise of many indigenous organisations which would otherwise have evolved into modernised organisations playing more relevant roles in community betterment in Singapore (Wong, 1998).

Besides the lack of enthusiastic support from the colonial administrators for the aforementioned indigenous organisations, it was noted that these organisations did not adapt quickly enough as Singapore began to modernise in the early twentieth century (Wong, 1998). Their leadership depended on traditional businessmen who were conservative. Not many changes were introduced in the organisations, which as a result became less effective channels for people to address their concerns. The younger Singaporeans having become more educated and egalitarian tended to be cynical about the efficiency of these indigenous organisations. Today some of these organisations are still operating marginally despite attempts being made to revitalise them (Vasoo, 1990, 1994).

With increasing tempo in Singapore's modernisation after the 1930s, the nature and types of social problems changed. These emerging social problems such as child labour, prostitution, destitution, drug addiction, divorces, child neglect, domestic violence and delinquency could not be tackled effectively by the indigenous organisations which lacked the resources and the organisational ability to meet the challenges. The colonial bureaucrats at that time felt that more non-sectarian and secular voluntary organisations have to be ushered to deal with the contemporary social problems. Such a thrust was thought to be feasible, as it would cater to specific client populations. As a consequence, between 1930 and 1970, there was an unprecedented growth in the number of secular formal voluntary organisations, which were affiliated to the then Singapore Council of Social Service, now known as the National Council of Social Service (NCSS).

The number of voluntary organisations affiliated to the NCSS have increased five-fold from 40 in 1960 to 207 today (NCSS, 1998/99). Of these affiliates, 50 organisations are funded by the Community Chest, which was set up in 1984 as a central fund raising body to meet the funding needs of charities. The voluntary welfare sectors activities are coordinated by NCSS, which is a national body through which the government communicates and interacts. The NCSS has over the years become a powerful and influential central machinery for encouraging citizen participation in voluntary work and influencing the delivery of social and welfare programmes.

The establishment of Community Chest under NCSS has given the voluntary welfare sector more concerted sense of purpose and direction in leading the voluntary organisations in Singapore (NCSS 1998/99). The Community Chest is now viable centralised machinery for fund raising. The number of charities supported by the Chest has increased from 18 in 1984 to 256 in 1999 (NCSS 1998/99). More than $250 million was raised since the inception of the Community Chest. The allocation to funded charities have increased each year and in 1998–99 about $36.2 million was disbursed to voluntary organisations serving the disabled ($21.8 million), the family ($3.3 million), children and youth ($2.4 million), the elderly ($3.8 million) and health and community needs ($4.9 million). The large disbursement was an accomplishment and indeed a good measure of public support for charitable activities (NCSS, 1998/99). It is very trying to raise such a large sum of funds but with the backing of many working Singaporeans, the funding targets set each year by the Chest have been realised and it reflects that Singaporeans do respond positively to play a role in community problem solving.

The development of Community Chest has attracted the involvement of many ordinary citizens and professionals in running the Chest and organising fund raising activities. Their active involvement has helped to widen the network of support from community groups, individuals and business enterprises. The continued existence of the Chest demands its ability to mobilise more workers to share the mission of the chest and to be able to witness that their monetary contributions are helping specific needy Singaporeans. It is therefore crucial for the Chest to be emplaced as a personable and helpful organisation, which engenders positive warmth for people making charitable contributions. Therefore any activities, which contribute to making the Chest impersonal, will erode its support base.

The Chest's main source of financial support comes from the most popular fund raising programme known as Social Help and Assistance Raised by Employees (SHARE). This method of raising fund is most innovative and cost-effective. Any working individuals can make monthly pledges through payroll, bank account or credit card deductions. In 1998 about $15.3 million was contributed by employees from 1773 firms, businesses, and industries (NCSS, 1998/99). The target of SHARE donors to reach is 400,000 and this represents about 25% of Singapore's working population (NCSS, 1996/97). There is still capacity to increase the SHARE donors and to achieve this, the Chest would have to plan a more personalised approach in reaching out to individuals in the various corporations by recruiting volunteer SHARE promoters at the different work settings.

Current services of the voluntary welfare sector

In Singapore, the voluntary welfare sector takes on the responsibility of providing services to overcome various human failures, which occur during different periods of life, particularly during childhood, adolescence and adulthood. The types of welfare services available are described briefly.

Welfare services for children

A great deal of work is being carried out by voluntary organisations for deprived children and the programmes are both preventive and remedial in nature. Children come into care because of different reasons. A child from a family may need care for a period while the mother is hospitalised for long term illness. Some may require institutionalisation because of desertion or death of parents and others may need specialised form of service for their behavioural problems.

The range of voluntary welfare services for children in Singapore includes:

(a) Counselling services:
These are services provided for children who present behavioural problems in their families. Organisations like the Singapore Children Society, the Children's Aid Society and the Students' Care Service are constantly being referred children who require counselling.

(b) Residential services:
Residential institutions cater for some children who are homeless through break up of their families because of divorce, separation, desertion or neglect. Residential institutions operated by the Salvation Army, Children Aid Society, Canossaville and others, continue to provide long and short term care for these group of children.

(c) Rehabilitative services for the handicapped
Children who are physically and mentally handicapped need special services, which will meet their needs. Many of them though limited by their physical and mental abilities can make remarkable progress and become useful members of society. A majority of the rehabilitative services are presently being undertaken by voluntary organisations. Associations like the Singapore Association for the Visually Handicapped, Singapore Association for the Hearing Impaired, Movement for the Intellectually Disabled of Singapore, Singapore Spastic Childrens Association, Red Cross Home for Disabled, the Bizlink provide facilities for care, training and employment of some of our physically and mentally handicapped children.

Welfare services for youth

More voluntary welfare organisations are assuming primary responsibility to provide welfare services for young people who require either guidance and advice or corrective training so that they can be helped to adapt in our society. These services can be primarily categorised into:

(a) Refractory children's service
Supervision and treatment of children and young persons who are found to be refractory are undertaken by some voluntary childrens organisations such as Singapore Children's Society and Marymount Vocational Centre. Counselling and guidance services are provided by these organisations.

(b) Residential services
Most of the residential services provided are for youths with behavioural difficulties. Some of them are Boys Town, Pertapis Home and Ramakrishna Mission Boys' Home.

Welfare services for adults

Some people are vulnerable to social problems when they are in their adulthood. The simple reason being, that they fail socially and personally to use resources in their environment; thus resulting in their inability to discharge their responsibilities. It is therefore necessary to provide some remedial and supportive welfare services to enable them to function effectively again.

Some of these services are:

(a) Counselling services
Social service centres, the Counselling and Care Centre and the Samaritans of Singapore, are providing some of the counselling programmes for adults who have personal and family problems.

(b) Residential services
Residential care for adults is primarily for those who are old and have no relatives to receive them. A wide range of residential services for the old are delivered by voluntary organisations such as the Little Sisters of the Poor, the Society of the Aged Sick, the St John's Home for the Aged, Villa Francis, Moral Home for the Aged Sick, Sree Narayana Home for the Aged Sick and other voluntary social and religious groups.

New developments in the voluntary welfare sector

In the recent years, further new developments have emerged in the voluntary welfare sector. Many new organisations are formed in response to the government's call for many helping hands in a coordinated effort at providing social services to the people. Such an emphasis helps to reach out further to families in need and others who remain isolated because of ignorance.

Development of Family Service Centres (FSCs)

Social service providers and community leaders have recently recognised that many problems encountered by individuals (e.g., drug abuse, school drop out, juvenile delinquency, divorce, destitution) have their roots in the family. The Committee on Destitute Families (1989) noted, "Destitution is a multi-causal phenomenon and would usually involve the interplay of many factors." In a survey of almost 200 families, the committee found that there were combinations of reasons that account for their respondents' destitution. These included family dysfunctions, irregular employment of heads of households, breadwinners admitted to prison or Drug Rehabilitation Centres (DRCs). A study by Yayasan MENDAKI (a local self help group) found that one-third of Malay drug addicts in Singapore were from broken homes with parents who were separated or divorce.

The Committee on Destitute Families was one of the three committees set up by the Advisory Council on Family and Community Life. The government set up the Council in 1989 to review the needs and aspirations of family and community. The second objective was to recommend policies and measures to enable Singaporeans to achieve a more satisfying family and community life (Advisory Council on Family and Community Life, 1989). The Council recognised that the family is the building block of society and thus every family unit should be preserved and kept strong, cohesive and supportive of its members.

Government policies have since been targeted at strengthening the family as a unit. In 1993 the government introduced the Small Families Improvement Scheme, to assist low-income families get out of the poverty cycle. One of the criteria of eligibility and continued participation in the scheme is that the family must stay intact. In 1994 the government introduced schemes that will "channel rights, and benefits and privileges, through the head so that he can enforce the obligations and responsibilities of family members" (National Day Rally, 1994). There are also other governmental policies relating to health and housing that aim at strengthening the family unit.

One of the key recommendations of the Advisory Council on Family and Community Life was the establishment of Family Service Centres (FSCs) in major housing estates to provide a wide range of family-oriented social services for the community.

The Council explained:

> We should strive to provide more family support service at the community level to help families cope with their family responsibilities and problems. We should mobilise the community to implement more preventive and developmental programmes for low income families in public housing estates. (Advisory Council on Family and Community Life, 1989, p. 28)

The FSC is to be a one-stop social service centre with easy access for the family. Following the above recommendations, the then Ministry of Community Development [recently named Ministry of Community Development and Sports (MCDS)], together with some voluntary and grassroots organisations set up 4 pilot FSCs from 1990 to 1992.

The National Council of Social Service (NCSS) describes the FSC as:

> a community-based centre, which provides integrated remedial, preventive and developmental services to help families cope with their responsibilities and problems. By making services accessible at the community level, it is hoped to develop families' resources, build community and support and responsibility and forestall problem by encouraging families to seek help early. (NCSS, 1994)

Following an evaluation of the performance of the four pilot FSCs by an MCDS appointed consultant, a tripartite relationship was established to facilitate the setting up and monitoring of more FSCs in major housing estates. MCDS will provide the funding for FSCs. This comes in the form of funding for 90% of capital expenditure and part of the operational costs. The private sector is also actively involved often through donations to the FSCs for the remaining 10% of capital expenditure. Such a funding support formula by the state has encouraged more VWOs to assist and support individuals and families in need. The NCSS will coordinate the FSCs' programmes on a nationwide basis. The NCSS also provides funding for the operational costs (often through the community chest). The Family Resource and Training Centre (FRTC) of the Singapore Association of Social Workers will provide support to FSCs in training and in consultancy for specific programme implementation (NCSS, 1994). Since its introduction in the early nineties, to date about 27 FSCs have been established and are serving families in different housing estates throughout Singapore. More are in the process of being established.

Development of self-help groups

Another recent development in the voluntary welfare sector in Singapore is the establishment of self-help organisations in response to the needs of the different ethnic communities. It was felt that some social issues could be better addressed at the ethnic community level taking into consideration the specific cultural context in which these issues surfaced. These organisations receive the full support from the government, often in the form of dollar-per-dollar financial support up to a certain amount. These organisations also receive financial support from members of their communities who are gainfully employed. Often this comes in the form of automatic monthly deductions from their salary. The establishment of the self-help groups is an excellent example of the relationship between the government and the voluntary sector in nation building. Often times these organizations are initiated from within the individual ethnic communities and the initiatives are supported financially by the government (through the dollar per dollar grant). The private sector completes the tripartite relationship with corporate funding or sponsorships. This is an interesting new initiative and one has to examine its main implications. In a multiracial setting such as that of Singapore, it is crucial to encourage VWOs to respond to specific needs and problems facing various ethnic groups, namely Chinese, Malays, and Indians. These efforts can in the longer term help to formulate social integration among the ethnic groups and hence strengthen the social health of the Singapore society.

(a) The Council for the Development of Singapore's Muslim Community (Yayasan MENDAKI) — The Malay self-help group

In the early 1980s, the Malay leaders realised that in order to improve the position of the Malays vis-à-vis the other ethnic communities in Singapore as well as to increase the potential for the members of the Malay community to contribute to nation building, they must address the problem of poor educational performance of Malay children. They acknowledged that education is the key to upward social mobility. Yayasan MENDAKI began in 1982 as the Council on the Education for Muslim Children, with the aim of improving the educational achievement of Muslim students.

In 1989, the Malay leaders felt that Yayasan MENDAKI could expand its role in other aspects of development. It was then incorporated as a charitable company with the mission of developing "a self-reliant, successful and morally-strong Malay/Muslim community within multiracial Singapore" (Yayasan MENDAKI, 1992, p. 8). Since then, MENDAKI has launched numerous programmes — economic, educational, social and cultural — to meet the needs of the Malay community and to enhance their potential to contribute to the development of the nation as a whole.

The success of MENDAKI's programmes has been documented especially in the area of education. Malay students have performed better in major examinations compared to their counterparts fifteen years ago. Also the proportion of Malay students in tertiary institutions has also recorded a stark increase since the early 1980s.

MENDAKI works very closely with the other Malay/Muslim voluntary organisations in Singapore. It now acts as an umbrella organisation, coordinating the different programmes and services provided by the different Malay/Muslim organisations. This would certainly ensure effective use of resources to achieve their mission.

MENDAKI also works closely with the private sector in delivering its services and scheme. For example, its economic development department works closely with the Development Bank of Singapore in managing the Islamic Trust Fund. Other collaboration with the private sector includes scholarships and training opportunities with members of the Malay community. However MENDAKI faces the challenge of winning the respect of other Malay/Muslim organisations in terms of its leadership role in enabling the Malay/Muslim community to make progress.

(b) SINDA (Singapore Indian Development Association) — The Indian Self-help Group

Similar to the development of MENDAKI highlighted earlier, the role of SINDA in addressing the educational underachievement of Indian students originated with the concern of some Indian Members of Parliament. An Action Committee on Indian Education was formed to study the causes of Indian students' underachievement. In 1991 SINDA was tasked to address the educational and socioeconomic issues facing Singapore's Indian Community. SINDA has since, developed a range of social service programmes to meet the above objectives. It provides tuition classes, parent outreach activities, counselling services as well as family life education seminars for Indian families. (Action Committee on Indian Education, 1991)

SINDA is vulnerable to being fractured because of competing interests of different Indian sub-groups. The Indian community in Singapore is heterogeneous and SINDA will increasingly need to find appropriate and acceptable strategies to galvanise different Indian organisations in Singapore to work for a common objective to uplift the social, economic and educational performance of the Indian community.

(c) CDAC (Chinese Development Assistance Council) — Chinese self-help group

The Chinese Development Assistance Council was also recently initiated to meet the needs of the Chinese underclass. The main focus of the council is the educational performance of Chinese students from low-income families. The council provides facilities and affordable educational services for these students in different housing estates in Singapore. Presently three such educational centres are in operation.

CDAC has an economy of scale to deliver its services effectively because of broad base support of the Chinese community. It has to convince the middle class Chinese that there is a significant Chinese underclass requiring assistance. CDAC will have to publicise the needs of specific target groups to enlighten the benefactors so that they will give more support to its programmes. The major task facing CDAC is to help revitalise existing traditional clan associations for more effective utilisation of their resources to assist the Chinese underclass. It has to be prepared to take the leadership role in finding various solutions to the problems faced by the Chinese underclass.

The voluntary welfare sector: Contributions and issues

The colonial administrator's lack of endorsement and support for early pioneering efforts of the voluntary welfare sector did choke the indigenous growth of voluntary efforts in community problem solving. However, these efforts were rekindled after self-government as social, economic and ecological changes in Singapore precipitated the need for voluntary response in establishing local organisations to tackle new problems arising from modernisation and change.

The voluntary welfare sector became a formidable front, besides the governmental sector, to enlist the participation of concerned citizens to lend a helping hand for the disadvantaged and displaced in the Singapore community. Since 1970, the voluntary welfare sector has become better organised into a national social movement in partnership with the government in helping people facing various difficulties such as the disadvantaged families and children, the disabled, the aged sick and youths at risk. Today, over 223,600 beneficiaries have been assisted by different voluntary organisations, affiliated to NCSS (NCSS, 1998/99). This is indeed a commendable nation building effort to mobilise and translate the desires of those more able to help the less able. This is community building as mutual help is being promoted through voluntary activities which are supported by better-endowed citizens. In the long term social harmony and cohesion is maintained because Singaporeans of various ethnic backgrounds share a common purpose to help their fellow citizens irrespective of their creed. Singapore society does not become fractured by frictions between uncaring able and the less able citizens. Singapore should avoid some of the dangers facing completely free market societies by creating social institutions which will selectively intercede in reducing the burdens of the least capable and endowed in our community.

Shared responsibility — The tripartite relationship

The voluntary welfare sector works in partnership with the government and the private corporations to find ways and means to assist the disadvantaged sector of the population. This tripartite approach is effective as the problems of the displaced, poor and disadvantaged are viewed as shared responsibilities of all parties concerned. In contrast, the voluntary welfare sector in many countries is constantly engaged in a confrontational approach to tackle the problems of the disadvantaged. This protracted difference between the government and the voluntary welfare sector does not make effective headway to solve social problems. More often than not, the disadvantaged and the poor end up in the worse of situation without having their problems remedied. To prevent this from happening in Singapore, the voluntary welfare sector, the government and the private corporations have accepted joint responsibility to develop a cooperative partnership. In this way all the parties have a part to play and the many helping hand principle is pursued. (Yap, 1991; *Singapore: The Next Lap*, 1991).

Many members of the society have benefited from the social services provided by the voluntary sector. The number of beneficiaries has increased over the years. This would not have been possible without the active support of the government and private sector.

The partnership between the three sectors however, seems predominantly focused on the role of fund providers and fund receivers. The voluntary sector is seen as largely receiving funds from the government and private sector to delivery its services. Both these sectors could be challenged to play a more active role in social service in the form of volunteer participation. Since volunteers form the backbone of many of the VWOs' effort, both the private and public sectors should work towards encouraging their employees to be active volunteer in VWO activities. This is even more crucial with a labour force participation rate of 65%, the bulk of potential volunteers are indeed members of the working force.

This will also increase efforts at improving social justice by encouraging the well off in the society to contribute and care for the less fortunate. Social justice refers to equity, equality, and fairness in the distribution of social resources (Flynn, 1995). Financial resources have been channelled from the government and private sector to the less fortunate through the voluntary sector. This is evident with 90% of Singaporeans today owning their own homes (MITA, 2000). Within each ethnic group, the tripartite relationship has also shown good results toward social justice. Besides funding however, the active participation in voluntary activities is a show of cohesion and a sense of responsibility towards fellow citizens. The challenge is to increase the participation rates of employees in both the private and government sectors.

Funding

Funding of the activities of voluntary welfare sector in Singapore is mainly obtained through public and private donations. It is estimated that the whole voluntary welfare sector including those agencies not affiliated to the NCSS require about $120 million annually to operate their services. This huge budget has to be raised through various fund raising activities and so far because of the healthy Singapore economy the funding target has been achieved without difficulty. With the Community Chest's centralised fund raising effort, the charities, which are benefiting have been given a new lease of organisational life. They can undertake new programmes to meet new community needs. This is indeed helpful to the community as emerging social problems are solved before they worsen.

The funding burdens of the voluntary sector are reduced as the government, believing in partnership, funds approved social and welfare projects on a 50% recurrent funding principle. For capital projects, 90% funding is considered. This commitment by the government enables the voluntary welfare sector to initiate relevant projects and reinforces the concept of cost sharing and partnership. Such a principle prevents over dependency of the voluntary welfare sector and reinforces equal responsibility. Moreover the voluntary welfare sector can now be more confident to respond to critical community problems, which require attention.

The centralised fund raising by the Chest has helped to rally the more able in the community to assist the less fortunate. Such a united fund raising effort has to be monitored carefully to ensure that fund raising efforts are cost effective. The cost of raising the charity dollar must be kept very low and overhead and other peripheral expenses must not be allowed to be more than 10% of the amount raised. Also the side effects of insatiable funding needs and over-budgeting of voluntary organisations, dependency and danger of depersonalisation of services and compassion fatigue of donors must be watched carefully. The danger facing united fund raising efforts is the possible temptation to misallocate funds to areas, which are not relevant to meet needs of people who require help. When this occurs, the whole fund raising machinery will collapse, as will be no public confidence for the organisations.

Professional and cost effective service delivery

With available funds, the challenge for voluntary welfare organisations is to ensure good professional inputs and cost effective services for their target groups. Management of these organisations have the civic accountability to continually evaluate and monitor the services delivered to avoid depersonalisation and even complacency. One of the related challenges is the composition of the management committees in these organizations. Many of them are volunteers who are willing to serve but do not have expertise to provide professional directions to the organizations that they are managing. In this sense, the private sector can play a more active role in the partnership. Professionals from the private sector can be encouraged to serve in the management of these organizations to ensure the effective and efficient service delivery and to enhance the tripartite relationship between the three sectors.

Promoting citizen participation

The participation of the voluntary welfare organisations in community problem solving negates welfarist approach in dealing with social diswelfares in society. The involvement of citizens in voluntary activities helps to promote mutual support among people and in the long term improves the social health of Singapore. All these opportunities available for citizens to be engaged in altruistic activities do produce social antigens in people and prevent them from becoming self-seeking, selfish and hedonistic. In short more citizen participation in social and welfare activities augurs well for the nation as it can contribute to the building of a more graceful society, which cares for its people irrespective of their background.

The voluntary participation rate in Singapore is still low when compared to other industrial nations. The current rate of volunteer participation in Singapore stands at 10% (Singh, Ong, & Vasoo, 1997). The government recendy set up the National Volunteer Center (NVC) to spearhead efforts at increasing the volunteer participation rate. While lack of time is often sighted as a reason for non participation, a recent study showed that there were other motivators and demotivators. Singh, Ong, and Vasoo (1997) found that motivators included a sense of compassion and the challenging nature of the tasks given while demotivators included lack of say in tasks scheduling and lack of resources within the organizations.

Corporate volunteerism

To enhance the tripartite relationship better, efforts are not targeted at increasing the corporate volunteerism rate. This is moving beyond the traditional financial donations that corporations contribute to the development of the welfare sector. The NCSS has launched the Corporate Community Involvement Programme (CCIP) to achieve this end (NCSS, 2000). Companies are matched with VWOs with regard to the latter's volunteer needs. The nature of corporate support range from setting aside a day in a year for volunteer events to allowing staff time-off to do volunteer work. Some companies have also contributed through their employment practices. There are those who actively employ members of the disabled community to give them the opportunity to function effectively in society and contribute to nation building.

Cooperation of self-help groups

In view of the parallel developments of the various self-help groups, it will be more urgent for the leadership of these organisations to come together from time to time to review how they can cooperate and share expertise and experiences. Through these exchanges various ways can be formulated collectively to help one another to address the concerns facing the underclass of their respective communities. This will strengthen community cohesion further and contribute to nation building.

Promotion of social responsibility

The voluntary welfare sector is not a social control mechanism. It is a recipe for the Singapore society to provide an avenue for the better of Singaporeans to discharge their social responsibilities in caring for the less better. Professionals and ordinary citizens sit on the management of voluntary organisations and they chart the work of their organisations.

The sector is also not an administrative mechanism that can be absorbed by the government. It functions as a conduit through which invaluable ideas and actions could be prescribed to solve problems facing the community.

Conclusion

The voluntary welfare sector, which comprises mostly nongovernmental organisations, has become a powerful and invaluable forum for promoting many helping hands tackling the problems of the disadvantaged sector of the population. The tripartite relationship it has established with the government and private corporation sector has successfully moved Singapore away from the welfarist model of meeting the needs of the less fortunate members of the society. The self-help model through effective partnership with the latter two sectors has contributed significantly to nation building as reflected in Singapore's economic success in the last three decades.

The voluntary welfare sector however, faces great challenges as it continues to play its role in serving the community. Most voluntary organisations will be facing an acute problem in the greying of its leadership. In order that they can remain viable and responsive, it will be pertinent to encourage younger professionals to be inducted into their leadership. The declining youth and increasing aging population do hold prospects as well as setbacks for voluntary work in Singapore. Less young will be available for leadership renewal. There will be retirees with expertise and they could be mobilised for useful voluntary activities.

The tripartite partnership among the voluntary sector government and private corporations has led to shared responsibilities in community problem solving. Mutual respect and sharing of expertise among these actors will help to forge a common direction to promote community betterment and nation building. With matching government grant for voluntary organisations more initiative will be taken quickly to tackle emerging social problems related to the family, aging population, delinquency, drug abuse, AIDS and affluence. It is anticipated that with the establishment of more voluntary organisations, there will be increased competition for funds. Voluntary welfare organisations will have to face the challenge of presenting the most cost effective service strategies in seeking funds for their operations.

The need to strengthen the tripartite partnership approach by reviewing jointly the social implications of the changing demographic patterns of Singapore population is crucial so that the ownership of the Singapore community's problem become a shared challenge. The development of this tripartite model in community problem solving is a fresh strategy to forge consensus and promote concerted efforts of all the three key sectors. This strategy does not create dependency as witnessed in the welfarist state where governments are seen to be the main provider of solutions to the community's concerns.

Most urgently, we must encourage more young people to participate in various voluntary activities. Only 10% of the population are involved as volunteers in various activities of non-governmental organisations. In doing so we can help to strengthen the soul of our nation. The unique ethnic make up of the nation is an asset for volunteerism to flourish. Indeed, volunteerism has been a core value in each of the ethnic groups. The participation of different ethnic groups to tackle their specific problems, can help to prevent problems of ethnicity and facilitate social integration. It motivates rather than negates the ethnic ethos of mutual help. It provides a forum for ethnic groups to come together to see how they can share resources for community problem solving. This is critical for Singapore's social and economic development. VWOs have positively responded to contribute in delivering services that enhance social integration among different social and ethnic groups.

References

Action Committee on Indian Education (1991). *At the crossroads: Report of the Action Committee on Indian Education*. Singapore.

Advisory Council on Family and Community Life (1989). *Report of the Committee on Destitute Families*. Singapore: Ministry of Community Development.

Advisory Council on Family and Community Life (1989). *Report of the Committee on Family and Community Life: Towards a Better Family and Community Life*. Singapore: Ministry of Community Development.

Cheng, L.K. (1990). Reflections on the changing roles of Chinese clan associations in Singapore. *Asian Culture*, 14, 57–68.

Flynn, J.P. (1995). Social justice in social agencies. *19th Encyclopaedia of Social Work*. Washington, D.C.: NASW Press.

Goh, C.T. (1994). *Prime Ministers National Day Rally Speech 1994*. Singapore: MITA.

Housing and Development Board (HDB) Annual Report (1995), (1999).

MCDS/NCSS (1999). *Guidelines to Setting Up FSCs. Singapore:* Ministry of Community Development and Sports & National Council of Social Service.

MITA (2000). *Singapore 2000*. Singapore: Ministry of Information and the Arts.

National Council of Social Service (NCSS) Annual Reports, 1983 to 1999.

NCSS (1994). Guide to the Setting Up of Family Service Centre for Voluntary Welfare Organisations. Singapore: NCSS.

Pang, S.Y. (1992). Housing Policy Changes in Singapore. In Low and Toh (eds), *Public Policies in Singapore*. Singapore: Academic Press.

Purcell, V. (1980). 2nd Ed. Chinese in Southeast Asia. Oxford: Oxford University Press for Royal Institute of International Affairs.

Randall, V. (1998). *Political Change and Underdevelopment: A critical introduction to third world politics*. Hampshire: Macmillan.

Singapore: The Next Lap. (1991). Singapore.

Singh, R., Ong, T.H., and Vasoo, S. (1997). *Volunteer Participation in Social Service and Welfare Organization*. Submitted to the Ministry of Community Development.

Taub, R.P. (1988). *Community Capitalism*. Boston: Harvard Business School Press.

Vasoo, S. (1990). Enhancing Citizen Participation in Voluntary Organisations: Some Issues and Challenges. Peter Hodge Memorial Lecture, Department of Social Administration, University of Hong Kong.

Vasoo, S. (1992). Some Emerging Social Issues in Singapore. In Azizah, K. and Lau, T.S. (Eds). *Malaysia and Singapore: Problems and Prospects*. Singapore: Singapore Institute of International Affairs.

Vasoo, S. (1994). Neighbourhood Leaders' Participation in Community Development. Singapore: Times Academic Press.

Vasoo, S. (1998). New directions in community development in Singapore: Some influencing factors and challenges. Paper presented at the ICSW Conference in July 1998, Jerusalem, Israel.

Wee, A (1983). The Singapore Council of Social Service: Some thought on its roles in the future. In SCSS *Twenty Five Years of Social Service Singapore*: Singapore Council of Social Service.

Weiner, M. and Huntington, S.P. (1987) (Eds). *Understanding Political Development: An analytic Study*. Boston: Little Brown.

Wong, A.K. and Yeh, S.H.K. eds (1985). Housing a Nation: 25 Years of Public Housing in Singapore. Singapore: Housing Development Board.

Wong, S.K. (1998). *"Huiguan21": Past, Present and Future of the Chinese Clan Associations in Singapore*. Paper presented at the 7th Malaysia-Singapore Forum, National University of Singapore.

Yap, M.T. ed. (1991). Social Services: The Next Lap. Singapore.

Yayasan MENDAKI (1992). *Annual Report*.

Chapter 19

Studying neighbourhood leaders' participation in residents' organizations in Hong Kong and Singapore: Some theoretical perspectives*

S. Vasoo[†]

Introduction

In the last few decades, a significant interest has developed among researchers in understanding fully the dynamics of neighbourhood

---

*From Vasoo, S. (1990). Studying neighbourhood leaders' participation in residents' organizations in Hong Kong and Singapore: Some theoretical perspectives. *International Social Work*, 33(2), 107–120. Reprinted with permission by International Social Work.

This paper consolidates earlier ideas on the participatory behaviour of people in social service agencies. The prevailing theoretical frameworks for studying the neighbourhood leaders' participative behaviour in residents' organisations are also touched.

[†]S. Vasoo is a Senior Lecturer at the Department of Social Work and Psychology National University of Singapore, Kent Ridge, Singapore.

leaders'[1] participation in various residents' organizations.[2] In both Hong Kong[3] and Singapore[4] researchers are becoming increasingly interested in the area. Such an interest has been generated by the fact that governments in both developed and developing nations have recognized the importance of mobilizing neighbourhood leaders for the betterment of the neighbourhood (UN, 1975).[5]

Despite increasing attention by Hong Kong and Singapore governments, the performance of residents' organizations in the respective settings depends to a large extent on their internal dynamics. Among these internal dynamics, satisfaction of the neighbourhood leaders is one of the key variables. This is because residents' organizations by the very nature of their work are expected to promote altruism. Hence, the involvement in these activities must necessarily produce satisfaction and psychic benefits to the neighbourhood leaders (Sharp, 1978: Kemper, 1980) who have to invest much time and effort.

Attrition rates are not uncommon in residents' organizations and these are due to the lack of satisfaction derived by the neighbourhood leaders in their participation. Neighbourhood leaders who are satisfied tend to be frequently involved in the activities of their organizations (Gidron, 1983) and they are more likely to continue with their involvement. As a consequence, the survival of residents' organizations is ensured and they provide a forum through which the neighbourhood problems are articulated.

---

[1] In the context of this study, the term 'neighbourhood leaders' is defined to cover chairmen, secretaries and treasurers of various residents' organizations, who are the principal office bearers.

'Participation' here refers to the action component of the neighbourhood leaders. It's sometimes used interchangeably with the term 'involvement'.

[2] This term refers to government sponsored organizations established to promote citizen participation. In the context of this study, it covers mutual aid committees (MACs) in Hong Kong and residents' committees (RCs) in Singapore.

[3] Hong Kong is a British colony but will cease to be so in 1997 when it will be returned to the People's Republic of China. It consists of Hong Kong Island, Kowloon peninsula and the New Territories on the Chinese mainland. It has a total land area of 1050 sq km.

[4] Singapore is an island city state situated at the tip of the west Malaysian peninsula and has a total land area of 620.5 sq km.

[5] The 'neighbourhood' is defined to include a block of public housing flats or a few blocks in a specific zone or area.

The satisfaction of the neighbourhood leaders' involvement is crucial as it not only enhances their roles in community development but also provides continuity of leadership. However, the satisfaction and continued involvement of the neighbourhood leaders are a result of the interplay of other social factors.

In recent years, it has become more obvious that many urban communities lack the inducements for the growth of residents' organizations. This is because urban neighbourhoods are more complex than they appear to be, and as such, residents' organizations are found not to have entrenched themselves so easily in a locality.

Most often, residents' organizations have to be induced into existence by governments or external agents to maintain dialogues and contacts with local residents. This need to maintain links with local residents is increasingly emphasized by most governments today.

It is now becoming evident in many developing countries, like Hong Kong and Singapore, that governments are making vigorous attempts to encourage the setting up of new forms of intermediaries in urban neighbourhoods. This is because the respective governments feel that they cannot rely on traditional structures or leadership. These have become ossified and less creditable in the eyes of the residents, namely the young. According to Esman (1978: 167),

> ... traditional and paternalistic structures have recently come under heavy strains and many have broken down. Patrons and kinfolk, even when reinforced by government, frequently cannot or will not accept their customary obligations to a growing number of impoverished and dependent persons. The latter are compelled to shift for other patrons or institutions to protect their interests.
>
> As societies modernize, traditional structures may lose their legitimacy — as well as their utility — especially among younger persons who have been exposed by modern education and mass media to egalitarian ideas and who are repelled by the special privileges enjoyed by traditional leaders, many of whom have been co-opted or corrupted by outside groups.

In the case of Hong Kong and Singapore, new forms of intermediaries have been initiated by the respective governments. Much governmental resource has been deployed to encourage the formation of residents' organizations to facilitate neighbourhood leaders' participation in community development.

The fact that residents' organizations, namely the Mutual Aid Committees (MAC) and Residents' Committees (RCs) have become a backbone for neighbourhood leaders to participate in community development in the various new towns of Hong Kong and Singapore, has prompted researchers to be interested in studying into their set-ups. Both the Hong Kong and Singapore governments have responded by establishing residents' organizations for residents to participate in dealing with their neighbourhood needs, articulate their concern, provide their views and suggestions on governmental policies directly or indirectly; and receive feedback from policy makers. The respective governments have invested considerable resources in terms of time, personnel and finance to establish these organizations. Since 1973, more than 3500 residents' organizations (i.e. MACs) have been set up in Hong Kong. In Singapore, about 300 residents' organizations (i.e. RCs) have been established since 1975. Such a phenomenal increase is an indication of the two governments' interest in reaching out to the masses to induce their participation in neighbourhood betterment.

In this article, the prevailing theoretical frameworks for studying the neighbourhood leaders' participative behaviour will be scrutinized and discussed, and a proposed theoretical framework for studying neighbourhood leaders' participation in residents' organizations in Hong Kong and Singapore will be presented.

Some prevailing theoretical frameworks

The study of social factors influencing neighbourhood leaders' participation in their residents' organizations is still underexplored. Both social and political science disciplines have contributed relevant knowledge for the development and adoption of various theoretical approaches. Of late, the social work field has added further conceptual understanding on the subject (Sanders, 1958; Biddle and Biddle, 1965, 1968; Ross, 1967; Perlman and Gurin, 1972; Brager and Specht, 1973; Rothman, 1974; Edwards and Jones, 1976) besides its many descriptive literatures on community development (Turner, 1968; Cary, 1970; Cox et al., 1970; Taylor, 1974; Henderson and Thomas, 1980, 1981).

Based on the political perspective, neighbourhood leaders' participation has been studied by applying two conceptual models. These are the technocratic and democratic models (Kramse, 1968; Carbonnel, 1977).

The technocractic model emphasizes government intervention through technocratic elites who encourage participation of the leadership through officially sponsored organizations. Such organizations may be directed from the top where power in decision making is usually concentrated. On the other hand, the democratic model views the importance of encouraging participation by allowing neighbourhood leaders to make decisions on issues which affect them. In this case, power in decision making is decentralized and vested in those who are directly involved at the bottom (Jones et al., 1978: 2)

The use of the two conceptual models as an analytical framework for the study has some shortcomings. It is limited to the analysis of power relations between elites and neighbourhood leaders in their interactions to promote neighbourhood improvement. However, an analysis of these relations and interactions is elusive and at times difficult. Moreover, their use as frameworks of neighbourhood leaders' participation has failed to provide insights into how social factors such as age, sex, occupation, residents' orientations[6] and social support conditions[7] affect the participative behaviour of neighbourhood leaders.

Another theoretical conception which has been widely applied is the 'balance theory', propounded by Litwak and Meyer (1967: 246–62). This theory, as described by Jones et al. (1978:8), does not support the notion that;

> ... both bureaucratic-sponsored involvement and grassroots protest are the primary strategies of increasing participation. Instead it assumes that both the bureaucracy and citizen groups have legitimate spheres of

---

[6] The term 'resident orientation' is defined as a degree of concern for promoting self-help of residents as well as representing residents on matters which affect their welfare in a neighbourhood.

[7] The term 'support conditions' refers to four primary elements. It includes the degree of co-operation among committee members, the degree of participation by residents, the degree of assistance in the form of administrative help and guidance given by government officials and the financial adequacy of the residents' organizations.

influence, and are individually capable of performing certain tasks but must collaborate in the public domain to achieve other common social goals.

The theoretical framework based on 'balance theory' has been used by Jones et al. (1978) in their study of neighbourhood associations. Although this theory is interesting it has been found to have some empirical limitations. First, neighbourhood leaders of bureaucratic-sponsored residents' organizations have a limited sphere of influence. Their parameters for involvement can be directed by bureaucratic officials. In this respect, the balance of power is often tipped in favour of the bureaucratic officials. Second, the theory does not take into consideration that the neighbourhood leaders' resident orientation can affect their participation in neighbourhood betterment.

Third, other correlates such as financial condition, residents' support, co-operation of committee members and government officials' support, are neglected by the theoretical approach in examining their influences on the participative behaviour of neighbourhood leaders.

Some studies have examined the neighbourhood leaders' participation using three different sociological models. They are the 'rational model', the 'natural systems model' and the 'power-politics model' (Gummer, 1978). In the rational model, the organization '... is conceived as an instrument, that is a rationally conceived means to the realization of expressly advanced group goals. Its structures are understood as tools deliberately established for efficient realization of these group processes' (Gouldner, 1959: 404). In the natural system model, the neighbourhood leadership group is seen as striving 'to survive and maintain its equilibrium, and thus striving may persist even after its explicitly held goals have been attained... The natural system is typically based upon an underlying organic model which stresses the independence of the component parts' (Gouldner, 1959: 404). The natural system model has so far been applied by Loy (1979) to the analyses of the residents' organizations in some housing estates in Singapore. The power-politics approach provides a framework to analyse the neighbourhood leadership group '... as essentially a political arena in which interest groups compete for the control of organizational resources' (Gummer,

1978: 354). This approach also provides insights into the internal factionalism and competition among neighbourhood groups which may have positive or negative effects on the relationship among the leaders and their efficacy (Crenson, 1974).

The above theoretical concerns based on a sociological perspective are directed at the examination of the organizational system in which the neighbourhood leaders are involved. Such analyses at a macro level generally neglect looking into neighbourhood leaders' social concern and the presence of social incentives which can influence their participation. The latter have been thought to be important in sustaining their participation (Bailey, 1974; Lamb, 1975; Rich, 1980). This is because they expect, in return for their services, social incentives either from within or outside their residents' organizations. In this respect, Rich's theoretical model of interest group leadership (1980: 570), which is a combination of both exchange theory and theory of collective goods, provides useful insights into the dynamics of participation by neighbourhood leaders. He viewed this model as

> ... A series of exchanges between leaders and non leaders and which leaders offer potential members some package of benefits in exchange for their support of the association. In turn, leaders receive contributions to be used in securing collective goods for the group and are allowed to keep any surplus of revenues over the cost of these goods. This surplus, along with a variety of benefits in symbolic and material exchanges with members, are viewed as the primary incentives keeping the leaders in their role.

Discussions of theoretical frameworks for the study of participative behaviour are scattered throughout various literatures. There are few known sources in which a comprehensive overview has been documented. So far, two comprehensive overviews have been collated, one by Tomeh (1973); and the other by Wandersman (1981). Tomeh singled out three theoretical approaches which would be relevant to the study of neighbourhood leaders' participation. They are:

(a) *Growth and function theory*. The focus is on evaluation of industrial society with special emphasis on the growth and functions of residents' organizations or other formal voluntary associations. Tomeh (1973: 91) pointed out that

> ... formal associations are seen as contributing in society by supporting the normative order or seeking to change it and implement important values. At the same time, such organizations may contribute to the social stability as adaptive mechanisms for traditional institutions, and their importance is further noted in terms of the role they play in various societal processes such as the distribution of power, decision making, opinion formation and socialization.

(b) *Socio-psychological theory*. Based on this theory, attention is paid to the underlying reasons for the attraction, interaction and sustenance of individuals in residents' organizations or other formal voluntary associations. As described by Tomeh (1973: 91):

> ... formal associations are viewed as integrative of the personality systems of their members. Thus, the function of the association on the personal level is to provide the individual with affectional support and other satisfactions formerly available to him in such traditional groups as the family, neighbourhood and church. More generally, the association allows individuals to transcend their immediate life situations and serves to integrate them with the broader community and society.

(c) *Organizational theory*. In this theory, the residents' organizations or associations are examined in terms of their organizational characteristics (such as objectives, structures and functions) and how these characteristics affect their membership. This framework, as summarized by Tomeh (1973: 92),

> ... considers of interest the structure of the association, the different processes of operation, the impact of the social setting upon the organisation, the pattern of relationships within the association, and the inter-relationships of various structural, organisational and ideological features.

Wandersman's (1981) comprehensive overview of the theoretical framework for the study of neighbourhood leaders' participation is the most recent. He specifies a number of important social dimensions associated with participation, including such aspects as 'who is participating, how people are participating and what are the effects of participation' (1981: 28). However, he warns that the framework 'should be considered as a map to major dimensions and the relationships rather than as a detailed theoretical model' (1981: 28).

In summary, his framwork is directed at studying the external and internal factors influencing the participation of people and the consequences of participation. All these aspects cover a number of major elements which include environment, ecological and social characteristics of the community, individual differences, parameters of participation, mediators, and effects of participation. These two comprehensive overviews of the theoretical frameworks are useful in giving initial ideas to researchers interested in studying social factors influencing the participation of neighbourhood leaders. Since the field of participation is so broad and elusive, each researcher must eventually define the parameters for their investigations. The parameters which are chosen are often influenced by the researcher's leanings and interest.

The proposed theoretical framework

In devising an appropriate theoretical framework for studying neighbourhood leaders' participation in residents' organizations in Hong Kong and Singapore, a number of related issues have to be considered. First, the area of investigation has to be concerned with neighbourhood leaders who have either been selected or co-opted into residents' organizations. They are engaged in voluntary activities aimed at improving the social or physical well-being of residents in their neighbourhoods. Unlike participation in profit-oriented organizations, the neighbourhood leaders do not receive any tangible benefits (Smith, 1980b: 34–75; Qureshi et al., 1979). In the light of this, profit motives in terms of monetary gain are least important in affecting their participative behaviour. What seems to be more crucial is the degree of the neighbourhood leaders' concern for promoting the welfare of the residents (resident orientation) with whom they have to interact regularly. Sills (1957) has delineated this degree of concern as 'other-oriented' and 'self-oriented'. People with either of these categories of concern are attracted to join voluntary organizations such as the residents' organizations.

Second, residents' organizations, unlike profit-orientated organizations, depend heavily on the commitment of their leadership to discharge their social functions. However, this commitment is affected by the presence or absence of social support conditions which are made up of tangible and intangible resources (Smith, 1981: 21–36). The tangible resource in this case is the funds available to the leadership, and the intangible resources include support given by the residents, members in the leadership and government officials. Furthermore, residents' organizations are established with an intention to improve the welfare of residents and the neighbourhood environment. As such they can only be viable provided their leaders who are particularly concerned about promoting the welfare of residents in the neighbourhood are accorded the necessary social support. Taking these issues into consideration and reviewing known theoretical frameworks which have been adopted in studying citizen or neighbourhood leaders' participation, it seems that a theoretical framework based on conditional participative theory is the most pragmatic framework to be employed for future studies. This theoretical framework is an extension of the general model of interest group leadership propounded by Rich (1980: 570). Although Rich's model is useful, it has shortcomings. First, it focuses mainly on social incentives as important variables in the maintenance of the neighbourhood leaders' participation in community development. The incentives the leadership may derive are the collective goods provided through the residents' organizations. These collective goods include the enjoyment of the role of leadership itself, and the selective benefits that are incidental to the role of the leader (Rich, 1980: 572). Second, the model that emphasizes social incentive neglects the neighbourhood leaders' resident orientation as an additional factor in influencing their participatory behaviour. This aspect is important because people who are involved in the leadership of residents' organizations have varying degrees of commitment to promote the welfare of residents. The higher their degree of commitment, the more support they expect in order to carry out their work.

The conditional participative theory is an uncomplicated and straightforward theoretical framework (see Figure 1). It places importance on two

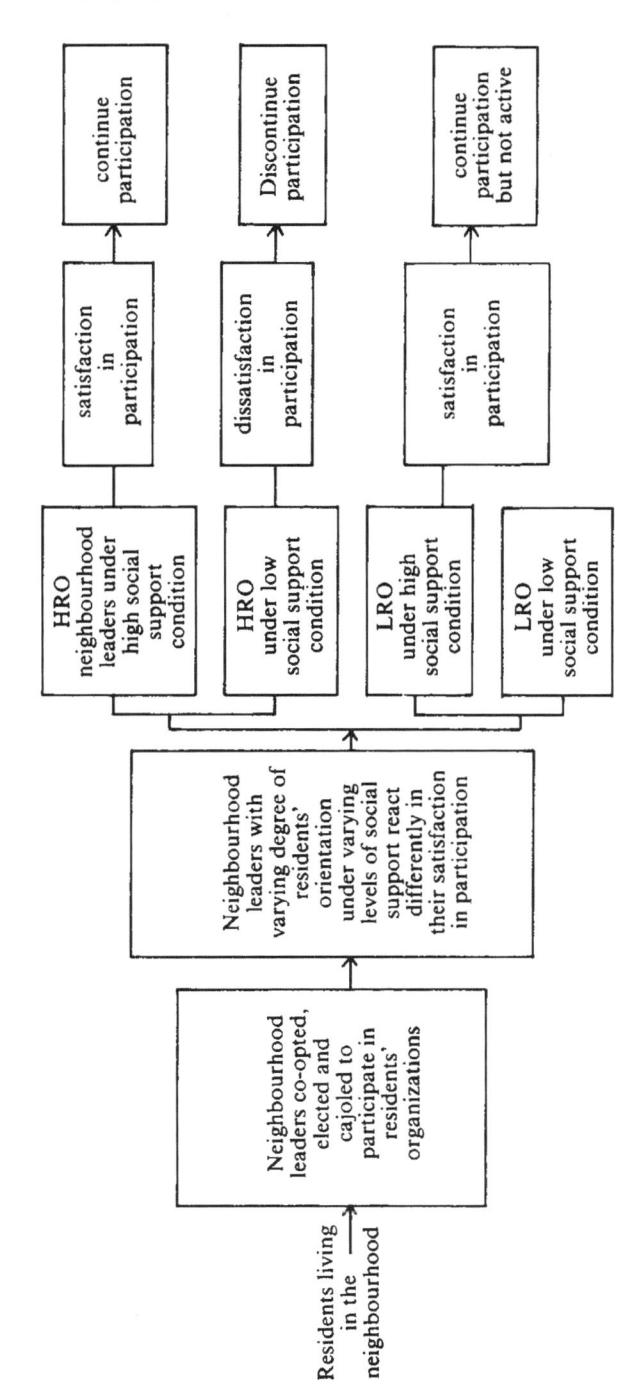

Figure 1. Resident orientation and social support conditions: Their effects on the neighbourhood leaders participation

conditions which have primary influence on the neighbourhood leaders' participative behaviour which include their satisfaction, frequency of involvement, and potential for continued participation. These two conditions are: (1) the neighbourhood leaders' degree of resident orientation, and (2) the conditions of social support available to them. Since residents' organizations are nonprofit-making formal organizations, the performance of their leadership is to a significant extent affected by the two conditions mentioned.

Generally neighourhood leaders in residents' organizations need social support in order to maintain their satisfaction in their participation. As this is the case, the perceived presence or absence of social support conditions is likely to affect their level of satisfaction, which in turn affects their participation. The satisfaction of neighbourhood leaders in their participation seems to be related to the presence of four interacting elements:

(a) the degree of involvement by residents in programmes organized by the neighbourhood leaders (residents' support);
(b) the usefulness of assistance provided by government officials in charge of the residents' organizations (official support);
(c) the degree of co-operation among committee members to carry out the work of the organization (committee members' support);
(d) the adequacy of funds (financial support).

All these elements determine the social support conditions in each of the residents' organizations.

However neighbourhood leaders' satisfaction in participation is not entirely dependent on the social support conditions they are exposed to. Their resident orientation appears to be an additional and equally important factor, directly or indirectly influencing their participative behaviour. Figure 1 indicates how the two conditional variables have implications for neighbourhood leaders' participation.

Residents' organizations tend to attract neighbourhood leaders with varying degrees of resident orientation. These neighbourhood leaders can be categorized loosely into two groups, those possessing high resident orientation (HRO) and those possessing low resident orientation (LRO). HRO neighbourhood leaders are motivated to improve the welfare of residents in the neighbourhood. However, they expect a high condition of social support in order to carry out their work effectively. When this expectation is met, they are likely to be satisfied. In the case of LRO neighbourhood leaders, who are more self-oriented, the low social support condition does not affect satisfaction in participation.

It is asserted that HRO neighbourhood leaders, as compared to those with LRO, tend to react differently under low conditions of social support. HRO neighbourhood leaders because of their motivation to promote the betterment of residents and the neighbourhood, can be easily frustrated if they find that the social support condition is poor in their organization. This appears to be so because they are unable to translate their altruistic intentions into reality.

Summary and discussion

The article has discussed the state of research on citizen and neighbourhood leaders' participation. It has explored the various theoretical frameworks adopted for studies on participation in formal voluntary organizations such as the residents' organizations. It has also described the conditional participative theory and supported the case for applying such as theoretical framework in studying neighbourhood leaders' participation in residents' organizations in Hong Kong and Singapore.

Empirical research interest in citizen and neighbourhood leaders participation in residents' organizations has increased recently. Most research in this field had been confined to understanding the reasons for the phenomenal growth of residents' organizations and the examination of socioeconomic characteristics of the participants. The focus on these aspects has at best provided insights into the nature and the types of residents' organization established and the characteristics of participants in such organizations. The limitation of this focus is obvious as it does not cast light on the dynamics of participation and the social factors influencing participative behaviour.

The conceptual frameworks generated for studying citizen and neighbourhood leaders' participation in residents' organizations have been confined to socio-psychological and organizational perspectives. These frameworks have engendered empirical difficulties as they have mainly examined a few significant variables related to the participants or organizations (Tomeh, 1973: Wandersman, 1981; Smith, 1980a: 8–33).

An increasing number of residents' organizations have been set up in urban public housing estates in Hong Kong and Singapore. This increase has come about as a consequence of government sponsorship to stimulate citizens to be involved in improving the social and environment conditions of their neighbourhoods. Without government sponsorship and encouragement such organizations would not take root in the urban neighbourhoods, because the urban milieu is not really conducive to the natural growth of neighbourhood organizations. As Taub et al. (1977: 426) elaborated, 'The changing scale of social organisation associated with accelerated rates of communication, transportation, and educational and occupational mobility has reduced the significance of the local neighbourhood as a source of social integration.'

The establishment of residents' organizations in Hong Kong and Singapore has attracted citizens with varying degrees of resident orientation (both 'self' and 'other' oriented) to exercise collective leadership. Given this situation, it would be inevitable to find in Hong Kong's and Singapore's residents' organizations a combination of leaders with different degrees of concern to promote the betterment of the residents in their neighbourhoods. These leaders who are involved in basically non-profit-making organzations are subjected to varying conditions of social support. These conditions will have an impact on their participative behaviour. Some studies have established that social support acts as both 'motivator' and 'satisfier' of those involved in voluntary service (Herzberg, 1966; Halpern, 1966; Gidron, 1983).

The theoretical framework based on the conditional participative theory has been proposed for studying neighbourhood leaders' participation in residents' organizations in Hong Kong and Singapore. This is because, unlike other theoretical approaches, it assesses the influence of social support and the neighbourhood leaders' resident orientation on the neighbourhood leaders' participative behaviour. These aspects have been unexplored in many earlier studies.

References

Bailey, Robert, Jr (1974) *Radical in Urban Politics*. Chicago: University of Chicago Press.

Biddle, W. and L.J. Biddle (1965) *The Community Development Process*. New York: Rinehart and Winston.

Brager, G. and H. Specht (1973) *Community Organising*. New York: Columbia University Press.

Carbonnel, Aurora (1977) *A Case for Citizen Participation: The Role of Citizen Participation in Development*. College of Public Administration, University of Philippines.

Cary, L.J. (ed.) (1970) *Community Development as a Process*. Columbia, MO: University of Missouri Press.

Cox, F.M., J. Erlich, J. Rothman and J. Tropman (eds) (1970) *Strategies of Community Organisation: A Book of Readings*. Itasca, II: F.E. Peacock.

Crenson, Matthew (1974) 'Organisational Factors in Citizen Participation', *Journal of Politics* 36: 356–78.

Edwards, Allan D. and Dorothy, G. Jones (1976) *Community and Community Development*. The Haque: Mouton.

Esman, M.J. (1978) 'Development Administration and Constituency Organisation', *Public Administration Review* 38(2): 166–72.

Gidron, B. (1983) 'Sources of Job Satisfaction Among Service Volunteers', *Journal of Voluntary Action Research* 12(1): 20–35.

Gouldner, A.W. (1959) 'Organizational Analysis', in Robert K. Merton, Leonard Bloom and Leonard S. Cottrell (eds) *Sociology Today*, New York: Basic Books.

Gummer, Barton (1978) 'A Power-Politics Approach to Social Welfare Organizations,' *Journal of Social Service Review* 52(3): 349–61.

Halpern, G. (1966) 'Relative Contributions of Motivator and Hygiene Factors to Overall Job Satisfaction', *Journal of Applied Psychology* 50(3): 198–200.

Herzberg, F. (1966) *Work and Nature of Man*. Cleveland, OH: World Publishing.

Jones, John F., K.F. Ho, B. Chau, M.C. Lam and B.H. Mok (1978) *Neighbourhood Associations in a New Town: The Mutual Aid Committees in Shatin*. Hong Kong Social Research Centre, The Chinese University of Hong Kong.

Kemper, T.D. (1980) 'Altruism and Voluntary Action', in D.H. Smith et al. (eds) *Participation in Social and Political Activities*, pp. 306–38. London: Jossey-Bass.

Kramse, Elliot (1968) 'Functions of a Bureaucratic Ideology: Citizen Participation,' *Social Forces* 16(2): 129–43.

Lamb, Curtis (1975) *Political Power in Poor Neighbourhoods*. New York: John Wiley.

Litwak, Eugens and Henry, C. Meyer (1967) 'A Balance Theory of Co-ordination between Bureaucratic Organisations and Community Primary Groups', in Edwin J. Thomas (ed.) *Behavioural Science for Social Workers*, pp. 246–62. New York: Free Press.

Loy, Jackson (1979) *'Residents' Committees in Singapore: an Exploratory Study'* an academic exercise, Department of Sociology, University of Singapore.

Perlman, R. and A. Gurin (1972) *Community Organising and Social Planning*. New York: John Wiley.

Qureshi, H.B., B. Davies and D. Challis (1979) 'Motivations and Rewards of Volunteers and Informal Care Givers', *Journal of Voluntary Action Research* 8(1–2): 47–55.

Rich, Richard C. (1980) 'The Dynamics of Leadership in Neighbourhood Organisation', *Social Science Quarterly* 60(4): 570–87.

Ross, M. (1967) *Community Organisation*, 2nd edn. London: Harper and Row.

Rothman, J. (1974) *Planning and Organising for Social Change*. New York: Columbia University Press.

Sanders, I.T. (1958) 'Theories of Community Development', *Rural Sociology* 23:1–12.

Sharp, E.G. (1978) 'Citizen Organisation in Policing Issues and Crime Prevention: Incentives for Participation', *Journal of Voluntary Action Research* 7: 45–58.

Sills, D.L. (1957) *The Volunteers: Means and Ends in a National Organisation*. New York: Free Press.

Smith, D.H. (1980a) 'Methods of Inquiry and Theoretical Perspectives', in D.H. Smith et al., *Participation in Social and Political Activities*, pp. 8–33. London: Jossey-Bass.

Smith, D.H. (1980b) 'Determinants of Individuals' Discretionary Use of Time', in D.H. Smith et al., *Participation in Social and Political Activities*, pp. 34–75. London: Jossey-Bass.

Smith, D.H. (1981) 'Altruism, Volunteers and Volunteerism', *Journal of Voluntary Action Research* 10(1): 21–36.

Taub, R.,G. Surgeon, S. Lindholm, P.B. Otti and A. Bridges (1974) 'Urban Voluntary Associations, Locality Based and Externally Induced,' *American Journal of Sociology* 83(2): 432–42.

Taylor, W.E.K. (1974) 'The Nature of Community Work', *Community Development Journal* 9(2): 20–5.

Tomeh, Aida K. (1973) 'Formal Voluntary Organisations; Participation, Correlates and Inter-relationship', *Sociological Inquiry* 43: 89–112.

Turner, J. (ed.) (1968) *Neighbourhood Organisation for Community Action*. New York: National Association of Social Workers.

United Nations (1975) *Popular Participation in Decision Making for Development*. New York: United Nations.

Wandersman, A. (1981) 'A Framework of Participation in Community Organisations', *Journal of Applied Behavioural Science* 17(1): 27–58.

Chapter 20

Grass-root mobilisation and citizen participation: Issues and challenges*

S. Vasoo[†]

Introduction

The importance of grass-root mobilisation and citizen participation need not be over-emphasized. Though consideration has been given to different ways of encouraging citizens to participate in social matters which affect their lives, this area is more often than not tread with care by those in control of various social and community programmes, projects and services. This is because grass-root mobilisation and citizen participation attract varied and at times divergent interests of various groups in the

---

*From Vasoo, S. (1991). Grass-root mobilisation and citizen participation: Issues and challenges. *Community Development Journal*, 26(1), 1–7. Reprinted by permission of Oxford University Press.

This paper reinforces earlier ideas of participation of people in grassroots activities. Further discussions on some of the consequential factors of grassroots mobilisation and citizen participation, particularly in the Asian region are deliberated and some approaches to strengthen participation are proposed.

A version of this paper was presented at the Asia Pacific Regional Conference of International Council of Social Welfare, September 4–9, 1989, Kuala Lumpur.

[†]S. Vasoo is Head and Senior Lecturer in Social Work and Psychology, National University of Singapore.

community.[1] In this discussion, grass-root mobilisation and citizen participation are seen to involve similar processes.

There is a growing body of literature pertaining to grass-root mobilisation and citizen participation. The United Nations has documented this aspect of work, based on its many country experiences and it has set the tone in influencing the efforts of various governments in promoting the involvement of their citizens.[2] Besides the United Nations contribution to knowledge on grass-root mobilisation and citizen participation, various voluntary action researchers have also attempted to throw more light on this subject.[3] To date, one of the most comprehensive efforts to compile the widely scattered literature in the field of grass-root mobilisation and citizen participation has been undertaken by Smith and Freedman.[4]

Grass-root mobilisation and citizen participation have been seen as a panacea to the problems arising from urban renewal and development. As Spiro and Liron state:

> It is expected to improve the quality of planning, to make programmes responsive to the desires and preferences of local residents, to reduce alienation, enhance the power of the low classes, improve communication between government and the people, encourage moderation and responsibility among the residents.[5]

---

[1] Arnstein, S. (1969), "A Ladder of Citizen Participation," *Journal of American Institute of Planners*, Vol. 35, 216–224.

[2] United Nations (1975), *Popular Participation in Decision Making*. New York, Department of Social and Economic Affairs.

[3] Batten, T. R. (1967), *The Non-Directive Approach in Group and Community Work*, London, Oxford University Press; Crenson, M. A. (1974), "Organisational Factors in Citizen Participation," *The Journal of Politics*, Vol. 36, 356–378; Cole, R. L. (1974), *Citizen Participation and Urban Policy Process*, Lexington Mass., D. C. Heath; and Edward, A. D. and Jones, D. G. (1976), *Community and Community Development*, The Hague, Moutton.

[4] Smith, C. and Freedman, A. (1972), *Voluntary Associations: Perspectives on Literature*, Cambridge, Mass., Harvard University Press.

[5] Spiro, S. and Liron, H. (1981), *Citizen Participation in Urban Research: An Appraisal*, A Working Paper.

On the other hand, grass-root mobilisation and citizen participation have also been criticized for their unintended consequences in that they have created conflicts and hindered the effective implementation of community programmes and services. Such negative consequences are the result of the dilemmas, for example the choice between trading off participatory democracy against the expertise of technocrats in decision-making, and vice-versa. It is often impossible to maximise benefits arising from both these value-laden preferences, and accomodations and compromises have to be found.[6]

Grass-root mobilisation and citizen participation are aimed at the promotion of the collective efforts of citizens to better their communities and the provision of opportunities for them to be involved in various aspects of governmental decision or planning processes. In summary, they may be said to be based on three major assumptions:

(i) Citizen participation is a democratic right;
(ii) Social justice is most likely to be attained when all citizens can effectively voice their interests;
(iii) Informed citizens must be involved in the governance of bureaucracies in order to keep institutions responsible to changing societal needs.[7]

Another commonly-quoted definition that has received global acceptance is the United Nations' version, which emphasizes grass-root mobilisation and citizen participation as;

> the processes by which the efforts of the people themselves are united with those of governmental authorities to improve the economic, social, and cultural conditions of communities, to integrate these communities into the life of the nation, and to enable them to contribute fully to national progress.

---

[6] Burke, E. M. (1968), "Citizen Participation Strategies," *Journal of American Institute of Planners*, Vol. 37, 90–91.

[7] Jones, J. F. (1978), *Neighbourhood Association in a New Town: The Mutual Aid Committees in Shatin*, The Social Research Centre, The Chinese University of Hong Kong.

> This complex process is made up of two essentials: It entails the encouragement of the participation by the people themselves in efforts to improve their level of living with as much reliance as possible on their own initiative; and the provision of technical and other services in ways which encourage initiative, self-help and mutual help and make these more effective.[8]

In short, grass-root mobilisation and citizen participation should in the long run encourage people to become more self-reliant in social and economic activities and be more participative in neighbourhood and community betterment. Having presented this broad overview of the subject area, it is appropriate to discuss some of the consequential factors of grass-root mobilisation and citizen participation, particularly in the Asian region, and to suggest some approaches to strengthen it.

Growth of grass-root organisations

It has been observed that as a result of increasing grass-root mobilisation and citizen participation, there has been a phenomenal growth in the number of grass-root organisations. This is due to a few pertinent factors. First, the massive relocation of people particularly into urban settings, new towns and cities in the Asian region, has created social consequences which if left unattended, would have repercussions not only to the welfare of residents but also the governments concerned. Social consequences such as the breakdown of traditional helping networks, the loss of effective communication channels between those who govern and the people, the feeling of alienation and anomie among residents, increasing pressure from residents for better urban services from local governmental bureaucracies, disgruntlement arising from residents whose needs are unmet as a result of relocation and the like, have provoked the respective governments to direct significant resources to encourage the formation of grass-root organisations. These intermediate organisations are established to provide solutions to deal with the effects of resettlement in urban areas.

---

[8] United Nations (1975), *Report of the United Nations' Seminar on Community Development and Social Welfare in Urban Areas*, Geneva, Economic and Social Affairs Commission.

Hence, grass-root organisations have taken the form of basic grass-root structures to mobilise the young who are socially active in urban neighbourhoods. However, it is not sufficient to merely have intentions to provide the young with the channels for participation. Such intentions must be translated into concrete actions to encourage them to be involved. More programmes to attract the young could be implemented and young residents should be given more opportunities for participation in grass-root leadership.[9]

Second, traditional institutions which in the past played an important mediatory role between the residents and the government have lost their effectiveness.[10] This is because their functions have not evolved to keep abreast with the changing needs of residents. They have become impotent in representing broader cross-sectional interests of residents and have hence lost their capacity to be effective channels to communicate with government bureaucracies in their respective settings. Their lethargy has precipitated the interests of governments in the Asian region to encourage alternative organisational forms such as residents' organisations, citizen's bureaux, neighbourhood councils and district committees. These are new form forms of grass-root organisations. Like other traditional institutions, these grass-root organisations also face the danger of becoming inactive. This problem is accentuated if more low-resident orientation[11] (LRO) grass-root leaders[12] dominate the leadership and, the respective governments do not give active support to grass-root organisations.

---

[9] This term, refers to various social and civic organisations such as residents' committees, citizens' consultative committees, citizens' bureaux, settlement organisations, rural committees, village committees, rural co-operatives and welfare organisations established to promote community development.

[10] Esman, M. J. (1978), "Development Administration and Constituency Organisation," *Public Administration Review*, Vol. 38(2), 166–172.

[11] The term "low resident orientation" (LRO) is defined as a low level of concern for promoting self-help of residents as well as representing residents on matters which affect their welfare in a neighbourhood.

[12] Grass-root leaders are those people who hold committee or executive positions in various social and civic organisations.

Increase in government sponsorship

Various governments in the region have adopted an interventionist approach to establish grass-root organisations as channels for participation in community development. Their efforts result in the formation of an elaborate network of grass-root organisations. As a consequence there is plenty of room to fill the void in grass-root leadership. Grass-root leaders are mobilised by the respective governments to encourage citizens' participation. Where grass-root leaders have been nominated by the authorities, skepticism arises and this attitude can be further reinforced if the respective governments do not provide avenues for direct dialogue with residents and other bona-fide groups on various matters of concern. The availability of these alternative channels will make citizens' participation more representative and thereby reduce skepticism among residents of the governments' intentions.

Government sponsorship of grass-root organisations may produce some counter-effects to community development, if the grass-root leaders rely heavily on government administrative bureaucrats to chart programme directions for their organisations. They can become insular by undertaking programmes which are, on the whole, standardised. In the long run, grass-root organisations and their leadership may suffer from alienation. It is therefore important for neighbourhood leaders to have the independence to redefine the objectives of their organisations and work in concert with various governmental structures to improve the delivery of urban services.

The continued reliance of grass-root organisations on a small leadership base can contribute to organisational inertia. This condition would stem from a lack of initiative of these leaders to create opportunities for residents to participate in decision-making. There is an apparent danger that the leadership may become omnipotent if it is assumed that it knows best the problems faced by residents.

Grass-root organisations can be conceived as administrative satellites through which citizens and their leaders can be mobilised to participate in improving the urban service-delivery systems. It is a device used by various governments to encourage local residents to take an active interest as volunteers in tackling urban problems. These problems, such as environmental deterioration, anomie, crime and psychological stress, will not be effectively solved by the administrative machinery of governments alone unless the support and co-operation of grass-root leaders and residents are harnessed.

Better representation of grass-root leaders

It appears that the leadership in grass-root organisations has a higher percentage of involvement of people with professional and technical background, than any other occupational status. The dominance by members of this group is as expected because they seem to have a high political efficacy — a characteristic that has been substantiated by other studies.[13] Their presence strengthens the leadership of grass-root organisations as their expertise could be tapped.

What appears more significant in the urban areas is that there is an under-representation of neighbourhood leaders with lower socio-economic status (SES), although the majority of their working population is engaged in production and service-related occupations. This could be attributed to the lack of tangible rewards which are important to meet their needs.[14]

The under-representation of people with lower SES in the neighbourhood leadership can hamper the work of grass-root organisations. This is particularly so when the current leadership is unable to reflect and respond to the needs of residents in the lower income group in the various neighbourhoods. This danger of a more biassed organisational outlook, reflecting the interests of elites, can be averted by the governments. This can be achieved by encouraging a good mix of people and SES to be involved in grass-root organisations.

Steps can also be undertaken to encourage more people with high resident orientation[15] (HRO) to take up leadership positions in grass-root

---

[13] Jones, J. F. *et al.* (1978), *Op. cit.*, p. 78; Yuen, Kathy, (1983), *Report of the Survey on Residents Opinions About Community Participation and the Residents' Committees*, Unpublished Report, pp. 12–13.

[14] O'Brien, D. J. (1975), *Neighbourhood Organisations and Interest Group Process*, Princeton, New Jersey, Princeton University Press.

[15] This term "high resident orientation" (HRO) is defined as a high level of concerns for promoting self-help of residents as well as representing residents on matters which affect their welfare in a neighbourhood.

organisations. When more grass-root leaders with these characteristics are attracted to be involved in grass-root organisations, they encourage them to be viable. This is because HRO grass-root leaders are motivated to represent the problems of residents.

Enhancing grass-root mobilisation and citizen participation

It seems that the enhancement of grass-root mobilisation and citizen participation in community development varies directly with the level of social support. Therefore, it is necessary to ensure that high social support conditions[16] are present all the time in grass-root organisations. This is important for the sustenance of the grass-root leaders' performance. High social support acts as an incentive or a motivator and it provides the impetus for them to discharge their responsibilities satisfactorily. Elsewhere, in other research,[17] job satisfaction has been also found to be significantly related to the presence of satisfiers.

The two social support elements, namely officials' and grass-root leaders' support are important in grass-root mobilisation and citizen participation. They appear to account for much of the support needed for activating the participation of grass-root leaders. This is because non-profit organisations like grass-root organisation have no tangible incentives to offer their grass-root leaders except for these two social support elements which play a significant part in sustaining their performance.

It is also interesting to note that low social support conditions have more serious effects on the motivation of HRO than on low resident orientation[18] (LRO) grass-root leaders.

---

[16] The term social support conditions refer to four elements. It includes the degree of co-operation among grass-roots leaders, the degree of participation by residents, the degree of assistance given by government officials and the financial adequacy of the grass-root organisations.

[17] Herzberg, F. (1966), *Work and Nature of Man*, Cleveland, Ohio, World Publishing Co.; Gidron, B. (1983), "Sources of Satisfaction Among Service Volunteers," *Journal of Voluntary Action Research*, Vol. 12, 21–35.

[18] Vasoo, S. (1987), "Residents' Organisations in the New Towns of Hong Kong and Singapore: Some Issues and Future Development," *Hong Kong Journal of Public Administration*, Vol. 9(2), 143–154.

Strengthening grass-root leadership and organisation

In order that the work of grass-root organisations can be strengthened and made effective, it is pertinent for grass-root leaders to identify factors which affect the efficiency and effectiveness of their organisations. The identification of relevant factors affecting the progress of their organisations and the manner in which systematic plans are devised to deal with them will determine whether their organisations will be viable. In short, we are talking about organisational performance appraisal, a subject which seems to be much neglected in the management of grass-root organisations. This is simply because the management of these organisations is viewed as a voluntary exercise based on ultruism. Grass-root organisations can become effective enterprises provided those who manage them are prepared to come to grip with and tackle issues which affect the performance of their organisations.

It is important for grass-root organisations to address these questions: "Are our programmes meeting the changing needs of our constituents?", "What are the costs and benefits of our programmes?", "What are the expected results of the programmes?" and "What kind of mechanism do we have to ensure the quality of the programmes?". Only when grass-root leaders begin to seriously consider answering these questions, can the grass-root organisations demonstrate the efficiency and effectiveness of its service delivery.

People who hold leadership positions in grass-root organisations are from various occupations. A significant number of them also hold executive positions in other civic organisations. This seems to be so because those who are active in one organisation are usually persuaded to assume leadership in another. This precarious situation has its consequences, although we may argue that they can still contribute their expertise. Firstly, confusion of role-identity may arise because these people are involved in too many organisations, which may have complementary or conflicting objectives. Secondly, the ability to give their best can be affected. Thirdly, their participation may be less forthcoming owing to their numerous commitments. Therefore, it is important for those in leadership positions not to be involved in too many organisations as this will affect their potential to be effective.

For grass-root organisations to be progressive, it must have a continuity of leadership and direction. Change in leadership style and management may be necessary and this can be instituted by coopting more people who have the experience to contribute towards organisational efficiency and goal attainment.

Many of those who lead in grass-root organisations are busy with their own commitments and some therefore may not be able to attend consistently the meetings of their organisations. The poor attendance of principal members at various meetings leads to their non-attachment to their organisations, which will in turn minimize their opportunities to obtain appropriate feedback important to their organisation' progress. This lack of feedback will ultimately affect their roles in enhancing the growth of their organisations.

In order to prevent some grass-root leaders from being over-burdened, it is essential to have a more equitable distribution of responsibilities so that there will be no over-loading on a few persons. Also, the distribution of duties will enable the leaders not only to be just involved in planning and administration but also in monitoring the results of their programmes. All these aspects, if implemented, can promote job satisfaction among grass-root leaders involved in voluntary action.[19] Functions such as mapping out new programmes, setting directions for a period of time and dealing with organisational blockages, form an essential responsibility of key leaders. Though these functions are less tangible, they are important components in determining the grass-root organisations' environment. Hence, these tasks should be incorporated into the job description of the leaders.

Conclusion

Grass-root mobilisation and citizen participation in grass-root organisations can be adversely affected, especially when HRO grass-root leaders perceive that they do not have high social support. They, by nature, being more inclined to be active, are often left to carry the burdens of their organisations. As a consequence, they become burnt-out leaders

---

[19] Gidron, B. (1983), *Op. cit.*

portraying various symptoms such as low satisfaction from achievements, lack of drive in discharging the mission of their organisations, feeling estranged and back-sliding in performance. To prevent HRO grass-root leaders from being burnt-out, it is essential that there be a more equitable distribution of organisational responsibilities.

More urgently, for any grass-root organisation to perform efficiently and effectively, skilled and competent manpower is essential. Many good and competent grass-root leaders and professionals must be attracted to be involved and more attempts should be made by the leadership to recruit them.

For grass-root organisations to remain effective, those who manage them must carry out an organisational diagnosis from time to time. It is only through such an exercise that it will be possible to identify specific areas which affect them and make decisions to solve the problems faced. With flexible organisational objectives and administrative support by respective governments for grass-root leaders, it is anticipated that the future work of grass-root organisations could be strengthened.

Chapter 21

Promoting voluntary efforts in meeting community needs in Singapore: Some challenges*

S. Vasoo[†]

The article discusses some issues confronting the participation of volunteers in the voluntary social and welfare service sector. It also identifies some of the changing social and demographic factors and how these factors are likely to influence the future developments in voluntary services. Some recommendations in ways to enhance volunteers' participation are considered.

---

*From Vasoo, S. (1992). Promoting voluntary efforts in meeting community needs in Singapore: Some challenges. *Asia Pacific Journal of Social Work*, 2(2), 25–37. Copyright © Department of Social Work, National University of Singapore, Singapore, reprinted by permission of Taylor & Francis Ltd, http://www.tandfonline.com on behalf of Department of Social Work, National University of Singapore, Singapore.

This paper was presented at the First Institute of Strategic and International Studies (ISIS) South-East Asia Roundtable on Social Development: Managing the Impact of Industrialisation, held in Kuala Lumpur, 20–21 January 1992.

Volunteerism issues which have been touched in previous writings are being revisited. This article examines some of the factors affecting participation in voluntary social and welfare organisations in Singapore, and discusses on the strategies taken by the voluntary social and welfare services to ensure viability to deliver services.

[†]S. Vasoo is Head, Department of Social Work & Psychology, National University of Singapore.

Introduction

Participation in voluntary social and welfare services in Singapore has been undergoing significant transformation in last five decades. Activities of clan and lineage organisations (Esman, 1978; Seah, 1979; Vasoo, 1991) have declined steadily despite recent efforts to encourage them to reform. In response to this situation, more formal voluntary social and welfare organisations have been and are being established to assist the disadvantaged sector of Singapore's community such as the disabled and sick, aged destitutes, individuals and families in distress, and children and youths in need of care and guidance. Also neighbourhood betterment activities undertaken by Residents' Committees in the public housing estates, have increased pointedly in the last decade. The Government's conscious policies in avoiding the welfarist model and emphasis on promoting self help through the provision tax exempt status, matching grant, land and capital cost, for selected voluntary social and welfare organisations, have contributed to the growth of voluntary efforts[1] in involving many helping hands to care for the unfortunate and less abled citizens. The Government in adopting such a thrust reiterates that:

> "Many helping hands is the Singapore's way of helping that small segment of our community who cannot keep pace with the rest of the population. They are found in every society, however affluent and progressive. Such families lag behind the rest of the population. They are in danger of becoming destitutes, despite a comprehensive social security net in the form of the Central Provident Fund which provides protection in old age, major illness, incapacity and premature death of a breadwinner."
> (Next Lap, 1991:17).

The promotion of voluntary efforts in the provision of social and welfare services will be subjected to more challenges in the near future as a result of a number of factors which either retard or facilitate the participation of volunteers. Some of the main factors include:

---

[1] This is defined as citizens' involvement in the activities of voluntary social and welfare organisations. These activities include voluntary services such as management and fund raising and personal help to people in need of help.

(a) competing demand for volunteers' time by various organisations; (b) impact of Singapore's aging population; (c) relocation and rehousing of people; (d) weakening of traditional organisations; (e) changing physical and social environment; (g) greying of organisational leadership and; (h) preventing the erosion of human values. This paper will firstly examine some of the implications of these factors on participation in voluntary social and welfare organisations in Singapore. Secondly, the paper will also discuss the strategies undertaken collectively by the voluntary social and welfare services to ensure viability to deliver services.

(a) *Demand for volunteers' time*
With improvements in working conditions, Singaporeans are having more leisure time. At least 50 per cent of the working Singaporeans have about 14 hours of leisure time per week. This is likely to be tapped by various social and welfare organisations. In the light that leisure time is limited, Singaporeans are likely to expand it in voluntary activities which are beneficial and useful (Olson, 1965; Smith, 1980). It is therefore important for voluntary social and welfare organisations to make their voluntary service programmes interesting and a growing experience for volunteers. Unless this is actively considered, they will not be able to attract and sustain volunteers. It has been found that organisations which offer mundane and routine voluntary service programmes cannot sustain the interest of volunteers longer than necessary (Gidron, 1983).

The participation of volunteers in Singapore's voluntary social and welfare services is still rather low. It has been found that only 6 per cent of the population between 15 and 55 years old are involved in voluntary work. This participation rate compares less favourably to other countries such as United States of America, Japan and United Kingdom, where participation rate is 39 per cent, 25 per cent and 12 per cent, respectively (VADC, 1990:9). In order to encourage more voluntarism, Volunteers' Month has been initiated to give more public recognition to volunteers and information about voluntary work.

(b) *Impact of an aging population*
In the near future the number of young volunteers will decline and this will affect the work of voluntary social and welfare organisations which rely on younger volunteers for active programmes. This is because one of

the most significant social phenomena facing Singapore in the immediate decade is population aging. The population aging trend is becoming conspicuous. In 1990, there were about 118,300 persons aged 60 years and above and by the turn of the century, the number will increase to 332,000 persons. It is estimated that about 25 per cent of Singaporeans will be above 60 years by year 2030.

However, the reduction of young volunteers could be augmented by mobilising older persons who will form the potential pool for volunteer manpower. Currently, few organisations have a comprehensive plan in tapping the rich experience and expertise of our retired senior citizens. It is therefore desirable for our organisations to identify various voluntary activities for their involvement.

(c) *Relocation and rehousing*

The rehousing of residents into public housing estates in the New Towns is one of the most significant social programmes successfully implemented by the PAP (People's Action Party) government in this century (Wong and Yeh, 1985). About 87 per cent of the population of 2.6 million people have already been housed in the Housing Development Board (HDB) flats (HDB, 1989/90). The rehousing of residents into New Towns has contributed to an improved living standard. The new living environment is a welcome change for the residents.

However, the success of housing residents in the newly designed environment cannot be measured in terms of the number of people rehoused or better layouts. It has to take into consideration whether the residents are also co-operating with each other to make their neighbourhoods a better place to live in. Since most people have been rehoused, neighbourhood co-operation is currently receiving more attention.

The massive relocation of people into public housing has had some social consequences for not only the residents but also the PAP government. Social consequences such as breakdown of traditional helping networks, need for more effective communication channels between policy makers and the residents, the feeling of alienation and anomie among residents, the increasing pressure from residents for better urban services have prompted policy makers to deploy resources to encourage the formation of Family Service Centres and Residents' Committees to deal with the abrasions arising out of high rise living.

(d) *Weakening of traditional organisations*
Traditional organisations such as clan and lineage associations, and guilds and mutual aid societies which have been playing an important mediation role between the residents and government in the past seem to have lost their effectiveness and credibility (Seah, 1979). They have become weak in representing broader cross-sectional interests of residents. They are no longer effective channels of communication between the policy makers and the government bureaucracies (Esman, 1978). As a consequence, the policy makers have been encouraging formation of new social and community organisations such as Citizen's Consultative Committees and Residents' Committees.

This approach has also been found to be of a rather limited utility. Participation in these social and community organisations depends upon two factors. One is support from the residents themselves. Another is the resident-orientation of the neighbourhood leaders. It has been found that effectiveness of these social and community organisations is most noticeable when neighbourhood leaders are high in both social support and resident-orientation (Vasoo, 1987).

(e) *Changes in physical and social environment*
We have developed many new town communities, and as such participation in voluntary services is likely to shift from institutional and welfare home settings to the neighbourhoods of housing estates. This direction will become more evident in the future as more voluntary social and welfare organisations are established to promote community based programmes to meet social and recreational needs of people. Volunteers and potential volunteers will find it more convenient to render their services in their own neighbourhood. They can be involved in wide ranging activities such as child care, befriending, youth guidance, and care for the aged.

Conserving our environment will be a serious issue of the future. As we look ahead we can see a rise in interest to conserve and prevent pollution of our environment. More volunteers will have to be mobilised to deal with environmental issues at local and national levels.

Singapore's social networks and contacts with our region could be further strengthened by making available volunteers with different professional expertise such as medicine, engineering, education and communication, to countries in the region. It will be timely to involve our young people for volunteer service overseas. The Singapore Council of Social Service and the Singapore International Foundation could look into organising such a programme for involvement of some our citizens in overseas volunteer programmes.

(f) *Greying of organisational leadership*

In the next two decades, many voluntary social and welfare organisations will be facing a greying leadership. There is a danger of gerontocracy pervading in the organisations and this may lead to organisational inertia, parochialism and lethargy. To remain viable and progressive, these organisations have to find ways to renew their leadership. Although it cannot be ignored that older leadership does provide organisational wisdom, the survival of people-oriented organisations, both in the public and private sectors, must depend on the readiness of the older leadership to prepare able younger citizens to manage them. It is indeed amusing to many outsiders that conscious efforts are undertaken in Singapore to induct the young into the managements of these organisations. However the renewal of leadership is still much slower than expected in the voluntary social and welfare service sector as there is some resistance to renewal and change.

(g) *Preventing the erosion of human values*

The social health of any progressive and vibrant society varies directly with the human values the members of the society cherish as well as their capacity to find social antigens to decadent values that erode moral and social responsibilities. Singapore is an open economy. The population is exposed to various information which have either positive or negative effects on outlook to life. They are more vulnerable to the erosion of human values. It is important, therefore, for Singaporeans to actively promote right kinds of social values as early as possible. The right time for this purpose is when a child begins school.[2] Such an emphasis in the school curriculum can facilitate helping behaviour. Values education, if carefully planned, can also encourage good citizenship. In the long run, it can prevent the citizens from becoming self-centred and uncaring.

---

[2]Values education in this context covers the teaching of ethics, moral codes and good citizenship.

More citizens with high social DNA are to be nurtured.[3] These people with the acumen for the promotion of public good are likely to further strengthen the foundations of our social and public institutions.

Enhancing volunteer participation

The enhancement of volunteer participation in voluntary social and welfare organisations varies directly with the level of social support. Therefore, it is necessary to ensure that high social support conditions are all the time present in organisations. This is important for the sustainment of volunteers' performance. High social support acts as an incentive or a motivator and it provides the impetus for them to discharge their responsibilities satisfactorily.

In the context of Singapore, voluntary social and welfare organisations face no difficulties in mobilising people to be involved. What seems to be the common problem is that they all face a high turn-over rate of volunteers. This is because volunteers are generally not assigned tasks which are enjoyable and demanding of their creative potentials. Consequently, they become dissatisfied. In order that job satisfaction of volunteers can be increased, there is an urgent need for voluntary social and welfare organisations to provide more opportunities for involvement of volunteers in programme planning and development (Gidron, 1983; Francis, 1985). It will be useful to set up a Volunteer Development Committee in various organisations to develop and sustain volunteers.

It is agreed that we must make volunteer participation dynamic. How do we achieve this? Should we allow it to take its own course and do nothing about it? Volunteer participation can be vibrant provided we all make periodical reviews of our organisational objectives. In reviewing our organisational objectives we will be better able to discover ways to strengthen our programmes to attract more young people. Through the delegation of responsibilities to the young, more ideas can be generated and meaningful activities could be implemented.

---

[3] People with high social DNA are those who have positive concern for residents' wellbeing and public good.

Strengthening partnership in voluntary service

In order that partnership in voluntary service can be strengthened and made effective, it is pertinent for management and professionals of voluntary social and welfare organisations to identify factors which affect the efficiency and effectiveness in utilising volunteers. The identifications of relevant factors affecting the participation of volunteers and the manner in which systematic plans are devised to deal with them will determine if their organisations' volunteer programmes will be viable. In short, we are talking about organisational appraisal of volunteer usage, a subject which seems to be much neglected in the management of organisations. This is simply because the running of these organisations is viewed as a voluntary exercise based on altruism. Voluntary social and welfare organisations can become effective enterprises provided those who manage it are prepared to come to grip with and tackle issues which affect volunteer involvement in their organisations.

It is important for management and professionals in voluntary social and welfare organisations to address these questions: Are our volunteer programmes meeting the changing needs of our constituents? What is the outcome of our volunteer programmes? and What kind of mechanism do we have to ensure the good quality of our volunteer programmes? Only when management, professionals and volunteers begin to seriously find answers to these questions, then can organisations demonstrate the efficiency and effectiveness of its volunteer programmes.

People who are volunteers in voluntary social and welfare organisations are from various occupations. A significant number of them also hold executive positions in other civic organisations. This seems to be so because those who are active in one organisation are usually persuaded to assume leadership in another. This precarious situation has its consequences, although we may argue that they can still contribute their expertise. Firstly, confusion of role-identify may arise because they are involved in too many organisations which may have complementary or conflicting objectives. Secondly, the ability to give their best can be affected. Thirdly, their participation may be less forthcoming owing to their numerous commitments. Therefore, it is important for those in leadership position not to be involved in too many organisations as this will affect their potential to be effective.

For voluntary social and welfare organisations to be progressive, it must have a continuity of leadership and direction. Change in leadership style and management may be necessary and this can be instituted by co-opting more people who have the experience to contribute towards organisational efficiency and goal attainment.

Many of those who lead in voluntary social and welfare organisations are busy with their own commitments and some therefore may not be able to attend consistently the meetings of their organisations. The poor attendance of principal members at various meetings leads to their non-attachments to their organisations which will in turn minimise their opportunities to obtain appropriate feedback from volunteers about their organisations' progress. This lack of feedback will ultimately affect their roles in strengthening voluntary service partnership.

In order to prevent volunteers and volunteer leaders from being over-burdened, it is essential to have a more equitable distribution of responsibilities so that there will be no over-loading on a few persons. Also, the distribution of duties will enable the volunteers as well as volunteer leaders not only to be just involved in planning and administration but also in monitoring the results of their programmes. All these aspects if implemented, can promote job satisfaction among volunteers and volunteer leaders involved in voluntary service.

Promoting care and share

The voluntary social and welfare services under the auspices of the National Council of Social Service, a national co-ordinating body for voluntary social and welfare organisations saw a need for its affiliates to join efforts to inform and persuade the public to contribute funds and volunteer service to charitable activities. As a result of this, a centralised fund raising body, the Community Chest of Singapore, was formed in 1983. The formation of the Chest was precipitated by a few concerns which had to be addressed so that the service delivery of the voluntary social and welfare organisations would not be affected.

Firstly, affiliated agencies of the National Council of Social Service were confronted by increasing competition in fund raising among them and smaller organisations faced increasing difficulties to compete for funds.

Secondly, it was felt that establishment of the Chest would relieve welfare organisations of the burdens of raising funds and they could concentrate more on improving their services.

Thirdly, the collective fund raising efforts by the Chest would reduce the number of times corporations and the public are approached for donations and as a result this would minimise aversive feelings about charitable givings.

Fourthly, the collective fund raising would be more cost effective and provide a more equitable system of fund distribution to affiliates.

Finally, the community would be encouraged to share the public burden of supporting the unfortunate and the less abled members. This is in line with the Government's policy to promote self-help and to avoid undue dependence on state intervention and provision of welfare handouts.

Arguments against a welfarist model have been advanced and strongly supported by the government because there would be a strain on national budget, increase in taxes to sustain various social security measures and the incentive for productive investments and work ethnics would be eroded (Wong, 1983). In view of this situation, we see a more decentralisation of care of the less fortunate from the government to greater community efforts.

This trend in involving the community is useful and hopefully it will humanise the care of the less fortunate. However, to be effective, some basic support from government in terms of grant matching financial, tax exemption, and facilities, is necessary as it would make government involvement more visible.

Growth of Community Chest

The Chest has become a viable forum for collective fund raising. It is now a household name. The number of charities supported by the Chest has increased from 18 in 1984 to 42 in 1991. Correspondingly, the funds required to support the work of these charities have also increased from $5 million in 1984 to $24 million in 1991. (Community Chest, 1991). It is indeed a trying task to raise such a large sum of funds but with the backing of many Singaporeans, the funding targets of the Chest have been achieved. This also reflects that Singaporeans do respond positively to worthy charitable activities and they are also 'others orientated'.

The Chest growth has attracted the involvement of many lay people and professionals who volunteer in the management of the Chest as well in its activities. Their participation has generated the development of a wider network of support from corporations, community groups and individuals. The survival of the Chest depends on whether the ordinary citizens, particularly workers are identified with its mission and they can visualise that their monetary contributions are helping specific groups in need. It is therefore important to project the Chest as a personable organisation, and moves to impersonality will weaken the support base.

More organisations are joining the Chest because they are allocated funds on the basis of deficit funding. They are given more or less guaranteed income, and allocation of funds are not influenced by any interested parties. This impartiality does help to enhance the credibility of the Chest.

Popular fund-raising methods

The Chest's most popular fund raising method is the SHARE (Social Help and Assistance Raised by Employees) programme and it is the main source of funds since 1988.

The SHARE programme receives monthly pledges through payroll, bank account or credit card deductions from employees. In the last seven years, 205,562 employees from 864 corporations are regular contributors and about $7 million is raised from the programme.

At this juncture about 20% of the working population are contributing and they are mostly the public sector employees. Their average contribution is $3 per month. This is the most cost-effective fund raising method.

The more manpower intensive methods of fund raising such as charity dinners, film premiers, walkathons, TV shows and donation draws are carried out from time to time. Sometimes these fund raising activities do not produce good returns if not carefully managed.

SHARE programme does have further mileage with the mobilisation of SHARE Executives from supportive companies which deploys their employees to help the Chest during the SHARE campaign month. As more SHARE Executives are recruited, the muplitier effects of fund raising would be realized. The SHARE Executive Programme need to be popularise and companies are beginning to see the long term benefits of being seen as good corporate citizens and an opportunity for the executives to be trained in community relations skills.

Some consequences of collective fund raising effort

The establishment of the Community Chest for centralised fund raising to support the voluntary social welfare services has given a new lease of organisational life to the benefiting organisations. They can pioneer new programmes to meet new community needs. Evidently, seven new projects related to the rehabilitation of the disabled, aged sick and counselling and protection of distressed families have been implemented since 1985. These would not have been possible without collective fund-raising efforts through the Chest.

New emphases and opportunities for participation in the voluntary social and welfare sector have emerged. Voluntary efforts are now directed towards the improvement of service delivery instead of dealing with punctuated worries about the financial inadequacy of agencies.

Centralised fund raising has attempted to rally community efforts to meet the needs of the less fortunate by institutionalising a system of public accountability among voluntary social and welfare organisations. On the other hand the side effects of such an approach are insatiable funding needs and overbudgeting by agencies, dependency and danger of depersonalisation of beneficiaries and compassion fatigue as a result of continuous request for donations.

Conclusion

Participation in the voluntary social and welfare services can be adversely affected especially if voluntary efforts are not given social support by volunteer leaders and staff. As a consequence high attrition rate of volunteers would be expected because they become burn-out. The partnership among volunteers, volunteer leaders and staff has to be strengthened.

Various pertinent factors influencing voluntary efforts in Singapore have been identified and elaborated. The declining young and increasing aged population hold both promise and setbacks for voluntarism in Singapore. Less young people will be available for leadership renewal in voluntary social and welfare organisations whilst on the other hand there will be a surplus of retirees whose talents and expertise could be fully tapped for voluntary activities.

The major milestone in the voluntary social and welfare service scene is the development of centralised funding undertaken by Community Chest. This has reshaped the manner of charitable contributions and will influence the service directions of voluntary social and welfare service sector. Competitions for donations will in future be between the Chest and other non-Chest funded agencies.

The policy emphasis on promoting self-help has led to more voluntary initiatives to provide services for the less abled and unfortunate persons in Singapore. In recent years many voluntary social and welfare organisations have been established in the neighbourhoods of housing estates to promote neighbourhood betterment programmes. For these organisations to be more viable, matching government grants could be considered.

More urgently, for voluntary efforts to be efficiently and effectively tapped, skilled and competent volunteer manpower is essential. Many good and competent professionals must be attracted to give a fresh impetus to the management of the voluntary social and welfare services.

References

Community Chest of Singapore (1991). Budget Facts and Figures 1991.
Esman, M.J. (1978). "Development Administration and Constituency Organisation." *Public Administration Review*, Vol. 38(2): 166–172.
Francis, G.R. (1985). "Motivating Volunteers to Participate" in Moore, L.F., *Motivating Volunteers*. Vancouver: The Volunteer Centre.
Gidron, B. (1983). "Sources of Job Satisfaction." *Journal of Voluntary Action*, Vol. 1(10), pp. 20–25.

Housing and Development Board (1989/90), Annual Report, Singapore.

Olson, M. (1965). *The Logic of Collective Action*. New York, Cambridge, Mass: Harvard Press.

Seah, C.M. (1979). Grassroots Leaders' Political Participation, 25th Anniversary Publication, Petir, People's Action Party, pp. 276–281.

Smith, D.H. (1980). "Determinants of Individual's Discretionary Use of Time," in Smith, D.H. et al. (eds.), *Participation in Social and Political Activities*. London: Jossey-Bass, pp. 34–75.

Vasoo, S. (1987). "Residents' Organisations in New Towns of Hong Kong and Singapore: Some Issues and Future Development," *Asian Journal of Public Administration*, Vol. 2: 143–145.

Vasoo, S. (1991). "Grass-root Mobilisation and Citizen Participation: Issues and Challenges," *Community Development Journal*, Vol. 26(1): 1–7.

Volunteer Action and Development Centre (VADC, 1990). Survey of Volunteer Manpower in Singapore.

Wong, A and Yeh, H. K. eds. (1985). *Housing A Nation*. Maruzen Asia, Singapore.

Chapter 22

Neighbourhood leaders' participation: Conclusions and implications*

S. Vasoo

Introduction

This chapter will draw some specific conclusions based on the macro and micro analyses of the information and data gathered through secondary information and the empirical research on neighbourhood leaders in the residents' organizations in Toa Payoh New Town. At the same time, the task would not be complete without suggesting the more important implications of the neighbourhood leaders' participation in community development.

---

*Reprinted with permission by the publisher from Vasoo, S. (1994). Conclusions and Implications. In S. Vasoo, *Neighbourhood Leaders' Participation in Community Development* (pp. 125–137). Singapore: Times Academic Press.

This is a selected chapter based on findings of the study done on neighbourhood leaders and their participative behaviour, particularly the neighbourhood leaders' satisfaction in their participation in community development in Toa Payoh New Town. The conclusion and implications seem to suggest the neighbourhood leaders with high resident orientations with given social support tend to be more retentive and driven to participate. For more details readers are encouraged to read the monograph.

Development of residents' organizations

It has been observed that a number of common factors have accounted for the development of residents' organizations in Singapore. First, the massive relocation of people, particularly into public housing estates in the new towns, has some social consequences, which if left unattended, would have repercussions not only to the welfare of residents but also the government concerned. Social consequences such as the breakdown of traditional helping networks, the loss of effective communication channels between those who govern and the people, the feeling of alienation and anomie among residents, the increasing pressure from residents for better urban services by local governmental bureaucracies, disgruntlements arising from residents whose needs are unmet as a result of relocation and the like, have provoked the Singapore government to direct significant resources to encourage the formation of residents' organizations. These intermediate organizations are established to provide solutions to deal with the effects of resettlement and high-rise living in public housing estates.

Second, about half of the residents in the new towns of Singapore are below 25 years old. In the future it is envisaged that they would form a rather articulate group which would demand more participatory democracy in the affairs of their neighbourhoods.

It would be a gross misjudgement of the government if appropriate channels are not devised for residents to participate in neighbourhood affairs. Hence, residents' organizations were crystallized as basic grassroots structures to mobilize the young who are socially active in the neighbourhoods of the new towns in Singapore. However, it is not sufficient to merely have intentions to provide the young with channels for participation. Such intentions must be translated into concrete action to encourage them to be involved. More programmes such as civic education, environmental conservation, credit union, neighbourhood social service, family-life education and volunteer leadership development, could be implemented to attract the young. Youth groups or committees could be set-up under the auspices of the residents' organizations to provide a new impetus and renewal of neighbourhood leadership.

Third, traditional institutions which in the past played an important mediatory role between the residents and the government have lost their credibility (Seah 1979). This is because their functions have not evolved to keep abreast with the changing needs of residents. They have become impotent in representing broader cross-sectional interests of residents and have hence lost their grounds to be effective channels to communicate with the government bureaucracies in the respective settings. Their lethargy has precipitated the Singapore government to encourage alternative organizational forms such as the residents' organizations. Like other traditional institutions, the residents' organizations in Singapore also face the danger of becoming inactive. This would be precipitated if more LRO neighbourhood leaders dominate the leadership and the respective governments do not give active support to residents' organizations.

Implications of government sponsorship

The Singapore government adopted an interventionist approach to establish residents' organizations as channels for participation in community development. This resulted in the formation of an elaborate network of residents' organizations in the neighbourhoods of various new towns. As a consequence there was plenty of room to fill the void in neighbourhood leadership. Neighbourhood leaders were appointed by the government to encourage citizens' participation. Critics have argued that such a co-optive process has given rise to doubts among some residents in Singapore about the authenticity of these neighbourhood leaders' intentions. Where neighbourhood leaders have been appointed by the authorities, such scepticism does arise and this attitude can be further reinforced if the government does not provide avenues for direct dialogue with residents and other bona fide groups on various matters of concern. The availability of these channels will make citizens' participation more representative and thereby reduce skepticism among residents of the government's intentions.

Government over-sponsorship of residents' organizations may produce counter-effects to community development if the neighbourhood leaders rely heavily on government administrative bureaucrats to chart programme directions for their residents' organizations. They can become insular by mainly undertaking programmes which are standardized. In the long-run, residents' organizations and their leadership may become dependent. It would be important for the neighbourhood leaders to redefine the objectives of their organizations and work in concert with various governmental structures to improve the delivery of urban services.

The continued reliance of the residents' organizations in Singapore on a small leadership base can contribute to organizational inertia. This condition would stem from a lack of initiative of these leaders to create opportunities for residents to participate in decision-making. There is an apparent danger that the leadership may become omnipotent if it assumes that it knows best the problems faced by residents.

A structured framework has evolved for grassroots level participation of residents. It also acts as a conduit through which anti-government or communist inspired activities can be dealt with. This strategy has been adopted by the government since independence. The challenges facing such an a channel of citizens' participation is its ability to reach residents who abstain from participating in residents' organizations.

The residents' organizations are conceived as administrative satellites through which citizens and their leaders can be urged to participate in improving the urban service delivery systems. It is a neighbourhood organization established to recruit voluntary manpower to tackle various problems confronting the urban setting. These problems such as environmental deterioration, anomie, crime and psychological stress will not be effectively solved by the administrative machinery of the government alone unless the support and cooperation of neighbourhood leaders and residents are harnessed.

Structure and organization

The residents' organizations are established with the initial assistance of the government bureaucrats, namely the Senior Community Development Officers in the Constituency Secretariat. The organization is centrally coordinated by the Field Division which is located in the People's Association. As a result of this centralization, all policies decided by the Field Division on the operations of the residents' organizations have a uniform impact. Such a centralized coordinating system has its pros and cons. It provides uniformity in the deployment of government resources and quick dissemination of government policies. On the other hand, the organizational variations in terms of their activities specific to the neighbourhood needs may be sacrificed for the sake of maintaining similarity in the structure and activities. It is indeed useful to ensure that flexibility is given to the residents' organizations to design organization structures which are relevant to their operational context. Innovative organization structures can encourage more residents' participation.

There is flexibility for residents' organizations to cooperate in carrying out joint activities and this encourages the initiatives of the neighbourhood leadership to cooperate at the inter-organizational level in dealing with issues affecting residents widely. The encouragement of cooperation among residents' organizations will lessen competition for financial resources and enable them to work together on specific issues affecting the various constituencies.

Characteristics of the neighbourhood leaders

Generally, the neighbourhood leadership in the residents' organization in Toa Payoh has a higher percentage of involvement by people with professional and technical backgrounds than other occupational area. The dominance by members of this group is as expected because they seem to have high political efficacy — a characteristic that has been substantiated by other studies (Jones et al. 1978:72–8; Yuen 1983:12–3). Their presence strengthens the leadership of the residents' organization as their expertise could be tapped.

What appears more significant in the new town setting is that there is an under representation of neighbourhood leaders with lower socio-economic status (SES) although the majority of their working population is engaged in production and service related occupations. The low representation of people with lower SES in the residents' organizations could be attributed to the lack of tangible rewards which are important to meet their needs (O'Brien 1975).

The under representation of people with lower SES in the neighbourhood leadership can hamper the work of the residents' organizations. This is particularly so when the current leadership is unable to reflect and respond to the needs of residents in the lower income group in the various neighbourhoods. The danger of a more biased organizational outlook reflecting the interests of elites can be averted by the government. This can be achieved by encouraging a good mix of people with low and high SES to be involved in the residents' organizations.

More neighbourhood leaders in the residents' organizations in Toa Payoh have high resident orientation. This can be attributed to altruistic interests prevalent among people who volunteer. On the other hand, there is a correlation between high resident orientation neighbourhood leaders and their past membership in school clubs in the new town. It appears that their past association with school clubs produced a socializing effect on their resident orientation which is viewed to play a role in influencing their participative behaviour.

In Toa Payoh, there is more middle-aged neighbourhood leaders. Both the young and middle-aged neighbourhood leaders in the new town have high resident orientation and are better educated. The level of education does influence the residents' orientation. Better education can make the neighbourhood leader more critical about prevailing organizational conditions which may hamper their performance in their residents' organizations.

The system of selection of neighbourhood leaders into residents' organizations as practised in Toa Payoh is based on the notion of free-will and interests to volunteer. In such an open system, neighbourhood leaders with either low or high resident orientation are attracted to be involved. It is sometimes difficult to predict how they would perform in their residents' organizations. However, despite this dilemma, it cannot be denied that steps can be undertaken to encourage more people with high residents' orientation to take up leadership position in the residents' organizations. When more neighbourhood leaders with this characteristic are attracted to be involved in the residents' organizations, they could help the organizations to be viable. This is because HRO neighbourhood leaders are motivated to represent problems of residents.

Neighbourhood leaders in community development

The neighbourhood leaders in Toa Payoh are actively involved in carrying out various activities to promote community betterment. The inactive state is confined more to those with LRO.

The neighbourhood leaders, especially those with HRO would form the driving force behind any activities for community betterment. This is partly because the objectives of their residents' organizations are sufficiently flexible to encourage innovations to improve the welfare of residents in the neighbourhoods. As a result, less frustrations are encountered by them in their participation.

The HRO neighbourhood leaders, unlike their LRO counterparts, are motivated by 'people oriented' desires. These neighbourhood leaders who have such traits require the necessary social support to sustain their participation.

Factors influencing community development participation

There is ample evidence from the results of the findings to suggest that Toa Payoh's neighbourhood leaders' participation in community development varies directly with the level of social support. Therefore, it is necessary to ensure that high social support conditions are present in the residents' organizations all the time. This is important for the sustenance of the neighbourhood leaders' performance. High social support acts as an incentive or a motivator (Herzberg 1966) and it provides the impetus for them to discharge their responsibilities satisfactorily. In some studies (Qureshi et al. 1979; Gidron 1983), it has been established that satisfaction in voluntary action is significantly related to the presence of support elements or satisfiers (Gidron 1983) such as task achievement, recognition, good interpersonal relations and working conditions and professional assistance.

The two social support elements, namely officials' and committee members' support are the most important of the four support elements identified. They appear to account for activating the participation of the neighbourhood leaders. This is because non-profit organizations like residents' organizations have no tangible incentives to offer their neighbourhood leaders except for these two social support elements which play a significant part in dictating their performance.

HRO neighbourhood leaders in Toa Payoh are more positively responsive to high social support conditions. This is because the HRO neighbourhood leaders by the very nature of their concern to better the welfare of residents in their respective neighbourhoods, expect high social support conditions to carry out their work effectively. High social support conditions are therefore important and have a motivating effect on the HRO neighbourhood leaders in the new town. To develop further from these findings, it can be surmised that HRO and high social conditions are universal factors enhancing satisfaction, frequency of participation and continuity in the work of residents' organizations.

It is also interesting to note that low social support conditions have different effects on the participative behaviour of HRO and LRO neighbourhood leaders in Toa Payoh. The LRO neighbourhood leaders are more dissatisfied than their HRO counterparts. This situation is contributed by the pressure asserted by the HRO neighbourhood leaders on the LRO neighbourhood leaders who have generally been found not to be performing as expected. As a consequence, the LRO neighbourhood leaders become dissatisfied.

Implications for specific areas

Finally, this chapter would be ill-conceived if it overlooked discussions on implications of the findings on three specific areas:

a) social or community workers interested in working with neighbourhood leaders in the residents' organizations in Singapore;
b) future research on neighbourhood leaders in residents' organizations; and
c) the future of the neighbourhood leaders' participation in community development.

Social or community workers and neighbourhood leaders

In Singapore, there has been a growing interest among trained social and community workers to be involved either as employees or volunteers in working with the neighbourhood leaders in the residents' organizations. There seems to be less scepticism but more optimism among trained social workers about the government's role in encouraging neighbourhood leaders' participation in community development.

The author recognizes that besides trained social or community workers, other human service professionals, such as psychologists, sociologists, ecologists, managers and lawyers, can contribute their expertise to the development of residents' organizations. However, the ensuing discussion will only focus on the roles that could be played by trained social or community workers.

The survey has ascertained that social support conditions do directly affect the participative behaviour of neighbourhood leaders. Consequently, this affects the performance of residents' organizations. To understand and take necessary measures to strengthen the internal dynamics of residents' organizations, it is important for the government departments in charge of residents' organizations in Singapore to engage the services of external consultants from time to time. This is because external consultants who have no vested interest in residents' organizations, can conduct objective organizational diagnosis and suggest recommendations to make residents' organizations more viable. So far, some consultants have been approached. It would be timely for the authorities to involve trained social and community workers in Singapore, as they have a long historical connection and experience in human service organizations. They also form the main professional force in these set-ups. Their diagnostic skills drawn from their work with individuals, groups and community would be relevant in the assessment of performance of residents' organizations. A diagnostic instrument to assess the objectives, reward and administrative system, structure, leadership, and resources of residents' organizations, would help to isolate obstacles in any or some of these areas. When neighbourhood leaders are enlightened about their organizational problems, they would be more motivated to find solutions. Solutions to overcome the obstacles could be drawn-up by the trained social and community workers in consultation with the neighbourhood leaders. In due course, the residents' organizations can be strengthened through a more insightful leadership.

Most of the activities organized by the neighbourhood leaders in Singapore are based on superficial information obtained from their limited contacts with residents or on their own assumptions. Hence, residents' participation in activities is limited to a small number of people. More residents could be motivated to be involved in activities, if the neighbourhood leaders become aware of the need to assess residents' viewpoints on various issues. Somehow, because of their lack of technical knowledge and expertise, they have neglected this important task which could provide relevant information to enable them to plan appropriate activities. The assistance of trained social and community workers could be solicited, particularly in designing surveys for the collection, collation, analysis and the presentation of data on a number of areas related to the neighbourhoods. This technical assistance will be valuable in helping the neighbourhood leaders. Otherwise with their limited experience, they will not be able to interpret and fully grasp complex information. Also, with the setting up of a sound information system on socio-economic characteristics of the neighbourhoods, the neighbourhood leaders will have easy access to information for organising appropriate activities.

Like most human service organizations, the residents' organizations are likely to face problems of either stable or declining resources (e.g. voluntary manpower, funds, facilities). Concurrently, they will also be confronted by more complex neighbourhood problems and demands. All these challenges may create dilemmas for the neighbourhood leaders, especially when they are volunteers who would have to contend with the limited discretionary time available to undertake various community activities. In this connection, social and community workers in Singapore can assist the neighbourhood leaders to deal with the dilemmas by encouraging them to draw up the priorities of their organizations. Simultaneously, they can explore with them the possibility of enlarging the base of participation in their organizations. This can be achieved by organizing task forces comprising residents who have a special interest in issues such as environment, crime prevention, town planning, transportation, housing policies, health and education. In doing this, the social and community workers can extend their expertise to spread the burdens of the neighbourhood leaders. More residents with HRO could be mobilized to participate in the various task forces of residents' organizations. At the same time, social and community workers could also encourage the organizational linkage between residents' organizations and other community groups or organizations to deal with broader issues of concern which are outside the purview of residents' organizations. It is felt that this inter-organizational cooperation and coordination when undertaken, will reduce unnecessary wastage of resources and competition among organizations serving the neighbourhoods.

In recent years, increasing emphasis has been given to the training of volunteers in social and welfare service organizations. In this respect, neighbourhood leaders have been given training especially centred on committee procedures. This training however is by itself inadequate to prepare them to be more effective leaders. It lacks concentration in equipping neighbourhood leaders with inter-personal, group processes and dynamics, management and intra-organizational skills. There is a case for the authority to strengthen its training unit urgently. Social and community workers with extensive experience in volunteer training can be requested to develop course modules for the training in the skills mentioned. The strengthening of the training unit will certainly enhance the effective management of residents' organizations.

Future participation in community development

Some discussion would be useful to attempt to address a few pertinent questions relating to the future of the neighbourhood leaders' participation in the Singapore context: will the neighbourhood leaders continue to be active under the prevailing conditions? What steps can be taken to enhance their participation? What will be the effects on their participation as a result of implementation of the Town Councils in Singapore?

The establishment of Town Councils,[1] will directly generate more enthusiasm among the neighbourhood leaders because they will have wider scope of responsibility and decision-making in the management of new towns. Some of them may be selected into the Town Councils and this will upgrade the status of the neighbourhood leaders. Consequently, the dynamics of leadership participation in residents' organizations will be

---

[1] The idea of Town Councils was mooted in 1985 and implemented in 1988. The Town Councils are responsible for the maintenance and management of common areas in housing estates, which used to be one of the HDB's roles in estate management. Such a move has direct implications for the residents' organizations.

more competitive. It cannot be excluded that political aspirants will find their way into residents' organizations and some of whom may be nominated to stand for general election by the government under the political leadership of the PAP.

It is envisaged that the future of neighbourhood leaders' participation in community development in Toa Payoh, will continue to be active, if not strengthened. This is because of the high social support conditions under which the neighbourhood leadership is operating. Besides this, the residents' organizations comprise of more HRO neighbourhood leaders who will remain a dominating force in the leadership. Such a leadership, comprising mainly of committed HRO neighbourhood leaders will by direct or indirect group pressure, weed out the LRO neighbourhood leaders who are unmotivated. In the long-run, more HRO neighbourhood leaders can be expected to be retained in the residents' organizations and with the given high social support conditions, the neighbourhood leadership will continue to be active.

The neighbourhood leaders tend to generally rely on guidance from Senior Community Development Officers. Such a dependency, can in the long-run negate 'self-help' and hinder initiatives to organize residents to be involved in dealing with neighbourhood issues. In order to enhance participation in community development, the primary objective of Senior Community Development Officers is to encourage neighbourhood leaders to improve their neighbourhoods on their own efforts together with the essential cooperation of various governmental authorities.

The survey also seemed to suggest that organizational activism in residents' organizations can be adversely affected, especially when HRO neighbourhood leaders perceive that they do not have high social support. They by nature being more inclined to be active, are often left to carry the burdens of their organizations. As a consequence, they burn out as leaders[2] exhibiting various symptoms such as low satisfaction from achievements, lack of drive in discharging the mission of their organizations, feeling estranged and back-sliding in performance. To prevent HRO neighbour-

---

[2] Burnt-out leadership is a common phenomenon in voluntary organizations. Burnt-out is defined as a process of wearing out or becoming exhausted through excessive demands in energy and resources.

hood leaders from burning out, it is essential that there be a more equitable distribution of organizational responsibilities. More urgently, residents' organizations must have a large majority of HRO neighbourhood leaders so that they can counter the effects of demotivation by LRO neighbourhood leaders. With this and flexible organizational objectives and administrative support by the government for the neighbourhood leaders, it is anticipated that the future work of residents' organizations could be strengthened. However, in the older housing estates, an entirely new phenomenon may emerge.

In Singapore, the older estates will have less active leadership. It therefore becomes necessary for the government to quickly upgrade these older housing estates by building better fiats so that a demographic balance could be maintained for renewal of effective neighbourhood leadership. It is predicted that many of the neighbourhoods leaders with better socio-economic backgrounds living in the older housing estates, will move into new and better housing estates. Such a mobility will most certainly affect the activities of residents' organizations.

Bibliography

Aldridge, M. 1979. *The British New Towns.* London: Routledge & Kegan Paul.

Anderson, Robert. 1971. Voluntary Association in History. *American Anthropologist* 73(i):209–22.

Anderson, Robert and Gallatin Anderson. 1959. Voluntary Associations and Urbanizations: A Diachronic Analysis *American Journal of Sociology* 65:265–73.

Bailey, Robert, Jr. 1974. *Radical in Urban Politics.* Chicago: University of Chicago Press.

Baird's, J.E., Jr. 1977. *The Dynamics of Organisational Communication.* New York: Harper and Row.

Banton, Michael. 1968. Voluntary Associations: Anthropological Aspects. *International Encyclopaedia of the Social Sciences.* Macmillan and the Free Press. 16:357–62.

Barker, E.W. 1970. *Housing and Development Board's First Decade in Public Housing, 1960–1969.* Singapore: Housing Development Board.

Batten, T.R. 1967. *The Non-Directive Approach in Group and Community Work.* Oxford: Oxford University Press.

Berkowitz, L. 1970. The Self, Selfishness, and Altruism. In Macauly, J.R. and Berkowitz, L. eds., *Altruism and Helping Behaviours.* New York: Academic Press.

Bernstein, B. Some Sociological Determinants of Perception. An Inquiry into Sub-Cultural Differences. In Fishman, J.A. ed., 1968. *Readings in the Sociology of Language.* The Hague: Mouton.

Biddle W.W and Biddle, L.J. 1965. *The Community Development Process.* New York: Holt, Rinehart and Winston.

———. 1968. *Encouraging Community Development.* New York: Holt, Rinehart and Winston.

Booth, Alan. 1972. Sex and Social Participation. *American Sociological Review* 37:183–92.

Brager, G. and Specht, H. 1973. *Community Organising.* New York: Columbia University Press.

Briscoe, C. and Thomas, D.N. 1977. *Learning and Supervision in Community Work.* London: George Allen and Unwin.

Byran, J.H. 1972. Why Children Help: A Review. *Journal of Social Issues* 28:87–105.

Carbonnell, Aurora. 1977. *A Case for Citizen Participation: The Role of Citizen Participation in Development.* College of Public Administration, University of Philippines.

Carry, L.J. ed., 1970. *Community Development as a Process.* Columbia: University of Missouri Press.

Chan, H.C. 1975. *Politics in a Administrative State: Where Has the Politics Gone?* Department of Political Science, University of Singapore.

———. 1975. *The Dynamics of One Party Dominance: The PAP at the Grassroots.* Singapore: Singapore University Press.

———. 1976. *The Dynamics of One Party Dominance: A Study of Five Singapore Constituencies.* Singapore: Singapore University Press.

———. 1979. *In Middle Passage the PAP Faces the Eighties.* Singapore: Chopmen Enterprises.

Chan, Phillip, S.S. 1975. *The Planning of a Satellite Town — Toa Payoh New Town.* An Academic Exercise, Department of Estate Management and Building, University of Singapore. 1975.

Cheah, H.B. 1978. *A Study of Poverty in Singapore.* An unpublished M.Soc.Sc. dissertation, University of Singapore.

Chen, Peter, S. J. 1976. An Ecological Study of Social Pathology in Singapore. *Sociology Working Papers No. 59.* Singapore: Department of Sociology, University of Singapore.

———. 1977. *Social Ecology of Singapore.* Singapore: Federal Publications.

———. 1977. The Power Elite in Singapore. In Shaw, K.E. *Elite and National Development in Singapore.* Tokyo: Institute of Developing Economics.

———. 1978. An Ecological Study of Social Pathology in Singapore. In Chen, Peter S.J. and Evers, Hans Dieter eds., *Studies in Asean Sociology.* Singapore: Chopmen Enterprises.

———. 1983. *Singapore: Development Policies and Trends.* London: Oxford University Press.

Chen, Peter S.J. and Tai Chin Lim. 1978. Urban and Rural Living In a Highly Urbanized Society. In Chen, Peter S.J. and Evers, Hans-Dieters eds., *Studies in Asean Sociology.* Singapore: Chopmen Enterprises.

Chiew, S.K. 1981. *Singapore National Identity.* Unpublished M.Soc.Sc. dissertation, University of Singapore.

Chng, M.C. 1975. *Human Territoriality in Singapore: Territorial Needs and Assumptions and HDB Designs.* Academic Exercise, Singapore: Department of Sociology, University of Singapore.

Choe, Alan F.C. 1973. Public Housing, Urban Renewal and Transformation of the Environment. *Towards Tomorrow: Essays on Development and Social Transformation in Singapore.* Singapore: National Trade Union Congress.

Chua, P.C. ed., 1973. *Planning in Singapore.* Singapore: Chopmen Enterprises.

Concericiao, J.F. 1969. A New Environment for Singapore. *Radio and T.V. Talks Series 11.* Singapore: Adult Educational Board.

Cox, F.M. et al. eds., 1970. *Strategies of Community Organisation: A Book of Readings.* Itasca, Illinois: F.E. Peacock Publishers, Inc.

Cox, F.M. et al. 1977. *Tactics and Techniques of Community Practice.* Itasca, Illnois. Peacock.

Crenson, M.A, 1974. Organisational Factors in Critizen Participation. *Journal of Politics* 39:356–78.

Dunham, A. 1970. *The New Community Organisation.* New York: Crowell.

Durkheim, Emile. 1933. *The Division of Labour in Society.* Translated by George Simpson. New York. Macmillan.

Ecklien, J.L. and Lauffer, A A. 1972. *Community Organisers and Social Planners.* New York: Wiley.

Edwards, Allan D. and Jones, Dorothy, G. 1976. *Community and Community Development.* The Hague: Mouton.

Elvin Mark. 1973. *The Pattern of the Chinese Past.* London: Methuen.

Esman, M.J. 1978. Development Administration and Constituency Organisation. *Public Administration Review* 38(2): 166–72.

Fairbank, John K. ed., 1957. *Chinese Thought and Institutions*. Chicago: University of Chicago Press.

Freedman, M. 1957. *Chinese Family and Marriages in Singapore*. London: HMSO.

———. 1960. Immigrants and Associations: Chinese in the Nineteenth Century, Singapore. *Comparative Study in Society and History* 3:25–48.

———. ed., 1970. *Family Kinship in Chinese Society*. Stanford. University of Stanford Press.

Gans, Herbert. 1962. *The Urban Villagers*. New York: Free Press.

Geiger, T. and Geiger, Frances M. 1973. *Tales of Two City-States: The Development and Progress of Hong Kong and Singapore*. National Planning Association, Studies in Development Progress, No. 3.

Gidron, B. Jan-Mar 1983. Sources of Job Satisfaction Among Service Volunteers. *Journal of Voluntary Action Research* 12(1):20–35.

———. 1980. Volunteer Workers: A Labour Economy Perspective. *Labour and Society* 5:355–65.

Goetschius, G.W. 1971. *Working with Community Groups*. London: Routledge and Kegan Paul.

Goh, C.T. 1980. *Kampong Eunos RC Seminar*. Souvenir Magazine.

———. 3 July 1983. Community Participation — The Key to the Security and Prosperity of Singapore. *National RC Conference*. Singapore.

Goh, K.S. 1972. *The Economics of Modernization*. Singapore: Asian Pacific Press.

Goode, E. 1966. Social Class and Church Participation. *American Journal of Sociology* 72:102–11.

Government of Singapore. 1991. *Singapore: The Next Lap*. Singapore: Times Editions.

Grummer, Burton. 1978. A Power-Politics Approach to Social Welfare Organisations. *Journal of Social Service Review* 52(3):349–61.

Gray, Paul. 1976. Voluntary Associations in Ghana. *Journal of Voluntary Action Research* 5(3–4):221–30.

Greer, Scott. Individual Participation in Mass Society. In Roland Young, ed., 1958. *Approaches to the Study of Politics*. Evanston: Northwestern University Press.

Hadley, R. and Webb, A. 1971. Young Volunteers in the Social Services. *Social Work Today* 2:21–5.

Hagedon, R. and Labovitz, S. 1967. An Analysis of Community and Professional Participation Among Occupations. *Social Forces* 46 (June):484–91.

———. 1968. Participation in Community Associations by Occupation: A Test of Three Theories. *American Sociological Review* 33:272–83.

Hall, Edward Twitchell. 1966. *The Hidden Dimension: Man's Use of Space in Public and Private Garden City*. London: Doubleday.
Halpem, G. 1966. Relative Contributions of Motivator and Hygiene Factors to Overall Job Satisfaction. *Journal of Applied Psychology* 50(3):198–200.
Hassan, R. 1975. Social and Psychological Implications of High Population Density. *Sociology Working Papers No. 47*. Singapore: Department of Sociology, University of Singapore.
Hassan, R. 1976. Public Housing. In Hassan, Riaz ed., *Singapore: Society in Transition*. Kuala Lumpur: Oxford University Press.
Hassan, R. 1977. *Families in Flats: A Study of Low Income Families in Public Housing*. Singapore: University of Singapore Press.
Heller, K. and Monahan, J. 1977. *Psychology and Community Change*. Homewoord, Illinois: Dorsey Press.
Henderson, P. and Thomas, D.N. 1980. *Skills in Neighbourhood Work*. London: Allen and Unwin.
———. eds., 1981. *Readings in Community Work*. London: George Allen and Unwin.
Herzberg, F. 1966. *Work and Nature of Man*. Cleveland, Ohio: World Publishing Co.
Ho, S.C. 1975. *Human Territoriality in Singapore: territorial needs and assumption in housing design*. Academic Exercise, Singapore: Department of Sociology, University of Singapore.
Hon, S.S. 1973. *The New Phase of Industrial Development in Singapore*. An Address to The Singapore Press Club, 23 March 1973, Singapore Government Press Statement.
Housing and Development Board (HDB). 1960. *Annual Report*. Singapore.
———. 1965. *Annual Report*. Singapore.
———. 1970. *Annual Report*. Singapore.
———. 1978. *Annual Report*. Singapore.
———. 1980. *Annual Report*. Singapore.
———. 1981. *Annual Report*. Singapore.
———. 1989 *Annual Report*. Singapore.
———. 1991. *Annual Report*. Singapore.
Housing and Development Board. 1965. 50,000 *Up: homes for people*. Singapore: Straits Times Press Ltd.
Howard, E. 1965. *Garden Cities of Tomorrow* (first published in 1898 as Tomorrow: a Peaceful Path to Real Reform). London: Faber.
Huntington, S.P. and Nelson, Joan M. 1976. *No Easy Choice: political participation in development countries*. Cambridge Massachusetts: Harvard University Press.

Inkeles, Alex. 1969. Making Man Modern: On the Causes and Consequences of Industrial Change in 6 Developing Countries. *American Journal of Sociology* 75:208–25.

Janowitz, M. 1967. *The Community Press in an Urban Setting.* Chicago: University of Chicago Press.

Johnson, Graham. 1975. Voluntary Association and Social Change: Some Theoretical Issues. *Journal of Comparative Sociology* 16 (1–2):51–63.

Jones, J. F. et al. 1978. *Neighbourhood Association in a New Town: The Mutual Aid Committees in Shatin.* Social Research Centre, Chinese University of Hong Kong.

Kasl, S. and Harburg, E. 1972. Perceptions of the Neighbourhood and the Desire to Move Out. *Journal of the American Institute of Planners* 38:318–34.

Kemper, T.D. Altruism and Voluntary Action, Smith, D.H. and Macaulay et al. eds., 1980. *Participation in Social and Political Activities.* San Francisco, California: Jossey-Bass Publishers.

Kerri, James. 1976. Studying Voluntary Association as Adaptive Mechanism: A Review of Anthropological Perspectives. *Current Anthropology* 17(1):23–47.

Kramse, Elliott, A. 1968. Functions of a Bureaucratic Ideology: Citizen Participation. *Social Forces* 16(2): 129–43

Lansing, J.B., Marans, R.W., and Zehner, R.B. 1970. *Planned Residential Environments.* Ann Arbor: Michigan Institute for Social Research, University of Michigan.

Lansing, John. B. 1966. *Residential Location and Urban Mobility: The Second Wave of Interviews.* Ann Arbor: Survey Research Centre, Institute for Social Research, University of Michigan.

Lawler, E.E. 1973. *Motivation in Work Organisations.* Monterey, California: Brooks-Cole.

Lee, K.Y. 1962. *Battle for Merger.* Singapore: Government Press.

———. 1965. *The Battle for Malaysia.* Singapore: Government Press.

———. 18 Feb 1970. *Hong Kong and Singapore — A Tale of Two Cities.* An address to the 75th Congregation for the Confemment of Honorary Degree, University of Hong Kong.

———. 20 January 1980. *Speech at the People's Action Party (PAP) 25th Anniversary Rally held at National Theatre.* Singapore.

———. 11 July 1981. *Speech at the inauguration of Tanjong Pagar Plaza and Everton Park Residents' Committees* at Everton Park, Singapore.

———. 17 November 1981. Excerpts from the Prime Minister's Discussions with PAP MPs.

———. 1981. RCs serve as Breeding Grounds of Leaders. *Speeches*. Ministry of Culture, 5(2):1–4.

———. 27 May 1982. *National RC Dinner Souvenir Magazine*. Singapore.

Lim, C.K. 1969. Growth of Central Singapore and Regeneration of the City. *Journal of the Singapore Institute of Architects*. July/August No. 35:2–23.

Lim, S. 1973. *Relocation, Social Networks and Neighbouring Interaction in a Block of Flats*. Academic Exercise, Singapore: Department of Sociology, University of Singapore.

Lim, S.S. July 1980. *The Role of Residents' Committees — Problems and Prospects*. An unpublished paper presented at the Seminar organized by HDB and RC Central Secretariat.

Linski, G.E. 1956. Social Participation and Status Crystallization. *American Sociological Review* 21:458–64.

Little, Kenneth. 1965. *West African Urbanization: A Study of Voluntary Association in Social Change*. Cambridge: Cambridge University Press.

Litwak, Eugene and Meyer, Henry C. A. 1967. Balance Theory of Co-ordination between Bureaucratic Organisations and Community Primary Groups. In Edwin J. Thomas ed., *Behaviour and Science for Social Workers*. New York: Free Press.

Liu, T.K. 1973. Reflection on Problems and Prospects in the Second Decade of Singapore's Public Housing. In Chua, P.C. ed., *Planning in Singapore*. Singapore: Chopmen Enterprises.

Liu, T.K. Design for Better Living Conditions. In Yeh, S. H. K. ed., *Public Housing in Singapore*. Singapore: Singapore University Press.

Loh, E.J. 1974. *Sociological Consequences of Internal Density on Personal and Family Relationships — A Case Study*. An Academic Exercise, Department of Sociology, University of Singapore.

Loh, S.S. 1980. *Integrated Planning and Implementation of Public Housing in Singapore — A Case Study*. Singapore Housing and Development Board.

Loring, W.C. Housing and Social Organisation. 1956. *Journal of Social Problems* 3:160–68.

———. 1964. Residential Environment, Nexus of Personal Interactions and Healthful Developments. *Journal of Health and Human Behaviour* 5:166–69.

Loy, Jackson, D.E. 1979. *The Residents Committees in Singapore*. An *Exploratory Study*. An Academic Exercise, Department of Sociology, University of Singapore.

Macrov, D. 1972. Work Patterns and Satisfaction in an Israeli Kibbutz: A Test of the Herzberg Hypothesis. *Personnel Psychology* 25:481–92.

Madge, John. 1968. Housing: Social Aspects. *International Encyclopedia of Social Sciences* 6:516–21. Macmillan: Free Press.

Maimon, Z. and Ronen, S. 1978. Measures of Job Facets Satisfaction as Predictors of the Tendency to Leave or Tendency to Stay with an Organisation. *Human Relations* 31(12): 1019–130

Milne R.S. and Diane K. Mauzy. 1990. *Singapore: The Legacy of Lee Kuan Yew.* Boulder and Oxford: Westview Press.

Ministry of Culture. 1978–82. *Speeches.* Singapore: Government Printer.

———. 1971. Some Social Implications of High Density Housing. *American Sociological Review* 36:18–29.

———. 1967. *Towards a More Just Society.* Singapore: Government Printing Office.

Nanyang University Geographical Society. 1970. An Abridged Report of the Geographic Survey on the Toa Payoh and Queenstown Housing Estates. *The Geographical Journal* 3.

Nellkin, D. 1974. *Jetport: The Boston Airport Controversy.* New York: Transaction.

O'Brien, D.J. 1975. *Neighbourhood Organisations and Interest Group Processes.* Princeton, New Jersey: Princeton University Press.

Olson, M. 1965. *The Logic of Collective Action.* New York, Cambridge, Mass: Harvard University Press.

Ong, Teck Hui. 1979/1980. *Community Living in Highrise Density Public Housing in Singapore.* Academic Exercise, Department of Building and Estate Management, National University of Singapore.

Ong, W.H. 1978. *The Economics of Growth and Survival.* Singapore: National Trade Union Congress.

Ooi, J.B. and Chiang, H.D. eds. 1969. *Modern Singapore.* Singapore University of Singapore Press.

Osborn, F.J. 1942. *New Towns after the War.* London: Dent.

———. 1954. Success of the New Towns. *Town and Country Planning* 22(131):117–18.

Osborn, F.J. and Whittick, A. 1969. *The New Towns: The Answers to Megalopolis.* London: Leonard Hill.

Palisi, B. 1965. Ethnic Generation and Social Participation. *Sociological Inquiry* 35:219–26.

Perlman, R and Gurtn, A. 1972. *Community Organising and Social Planning.* New York: John Wiley and Sons.

Phoon W.D. et al. 1976. A Preliminary Study of the Health of a Population Staying in Apartments of Varying Sizes. Singapore. *Annals of Tropical Medicine and Parasitology* 70(2):232–46.

Quah, J.S.T. 1975. *Administrative Reform and Development Administration in Singapore: A Comparative Study of the Singapore Improvement Trust and the Housing and Development Board.* Ph.D. Thesis, Fonda State University.

Qureshi, H., Daviers, B., Challis, D. 1979. Motivations and Rewards of Volunteers and Informal Care Givers. *Journal of Voluntary Action Research* 8(1–2):47–55.

Residents' Committee (RC) Central Secretariat. 1980. *Handbook on RC Rules and Regulations.* Singapore.

Residents' Committee (RC) Central Secretariat. Mar 1982. *Monthly Report.* Singapore.

Rich, Richard C. 4 March 1980. The Dynamics of Leadership in Neighbourhood Organisation. *Social Science Quarterly* 60(4):47–55, 570–87.

Riches, G. Spring 1971. A Process of Community Development Functions of Community Centres in Hong Kong and Singapore. *International Review of Community Development* Nos. 25–26.

Riches, G. 1978. *Community Centres in Singapore and Hong Kong.* Centre for Asian Studies, University of Hong Kong.

Rose, A.M. 1962. Nation and Participation: A Comparison of Group Leaders and the Mass. *American Sociological Reveiw* 27:834–38.

Ross, M. 1967. *Community Organisation.* London: Harper and Row.

Rothman, J. 1974. *Planning and Organising for Social Change.* New York: Columbia University Press;

Sanders, I.T. 1958. Theories of Community Development. *Rural Sociology* 23:1–12.

Savage, Victor. 1973. *Intra-Urban Residential Mobility — A Case Study of Neighbourhood Three, Toa Payoh.* An Academic Exercise, Department of Geography, University of Singapore.

Schmidt, J.F. and Rohrer, W.C. 1956. The Relationship of Family Type to Social Participation. *Marriage and Family Living* 18:224–30.

Scott, J.C., Jr. 1957. Membership and Participation in Voluntary Associations. *American Sociological Review.* 22:315–26.

Seah, C.M. 1973. *Community Centres in Singapore: Their Political Involvement.* Singapore: Singapore University Press.

———. 1978. Grassroots Political Participation in Singapore. *Petir 25th Anniversary Issue: 1954–1978.* Singapore: People's Action Party.

Sharp, E.B. 1978. Citizen Organisation in Policing Issues and Crime Prevention: Incentives for Participation. *Journal of Action Research* 7(1–2):45–58

Sills, D.L. 1957. *The Volunteers. Means and Ends in a National Organisation.* Glencoe. Free Press.

Singapore, Dec 1978. *Hansard* 38(1):50–51. Singapore Parliamentary Proceedings.
Singapore People's Association. 1980. *Annual Report.* People's Association.
Singapore Police Force. 1980. *Annual Report.* Singapore: Ministry of Home Affairs.
Singapore Statistics Department. *Singapore Census 1947.* Singapore: Singapore National Printer.
———. *Singapore Census 1957.* Singapore: Singapore National Printer.
———. *Singapore Census 1980.* Singapore: Singapore National Printer.
———. *Household Expenditure Survey, 1987–88.* Singapore National Printer.
———. *Singapore Census 1990.* Singapore: Singapore National Printer.
Smith, Constance and Freedman, Anne. 1972. *Voluntary Associations: Perspectives on the Literature.* Cambridge, Massachusetts: Harvard University Press.
Smith, D.H. 1966. A Psychological Model of Individual Participation, Applications to Some Chilean Data. *American journal of Sociology* 72:249–66.
Smith, D.H. 1981. Altruism, Volunteers and Volunteerism. *Journal of Voluntary Action Research* 10(1):21–36.
Smith, D.H. and Reddy, R.D. 1972. An Overview of the Determinants of Individual Participation in Organised Voluntary Action. In D. H. Smith, R. D. Reddy, and B. R. Baldwin eds., *Voluntary Action Research.* Lexington, Mass, Heath.
Smith, D. H. and Reddy, R. D. 1972. Contextual & Organisational Determinants of Individual Participation in Organised Voluntary Action. In D.H. Smith, R.D. Reddy and B.R. Baldwin eds.. *Voluntary Action Research.* Lexington, Mass, Heath.
———. 1980. Methods of Inquiry and Theoretical Perspectives. In Smith D. H. et al. *Participation in Social and Political Activities.* London: Jossey-Bass.
———. 1980. Determinants of Individuals' Discretionary Use of Time in Smith D.H. et al. *Participation in Social and Political Activities.* London: Jossey-Bass Publishers.
Sommer, Robert. 1969. *Personal Space: The Behavioural Basis of Design.* Eaglewood Dliffs, New Jersey: Prentice-Hall.
Staub, E. 1975. *The Development of Prosocial Behaviour in Children.* Morisstown, New Jersey: General Printing Press.
Staub, E. and Feinberg, H.K. 1980. Socialization and Prosocial Behaviour in Children. In Smith, D.H., Macanlay, J. et al. *Participation in Social and Political Activities.* London: Jossey-Bass Publishers.
Sussman, M.B. Activity Patterns of Post-Parental Couples and their Relationship to Family Continuity. *Marriage and Family Living* 17:338–41.

Tai Ching Ling Relocation and Population Planning: A Study of the Implication of Public Housing and Family Planning in Singapore. In Acre, W.F. and Alvarez, Gabriel, eds., 1983. *Population in Southeast Asia.* Singapore: Institute of Southeast Asian Studies.

Tai Ching Ling and Chen, Peter. 1982. *Housing As a Basic Need.* Singapore: Maruzen Asia.

Tan, Roney K.L. 1972. *The Impact of Relocation of HDB Tenants — A Case Study.* M. Soc. Sc. Thesis. Singapore. Department of Sociology, University of Singapore.

Tan, T.B. Estate Management. Yeh, Stephen, K.S. eds., 1975. *Public Housing in Singapore.* Singapore: Singapore University Press.

Taub, Richard P. et al. 1977. Urban Voluntary Associations Locality Based and Externally Induced. *American Journal of Sociology* 83:425–42.

Tay, K.S. Public Housing in Singapore. 1969. *Rumah* 8:37–42.

Taylor, W.E.K. 1974. The Nature of Community Work. *Community Development Journal* 9(2).

Teh, C.W. Public Housing in Singapore. The Singapore Improvement Trust. 1961. *Rumah* 4:5–9.

———. 1963. Public low-cost and low-rental Housing in Singapore. *Ekistics* 16(93):88–91.

———. 1967. *Design and Planning of Public Housing in Singapore.* Second Afro-Asian Housing Congress. Singapore. Also published in Cairo: Afro-Asian Housing Organisation.

———. Public Housing. Ooi, J. B. and Chiang, H.D. eds., 1969. *Modern Singapore.* Singapore: University of Singapore.

———. Public Housing — the Next Efforts. In Conceicao, J.F. ed., 1969a. *A New Environment for Singapore.* Radio and T.V. Talks Series 11. Singapore: Adult Education Board.

———. Public Housing in Singapore: An Overview, in Yeh, S.H.K. ed., 1975. *Public Housing in Singapore.* Singapore: Singapore University Press.

Thung, S.N. Needs and Community Services in Housing Estates. Seminar Proceedings. Oct 1977. *Social Well-Being Through Community Participation: The Contribution of Social Work.* Singapore.

Tomeh, A.K. 1973. Formal Voluntary Organisation Participation, Correlates and Interrelationships. *Sociological Inquiry* 43:89–22.

Tonnies, Ferdinard. 1957. *Community and Society.* Translated and edited by Charles P. Loomis. East Lansing: Michigan State University Press.

Turner, J. ed., 1968. *Neighbourhood Organisation for Community Action.* New York: National Association of Social Workers.

United Nations. 1975. *Popular Participation in Decision Making for Development.* New York.

Wandersman, A. 1981. A Framework of Participation in Community Organisations. *Journal of Applied Behavioural Service* 17(1):27–58.

Warren, R.B. and Warren, D.I. 1977. *The Neighbourhood Organisers Handbook.* Notre Dame: University of Notre Dame Press.

Western, J.S. et al. 1973. Housing and Satisfactions With Environment in Singapore. *Sociology Working Papers* No. 13. Singapore: Department of Sociology, University of Singapore.

Wilner Daniel, M. et al. 1962. *The Housing Environment and Family Life: A Longitudinal Study of the Effects on Housing and Morbidity and Mental Health.* Baltimore: John Hopkins Press.

Wilner Daniel, M. and Baer, W.G. 1970. *Sociocultural Factors in Residential Space.* Mineograph. Department of Health, Education and Welfare and the American Public Health Association, USA.

Winsborough, H.H. 1965. The Consequences of High Population Density. *Law and Contemporary Problems* 31:120–6.

Wong, Aline K. 1974. *The Social Implications of High-Rise Living.* Proceedings of the Conference on Tall Buildings. Kuala Lumpur: Institution of Engineers.

Wong, Aline and Yeh, Stephen H.K. eds., 1985. *Housing A Nation: 25 Years of Public Housing in Singapore.* Singapore: Housing Development Board.

Yap, M.T. 1975. *Privacy and Neighbourliness.* Academic Exercise. Singapore: Department of Sociology, University of Singapore.

Yeh, S.H.K. and Lee Yoke San. 1968. Housing Conditions in Singapore. *Malayan Economic Review* 13(1):11–38.

Yeh, S.H.K. 1972. *Homes For the People: A Study of Tenants' Views on Public Housing in Singapore.* Singapore: Government Printing Office.

Yeh, S.H.K. Mar 1972. Some Trends and Prospects in Singapore's Public Housing. *Ekistics* 33(196).

Yeh, S.H.K. and Tan, S. L. 1974/75. Satisfaction With Living Conditions in Public Housing Estate in Singapore. *Journal of the Singapore Institute of Planners* 4(1): 72–84.

Yeh, S.H.K. Housing Conditions & Housing Needs. In Yeh, S.H.K. ed., 1975. *Public Housing in Singapore.* Singapore: Singapore University Press.

Yeh, S.H.K. ed., 1975a. *Public Housing in Singapore: A Multi-disciplinary Study.* Singapore: Singapore University Press.

Yeung, Yue Man and Yeh, S.H.K. A Review of Neighbourhoods and Neighbouring Practices. Yeh, Stephen H.K. ed., 1975. *Public Housing in Singapore.* Singapore: Singapore University Press,

Yeung, Y.M. and Yeh, S.H.K. Life Styles Compared: Squatters and Public Housing Residents. Yeh, S.H.K. ed., 1975a. *Public Housing in Singapore.* Singapore: Singapore University Press.

Yuen, Kathy. Dec 1983. *Report of Survey on Residents' Opinion About Community Participation and the Residents' Committees.* Singapore.

Part 6

Examining Social Issues and Social Development

Chapter 23

The development of new towns in Hong Kong and Singapore: Some social consequences*

S. Vasoo[†]

New Towns have become a common feature in Hong Kong and in Singapore (Housing Authority 1984/85; Housing and Development Board 1984/85).[1] Since the 1960s, both the Hong Kong and Singapore governments have

---

*From Vasoo, S. (1988). The development of new towns in Hong Kong and Singapore: Some social consequences. *International Social Work*, *31*(2), 115–134. Reprinted with permission by *International Social Work*.

This article looks at the social consequences and challenges of rehousing residents in the public housing estates of the new towns in Hong Kong and Singapore.

[†]S. Vasoo is a Senior Lecturer in the Department of Social Work and Psychology, National University of Singapore, Kent Ridge, Singapore 0511.

International Social Work (SAGE, London, Newbury Park, Beverly Hills and New Delhi), Vol. 31 (1988), 115–133.

[1] New Towns are self-contained public housing estates which have a population of more than 150,000 people. These have been and are being developed by the governments of Hong Kong and Singapore to solve the housing needs of the growing population in the respective countries. Singapore is an island state situated at the tip of the West Malaysian peninsula and has a total land area of 620.5 km^2. Hong Kong is at present a British colony but will cease to be so in 1997 when it will be returned to the People's Republic of China. It consists of Hong Kong Island, Kowloon peninsula and the New Territories on the Chinese mainland. It has a total land area of 1050 km^2.

found it necessary to develop New Towns to house their growing populations. The growth of the population in the post-war years has been remarkable in both countries. In Hong Kong, between 1951 (2.01 million) and 1981 (5.13 million) the population increased by 3.12 million (H.K. Census 1981). With regard to Singapore, between 1947 (0.94 million) and 1980 (2.41 million) the population increased by 1.47 million (Singapore Census, 1980). Such a steep increase in population has resulted in overcrowding of the city and central areas in both countries. (Sit, 1981: 142; Teh, 1975: 4). This situation reached an intolerable limit in the early 1960s (Drakakis-Smith, 1973: 39–56; Yeh, 1975: 27–37), resulting in insufficient land for accommodation, sprawling squatter settlements and deteriorating environmental conditions and threatening outbreaks of contagious diseases. In the face of this explosive demand for shelter, both the governments of Hong Kong and Singapore decided to defuse the situation by developing New Towns in outlying areas to accommodate people in low-cost housing.

Development of these new towns was based on the experiences gained by Britain, the fore-runners of massive new town programmes (Aldridge, 1979: 1–19). The idea of new towns as a panacea to British urban problems was first mooted by Ebenezer Howard (1965) and F.J. Osborn (1942, 1954). Their contributions, and the British approach to new town developments, influenced the way Hong Kong and Singapore responded to the over populated urban city centres.

This response was, essentially, to decant people into new towns in the respective countries. This seemed to be the most effective strategy and in order to attract as many people as possible into the new towns, the governments had to ensure that these towns were self-contained communities with adequate facilities to support social life and interaction.

The development of new towns by the governments of Hong Kong and Singapore may be viewed as an attempt not only to meet the housing needs of their people but also to maintain social and political stability.

To date about 40 percent of Hong Kong's population and 80 percent of Singapore's live in the new towns and the various public housing estates. The resettlement of such a sizeable proportion of people in the two countries has generated a concern to find ways in which the residents' needs and problems could be understood so that various measures could be adopted to help them adjust and adapt more effectively to their high-rise environment.

However, this rapid development of new towns has brought with it social consequences and challenges. These social consequences and challenges concern the social integration of people who have been rehoused, the building of relationships and support networks among residents, the psycho-social adjustments of residents, the relationship between residents and the government as represented by local bureaucracy, the willingness of the government to accept residents' feedback, the response of the government to the needs of the residents and the availability of avenues for residents to seek redress for their problems. Such substantive matters, if left unattended, would have undesirable implications for the government as well as for the well-being of the residents who have to establish new roots in the public housing estates of the new towns.

Admittedly, these unintended social consequences have impressed upon the respective governments the need to initiate appropriate administrative actions. In response to the social consequences arising from rehousing people in the new towns, to the need for residents to be involved in dealing with the problems of their neighbourhoods and in recognition of the need for effective communication between residents and government on matters of social concern, the Hong Kong and Singapore governments have found it necessary to initiate organizations through which residents living in the new towns could be mobilized to participate in and attend to the welfare of their neighbourhoods.

This article focuses mainly on some of the consequences of rehousing residents in the public housing estates of the new towns in Hong Kong and Singapore.

Some consequences of rehousing people in new towns

There is no doubt that rehousing has had both positive and negative effects on the social and psychological well-being of the residents. Many scholars and researchers have conducted studies on the social consequences of living in the high-rise environment of new towns. Some of these studies (Loring, 1956, 1964; Hall 1966; Lansing, 1966; Bernstein, 1968; Madge, 1968; Sommer, 1969) have identified negative effects, while others (Wilner 1962; Winsbrough, 1965; Wilner and Baer, 1972; Mitchell, 1971) have found no adverse consequences on social life.

New Town residents are expected to cope with their environment and as a result they respond in different ways. A number of articles on urban communities have highlighted the endogenous processes resulting in the formation of voluntary organizations which have been used by residents as vehicles for social integration and for counteracting the abrasive social situation. It has been argued that given the complexities of the urban communities, the urban environment is not conducive to social integration (Taub et al., 1977: 426).

Since the new town environments of Hong Kong and Singapore are urbanized communities, comprising mostly residents living in high-rise public housing flats, it would be interesting to throw some light on the attempts by residents and governments to facilitate the social integration of the community. Before probing into this particular aspect, it could be useful to take note of the views on the response of the urban communities in the new towns to organizing and integrating the residents.

Urban communities are said to be less responsive to collective action and to the mushrooming of voluntary organizations. This is because the social system is not highly structured and outside agencies that need to communicate with the residents must sponsor or even create secondary associations for the local residents (Taub et al., 1977). It seems that the urban communities do not provide the culture necessary for the growth of voluntary associations.

Some social consequences in the Hong Kong context

There seem to be very few known studies on the social consequences of residents living in high-rise public housing estates in the new towns. A cursory survey of the literature pertaining to this aspect indicates that research has been centred on the examination of housing policies, housing problems and the development of housing in Hong Kong. Most of the studies, undertaken by urban geographers, have looked into the spatial and ecological distribution of the population in public housing, the economic analysis of housing and the genesis of new towns (Dwyer, 1971; Prescott, 1971; Wigglesworth, 1971; Drakakis-Smith, 1973; Pryor, 1973; Wong, 1978; Sit, 1980, 1981; Choi, 1977; Law, 1982; Leung, 1980; Wong, 1982). All have scarcely dealt with the social consequences.

Only two large scale studies on the social consequences of life in public housing schemes were published: one by Mitchell (1969, 1971), and the other by Millar et al. (1981). Both were concerned, among other things, with the quality of life of the residents. Some of the respondents in these studies were residents living in high-rise public housing estates and as such the findings are helpful for the researcher to draw some general conclusions about the social implications of people living in the new towns. In addition, there are three smaller studies (Kan, 1974, 1975; Wong, 1978) and they provide some insights into the socio-economic characteristics and neighbourly interaction of residents and their utilization of facilities and services. These studies and those by Mitchell (1969, 1971) and Millar et al. (1981) will form the basis from which to draw inferences on the social adjustment of residents living in the new towns.

Household density in the public housing estates of the new towns is high and the average household size is about five persons. Although household densities are high they do not have any effect on the emotional state of the members of the household. Mitchell (1971: 1) observed that:

> High densities are to have very little effect on individuals and families although there is a suggestion that congestion is a potentially significant stress.

However, the spatial features of housing do affect the pattern of social relationship. Mitchell (1971: 3) found that:

> Floor levels are significant in Hong Kong simply because it is more difficult for residents on the upper stories of the multi-storey building to move about and to get away. Consequently they are forced to have close social relationship with the other members in their dwelling unit.

Neighbourliness is high in Resettlement blocks[2] and Housing Authority blocks.[3] Kan (1974: 35) found that Resettlement blocks have the highest score of neighbourliness, followed by residents living in Housing

---

[2] Resettlement blocks are six-storey H-shaped buildings with flats of varying sizes between 11.1 m^2(120 ft^2) and 22.2 m^2(240 ft^2). Communal facilities such as toilets and bathrooms were built during the early phase of the public housing programme to resettle people. They are known as Type B public housing.

[3] Housing Authority blocks have flats of better design and larger floor space, ranging from 24.1 m^2 to 40 m^2(259 ft^2 to 431 ft^2). The flats have self-contained facilities and are known as Type A public housing.

Authority blocks. The duration of their residence is related to the degree of neighbourliness.

Community integration is found to be rather low among residents. Kan (1974: 60) observed that:

> Two-thirds of the respondents think it is not right to intrude into another's private life though 28.1% say they will do so depending on the situation. Among the latter, 59.8% will do so when they think that their interference will bring fruitful consequences and do justice to the party concerned. The rest will not bother.

Further, estate officers who are involved in the management of public housing estates have assessed that residents are generally not committed to participating in the affairs of their neighbourhood and that there is an atmosphere in the affairs of the neighbourhood and the residents (Kan, 1974: 60). However, the estate officers' picture of residents' interest in building a cohesive community and promoting mutual help is not always gloomy. Views among officers on this aspect seem to be divergent, and slightly more than half of them think that community cohesiveness is weak (Kan, 1974: 6).

The high-density high-rise public housing in the new towns makes an impact on the lives of children. Families with more children tend to be freer in their supervision of children and to give them greater freedom to leave the house so as to reduce the density in the household. As a consequences of this, the children become more vulnerable to delinquent activities (Mitchell, 1969: 291–300; 1971: 4). In the most recent bio-social survey by Millar et al. (1981: 272) on maladjustments as measured by the Langer scale by housing type, it was found that:

> Residents living in resettlement estates have the highest scores in maladjustment and mental disturbance and with the lowest score for life enjoyment.

These findings suggest that some aberrations and social dysfunctions are faced by individuals and families living in public housing estates and these draw the attention of the policy-makers and administrators to the need to find ways to make social life better in the estates of the new towns.

One concern among residents living in these public housing estates is the security of the neighbourhood. Residents seem to be alarmingly concerned about crime in their locality. It has been found that fear of crime seems to be more prevalent among residents living in resettlement and low-cost housing estates (Millar et al., 1981: 308–10). Hence, feelings of insecurity among these residents are related to the crime situation in their neighbourhood and they have become rather phobic about crime. Consequently people are afraid or more reluctant to use public facilities. This psychological state has been noted by Kan (1975: 29).

By 1974 the rate of violent crime had increased five-fold (86.4 per 100,000 persons) when compared to 1960 (17.5 per 100,00 persons), and the community reacted by pressing the government to take action to reduce crime, especially in the housing estates (Millar et al., 1981: 306). As a result there was a joint effort by the government and the residents to establish residents' organizations to combat the growing crime problems.

On the whole residents in Hong Kong's new town environment are not highly integrated and are said to be passive in taking an interest in meeting the communal needs of their neighbourhoods. This docility is in part due to utilitarianistic familialism,[4] a predominant Chinese attitude. They prefer to tolerate inconveniences and frustration rather than to deal with them and it is common for them to keep to the family circle, to relatives and to clansmen (Kan, 1975: 43).

With regard to the physical aspect of adjustment to the new towns, the residents have assessed their living conditions to be better than in the past. Generally, the residents have found the basic provision and the present residential environment as a whole to be satisfactory (Leung, 1980: 348–92).

Based on the available findings on the social adjustment of residents in the public housing estates of Hong Kong's new towns, it could be

---

[4] See Lau, S. K. (1981) 'Utilitarianistic Familism: The Basis of Political Stability', in Y. C. King Ambrose and R. P. L. Lee (eds) *Social Life and Development in Hong Kong*, The Chinese University of Hong Kong. He defined the term as 'a normative and behavioural tendency of an individual to place his familial interest above the interests of society or any of its component individuals and groups in such a fashion that the furtherance of his familial interests is the primary consideration. Moreover, among the familial interests materialistic interests take priority over all other interests.'

inferred that the social environment has generally not been conducive. This is due to the strains produced by the congested housing estates, personal insecurity, the increase in criminal offences and the impersonality of the residents. The scenario as described by Kan (1974: 62) was prevalent in the early 1970s. She observed:

> In addition to strains produced by the congestion of housing estates, there are crippling fears of daily insecurity and alarming increase of criminal offences, formidable dirt and rubbish and public indifference to general squalor. There is a trend towards attitudes of self-defence and self-preservation among residents.

It can also be concluded that the surge in rehousing people in new towns in the 1960s and 1970s has brought improved housing conditions but not without great social and personal costs (Mitchell, 1969: 46). Socially it has to some degree affected the social integration of the urban communities (Mitchell, 1969: 446).

The new town environment has in a way hampered the growth of indigenous organization. There has been no remarkable response by residents to come together to initiate formal or informal organizations to deal with some of the social consequences they are facing or have faced. Residents have remained generally docile and not very motivated to act in circumventing some of the aberrations of the urban milieu. Some of the older residents tried to implant Kaifong associations[5] in the 1960s but without much success (Wong, 1970; Lau, 1981). The associations failed to attract the support of residents, who doubted its efficacy in serving them, and their functions were overtaken by social and political changes which made their role redundant. Today they exist in name only, their buildings unattended and without life, though some die-hard officials futilely continue to try to salvage their organizations.

After the late 1960s, the new towns in Hong Kong saw an upsurge in the growth of formal organizations. These organizations, such as

---

[5] Kaifong associations are mutual aid organizations. The first was registered in 1949 under the Community Development Section of the Social Welfare Office. Educational, welfare and recreational activities have been conducted by these associations.

community centres, community halls and voluntary welfare bodies, were affiliated to the Hong Kong Council of Social Service and are the efforts of people who are not residents of the new towns.

The government by then had become urgently aware of the social consequences of its rehousing programmes for the new town residents and the need to maintain social and political stability in the new town communities. This need was recognized through the lessons the government had learned from the Kowloon riots in 1966. One of the main lessons learned was that the government had to find effective mechanisms to keep in touch with the common man and his aspirations, in fact to feel the pulse of the community. The government failed to realize this until after the riots because it was dependent on a small group of economic elites (Kuan, 1979; 165–6), on displaced traditional organizations and on the near-defunct Kaifong associations (Leung, 1982: 161), which all had limited contact and support in the communities in the urban city areas and new towns.

Since the 1970s, the government has begun to take initiatives to encourage the establishment of social and localized institutions, one of which, the residents' organizations, is on a significantly grand scale in urban areas. Also, the government's move to establish public housing estates has opened up a new arena for the involvement of local residents in neighbourhood affairs in the various new town settings.

Some social consequences in the Singapore context

In the 1960s, the literature on Singapore's public housing dwelt mainly on the development of public housing, on housing problems and conditions, on housing programmes and designs and on urban renewal (Teh, 1961, 1963, 1967, 1969, 1969a; Choe, 1967, 1973; Yeh and Lee, 1968; Concenciao, 1969; Lim, 1969; Tay, 1969). The literature, written mainly by architects and planners, made no attempt to examine the social adjustment and responses of residents in the new towns. This could be partly due to the fact that the development of public housing was in its early stages. It was not until the 1970s that more studies on the social adjustment of residents in public housing covering such aspects as social and psychological implications of high-density living, social relationships and interaction of residents, residents' views on public housing and ecological distribution of social pathology were thought to be needed (Tan, 1972; Yeh, 1972a, 1972b, 1975a; Lim, 1973; Western et al., 1973; Loh, 1974; Wong, 1974; Chng, 1975; Hassan, 1975, 1977; Ho, 1975; Yap, 1975; Yeung and Yeh, 1975, 1975a; Chen, 1976, 1977, 1978; Phoon et al., 1976; Chen and Tai, 1978). These studies were undertaken by social researchers, most of them sociologists. Except for the studies by Yeh (1972a) and by Hassan (1977), most of these studies were conducted on a small scale.

Based on the two large scale studies, some inferences on the social adjustments of the new town residents in Singapore are discussed. Where possible the discussion will be supplemented by findings from some of the relevant small scale studies, as well.

The living conditions of the residents in the new towns have improved since their rehousing. Since most of them were originally from squatter areas and congested private tenement housing, the impact of this rehousing on them was significant. The 1968 and 1973 surveys (Yeh, 1972a, 1975) of residents living in these public housing estates revealed a general improvement in living conditions and a considerable change in the households.

Although there have been significant changes in the living conditions of families who have moved into the public housing estates, they have indicated a fairly high level of satisfaction with the changes (Yeh, 1975: 337). Further, households who were resettled, as compared to those who voluntarily moved in, were equally satisfied with the changes, if not more so (Yeh, 1975: 349).

These findings on the high level of satisfaction with the changes have been qualified by a number of other researchers (Tan, 1972; Lim, 1973; Hassan, 1976, 1977), who found that the lower-income groups were more adversely affected by rehousing. Hassan (1976: 251) asserted that:

> The adverse economic consequences particularly for the lower income group, seriously affected other areas of their family and social life . . . The evidence collected in a recent survey on the impact of relocation of the family indicates that, at least for poor families, the increase in household expenditure results in trimming of expenses on the household activities. The two areas where expenses are frequently trimmed as a

result of high cost of living are food and children's education. Given the already low expenses on these items, further acts have serious implications for children's schooling and their performance in school as well as health of family members, particularly of the children.

Having highlighted some observations on the living conditions of residents, it would be appropriate at this point to discuss the psychosocial effects of rehousing people in high-rise public housing in the new towns and to cite some relevant findings to elaborate on this area of discussion.

Families with higher household density are more vulnerable to stress. This is due to the lack of useable space within the households. Hence, families living in a limited floor area, particularly those in one room flats, have been found to be more exposed to stress. Hassan's study (1975: 10–12) revealed that:

> High internal density, as measured by the number of square feet per person in the flat, appears to be positively correlated with the worry index... The evidence shows that larger families (six persons and above) have higher scores on the worry index.

Families living on higher floors (between floors six and twelve) face more strain and stress than those who live on lower floors. This is because members on higher floors are more restrained by the height and find it difficult to leave the flat when they face tensions (Hassan, 1975: 12).

High household density affects the parent–child relationship. Children from high-density homes tend to be less confined to their households and to inadvertently receive little supervision from their parents when they are outside in the environment. Such children, especially those from the lower income group, are more exposed to delinquent activities (Hassan 1975: 12). This observation is supported by Chen (1977: 16).

Prior to relocation, most of the new town residents came from various ethnic enclaves in the city and urban areas, from squats and from dilapidated old tenement housing where there was more sharing of communal facilities and social interaction. Now they live in self-contained Housing and Development Board flats which make them insular and impersonal in their behaviour. Chng (1975) and Lim (1973) in their studies found that neighbourly interaction was limited, selective and lacked the feeling of community sentiments. Besides being disengaged from their old social networks, the residents would need to incur some personal cost to establish a new network of social relationships. Given the more anonymous environment of their neighbourhood, and when pushed by stress and pulled by autonomy, people in high-density high-rise public housing tend to withdraw into a private world, thereby creating a spatial environment which is characterized by an inward-looking attitude, impersonality, individualism, apathy and sense of general insecurity (Hassan, 1976: 260).

In addition to being apathetic, the residents of the housing estates in the new towns are from time to time troubled by vandalism and fear of crime. However, this concern is not as glaring because most estates are not crime infested (Singapore Police Force, 1980).

Having discussed the social adjustments of residents in the new towns, it would be appropriate to draw a few inferences based on the various findings.

The creation of new towns, followed by the decantation of people to these places, has certainly hastened the breakdown of the extended family structure. More than 70 percent (HDB 1980) of residents are nuclear families and such a family structure would have to rely more on the help of formal or informal groups rather than kin groups. At the same time social support networks do not emerge so readily because residents are inward looking and need prodding to form networks of social support.

The rehousing of residents in new towns has contributed to an improvement in their conditions and the new living environment is certainly a welcome change for the residents. However the success of housing residents in a newly designed environment cannot be measured in terms of the number of people rehoused and the better physical layouts alone; it must take into consideration whether the residents are co-operating to make their neighbourhood a better place to live. This latter aspect has yet to receive more support from the residents.

The relocation of people into new towns has imposed upon the government the need to find more effective strategies to manage and deliver urban services efficiently to the people in the various housing pockets, as well as to keep in touch with the views and needs of the people who are more articulate.

The various studies cited have revealed that people who have been resettled in new towns are less interactive and neighbourly. This situation, coupled with the feeling of loss of community, may have affected the development of community attachment among residents. Absence of community attachment can retard the process of participation by the residents in the maintenance of their social and physical environment (Hassan, 1976: 262). This lack of interest in the maintenance of their social and physical environment can create various pathologies, some of which have already been identified.

About 45 percent of the population living in new towns are children and young persons (HDB, 1978) who are being or are already socialized in the high-rise environment. This situation raises some concern. Firstly, if the young are not encouraged to be interested in the welfare of their neighbourhoods, they are likely to adopt the same attitudes as their parents and may become more parochial in their outlook. Secondly, as the young are now more literate and educated, they are likely to demand better urban services and facilities and if such demands fail to be met, they can become rather disruptive to the well-being of the neighbourhoods. Finally, if the young are denied the opportunity to care for their environment, they would be less rooted in their neighbourhood and would become less committed to building a close-knit community.

About 15 percent (HDB, 1980) of public housing in the new towns are rental flats primarily occupied by the lower-income group. There is evidence to suggest that this sector of residents is more vulnerable to social dysfunctions (Hassan, 1976, 1977) and therefore would require more attention from the policy-makers and the local bureaucracies.

Singapore's new town environment has generated some spontaneous efforts among residents to initiate formal organizations to deal with the social consequences of rehousing. In the early 1960s Queenstown and Toa Payoh New Towns' residents witnessed the establishment of Residents' Associations. These Associations were formed by residents who were interested in promoting social and recreational activities and in recommending neighbourhood improvements to the HDB. Initially, the Associations were able to attract some residents to be members, but membership did not increase in the process of time. This was due to a lack of awareness among residents and the inability of the Associations to dispense benefits to members which were exclusive and were not enjoyed by non-member residents living in the same neighbourhood. Besides, the complexity of the new town environment reinforced the residents' feeling of distrust in the Associations' credibility.

Together with the lack of support from residents, the lack of financial resources, the difficulties in securing premises to operate in the new towns and the inadequate administrative support for communicating with as many residents as possible made the Associations operationally ineffective. Eventually, in the early 1970s, they ceased to exist. Indigenous efforts to organize residents became rare and were unheard of in the new towns of Singapore.

During the last two decades the new towns in Singapore saw a number of formal organizations being established under the auspices of the government. By the late 1970s, most of Singapore's old communities had been restructured through the government's provision of new housing for the people. The pragmatic efforts by the government to rehouse people in the various new towns have had both intended and unintended consequences in the social life of the residents. Some of these consequences have been discussed, and attempts were made by the government to set up local social institutions such as the community centres and citizens' consultative committees[6] to deal with the needs and problems faced by residents living in the new towns. These institutions were the translation of the government's desire to keep in touch with the grass-roots level of society. They were intended to obtain views to reshape government policies, including housing for people and better social integration of the residents who belong to different ethnic groups. At the same time they were designed to meet the challenges of the growing social complexities in the nature and extent of the problems of residents in the new town neighbourhood. However, they are now becoming less effective in mobilizing and enhancing the involvement of the residents. As a result, the government has had to plan new approaches in reaching residents at the grass-roots,

---

[6]These are intermediate organizations comprising local citizens who are appointed by the government to maintain a channel of communication between the people living in a constituency and the various governmental authorities.

namely the residents' committees which provide a new channel for the participation of residents in community development.

Besides government-induced formal organizations, the voluntary welfare organizations also play a part in delivering services to specific target groups who have been found to be in need of help. However, the role played by the voluntary welfare organizations under the Singapore Council of Social Service, in developing formal voluntary organizations has been rather limited and has centred mainly on the delivery of services to the disadvantaged groups.

In appraising the auspices under which most of the formal organizations have been introduced, it can said that the new town environment has not inspired the establishment of indigenous residents' groups or organizations.

Summary and discussion

The discussions in this article have suggested that the development of new towns in Hong Kong and Singapore has correspondingly precipitated some social consequences. These consequences have prompted the respective governments to act by encouraging the establishment of residents' organizations as a means to counteract some of the problems faced by residents living in the high-rise environment. The rehousing of many people who needed housing can be seen as a socio-political decision and the implementation of such a decision has created other social challenges which require the attention of the Hong Kong and Singapore governments. These challenges, namely the prevention of the breakdown of the social structure, the loss of effective communication between the government and the people, the pressure arising from the demands of rehoused residents on the services provided by local governmental bureaucracies, e.g. the estate office, and other government bureaucracies dealing with environmental and urban services, would have to be dealt with. Coupled with these challenges, the increasing aspiration of relocated residents for a higher standard of urban services, the potential misinterpretation of governmental policies by rehoused residents and its attendant implications, the disruptive dangers arising from disgruntled residents whose needs are not met as a result of resettlement and their potential threats to neighbourhood stability are other added problems to which the two governments have to find amicable solutions.

The solutions adopted by the two governments in the face of the challenges, particularly in trying to provide low-cost public housing, merits discussion. The actions taken by them have created an almost complete reorganization of the social structure of their societies. The large scale decantation of people into the new towns has brought about the need for the governments to rethink ways to reach the residents, and as a result, the two governments have encouraged the establishment of residents' organizations in the new towns to work towards a better neighbourhood and to promote community development. Residents' organizations have been thought of as one of the strategies to enlist the support of residents to care about their neighbourhood. In short, they are to facilitate the process of social integration.

Generally, the relocation of people in the new towns of Hong Kong and Singapore has brought about more or less similar social implications, such as the lack of neighbourliness and mutual support among residents, loss of control in the supervision of children, increase of stress in households with high internal density, insularity and impersonality among residents, and the lack of concern for their physical and social environment (Mitchell, 1969; Kan, 1974; Chen, 1977; Hassan, 1977). These social implications tend to suggest that the communities in the new towns can be described in Janowitz's (1967) term, as a 'community of limited liabilities'. This situation is enhanced by a number of factors. Firstly, the residents' personal and social needs are fulfilled by groups and networks outside their community, e.g. working colleagues, professional groups and clubs, friendship groups, etc. Secondly, residents, particularly those who are young adults, expect to move to better accommodation in other areas. Under such circumstances they are unlikely to be rooted in and committed to their present community, which is perceived as a place for transit. Thirdly, there are less opportunities for residents to be mutually dependent as the family and the kin group serve to meet most of their social needs and the essential services are obtainable from impersonal sources. Although the existing findings on social implications of high-rise living in the new towns of Hong Kong and Singapore imply that the new town is a community of limited liabilities, it does mean that the new town residents are docile and cannot be encouraged to participate in affairs affecting their neighbourhoods. The residents can be organized, however, to take an active role to mitigate some of the depersonalizing influences (Warren and Warren, 1977: 151–7).

One major factor which accounts for the difference in attitudes to the environment between new town residents in Hong Kong and Singapore is that most new town residents in Singapore are home owners and as such they have a stake in ensuring that their environment is safe and clean. In the case of Hong Kong, the residents are mostly living in rental flats and they tend to be less bothered about the state of their external environment.

The new towns of Hong Kong and Singapore do not have the culture for the germination of indigenous voluntary organizations. If there are any locally based voluntary organizations, such organizations have been induced either by the government or by other external agents from the voluntary welfare sector.

References

Aldridge, M. (1979) *The British New Towns.* London: Routledge and Kegan Paul.

Bernstein, B. (1968) 'Some Sociological Determinants of Perception: An Inquiry into Sub-Cultural Differences', in J.A. Fishman (ed.) *Readings in the Sociology of Language*, pp. 223–39. The Hague: Mouton.

Chen, Peter S. J. (1976) 'An Ecological Study of Social Pathology in Singapore', *Sociology Working Papers No. 59*, Singapore: Department of Sociology, University of Singapore.

Chen, Peter S. J. (1977) *Social Ecology of Singapore.* Singapore: Federal Publications.

Chen, Peter S. J. (1978) 'An Ecological Study of Social Pathology in Singapore', in Peter S. J. Chen and Hans Dieter Evers (eds) *Studies in Asean Sociology,* pp. 367–87. Singapore: Chapmen Enterprises.

Chen, Peter S. J. and Tai Chin Ling (1978) 'Urban and Rural Living in a Highly Urbanized Society in Peter S. J. Chen and Hans-Dieter Evers (eds) *Studies in Asean Sociology,* pp. 406–21. Singapore: Chapmen Enterprises.

Chng, M. C. (1975) *Human Territoriality in Singapore: Territorial Needs and Assumptions and HDB Designs*, Academic Exercise, Singapore: Department of Sociology, University of Singapore.

Choe, Alan F. C. (1967) *Slum Clearance and Urban Renewal in Singapore*, Paper presented at Afro-Asian Housing Congress, Singapore. (Papers — Vol. 1) Docs 1–3.

Choe, Alan F. C. (1973) 'Public Housing, Urban Renewal and Transformation of the Environment', in *Towards Tomorrow: Essays on Development and Social Transformation in Singapore*, pp. 25–39. Singapore: National Trade Union Congress.

Choi, C. Y. (1977) 'Urbanization and Redistribution of Population: Hong Kong — A Case Study', *Patterns of Urbanisation* 1: 239–87.

Concenciao, J. F. (1969) *A New Environment for Singapore*. Radio and TV Talks Series 11. Singapore: Adult Educational Board.

Drakakis-Smith, D. W. (1973) *Housing Provision in Metropolitan Hong Kong*. Hong Kong: Centre of Asian Studies, University of Hong Kong.

Dwyer, D. J. (ed.) (1977) *Asian Urbanization: A Hong Kong Casebook*. Hong Kong: Hong Kong University Press.

Hall, E. T. (1966) *The Hidden Dimension; Man's Use of Space in Public and Private Garden City*. London: Doubleday.

Hassan, R. (1975) 'Social and Psychological Implications of High Population Density', *Sociology Working Papers No. 47*. Singapore: Department of Sociology, University of Singapore.

Hassan, Riaz (1976) 'Public Housing', in R. Hassan (ed.) *Singapore: Society in Transition*, pp. 240–68. Kuala Lumpur: Oxford University Press.

Hassan, R. (1977) *Families in Flats: A Study of Low Income Families in Public Housing*. Singapore: University of Singapore Press.

HDB (Singapore Housing and Development Board) (1978) *Annual Report*.

HDB (Singapore Housing and Development Board) (1980) *Annual Report*.

HDB (Singapore Housing and Development Board) (1984/85) *Annual Report*.

Hong Kong Housing Authority (1984–5) *Annual Report*.

Howard, E. (1965) *Garden Cities of Tomorrow* (first published in 1898 as 'Tomorrow: A Peaceful Path to Real Reform'). London: Faber.

Janowitz, M. (1967) *The Community Press in an Urban Setting*. Chicago: University of Chicago Press.

Kan, Angela (1974) *A Study of Neighbourhood Interaction in Public Housing: The Case of Hong Kong*. Hong Kong: The Chinese University of Hong Kong, Social Research Centre.

Kan, Angela (1975) *Implications of Concentrated Utilization of Local Facilities and Services in Public Housing Estates in Hong Kong*. Hong Kong: The Chinese University of Hong Kong, Social Research Centre.

Kuan, H. C. (1979) 'Political Stability and Change in Hong Kong', in B. L. Tsong, R. P. L. Lee and U. Simonis (eds) *Hong Kong Economic, Social and Political Studies in Development.* Folkstone, UK: Dawson.

Lansing, John B. (1966) *Residential Location and Urban Mobility: The Second Wave of Interviews.* Ann Arbor: Survey Research Centre, Institute for Social Research, University of Michigan.

Lau, S. K. (1981) 'The Government, Intermediate Organisations and Grass-roots Politics in Hong Kong'. *Asian Survey* 21(8): 865–84.

Law, C. K. (1982) 'A Partial Economic Analysis of the Public Housing Policy of Hong Kong', in J. Y. S. Cheng (ed.) *Hong Kong in the 1980s.* Hong Kong: Summerson Eastern Publishers.

Leung, C. B. (1982) 'Community Participation: From Kai Fong Association, Mutual Aid Committees to District Board', in J. Y. S. Cheng (ed.) *Hong Kong in the 1980s*, pp. 152–70. Hong Kong: Summerson Eastern Publishers.

Leung, C. K. (1980) 'Urbanization and New Towns Development', in C. K. Leung, J. W. Cushman and Gungwu Wang, *Hong Kong: Dilemmas of Growth*, pp. 289–308. Canberra: The Australian National University.

Lim, C. K. (1969) 'Growth of Central Singapore and Regeneration of the City', *Journal of the Singapore Institute of Architects* 35: 2–23.

Lim, S. H. (1973) *Relocation, Social Networks and Neighbouring Interaction in a Block of Flats.* Academic Exercise. Singapore: Department of Sociology, University of Singapore.

Loh, E. J. (1974) *Sociological Consequences of Internal Density on Personal and Family Relationships — A Case Study.* Academic Exercise, Singapore: Department of Sociology, University of Singapore.

Loring, W. C. (1956) 'Housing and Social Organisation', *Journal of Social Problems* 3: 160–8.

Loring, W. C. (1964) 'Residential Environment, Nexus of Personal Interactions and Healthful Developments', *Journal of Health and Human Behaviour* 5: 166–9.

Madge, John (1968) 'Housing: Social Aspects'. *International Encyclopaedia of Social Sciences*, Vol. 6, 516–21. Macmillan and Free Press.

Millar, S. et al. (1981) *The Ecology of a City and its People: The Case of Hong Kong.* Canberra: Australian National University Press.

Mitchell, E. E. (1969) *Levels of Emotional Strains in Southeast Asian Cities — A study of Individual Responses to the Stresses of Urbanization and Industrialization*, Vols. 1 and 2, A Project of Urban Family Life Survey, Hong Kong.

Mitchell, R. E. (1971) 'Some Social Implications of High Density Housing' *American Sociological Review* 36: 18–29.

Osborn, F. J. (1942) *New Towns after the War.* London: Dent.

Osborn, F. J. (1954) 'Success of the New Towns', *Towns and Country Planning* 22(131): 117–18.

Phooh, W. D. et al. (1976) 'A Preliminary Study of the Health of a Population Staying in Apartments of Varying Sizes', *Singapore Annals of Tropical Medicine and Parasitology* 70(2): 232–46.

Prescott, J. A. (1971) 'Hong Kong: The Form and Significance of High Density Urban Development', in D. J. Dwyer (ed.) *Asian Urbanization, A Hong Kong Casebook*, pp. 12–19. Hong Kong: Hong Kong University Press.

Pryor, E. G. (1973) *Housing in Hong Kong.* Hong Kong: Oxford University Press.

Singapore Police Force (1980) *Annual Report*, Ministry of Home Affairs.

Singapore Census (1980), Singapore: National Printer.

Sit, V. F. S. (1980) 'Hong Kong's New Towns Programme and its Regional Implications', in C. K. Leung, J. W. Cushman and Gungwu Wang (eds) *Hong Kong: Dilemmas of Growth*, pp. 397–417. Canberra: Australian National University.

Sit, V. F. S. (ed.) (1981) *Urban Hong.* Hong Kong: Summerson Eastern Publishers.

Sommer, Robert (1969) *Personal Space: The Behavioural Basis of Design.* Englewood Cliffs, NJ: Prentice-Hall.

Tan, Roney, K. L. (1972) *The Impact of Relocation of HDB Tenants — A Case Study*, M.Soc.Sc. thesis. Singapore: Department of Sociology, University of Singapore.

Taub, Richard P. et al. (1977) 'Urban Voluntary Associations Locality Based and Externally Induced,' *American Journal of Sociology* 83: 425–42.

Tay, K. S. (1969) 'Public Housing in Singapore', *Rumah* 8: 37–42.

Teh, C. W. (1961) 'Public Housing in Singapore. The Singapore Improvement Trust', *Rumah* 4: 5–9.

Teh, C. W. (1963) 'Public Low-Cost and Low-Rental Housing in Singapore', *Ekistics* 16(93): 88–91.

Teh, C. W. (1967) *Design and Planning of Public Housing in Singapore*, Second Afro-Asian Housing Congress, Singapore. Also published in Cairo: Afro-Asian Housing Organisation.

Teh, C. W. (1969) 'Public Housing', in J.B. Ooi and H. D. Chiang (ed.) *Modern Singapore*, pp. 171–80. Singapore: University of Singapore.

Teh, C. W. (1969a) 'Public Housing — the Next Efforts', in J. F. Conceicao (ed.) *A New Environment for Singapore*, pp. 17–25. Radio and TV Talks Series 11. Singapore: Adult Education Board.

Teh, C. W. (1975) 'Public Housing in Singapore: An Overview', in S. H. K. Yeh (ed.) *Public Housing in Singapore*, pp. 1–21. Singapore: Singapore University Press.

Warren, R. B. and D. I. Warren (1977) *The Neighbourhood Organisers Handbook*. Notre Dame: University of Notre Dame Press.

Western, J. S. et al. (1973) 'Housing and Satisfactions with Environment in Singapore', *Sociology Working Papers, No. 13*, Singapore, Department of Sociology, University of Singapore.

Wigglesworth, J. M. (1971) 'The Development of New Towns', in D. J. Dwyer (ed.) *Asian Urbanization: A Hong Kong Casebook,* pp. 48–69. Hong Kong: Hong Kong University Press.

Wilner, Daniel M. (1962) *The Housing Environment and Family Life: A Longitudinal Study of the Effects on Housing and Morbidity and Mental Health.* Baltimore: Johns Hopkins Press.

Wilner, Daniel M. and W. G. Baer (1972) *Sociocultural Factors in Residential Space.* Mineograph, Department of Health, Education and Welfare and the American Public Health Association, USA.

Winsborough, H. H. (1965) 'The Consequences of High Population Density', *Law and Contemporary Problems* 31: 120–6.

Wong, Aline K. (1970) 'Chinese Voluntary Associations in South East Asian Cities and the Kaifunds in Hong Kong', *Journal of the Hong Kong Branch of the Royal Asiatic Society* 11: 62–73.

Wong, Aline K. (1974) *The Social Implications of High-Rise Living.* Proceedings of the Conference on Tall Buildings, Kuala Lumpur, Institution of Engineers.

Wong, K. Y. (1982) 'New Towns — The Hong Kong Experience', in J. Y. S. Cheng (ed.) *Hong Kong in the 1980s.* Hong Kong: Summerson Eastern Publishers.

Wong, Luke S. K. (1978) *Housing in Hong Kong: A Multidisciplinary Study.* Hong Kong: Heinemann Educational.

Yap, M. T. (1975) *Privacy and Neighbourliness.* Academic Exercise, Singapore: Department of Sociology, University of Singapore.

Yeh, S. H. K. and Lee Yoke San (1968) 'Housing Conditions in Singapore', *Malayan Economic Review* 13(1): 11–38.

Yeh, S. K. H. (1972a) *Homes for the People: A Study of Tenants' Views on Public Housing in Singapore.* Singapore: Government Printing Office.

Yeh, S. H. K. (1972b) 'Some Trends and Prospects in Singapore's Public Housing', *Ekistics* 33 (196).

Yeh, S. H. K. and S. L. Tan (1974) 'Satisfaction with Living Conditions in Public Housing Estate in Singapore'. *Journal of the Singapore Institute of Planners* 4(1): 72–84.

Yeh, S. H. K. (1975) 'Housing Conditions and Housing Needs', in S. H. K. Yeh (ed.) *Public Housing in Singapore.* Singapore: Singapore University Press.

Yeh, S. H. K. (ed.) (1975a) *Public Housing in Singapore: A Multidisciplinary Study.* Singapore: Singapore University Press.

Yeung, Yue Man and S. H. K. Yeh (1975) 'A Review of Neighbourhoods and Neighbouring Practices', in Stephen H. K. Yeh (ed.) *Public Housing in Singapore*, pp. 262–180. Singapore: Singapore University Press.

Yeung, Y. M. and S. H. K. Yeh (1975a) 'Life Styles Compared: Squatters and Public Housing Residents', in S. H. K. Yeh (ed.) *Public Housing in Singapore*, pp. 302–24. Singapore: Singapore University Press.

Chapter 24

Some emerging social issues in Singapore*

S. Vasoo[†]

The social landscape of Singapore has been undergoing a rapid transformation over the last three decades. This transformation has been facilitated by a number of social, economic and political factors. Some of the broader social issues underlying the changes in the social landscape of Singapore are identified here. Some of the emerging social problems and issues that are likely to confront Singapore in the next 25 years are also discussed.

Relocation and rehousing

New towns have become a common feature in Singapore.[1] Since the 1960s, the Singapore government has found it necessary to develop new

---

*Reprinted with permission by the publisher from Vasoo, S. (1992). Some Emerging Social Issues in Singapore. In K. Azizah & T. S. Lau (Eds.), *Malaysia and Singapore: Problems and Prospects* (pp. 97–122). Singapore: Singapore Institute of International Affairs.

This write-up discusses the changes in Singapore's social landscape and some of the more pertinent social issues and problems such as the impact of population ageing, re-employment of retirees, increasing financial burdens of health care systems and potential erosion of human values. The comments in this paper cover a collection of views and analyses undertaken in earlier years.

[1] New towns are self-contained public housing estates which have a population of more than 150,000 people. These have been and are being developed by government to solve the

towns to house the growing population. To decant people into new towns, the government has ensured that the new towns are self-contained communities with adequate facilities to support social life and interaction.

The rehousing of residents into public housing estates in the new towns is one of the most significant programmes successfully implemented by the People's Action Party (PAP) government in this century.[2] About 87% of the population of 2.6 million people have already been housed in the Housing and Development Board (HDB) flats.[3] The rehousing of residents into new towns has contributed to an improved living standard. The new living environment is a welcome change for the residents.

However, the success of housing residents in the newly designed environment cannot be measured in terms of the number of people rehoused or better layouts. It has to take into consideration the social consequences and challenges facing the residents but also the PAP government. These social consequences and challenges concern the social integration of people who have been rehoused, the building of relationships and support networks among residents, the psycho-social adjustments of residents, the feeling of alienation and anomie among residents, the relationship between the residents and government represented by local bureaucracy, the willingness of the government to accept residents' feedback, the response of the government to the needs of the residents and the availability of avenues for residents to seek redress for their problems. The increasing pressure from residents for better urban services have prompted policy makers to deploy resources to encourage the formation of various social and community organisations to deal with the abrasions arising out of high rise living.

Families with higher household density are more vulnerable to stress. This is due to the lack of useable space within the households. Hence, families living in limited floor area, particularly those in one room flats, have found to be more exposed to stress. Hassan's study revealed that high

---

housing needs of the growing population. Housing and Development Board, *Annual Report*, 1984/85.

[2] Wong, Aline K., and Stephen H.K. Yeh (eds.), *Housing a Nation: 25 Years of Public Housing in Singapore*, 1985.

[3] Housing and Development Board, *Annual Report*, 1989/90.

internal density, as measured by the number of square feet per person in the flat, appears to be positively correlated with the worry index. Families living on higher floor (between 6 and 12 floors) face more strain and stress than those who live on the lower floors. This is because members on higher floors are more restrained by the height and find it difficult to leave the flat when they face tensions.[4]

High household density affects the parent-child relationship. Children from high density homes tend to be less confined to their households and inadvertently receive little supervision of their parents when they go to the environment outside. Such children, especially those from lower income group become more exposed to delinquent activities. This observation is supported by Chen.[5]

Prior to relocation, most of the new town residents came from various ethnic enclaves in the city and urban areas, squatters and dilapidated old tenement housing where there was more sharing of communal facilities and social interactions. Now they live in self-contained HDB flats which make them insular and impersonal. Chng and Lim in their studies found that neighbourly interaction was limited, selective and lacked the feeling of community sentiment.[6] Besides being disengaged from their old social networks, it would incur some personal costs for the residents to establish a new network of social relationships. Given the more anonymous environment of their neighbourhood and when pushed by stress, or pulled by autonomy, people in high density high rise public housing tend to withdraw into a private world, thereby creating a spatial environment which is characterised by inward looking attitude, impersonality, individualism, apathy and a sense of general insecurity.[7]

---

[4] Hassan, R., 'Social and Psychological Implications of High Population Density', *Sociology Working Paper No. 47*, 1975, pp 10–12.

[5] Chen, P.S.J., *Social Ecology of Singapore*, 1977, p 16.

[6] Chng, M.C., Human Territoriality in Singapore Territorial Needs and Assumptions and HDB Designs, an Academic Exercise: Department of Sociology, NUS, 1975. Lim, S.H., Relocation, Social Networks and Neighbouring interaction in a block of flats, an Academic Exercise: Department of Sociology, NUS, 1973.

[7] Hassan, R., 'Public Housing' in Riaz Hassan (ed.), *Singapore: Society in Transition*, 1976, p 260.

In addition to being apathetic, the residents of the housing estates in the new towns are from time to time troubled by vandalism and fear of crime. However, this concern is not as glaring because most estates are usually safe and not crime infested.[8]

From the various studies cited, it has come to light that people who have been resettled in new towns are less interactive and neighbourly. This situation, coupled by the feeling of loss of community, may have affected the development of community attachment among residents. The absence of community attachment can retard the process of participation of the residents in the maintenance of their social and physical environment.[9] The ramifications for lack of interest in the maintenance of their social and physical environment can create various pathologies, some of which have already been identified.

About 45% of the population living in new towns are children and young persons[10] who are being or are already socialised in the high rise environment. This situation raises some concern. Firstly, if the young are not provided with the right channels to be interested in the welfare of their neighbourhoods, they are likely to adopt the same attitudes as their parents and may become more parochial in their outlook. Secondly, as the young are now more literate and educated, they are likely to demand better urban services and facilities and if such demands fail to get communicated, they can be rather disruptive to the well-being of the neighbourhoods. Finally, if the young are denied the opportunities to care for their environment, they would be less rooted to their neighbourhood and would become less committed to build a closely-knitted neighbourhood.

About 4.67% of the public housing in the new towns are one room flats, which are primarily occupied by the lower-income group.[11] There is evidence to suggest that this sector of residents is more vulnerable to social dysfunctions (Hassan 1976, 1977) and therefore would require more attention from the policy makers and the local bureaucracies.[12]

---

[8] Ministry of Home Affairs, *Annual Report*, 1980.
[9] Hassan, R., *Families in Flats: A Study of Low Income Families in Public Housing*, 1977, p 262.
[10] Housing and Development Board, *Annual Report*, 1977/78.
[11] *ibid.*, 1989/90.
[12] Hassan, 'Public Housing, 1976: Hassan, 'Families' 1977.

Weakening of traditional organisations

Traditional organisations such as clan and lineage associations and guilds and mutual aid societies which have been playing an important mediation role between the residents and government in the past seem to have now lost their effectiveness and credibility.[13] They have become weak in representing broader cross-sectional interests of residents. They are no longer effective channels of communication between the policy makers and the government bureacracies.[14]

Singapore's new town environment has generated some spontaneous efforts among residents to initiate formal organisations to deal with the social consequences of rehousing. In the early 1960s Queenstown and Toa Payoh New Towns' residents witnessed the establishment of Residents' Associations. These Associations were formed by some residents who were interested to promote social and recreational activities and recommend neighbourhood improvements to HDB. Initially the Associations were able to attract some residents to be members, but membership did not increase overtime. This was due to the lack of awareness among residents and the inability of the Associations to dispense exclusive benefits to members other than those enjoyed by non-member residents living in the same neighbourhood. Besides, the complexity of new town environment reinforced the residents' feeling of distrust in the Associations' credibility. Together with the faltering support from residents, the lack of financial resources, the difficulties in securing premises to operate in the new towns and the inadequate administrative support to communicate with as many residents as possible, the Associations became operationally ineffective. In the end they ceased to exist in the early 1970s. Indigenous efforts in organising residents became rare and unheard of in the new towns.

As a consequence, the government has been encouraging the formation of new social and community organisations. During the last two decades the new towns in Singapore saw a number of formal organisations being established under the auspices of the government.

---

[13] Seah, Chee Meow and Soeratno Partoatmodjo (eds.), *Higher Education in the Changing Environment: Case Studies: Singapore and Indonesia*, 1979.
[14] Esman, Milton J., Ethnic Conflict in the Western World, 1977.

By the late 1970s, most of Singapore's old communities had been restructured through an increasing tempo by the government to provide housing for people. The pragmatic efforts of the government to rehouse people in the various new towns have both intended and unintended consequences in the social life of the residents. Attempts have been made by the government to set up two local social institutions such as the community centres/ clubs and citizen's consultative committees[15] to deal with the needs and problems faced by residents living in the new towns. These institutions have been the translation of the government's desire to keep in touch with the grassroots level of society. They are intended to obtain views to reshape government policies including housing for people and better social integration of the residents who belong to different ethnic groups. At the same time they are designed to meet the challenges of the growing social complexities in the nature and extent of the problems of residents in the new town neighbourhood. However, they are becoming less effective in mobilising and enhancing the involvement of the residents. As a result, the government has to plan new approaches in reaching residents at the grassroots, namely the residents' committees to provide a new channel for the participation of residents in community development.

Besides government induced formal organisations, the voluntary welfare organisations also play a part in delivering services to specific target groups who have been found to be in need of help. However, the role played by the voluntary welfare organisations under the Singapore Council of Social Service to develop formal voluntary organisations has been rather limited and centred mainly on the delivery of services to the disadvantaged groups.

In fact, the approach to encourage the formation of new social and community organisations by the policy makers has also been found to be of a rather limited utility. Participation in social and community organisations depends upon two factors. One is support from the residents themselves. Another is the resident orientation of the neighbourhood leaders. It

---

[15] These are intermediate organizations comprising of local citizens who are appointed by the government to maintain a channel of communication between the people living in a constituency and the various governmental authorities.

has been found that success of social and community organisations is most noticeable when neighbourhood leaders are high in both social support and resident orientation.[16]

Changing socio-ecological environment

Singapore's socio-ecological environment has been changing rapidly. In the last 25 years, the demographic patterns have changed due to changing fertility trends and population policies. The physical environment and skyline have been reshaped; the population has been redistributed into various new towns. In addition, expectations and demands of the younger generation of population for better social service provisions (for example, housing, education, health, transportation and entertainment) have risen sharply.

The demands, if not mediated, would increase the financial burden on Singapore. Other alternative strategies of meeting the demands are being devised. It is not surprising, therefore, to see an increase in governmental emphasis on corporatisation and restructuring of some social provisions such as health and education. Government is also encouraging citizens to set up more self-help organisations such as Family Service Centres to deal with social problems and emerging community needs. Through these citizens' initiatives, it is hoped that financial resources will be used effectively and service efficiency increased. In the government's pursuits of restructuring and privatisation of the public sector, it is important that social provisions be priced in a range which is within the reach of the ordinary working class.

In the next two decades, many social and community organisations will be facing a greying leadership. There is a danger of gerontocracy pervading in the organisation and this may lead to organisational inertia, parochialism and lethargy. To remain viable and progressive, these organisations have to find ways to renew their leadership. Although it cannot be ignored that older leadership does provide organisational wisdom, the survival of people-oriented organisations, both in the public and private sectors, must depend on the readiness of the older leadership to prepare

---

[16] The term low resident orientation (LRO) is defined as low level of concern for promoting self-help of residents as well as representing residents on matters which affect their welfare in a neighbourhood.

able younger citizens to manage them. It is indeed amusing to many outsiders that conscious efforts are undertaken in Singapore to induct the young into the managements of many public and statutory organisations. This process has brought about a smooth social transition and continuity from one generation to another without any disruption, contrary to what is normally experienced in most developing countries.

Some emerging problems are expected to surface in the next decade as a result of the demographic changes, changing value orientation, declining fertility and socio-ecological changes. These problems include impact of our ageing population, re-employment of retirees, erosion of human values, competing demand for discretionary time, economics of health care and emigration.

One of the most significant social phenomena of the future is population ageing in Singapore. In Singapore where the average life expectancy at birth is about 74 years, it is appropriate to consider the elderly population as comprising those who are 60 years and above. Although there is presendy no official retirement age, there appears to be an implicit recognition that the retirement age should be raised from the previous 55 years to 60 years.

The population ageing trend has been conspicuous. In 1970, there were about 118,300 persons aged 60 and above. The number increased by 47% to 173,000 in 1980. By the turn of the century, the number will rise to about 332,000. It has been estimated that 25% of Singaporeans will be above 60 years by 2030.[17]

A major challenge which will confront Singapore in the future has been identified by the government as the ageing of its population, expressed as the expected dramatic increase in the number of elderly persons and in the relative proportion of the elderly to the other age groups. While the aged population in Singapore is relatively small (8.6%) compared to most developed countries (11.4%), demographers in Singapore have predicted a sizeable increase in this age group in the next 50 years.[18]

---

[17] Cheung, Paul and S. Vasoo, *Country Study on the Elderly Singapore,* Paper commissioned bt the Economic and Social Commission for Asia and the Pacific, 1989.

[18] These figures are based on those aged 65 years and above. Binstock, R.H., W.S. Chow and J.H. Shultz, *International Perspectives on Ageing: Population and Policy Challenges,* United Nations Fund for Population Activities, 1982.

This trend, shared by other newly industrialising countries, is anticipated to result in a broad-based transformation of the society, requiring adjustments and adaptations at all levels. This would significantly alter the dependency ratio between the young and the old.

Two implications have received particular emphasis. First, concern is expressed on whether ageing of the population will increase the dependency ratio on the state for welfare and financial assistance. A related question is whether the traditional caring institutions will remain intact given the rapid social changes that Singapore is experiencing. Second, concern is also expressed on the economic implications of population ageing and its potential impact on the economy's future development.

Increasing awareness of issues of the elderly in Singapore has been generated as early as the 1970s. At least seven studies were conducted on the elderly during that time. In the 1980s, the number of studies have increased significantly. Even before the beginning of 1985, there were at least ten known studies, one of which was 'Social Policy and the Elderly' conducted by the Singapore Council of Social Service.[19] In addition, the appointment of two high-level committees in 1982 and 1988 to review the problems arising from population ageing reflected this concern. There was also an awareness that the rapidity of the ageing process and its consequences are related to, if not an outcome of, the policies implemented in the past. The two committees, chaired by Cabinet Ministers and comprised representatives from various sectors, were therefore given the task of reviewing the policy options and recommending policy changes. These two committees, as well as other initiatives, marked the beginning of Singapore's effort to plan for an ageing society. On the other hand, the report of the Committee on problems of the Aged, or commonly known as the Howe Report, further opens a gate for more public attention and debate on issues facing the elderly.[20]

The national infrastructure dealing with population ageing will be described at two levels: policy formulation and programme implementation. Three general features of the infrastructure deserve special mention

---

[19] Chen, P S.J, *Survey of Sociological Study in Singapore Society,* 1982.

[20] Ministry of Health, *Report of the Committee on the Problems of the Aged*, Singapore, 1984.

at the outset. First, population ageing and its implications have been accorded high political emphasis. The ruling political party has explicity mentioned population ageing as an important issue in its agenda for national discussion. As a result, efforts in policy formulation and programme implementation have benefitted from such political patronage. Second, Singapore is a relatively small place and an extensive network of government and non-government organizations are already in place. Thus, it is possible to exploit what is already in existence in the creation of a support infrastructure for the aged. Third, the growing affluence of Singapore makes it possible for the government and the society to divert resources to the programmes and services for the elderly, leading to a rapid expansion of the formal support network.

Policy formulation

In the 1970s, the concern for the welfare of the immigrant aged led to the establishment of a number of services catering to the special needs of this group. Such services were formulated by the then Ministry of Social Affairs in conjunction with the Singapore Council of Social Service. Although they attracted much attention, planning efforts were essentially sectoral and services were treated as an extension of the existing social welfare schemes

In the 1980s, the concern has broadened as the implications of population ageing were made known. The fact that the problems of the aged will not disappear along with the passage of the group of immigrants, destitute aged led to serious reviews of the issue. In June 1982, the appointment of a high level 13-member committee marked the beginning of the government's efforts to understand the implications of population ageing and to implement appropriate counter-measures.

The Committee on the Problems of the Aged was chaired by the then Minister for Health. In its deliberations, the Committee took the problems of old age beyond the realm of humanitarian and social welfare concerns. It took note of the long term impact of population ageing and its ramifications. As a result, the Committee stressed the potential contributions of the elderly to the society and the importance of incorporating them in socio-economic development, while concurrently acknowledging and meeting their special needs. To assist in its deliberations, the Committee commissioned the National Survey on Senior Citizens in 1983,[21] providing updated information from an earlier study conducted in 1976.[22]

The report of the Committee was finalized and released in March 1984. Several controversial policy recommendations such as raising the aged eligible for provident fund withdrawal and legislations on filial piety lead to much public outcry and discussion. However, the bulk of the Committee's recommendations were accepted. The major ones included the change in provident fund contribution rates for older persons to generate employment for older workers, legislation on minimum standard of aged homes, increased aged dependants' relief under the Income Tax Act and measures to foster family and intergenerational cohesion.

To implement the report's recommendations, several committees were established with members drawn from relevant ministries, statutory boards, institutions of higher learning and non-government agencies. The Co-ordination Committee to implement the Report on the Problems of the Aged was set up in August 1985 under the Ministry of Community Development (formerly the Ministry of Social Affairs) to evaluate and oversee the implementation of the report's recommendations. The Committee to Co-ordinate the Development Programmes and Activities was formed in January 1986 in the Ministry of Community Development to promote, direct and supervise the implementation of the recommendations in respect of health and recreational needs and social services and institutional care by government and non-government agencies. The Committee on Public Awareness on Ageing was set up to spearhead a public education and awareness programme in the Ministries of Community Development and Communication and Information to educate the public with a view to projecting a more wholesome image of senior citizens. The Public Awareness Programme on Ageing was launched in November 1987

---

[21] The National Survey on senior citizens was conducted jointly by the then Ministry of Social Affairs and the Ministry of Health for the Committee on the Problems of the Aged in 1983. The survey was based on 5,538 persons aged 55 years and above and who were living in private households.

[22] This refers to a survey sponsored by the Ministry of Health in 1976 and published in 1982 by Peter Chen, entitled The Elderly in Singapore.

with the establishment of a tripartite Task Force on the Employment of the Elderly in the Ministry of Labour. The task force comprising employers, government and union representatives would study the need to provide counselling for and retraining of older workers.

Recognising that population ageing is also a demographic problem, the government established in 1984 an Inter-Ministerial Population Committee (IMPC) to undertake a comprehensive review of Singapore's population trends and to make recommendations on policy measures to arrest the declining fertility rate and to bring about the desired population size and composition. Chaired by the Permanent Secretary of the Ministry of Health and reporting to the First Deputy Prime Minister, the members of the IMPC comprised Permanent Secretaries of relevant government ministries. Following the IMPC's recommendations, Singapore's population policy was revised in 1987. The Committee, assisted by the Population Planning Unit, continues to monitor Singapore population trends.

In June 1988, the Advisory Council on the Aged, headed by the Minister for Home Affairs, was formed to undertake a comprehensive review of the status of ageing in Singapore. Its term of reference, inter alia, include the review of programmes and services available to the aged, to examine the premises, assumptions and policy recommendations contained in the 1984 Report on the Problems of the Aged, to suggest ways to enable the aged to work beyond age 55 and finally to examine how families can be helped to look after their aged dependants.

The Advisory Council appointed four committees to look into the specific issues of concern. The four committees were: Committee on Community-Based Programmes for the Aged, Committee on Attitudes Towards the Aged, Committee on Residential Care Programmes for the Aged and Committee on Employment for the Aged. The composition of the members of the Advisory Council and the committees included experts from government ministries, statutory boards and voluntary organisations who were concerned with the provision and planning of services for the aged.

In September 1988, the reports of the four committees were reviewed by the Council and subsequently submitted for the consideration of the government. One of the key recommendations proposed by the Council was that a National Council on Ageing should be set up with the character and authority of a statutory board to effectively plan and co-ordinate policies and programmes for the elderly. Other proposals included raising the retirement age from 55 to 60 as continued employment provides a sense of worth, dignity and financial independence to the elderly; adjusting the seniority-based wage system so that more older people will be employed; expanding and strengthening public education programmes on the aged and ageing so that the right attitudes towards the aged could be inculcated; making land available for voluntary organisations to set up homes for the aged, lengthening the term leases for homes; studying the feasibility of providing health and medical services for the frail elderly living in their own homes; and increasing the dependency tax rebate for families who look after the aged.

A national policy on ageing in Singapore is therefore taking shape after these successive policy reviews. Two characteristics are worth noting in the policy formulation process. First, these Committees have the benefit of representation from various sectors. This has the advantage of receiving diverse inputs and making implementable decisions. Historically, cross-sectoral representation has worked well in the local context and it is the standard feature in Singapore's government problem solving approach. Second, the Committees were given much publicity. Public awareness of the issues were heightened, especially when controversial recommendations were made. The enhanced discussion on policy changes by the public reflect an increasing emphasis on social care of the elderly in Singapore. Public inputs have thus become an important consideration in both the Committees' deliberations.

Programme implementation

The programmes and activities for the elderly are co-ordinated through three principal organisations: the Ministry of Community Development, the Ministry of Health and the Singapore Council of Social Service. The two Ministries, in addition to the provision of direct services, provide overall guidance in planning for welfare and health services respectively. The Singapore Council of Social Service plays a co-ordinating role among non-government organisations and helps in representing their views to the government. A total of 26 voluntary and religious organisations affiliated to the Singapore Council of Social Service are currently providing services to the elderly. In addition, other ministries or statutory bodies may also be responsible for certain schemes concerning the elderly, such as the HDB. Taken together, the services offered by government and non-government organisations are comprehensive.[23] Basically, provision of social service for the elderly can be categorised into formal and informal care. Formal services for the elderly in Singapore include community based services and residential care. Informal services are support given by the family or friends of the elderly.

Presently, the community based services available in Singapore include the home nursing service, befriending service, senior citizens' or retirees' club, day care centre, and free or cheap meal service. While existing community based services should be developed further, other forms of services for the elderly such as telephone contact service, home-help service, neighbourhood mobilisation scheme, pre-retirement courses, health centre, and support for family care-givers should also be explored and possibly introduced to provide a broad based service.

Residential care includes the aged homes, nursing homes, community homes and commercial homes. The provision of social services to the elderly is particularly important in view of the rising number of elderly in the community, the smaller size of the family and more women entering the labour force. The routine of the family would be greatly disrupted when an elderly member becomes weak and requires regular attention. In addition, the large number of elderly (11,044) who live in one-person household suggests the vulnerability of this group in times of need and sickness. In Singapore, with only 2% of the elderly living in institutions, the family's role in ensuring the well-being of the elderly is of paramount importance. In a rapidly changing society, the family is also subjected to numerous competing demands that might affect its capability and willingness in the provision of care.

The National Survey on Senior Citizens in 1983 showed that about 5% of non-institutionalized elderly lived alone, with the remaining living

---

[23] Vasoo, S. and B.H. Tan, *The Status of Ageing in Singapore,* Unpublished manuscript, Singapore Council of Social Service, 1985.

in households mainly with immediate relatives. The finding was re-affirmed in a 1986 survey,[24] noting that the elderly tended to live with immediate family members. The same survey also showed that the elderly enjoyed reasonably good accomodation with 98% observed to be living in satisfactory living conditions in terms of sleeping arrangement, accessibility to facilities and cleanliness. It was also found that home ownership was high and two thirds of the elderly lived in households with monthly income exceeding $1,000/-. Questions were asked in the surveys about preferred living arrangement. It was found that there was a distinct and overwhelming preference among the elderly to live with their children, in particular, their married children. The choice of co-residence appears to be culturally influenced: the Chinese and Indians preferred to live with their married sons while the Malays preferred their married daughters. The surveys also found an overwhelming reluctance among the elderly to stay in old folks' homes, as was expected. The findings from a number of studies have shown that most of the elderly with immediate relatives (spouse, children and grandchildren) would have little problems in obtaining support in times of need.[25] They were also found to be engaged in meaningful interactions with the children they lived with and maintained frequent contacts with children who were living apart. The respondents were also confident that they could rely on their family for help when they were ill or when fhey had other problems. No evidence has been found to suggest that the family, as an institution, is shirking its responsibilities. However, several changes could restrict the effectiveness of the family as the primary source in the future. First, the increasing involvement of married women in the labour force could reduce the availability of care givers within the family. In 1980, the labour force participation rate of married women in the 30 to 40 age group was 33%. This has increased to 46% in 1988. With the shrinking of family size, there are also likely to be less persons to share out the responsibility of care. In the 1960s, a woman

---

[24] The survey on the Aged Living in the Community was conducted by the Ministry of Health in 1986. The survey was based on 1,013 persons aged 60 and over and who were living in private households.

[25] Cheung, Paul, *The Transition of the Social Support Systems for the Aged in Singapore. Emerging Patterns and Policy Options*, 1988.

tended to have about six children in her life time. This dropped to about four children in the 1970s and to about 2.5 in the 1980s. There is also concern about the younger generation, who may not be as filial towards their ageing parents. The decline in family size, coupled with increasing external commitments and value changes of the family members could erode the coping capability of the family in the care for an aged sick. These changes suggest that the formal support system may have an important role to play in the future. Therefore, to encourage the family to care for its elderly members to the fullest extent possible, the government has introduced measures which included the intergenerational co-residence, income tax relief, moral education programme, community based services and legislation. In the intergenerational co-residence, married children and their parents are allowed to apply adjoining HDB flats. Their applications will also be given priority in allocation. Also, for a person who is caring for an elderly dependant, a $3,500 income tax relief is given from Year of Assessment 1991, provided that the latter is not earning more than $1,500 a year. Moreover, children can claim tax relief of up to $6,000 a year for the equivalent sum of money they have contributed to their parents' Central Provident Fund (CPF) account.

In addition to the family support and community based services, financial support services are also available. The public assistance scheme under the Ministry of Community Development provides monthly allowances ranging from $140 for single person households to $400 for four person households. At present, about 2,833 persons aged 60 and above are receiving direct financial assistance. In addition, voluntary organisations also render assistance in cash and kind to the financially distressed. Churches, temples, charitable foundations and various community service groups provide ad hoc aid such as *hong bao* and food to the needy elderly during the festive seasons. However, the various financial schemes lack co-ordination to ensure efficient and effective distribution of financial resources. The old age financial security for Singaporeans is provided principally through the CPF scheme, whereby monthly contributions are made by both employees and employers. At present, the rates of contribution is 17.5% for employers and 22.5% for employees. The scheme is run by a statutory board and guaranteed by the government. Contributors can also draw on the fund for approved purposes, such as purchase of property, payment of medical expenses and other investment ventures. The principal sum plus interest can be withdrawn at age 55, except for a sum of $30,000 which can only be withdrawn after the age of 60. This is to provide an added protection for financial well-being in old age against squandering of the savings. Part of the CPF is channelled into a Medisave account which can only be drawn for medical expenses. At present, the cap for the Medisave account is set at $15,000

To help reduce the burden of care on the family, services such as home visiting, day care and respite care are being offered. The government has also launched various initiatives to promote as much community involvement in these services as possible. Two objectives are emphasized. First, the elderly should be kept fit and healthy, capable of full participation in the mainstream of community life. Second, the aged sick are to be provided supportive services which will enable them to live with their families for as long as possible.

The Committee on the Problems of the Aged recommended that laws be passed to impose on children the obligation to care for their elderly parents. No legislations have been instituted and the Advisory Council on the Aged has also advised against it. However, the government is prepared, if necessary, to institute legal protections for the welfare of the elderly if the family is abdicating its duties.

Are these measures likely to be effective in fostering greater family support? These measures reflect to a large extent cultural emphasis on the importance of the family and are therefore consistent with general sentiments. However, these are essentially passive measure's designed to maintain rather than to foster families ties. The moral education programme is therefore special as it takes a proactive role to inculcate specific filial attitudes. Whether such an intervention can help to stem the influence of Westernization remains to be seen. However, education of this nature may help prepare the young to accept the challenge of caring for their aged parents.

Community participation and involvement

A major planning principle put forward by the Committee on the Problems of the Aged is the recognition of the potential contribution of the elderly to the society and their own welfare. This principle came through clearly in the Committee's report and was again endorsed by the Advisory Council on the Aged. Singapore is likely to have a quarter of its population aged 60 and over, and it is clear that this vast amount of human resources must be tapped if Singapore is likely to maintain its economic prosperity. Harnessing the contributions of the elderly is however easier said than done. Age-old prejudices often cast the elderly in poor light and the emphasis is mainly placed on their problems rather than their potential contributions. The developmental emphasis of the government's approach is therefore encouraging.

Recognising that contribution is possible only through participation, the two national planning committees have given prominent attention to three aspects of participation, ie. health maintenance, community activities and gainful employment.

Health is often the critical factor in a person's adjustment in old age. While old age is not necessarily a time of ill health and disability, a variety of chronic illnesses do occur more frequently among the elderly than among the younger persons. In Singapore, the large majority of the elderly enjoy reasonable good health and lead independent lives. But they are also disproportionately large consumers of medical care. In 1986, the elderly accounted for 18% of all admissions into government hospitals while forming only 8% of the population. In absolute numbers, the admission statistics showed an impressive rise of 79% from 23,000 in 1977 to 40,000 in 1986. It is projected that by end of the century, their admissions would increase to at least 30% of total admissions. To reduce the level of morbidity among the elderly, the role of primary health care has been emphaiszed. Three aspects, namely the health education, health screening and self-help groups have been promoted thus far.

Participation in community activities is an indication of the elderly's integration in the society, beyond the confines of the family. Greater involvement in the community, especially in age integrated activities, signifies a respectable status accorded to the elderly. Conversely, social isolation of the elderly reflects a poor image of the elderly among the younger generation. Community participation of the elderly can be grouped into two types: age segregated or age integrated. The rapid proliferation of Senior Citizens' Clubs encouraged by the government is one example of the former. These clubs offer recreational programmes, health screening, keep fit activities and opportunities for community services to senior citizens. At present, there are 166 such clubs with a membership of about 47,600, run mostly by government or para-government organisations. Among the few non-government run clubs, the Singapore Action Group of Elders (SAGE) is the largest with a membership of about 1,500. Such age segregated clubs meet certain needs of the elderly. They provide a contact point for meeting and making friends and a forum for exchange of opinions and experiences. They, unfortunately, also segregate the elderly from the other age groups. The establishment of a network of Senior Citizens' Clubs may therefore heighten the awareness of the elderly as a distinct social group. Thus far, these clubs are not linked to form a larger organisational base. The National Council of Ageing, proposed by the Advisory Council on the Aged could conceivably provide the linkage to these clubs, effectively organising them into a potentially potent self-interest group. On the other hand, to what extent are the elderly involved in age integrated activities? This is difficult to assess, as empirical evidence are scarce. In a 1987[26] in a report on the support systems of the elderly, sponsored by the United Nations University, it was found that the most common avenue of participation is through religious activities. Apart from these, the study found that the higher the educational attainment, the greater the involvement in formal organisations. By and large, however, such involvements were not extensive, suggesting very strongly that avenues have to be developed for the elderly to be more involved in age integrated activities. Reasons for non-involvement included being too busy with household chores, lack of interest and lack of opportunities. It should be stressed that the potential for the elderly to participate in community services has yet to be realised. This group clearly possesses varied experience and talents that could be tapped by the community for specific projects. At present, elderly persons are involved in ad hoc community activities. More could be encouraged to join in such community services as childcare, home nursing, crime prevention, befriending, teaching and home help. The Volunteers Development Programme of the Singapore

---

[26] The study was conducted by the National University of Singapore, sponsored by the United Nations University, Japan,

Council of Social Service is currently exploring the recruitment of elderly volunteers.

It has been the emphasis of the government that the elderly should be encouraged to work for as long as possible in order to maintain mental alertness and financial independence. Moreover, in labour-short Singapore, the elderly constitute an important source of labour supply. However, as noted earlier, there has been a gradual decline in their labour force participation rates in the past five years.

Re-employment of retirees

In 1989, it was estimated that 58% of those between 55 years and 59 years were economically inactive in Singapore. Among those above 60 years, 82% were economically inactive. The labour force participation rate of these two age groups are no doubt low. There is an urgency to encourage more older workers to be retrained in our work force.

The number of people in the retirement age group is on the increase. It is projected that by the end of 1990s, there will be 230,000 persons in the retirement age group, that is, between 55 and 64 years. With such an increasing number of retirees coming on stream, it is a challenge to both the public and private sectors to establish a more specialised service for retraining and re-employment of the retirees.

In view of the future shortage of manpower and slow increase in population, there are pressing demands from the trade unions and retirees to extend retirement age from 55 to 60 years.

The Advisory Council on the Aged, in its deliberations, was aware of the urgent need to promote greater economic participation of the elderly and arrived at four broad recommendations, i.e. raising of retirement age, changing the wage system, increasing employment opportunities and training and retraining.

The Council was of the view that the customary retirement age at 55 should be raised to 60. This increase should be done through negotiations between employers and employees, taking into consideration the special needs and circumstances of each economy or job. However, the government has since indicated that such negotiations may be too slow to bring about changes in retirement age. Inspite of the government's urging, only 65% of unionized companies and 25% of non-unionized companies in the private sector have done so in 1990. The employers were apparently concerned with the unsuitable nature of the work, the high cost and lower productivity of employing older workers. In a survey conducted by the Ministry of Labour in 1988, it was found that 47% of the companies with retirement age below 60 reported that it was impractical to revise their retirement age.[27] Among them, 56% gave the reason of unsuitable work and about a third each indicated high cost, lower productivity and less feasibility in employment as reasons. The Ministry of Labour, therefore, announced in March 1989 that retirement age will be raised to 60 by 1992. The three-year grace period is to allow companies to make necessary adjustments.

The Council also noted that wages in Singapore are largely based on seniority. Consequently the wage bill for an older worker is far greater than a new entrant, even if they are employed in the same job. As an inducement to encourage employers to retain older workers, the government has reduced the rate of Provident fund contributions for older workers. To further facilitate the expansion of employment opportunities, the Council advocated fundamental adjustments in the wage system, taking into account considerations such as the salary to be tied to the worth of a job, salary scales to be shortened, costly fringe benefits tied to seniority to be reduced and staff to be rewarded through one-off bonuses rather than through basic wage increments.

To increase the employment opportunities, the Council urged employers to allow greater options such as part-time work, flexitime work, working at home or working on alternate days. The Ministry of Labour's Employment Service Department will provide special assistance to older workers in job placements.

The Council recognised that one obstacle to continued employment for older workers is their inadequate or outdated skill level. It urged the Skill Development Fund, a statutory body financing skill training, to develop special schemes for older workers and to provide special subsidy to employers in retraining their older workers. It is foreseeable in the

---

[27] The survey on retirement policy was conducted by the Labour Relations Department of the Ministry of Labour in 1988. The survey was based on 711 unionized companies and 36 unions.

future that training programmes for the older workers will be developed by various local training institutes.

Will these measures taken together halt the decline of the elderly's labour force participation rate? The answer to this question is contingent on a number of factors. First, it is clearly essential that these measures are fully implemented. While the government can take steps to encourage the employment of older workers, the employers themselves must see the advantage of hiring them. Reluctance on the part of the employers will not help to generate work opportunities. Second, the attitudes of the older workers may be changing such that leisure is increasingly valued over continued employment. If this is the case, then, Singapore may follow the example of many developed countries where the participation rates of older workers drop steadily regardless of employment opportunities.

It is important to note that the retention of retirees affects job openings for the young. The problems of re-employing the aged and of the resulting frustrations in the young both deserve serious consideration.

Erosion of human values

The social health of any progressive and vibrant society varies directly with the human values the members of the society cherish as well as their capacity to find social antigens to decadent values that erode moral and social responsibilities. Singapore is an open economy. The population is exposed to various information which have either positive or negative effects on their outlook to life. They are more vulnerable to the erosion of human values. It is important, therefore, for Singaporeans to actively promote right kinds of social values as early as possible. The right time for this purpose is when a child begins school.[28] Such an emphasis in the school curriculum can facilitate helping behaviour. On moral education programme, the government has initiated changes in the school curriculum to strengthen traditional family values and inculcate filial piety and respect for the elderly. For example, an annual Senior Citizens' Week is being organised to promote the contributions and status of the elderly. A

---

[28] Values education in this context covers the teaching of ethics, moral codes and good citizenship.

family life education programme has also been implemented to promote harmonious family living. Values education, if carefully planned, can also encourage good citizenship. In the long run, it can prevent the citizens from becoming self-centred and uncaring.

More citizens with high social DNA are to be nurtured.[29] These people with the acumen for the promotion of public good are likely to further strengthen the foundations of our social and public institutions.

With improvements in working conditions, Singaporeans are likely to have more discretionary time which can be tapped by many social and community organisations. As discretionary time is rather limited, Singaporeans are likely to spend it in voluntary activities which are beneficial and useful to them. There is always a danger that they may participate less in altruistic activities for they have to first meet their own economic necessities. It is, therefore, crucial for social and community organisations to make their voluntary service programmes interesting and satisfying experiences for the participants.

Economics of health care

In recent years, the issue of rising cost of health care in Singapore has been a subject of public debate. This has been generated by the Government's move to restructure and privatise public hospitals and the general concern among consumers of the increasing cost in health care. Though the total expenditure on health care in Singapore is still well below 3% of the GDP and the current level of health care expenditure is still considered low by western standards. The concern is not symptomatic, although it should be noted that in the last 15 years, government recurrent expenditure on health care has increased by three-fold in nominal terms, well exceeding the economic growth. It is precipated by a significant increase in consumer price index for health care which has risen to 20% over the last 5 years. The private per capital expenditure on health has increased from $100 in 1976 to over $300 in 1986. Health care expenditure will also increase steeply, especially with our ageing

---

[29] People with high social DNA are those who have positive concern for the residents' well-being and public good.

population. As people become more affluent and better educated, the demand for better health care services will increase. The important issue is that the increasing expectation for health care must be balanced with affordability.[30]

It is envisaged that there will be more concerted efforts by the Government to implement various cost containment measures, such as curtailing the increasing demand for health care, promotion of primary health care, regulating the supply of health services, reduction of subsidies for those who can afford, establishment of community hospitals, cost-control on high-tech medicine and efficient use of health care professionals.

Increasing demand for health care is inevitable due to advances in medical technology, longer life expectancy, population ageing, increasing affluence and education and hence expectation of the people. In 1957, the life expectancy at birth was only 64 years. Today, it is 74 years. In fact, improvements in life expectancy among the elderly, particularly among the male elderly, have been much greater than that of the general population.

However, what people really want is good health and not good health care. As the major provider of health services to the population, responsible for about 70% of the total hospital care and 30% of primary health care, the government could lead in setting realistic standards of health care by regulating the amount of cost that the public is willing and can afford to share. This could help in dampening or slowing down the demand for better health care and services so that it would not be incompatible with our economic growth. Moreover, the government could also help to contain the increasing cost of health care by improving productivity in the public health services and encouraging competition among the health care providers in both the public and private sector. On the other hand, the provision of an efficient preventive health care and frontline curative services through the primary health care services plays an important part in keeping the population healthy and curtailing the demand for health care. The comprehensive immunisation programmes would help to prevent

---

[30] Low, Puk Yeong, *Cost Containment: The Government's Role*, paper presented at the seminar on Economic Issues in Health Care, 1988.

many serious infectious diseases. Early detection and treatment of serious conditions could reduce the need for costly hospitalisation. The government could continue to ensure that the primary health care services are easily available to the population. Further, careful consideration has to be taken to ensure that there are sufficient subsidized classes of bed (B2 class and C class) for those who are in the low income group. Otherwise, this group would find health care less accessible and they would delay in seeking treatment. This could add to further cost increase in health care. On health financing, the policy decided by the government is the Medisave Scheme, which aims to build the individual's financial resources so that those who fall sick would have the means to pay for their health care, especially in his old age. Being the individual's personal saving, incentives have already been provided for him to stay well and use the Medisave wisely.

Emigration problem

Emigration of some young adult Singaporeans is a new emerging problem. As Singapore maintains an 'open door' policy, there is no administrative controls for emigration from Singapore. With the increase in regional economic co-operation and growing investments of Singapore companies overseas, there is an emerging flow of temporary emigration of managers and skilled workers. Singaporeans emigrating to the West have also become noticeable in recent years as some of the developed countries have relaxed their immigration policies. The trend of migratory flows of Singapore could be seen within a framework of growing regional and international economic exchanges of which labour exchange is becoming an important aspect. In general, Singapore benefits from the supply of skilled and unskilled labour from the region while the region benefits from the provision of technicians, professionals and investment by Singapore firms.

There are four main reasons for Singaporeans to leave Singapore, namely, the homeland emigration where the emigrants return to the countries of origin; emigration for family reunion where Singaporeans who have married foreign spouses may choose to stay overseas and eventually settle there; emigration for better living arising from political or social reasons and economic emigration where the Singaporeans leave Singapore to take up overseas employment for better career prospects, higher returns and other benefits.[31]

It is estimated that the number of people who have emigrated between 1986 to 1990 ranged from 5,040 to 6,320 persons.[32] Many of those who have migrated were economic migrants with professional and technical skills. This outflow of people, though small, deplete the local pool of talent. To stamp the outflow, it is necessary that more educational and career opportunities be made available to children of the potential emigrants.

It must be reiterated that Singapore cannot afford to face a prolonged economic down turn. When this happens, we could see a greater exodus of people as the world has become an arena for inter-migration.

Conclusion

In summary, Singapore's social landscape has indeed undergone significant changes as a result of demographic transition, relocation and rehousing, urban development and city planning and compressed modernization. Some of the more pertinent social issues and problems are the impact of population ageing, reemployment of retirees, increasing financial burdens of health care systems and potential erosion of human values. The challenges confronting policy makers and the Singapore community are to provide proactive and cost-effective solutions.

---

[31] Cheung, Paul, *Social and Economic Implications of Singapore's Immigration and Emigration Patterns*, report presented at the International Conference on Migrations, Singapore, 1991

[32] *ibid.*

Chapter 25

Social policy based on assets: The impact of Singapore's Central Provident Fund*

Michael Sherraden, Sudha Nair, S. Vasoo,
Tee Liang Ngiam, and Margaret S. Sherraden[†]

The Central Provident Fund (CPF) of Singapore is the world's most extensive example of social policy based on assets. It stands in marked contrast to Western welfare states, where social policy is based primarily on

---

*From Sherraden, M., Nair, S., Vasoo, S., Ngiam, T. L., & Sherraden, M. S. (1995). Social policy based on assets: The impact of Singapore's Central Provident Fund. *Asian Journal of Political Science*, *3*(2), 112–133. Reprinted by permission of the publisher (Taylor & Francis Ltd, http://www.tandfonline.com).

This paper provides a perspective of research findings regarding how Singaporeans view the effects of the Central Provident Fund and its impact as Singapore's primary social policy instrument for financial security in retirement. The work is an early analysis of financial security in old age.

[†]Michael Sherraden, Ph.D., is Director, Center for Social Development, Washington University, St. Louis, Missouri, USA; Sudha Nair is Executive Director, Ang Mo Kio Social Service Centre, Singapore; S. Vasoo, Ph.D., is Head, Department of Social Work and Psychology, National University of Singapore; Ngiam Tee Liang, Ph.D., is Senior Lecturer, Department of Social Work and Psychology, National University of Singapore; and Margaret S. Sherraden, Ph.D., is Assistant Professor, Department of Social Work, University of Missouri at St. Louis. Support for this study has come from the US Information Agency (Fulbright Fellowship Program), The Rockefeller Foundation, Washington University in St. Louis, and the National University of Singapore.

income transfer through social insurance and public aid. The perspectives underlying these two types of policies could hardly be more different. In the West, social policy is thought of as income for consumption that the population is able to enjoy because the economy is productive enough to be taxed for social spending. In Singapore, most "social policy" (this phrase is relatively uncommon in public discourse in Singapore) is financed out of CPF's individual asset accounts and social policy is better integrated with economic policy. Because of the merging of social and economic interests in CPF, it is particularly useful to ask: What are the social impacts?

This topic has been somewhat overlooked in the past. A number of scholars have written generally about CPF as a social security or social welfare system.[1] Others have addressed accountancy issues such as contribution rates, partitions into accounts, or interest rates;[2] coverage and

---

[1] Mukul G. Asher, *Social Adequacy and Equity of the Social Security Arrangements in Singapore,* Occasional Paper No. 8 (Singapore: Centre for Advanced Studies, National University of Singapore, 1991); N.W.S. Chow "Social Security Provision in Singapore and Hong Kong", *Journal of Social Policy,* Vol. 10, No. 3 (1981), pp. 353–356; Catherine Jones, "Hong Kong, Singapore, South Korea, and Taiwan: Oikonomic Welfare States", *Government and Opposition,* Vol. 25, (1990), pp. 446–462; K. Kalirajan and Paitoon Wiboonchutikula, "The Social Security System in Singapore" in Amina Tyabji (ed.), *Social Security Systems in ASEAN,* special edition of *ASEAN Economic Bulletin,* Vol. 3, No. 1, (1986), pp. 129–139; Liew Kian Siong, *The State of Welfare in Singapore,* M.Soc. Sci. thesis, Department of Sociology, National University of Singapore, 1992; Linda Y.C. Lim, "Social Welfare", in K.S. Sandhu and Paul Wheatly (eds.), *The Management of Success: The Moulding of Modern Singapore* (Singapore: Institute of Southeast Asian Studies, 1989), pp. 171–197; Monika Queisser, "Social Security Schemes in South-East Asia", *International Social Security Review,* Vol. 44, No. 1/2 (1991), pp. 121–135; Tay Boon Nga, "The Central Provident Fund: Operation and Schemes", in Linda Low and Toh Mun Heng (eds.), *Public Policies in Singapore: Changes in the 1980s and Future Signposts* (Singapore: Times Academic Press, 1992), pp. 264–281.

[2] Central Provident Fund Board, *Annual Reports* (Singapore: Central Provident Fund Board, 1955–1992); Central Provident Fund Study Group, National University of Singapore, *Report of the Central Provident Fund Study Group,* special issue of *The Singapore Economic Review,* Vol. 31, No. 1 (1986); Antal Deutsch and Hanna Zowall, *Compulsory Savings and Taxes in Singapore* (Singapore: Institute of Southeast Asian Studies, 1988); Amina Tyabji, "Financing Social Security", Paper presented at a conference on the Fiscal System in Singapore, National University of Singapore, February 1990.

adequacy issues;[3] microeconomic effects on households and businesses;[4] macroeconomic impacts of CPF;[5] and particular policy areas, such as ageing,[6] housing[7] and health care.[8] However, in these studies, there has not

---

[3] Asher, op. cit. (1991); Liew, op. cit. (1992).

[4] Lawrence B. Krause, Koh Ai Tee and Lee (Tsao) Yuan, *The Singapore Economy Reconsidered* (Singapore: Institute of Southeast Asian Studies, 1987); Wee Chow Hou and Han Sin Bee, "The Central Provident Fund — Some Micro and Macro Issues", *Singapore Management Review*, Vol. 5, No. 2 (1983), pp. 35–52.

[5] Mukul G. Asher, "Economic Effects of the CPF Scheme", *Singapore Business Yearbook* (1983), pp. 25–35; Central Provident Fund Study Group (1986); Goh Keng Swee, *The Practice of Economic Growth* (Singapore: Federal Publications, 1977); Lim Chong Yah, *Policy Options for the Singapore Economy* (New York: McGrawHill, 1988); Cedric Pugh, "Public Policy, Welfare and the Singapore Economy", *Annales de L'Economia Publique Socials et Cooperative*, No. 4 (1984), pp. 433–455; Parthasarrathi Shome and Kathrine Anderson Saito, *Social Security Institutions and Capital Creation: Singapore, the Philippines, Malaysia, India and Sri Lanka* (Kuala Lumpur: Sritua Arief Associates, 1985).

[6] Paul Cheung, "Population Ageing in Singapore", Paper presented at the WHO-MOH Joint Workshop on Healthy Ageing, Singapore, October 1992; Republic of Singapore, Ministry of Health, *Report of the Committee on the Problems of the Aged* (Singapore: Government Printer, 1984); Republic of Singapore, *Report of the Advisory Committee on the Aged* (Singapore: Government Printer, 1989).

[7] Chua Beng Huat, "Public Housing Policies Compared: U.S., Socialist Countries, and Singapore", Paper presented at the 83rd annual meeting of the American Sociological Association, Atlanta, 1988; Goh Keng Swee, *Urban Incomes and Housing: A Report of the Social Survey of Singapore, 1953-54* (Singapore: Government Printer, 1956); Lee E. Goh, "Planning that Works: Housing Policy and Economic Development in Singapore", *Journal of Planning Education and Research*, Vol. 7, No. 3 (1988), pp. 147–162; Cedric Pugh, "Housing in Singapore: The Effective Ways of the Unorthodox", *Environment and Behavior*, Vol. 19, No. 3 (1987), pp. 311–330; Augustine H.H. Tan and Phang Sock-Yong, *The Singapore Experience in Public Housing*, Occasional Paper No. 9, Centre for Advanced Studies, National University of Singapore (Singapore: Times Academic Press, 1991); Martin Tracy, reporting for the Committee on Provident Funds, *Experience of Provident Funds in the Provision of Housing and Scope for Improvement*, Report at the XXIVth General Assembly (Geneva: International Social Security Association, 1992); Aline Wong and Stephen H.K. Yeh (eds.), *Housing a Nation: 25 Years of Public Housing in Singapore* (Singapore: Maruzen Asia for the Housing Development Board, 1985); Stephen H.K. Yeh (ed.), *Public Housing in Singapore* (Singapore: Singapore University Press, 1975).

[8] Phau Kai Hong, *Privatisation and Restructuring of Health Services in Singapore*, Occasional Paper No. 5 (Singapore: Institute for Policy Studies, 1991); Republic of Singapore, *Towards Better Health Care: Report of the Health Care Review Committee* (Singapore: Government Printer, 1992); Toh Mun Heng and Linda Low, *Health Care*

yet been a careful assessment of how CPF has been used by Singaporeans and its impact as Singapore's primary social policy instrument.

Study methods

Several study methods were employed in Singapore: (1) review of all available documentary evidence; (2) interviews with policy-makers, CPF program officials and CPF scholars; (3) analysis of macro program data provided by the CPF Board; (4) focus group discussions with different segments of the Singapore population by race/ethnicity and income levels (11 groups); and (5) a face-to-face in-home survey with a random sample of CPF members (N = 356, response rate 79.1 per cent). These multiple research approaches have been important in order to "see" the CPF from different perspectives and obtain a balanced overall understanding. This article is a brief summary of some of the overall research findings regarding social impacts and how Singaporeans view the effects of CPF.

Social impact

In a fundamental sense, CPF policy can best be understood by what it does for members, and what it does for members can be represented by how CPF funds are used. In turn, use of funds can be tracked by annual withdrawals for different purposes. In a word, CPF's social impact is reflected in the pattern of withdrawals. This is not policy as someone may have intended, but policy as it *actually operates* in Singaporean households and communities. In this section, we look at withdrawals by function.

Withdrawals in a given year

We turn first to withdrawals in a given year. Table 1 summarizes net withdrawals in 1993, showing the amount and percentage for each major

---

Economics, Policies and Issues in Singapore, Centre for Advanced Studies, National University of Singapore (Singapore: Times Academic Press, 1991).

Table 1. Total CPF withdrawals (net of refunds), 1993, millions of dollars

Category and Scheme	Amount (S$)	Per Cent of Total
Lump Sum Provident Fund*		
Age 55	927.9	8.5
Leaving Singapore	178.0	1.6
Death and Disability	81.1	0.7
Income Protection		
Minimum Sum	122.3	1.1
Housing		
Public Housing	1,821.8	16.6
Residential Properties	1,687.6	15.4
Health Care		
Medisave	250.2	2.3
Insurances		
Home Protection	62.8	0.6
Dependent Protection	57.3	0.5
Medishield	41.9	0.4
Education		
Education	27.5	0.3
Investments		
Non-Residential Property	47.0	0.4
SBS Shares	(2.8)	(0.0)
Investment	4,129.3	37.7
Special Discounted Shares	1,512.0	13.8
TOTAL	10,943.9	100.0

*Lump Sum category refers to provisions in Section 15 of CPF Act.

Source: Annual Report 1993, CPF Board.

scheme. The total withdrawn during 1993 was S$10,943.9 million. Of this total, it is most striking that share investment (Investment Scheme and Special Discounted Shares Scheme) accounted for 51.5 per cent of the total. This was a dramatic change from 1992, spurred by 1993 changes in rules and incentives for share investments in CPF. As of 1993, CPF has become a major engine for share ownership by the Singapore population.

The two housing schemes (Public Housing and Residential Property) accounted for 32.0 per cent of all withdrawals. The original lump sum provident fund schemes (Age 55, Leaving Singapore, Death and Disability) together accounted for only 10.8 per cent of withdrawals. In other words, as measured by dollars withdrawn during 1993, the impact of housing schemes was about three times as great as that of the lump sum provident fund.

Making up a smaller proportion of total withdrawals is the health care scheme (Medisave) at 2.3 per cent. The remainder of the schemes make up still smaller percentages: insurances (Home Protection, Dependents' Protection, and Medishield) accounted for 1.5 per cent; income protection (Minimum Sum) accounted for 1.1 per cent; and the Education Scheme accounted for only 0.3 per cent.

Overall, we can say that what today's CPF does foremost for Singaporeans is share investment and housing. Old age security, at this time, plays a distant tertiary role (although share investment and housing can also be considered important forms of old age security). Health care comes next, while insurances, income protection, and education are relatively minor schemes in terms of dollars spent.

Withdrawals by social objective

It may be helpful to summarize CPF withdrawals over time. In keeping with the central theme of this paper, we now look at CPF withdrawals not exactly by types of schemes, but rather by the general social objective which they seek to promote. Taking this viewpoint requires us to rearrange schemes into slightly different categories: retirement, family protection, health care, housing, investments and education. Table 2 presents annual withdrawals in these categories between 1960 and 1993.

This table provides the single most concise summary of "what CPF has been doing for Singaporeans" since it began 40 years ago under the British Colonial Government. First we can look at total withdrawals, which grew from a mere $3.9 million in 1960 to a three thousand-fold

Table 2. Summary of annual CPF withdrawals* by social objective,** 1960–1990, millions of dollars (percentages)

Year	Retire	Security	Housing	Invest	Health	Educ	Total
1960	3.4 (87.2)	0.5 (12.8)	— (100.0)	—	—	—	3.9
1965	8.0 (86.0)	1.3 (14.0)	— (100.0)	—	—	—	9.3
1970	19.6 (43.5)	2.6 (5.7)	22.9 (50.8)	— (100.0)	—	—	45.1
1975	72.7 (33.5)	9.8 (4.5)	134.8 (62.0)	— (100.0)	—	—	217.3
1980	237.2 (30.4)	19.0 (2.4)	520.9 (66.9)	1.9 (0.2)	— (100.0)	—	779.0
1985	652.6 (19.4)	94.0 (2.8)	2,566.4 (76.4)	2.6 (0.1)	43.9 (1.3)	— (100.0)	3,359.2
1990	1,025.5 (25.9)	83.1 (2.1)	2,259.1 (57.2)	332.3 (8.4)	240.1 (6.1)	11.9 (0.3)	3,952.0 (100.0)
1993	1,228.2 (11.2)	201.2 (1.8)	3,509.4 (32.1)	5,685.5 (52.0)	292.1 (2.7)	27.5 (0.2)	10,943.9 (100.0)

*Includes all withdrawals of money that actually reaches the CPF Board. Does not include money withheld at the company level for the CoWEC scheme, nor any non-CPF collections.

**For the purposes of this table, the social objectives listed are comprised of the following CPF schemes:
    Retirement = Age 55, Minimum Sum, Leaving Singapore
    Family Security = Death, Disability, Home Protection, Dependent Protection
    Housing = Public Housing, Residential Properties
    Investments = SBS Shares, Non-Residential Properties, Investment, Special Discounted Shares
    Health = Medisave, Medishield
    Education = Education

Source: Annual Reports, CPF Board.

increase of $10,943.9 million in 1990 (the total figure is slightly different, depending on which CPF Board figures one uses). In 1990 (before investments played a major role in CPF withdrawals) the total CPF withdrawals were about 6.9 per cent of GDP. Looking at this figure in terms of "social impact", it was more money than the Singapore Government spent for all recurrent expenditures in "social and community policy" (including education, health, community development, information and the arts, environment and public housing) during the same year. Therefore, as measured by dollars applied, CPF has by far the greatest impact of any domestic social policy. It casts a very large shadow over everything else.

Turning next to what social objectives were being addressed by CPF withdrawals (Table 2), in 1960 and 1965, in keeping with the original provident fund concept, more than 85 per cent of the withdrawals were for retirement and the remainder for family security.

By 1970, a dramatic change was occurring. The Public Housing Scheme had been introduced in 1968, and by 1970, it already represented 50.8 per cent of all CPF withdrawals. This figure rose to a remarkable 76.4 per cent by 1985. Thus, when CPF outgrew its narrow provident fund beginnings, the simple retirement fund — often derided as "coffin money" — took wing and facilitated a huge housing programme, transforming Singapore in the process, both physically and socially. We do not have space in this report to describe housing policy in detail. However, the amount of expenditure compared to GDP, and the substantial transformation of rural kampung areas and urban slums into high rise apartments, more than 90 per cent owned by Singaporeans, must qualify Singapore's housing policy, on a per capita basis, as one of the most comprehensive ever undertaken.

From 1970 to 1985, retirement played an ever declining role relative to housing, although absolute withdrawal amounts continued to rise. With a changing age structure, however, this pattern was reversed by 1990, when retirement accounted for 25.9 per cent of all withdrawals. As the population continues to age, withdrawals for retirement are likely to rise during coming decades.

Family security has continued to decline in relative emphasis, falling to 1.8 per cent of withdrawals by 1993. With increasing general health of the population and decreasing physical danger in employment for Singapore citizens, family security withdrawals will probably continue to remain at modest levels in the years ahead.

Investment started with the SBS Shares Scheme in 1978, but accounted for only 0.2 per cent of all withdrawals by 1980 and an even smaller 0.1 per cent by 1985. However, after the Non-Residential Properties and Investment Scheme was introduced in 1986, this category leaped to 8.4 per cent of all withdrawals by 1990, the third largest category of withdrawals after housing and retirement in that year. With the 1993 introduction of the Shares Top-Up and Enhanced Investment Schemes, withdrawals for investment exploded to 52.0 per cent of all withdrawals during that year.

Next, we can look at more recent objectives of CPF — health care and education. In health care, Medisave was a new programme in 1985, accounting for only 1.3 per cent of withdrawals during that year. By 1990, Medisave had grown in importance and had been joined by Medishield. Together, these two health-related schemes accounted for 6.1 per cent of withdrawals in 1990. It is noteworthy that increases in CPF health withdrawals moderated between 1990 and 1993, rising only about 21.7 per cent in nominal dollars, and falling to 2.7 per cent of total CPF withdrawals in 1993. Singapore is highly determined to keep health expenditures low and CPF withdrawals for health care reflect this policy emphasis.

Within CPF, the social objective of education is addressed only by the Education Scheme which began in 1989. This scheme is restrictive, as only a portion of the population goes on to tertiary education in Singapore. Therefore, compared to most other uses of CPF, withdrawals are rather small. In 1993, the Education Scheme accounted for only 0.2 per cent of CPF withdrawals.

A note on Edusave

Also of interest is a CPF-like scheme called Edusave. In December 1990, having recently assumed the Prime Minister's Office, Goh Chok Tong announced Edusave saying, "I want to give everybody a chance to appear at the same starting line, regardless of his financial background ... I have come up with the Edusave programme because I want to temper our meritocratic, free market system with compassion and more equal opportunities".[9] He called Edusave "an investment in our children". Significantly, if the money is not used by completion of O Level (the equivalent of high school), the balance goes into the CPF Ordinary Account. Thus, it seems quite possible that Edusave will be integrated with CPF in the future.

---

[9] Straits Times, 18 December 1990.

Edusave is a major departure because (1) virtually all young people will have accounts which can later be transferred to a CPF Ordinary Account; and (2) the Government is making universal deposits that are not tied directly to employment. These are very important policy precedents. Although deposited amounts are currently modest, the Edusave structure opens the door toward a truly universal CPF with multiple funding channels. In 1995, this potential became apparent as the Government announced matching grants to community groups who raise money for Edusave accounts for children in the community.

Singaporeans' views on the Central Provident Fund

No previous study has asked Singaporeans what they think about the CPF, what they think of the various schemes and what they think of CPF operations and services. This section presents a summary of focus group discussions.

A total of 11 focus groups with different segments of the Singapore population were conducted; all were homogeneous, usually by race/ethnicity or income, but there was also one group of single mothers and one group of elderly persons.

From the 11 groups, 831 distinct comments were recorded and retained for analysis. These 831 comments met two simple criteria: (1) each was clearly and directly related to some aspect of CPF, and (2) each made a consistent point. For the most part, this section simply reports the views of focus group participants as they expressed them. Comments are under particular headings to illustrate main themes.

Overall results

Looking first at overall sentiment about CPF, comments can be sorted into two categories: those that tend to be favourable, and those that tend to be unfavourable (Table 3).

Altogether, there are 520 positive or neutral comments (63 per cent of the total). For discussion purposes, and although it is a rough approximation, we lump these together as "favourable" comments.

Social policy based on assets 495

Table 3. Focus group comments: Overall results

Comments directly or implicitly favourable	
Generally positive	466
Neutral but accepting	54
Total favourable	520
Comments directly or implicitly unfavourable	
Raising a concern	221
Offering a suggestion	90
Total unfavourable	311
Total comments	831

On the other hand, there are 311 concerned or suggestive comments (37 per cent of the total). For lack of a better term, these are lumped together as "unfavourable". A word of clarification is in order: many of the concerns and suggestions are offered by participants not as empty complaints, but from a generally positive outlook on CPF. Those who raise concerns or offer suggestions usually do so from a position of overall support. Also, our impression in leading the focus groups is that CPF is extremely popular among Singaporeans; the underlying sentiment is an almost bedrock support. But we have encouraged participants to speak up, and they have obliged us. They tell us what is on their minds and it is sometimes about a perceived need for improvement. Therefore, one way to think about the "unfavourable" category is "things that might be improved about CPF".

Becoming more specific, comments can be broken down into three categories of main topic: policy, operations, and effects (Table 4).

CPF policy draws the most comments, with 475 (57 per cent of the total) and these are slightly more favourable than unfavourable. The next largest category is CPF effects, with 253 comments (30 per cent of the total); these comments are distinctly more favourable than unfavourable at a ratio of almost 5:1. CPF operations is the least discussed category, with 103 comments (12 per cent of the total), and these are more favourable than unfavourable at a ratio of about 3:2. In this article, we examine only those comments on CPF effects.

Table 4. Comments on policy, operations and effects

Comments on CPF policy	
Favourable	250
Unfavourable	225
Total policy	475
Comments on CPF operations	
Favourable	60
Unfavourable	43
Total operations	103
Comments on CPF effects	
Favourable	210
Unfavourable	43
Total effects	253
Total comments	831

Table 5. Comments on effects of CPF

Effects on individuals	
Favourable	124
Unfavourable	20
Effects on families and households	
Favourable	87
Unfavourable	37
Effects on economy and society	
Favourable	42
Unfavourable	17
Total comments*	290

* The total does not equal the total comments on effects on Table 4 because some comments refer to more than one effect and these are included here in more than one category.

Effects on individuals

About half of all the comments on effects of CPF refer to effects on individuals, which we examine first. CPF is designed as a "pro-work" policy, that is, benefits come only with employment, and when asked, some say that CPF does indeed make them work harder and may be more effective in this regard than a social insurance scheme:

> *I'll work harder. I will only get more CPF by working more.*

> *If I work hard, if my employer appreciates my effort, he will promote me and I'll be getting a higher salary. Although the percentage [of CPF contribution] is the same, it will be based on a higher salary, so I get more money. So it does motivate me to work harder.*

Another theme is that CPF encourages people to plan for the future:

> *People plan for the long term with CPF because, since they cannot withdraw the money now, they are forced to think long term.*

> *With CPF, you can plan your future wisely too.*

> *It makes me plan for my old age, taking into consideration the amount I will have in my CPF account.*

Turning to more psychological effects, some say that CPF increases their self esteem:

> *It has helped increase our self esteem. From living in attap* [thatched roof] *houses, we now live in brick homes.*

> *All our needs are taken care of so we feel good about ourselves.*

The most common type of comment is that CPF increases one's sense of security:

> *I feel more secure.*

> *If we do not have CPF, what will our life be like? There is a sense of security.*

> *When I am old and too weak to work, I will not feel so helpless because I still have some money in my CPF account.*

Closely related to security, another theme is independence:

> *You do not have to depend on children to support you. This independence makes you feel good.*
>
> *With CPF, the old folks can depend on themselves.*
>
> *It takes the burden off the young. Because their parents have CPF, they can live their own lives.*

Other discussants emphasize more directly the economic effects of CPF:

> *You feel richer.*
>
> *Unconsciously a pool of money will be collected from your salary and it can be used for business, investment, shares, education and insurance. Although only a small sum of money is collected from your salary each month ... but a drop of water, a grain of sand, makes a mighty ocean and a pleasant landing.*

Others note benefits over pensions schemes, particularly in relation to freedom and control at the workplace:

> *CPF is better than the pension scheme because you know exactly how much you will be receiving, whereas in the pension scheme, you don't.*
>
> [CPF compared to pension]: *When I have the pension, I'm tied to the company. It doesn't give me a chance to say let's look at greener pastures, or let me think about, let's say I want to go to another company, you know for improvement or otherwise, but I'm tied to this company. I don't want that hung over my neck.*

On the other hand, not all CPF effects on individuals are seen as positive. By far the most common type of dissatisfaction at the individual level is the problem of waiting so long for the money and not being able to spend it sooner:

> *I will not be satisfied until I reach my retirement age.*
>
> *If you have 20 years to go before 55 years old, you will think it is a long wait.*
>
> *We do not even know whether we can live that long to see our CPF.*

It is possible that, for some, this has a negative effect on work behaviour:

> *They end up working less because they have so much deduction. They say, "If I work overtime, my money goes there. No point me working."*

Others express concern that the money might not be there when they reach 55:

> *Yes, I think a lot because to reach 55, my way is still a long way more. Tomorrow we may lose, everything is gone.*
>
> *Yes, I have a friend who will ask me what will happen if suddenly your money is not there.*

One concern is the handling of the lump sum as a major financial responsibility:

> *If you are given a lump sum from CPF, you must be able to manage this lump sum properly. If not, the money would just go.*
>
> *Yes, there is a big lump sum, but there is a fear of spending it all.*
>
> *... so they give me one whole lump sum. Now it is up to me. Well, I'm no god to judge how long I'll live.*

On the other hand, others argue that CPF should give more responsibility to people much earlier in their lives, that it is protecting Singaporeans too much:

> *CPF provides a wrong sense of stability. You assume the rate of savings and returns. With this false assumption, some would engage in speculative ventures which might prove to be a loser.*

Another viewpoint is that CPF may in fact have an adverse effect on saving:

> *CPF has spoiled the people, giving them a false sense of security. Even among the lower income families, people do not think it is necessary to save because they think that CPF would take care of them in their old age ... It is affecting people's savings negatively.*

Effects on families and households

Some Singaporeans point to general economic effects of CPF on the family and household:

> *... helps us increase our standard of living.*
>
> *We don't have to worry about the house payment.*
>
> *We bought shares through CPF. Otherwise I wouldn't be able to have any shares. Thirty years ago, ten years ago, we don't dream of it.*

But the majority of favourable comments about families and households (66 per cent of the total) relate, in one way or another, to children:

> *We are planning to buy a house because we are now renting and the house will never belong to us. A purchased house has better benefits. Our children will have a house. We have the CPF and we might as well buy the house for our children's future.*
>
> *Well, they inherit the money when we go, so they are very better off.*
>
> *If you were to go and see Moses halfway* [die before you are old], *it'd benefit your dependents. Somehow or other the money would still be there and would not go to waste.*

However, focus group participants do raise some concerns about CPF and family life. Economic and social concerns are of several types. One is the hardship effect on low income families:

> *Children may be worse off in lower income groups* [due to lower disposable income and less consumption].

Perhaps surprisingly, another type of concern is that CPF gives the wrong message to members and they no longer save on their own. This is seen not merely as a financial issue, but a matter of proper values:

> *The security induced by CPF prompts people to spend their income on family and children. This trend of not saving so much is worrying because it is reshaping our values. The Chinese used to have the virtue of saving for their children, as it means doing something good for oneself too. Security is no doubt produced by CPF, but people should also save.*
>
> *With CPF, it would affect the children's spending habit. Spending more money on children would spoil them and spoil the cultivation of the thrifty values.*

One person sees negative effects on the extended family as CPF makes older people more independent:

> *With the total package of CPF, housing policies and funds for home ownership, the family unit is being broken down. Because they could all afford their own place, children do not want to live with their parents or take care of them. If we did not have CPF, this might not happen.*

One person even sees distortions in how some Singaporeans may look for a mate:

> *CPF has created a social phenomenon that the ideal man would be aged 55 to 60, that's when he is getting his CPF, for there's money to be spent... In a way, it has affected family relations and mate-finding.*

A different type of concern is that CPF generates family conflict over the money:

> *Parents' CPF withdrawal coincides with children's needs to set up their own family and this pressurizes parents to loan money to the children. Problems arise when the children do not pay back.*
>
> *Maybe it* [the CPF lump sum] *will be cheated by your children? Or they may fight among themselves for the bigger share? That will be terrible!*

Macro effects on the economy and society

Although the focus group leaders did not ask questions about the effects of CPF on Singapore in general, a rather substantial number of comments address these "macro" effects of CPF on the economy and society. One type of comment refers to stabilizing social effects of CPF, particularly regarding home ownership:

> *CPF has allowed Singapore to remain stable; we don't think of migration.*
>
> *In addition, home ownership allows the government to institute any plans they have for their citizens, easily* [this is said in an approving tone].

But other social effects of CPF are not viewed as positively. A number of discussants respond to a question about whether CPF encourages migration out of Singapore:

> *Anyone leave to collect CPF? Yes, we know of such people.*
>
> *I think CPF will certainly not hold people back but may increase their chance of migrating if they have a lot of money in their CPF account. This is because when you migrate, you can withdraw all the money in your CPF account, which may be enough for you to have a very good life in another country.*

While some of the above sociological effects of CPF are no doubt important, macroeconomic effects may have greater long-term impact. Favourable comments are listed below. One type of comment emphasizes positive impacts on savings, investment and economic growth:

> *It is about the right* [CPF contribution] *rate, 40 per cent of savings. Surveys show that Singapore is one of the highest saving nations in the whole world.*
>
> *In the Singaporean context, definitely CPF is good and it has actually been the engine of the economic growth in the funds which gave the construction industry a boom, gave workers a better standard of living, and it has also been a source of cheap funds for lots of infrastructure*

projects in Singapore. So on the macro view, CPF has done an outstanding job in the Singapore context.

Another type of comment views CPF as a tool to actively manage macroeconomic issues:

As people live longer, more illness. With the high health cost, it would definitely be a drain to the country's resources [if some health care were not "self-funded" through CPF].

As for my own theory as to why the government is coming up with schemes and programmes that encourage us to spend the CPF money like investing in stocks and shares, private properties and such, which is going to take you a long time to pay up.

So, when you reach your 55 years, your cash balance would not be that great, as most of your cash is tied up in stocks and shares and properties which are not easily liquidated. This is because a great amount of cash that would be pumped into the economy which would fuel consumerism. This would then lead to inflation and people would be unhappy about it ... We should congratulate the government for anticipating such a problem.

Some discussants emphasize that the benefit of CPF is mutual, to the individual and to the nation and "government" [the latter term is sometimes used to refer not only to government, but to society and the economy as well]:

And with CPF the benefit is not only to the individual. It transcends the individual to the nation as well. That's a bigger benefit ...

But then again from our contribution, there's a lot of money being invested by the government. That's a fact, that's why it also boosted the economy. Till you reach 55, there's a lot of money invested, our contribution by the CPF to the government. There's a lot of interest gained. In terms of the government, it is their benefit. From our contribution, I'm sure they're not dumping it somewhere stagnated. They're investing it, that's a fact. That's why we're prospering. As I said, it benefit both sides. It benefit us because we're given home ownership, we're given a form of saving. It also benefit the government. So in this move, it benefit both parties. It's good for both.

But not all observations on macroeconomic impacts are favourable. One strong concern is the effect of CPF on business competitiveness:

I think CPF is a cost-factor in business operation because it's an add-on to the bill straight off.

There's no need to put so much money into a controlled, compulsory type of funding mechanism if the money could be used for speculative purposes. It's defeating itself. Meanwhile, the escalating cost of doing business here is forcing companies to go overseas and you are still forcing people to save more. You should just correct and cut back.

On a somewhat related theme, others think that CPF, due to its 100 per cent portability, has a negative effect on employees' commitment to the employer and company. Sometimes they suggest some form of vesting:

... the way CPF is done in Singapore does not generate much loyalty among the employees.

I see the way CPF is practised in Singapore, there's no doubt the employees benefit a great deal. But it has resulted in bad work ethics among the employees. Because of the compulsory nature of CPF, the average employee is not worried. This has contributed to job-hopping among the younger generation of workers. Whether they would work harder or not, I don't know, but they have no loyalty to the employers.

Another person suggests that so much CPF money going into home purchases that it is pushing up the price of housing:

For example, the price of house [is rising] too. Maybe it is because everyone is using CPF to buy a house, that's why the price has increased so tremendously.

Focus group summary and conclusions

The strength of the focus group method is that we can see the issue clearly from the participants' perspectives. The language is not always perfect — grammar may not be precise, "Singlish" is common, metaphors are occasionally mixed. Nonetheless, comments tend to be very clear.

Overall, Singaporeans are pleased with CPF. The tone of all focus groups is generally positive and favourable comments considerably outnumber unfavourable comments. Again, we would emphasize that much of what is here called "unfavourable" can be understood as constructive criticism and suggestions in an atmosphere of general support. Perhaps the single most important finding in focus groups is that Singaporeans think the CPF has extremely positive effects. Overall they think it has positive impacts on individuals, family life and the nation as a whole.

Participation in CPF and effects of asset accumulation

We turn next to results of a structured survey of CPF members. Our primary interest in this section is the effects of asset accumulation in CPF accounts.

Plans for using the CPF lump sum

Because the original purpose of CPF was a lump sum retirement benefit and in the public's mind CPF is still largely defined this way, it is important to ask members what they intend to do with the lump sum at retirement.

In descending order of importance, members say they will use the lump sum for living expenses (4.5 on a 5-point scale), medical care (4.4) and savings (4.3). These are in line with the major purposes of CPF. We did not ask about housing because, by age 55, the vast majority of CPF members already own a home.

The next group of lump sum uses, in descending order of importance, are children's education (3.8), travel (3.4), children's marriage (3.2), helping children with business or other investment (3.1), giving money to voluntary organizations (3.1), renovating the residence (3.0), giving money to religious organizations (3.0), paying off loans (3.0) and upgrading the residence (2.9). The main themes here are taking care of children, giving money to voluntary or religious organizations and improving the personal residence.

Table 6. Plans for use of lump sum at age 55 (N = 365)

Type of Use	Rating (5 Pt. Scale)
Living expenses	4.5
Medical care	4.4
Savings	4.3
Children's education	3.8
Travel	3.4
Children's marriage	3.2
Helping children with investment	3.1
Giving to voluntary organizations	3.1
Renovating residence	3.0
Giving to religious organizations	3.0
Upgrading residence	2.9
Investing in residential property	2.7
Investing in shares	2.7
Investing in an annuity	2.6
Starting a business	2.6
Buying furniture	2.4
Investing in an existing business	2.4
Religious pilgrimage	2.2
Own education	2.2
Purchase automobile	2.0
Migrate from Singapore	1.8

The next group, somewhat more negative than positive, in descending order of importance, are investing in residential property (2.7), investing in shares (2.7), buyingan annuity (2.6), starting a business (2.6), buying furniture (2.5) and investing in an existing business (2.4). The main theme here is investment.

The final group of responses, ranking rather low, are to use the lump sum for a religious pilgrimage (2.2), the member's own education (2.2), purchase of a car (2.0), and to migrate out of Singapore (1.8). Explanations are straightforward. Pilgrimages are practiced mostly by Muslims. By age

55, most people are not thinking about their own education. Only a minority of Singaporeans own cars, which are expensive and not necessary for living in Singapore. And, in distinct contrast to earlier periods in Singapore's history, most people do not anticipate migrating, even at retirement.

Satisfaction with CPF

When asked how satisfied they were with CPF overall, respondents are remarkably positive, averaging 4.1 on a 5-point scale. Only one out of 356 says he or she is very dissatisfied and 12 others say they are dissatisfied. The remaining 343 (96.3 per cent) are positive or neutral. A solid 119 (33.4 per cent) say they are very satisfied.

When asked what they think is the best or most important thing about CPF, 30.6 per cent say something about savings and security; 20.5 per cent mention only retirement security; 15.4 per cent mention only housing; 11.8 per cent mention multiple specific uses of CPF; 9.8 per cent mention other factors; and 11.8 per cent give no response.

Specific effects of CPF participation

Next, we asked about specific effects of participating in CPF. Roughly in order of magnitude of effect, respondents say that CPF makes it more likely that they will own their flat (2.8 on a 3-point scale), and get better health care (2.5). Thus, these primary policy objectives of CPF are being fulfilled for most participants.

Turning to psychological effects, respondents say that their participation in CPF makes it more likely that they feel confident about the future

Table 7. Satisfaction with CPF (N = 356)

Very Satisfied	119	33.4%
Satisfied	53	43.0%
Neutral	71	19.9%
Dissatisfied	12	3.4%
Very Dissatisfied	1	0.3%

(2.6), feel secure (2.6), will be independent in old age (2.6), feel in control of their life (2.4) and have a happy family life (2.3).

When it comes to planning, respondents say that CPF makes it more likely that they will make educational plans for their children (2.4) and plan for their retirement (2.4). CPF is intended to be a pro-work policy and respondents confirm that participation in CPF makes it more likely that they work hard on their jobs (2.4) and stay employed (2.3). CPF is also intended, in part, as a nation-building policy to strengthen attachments to Singapore and respondents confirm that CPF makes it more likely that they will stay in Singapore, i.e. not migrate (2.3). Ranking lower, but still with a positive effect are investment effects of CPF: owning other residential property (2.1), owning shares of stock (1.8), starting a new business (1.7) and investing in an existing business (1.7).

Finally, effects on family formation appear to be weak. Participants do not frequently say that CPF makes it more likely that they will get married at an earlier age (1.6), or have more children (1.5). Looking at intergenerational effects, 68.5 per cent of respondents say that their children are better off because of CPF, while only 0.3 per cent (1 respondent) says that children are worse off. The remaining 31.2 per cent say neither or give no opinion (people with no children usually give no opinion).

Specific effects of home ownership

Turning to specific effects of home ownership, one of the highest ranking sets of responses relates to increased effort to maintain the property. Respondents say that home ownership makes it more likely that they will keep the residence neat and clean (2.8 on a 3-point scale), repair and maintain the residence (2.7), renovate the residence (2.7) and pay attention to property values (2.5).

Psychological effects also rank high. Home ownership makes it more likely that Singaporeans feel confident about the future (2.7), will be independent in old age (2.7), feel secure (2.7), feel in control of their lives (2.5) and have a happy family life (2.5).

Turning to work effects, respondents say that home ownership makes it more likely that they will stay employed (2.5), and work hard

Table 8. Effects of CPF participation (N = 356)

Type of CPF Effect	Rating (3 Pt. Scale)
Own One's Flat (Residence)	2.8
Feel Confident About Future	2.6
Feel Secure	2.6
Be Independent in Old Age	2.6
Get Better Health Care	2.5
Feel in Control of One's Life	2.4
Make Educational Plans for Children	2.4
Plan for Retirement	2.4
Work Hard on One's Job	2.4
Stay Employed	2.3
Have a Happy Family Life	2.3
Stay in Singapore (Not Migrate)	2.3
Own Other Residential Property	2.1
Own Shares of Stock	1.8
Start a Business	1.7
Invest in Existing Business	1.7
Get Married at an Earlier Age	1.6
Have More Children	1.5

on their jobs (2.5). Home ownership also makes it more likely that CPF members will make educational plans for the children (2.4), and stay in Singapore, i.e. not migrate (2.4). As for effects on social relations in the community, responses are somewhat lower, but still positive. CPF members say that home ownership makes it more likely that they will be friendly with neighbours (2.3) and be respected in the community (2.2). However, social ties to organizations are less affected by home ownership. Fewer respondents say that home owning makes it more likely that they will become active in voluntary organizations (1.8), or become active in grassroots (political) organizations (1.6). Finally, effects on family formation also appear to be weak. Not many respondents say that home owning makes it more likely that they will have more children (1.6).

510 *Collected Readings on Community Development in Singapore*

Table 9. Effects of home ownership (N = 356)

Type of Home Ownership Effect	Rating (3 Pt. Scale)
Keep the residence neat and clean	2.8
Repair and maintain the residence	2.7
Renovate the residence	2.7
Feel confident about the future	2.7
Feel secure	2.7
Pay attention to property values	2.5
Feel in control of one's life	2.5
Have a happy family life	2.5
Stay employed	2.5
Work hard on one's job	2.5
Make educational plans for children	2.4
Stay in Singapore (not migrate)	2.4
Be friendly with neighbours	2.3
Be respected in the community	2.2
Be active in voluntary organizations	1.8
Be active in "grassroots" (political) organizations	1.6
Have more children	1.6

Discussion of survey results

CPF is viewed primarily as a savings and retirement scheme, even though the major use of funds to date has been for housing. This may indicate that even though most CPF resources are tied up in housing, these resources are still viewed by CPF members as security for retirement. The move toward reverse mortgages announced in January 1994 is consistent with this interpretation, allowing Singaporeans to use their housing assets without moving from the residence.

Although most CPF assets are currently tied up in housing, this pattern may change in the future. Uses of CPF are likely to shift as greater funds accumulate, the population ages and home ownership increasingly occurs through intergenerational transfer. Therefore, it remains important to ask Singaporeans what they intend to do with their lump sum at retirement. Responses to these questions should be encouraging to Singaporean policy makers. Other than living expenses and health care, saving ranks very high, as does improving the personal residence. Other real property and share investments rank low. But human and social investments rank high. These human and social investments include helping the next generation and giving money to religious and voluntary organizations. The only significant consumption use (other than living expenses and health care) is travel at age 55, which tends to be popular. Purchases of durable goods (furniture or car) are planned by relatively few members.

As regards specific impacts, respondents give very high marks to CPF across a broad range of economic, psychological and social effects which we list here in approximately descending order of importance. Foremost, CPF is viewed as an effective vehicle for providing housing and health care. A number of positive behavioural effects are also indicated, particularly in taking care of property, planning for the future and working. Psychological effects of asset holding — greater confidence, increased security, a sense of control — are also noteworthy. Social effects are somewhat less prominent in stronger community relations and not migrating from Singapore.

Several types of hypothesized effects do not receive much support in the findings. These include limited impact on social attachments to voluntary and political organizations and limited impact on family formation (getting married at earlier ages and having more children). Indeed, although we did not test this, it is possible that CPF actually has a negative impact on family formation because of the greater opportunity cost (foregoing CPF accumulations) for women who interrupt employment for child rearing. However, when asked about intergenerational effects of CPF, the vast majority of respondents say that children are better off. From focus groups, we know that the reason is greater asset accumulation and the opportunities this will provide to the next generation.

Also ranking low in effects are all types of investments other than the personal residence. However, with the expansion of CPF into the Enhanced Investment Scheme and the Shares Top-Up Scheme for Telecom shares (and presumably successor subsidized share schemes in future privatizations), it is likely that this pattern will be altered in the future. Senior

Minister Lee Kuan Yew and Prime Minister Goh Chok Tong have discussed the importance of asset building and stakeholding. Following the success of home ownership, Singapore's leaders have announced share ownership as the next undertaking in asset accumulation across the population.

One might expect certain unfavourable effects of CPF as well. As a theoretical matter, the greatest of these would be the consumption that is foregone by saving such a large percentage of income. Indeed, 38.5 per cent of respondents say that making CPF contributions causes at least some financial difficulty. Discontent may also be suggested in the call for greater flexibility in use of funds. On the other hand, we find strong general support for investment as opposed to consumption in use of CPF funds, both before and after age 55.

Conclusions

By far the most important social impact of CPF to date has been in housing. As Senior Minister Lee Kuan Yew said in an interview for this study, the 1968 decision to use CPF funds to promote home ownership was intended to help Singaporeans identify with the nation and to fight for the country should that become necessary. There is little doubt that widespread home ownership has had a major impact on social stability. Assets in housing have enabled most Singaporeans, even those with low incomes, to become stakeholders.

The positive psychological impact of CPF is also noteworthy. Confidence, security, control and independence rank high as effects of CPF. We know from focus group discussion that Singaporeans feel empowered by CPF. In a sense, their social policy decisions are "in their hands" and they generally like it that way. However, those who have very small CPF balances are concerned that this will not be enough.

There is a question about the impact of CPF on family formation and child bearing. It is noteworthy that "have more children" ranks at the bottom of the list of possible effects of CPF participation and also at the bottom of the list of possible effects of home ownership. Most Singaporeans do not see any connection between CPF and decisions to have children. Indeed, there is nothing in the structure of CPF that promotes childbearing. Moreover, the added economic incentive of CPF probably makes some women reluctant to leave the workforce to bear and raise children. Given Singapore's low birthrate, this may be a matter of concern to policy makers.

As we look to the future, the next generation of Singaporeans will inherit substantial wealth in homes, shares and CPF cash balances. It is likely that CPF schemes will continue to expand as these resources grow, coverage and adequacy will very likely continue to improve and social impacts will become even more pronounced and varied than in the past.

Chapter 26

Singapore: Social development, housing and the Central Provident Fund*

S. Vasoo[†] and James Lee[‡]

The high rates of economic growth and significant improvements in standards of living recorded in East-Asian nations such as Singapore in recent decades has attracted increasing attention from social policy scholars in the industrial countries. Many believe that the experiences of these countries offer useful lessons for the Western welfare states. This article examines social security and housing policies in Singapore and shows how both were an integral part of a wider commitment to promote economic development. The article suggests that Singapore provides a

---

*Reprinted with permission by the publisher from Vasoo, S., & Lee, J. (2001). Singapore: Social development, housing and the Central Provident Fund. *International Journal of Social Welfare*, *10*(4), 276–283. Copyright © John Wiley & Sons Ltd and *International Journal of Social Welfare*.

This paper examines social security and housing policies in Singapore and shows how it is possible to integrate both with economic policies that promote development, offering useful lessons for the Western welfare states. Some of the ideas are a reflection of earlier points made on issues related to asset building.

[†]Department of Social Work and Psychology, National University of Singapore, Email: swkhead@nus.edu.sg

[‡]Center for Comparative Public Management and Social Policy, City University of Hong Kong

good example of a developmentalist approach to social welfare that successfully harmonises economic and social objectives.

Keywords: Singapore, housing policy, social security, social development, Central Provident Fund

In the last two decades, the European welfare states have been criticised for failing to address problems of unemployment and poverty. It is also claimed that Western welfare statism is too expensive, and that it has harmed economic development (Feldstein, 1974; Mishra, 1984, 1990; Pierson, 1995; Buti, Franco & Pench, 1999). In many industrial countries, government programmes have been trimmed down or privatised.

On the other hand, poverty and deprivation remains endemic in the developing countries of the Global South. The governments of these countries are not able to allocate sizable resources to the social services even though the need for government assistance is great. It is generally agreed that these countries cannot afford the comprehensive social services provided in the industrial nations. Attempts by some political leaders to expand the social services to meet the pressing social needs of the developing countries have not been very successful.

East Asian nations such as Hong Kong, South Korea, Singapore and Taiwan (the so-called 'tiger economies') lie between these two extremes. Although these countries were economically underdeveloped at the time of the Second World War, they experienced rapid economic development during the latter decades of the last century and today, their citizens enjoy high standards of living.

The East-Asian countries are characterised by a high level of state intervention in social welfare and yet they have experienced rapid economic growth. Social policy in these countries has developed rather differently from that in either the Western welfare states or the developing nations of the Global South. Perhaps the most important feature of social welfare in these countries is that social policies have not been divorced from the larger economy as has been the case elsewhere. Social goals have been met by integrating social welfare with economic development.

The social policies of these countries have attracted attention from several social policy scholars who believe that there is a distinctive East Asian model of social welfare (Goodman, White & Kwon, 1998). The existence of an East Asian welfare model challenges the theoretical parsimony of the three worlds of capitalism model (the liberal, conservative and social democratic) suggested by Esping-Andersen (1990) a decade ago. It also offers insights into the viability of a normative approach to social welfare known as developmentalism. As articulated by Midgley (1995, 1997), this approach urges the harmonisation of economic and social policy. Developmentalists believe that social welfare can best be promoted when governments implement macroeconomic policies that promote sustainable, people-centred economic development and, at the same time, formulate social policies that invest in people's capabilities to participate effectively in the productive economy. It avoids the emphasis on unilateral income transfers in Western welfarist thinking and rejects the notion that the market alone can ensure prosperity for all.

Since independence in 1965, Singapore has experienced an economic and social transformation. It has been transformed from a dependent colonial territory to one characterised by wealth and opportunity. Good housing, income security for old age, good primary health and universal education have all somehow been achieved without impeding productivity and economic development. This fact has intrigued many, but also has its critics who believe that the country's success has been overrated (Tremewan, 1998).

The twin goals of economic development and social welfare, which have been pursued in Singapore over the last forty years offers insights into the developmental model of social welfare. Singapore's experience also sheds light on and the potential of the developmental model to provide a new rationale for social policy in both the developing and the industrial nations. The experience of Singapore suggests that it is possible to integrate social policies that promote housing and social security with economic policies that promote development. The main argument is that, given a right mix of social policies and appropriate institution arrangements, economic development can be harnessed to achieve social ends.

Social policy in Singapore

Singapore is an island city-state of 648 square kilometres located at the tip of the Malaysian Peninsula. The country has a population of 3.89 million.

The island was colonised by the British in 1819 and served for 140 years as a trading port. The colonial administrators adopted a laissez-faire approach to the economy but at the same time, created a strong administrative system. The trading economy grew slowly and few resources were deployed for social purposes. This was in keeping with British colonial policy that minimised government expenditure, and required that local needs be funded through local resources.

Singapore was occupied by the Japanese army during the Second World War, shattering the myth of British imperial invincibility. At about this time, radical nationalists, socialists and communist began to agitate for independence from British rule (Lee, 1988). Their campaigns came to fruition in 1965 when, after a brief period of federation with Malaysia, Singapore secured sovereignty under the People's Action Party (PAP). Leading members of the Party had been influenced by British Fabian socialist ideas and faced with economic challenges and competition from communist rivals, they committed themselves to strong, centralised government. They also built on the British administrative tradition bequeathed during the colonial period and implemented a series of economic and social policies that had a profound effect on the country's subsequent development.

From the beginning, the People's Action Party focused its attention on economic development and little resources were allocated for social welfare. In addition, the Party leadership took a different approach to social policy from that adopted in Britain and other European nations. Instead of using social policy as a means of addressing social needs and redistributing income, the Party implemented social policies that were intended to serve the interests of economic development. Its two major social policy initiatives were public housing and social security.

Following the creation of the Housing Development Board (HDB) in 1960, public housing expanded rapidly and constitutes, together with Hong Kong, one of the most extensive housing programmes ever created. Following a subsequent commitment to home ownership, more than 80% of Singaporeans now live in dwellings built by the government. The social security system is very different from that in Europe and elsewhere. There is no social insurance and instead, the government has promoted the expansion of a mandatory savings scheme known as the Central Provident

Fund (CPF). This scheme had been introduced during colonial times. A small, residual social assistance scheme also operates to help the most conspicuously needy for limited periods of time.

Housing and social security have helped foster Singapore's spectacular economic success, which was based on a policy of export-oriented industrialisation. Despite periods of economic difficulty, Singapore has recorded rates of economic growth of around 9% per annum for most of the period following independence. Also, as shown in Table 1, Singapore

Table 1. CPF contribution rate (%).

Year	Employer	Employer Weight	Medisave	Gross Rate
1955	5	5		10
1968	6.5	6.5		13
1970	8	8		16
1972	14	10		24
1973	15	11		26
1974	15	15		30
1977	15.5	15.5		31
1978	16.5	16.5		33
1979	20.5	16.5		37
1982	22	23		45
1984	25	25	6	
1985	25	25	6	50
1986	10	25	6	35
1989	15	23	6	38
1992	18	22	6	40
1995	20	20	6	40
1997	20	20	6	40
1999	10	20	6	30*
2000	14	20	8	34**

*Singapore was hit by the Asian financial crisis and as such the gross CPF contribution was reduced.
**The Singapore economy improved and therefore CPF was increased upwards again.

Source: Low L, Aw TC (1997). Housing a healthy, educated and wealthy nation through the CPF (p. 34) Singapore Annual Reports 1999; 2000.

has made important gains in the well-being of its people. GNP per capita rose from US$11,710 in 1989 to US$22,828 in 1999. The savings rate has been high and inflation has been low. Unemployment is also low and more than 60% of the work force participates in the CPF scheme.

Of course, Singapore has not been immune from economic crises. In 1985 there was a recession due to property speculation and high inflation compounded by falling exports. In 1997, Singapore was again hard-hit by the Asian economic crisis. Singapore's economic growth shrank from an average of 10% since 1989 to 0.4% in 1998. However, in both cases, the government has responded and managed to continue the long-term drive for economic and social development (Goh, 2000).

These achievements are the result of effective governance and prudent planning under a stable political regime (Vasil, 2000). It is also the result of the deliberate use of social policy to promote economic development. The importance of adequately housing workers was stressed from the outset. The potential of the Central Provident Fund to support economic development was also recognised. The use of these social programmes as 'productivist' measures (Midgley, 1995) has been a key element of Singapore's economic and social development.

The Central Provident Fund

The Central Provident Fund (CPF) was created in 1955 by the British colonial administration to provide retirement security for workers. Similar schemes were created in many other parts of the British Empire. Although Britain had created a comprehensive social insurance programme for its own workers, a lack of resources engendered an alternative policy approach for the colonies. Both employees and employers were required to contribute to the scheme and originally, a contribution of 10% of the payroll was imposed. The contributions were invested in an individual retirement account that could only be withdrawn when the employee reached the age of 55 years. However, it was subsequently amended to allow flexibility of the contribution ratio. Contributions were later increased to 25% from both employer and employee but were later reduced to 20%.

Although the CPF was originally intended as an old-age retirement scheme, its role was extended to permit the withdrawal of savings for other purposes, the most important of which was the purchase of a home. Subsequently, withdrawal was permitted to meet the costs of higher education, medical care and health insurance. Singaporeans can now also use their CPF savings for investment in the equity market. However, while a number of options for utilising savings have been created, Sherraden and his colleagues (1995) report that the purchase of government housing remains the primary major form of savings utilisation. In addition, the purchase of a home is viewed by many Singaporeans as an effective means of income protection in old age. Housing and social security are thus inextricably linked in Singapore's social policy. While provident funds in other countries usually function only to provide retirement income, Singapore's CPF 'Facilitated a huge housing program, transforming Singapore in the process both physically and socially' (Sherraden, 1997: 48).

While the Central Provident Fund was originally intended to mobilise savings for old-age retirement, its expansion into housing and other activities fostered and supported the government's strong commitment to economic and social development. It also differed from the pooled-risk system of Western welfare states where social security benefits are not directly linked to personal contributions. The CPF has been designed to help people become more self reliant (Central Provident Fund, 1998). The idea is that the financial burden of social security should remain within a generation and not to be shifted to the younger generation. The advantage of such a system is that when a society ages, the increasing burden of care of the elderly will be borne by individuals and families with savings, and not be shifted to the state.

Sherraden (1997) reports that in the mid-1990s, the CPF had about $52 billion in its member accounts. About $10 billion is deposited annually and about the same amount is withdrawn. The contribution rate was 18.5% of the payroll for employers and 21.5% of wages from employees. These rates are high by international social-security standards but the government has indicated that it will seek to lower them in the future. Avoidance has become a problem and as the country attracts more migrant workers, a growing proportion of the labour force is not protected by the scheme. Another interesting development is that withdrawals are increasingly being used to invest in equities. Whether this trend will continue as equity markets face increasingly difficulties remains to be seen.

Opinion research conducted by Sherraden and his colleagues (1995, 1997) reveals that Singaporeans are very satisfied with the CPF. It is interesting that those interviewed expressed a strong preference for the provident fund approach rather than social insurance, which many regarded as unfair because it pools risks and redistributes resources to those with lower incomes. Surprisingly, even those in lower income groups disliked the re-distributive implications of social insurance despite the fact that they themselves would benefit most from a programme of this kind. The CPF, it seems, is deeply culturally institutionalised. The research reveals that what began as a colonial provident fund has now become highly accepted as a means of asset accumulation, and that asset accumulation has become a strongly held cultural value. As Sherraden (1997: 53) notes, the next generation of Singaporeans will 'inherit substantial wealth in homes, shares and CPF cash balances'. Although it is not possible to speculate how this will translate into future consumption and savings decisions, housing and home ownership will continue to be high on the agenda.

The Housing Development Board and housing policy

Since the 1960s, when Singapore's Housing Development Board was established, the country's public housing programme has grown to become one of the largest in the world. Public housing is comprised of apartments produced and sold by the state. These apartments range from two to five rooms, mostly in high-rise buildings. The programme caters for the housing needs of both the working class and the majority of the middle class. The private housing market remains relatively small and is only comprised of about 10% of the total housing stock. It caters for the upper middle class and the very rich.

Each Singaporean citizen is permitted to purchase a government-built dwelling on two occasions. This policy stimulates the development of an active resale market for government dwellings when families decide to upgrade. Housing mobility through upgrading to larger units is encouraged and supported by the government. Lee Kuan Yew (2000) has stated

Table 2. Social and economic indicators of Singapore (1989, 1994–1999)

Year	Per Capita GNP S$ US$1 = S$1.74	GDP Growth %	Gross National Savings $M	Inflation %	Unemployment Rate %	% of Labour Under CPF	Public Home Ownership (%)	Infant Mortality (%)
1989	20,381.5	9.6	26,144.8	2.4	1.9	69.4	79	6.3
1994	32,424.7	11.4	53,114.3	3.1	1.9	67.3	80	4.1
1995	35,021.9	8.0	61,328.7	1.7	2.0	67.2	81	3.8
1996	36,735.1	7.5	66,997.4	1.4	2.2	66.3	81	3.6
1997	39,923.9	8.4	80,314.5	2.0	1.7	65.3	81	3.6
1998	38,418.0	0.4	80,626.9	–0.3	2.3	62.0	82	4.1
1999	39,721.4	5.4	83,567.9	0.0	3.3	62.0	82	3.2

Source: *Yearbook of Statistics 2000*, Singapore Department of Statistics.

that home ownership was an important element of his government's housing policy:

> My primary preoccupation was to give every citizen a stake in the country and its future. I want a home-owning society. I have seen the contrast between blocks of low cost rental apartments, badly misused and poorly maintained, those of house-proud owners, and was convinced that if every family owned its home, the country would be more stable. (Lee, 2000: 95–96)

This goal was largely achieved through linking the programmes of the Housing Development Board (HDB) and the CPF. In an important decision in 1968, the government passed legislation that permitted CPF savings to be used for home ownership. Unlike many other countries, the government was able to achieve a high rate of home ownership without having to allocate a high proportion of general revenues to the programme. By using their own savings to purchase housing, a major challenge to government financing home ownership was overcome.

In its early years, the CPF served the purpose of home financing extremely well. While most workers rented apartments, many more used the savings accumulated in their CPF accounts to purchase their homes. As shown in Table 3, the home-ownership rate reached 90% in 1995. Most

Table 3. Singapore housing indicators

Year	Total No. of Dwellings	Private Housing (%)	Public Flats for Sale (%)	Home Ownership Rate (%)
1970	306,000	16	38	29
1980	467,000	13	70	59
1990	781,000	13	79	88
1995	857,000	14	81	90
1996	874,000	15	82	87
1997	910,000	14	82	86
1998	955,000	16	81	85
1999	1,007,311	18	82	86

Source: *Singapore Annual Report 1999* and *Yearbook Statistics 2000*.

of these homes were built by the government. In more recent years, however, some more affluent owners of public housing have purchased homes in the private sector by capitalising their public housing assets. The HDB works on both market and institutional principles, seeking to maximise the developmental advantages of housing investment. HDB flats are sold to Singaporeans at competitive prices and yet, since HDB practically controls more than 80% of the middle-class housing market, it faces less competition and naturally monopolises. In normal market situation, house prices easily appreciate as a result of market failure as private developers monopolise supply. However, since it is also in the interest of the Singaporean government to maintain stable house prices for the sake of political legitimacy, the role of the state is thus to ensure that house prices appreciate healthily.

In analysing Singapore's housing policy, it is important to recognise first, that housing in Singapore has always been highly commodified and that it does not carry the 'social housing' connotation as in many Western countries. While the public-housing sector in many of these countries is relegated to the provision of rented shelters, public housing in Singapore is about stakeholding, privilege and status. Housing is marketed as a commodity and most Singaporeans can have access to housing through their CPF savings.

Second, Singapore's housing policy enhances social integration as different income and ethnic groups are housed together, and thus live and interact with one another. This agenda for social integration is critical as Singapore is a multi-racial society, and the need to prevent the creation of ethnic ghettos has been an important policy objective. Whereas the label of social exclusion and marginalisation has often been attached to public housing in Western societies, the case of Singapore suggests the contrary. Sherraden, Nair, Vasoo and Ngiam (1995) argued that the Singaporean housing system has allowed a social configuration that facilitates empowerment and inclusion. Housing is both a personal and a national asset.

Third, housing in Singapore is fully integrated with economic development. Earlier provision of public housing tended to emphasise the improvement of housing standards while its later development focused more on community identity and asset appreciation (Chua, 1997). The flexibility of housing policy designed to adapt to changing economic and social circumstances is revealed in the words of the current Prime Minister, Mr Goh Chok Tong (1994: 14–15) who said:

> We have been rewarding Singaporeans for many years. The biggest prizes are the 600,000 HDB flats which 90% of Singaporeans own. Now HDB is buying back three-room flats and reselling them at a discount to help the poorer Singaporeans to own their flats. Actually, our HDB residents have done very well. For example, one in three HDB homes have air-conditioners. One in five have personal computers. These are not essential items like telephones or refrigerators. Yet their ownership rate has increased by three times from 1987. It is the single biggest asset for most people, and its value reflects the fundamentals of the economy.

As this statement suggests, meeting the changing housing needs of the population in Singapore is given high priority. The government has sought to develop a housing programme that is commensurate with the increasing demand for a better-quality living environment as the economic status of the population rises. The idea of a housing ladder has been firmly incorporated in the housing system. The government has encouraged people in 2–3 room units to upgrade, so that dwellings can be redeveloped for further HDB housing programmes.

The government also recognises that with growing affluence, people tend to have higher housing aspirations. Since the early 1990s, HDB flats have appreciated two to threefold in value. Many Singaporeans want to capitalise on their first HDB flats and upgrade by using their second opportunity to purchase. While it is not the government's policy to encourage speculation, the spirit of asset appreciation is embedded in the presence of a mature resale market.

Social policy and economic development

Few other countries have used social security and housing policy to serve the goal of economic development to the extent of Singapore. The Western welfare states have tended to separate economic and social policy and have used social welfare to promote social rather than economic goals (Midgley, 1995). In many Western industrial countries, social policy is designed to subsidise incomes and transfer resources to the poor. Redistribution is an important social policy goal (Midgley, 1999).

In Singapore, on the other hand, social policy is primarily designed to facilitate economic development. This does not mean that social programmes do not seek to meet social needs. Indeed, there is substantial evidence to show that social policy in Singapore has contributed significantly to improving standards of living. But, in meeting social needs, the government has ensured that social policy does so within the context of contributing to the country's overriding goal of maintaining high rates of economic growth.

For example, by directly linking housing and social security with the economy, the government used social policy to promote macroeconomic objectives. It has been able to use the CPF not only to mobilise savings for retirement and home purchase but to control prices. When the state is the largest land developer, and has an 85% share of the market, it is possible to maintain stable house prices. From a political perspective, this engenders trust from the people to invest in public assets and facilitates political legitimacy. From a citizen's perspective, stable house prices guarantee a future asset income-stream and economic security. From an economic viewpoint, stable house prices ensure stable asset appreciation.

The government also furthers the goal of sharing profits from real-estate investment with homeowners. When housing is left entirely to the free market and when monopolistic tendencies prevail, home ownership can be risky. This problem has been demonstrated in Hong Kong's highly speculative housing market in the last two decades (Lee, 1999). Whereas developers in Hong Kong have always managed to reap a major share of economic growth in the last two decades through investing in the real-estate market, the Singapore HDB and CPF system has created a mechanism to ensure that real-estate investment returns are more widely spread out among the people. This explains why property tycoons in Hong Kong have always been key players in economic development, while similar domination has not occurred in Singapore.

The government has also used social policy to control inflation. Having realised the potential of social security and the public housing sector to influence consumption and expenditure, the government carefully manipulated the rate of CPF contributions. In the words of Lee Kuan Yew:

> Once workers got used to a higher take home pay, I knew they would resist any increase in their CPF contribution that would reduce their spendable money. So, almost yearly, I increased the rate of CPF contributions, but such that there was still a net increase in take home pay. It was painless for the workers to keep inflation down. (Lee, 2000: 97)

It is apparent that Singapore has been able to use social policy to control inflation when workers have surplus purchasing power. Clearly the state helped to pave the way for a managed approach to consumption by influencing consumption behaviour through social programmes.

In addition, the combined effect of a culture of property-owning and economic prosperity has spurred an extraordinary demand in home ownership that has, in turn, stimulated more investment in the housing sector (Lee, 1999). Home purchase incurs huge expenditures and thus requires a high saving ratio. In 1999, gross domestic savings comprised 50% of Singapore's GDP. CPF savings undoubtedly form a major part of this savings rate. When these savings are translated into individual home ownership they store wealth for the future. It is for this reason that Low (1997) has argued that

Singapore's housing policy constitutes a long-term social security plan where wealth stored in housing can be realised in old age.

Singapore: A social development state?

These observations are consonant with the normative position outlined in developmentalist social policy thinking as articulated by Midgley (1995, 1999) which advocates the harmonisation of social interventions with economic development efforts, and the purposeful use of social policy to promote development goals. It also requires that economic development should result in tangible improvements in social well-being through social development. The theory proposes the adoption of a fully-integrated national development strategy that combines economic and social policies to promote a process of sustainable, people-oriented development that brings about improvements in standards of living for all. The account of social policy in Singapore provided in this article is not only compatible with the developmental model of social welfare but suggests that it is a viable one.

Other East Asian nations have also, it seems, adopted social policies that are in keeping with developmentalist thinking. Certainly, several of these countries regard housing as an important component of economic development. Castells, Goh and Kwok (1990) argued that public housing policy in both Singapore and Hong Kong during the 1970s provided important social wages for the workers to regenerate productivity. The provision of home ownership to the population helped enhanced the work ethic and reinforced family responsibility. Housing policy also has a direct link to economic growth since housing investment constitutes a substantial portion of the GDP through fixed capital formation (averaging 8–10%).

However, despite its accomplishments, Singapore should not be regarded as an unequivocal success, or as some sort of Utopia where all social problems have been solved and where everyone enjoys a harmonious and contented life. Indeed, social policy in Singapore has been subjected to critical analysis by several scholars who have questioned the tendency to present Singapore's social achievements in a highly favourable way. Several have argued that social policy in Singapore is driven by the state's desire to establish and maintain political legitimacy and control. Social policy in Singapore, they contend, is essentially about politics, and not about welfare, asset appreciation or economic development.

Chua (1997) argues that the Singaporean housing system has sought to depoliticise the population by exchanging social goods for political legitimacy. The need to create ideological consensus through the provision of good housing has been an overriding goal. But, he claims, it will never be completed, and hence the desire to improve housing by the state continues. Tremewan (1998) is more critical of the way the government has used social policy not only to secure political control but to subjugate the population to a workfare regime in which people are cajoled into being mere cogs in the state's productivist system.

Other critics have challenged the notion that Singapore and the other East Asian countries are developmental states committed to promoting economic development and the welfare of their citizens. Chan, Clark and Lam (1998) reject the argument that the East Asian countries have fared all that well in socio-economic performance during the last decade or that their achievements have been the result of orchestrated statism. They suggested that the East Asian experience has been the product of eclecticism and pragmatism rather than a highly articulated commitment to developmentalism. In addition, the role of the state has changed over time creating new challenges and opportunities.

These arguments are particularly relevant in the aftermath of the recent Asian financial crisis, which shows that the East Asian countries are also vulnerable to the effects of global capital finance. If the state fails to maintain a stable level of house prices and a steady rate of economic growth, social equilibrium will be adversely affected. This happened in Hong Kong and the other East Asian countries after the crisis. However, Singapore's housing market has thus far proved to be very resilient. In a globalising world, no country can be totally independent of international economic disturbances. However, since Singapore is based on integration and consensus, it was able to absorb some of the economic turbulence through wage-cuts, labour-market adjustments and careful monitoring of the CPF contribution rates. The tripartite relationship forged among the state, entrepreneurs and labour has thus made it possible to reach a consensus and to adjust more swiftly. It cannot be denied that Singapore and the other East Asian countries have succeeded in raising standards of living for most of their citizens through rapid and sustained economic growth and social development policies. Whatever the drawbacks of the current system, the government of Singapore has built more public housing than most other countries. Similarly, it has achieved high standards of education, low unemployment, low crime and, in terms of other social indicators, its achievements are considerable.

The experience of Singapore raises interesting questions about the purpose of social policy. Is social policy intended to achieve social equity through massive redistribution? Or is it seeking social equity and growth simultaneously through mixing personal and collective interests? In the East Asian context, social policy does not seem to be concerned with redistribution. In these countries, redistribution is largely dependent on economic growth, personal saving and consumption planning. Equity is judged on the basis of how an individual participates in and benefits from economic progress. The emphasis is on direct participation rather than a passive benefit through collective redistribution. In the case of Singapore, home ownership and managed life savings through the CPF have been used as major instruments of social policy.

The Singapore experience suggests that social welfare can be promoted in ways other than that adopted in the Western welfare states. It is based on a different relationship between the state and people. Other than being an interesting example of the social development model, it offers future opportunities to examine the role of institutional mechanisms for promoting distributive justice and social welfare more closely.

References

Buti M, Franco D, Pench L, eds. (1999). *The welfare state in Europe: Challenges and reform.* Cheltenham, UK, Elgar.

Castells M, Goh L, Kwok R (1990). *Shekkipmei syndrome: Economic development and public housing in Hong Kong and Singapore.* London, Pion Press.

Central Provident Fund Board (1997, 1998, 1999). *Annual Reports.*

Central Provident Fund (1995). *The CPF story.* Singapore.

Chan S, Clark C, Lam D (1998). *Beyond the developmental State: East Asia's political economics reconsidered.* London, Macmillan.

Chua BH (1997). *Political legitimacy and housing: Stake holding in Singapore.* London, Routledge.

Chua BH (2000). Public housing residents as clients of the state. *Housing Studies* 15(1): 45–60.

Esping-Andersen G (1990). *Three worlds of welfare capitalism.* Oxford, Polity Press.

Esping-Andersen G (1999). *Social foundations of postindustrial economies.* Oxford, Oxford University Press.

Feldstein M (1974). Social security, induced retirement and aggregate capital accumulation. *Journal of Political Economy* 83(1): 74–75.

Goh CT (2000). *Speech at National Day Rally 2000.* Ministry of Information and the Arts, Singapore.

Goodman R, White G, Kwon H (1998). *The East Asian welfare model: Welfare Orientalism and the state.* London, Routledge.

Gough I (2000). *Welfare regimes in East Asia and Europe.* Paper presented to the Annual World Bank Conference on Development Economics Europe 2000, Paris, 27 June.

Jacobs D (2000). Low public expenditures on social welfare: Do East Asian countries have a secret? *International Journal of Social Welfare* 9(1): 2–16.

Lee Kuan Yew (1998). *The Singapore story.* Singapore, Singapore Press Holdings.

Lee Kuan Yew (2000). *From third world to first: The Singapore story: 1965–2000.* New York, Harper and Collins.

Lee, KC (1999). *Home ownership and social change in Hong Kong.* London, Ashgate.

Low L, Aw TC (1997). *Housing a healthy, educated and wealthy nation through the CPF.* Singapore, Times Academic Press.

Midgley J (1995). *Social development: The developmental perspective in social welfare.* London, Sage.

Midgley J (1997). *Social welfare in global context.* London, Sage.

Midgley J (1999). Growth, redistribution and welfare: Towards social investment. *Social Service Review* 77(1): 3–21.

Ministry of Information and the Arts and Lianhe Zaobao (1999). *Singapore annual report* 1999.

Mishra R (1984). *The welfare state in crisis.* London, Wheatsheaf.

Mishra R (1990). *The welfare state in capitalist society.* Hempstead, UK, Wheatsheaf.

Pierson P (1995). Fragmented welfare states — federal institutions and the development of social policy. *Governance* 8(4): 449–478.

Sherraden M (1997). Provident funds and social protection: The case of Singapore. In: Midgley J, Sherraden M, eds. *Alternatives to social security: An international inquiry*.

Sherraden M, Nair S, Vasoo S, Ngiam TL (1995). Social policy based on assets: the impact of Singapore's central provident fund. *Asian Journal of Political Sciences* 3(2): 112–133.

Shin DM (1999). Economic policy and social policy: Policy linkages in an era of globalization. *International Journal of Social Welfare* 9(1).

Singapore (2000). *Yearbook of Statistics 2000*. Singapore Statistics Department.

Tang KL (1999). Planning for the unknown: Social policy making in Hong Kong 1990–1997. *International Journal of Sociology and Social Policy* 19(1/2): 27–56.

Titmuss R (1974). *Social policy: An introduction*. London, Allen & Unwin.

Tremewan C (1998). Welfare and governance: public housing under Singapore's party-state. In: Goodman R, White G, Kwon H, eds. *The East Asian welfare model: Welfare orientalism and the state*. London, Routledge.

Vasil R (2000). *Governing Singapore*. Australia, Allen and Unwin.

Yuen B, Teo HP, Ooi CL (1999). *Singapore housing: An annotated bibliography*. Housing Policy and Development Research Unit, National University of Singapore.

Chapter 27

Implementing socioeconomic measures to tackle economic uncertainties in Singapore*

S. Vasoo[†] and Kwong-leung Tang[‡]

Since its independence in 1965, the government of Singapore has played a key role in orchestrating the political, social, and economic development of the city-state. Faced with the challenge of recent economic downturn, the government has reacted positively through the introduction of a number of socioeconomic measures to alleviate the plight of needy people. The main thrust of the social and economic measures implemented is to strengthen the citizens' capacities. The government thus sees human capital development even in the context of economic downturn as the critical factor to further social and economic development. Overall, policymakers in Singapore put emphasis on individual

---

*Reprinted with permission by the publisher from Vasoo, S., & Tang, K.-l. (2002). Implementing socioeconomic measures to tackle economic uncertainties in Singapore. *Journal of Comparative Asian Development, 1*(2), 151–170. doi: 10.1080/15339114.2002.9678358.

This article examines how the Singapore government, in the wake of the Asian financial crisis had introduced social and economic measures to stimulate the economy while meeting retirement and social needs. The ideas and views have been earlier sounded and further insights on the social policy response are presented.

[†]National University of Singapore

[‡]University of Northern British Columbia

responsibility and familial support, while giving primacy to the harmonization of social and economic development.

"The government, on its part, will ensure that every Singaporean has equal and maximum opportunity to advance himself, while providing a social safety net to prevent the minority who cannot cope, from falling through. This way, we can have an enduring social compact where the able can do very well, and we can use some of the wealth generated by them to subsidise and help the less able." — Prime Minister Goh Chok Tong's National Day Rally Speech (August 19, 2001).

The government of Singapore has taken a particular view of the nexus between political and social development. It believes that many governments have given in to interest groups which placate for more state subsidies for various social provisions such as unemployment benefits, social assistance, health care, maternal and child allowances, and so forth. This is because political groups want to stay in power through gaining popular support by giving more goodies to their people. Popular measures can win votes, but they do not necessarily solve the countries' economic problems with more public spending (Vasoo & Lee, 2001). In the long run, countries could easily run into huge public debts that will have to be borne by its citizens. As a consequence, resources of the countries and their people will be depleted as public expenditure outstrips income by manifolds. The better endowed and the talented will leave and these countries become debt-ridden. Some countries are at the verge of economic breakdowns or bankruptcy. Furthermore, the government of Singapore has been critical of its colonial master for a long time. When Singapore was under British rule from 1819 to 1958, no attention was paid to the development of a comprehensive social security program as there was limited economic development. British rule was predicted to end in due course as the drive for self-rule and independence had already gathered momentum.

If this British model of welfare that emphasized comprehensive social protection for the people was prescribed, the government of Singapore contends that its social and economic development would have taken a different turn. It would have been left with a legacy of the "welfarist model" that is predicated upon the dominance of social rights and massive state intervention in social services. To the government, this was not a panacea to solve the serious problems of poverty, unemployment, environment, and housing which surfaced toward the end of the colonial era (Vasoo & Lee, 2001). An alternative policy option was made in place of the British social security system to meet financial needs of old age and retirement.

Since its self-government in 1959 and independence in 1965, the social and economic landscape of the island city-state has changed progressively under the People's Action Party (PAP). Better housing, security, health, education, environment, and employment opportunities have been achieved because of stable and effective political leadership (Lee, 1998). The government of Singapore argues that, unlike many other countries, stable leadership had been and is a precursor to and the backbone for Singapore's economic and social progress. Without such leadership, the government contends, no society (not even Singapore) will be able to move ahead in its social and economic development (Lee, 2000).

This conclusion could be supported in large part by an examination of the per capita income of its population. In 1959, Singapore's per capita GNP was US$400 and in 1999, after 40 years of PAP rule, its per capita GNP rose to US$21,000 (S$39,721). This 50-fold increase in per capital GNP and other achievements such as low inflation, increase in life expectancy, low infant mortality, reduced crime rate, and more volunteers' involvement (Singapore Yearbook of Statistics, 2000) are indeed mind boggling. Singapore has become a highly developed and free-market economy, enjoying one of the highest per capita GDP in the world (Ministry of Information and the Arts, 2001). Before the Asian financial crisis, it was the object of emulation for both developing and developed countries. These are the result of prudent and effective governance under stable political conditions led by indigenous leaders who are responsive to various social and economic challenges (Vasil, 2000).

However, Singapore's road to development has never been smooth. It was affected by a recession in 1985 as a result of property speculation and high domestically driven inflation compounded by low external demands for goods and services. In response, the government of Singapore took radical measures to deal with property speculation and revitalize the economy by various cost-cutting measures, including a reduction of 15% Central Provident Fund (CPF) contribution by employers. This helped to stimulate Singapore's economy and made exports more competitive. Economic growth was robust again.

Following the Asian financial crisis in 1997, Singapore was badly hit. No country in Asia was spared from serious economic downturns. Its domestic economic growth drastically dipped to 0.3% in 1998 from 7.8% in 1997. At one time, unemployment rose to 4.5%, its highest level since the last recession in 1986. Not long after, it experienced a short spurt of growth, with the economy posting a 9% growth. In July 2001, however, second-quarter economic data indicated yet again that Singapore's economy had slipped into another recession. In mid-2001, the government quickly cut its growth forecast for the year 2001 downward to 0.5%–1.5% (*Far Eastern Economic Review*, August 9, 2001). The latest official figure pointed to a decline of 2.2% for the whole year. Concomitantly, unemployment was on the rise. It was estimated by some that 20,000 workers would be entrenched in 2001.

Faced with its greatest economic challenge, the government of Singapore fought back. In the wake of the Asian financial crisis, it imposed a number of measures to cut business costs and stimulate domestic demands. Various pragmatic socioeconomic measures were put in place to help turn the economy around since Singapore's open economy is vulnerable to social, economic, and political turmoil in the Asian region. Singapore's economy cannot be fully buffered from external social, political, and economic factors. Proactive social and economic policies were introduced. Further restructuring of the economy to knowledge based and life science industries, promotion of financial services and high-technology manufacturing were also put on the pipe-line. In keeping with these efforts, the government deployed more resources to education, promoting skills-training of manpower, retraining of older workers, attracting skilled overseas workers, and providing tax incentives for high value-added, high-technology companies (Goh, 2000). With such policy measures, the government of Singapore hoped that Singapore would be able to resume its social and economic development based on building the individual's self-reliance and personal assets. Workers are motivated to work, which in turn contributes to economic prosperity. The government hoped to avoid state welfarism that could easily erode work ethics as well as undermine social and personal responsibility.

Among these measures, an important one involved the cuts to employer's contribution to the CPF. The cutting of CPF has never been used before as a measure to deal with economic downturn. It was seen as an antidote used only as a last resort to quickly stimulate Singapore's economy by making its goods and services more competitive. As such, the government saw it necessary to look at this option recently when faced with serious economic downturn.

This paper will look at how the government of Singapore has made use of its CPF to meet the dual purposes of addressing economic downturn while meeting retirement and other social needs. We argue in this paper that the government has played a most dynamic role in the wake of the Asian financial crisis, adjusting its retirement scheme and introducing social and economic measures to stimulate the economy and meeting social needs. Some of these significant measures will be highlighted and discussed.

Central Provident Fund as socioeconomic leverage

The Central Provident Fund Act was implemented in 1955 by the British colonial government. Both employees and employers were then required to make monetary contribution to this fund which could only be withdrawn at 55 years of age. The CPF contribution started off modestly with a rate of 10% contribution which made up of equal contribution from employees and employers (CPF, 1995). The CPF Act was subsequently amended and the contribution by employees and employers were raised to 25% each at one stage. It became a forerunner for development of a number for schemes to cover housing ownership, financial provision for old age, medical care, and health insurance.

Essentially, CPF is the main old-age, compulsory savings scheme in Singapore. A ceiling on contributions is imposed. The monthly contributions are subject to a maximum of S$1,200 for the employer and S$1,200 for the employee, based on a salary ceiling of S$6,000 a month, beyond which no CPF is payable. The CPF scheme was extended to all self-employed persons earning a net trade income of more than S$2,400 a year in July 1992. By contributing 6% to 8% (depending on age) to the Medisave Account, self-employed people are able to enjoy healthcare benefits as other working members. There is no income tax on contributions, interest, or withdrawals.

There are three accounts for each contributing member: the Ordinary, Medisave, and Special Accounts. The most important is the Ordinary Account where savings can be used for housing, approved investments, insurance, education, and transfers to top-up parents' Retirement Accounts. Medisave Account savings are for meeting hospitalization expenses and certain approved outpatient treatments such as hepatitis-B vaccinations, renal dialysis, and chemotherapy. It can also be used to buy MediShield and MediShield Plus and approved private medical insurance under Private Medical Insurance Scheme. Savings in the Special Account are reserved for old age and contingency purposes.

As noted above, the CPF scheme started off modestly with 10% contribution rate from both employees and employers, but it was later changed to allow flexibility to meet changing economic conditions. In 1982, contributions were raised to 25% and this was reduced to 20% in the mid-1990s. Though the CPF served as a retirement program, it was gradually extended to allow contributors' withdrawal of savings for other purposes. People can use their CPF savings for investment in the equity market for asset appreciation. This flexibility to allow CPF members to invest part of their savings came about as a result of popular requests to obtain more financial returns on funds rather than a fixed interest rate.

Since its inception, the CPF program has been development oriented (Vasoo & Lee, 2001). It has been designed to enhance economic activities of people as well as make people more self-reliant to meet their social needs (CPF, 1998). The program encourages individual savings. It is not a pooled risk, unlike other social security systems where contributions are pooled together to support one's social and healthcare needs.

CPF is essentially an individual saving account. The idea is that the financial burden of social security should remain within that generation and not to be shifted to the young. Thus the CPF program represents an attempt by the government of Singapore to use earmarked forced savings to finance social goods such as provision for old age, housing, and medical care (Asher, 1985). This program is an embodiment of individual responsibility, allowing working people to save their earnings and invest them in a wide range of programs (public housing, investments, insurance, hospital expenses, retirement, etc.). In other words, CPF would ensure that the retirement needs of the workers would not become a burden on the state.

According to the government, the advantage of such system is that when facing an aging society, increasing financial burden of elderly care should be shouldered by the individuals. The government of Singapore held the belief that income growth would be the key to meeting social objectives and welfare for the entire population. Over time, needs such as housing, income security for old age, primary health, and education have been met without huge government spending on welfare.

CPF and the economy

At all times, there has been a high national saving ratio in Singapore. Some 60% of the work force participated in the CPF scheme as unemployment had remained low. These achievements resulted from prudent planning and effective governance. Since its inception, the CPF contribution rate had been gradually climbing up. Although contributions from employees and employers constitute the primary source of savings for this program, it is centrally administered (Low & Aw, 1997). The CPF Board that administered the fund is a statutory body. Despite the independent nature of these statutory bodies, the state is able to wield considerable influence over the policy and structure of the fund. This has the advantage of having external economies of scale and lowered administrative costs.

The CPF contributions on the part of the employers represent one form of cost for the employers. Also, revisions of employer's contributions could greatly affect the level of savings in the account. In time of economic recession, the PAP wished to reduce the financial burden of the employers. In the history of CPF, twice (during the 1985 recession and recent Asian financial crisis) did the PAP reduce employer's contributions in order to lower cost of labor. A cut in CPF payments was a key move by the government to help slash business costs to keep the city-state competitive.

Singapore faced a recession in 1985, fuelled in large part by property speculation and high inflation. The government of Singapore then took a determined stand to regulate property market and stimulated the economy through cost-cutting measures. Above all, the contribution rate for CPF by

Table 1. CPF contribution rate (%) (1995–2000)

Year	Employer	Employee	Medisave Weight	Gross Rate
1955	5	5	—	10
1982	22	23	—	45
1984	25	25	6	50
1985	25	25	6	50
1986	10	25	6	35
1989	15	23	6	38
1992	18	22	6	40
1995	20	20	6	40
1997	20	20	6	40
1999	10	20	6	30
2000	14	20	8	34

Source: Adapted from Vasoo and Lee (2001).

employers was reduced from 25% to 10% (see Table 1). This helped businesses to cope with the recession by reducing labor costs. This policy was effective and the economy was on the upswing again. As noted above, Singapore was hit by the Asian financial crisis in 1997 and as such the CPF contribution was again reduced to 10% in 1999, though the Confederation of Industries wanted to cut employers' contributions to be trimmed down from 20% to 5% (*Asiaweek*, November 13, 1998). Inevitably, lower employers' contributions for a prolonged period of time could somewhat undermine the financial capacity of each member to meet his social needs.

After Singapore's economy improved, the CPF was restored to 14% in 2000. However, the economic recovery was short-lived: the full employers' CPF contribution was stalled following yet another economic recession in 2001. Singapore faces another tough economic challenge. The government of Singapore fought back by again instituting cost cutting measures that have immediate impact on the economy. The National Trade Union Congress (NTUC) urged all workers to continue the support the reduced employers' CPF contributions rate.

The cutting of CPF has never been used repeatedly as a measure to deal with economic downturn. Policymakers feel that this is an effective antidote to quickly stimulate the Singapore economy by making its good and services more competitive. Coincidentally, the government of Singapore decided the stalling of the restoration of the rate of CPF contribution as the recession came back in 2001. This is crucial because of the need to prevent more job loss by the hollowing out of manufacturing industries to countries with cheaper manpower and make exported electronic goods more marketable. This would attract more high technology investments to Singapore to create new areas of employment.

The adjustments of CPF (cutting and the restoration) are necessary economic leverages to keep in tandem with the changes in the economic conditions confronting Singapore from time to time. More importantly, the government, workers, and the employers came to realize the need of a strong symbiotic relationship to weather unexpected economic downturns. Such a relationship becomes very important to deal with the vagaries the globalization of economies. Strong tripartite relationship will make a country more socially and economically viable.

Healthcare measures as cost containment

In Singapore, the ageing population will gradually impose more burdens on healthcare provisions. The elderly who are better educated and endowed will be more vocal and lobby for higher concession for using health services. The establishment of pressure groups among the elderly is likely to increase the competition for health resources. Such a situation has to be responded by policymakers (IMC Report, 1999).

Healthcare delivery in Singapore has undergone major reforms in the last 15 years. This is due to increasing government expenditure in the provision of health services. Most policymakers have been confronted by a dilemma, namely the need to maintain the affordability of health services for the general population and to contain the escalating healthcare cost. In short, health cost has to be seen and felt to be reasonable. Healthcare, whether needed or not, has become a focus of concern to families.

Reforms in healthcare were initiated to find solutions to improve the health services and contain the long-term increase in cost and government subsidies in the provisions of health care. Different policy strategies were adopted by the Ministry of Health to tamper the demand and contain the healthcare cost. Policy measures based on the principles of personal responsibility for health and tripartite partnerships comprising individuals, government and employers have been formulated. Under various plans (the first started in 1983 and the most recent in 1993), efforts were initiated to restructure the healthcare system and tackle a number of underlying concerns in the healthcare scene (Ministry of Health, 1993). Problems that are tackled included the prevention of unnecessary consumption and waste, the retention of good healthcare professionals, the recruitment of talented for consultancy services, the decentralization of healthcare, stronger emphasis on preventive medicine than tertiary care, and the reduction of overstay of elderly in hospitals.

Co-payment of healthcare cost and rationing of medical care are the main policy thrusts besides the restructuring of the hospitals. They are aimed at increasing the accountability for government funds allocated. The policy measures start to produce tangible results and have received positive feedback from the public and patients.

The healthcare policy measures are driven by a few fundamental principles that center primarily on curbing over-consumption and induced demands of health services. Unless over-consumption of healthcare is tackled effectively, the problem of increasing healthcare cost will not be solved. The underlying assumption is that consumers are required to make co-payment for their usage of healthcare services. Such payments are based on the class of medical care the patients have opted for. The better the ward class, the higher the medical charges. The emphasis on co-payment for medical care has not only elevated their awareness of the medical costs but also made consumers more cautious about their demands for medical treatments.

Individuals are encouraged to be responsible for looking after their own health. They have to save for their healthcare needs (Lim, 1997). Individual responsibility is a motivating factor for maintaining good health behavior. The more one keeps oneself healthy, the less one needs to spend his savings in the CPF. This will avert an over-reliance on state welfare and medical insurance.

There is a basic package of health services for any citizen who requires medical care. Such a package will be met by various financial mechanisms organized by the state to meet the unsubsidized part of the hospitalization cost (Lim, 1997). It is a decently good medical service that is within the reach of even the poorest in the community. The last premise is based on the motion that healthcare provision should be subjected to competition between the public and private sectors. Market forces are allowed to influence the delivery of health care so that more efficient and better services are provided to the consumers. Where necessary, the government of Singapore would intervene to ensure that healthcare cost is kept within the access of the ordinary consumers. Any anticipated runaway increase in medical cost is tackled quickly by government's provisions of medical manpower, medical supplies, facilities, and funding.

These are three specific healthcare policy measures implemented under the health reform plans. They are easily managed and not cumbersome to administer. At the same time, no new administrative structure or bureaucracy has been established to implement the policy measures namely, the Medisave Account (which is a part of CPF saving), the Medishield, and the Medifund. The unique feature about Medisave is that intergeneration transfers are allowed. It can be used to cover the hospitalization expenses and other medical treatments of family members including relatives who all have either no or low Medisave funds. Such an extended coverage of Medisave for the kin group does strengthen mutual support and strengthen familial bonds. Even distant relatives could be supported by the Medisave if it is established that they have no means to pay for their hospitalization cost.

However, to allay some of the concerns of the elderly, there had been some important recent changes to the Medisave scheme, which considerably reduces the healthcare expenses for older and disabled people. First, the government introduced the CPF's top-up scheme and the Medishield Scheme for the Elderly in 2000. The top-up went to those above 21 who contributed at least $100 to their CPF accounts. At the same time, the MSE would help older people, aged 61 to 69, by paying for 2 years of basic Medishield premiums. Those aged 70 and above would receive a Medisave top-up equivalent to 2 years of basic Medishield premiums, provided they have a Medisave account. However, some 44,000 older Singaporeans missed out the first time, because they did not have Medisave accounts or they did not sign up for Medishield (Ministry of Health, 2000)

A new low-cost insurance plan paid for out of Medisave was implemented. It would give older people who became disabled $300 a month for a maximum of 5 years. ElderShield was for Singaporeans and permanent residents who are between 40 and 69 years old (*Straits Times*, August 24, 2001). Over-40s get a Shield against disability). They must not already have disabilities. The government made it an opt-out scheme, so it could cover as many elderly persons as possible.

Prime Minister Goh referred to this program in his National Day Rally speech (2001) as a move to help the elderly to have access to medical care. He noted that the population in Singapore has been graying. In 2000, it was estimated that some 234,500 people were 65 or older. This would leap to 798,700 by 2030. The government believed that some 8% of them would need help in daily living.

CPF members (between 40 and 69 years old) could opt out of the plan. Otherwise, premiums would be deducted automatically from their Medisave accounts. At 65, members decide to stop their ElderShield contributions but they can make claims if they later become disabled. Those who begin on ElderShield at 40 would pay a yearly premium of between $100 and $150. Those who join at a later age will pay a higher premium. Those 65 years or older when the plan is launched would get the subsidy for 10 years; 64-year-olds for 9 years, and so on. Those who are 56 years old would receive the subsidy for a year. Those with too little funds in Medisave might draw on the Medisave accounts of their spouse, children or grandchildren. They might also top up their accounts with cash.

An interim plan has been devised to cover those who are at age 70 or older, or who cannot qualify for coverage because of existing disabilities. They need not pay the premiums but they may also receive payouts for up to 5 years if they qualify. Their eligibility rests upon their family's monthly income and the size of family. It is estimated that this plan would cover half the population. These two schemes would cost the government over S$400 million. The healthcare plan is a proactive social measure devised to tackle the anticipated heavy healthcare cost of the burgeoning graying population of Singapore.

Supportive socioeconomic initiatives

It seems obvious to the government that wage freeze and adjustments to the contribution rate to the CPF was insufficient when confronting the Asian financial crisis. The government of Singapore felt the urgency to introduce other measures. In 1998, it introduced an S$2 billion package of tax rebates and other measures. Later, the policymakers announced an S$10.5 billion cost-cutting package comprising wage cuts and corporate tax rebates (Hu, 1998). Some other measures were taken to reduce salaries and overall labor costs were estimated to be lower by 5%–8%. It was estimated that all the cost-cutting efforts yielded a 15% reduction in corporate costs. The government bolstered the fiscal stimulus by increasing outlays on infrastructure, providing rebates on property tax, and expanding credit for small businesses (Hansard, 2001). The government also committed strongly to use budgetary resources and surpluses to improve its human capital (Ngiam, 2000). This principle was put into practice over the years in an ad hoc fashion, including a CPF top-up, an HDB service and conservancy rebate, and worker upgrading program.

When the economy started to worsen in mid-2001, the government quickly announced a S$2.2 billion off-budget package to help businesses and individuals cope with the economic downturn. This was soon followed by another off-budget package introduced in the third quarter of the year (*Straits Times,* August 15, 2001). The government assessed that this recession was the most severe it faced since the independence. The unemployment rate was predicted to be about 5% by the middle of 2002. If true, this will be the worst recession faced in the last two decades.

Attempting to lessen the adverse impacts of the recession, Prime Minister Goh Chok Tong revealed some other policy measures in his National Day Rally Speech 2001. It was dubbed by critics as a new social compact. In his speech, Goh indicated that the government would share the fruits of economic growth with the people to enable them to meet the challenges of economic restructuring. It was necessary for the government to provide senior citizens with insurance against chronic disease. Common people would also be helped to cope with economic structuring. There was also a need to narrow the income gap.

Some guiding principles underlying the social development of Singapore were suggested by Goh (2001). First, the government would continue subsidizing basic services of housing, education and healthcare. Second, his government would "distribute part of the budget surpluses back to Singaporeans, to enhance their assets as well as to help them defray essential expenses." Goh suggested that each Singaporean would get "New Singapore shares." This represented Singapore's "new social compact": a move to care for the less privileged even in times of economic hardship. Finally, the government would give support to people and corporate sectors that are involved in charity, philanthropy, and volunteerism. Thus the government planned to grant Institution of Public Character status to private foundations that support charitable activities.

All in all, Prime Minister Goh promised more government input in economic and social development. On the economic front, the government would adopt these strategies: reaching out to new markets, encouraging entrepreneurship, fostering a culture of innovation, making structural adjustments, and recruiting global talent. On the social welfare front, the government continues to emphasize self-reliance but it also sees the need to increase social security.

As noted, the government introduced the second off-budget stimulus package to stimulate its economy. Some S$11.3 billion were involved. These included S$3 billion in tax cuts for companies and individuals, S$2.7 billion in the form of New Singapore Share, and over S$800 million in grants to retrain workers. It would result in a government budget deficit of $4 billion in 2001. The government would have to dip into its reserves to finance these projects.

Program-wise, some S$698 million were allocated as grants and relief given to support the poor to provide help to their mortgages, utilities bills, and hospital fees. A new Economic Downturn Relief Scheme was created for those who had lost the job. Some S$20 million would be given to the grassroots groups to provide for food, children's school, and transport fees. Another important thrust of the package is to help retrenched workers, including executives, to find new jobs. The idea of New Singapore Shares was innovative: those who were less well-off would receive more shares that could be converted for cash (Hansard, 2001).

Deputy Minister Lee Hsien Loong (Hansard, 2001) estimated that the second package worked out to benefit about S$2,000 to S$3,000 for each household. Specifically, the government suspended land sales, lifted restrictions on housing loans for foreigners, and removed the capital gains tax on properties sold within 3 years to assist homeowners. The package also included reduced tuition fees, rents, utility, and medical charges that benefit every citizen in one way or another. All the ministers and senior civil servants took a 10% pay cut for one year.

Despite these most-needed remedies, the government warned people against a diminished personal responsibility to fend for themselves. It also encouraged the people to adopt a more realistic attitude when seeking employment. Senior Minister Lee Kuan Yew cautioned older workers they needed to take on less attractive service-sector jobs, noting: "Older workers who are not bale to retrain to do these new jobs will have to switch to completely different work in the service sector where conditions of work and pay will not be equal to those in their old jobs" (*Straits Times,* August 18, 2001).

Criticism of the government efforts

Despite these quick responses by the government, there have been some criticisms from opposition parties. For instance, the Singapore Democratic Alliance "doubts the sincerity of the PAP" in bringing about a new deal. After Goh (2001) spoke of a new "social compact" between the government and less well-off Singaporeans to help them share in the country's wealth, an Alliance of opposition parties has called Prime Minister Goh's National Day Rally speech an "election speech" without solutions for Singapore's current economic ills (*Straits Times*, August 22, 2001). However, judging all the policy initiatives, this claim is not grounded, as the government of Singapore indeed had taken a concrete step to support the economy and assist the people to meet economic austerity.

In contrast, the Hong Kong SAR government has done much less after the Asian financial crisis when compared with the government of Singapore in meeting social needs. For instance, Unionist legislators urged the Hong Kong government to spend HK$41.6 billion from its reserves to boost the economy and create 30,000 jobs (*South China Morning Post*, August 24, 2001). The money was less than one-tenth of the government's HK$430 billion financial reserves. The spending package proposal included HK$10 billion for a training scheme; HK$10 billion to speed up infrastructure projects and create jobs; and a 30% reduction in public housing and market rents. This proposal fell on deaf ears.

Supporting the vulnerable a shared social responsibility

In retrospect, an important piece to social policy in Singapore is the reliance on voluntary action. Voluntary welfare sector is one of the key players in helping the more vulnerable groups. Concerned citizens are encouraged to lend a helping hand for the disadvantaged and displaced in the Singapore community. Since 1970, the voluntary welfare sector has become better organized into a national social movement in partnership with the government in helping people facing various difficulties such as the disadvantaged families and children, the disabled, the aged sick, and youths at risk.

As of December 2001, about 240,641 beneficiaries have been assisted by different voluntary organizations that are funded by Community Chest, the fundraising arm of the National Council of Social Service. Some S$34 million was disbursed to meet the funding needs of 111 programs run by various funded charities of the Chest. This is indeed impressive effort by the voluntary sector to mobilize those more able to help the disadvantage. Increasingly, there are competitions for funds as other social and civic groups are also appealing for public donations for their programs. However, it is encouraging to note that the Singapore public is generous as long the appeals are for worthy charitable causes. The concept of "many community helping hands" is being promoted through voluntary activities which are supported by better-endowed citizens.

In meeting the needs of the poor and the disadvantaged groups in Singapore, several sectors are mobilized to be involved: the voluntary welfare sector, the government, and the private businesses. This tripartite partnership represents reasonable and broad-based efforts to support the disadvantaged sector of the population. The burdens of care do not fall onto the shoulder of government alone. It becomes a shared social responsibility of all key players. As can be seen in a number of countries, the voluntary welfare sector is constantly struggling to find funds to meet the ever-increasing needs of the poor and disadvantaged groups. In frustration, they adopt a strident approach to fight for funds to alleviate the problems of these groups. Such an adversarial stance between the government and the voluntary sector can produce negative outcomes and the problems remain unresolved. In the end, the disadvantaged groups may become adversely affected. On the contrary, "the many helping hands" approach adopted in Singapore where the voluntary, corporate and the government sectors work in partnership has shown remarkable results in dealing with the disadvantaged and the disabled (Yap, 1991).

In the current economic downturn, various government and nongovernment agencies have put in place a slew of measures to help the poor and needy. The Ministry of Community Development and Sports (MCDS) has provided long-term financial help through the public-assistance scheme. A sum of $230 a month is given to a single-person household and $670 to a household of four or more persons. Lower income families living in rental flats can also turn to the rental and utilities assistance scheme for help. The government announced under the second off-budget package that it would raise the subsidy amounts and the income eligibility criteria for this scheme. The MCDS will also extend temporary financial assistance to lower-income HDB flat owners who faced difficulties paying utilities and maintenance charges.

In early 2002, the government said that utilities rebates of S$350 would be given to households in one- to three-room HDB flats, S$300 to those in four-room flats and S$250 to five-roomers. More attention would be paid to the lower income groups living in smaller flats. Those living in one- and two-room flats were given rental rebates of between S$8 and S$12 per month and service and conservancy rebates of S$7 to S$8. The government's Small Families Improvement Scheme aims to help low-income couples upgrade themselves by keeping their families small and concentrating their resources on bringing up their children. Under the scheme, up to S$16,000 will be given as a conditional housing grant and the child would receive S$400 to S$1,200, based on the child's education level. Needy pupils can get a 50% waiver of miscellaneous fees, full waiver of school fees and a textbook grant or an annual bursary. Childcare and student-care fees are also subsidized.

Various community self-help groups are pitching in too. Organizations such as the Singapore Indian Development Association, Malay/Muslim self-help group, MENDAKI, and Chinese Development Association Council have waived tuition for needy students, disbursed bursaries and helped many students buy school books this recession. Many grassroots organizations such as the Citizens' Consultative Committee and Residents' Committee have raised funds to help children of retrenched workers pay for school fees, stationery, and textbooks. At the neighbourhood level to help families get back on their feet, various Community Development Councils have introduced a temporary relief scheme, which includes ready cash, food vouchers and money to pay for children's school books, meals and transport.

These are notable efforts. In hospitals, patients in Class C wards are subsidized heavily. Medifund, has been set up by the government to help pay the medical expenses of the poor. Under the second off-budget package, as noted above, the government also announced a 10% rebate to be given to all class B2 and C hospital bills, and on subsidized day surgery. Retrenched Singaporeans would enjoy a 50% reduction in hospitalization bills.

A new innovative scheme to help retrain older or retrenched workers to make them more employable in the restructuring of the industries has been devised. Workers who undergo retraining would get up to S$2,000 a month. Supports are also be given to firms that encourage training unemployed workers to undergo retraining will now be able to get up to S$2,000 month in wage support while they prepare for new job. This assistance will be given for 6 months to enable workers to tide over while they are picking up new skills. This has been increased from the previous limit of S$600 a month (for 3 months only). These new limits are part of the Enhanced People for Jobs Traineeship Programme, under which companies that hire unemployed older workers can claim more financial support to run training programs to train these workers. The new S$2,000 ceiling for the "half pay" while retraining means that more workers will be able to take it up, including skilled workers and management staff.

The People for Jobs Traineeship Programme is managed by the Ministry of Manpower (MOM) with an objective to encourage companies to hire older workers. It was introduced as a pilot program. There are currently 60 companies participating in it. Companies are required to put in place a mentorship or traineeship arrangement to help retrain the workers they take on. The move to increase financial support for the program comes in the wake of more management staff and skilled workers being laid off. The program will cost S$200 million and will cater to some

20,000 trainees. Training and skills upgrading is crucial, if workers wanted to keep their job in the new economy.

In all, the government has planned to spend a total of S$809 million to encourage and fund training programs. Unemployed workers who plan to take up training courses to improve themselves will get support from the government. For those who take full-time training courses, the training allowance under the Skills Redevelopment Programme (SRP) will increase from the current S$600 a month to 75% of the worker's last-drawn salary, or S$1,000 a month, whichever is lower. Those on part-time courses will also receive S$5.70 per hour, up from the current S$3.80 per hour. The changes in the workers' training allowance are to encourage the retrenched older workers to acquire relevant new skills.

Employers who encourage a training culture in their companies will not be left out either. Those who send workers for training will receive absentee payroll support of between S$6.10 and S$6.90, depending on the age of the worker in service. The Skills Development Fund was set up to boost efforts in promoting skills upgrading, particularly in certifiable skills. It is expected to support 1.9 million training places in total over 3 years. The Education and Training Fund run by the NTUC that is closely tied to the government, will also get a boost of S$15 million, bringing the fund to a total of S$55 million. There have been queries on the usefulness of the retraining programs were effective. The results of surveys conducted by the MOM and the NTUC last year proved positive. Three out of four retrenched workers who took up full-time SRP training were able to secure employment within three to 6 months after their retraining.

Balancing political, social, and economic development

From the foregoing discussion, it can be seen that the PAP government has played a key role in orchestrating the political, social, and economic development of Singapore. Often, what Singapore conjures up in the minds of many people is the existence of a paternal state (Mirza, 1986). Since its independence in 1959, the government of Singapore has been dominated by a single political party, the PAP, which has been noted for having centralized control over the economy and imposing strong actions on disruptive social and political activities (Enricht, Scott, & Dodwell, 1997; Tan, 1995). It has managed the economy with firm policies and has relied on overseas multinationals to build the economy. This is reflected in the scale of state spending, the activities of state-owned enterprises, and even in the rate of national savings (Mirza, 1986).

Paradoxically, such an intrusive role is also discernible in the government's social policy reforms that are targeted at restricting state involvement (Deyo, 1992): "Large industry-wide unions were decentralized and house unions were encouraged. Some social insurance programs were partially decentralized to firms ... while educational and welfare programs, and later, medical coverage, devolved to firms." These changes are expected to provide the private and restructured public sectors the flexibility to deliver more cost effective services.

If the state has played a major role in the economic and social development of Singapore in the past (Dixon & Drakakis-Smith, 1993; Wilson, 1978), it has not changed its position, as exemplified in the recent budget speech of the government by Richard Hu (2000) who stated that it is "a deliberate policy to keep the public sector lean and trim, avoiding welfarism and confining Government's role to one of providing basic public goods and services, thus freeing more manpower and financial resources to the private sector as the engine of growth."

Socially and politically, the downside of a paternal state has been well documented: much regulation, less freedom of choice and information, more state paternalism, and greater favoritism toward state companies (Enricht et al., 1997; United Nations Development Project, 1991). Despite these arguments, many Asian states that have major central control have made economic progress. The PAP government has defended its interventionist rule by relating centralized control to economic growth, arguing that the former is a prerequisite for capitalist development and attracting foreign investments. Lee Kuan Yew, the former prime minister, once remarked that "authoritarian arrangements are essential to economic success" (cited in Hitchcock, 1998).

To the government, a second necessary condition for economic growth is the restriction of state intervention in social welfare. Essentially, social welfare is regarded as an inhibitor of economic growth. The small budget for public assistance and the absence of other social programs like unemployment insurance, coupled with the strong economic growth in Singapore, has given the government some ammunition to justify its position. However, as noted above, this official argument is not totally comprehensive, considering the massive investments of the government in social development provisions (i.e., education, health, and housing) between 1960 and 1990 that had some impact on the growth of the economy. These provisions have been considered as social development and nonconsumptive. Government investment in low-cost public housing, education, and medical care has kept the cost of living down and preempted demands for wage increases in spite of the long hours of work which most workers had to endure (Castells, 1992; Tan, 1995). Socially, the government could afford to do more but it refrains from doing so. Hence, any rise in the standard of living has to wait for improved economic performance. The upshot of this has been the presence of some social problems such as drug abuse, suicide, and increasing marital breakdowns in this small but advanced economy.

Ideologically, the "welfarist model," covering such institutions as full employment policy, the provision of public assistance, and unemployment benefits, is considered by Singapore's government to erode work ethics, which has to be shunned at all costs. As a mature economy and a developed society, there is high acceptance for private ownership and property rights. The market is seen to be the ultimate arbiter of economic outcomes.

The worldwide trend toward marketization of social security appeals to the PAP government. Not surprisingly, the government is pursuing a privatization strategy and aims to privatize a number of government-owned enterprises. Most notable are its efforts to cut back health spending and encourage people to fend for any medical contingency, and its attempt to implement the liberalization of the CPF that has been used an effective economic and social leverage. The adoption of western welfare state model is seen to create social and economic breakdowns in many developed and developing countries and this has deterred Singapore from getting into the welfare whirlpool that generates dependency (Goh, 1996). The CPF is not a welfare mechanism for redistribution of wealth. It only has encouraged people to be productive.

In Singapore, much attention is focused on reliable and honest people to manage social and public institutions that cater for public good (Vasil,

2000). It is most interesting to witness that the Singapore government, unlike governments in many countries, shares its accumulated assets with every Singaporeans. This helps to give each Singaporean a social and economic stake in country. Also, individuals are urged be self-reliant. Each family is given a decent shelter and its members are educated to their best abilities as human capital is the main resource to further social and economic development (Midgley & Tang, 2001).

Conclusion

In Singapore, policymakers are very conscious that the individual and his family's resolve to deal with social and personal setbacks are not weakened by to state subsidy and over-indulgence. The main thrust of the social and economic measures implemented so far (and even those during the current economic downturn) are to strengthen the citizens' capacities to deal with competing demands. In short, these various measures, as implemented, are premised on the assumption that they do not undermine the coping function of a family in the context of changing times. Almost all the social and economic packages used to tackle the challenge of the economic recession do not promote dependency on the state. State welfarism that is commonly practiced in Western developed countries is avoided by the government of Singapore, since the government believes that these measures adopted have been reported to be economically unsustainable as national expenditure outstripped income. Many of these governments find it politically difficult to cutback their social security benefits that become part of the psyche of its people and these benefits often become financial minefields to succeeding governments (Vasoo & Lee, 2001).

The government of Singapore believes in the creation of viable social institutions that allow the harmonization of social and economic objectives and enable individuals to work productively and obtain an income that will meet his and family's needs. Singapore's responses to recent economic setback have been marked by an equal emphasis on both social and economic development objectives. It is hoped by the government that as it had been in the past, the current package of measures will produce the same socially desirable outcomes and improvements to the quality of life of Singaporeans affected by the economic recession. These social and economic measures also seek topromote a tripartite system which requires the individuals, the state and the employers to share the cost for the delivery of social service provisions. This is indeed a unique partnership that reduces public burden, reinforces social responsibility, prevents state dependency and encourages personal and family responsibilities.

Given its land scarcity and vulnerability as a small nation-state, social policies in Singapore are aimed at building a harmonious, caring, and cohesive society. The rapid socioeconomic changes due to economic globalization together with a changing demographic profile pose a number of challenges to the stability and well-being of families. Indeed the ageing of Singapore's population will be acute. There will be fewer younger family members in the households. This will definitely stretch the family's ability to provide adequate care and attention to its elderly family members. Some families will need more support from the community when they cannot mobilize enough assistance from amongst its kin groups. The burdens of care are likely to increase (Vasoo, Ngiam, & Cheung, 2000). Social policies to deal with population ageing will have to be put in place to deal with the challenges facing the family with elderly members (IMC Report, 1999).

References

Asher, M. G. (1985). *Forced saving to finance merit goods: An economic analysis of the Central Provident Scheme of Singapore* (Working paper No. 36). Canberra: Australian National University Centre for Research on Federal Financial Relations.

Castells, M. (1992). Four Asian tigers with a dragon head: A comparative analysis of the state, economy and society in the Asian Pacific Rim. In R. Appelbaum & J. Henderson (Eds.), *State and development in the Asian Pacific Rim* (pp. 33–70). Newbury Park, CA: Sage.

Central Provident Fund (1995). *The CPF story.* Singapore: Author.

Central Provident Fund (1998). *Annual report.* Singapore: Author.

Deyo, F. (1992). The political economy of social policy formation: East Asia's newly industrialized countries. In R. Appelbaum & J. Henderson (Eds.), *State and development in the Asian Pacific Rim* (pp. 289–306). Newbury Park, CA: Sage.

Dixon, C., & Drakakis-Smith, D. (1993). *Economic and social development in Pacific Asia.* London: Routledge.

Enricht, M. J., Scott, E. E., & Dodwell, D. (1997). *The Hong Kong advantage.* Hong Kong: Oxford University Press.

Goh, C. T. (1996). *Prime minister's national day rally speech.* Singapore: Ministry of Information and the Arts.

Goh, C. T. (2000). *Prime minister's national day rally speech.* Singapore: Ministry of Information and the Arts.

Goh, C. T. (2001). *Prime minister's national day rally speech.* Singapore: Ministry of Information and the Arts.

Hansard (2001). *Singapore Parliamentary Proceedings on Tackling the Economic Downturn.* Vol. 73, no. 23.

Hitchcock, D. (1998). Cultural side of the Asian crisis. *Straits Times, Perspective,* April 15.

Hu, R. (2000). *Ministry of Finance, Budget statement.* Singapore: Ministry of Finance.

Inter-Ministerial Committee (1999). *Report of the Inter-Ministerial Committee on the ageing.* Singapore: Population Singapore.

Lee, K. Y. (1998). *The Singapore story.* Singapore: Singapore Press Holdings.

Lee, K. Y. (2000). *From the Third World to the First: The Singapore story 1965–2000.* Singapore: Singapore Press Holdings.

Lim, J. (1997). Health care reform in Singapore: The Medisave scheme. In T. M. Tan & S. B. Chew (Eds.), *Affordable health care* (pp. 277–285). Singapore: Prentice Hall.

Low, L., & Aw, T. C. (1997). *Housing, a healthy, educated and wealthy nation through the CPF.* Singapore: Times Academic Press.

Midgley, J., & Tang, K.-L. (2001). Introduction: Social policy, economic growth and developmental welfare. *International Journal of Social Welfare, 10*(4), 244–252.

Ministry of Health (1993). *Health care plan.* Singapore: Author.

Ministry of Health (2000). *Medisave pamphlet.* Singapore: Author.

Ministry of Information and the Arts (2001). *Singapore.* Singapore: Author.

Mirza, H. (1986). *Multinationals and the growth of the Singapore economy.* London: Croom Helm.

Ngiam, T.-L. (2000, January). *Globalisation, competitiveness and a greying population: The challenge for social security in Singapore.* Paper presented at the Asia Regional Conference on Social Security, Hong Kong.

Singapore Yearbook of Statistics (2000). Singapore: Singapore Statistics Department.

Tan, G. (1995). *The newly industrializing countries of Asia.* Singapore: Times Academic Press.

United Nations Development Project (1991). *Human development report 1991.* New York: Oxford University Press.

Wilson, H. E. (1978). *Social engineering in Singapore.* Singapore: National University of Singapore Press.

Vasil, R. (2000). *Governing Singapore.* St. Leonards, New South Wales, Australia: Allen & Unwin.

Vasoo, S., Ngiam, N. L., & Cheung, P. (2000). Singapore's ageing population: Social challenges and responses. In D. R. Phillips (Ed.), *Ageing in the Asia-Pacific regions: Issues, policies and future trends* (pp. 174–193). London: Routledge.

Vasoo, S., & Lee, J. (2001). Singapore: Social development, housing and the Central Provident Fund. *International Journal of Social Welfare, 10(4),* 276–283.

Yap, M. T. (Ed.). (1991). *Social services: The next lap.* Singapore: Academic.

Chapter 28

Achieving social development and care through the Central Provident Fund and housing in Singapore*

S. Vasoo and James Lee

Introduction

We are now seeing that in many developing and developed economies that an offer of a generous social security provision package is becoming an attractive socio-political agenda for various governments. Promises of highly subsidised social service and security provisions such as old age pensions, health care needs, housing, and education are made by governments in power as it has good voter appeal. However, many of the governments fail to keep their promises as the tide of rising cost in continuing with the generous social service and social security provisions is not stoppable except that it could be absorbed by increasing government

---

*Reprinted with permission by the publisher from Vasoo, S., & Lee, J. (2006). Achieving Social Development and Care Through the Central Provident Fund and Housing in Singapore. In S. Vasoo & N. T. Tan (Eds.), *Challenge of Social Care in Asia* (pp. 164–182). Singapore: Marshall Cavendish Academic.

This paper examines the East Asian Welfare Model and discusses the case study of Singaporean housing and the Central Provident Fund as mechanisms to achieve social development and social care objectives.

subsidy and charges. However, giving higher and higher subsidy for various social provisions is not an effective long-term solution as government expenditure has to be met by introducing more direct or indirect taxes. Therefore without corollary increase in state income, many governments come under pressure to roll back the social service provisions. In recognition of this dilemma, policy makers have to take into serious consideration the social development perspectives in policies which have generally been neglected. It is an important precursor for development in any society. Social development places high premium on ownership, co-payment and sharing, productivity and self worth and dignity. Welfare systems have been and are being criticised for failing to address the problems of removing poverty and widespread unemployment. The state welfarism has expanded and it is now too rigid and expensive as social development objectives have been compromised or neglected. Hence, many governments face enormous problems of financial sustainability and even consider state welfarism to be antithetical to social and economic development because instead of promoting self-help, dependency of people is enhanced because people's capacity to manage their lives and social needs have been eroded. Social development objectives of economic policies have been displaced by welfarist drives which are high subsidy driven leading to high inefficiency and waste. As a consequence, there are increasing pressures for policy makers to take action to either trim or change the state welfarism efforts. On the other hand, making end users bear the whole cost of various services can make it less affordable and this is not a solution either. Policy makers have to moderate the increasing demand for services as runaway demands coupled by public pressure for increase in subsidy can dislocate governments in due course. These and other related issues on the crisis of state welfare have converged into a burgeoning subject, now known as 'the search for an East Asian model of social and welfare development' (Goodman et al., 1998). Such a model emphasises on social development objectives and promote social care through formal and informal sectors.

This paper examines the prospects of this Asian effort based on the unique experience of the housing and income protection system to enhance social and economic development in Singapore. The main focus of the discussion is to examine why and how a massive public home ownership programme (86 percent of Singaporeans own homes built by the government) is both possible and sustainable to achieve social development objectives. The argument is that, given an appropriate level and mix of social institutions and policies, it is possible to harmonise both the social and economic development equations. To do so it requires some new understanding of the role of the state in (a) building institutions and mechanisms to promote social development objectives through the productive rather than consumptive means; and (b) regulating the dynamics between social policies and changing social needs with a view to discourage a mentality for high subsidy or free public sector services. All these point to the prospect of a social developmental model in the promoting of welfare as suggested by Midgley (1995) in the mid 1990s.

The rhetorical niceties of welfare state have often been used as political baits by various political groups to appeal to the masses for support. Indeed the most severe criticisms of the 'welfare state controversy' have come from the economist camp because the economic realities that many welfare states will run into deep economic troubles in the near future because their public expenditure will be more than their income. Proponents of the state welfarism have been either politically bias tended to treat the relationship between welfare state and the economy as something taken for granted. Many of them have neglected the buffet syndrome effects generated by state welfarism. However, states adopting social development objectives in their social and welfare provisions have made positive socio-economic progress. In fact, we know from experience that different social policies impact differently on the economy and therefore could not be lumped together and be treated as simply one conglomerate of social programmes. We can say at this stage the effect of purist welfare state policies based on heavy unilateral transfers in the form of subsidies can be disastrous to social and economic development. All we can see is that it might have failed to achieve an optimum level of social configuration, or that a wrong choice has been made on the allocation mechanism. In promoting social development we briefly present the debates on the East Asian Welfare Model and then discuss the Singaporean housing and the Central Provident Fund as a case study of the successful application of social development and social care objectives to achieve societal welfare.

East Asian welfare model: State intervention and incrementalism

While going through Atkinson's (1999) critique on the welfare state debate, which was largely based on Nordic experiences, and also the initial attempt by Goodman et al. (1999) on identifying an East Asian welfare regime, a striking affinity is apparent in their findings. In the case studies of Singapore, South Korea, Hong Kong, Taiwan, and Japan, Goodman et al. (1998) discovered a number of interesting similarities amongst these high growth Asian countries. First, although some social policy observers remain sceptical (Jacobs, 1999), the absolute level of social expenditure among these countries is generally accepted as comparatively lower than European welfare states as their level of state intervention through social welfare remains visible. While the mechanism of welfare allocation varies tremendously amongst these countries, the state always plays a key role in social regulation for allocation of social policy goods. In their assessment, Goodman et al. (1998, p. 13) argued that East Asian Welfare when examined closely and bearing in mind that other non-financial means or mechanisms in

> ... any view that measured the welfare role of the state purely by financial indicators would be misleading because it ignores the ways (or the regulatory mechanisms) in which the state has acted pervasively in East Asia to achieve welfare goals by other means, most notable is the strategic role of the states in directing a process of economic development with distributive as well as growth objectives.

Second, the notion of a state-provided or guaranteed welfare as a social right is only marginally developed. In its place, the family, the firm as well as social institutions play a significant role in terms of sharing social risks and social goods, although different social trajectories reflect a different mix/mode of institutional structures. This is particularly relevant to Northeast Asian city-states such as Hong Kong (Tang, 1999) and South Korea (Gough, 2000). The concept of comprehensive welfare planning is thus less preferred than pragmatism and incrementalism. Welfare is seen as a privilege rather than a social right (Lee Kuan Yew, 2000).

The state is a board of trustees while the people are the clients of the state (Chua, 2000). But strong state intervention and incrementalism in social policies are not new to Western welfare states observers. Equally, institutionalism is nothing novel to welfare state theorists. More importantly it is the will of policy makers to exercise collective decisions which though at times unpopular but are beneficial for the long term well being of the society.

There are a few aspects that make East Asian states unique. Our discussions have thus far identified two key directions. First, the institutional structure matters should be included in the East Asian welfare model. Second, we should consider the views strongly suggested by Atkinson (1999). Since the nature and impact of social programmes differ tremendously, it is therefore important when studying East Asian welfare model to pay attention to the choice and mix of social programmes and the reasons underlying such choice (Gough, 2000). Henceforth, the Singaporean housing and CPF systems were chosen as a focus of analysis since it is a unique example of how institutional structure can facilitate the attainment of socio-political as well as economic progress.

Achieving social development objectives

Singapore's public housing programme which started only in 1960, has now grown to become one of the largest in the world and has contributed to both social care and development objectives. To many western observers, the whole achievement of public housing in Singapore is spectacular and leaves many wondering the accomplishment. Public housing categorically refers to subsidised sale flat produced and sold by the state to some 86 percent of its people. It ranges from 2–3 rooms high-rise flats to 4–5 rooms luxurious apartments, catering for the housing needs of the working class as well as a majority of the middle class. The private housing market takes up only about 10 percent of the total housing stock and is largely confined to top end housing for the middle upper and the very rich. Singaporean citizens have each two opportunities to purchase government built flats. This stimulates the development of an active resale market for government flats when households decide to upgrade to bigger flats. In his latest memoir, Lee Kuan Yew (2000) was crystal clear about home ownership and achieving social development goals and he stated:

> my primary preoccupation was to give every citizen a stake in the country and its future. I want a home-owning society. I have seen the contrast between blocks of low cost rental apartments, badly misused and poorly maintained, those of house-proud owners, and was convinced that if every family owned its home, the country would be more stable.

How was this achieved? This was largely due to Lee's (2000) vision and through the successful fusion of two extremely ingenuous institutions: namely, the Housing Development Board (HDB) which commenced the public home ownership programme in 1964 and has since developed itself into one of the largest public developers in the developed world. Since about more than 86 percent of the population are housed in home ownership scheme, it is anticipated that future demand for flats is likely to slow down as a result of the falling population growth. The danger of the decline in Singapore's population will have implications for not only the resale market of flats but also on demand for new flats. This is an enigmatic situation where Singapore is the only industrial capitalism in the world who has physically achieved about 90 percentage home ownership. Not simply that. The HDB has been successful in producing a ladder of public owner-occupation flats with sufficient intra-system mobility, as well as a quality which is at par with any private housing markets in East Asia. The irony is when the demand for both quality living and ownership has been fully satisfied, the incentive for new housing demand would progressively decline. Singapore will face an 'aged housing system' much earlier than an 'aged population'. Henceforth, the ultimate challenge for the State is low to maintain (1) a healthy scarcity in the housing system so that the system would not be ageing so quickly; or (2) a restructuring of the current tenure system in both the public and the private sector, either way implies a retracking of the current full home ownership policy.

Central Provident Fund (CPF) as a social development mechanism

Another anchor social development mechanism is the establishment of a compulsory savings institution — the Central Provident Fund (CPF), which was initiated during the colonial period in 1955, aiming at providing some form of retirement benefits but incurring little financial risks. In the beginning the rate of contribution was kept at a low 5 percent for workers and a matching 5 percent from employers. The major part of the CPF savings could only be withdrawn at 55. At first workers did not put much faith into the scheme. But when the government changed its legislation in 1968, allowing people for the first time to withdraw their savings for the 20 percent down payment at that time in home purchase, it became a success because of appropriate mix of social objectives in housing policies. The government was able to achieve a higher rate of home ownership without risking a high level of state funding, since people are merely using their own savings. This also solved one of the major obstacles in the promotion of home ownership normally encountered by other developing economies which face difficulties to mobilise vital developmental funding for home finance. CPF achieves other social development objectives. Besides the use of CPF for payment of housing and old age retirement needs, the Fund's usage has diversified since its early inception. This is because an individual account holder has accumulated a respectable amount of personal saving and as such the Fund has evolved other social schemes to cater for healthcare (Medisave), child education (CPF for Education), and private investments. The diversification of CPF usage is in response to reduce reliance on the state to meet mainly old age retirement and healthcare needs. All these need aspects can become acute in future with the aging population. The total compulsory monthly individual CPF saving comprising both employer and employee contributions in its peak at one time amounted to 50 percent but has since been revised to 33 percent now (see Table 1).

The diversification of usage does protect the individual against some social risks and the scheme does incur any government financial outlay. It has been argued that although CPF is useful as an asset building scheme but when much of the individual's funds has been placed on housing

Table 1. CPF contribution rate (%)

Year	Employer	Employee	Medisave* Weight	Gross Rate
1955	5	5	—	10
1968	6.5	6.5	—	13
1970	8	8	—	16
1972	14	10	—	24
1973	15	11	—	26
1974	15	15	—	30
1977	15.5	15.5	—	31
1978	16.5	16.5	—	33
1979	20.5	16.5	—	37
1982	22	23	—	45
1984	25	25	6	50
1985	25	25	6	50
1986	10	25	6	35
1989	15	23	6	38
1992	18	22	6	40
1995	20	20	6	40
1997	20	20	6	40
1999	10	20	6	30**
2000	14	20	8	34***
2001	14	20	8	34
2002	16	20	8	36
2003	13	20	6–8	33****
2004	13	20	6–8	33

*Medisave was not introduced until 1984.

**Singapore was hit by the Asian monetary crisis and as such the gross CPF contribution was reduced.

***The Singapore economy improved and therefore CPF was increased upwards and this will be restored in due course.

****CPF reduced to meet global competition and economic restructuring.

Sources: Low, L. and T. C. Aw. (1997) Housing a healthy, educated and wealthy nation through the CPF, p. 34 and Singapore Annual Reports 1999; 2003; Singapore CPF Annual Report 2003; CPF Contribution Rate Booklet (Jan 2004).

which is a fixed asset, the danger is that the individual will have less cash at his disposal for his old age. Hence there is an urgency to re-examine the current CPF and housing policies to ensure that the old will have some funds to see through his old age besides just counting on his children to help. Otherwise, the individual account holder will have a property but not sufficient cash for retirement needs unless he sells his property. For such an individual, the CPF and Housing authorities can devise a scheme to buy back the flat under the step down replacement scheme or place the property under a reverse mortgage scheme.

The CPF investment scheme can be risky for individuals who do not have transparent or true information about various investment products in the market. Such lack of information can place the individual at a danger of losing his savings. It will be timely for CPF authority to provide investment advisory services to retirees who are less informed.

While it remains polemical whether a form of compulsory saving plan for all working population should be instituted by the State, it is clearly evident that Singaporean citizens seem to enjoy being homeowners in as early as the mid 1960s. Home ownership rate reached 90 percent in 1995 (see Table 2) and has since been slightly reduced because some wealthier public housing homeowners have shifted to the private sector when they manage to capitalise their HDB housing assets. The government carefully monitored the rate of CPF contributions in its early years and made quite progressive increases in contribution rate since 1968. Contribution rates were carefully determined to reflect income level, household consumption and price level. In the words of Lee Kuan Yew (2000, p. 97):

> Once workers got used to a higher take home pay, I knew they would resist any increase in their CPF contribution that would reduce their spendable money. So, almost yearly I increase the rate of CPF contributions, but such that there was still a net increase in take home pay. It was painless for the workers to keep inflation down.

It is apparent that Singapore does not want to face inflation when workers have surplus purchasing power. Clearly the State helps to pave the way for a managed life long consumption pattern where it seeks when possible to influence consumption behaviour through social programmes.

Table 2. Singapore housing indicators

Year	Home Ownership (HDB) Rate (%)	Total HDB Public Flats
1970	29	—
1980	59	—
1990	88	—
1993	89	655,487
1996	87	—
1997	86	—
1998	91	790,898
1999	92	823,760
2000	93	846,649
2001	93	863,552
2002	94	866,071
2003	94	874,183

Sources: Singapore Annual Report 1999 and Year Book and Statistics 2004.

Hence, CPF which is essentially a national personal savings institution is bein used as a macro economic tool to promote social and economic well being? Clearly one can argue that the workability of such a system requires a good degree of social management and consensus as well as a continuous level of economic growth. Without sustained economic growth, it will be difficult to allocate resources to areas of human capital development such as housing, education, and health. Nevertheless this does not preclude the necessity for an appropriate policy choice and a right governing mechanism. Western welfare states had evolved a sophisticated system of collective welfare through the principle of pooled risk. The swinging changes as a result of popular politics and the pandering to various interest groups do create difficulties and intractable problems of welfare dependency. As a result, the State makes more individuals dependent and incur serious public debts and economic drawbacks. Also, the other consequence is that the State shares all the financial risks while the most disadvantaged social groups are susceptible to social risks. The choice of risks and how to share them out thus matter. In the final analysis, individuals must be made accountable for the choice of their risks.

The HDB as a public organisation combines the ethos of an efficient bureaucracy and the flair of a modern day developer. The degree of Singapore's commitment in the provision of housing could be clearly felt in the words of its Prime Minister, Mr. Goh Chok Tong (1994, pp. 14–15):

> We have been rewarding Singaporeans for many years. The biggest prizes are the 600,000 HDB flats which 90 percent of Singaporeans own. Now HDB is buying back three-room flats and reselling them at a discount to help the poorer Singaporeans to own their flats. ... Actually, our HDB residents have done very well. For example, one in three HDB homes has air-conditioners.
>
> One in five has personal computers. These are not essential items like telephones or refrigerators. Yet their ownership rate has increased by three times from 1987. It is the single biggest asset for most people, and its value reflects the fundamentals of the economy.

Meeting housing needs and the promotion of home ownership are thus considered political goals in Singapore at least on two grounds. First, the state seeks to develop a housing programme that commensurates with the growing demand for a better quality living environment. The idea of a housing ladder has been firmly incorporated in the housing system. The government is now encouraging people in 2–3 room flats, which was popular in the 1970s, to upgrade, so that precious land could be redeveloped for further HDB housing programmes. To meet the needs of the emerging professional class, the government also established the Housing and Urban Development Corporation (HUDC) in 1979 and later encouraged the setting up of the executive condominium scheme to cater for the housing needs of those up-and-coming young executives who are not eligible for the ordinary HDB flats and yet find private housing unaffordable.

Second, the state also recognises that with growing affluence, people tend to have a higher aspiration on housing needs as well as an investment asset where they can meet their 'future' retirement needs. (Sherraden et al., 1995). Since the early 1990s, HDB flats have appreciated two to threefold in value. Many Singaporeans wanted to capitalise on their first HDB flats and seek to upgrade for better housing by means of their second opportunity to purchase flats from the government. While it is not the state policy to encourage speculation on public flats, the spirit of asset appreciation is embedded in the presence of a mature secondhand market. To some extent a high aspiration for improved housing as well as a steady growth in the economy tend to fuel housing speculations, as was the case of Hong Kong before 1997. Indeed Lee Kuan Yew (2000) regretted not to have used effective policy measures in the earlier days to thwart excessive housing demands when the property market became too buoyant.

Achieving specific social care objectives

Since the implementation of home ownership scheme by HDB, a number of social care projects or programmes have been carried out and the more significant outcomes and projects will be highlighted to support the outcomes of CPF and housing schemes which can be considered as two of the major Singapore social policies enhancing social and human capital development. Social care projects and programmes have strengthened the community bonding and support among residents and improved the social health of the neighbourhoods of housing estates in Singapore. More residents are coming out to participate in formal and informal non-governmental and governmental social groups and organisations to provide social, educational, and recreational needs of residents. Help for vulnerable individuals and families are also provided by those who are better provided — in short, a community support network to cushion those affected by personal, social, and economic crises and uncertainties.

The formation of neighbourhood organisations such as residents' committees, community clubs, social and recreational groups, and citizens' consultative committees has helped to build up formal social care networks in the various housing estates (Vasoo, 1994). These community groups formed on a basis of self help or through the encouragement of government bodies such as the Peoples Association (Vasoo, 2002) have come about as a response to deal with urban anomie and impersonality. The various social, educational, and recreational activities organised by the respective community groups promote better understanding and relationship among residents.

To assist the vulnerable families and strengthen family relationships, many Family Service Centres (FSCs) have been formed by Voluntary Welfare Organisations (VWOs). These organisations are managed by volunteers together with professional social workers and their operations are funded by the Government, Community Chest of Singapore and private sectors. This tripartite relationship fosters shared responsibilities and the commitment to social care is spread out to as many parties as possible. Such a strategy does not create dependency and the needs of the vulnerable are tackled by the collective efforts of the community.

The most recent social care body, namely the Community Development Councils (CDCs) have been ushered and there are at the moment five Councils headed by Mayors. These Councils which come under the aegis of People's Association are involved in mobilising residents, corporations, community groups and VWOs to be engaged in community building and community problem solving. The longer term outcomes will be to bring social assistance and care programmes such as public and medical fund assistances nearer to people and to give a more human touch to the help extended by government agencies. Social help and care is decentralised and made more accessible to people and those who are more able are encouraged to be involved to assist those in need. It is hoped that social care will find its roots and permeate into the localities of the various housing neighbourhoods.

Some implications on social development and care

In analysing the Singapore housing policy experiences a few important social objective issues could be teased. Firstly, housing in Singapore has come a long way from mere provision of simple shelter for the masses in the past to wealth accumulation for the future. As seen in many countries, housing policies are relegated to the mere provision of rented shelters and there is no ownership stake in their public housing schemes. Hence, rental housing policies adopted by many governments have detrimental effects and retards social development objectives which if promoted would give ownership and control to consumers. In line with economic growth and social development objectives, the welfare element of public housing is de-emphasised. In fact the Singaporean government considers housing more of a privilege rather than welfare. Housing is marketed as asset accumulation and all eligible Singaporeans can have access to it but there is an affordable cost they must bear through their CPF savings. This even makes the low-income families proud home owners and encourages them to upgrade their housing from two-room flats to five-room flats or executive apartments. Singapore's housing policy enhances social integration as different income and ethnic groups live and interact with one another. Such an agenda for social integration is critical as Singapore is a multiracial society and the need to prevent ethnic ghetto is an important social development objective to achieve. Whereas western societies have often attached the label of social exclusion and marginalisation to public housing, the case of Singapore suggests the contrary. Sherraden et al. (1995) argued that the Singaporean housing system has allowed a social configuration that facilitates empowerment and inclusion.

It is both a personal asset and a national asset. Secondly, housing in Singapore is fully integrated with economic development in a dynamic sense. Earlier provision of public housing tended to emphasise on the improvement of housing standards while later development focused more on community identity and asset appreciation (Chua, 1997). Heavy regulation in land supply and housing also enables a stable housing market with the CPF acting as an important facilitator for housing finance as well as a useful macroeconomic tool to influence consumption behaviour. Thirdly, social policies in western states seem to concentrate on the encouragement of consumptive rather than on productive behaviours. Such a policy perspective does in the longer term create liabilities for these states as they have to find more funds to deliver various social and welfare provisions including health, education, and housing. Consumers become dependent and their needs become insatiable because they contribute the least payment for the services. Therefore those who work hard are penalised because they have to pay for services which they do not consume. This is not the case as in Singapore's housing ownership scheme through CPF policy which has also helped to reduce the propensity to not only misallocate economic resources but also prevented the deterioration of liveable environment, family breakdown, property speculations, and unemployment.

These few perspectives as identified do reflect the ethos of a new body of social policy theory which places a premium on social development. The Social Development Model developed by Midgley (1995) in the mid 1990s encapsulated the spirit of harmonising social interventions with economic development efforts. It required that economic development should result in tangible improvements in social well being through social development which should embody a fully-integrated national strategy which is, process-oriented, goal-oriented and above all, the success of which must depend on whether or not an appropriate set of institutions has been developed over time (Midgley, 1995, pp. 140–148).

In the case of Singaporean housing, the HDB works on both market and institutional principles, seeking to maximise the developmental advantages of housing development. HDB flats are sold to Singaporeans at competitive prices. Since HDB practically controls 80 percent of the middle class housing market, it faces less competition and naturally monopolises. In normal market situation, house prices easily appreciate on monopolistic grounds by private developers as a result of market failure. However, since it is also in the interest of the Singaporean government to maintain a stable house price regime for the sake of political legitimacy, the role of the state is thus mediational and interventive when necessary. This situation does not apply to a private developer who only cares about profit maximisation.

The use of the CPF for housing ownership is another important policy development. When the society desires a high rate of home ownership and a stable long-term income stream, what better alternatives could there be better than to marry home ownership with personal/household savings. Stored wealth with stable appreciation of housing asset can lead to a steady life-long income stream and hence a reduction of the future financial burden on state. However, the greatest worry for the Singaporean government is house price fluctuations. If the state fails to maintain a stable level of house prices and a steady rate of economic growth, the present form of social equilibrium would be affected. While the solution for endogenous disturbance such as demand and supply shortfalls could somehow be remedied by a monopolistic control on the market, the greatest fear lies in exogenous economic factors, such as the 1997 Asian economic crisis and its aftermath. It is a strongly held view of policy makers that sustained economic growth through productive manpower is essential to upgrade the quality of life.

Singapore home ownership policy does motivate residents to be productively employed and their work ethos not eroded. In a globalising world, no one country could manage to be totally independent of any economic disturbances on an international scale. However, since the Singaporean system facilitates integration and consensus, the system was capable of absorbing some of the economic vibrations through wage-cuts, labour market adjustments, and careful monitoring of the CPF contribution rates during economic crisis. The tripartite relationship forged among the State, entrepreneurs, and labour has made it possible to reach a consensus in formulation and implementation of policies which achieve both economic and social development objectives.

Some issues and challenges of the public goods social institutions

The Singaporean housing and the CPF systems are not without their critics. Two broad strands of criticisms have emerged. Firstly, there are those who argue that the Singaporean housing system is driven by the desire of the state to establish political legitimacy. It is essentially about politics, not welfare or asset. However, it could not be denied that good politics has made it possible for 82 percent of the population to be homeowners. Chua (1997) suggested that the Singaporean housing system was really driven by a process of depoliticisation where social goods are exchanged for political legitimacy. The process to build up ideological consensus through the provision of good housing will thus never be complete, and hence the desire to improve housing by State continues.

Tremewan (1998), arguing along similar legitimacy line but was more critical of the entire shift of the nature of social policy — from income redistribution to managed lifetime consumption. CPF is not a welfare mechanism for redistribution of wealth. If it is, then Singaporeans would become indebted, but fortunately, CPF was formulated right from the start as a savings for old age and other social support. CPF does not encourage intra-class or intra-generational transfer and is at best one big State saving bank with lots of conditions for withdrawal. Low and Aw (1997) pointed out that since CPF is not a Pay-as-you-go (PAYG) system and is often fully funded, it is therefore not a pooled risk system like most European systems. In some ways, CPF is said to be tied to employment and it is work-performance related and hence the social objective outcome is to motivate people to continue working and have positive work ethics. A worker taps his own CPF savings which includes the accumulated interest. Unlike other pension schemes the worker draws down on his own savings and as such he is also motivated to be productive as his employer will be expected to contribute an equal amount of CPF contribution. The unemployed is not covered by CPF and therefore they are motivated to work if they can. Nonetheless, the dynamism of the CPF has already proved its sustainability through changes in legislations to allow for investment, medical care, housing, insurance coverage, and funding for education. The second strand of criticism seeks to challenge the whole notion of the social development. Chan, Clark and Lam (1998) dismissed the argument that East Asian states fared well in socio-economic performance in the last decade as purely the result of orchestrated statism. They suggested that East Asian stories are often the product of eclecticism and that we should always try to move beyond the developmental state.

These and other criticisms prompt us back to the fundamental social policy question: what are the purposes and nature of social policy? Are we seeking social equity through redistribution as a result of accepting certain forms of capitalism? Or is it about the creation of good social institutions with desirable social objectives that allow social and economic objectives to integrate; that enable individuals to work productively and yet be able to manage their income and consumption rationally over a lifetime? In the East Asian context, the social policies do not follow the premises of first question. The second proposition is more reflective of the social policy thrusts. We have shown in Singapore's case example that with a careful mix of housing and CPF savings, the social and economic development objective could be achieved. This approach has worked best for Singapore and produced socially desirable outcomes and improvements to the quality of social life. More importantly, it is evidenced that 86 percent of the population is housed in property owned and positive social development objectives such as social and ethnic integration, improved physical environment, family cohesion, and employability have been attained.

However, with the move towards a more globalised world economy, it is anticipated that Singapore's working population will face immense challenge in maintaining low unemployment rate of 3 percent. The Singaporean work world will be affected more by external factors such as regional, social, and political instability and low competitive wage cost and productive labour force. These factors can cause job loss particularly amongst older and less skilled workers and structural unemployment will surface. To mediate and reduce these problems the CPF policy will have to be flexible and respond to mutual interest of workers and employers. CPF contributions by both employees and employers will have to reflect the prevalent economic realities and vary with economic growth and employability. There can be future threats of prolonged unemployment of older workers and the problems of income maintenance will emerge. CPF policies cannot avoid addressing these issues such as graduated release of CPF funds, use of CPF for private unemployment insurance, and short term advance payment based on minimum household needs.

Conclusion

Based on the social and economic indicators as listed in the Table 3 below, it could be shown that in the past decade, Singapore has made both quantitative and qualitative achievements in the well being for its people. The GNP per capita rose from S$28,535 in 1993 to S$37,555 in year 2003 and 82 percent of the population are homeowners. This 50-fold increase in per capital GNP and other achievements such as low inflation, increase in life expectancy, low infant mortality, reduce crime rate, and more volunteers' involvement, are indeed mind boggling and these are results of prudent and effective governance under stable political conditions led by able political leadership which is responsive to various social and economic challenges (Vasil, 2000, pp. 202–252).

Social policies in Singapore have been transformed in the last three decades from one which is based on a highly subsidised system to one promoting a tripartite system which requires the individual, State and the

Table 3. Economic and social indicators (1993–2004)

Year	Per Capita GNP S$ US$ = S$1.74	Measures of Inflation (%)	Unemployment Rate (%)	CPF Contributions in Labour Force (%)	Life Expectancy Years	Public Flat Home Owner-ship (%)	Infant Mortality Rate Per 1,000 Live Births (%)	Gross Rate Per 100,000 Population Crime
1994	32,424.7	3.1	1.9	67.3	76.3	80	4.1	1,451
1995	35,021.9	1.7	2.0	67.2	76.4	81	3.8	1,401
1996	36,735.1	1.4	2.2	66.3	76.6	81	3.6	1,305
1997	39,923.9	2.0	1.7	65.3	77.4	81	3.6	1,228
1998	38,418.0	-0.3	2.3	62.0	77.4	82	4.1	1,278
1999	39,721.4	0.0	3.3	62.0	77.6	82	3.2	1,005
2000	39,599	1.3	3.5	58.1	78.1	82	2.5	807
2001	37,364	1.0	2.8	59.9	78.4	82	2.2	704
2002	37,834	-0.4	4.3	60.3	78.7	83	2.5	768
2003	37,555	0.5	4.6	59.7	78.9	82	2.2	802

Source: Yearbook of Statistics 2004, Singapore Department of Statistics.

employer to share the cost for the delivery of social service provisions. Such an emphasis reinforces the social commitment. It prevents state dependency and encourages personal ownership and accountability. Most importantly, individuals are encouraged to save, be self-reliant as far as possible and be a stakeholder in the public assets of Singapore. It is only through surplus asset accumulations and savings that one can invest in human capital to further social and economic development. The most important thing is that it has opened up a theoretical possibility in understanding the need to promote social development objectives, both for East Asia and perhaps also the West where state welfarism is prevalent. In a changing global economy it is important to devise progressive and responsive social and economic policies with emphasis on social development to deal with the vagaries of life.

References

*This is a revised version of the paper presented at the International Conference on Asset Building and Social Development at the Shandong University, China, 9 September 2004.

Central Provident Fund Board, 1997–2003 Annual Report(s).

Chan, S., Clark, C. and Lam, D. (1998). *Beyond the Developmental State: East Asia's Political Economics Reconsidered.* London: Macmillan.

Chua, B. H. (1997). *Political Legitimacy and Housing: Stake holding in Singapore.* London: Routledge.

Chua, B. H. (2000). Public Housing Residents as Clients of the State. *Housing Studies*, Vol. 15 (1), pp. 45–60.

Esping-Andersen, G. (1990). *Three Worlds of Welfare Capitalism.* Oxford: Polity Press.

Esping-Andersen, G. (1999). *Social Foundations of Postindustrial Economies.* Oxford: OUP.

Goh Chok Tong. (1994). National Day Rally 1994. Ministry of Information and the Arts, Singapore.

Goodman, R., White, G. and Kwon, H. (1998). *The East Asian Welfare Model: Welfare Orientalism and the State.* London: Routledge.

Gough, I. (2000). Welfare Regimes in East Asia and Europe. Paper presented to the Annual World Bank Conference on Development Economics Europe 2000, 27 June in Paris, France.

Jacobs, D. (2000). Low Public Expenditures on Social Welfare: Do East Asian Countries have secret? *International Journal of Social Welfare*, Vol. 9 (1) pp. 2–16.

Lee, K. C. (1999). *Home Ownership and Social Change in Hong Kong.* London: Ashgate.

Lee Kuan Yew. (2000). *From Third World to First: The Singapore Story: 1965–2000,* New York: Harper and Collins.

Lindbeck, A., Molander, P., Persson, T., Petersson, O., Sandmo, A., Weedenborg, and Thygesen, N. (1994). *Turning Sweden Around.* Cambridge: MIT Press.

Low, L. and Aw, T. C. (1997). *Housing, a Healthy, Educated and Wealthy Nation through the CPF.* Singapore: Times Academic Press.

Midgley, J. (1995). *Social Development.* London: Sage.

Ministry of Information and the Arts, 1997, 1998, 1999. Singapore.

Sherradden, M., Nair, S., Vasoo, S. and Ngiam, T. L. (1995). Social Policy based on assets: the impact of Singapore's central provident fund. *Asian Journal of Political Sciences*, Vol. 3 (2), pp. 112–33.

Shin, D. M. (1999). Economic Policy and Social Policy: Policy Linkages in an Era of Globalization. *International Journal of Social Welfare*, Vol. 9 (1).

Tang, K. L. (1999). Planning for the Unknown: Social Policy Making in Hong Kong 1990–1997. *International Journal of Sociology and Social Policy*, Vol. 19 (1/2) pp. 27–56.

Ministry of Information and the Arts and Lianhe Zaobao, 1999. Singapore Annual Report 1999.

Singapore Yearbook of Statistics 2004. Singapore Statistics Department, 2004.

Titmuss, R. (1974). *Social Policy: An Introduction.* London: Allen & Unwin.

Tremewan, C. (1998). Welfare and governance: public housing under Singapore's party-state. In R. Goodman, G. White, and H. Kwon (Eds.), *The East Asian Welfare Model: Welfare Orientalism and the State.* London: Routledge.

Vasoo, S. (1994). *Neighbourhood Leaders Participation in Community Development.* Singapore Academic Press, 1–20.

Vasoo, S. (2002). New Directions of Community Development in Singapore. In N. T. Tan and K. Mehta (Eds.), *Extending Frontiers: Social Issues and Social Work in Singapore.* Singapore: Eastern Universities Press, pp. 20–36.

Yuen, B., Teo, H. P., and Ooi, C. L. (1999). *Singapore Housing: An Annotated Bibliography.* Housing Policy and Development Research Unit, National University of Singapore.

Chapter 29

Singapore: Social investment, the state and social security*

James Lee and S. Vasoo

Robert Wade's (1990) study of South Korea, Taiwan and Japan in the late 1980s resulted in a better understanding of East Asian developmentalism as the 'governed' or 'guided' market and further invigorated the study of the 'developmental state' since Johnson's (1982) formative study of economic development in Japan. Despite the fact that the diversity of the developmental experiences in East Asia defies easy generalization, one pivotal element is the centrality of the role of the state in fostering economic growth and development. Developmental theorists have pointed to two linked and yet quite independent issues: first, the capacity of government, or what Evans (2006) termed 'bureaucratic capacity' to respond to changing circumstances both within and outside the national economy; second, the degree to which institutional arrangements are capable of being fully integrated, or simply put, whether state institutions are capable of synergizing with social institutions in such a way as to foster growth.

---

*Reprinted with permission by the publisher from Lee, J., & Vasoo, S. (2008). Singapore: Social Investment, the State and Social Security. In J. Midgley & L. T. Kwong (Eds.), *Social Security, the Economy and Development* (pp. 269–286). New York: Palgrave Macmillan Press.

This paper examines the nature of institutional arrangements that aim to facilitate integration between social investment and social welfare, using the unique case study of Singapore's housing system. Various issues on policy response based on previous work are addressed.

A developmental state with strong state capacity could stifle such synergy while one with low state capacity could foster chaos, either way failing to attain developmental objectives. This chapter will focus on the second element — institutional arrangements that aim to facilitate integration. In particular, the unique case of the integration between social investment and social welfare will be examined. This is the case of the Central Provident Fund and the public housing system in Singapore. This example is unique in two respects. First, the social security system of Singapore is fully integrated with the housing system resulting in a first-level integration within the welfare system. Second, the welfare system is integrated with the economic system largely through capital formation, housing investment, mass housing consumption, using asset appreciation as an incentive to maintain a second-level integration and also boosting the economy and employment through an expanding construction sector.

This chapter examines the nature of these institutional arrangements and demonstrates through a case study how Singapore's housing system contributes towards understanding the feasibility of socio-economic integration (Vasoo and Lee, 2001). The chapter begins with a brief description of Singapore's economy and its social security system. It then examines Singapore's economic development with reference to housing and social security by focusing on the two levels of integration mentioned earlier. The chapter concludes with a discussion on a number of issues and challenges facing Singapore arising from these institutional arrangements.

Singapore: Basic facts and the social security system

In the middle of the twentieth century, Singapore was a small tropical city with high humidity, plenty of marshland and a population of about one million people, mostly of Chinese descent. However, by 1980, the country emerged as one of the new economic powers of East Asia with a per capita GDP of US$6,865 and a population of 2.4 million (see Table 1). In 2005, Singapore had a per capita GDP of US$44,738 (ranked 5th in the 2006–2007 *Global Competitiveness Index*) and a population of 3.54 million. Since the early 1960s, public housing has been developed specifically to advance social and economic development. What are the factors responsible for this dramatic change since Singapore became an independent country in 1965?

Table 1. Key macroeconomic indicators on Singapore 1960–2005

	1960	1970	1980	1990	1999	2001	2003	2004	2005
Population (thousands)	1646	2075	2414	3016	3894	3325	3438	3484	3544
GDP (at 2000 price)	6710.8	16057.5	37631.7	76996.4	145229.8	156006.3	167549.3	182301.1	194371.3
GDP growth rate	—	13.7	9.7	9.2	7.2	−2.4	3.1	8.8	6.6
GDP per capita	1306	2789	10405	21915	35371	37014	38434	42833	44738
Gross fixed capital formation (at 1990 price)	—	6.9bn	19.2bn	32.7bn	68.5bn	—	40.3bn (2000 price)	44.4 (2000 price)bn	44.4bn (2000 price)
Inflation rate	0.3	0.4	8.5	3.4	0.4	1.0	0.5	1.7	0.5
Total labour (thousands)	471.9	650.9	1115.3	1537.0	1911.6	2330.5	2312.3	2341.9	2594.1
Unemployment rate	—	—	—	—	2.8	2.7	4.0	3.4	3.1
Annual growth in ext trade %	—	—	—	12.4	6.2	−7.3	20.5	21.0	9.4
Govt. debts	—	—	—	51.4bn	125.8bn	148.9bn	169.3bn	186.6bn	200.0bn

Note: Values here are in Singapore dollars millions (S$mn) and billions (bn).

Source: Author's computations based on statistics Singapore (various years). http://www.singstat.gov.sg/papers/economy.html#other%20econ

One explanation is that Singapore has the right combination of leadership, vision, development strategy and high quality labour. Henry Kissinger emphasized the role of leadership. In the Foreword to Lee Kuan Yew's memoir *From Third World to First*, he states 'As the main British naval base in the Far East, Singapore had neither the prospect nor aspiration for nationhood ... but history shows that normally prudent, ordinary calculations can be overturned by extraordinary personalities' (Lee, 2000, p. x). However, despite its importance, leadership is only one factor and vision and strategy, or more accurately, the institutional arrangements that combine them need to be considered.

For Singapore, the beginning of one such institution was purely accidental. When introduced by the British colonial government in the 1950s, the social security retirement system was never meant to be run as it is today. The Central Provident Fund (CPF) began as a self-funding savings scheme or a save-as-you-earn (SAYE) system rather than a pay-as-you-go (PAYG) system. The self-funding model was similar to provident funds created by the British for their colonies for good political reasons. This model ensured that British funds would not be drained to meet the colony's social security needs. The Singaporean provident fund turned out to be a valuable bequest when the People's Action Party (PAP) government took over in 1965. From the beginning, the CPF scheme was designed to provide retirement pensions. Despite pressures from workers who wanted to be able to withdraw their savings should they fall ill or become unemployed, the government stood firm insisting that savings could only be withdrawn upon retirement. However, the rule was subsequently liberalized in the late 1960s when a home ownership scheme was introduced to allow people to finance the purchase of public housing with their CPF savings.

Since then, the provident fund has been slowly adapting to the changing needs of an increasingly affluent population. Singaporeans can now use their provident fund accumulations for various purposes, including retirement, health care, meeting the costs of higher education and even investments. However, the most salient features of the scheme have remained intact since its creation in 1955. It is compulsory for all employees and is non-redistributive. The Central Provident Fund has three separate accounts. First, the Ordinary Account, which is used for retirement, buying a home, buying insurance, investment and education. Second, the Medisave Account, which can be used to pay hospital bills and approved medical insurance; and third, the Special Account, which is reserved for old-age contingencies.

It can be seen from Table 2 that the employers' contribution had stabilized at 13 per cent since 2003, but recently it was increased to 14.5 per cent. In July 2007, the total contribution rate was 34.5 per cent, with

Table 2. CPF contribution rate (per cent)

Year	Employer	Employee	Medisave	Total
1955	5	5	—	10
1968	6.5	6.5	—	13
1970	8	8	—	16
1972	14	10	—	24
1973	15	11	—	26
1974	15	15	—	30
1977	15.5	15.5	—	31
1978	16.5	16.5	—	33
1979	20.5	16.5	—	37
1982	22	23	—	45
1984	25	25	6	50
1985	25	25	6	50
1986	10	25	6	35
1989	15	23	6	38
1992	18	22	6	40
1995	20	20	6	40
1997	20	20	6	40
1999	10	20	6	30
2000	14	20	8	34
2002	16	20	6–8.5	36
2003	13	20	6–8.5	33
2004	13	20	6–8.5	33
2005	13	20	6–8.5	33
2006	13	20	6–8.5	33

Source: Author's computations based on Singapore Annual Reports various years and Singapore CPF Annual Report various years.

14.5 per cent coming from the employer and 20 per cent from the employee.[1] The recent increase of 1.5 per cent in the employers' contribution represents a favourable assessment of the country's future economic performance and is seen as an afforded contribution designed to protect workers' future. The percentage contribution rate also changes with age. Elderly people contribute only 12.5 per cent after the age of 55 years and 7 per cent after 60 years regardless of their income level. Monthly contributions (in Singapore dollars) are subject to a maximum of $600 for the employer and $1,200 for the employee, based on a salary ceiling of $6,000 a month. Although contributions to the Ordinary Account are not mandatory for the self-employed, many do contribute in order to enjoy the tax break and the benefit of setting aside funds for old age. However, self-employed people are required to contribute 6 per cent of their annual net trade income to their Medisave Accounts on a monthly basis.

Each member's savings account earns a market-linked interest rate, which is based on the 12-month fixed deposit and month-end savings rates of four major local banks. The rate is revised every three months. The programme guarantees members a minimum interest rate of 2.5 per cent. Savings in the Ordinary and Special Accounts earn an additional 1.5 per cent above the normal rate of interest, because they are used for retirement and longer-term savings purposes. Earned interest is tax free.

It is of course possible to challenge the fundamental organizing philosophy of the Central Provident Fund and conclude that Singapore is merely operating a large paternalistic saving bank with rules and restrictions on withdrawal and consumption, and that it is nothing like a traditional social security scheme that embodies the advantages of pooled risk and social justice. From the perspective of neoliberal economics, it might even be argued that the Singaporean arrangement is detrimental to the general welfare of the population, because consumption is orchestrated by the state and hence thwarts individual choice and self-determination in the disposition of wealth. However, these questions need to be answered on the basis of empirical evidence and, in this regard, several economic

---

[1] http://mycpf.cpf.gov.sg/Members/Gen-Info/Con-Rates/ContriRa.htm, 19/06/2007

studies by economists provide some useful insights which are discussed in the next section.

Social security and economic development in Singapore

For many economists, grappling with the relationship between social security and economic development has been a difficult one. Social security has been a major component of Western welfare states since Chancellor Bismarck launched the first state-run social insurance programme in Germany in the late nineteenth century. However, the question of whether social security is compatible with economic growth only emerged in the past three decades when the global economy became more volatile and inter-connected. Is social security expenditure harmful to economic growth? How compatible are social security expenditures and economic development? In the early 1960s, very few economists were interested in the compatibility issue conceptually or theoretically. Full employment, rising real wages and state pensions, augmented by adequate child benefit, were assumed to be able to eliminate poverty. Social security was regarded as a technical topic best left largely to those specializing in social policy. Since then, the situation has changed as welfare state performance has been extensively studied by economists. Research on unemployment insurance, invalidity benefits, the funding of pensions and other economic aspects of social security have been studied by both macroeconomists and microeconomists and many are quite divided over the issue of whether social and economic policy are compatible.

Martin Feldstein (1974, 1976) was one of the earliest opponents of the incompatibility thesis. He examined two types of social security spending — retirement pensions and unemployment insurance — and concluded that both had adverse effects on economic development. He argued that the 'social security programme in United States consumed approximately half of the personal savings, implying that it substantially reduced the stock of capital and the level of national income' (Feldstein, 1974, p. 22). He also suggested that 'unemployment insurance encourages temporary layoffs and that a reform of it could substantially lower the permanent rate of unemployment' (Feldstein 1976, p. 956). In his more recent work, Feldstein (2005) claimed that many social security programmes appear to be redistributive but that, in fact, most social security benefits go to middle- and higher-income households.

While Feldstein focused on the non-saving effects of social security, other economists focused on the problems of the pay-as-you-go social security system. Ehrlick and Zhong (1998) suggested that social security would soon face financial collapse as a result of a slow down in labour productivity and a continuously aging population. Thus, the general disposition of contemporary debates on social security is towards privatization and the individualization of social security accounts. However, one of the weaknesses of the incompatibility approach is that most studies are based on regression analyses, meaning that cultural and institutional variables are either assumed to be constant or are otherwise taken for granted. Accordingly, findings based on time series data run the danger of yielding relatively static and crude results.

Proponents of the incompatibility thesis make varied arguments. While some are clear that there is a trade off between economic growth and social welfare, others tend to suggest that the problem is really associated with the suitability or workability of institutional arrangements and of integrating seemingly unrelated policy domains. On the other hand, some economists believe that there is no fundamental contradiction between social security and economic development. In the words of a pro-compatibility economist, Anthony Atkinson (1999, p. 4), 'it is now widely realized that social and economic policy are inextricably intertwined. It makes no sense to discuss economic and social policy in isolation. To a considerable extent, the present problems of the welfare state are the result of economic failures.' Even anti-compatibility economist like Martin Feldstein agrees that there are two legitimate economic reasons for providing social insurance: the first is the presence of asymmetric information that weakens the functioning of private insurance, and hence explaining why the state needs to assume some responsibility of provisions; and the second is 'the inability of the government to distinguish between those who are poor in old age because of bad luck or a lack of foresight from those who are intentionally "gaming" the system by not saving' (Feldstein, 2005, p. 7).

A gap in social policy analysis: Social investment and social development

Outside the realm of economics, social policy analysts are also interested in studying the impact of social security expenditures on the economy. Primarily, their focus has been on its structure, coverage, strategies and methods of financing (Dixon, 1999). They assume that social security expenditure is essentially concerned with consumption and that its investment effect is negligible. Midgley (1994, 1995, 1997, 1999) was one of the first to suggest that social expenditures could and should be viewed as part of society's investment portfolio and should not, therefore, be considered as consumption. He believed that the neglect of the investment impact of social expenditures is partly the result of a strong ethical tradition in British social policy in the post-Second World War era when the welfare state was premised on the ideal that the government should distribute welfare resources collectively irrespective of its impact on economic development. Nonetheless, this does not mean that the main proponents of redistributive social policy were dismissive of social policy's impact on the broader economy. For example, Richard Titmuss's (1962) study of British income redistribution statistics insisted that the social, political and economic dimensions were interrelated.

The study of social policy took a turn in the 1970s when the oil crisis triggered a sea change in the world economy From a post-war social consensus about welfare expansion, social policy development was hijacked by economic recessions and took on a different trajectory. Stability began to evaporate in the 1970s and 1980s as governments sought to rationalize welfare through privatization. Market liberalism and neoconservative political practices soon became important aspects of government action. Towards the end of the twentieth century, Western scholars had shifted their focus from the study of welfare-state expansion to analyzing its regress. The study of European welfare-state retrenchment has now become a growth industry (Korpi, 2003).

Almost parallel with this development, was a strand of social policy studies that sought to review the role of social investment in social policymaking. The idea that social expenditures, when properly integrated with the economy, bring positive impact to growth slowly gathered momentum in the 1990s. Social expenditures here refer to a broad spectrum of social policies, including public housing, education and health. How various social policy domains interact with each other, and how they collectively affect macroeconomic development thus forms new focus of policy studies. Originating in the field of development studies in the 1960s and the 1970s, social investment was seen as a concerted effort by the governments of the developing countries to concentrate limited human and capital resources on economic development. Midgley's work, which was mentioned earlier, highlights 'the need to integrate economic and social policy because social expenditures in the form of social investment do not detract from but contribute positively to economic development' (Midgley and Tang, 2001, p. 246). From this perspective, social development is selective rather than universal, inclusive rather than exclusive in that it emphasizes social interventions that transcend remedial and maintenance-oriented approaches by implementing programmes that draw previously marginalized people into the mainstream of the economy. 'In a strict sense, social development cannot take place without economic development and economic development is meaningless if it fails to bring about significant improvements in the well-being of the population as a whole' (Midgley, 1997, p. 181).

The developmental approach in social welfare thus challenges the basic neoliberal argument that social programmes are harmful to growth. In addition, the United Nation Research Institute for Social Development (UNRISD) has also revived in recent years its interest in the contribution of social policy to economic and social development. In a recent paper, Mkandawire (2001), Director of UNRISD, argues that social policies can be used to enhance social capacities for economic development. In addition, there is also a revival of interest in growth economics and the emergence of the so-called 'new growth theories' which recognize that social development contains crucial instruments for economic development. These ideas will be explored with reference to Singapore and, particularly, its housing and social security policies.

First-level integration: Integrating housing and social security

Singapore's public housing programme was launched in the 1960s, and it has now grown to become one of the largest of its kind in the world today. Many Western observers believe that the Singapore's achievement in the field of housing has been spectacular, but others have questioned the desirability and sustainability of such high level of state involvement (Chua, 2003; Yeung, 2003). In Singapore, public housing generally refers to the dominant state-subsidized home ownership sector. The state produces and distributes 86 per cent of the housing stock mainly in the form of for-sale residential flats, perhaps the largest share by any modern government. It provides one of the most sophisticated housing ladders in East Asia in terms of housing choice and quality. The Singapore housing system has effectively achieved a monopolistic position, to the extent that private housing constitutes only a very small percentage of the housing market (10 per cent), largely confined to top-end housing for the very rich. Singaporeans have two lifetime opportunities to purchase government-built flats, and this right is confined to nationals only. In the early 1980s, people nearing retirement capitalized on house-price inflation and used their gains to buy in the private housing market, thus fuelling speculative activities, something that former Prime Minister Lee Kuan Yew (2000) regretted in his memoir. He noted that as property prices rose, everybody wanted to make a profit on the sale of their homes and then upgrade to the biggest home they could afford. Instead of the government choking off demand by charging a levy to reduce windfall profits, it accommodated the citizenry by increasing the availability of new homes. Unfortunately, this decision aggravated the real estate bubble and made it more painful when the currency crisis struck in 1997.

However, from a broader perspective, a second chance to purchase a government flat stimulates the development of an active resale market, thus providing much needed impetus to the economy. This was achieved by fusing two ingenuous institutions: namely, the Housing Development Board (HDB) and the Central Provident Fund (CPF). The HDB, which commenced the public home ownership programme in 1964, has since become one of the largest public developers in the world. The board was already in place prior to independence. The provident fund was initiated during the colonial period in 1955, and it aimed to provide some form of retirement benefits but incurring little financial risks for the government. In the beginning, the contribution rate was kept at a low 5 per cent for workers and a matching 5 per cent from employers. However, in 1984 the contribution rate reached its peak of 25 per cent totalling 50 per cent of the payroll. The rate has since gone down and has stabilized at 13 per cent for employers and 20 per cent for employees (Table 2). However, for new residents to Singapore, the contribution rate is maintained at 5 per cent for the first two years' of residence to allow them to adjust to the job market. Originally, the major part of the accumulated savings could only be withdrawn at the age of 55 for retirement purposes. In 1968–1981, however, provident fund rules were modified to allow savings to be withdrawn earlier for a down payment on a home, stamp duties and other related costs.

At first, Singaporeans did not show much enthusiasm for home ownership. This was largely because few could afford to purchase private homes. However, when the government changed the legislation in 1968 to allow members to use their provident fund savings as a downpayment for housing, the sales of Housing Board flats increased significantly. In 1981, the rules were further relaxed to allow withdrawals to be used to finance mortgage repayment for private housing. As was mentioned earlier, the rules for the use of CPF savings have since been augmented further to allow for the creation of healthcare (Medisave) and education (Edusave) accounts. The diversification of the use of CPF savings is intended not only to reduce reliance on the state to meet old-age retirement and healthcare needs but also to boost investment. From Table 2, it can be seen that the rate of contribution has been used as a leverage mechanism to regulate investment and consumption. From 1997 to 1999, the contribution rate was cut from 40 per cent to 30 per cent, largely to boost consumption after the East Asian financial crisis. Using Keynesian ideas, the government's policy reflects the view that economic contraction requires a boost in consumption and that savings should not be encouraged.

In operational terms, the government provides development loans and annual grants to finance the Housing Development Board. This funding comes largely from the Central Provident Fund. This takes the form of government bonds at a fixed interest rate, thus explaining why Singapore has debt servicing even during a time of positive economic growth (see Table 1). The circuit of capital is completed by the Central Provident Fund providing loan repayments to the Housing Development Board on behalf of public housing buyers. The essence of this phase of the circuit of capital is the integration of the individual saving function with the collective housing investment function, thus enabling the possibility of mass mobilization in effective consumption which is an essential condition for growth. Housing here fulfilled two important roles: the mass satisfaction of both spatial needs and investment needs (DisPasquale and Wheaton, 1996). The Housing Development Board mortgage interest rate is pegged at 0.1 per cent above the Central Provident Fund interest rate, which is generally about 2 per cent below the market mortgage interest rate provided by commercial banks. The advantage of the first circuit is that it overcomes the problem of market failure in terms of low-income housing finance which is encountered by most countries.

Second-level integration: Capital formation and growth

The second circuit of capital concerns a more complex interaction of the housing sector with the wider economy. However, what is demonstrated here is at best a partial view of the effects of housing investment in the second circuit of capital. First, housing investment forms an important part of fixed capital formation. For the period 1976–1997, an average of 9 per cent of Singapore's GDP was devoted to housing construction each year, while comparative figures for the United States and the United Kingdom were less than 4 per cent (Phang, 2001). In 1965–1998, the construction sector grew at a rate of 9.4 per cent, exceeding the average GDP growth of 8.8 per cent. Of the roughly one million housing units that were built, 82 per cent are attributable to public sector developers. The domination of public housing construction means that government housing policy has a direct impact on the creation of employment for construction workers and hence its direct effects on income and social well-being. According to the Economic Survey of Singapore 2006 (MTI, 2007), the construction sector continued to grow by 4.7 per cent in the final quarter of 2006, slightly lower than the 5.8 per cent rate of growth in the previous quarter. Although the construction sector suffered during the 1999–2004 period as a result of the East Asian financial crisis, it has rebounded in the past two years as a result of the continued recovery of the Singapore economy.

Second, the link between housing and social security also has a direct effect on the development of the housing loan market. For a long time, the Housing Development Board did not only provide concessionary housing interest rates for eligible Singapore citizens but also provided 'market rate' loans to those who were not eligible for low interest loans, thus playing the role of a commercial bank. During the peak of the Board's mortgage business, it took up 66 per cent of the market share (Phang, 2001, p. 451). Including the 10 per cent market share of the then Post Office Savings Bank — Credit POSB, the government practically monopolized three quarters of the mortgage market since 1986. It should be noted that the bank is a subsidiary of the Development Bank of Singapore (DBS).

The extension of Central Provident Fund for private housing finance has also led to rapid growth of housing loans from commercial banks. These increased from 6 per cent in 1975 to 37 per cent in 1995. As was mentioned earlier, the Post Office Saving Bank — Credit POSB, has also played a major role in providing housing loans. Other commercial banks have also participated in granting loans to buyers of public housing flats.

The involvement of commercial lenders has been on the increase since the turn of the new century as the government progressively shifts to a policy of liberalization in equity markets. In 2003, the government decided that the Housing Development Board should stop providing market rate loans, and housing loans should more appropriately be provided by commercial banks. In the words of Mr Mah Bow Tan, Minister for National Development, 'with such change, now the HDB can better fulfil its core responsibility, which is to provide basic affordable housing to the majority of Singaporeans. As a general rule, HDB should consider allowing the private sector to take over those functions which extend beyond its core responsibility' (Mah, 2005). However, this move by the government only serves to confirm and expand the role of the housing sector in the development of the country's financial market. This is why I have coined the phrase, second circuit of capital, which seeks to integrate the Central Provident Fund and the Housing Development Board system with larger economy. Through the Central Provident Fund's loan payments on behalf of buyers, financial institutions and commercial banks are able to strengthen their credit portfolio and, in turn, provide loans to private housing buyers. At the same time, private developers also benefit indirectly from the increased credit facilities provided by commercial banks. Given the intimate relationship between the Central Provident Fund and the financial sector, any interest rate change or contribution rate change would have an impact on the stability of the mortgage market. In other words, the government is perfectly capable of using policy instruments to either stabilize or destabilize the financial market. This, to some extent, explains why housing prices in Singapore are always comparatively more stable when compared to other Asian housing markets such as that of Hong Kong or Taiwan.

Issues and challenges

The two levels of economic integration described above assume that the economic environment is relative stable. However, once economic fluctuations are taken into account, the CPF and HDB configuration will be subject to dynamic challenges which require policy intervention. For example, since 2003, in order to boost a rather lacklustre property sector, the HDB has extended credit to low-income families and it has also capped the mortgage loan ceiling at 90 per cent. Second, also starting from 2003, owners of HDB flats who have occupied them for 15 years or more were permitted to sublet their flats irrespective of whether the flats were bought directly from the HDB or from the resale market. The objective of this policy is to provide homeowners greater flexibility to monetize their asset and to provide income for their retirement.[2] Homeowners in financial difficulty will then be able to generate some income from their flats to meet their retirement needs.

This policy will also stimulate the private rental market and provide more affordable housing to those who are unable to purchase a home.

---

[2] HDB Website: http://www.hdb.gov.sg/fil0/fil0296p.nsf/PressReleases/373FB45C96555B 1F4825708300208BFl?OpenDocument, 21/6/2007

Third, by relaxing the closed HDB and CPF housing finance circuit, it is anticipated that more commercial lenders will be engaged in home financing in the long run. This development will eventually change the HDB's role both as the builder and financer of public housing. All these policy adaptations suggest that the Singaporean model is not aiming to establish a static equilibrium but one that is dynamic and flexible. The integration of social policy and economic policy requires dynamic adaptations. Institutional arrangements must be able to adjust to suit a continuously changing socio-political situation.

Another challenge for public housing is its role in the *social integration* of the country's various ethnic groups, namely the Chinese, Malay, Indian and Eurasian people. Obviously, attempts at economic and social policy integration would fail if the country is faced with frequent disintegrating ethic conflicts. The government recognizes that social integration is a precondition for economic and social prosperity. Singapore's housing policy enhances social integration by requiring that different ethnic groups live and interact with one another. This policy also aims at integrating different income groups. However, the government also recognizes that it is insufficient to just require different ethnic groups to live in physical proximity to one another. Accordingly, education and various community programmes have been organized so that different ethnic groups interact in many different settings and learn to appreciate cultural diversity. Efforts to prevent racial discrimination through legislative prohibitions have also been introduced. The government takes pride in asserting that Singapore is a multiracial society, and its future development is dependent on the maintenance of racial harmony and social cohesion. All of these measures prevent social fractures that impede economic development.

It has been argued that CPF is useful as an asset building mechanism, but when so much of the individual's resources have been invested in housing, the danger is that Singaporeans will have less cash at their disposal during old age. Singaporeans have become 'asset rich, but cash poor'. To improve this situation, the government now promotes what is known as the step down replacement scheme or a reverse mortgage scheme that allows citizens to realize their asset value during old age. Stored housing wealth with stable appreciation can produce a life-long income stream and hence a reduction of dependency on state elderly welfare. However, the greatest worry of the Singaporean government is another international financial crisis. If the state fails to sustain a stable level of house prices and a steady rate of growth, the present social equilibrium would be seriously disrupted. Although the government is able to manage internal disturbances such as fluctuations in demand and supply through its control of the market and other economic policies, the greatest challenge lies in exogenous economic factors which are beyond its control.

In a globalizing world, no country can be totally independent of the effects of international economic disturbances. However, since the Singaporean system promotes integration and consensus, it is capable of absorbing economic vibrations through wage-cuts, labour market adjustments and careful monitoring of the CPF contribution rates during economic crisis. The tripartite relationship forged among the state, entrepreneurs and labour has made it possible to reach a consensus in formulating and implementing policies that achieve both economic and social development objectives.

Singapore is an interesting but unique case of East Asian developmentalism. Unlike the other East Asian tiger economies, it uniquely integrates housing and social security and, as was shown earlier, the integration of economic and social policy is seen through the two levels of capital circuits operating under conditions of dynamic equilibrium, with policy adaptations being made over a sufficiently long time scale. However, no attempt will be made here to generalize the Singaporean example and to ask whether it is one that other countries can emulate. The question of whether certain institutional arrangements might work on other societies is not only dependent on the integration process but also on cultural, political and other forces. People not familiar with Singapore are often amazed at the efficiency and effectiveness of government and the level of consensus which few other regimes enjoy in terms of policy formulation and implementation. But, obviously, there are unique political, social and cultural forces at work. In terms of bureaucratic capacity, the government of Singapore has been able to mobilize political support, foster national cohesiveness in the face of ethnic diversity and promote bureaucratic efficiency. It has also been able to exercise a laboratory like level of control. This has permitted it to experiment with public policy changes. Another aspect is the fact that Singapore is small by international standards. This makes governance much easier, and it also permits the government to mobilize the population and exercise social control. Obviously, the levels of integration discussed earlier are facilitated by size of the economy and by state effectiveness and must be understood within this context.

Nevertheless, three generalizations can be drawn from the Singaporean case. First, the integration of economic and social policy is possible when governance creates favourable institutional arrangements. This requires dynamic and creative leadership and, as such, the role of state matters a great deal if developmentalist goals are to be achieved. Second, social security configuration must move beyond its traditionally narrow focus to link with other social policy domains if it is to promote economic development. The inter-sector integration of social policies and programmes is thus a new and vital area for policy development and also for social policy research, particularly in the development context. Third, developmentalism in Singapore has been transformed in the past three decades from one which was based on a highly state-subsidized system to one promoting a tripartite system with some similarities to the European corporatist model requiring worker organizations such as the unions, the employers and the state to coordinate for optimal social provisions. The question here is whether the success of the Singaporean system points to the possibility of a global trend in social policymaking based on integration and corporatism as opposed to one based on fragmentation and liberalism which has characterized much of the social security policy so far.

Bibliography

Atkinson, A. B. (1999). *The Economic Consequences of Rolling Back the Welfare State.* Cambridge, MA: MIT Press.

Chua, B. H. (1997). *Political Legitimacy and Housing: Stakeholding in Singapore.* London: Routledge.

Chua, B. H. (2003). 'Maintaining Housing Values under Conditions of Universal Home Ownership', *Housing Studies*, 18(5), 765–780.

CPF Story (2006). Central Provident Board: Singapore.

DisPasquale, D. and Wheaton, W. (1996). *Urban Economics and Real Estate Markets.* New York: Prentice Hall.

Dixon, J. (1999). *Social Security in Global Perspective*. Westport, CT: Praeger.

Doling, J. (1997). *Comparative Housing Policy*. London: Macmillan.

Elrlick, I. and Zhong, J.G. (1998). 'Social Security and the Real Economy: An Inquiry into Some Neglected Issues', *AEA Papers and Proceedings*, May 1998, 151–158.

Evans, P. (1995). *Embedded Autonomy: States and Industrial transformation*. Princeton, NJ: Princeton University Press.

Evans, P. (2006). 'What Will the 21st Century Developmental State Look Like? Implications of Contemporary Developmental Theory for the State's Role', Paper presented at the Conference on *The Changing Role of the Government in Hong Kong*, Department of Sociology, Chinese University of Hong Kong.

Feldstein, M. B. (1974). 'Social Security, Induced Retirement and Aggregate Capital Accumulation', *Journal of Political Economy* 83(4), 447–475.

Feldstein, M. B. (1976). 'Temporary Layoff in the Theory of Unemployment', *Journal of Political Economy*, 84(5), 937–957.

Feldstein, M. B. (2005). 'Rethinking Social Insurance', *American Economic Review*, 95(1), 1–24.

Johnson, C. (1982). *MITI and the Japanese Miracle: The Growth of Industrial Policy* (1925–1975). Stanford: Stanford University Press.

Korpi, W. (2003). 'Welfare State Regress in Western Europe: Politics, Institutions, Globalization and Europeanization', *Annual Review of Sociology*, 29(4), 589–609.

Lee Kuan Yew (2000). *From Third World to First: The Singapore Story, 1965–2000*. New York: Harper and Collins.

Low, L. and Aw, T. C. (1997). *Housing a Healthy, Educated and Wealthy Nation Through the CPF*. Singapore: Institute of Policy Studies.

Mah (2005). Speech by Minister of National Development Mr. Mah Bow Tan at the Ministry of Manpower on 19 July 2005. Available from website http://www.mom.gov.sg/publish/momportal/en/press_room/mom_speeches/2005/20050719-speechbymrmahbowtanministerfornationaldevelopment-minist.html, on 27 December 2007.

Midgley, J. (1994). Defining Social Development; historical trends and conceptual formulations, *Social Development Issues*, 16(3), 3–19.

Midgley, J. (1995). *Social Development: The Developmental Perspective in Social Welfare*. London: Sage.

Midgley, J. (1997). *Social Welfare in Global Context*. London: Sage.

Midgley, J. (1999). 'Growth, Redistribution and Welfare: Towards Social Investment', *Social Service Review*, 77(1), 3–21.

Midgley, J. and Tang, K. L. (2001). 'Social Policy, Economic Growth and Developmental Welfare', *International Journal of Social Welfare*, 10(4), 244–252.

Mkandawire, T. (2001). Social Policy in a Development Context. Social Policy and Development Paper No. 7, June 2001.

MTI (2007). *Economic Survey of Singapore 2006.* Singapore: Ministry of Trade and Industries. Available from website: http://app.mti.gov.sg/data/article/7062/ doc/ESS_2006Ann_FullReport.pdf

Phang, S. Y. (2001). 'Housing Policy, Wealth Formation and the Singapore Economy', *Housing Studies,* 16(4), 443–459.

Quigley, J. (2001). 'Real Estate and the Asian Crisis', 10(2), 129–161.

Titmuss, R. M. (1962). *Income Distribution and Social Change.* London: Allen & Unwin.

Vasoo, S. and Lee, J. (2001). 'Singapore: Social Development, Housing and the Central Provident Fund', *International Journal of Social Welfare*, 10(4), 276–283.

Vasoo, S. and Lee, J. (2006). 'Promoting Social Development Through Integration of the Central Provident Fund and Public Housing Schemes in Singapore', *Social Development Issues*, 28(2), 71–83.

Wade, R. (1990). *Governing the Market: Economic Theory and the Role of the Government in East Asian Industrialization.* Princeton, NJ: Princeton University Press.

Yeung, H. (2003). 'Managing Economic (In)security in Global Economy: Institutional Capacity and Singapore's Development State', http://course.nus.edu.sg/course/geoywc/henryht. Accessed 17 February, 2007.

Chapter 30

Investments for social sector to tackle some key social issues*

S. Vasoo[†]

Introduction

By the next Singapore 100 (SG100), there will be some key emerging social issues which will need special attention and require new social innovative approaches for human capital development. More future social investments in terms of fund allocation, deployment of better qualified and committed social service personnel, improved facilities, enlarging volunteer base, value adding social policies and outreach service delivery can be deployed earlier to the social sectors to act as social antibodies to build the resilience of vulnerable working-class families who may slip down the ladder to achieve their human potential. We can no longer label the deployment of social and financial resources as welfarist because the focus will be on development of socioeconomic and psychological

---

*Reprinted with permission by the publisher from Vasoo, S. (2018). Investments for Social Sector to Tackle Some Key Social Issues. In S. Vasoo & B. Singh (Eds.), *Critical Issues in Asset Building in Singapore's Development* (pp. 21–35). Singapore: World Scientific.

The article discusses some key emerging social issues requiring special attention and highlights that the social investment efforts to tackle these issues should encourage self-help and influence people to take ownership of the various initiatives delivered in the neighbourhoods in partnership with a number of groups. Much of the issues raised are a collation of ideas surfaced in earlier analyses.

[†]Associate Professorial Fellow, Department of Social Work, NUS.

potential of working-class families with children and other vulnerable groups who face difficulty to cope with increasing cost escalation in meeting the demands to cope with their livelihood. This working-class sector of the Singapore population is not small and comprises of the 1st to the 50th decile household groups who are motivated to improve but face constraints beyond their social control to better their lives which in turn do have impact on their children's future. To simply put it, they are people who are employed but these individuals do not earn sufficient wages to help them tide over a sustainable period of time. Similarly, these households find it tough to enable their children to acquire relevant skills to prepare them to be productive and be future ready for a more competitive global economy. The average monthly income of these household groups is between S$494 and S$2,155[1] and most of them live in one- to three-room public flats. These affected families are more likely to face marginal growth in income because of new disruptive economies and the effects of increasing competitive wages from emerging economies in the region. The workers in the labour-intensive and manufacturing sectors and the older middle-level management, professional and technical employees are likely to face economic and social setbacks.

The inability to be versatile in analysing the emerging social issues and the outcome of the service delivery in the social sectors can prevent social policy makers to acquire better insight to anticipate social issues for effective management of social problems, resources and services.[2] Social analytics skills will be required if administrators can play a meaningful role in community problem solving in the coming years. At this juncture, there are lots of information available from the private, non-governmental and governmental sectors but these are kept under close private purview and not shared or coordinated. There is a wealth of information in the private and public archives that could be shared for more effective community problem solving. Unless there is a cooperative spirit of sharing of data for finding better solutions to deal with new social and economic

---

[1] Department of Statistics Singapore, *Yearbook of statistics* (Singapore: The Author, 2015).
[2] S Vasoo, "New directions of community development in Singapore", in Ngoh Tiong Tan and Kalyani Mehta (eds.), *Extending frontiers: Social issues and social work in Singapore* (pp. 20–36) (Singapore: Eastern University Press, 2002).

challenges, we will be no better in the long run as the data gather dust and the societal issues are less innovatively dealt with. With the saying "old wines in new bottles", the approach and solution will be more or less the same.

Social challenges and social investments

There are some major social issues that policy makers must keep a keen eye on and these require the employment of social analytics to appreciate how social issues will surface and their impacts on the socioeconomic and political landscape of Singapore. In having a good grasp on the emerging social issues, policy makers will then be able to plan realistic and realisable social programmes to tackle them. Attempts will be made in this paper to touch on some major issues that are likely to emerge. The case for further social investments to act as social antibodies in the context of Singapore is advocated to build and strengthen the social capital of those vulnerable families living in 292,344 units of one- to three-room public housing flats. This accounts for about 30.2% of the total number of 968,856 flats of various room types allocated to families in the various Housing and Development Board (HDB) estates.[3] The People's Action Party (PAP) government having decently housed almost about 82% of Singapore's population[4] to live in good public housing which is a landmark international record, must get HDB to re-examine its role of not just dwelling only on estate management,[5] but also place more emphasis on its role in social management by initiating the setting up of a social management unit in each HDB Branch to identify at the frontline vulnerable families for follow-up support in concert with Family Service Centres (FSCs) and other community and social service organisations. The challenge will be for HDB to find how it can also deal with the emerging social issues facing the major bulk of vulnerable families living in the HDB heartland. Identifying the factors that make vulnerable

---

[3] Housing and Development Board, *HDB Annual Report 2014/15* (Singapore, 2015).
[4] Housing and Development Board, *HDB Annual Report 2014/15*.
[5] Beng Huat Chua, "Navigating between limits: The future of public housing in Singapore", *Housing Studies*, 29(4), pp. 520–533, 2014.

families fall through the social crack will be useful for various social and community organisations to strengthen the capacity of vulnerable families. Any early intervention efforts such as education, finance, accessibility to social services, employability, health enhancement and skills development, can help towards levelling up these families and prevent serious social and economic divisions in Singapore society.[6]

Meeting issues facing working class families and implications

During the last decade, Singapore society is seeing a widening income gap and there is a sector of new poor being trapped in low wage due to depressed salaries arising from imported cheap labour and low skills.[7] This sector of the population requires closer attention because the children of these families are likely to be disadvantaged as they will not be able to acquire the numeracy and literacy levels required to start them off in primary schooling. This is because parents do not have the educational capacity to prepare their children who are normal but not educationally ready in numeracy and literacy to level up with their counterparts whose parents are more educated or schooled. These new poor families have both family and social difficulties which unless addressed early can lead to various social breakdowns. Here, the FSCs can work in concert with various community groups with the support of the Ministry of Education (MOE) and Ministry of Social and Family Development (MSF) to initiate early social and educational intervention programmes such as family mentoring, counseling, family life education, educational head start, care networks, income supplement projects and early reading. When more children in the low-income families are reached out to benefit from early supportive education and literacy programs, they will

---

[6] Kwong Ping Ho, "Towards a more equal, self-reliant society", in Soon Hock Kang and Chan-Hoong Leong (eds.), *Singapore perspectives 2012: Singapore inclusive: Bridging divides* (pp. 101–107) (Singapore: World Scientific Publishing, 2012).

[7] Irene Y.H. Ng, "Multi-stressed low-earning families in contemporary policy context: Lessons from Work Support recipients in Singapore", *Journal of Poverty, 17*(1), pp. 86–109, 2013.

be better prepared for schooling to develop their potential. The community and policy makers can assist by allocating more resources to militate against the loss of opportunities to enable many low-income children who otherwise may become ill-equipped to benefit from education and skills training opportunities. In the longer term, the social divide can be further widened when more of low-income children fail to acquire the knowledge and skills that can prepare them to earn a livelihood not only in Singapore but also globally. When the social gap widens, the consequences will not be good for the Singapore community as a divided community may be socially unhealthy to Singapore with more frustrated intergenerational younger families.[8]

The Gini coefficient based on per household member after taking into account of government transfers is 0.412.[9] This income gap can widen further in the future when wages get depressed. One of the more serious consequences for not tackling the income divide will be the confounding effects of ethnicity and low income. Therefore, policy makers must be sensitive to moderate the economic market to reduce the widening social divisions in our Singapore society.[10] There must be more visible hand of the government to moderate and implement some effective forms of redistributive justice with an economic heart, particularly in education, healthcare, housing and workfare for lower skilled workers.[11] Unless members of the public feel the impact in their social and economic lives, current policy makers will lose their credence and more contending policy opinion makers will surface to provide other populist options for the working class. As a consequence, there will be more social fractures within the society and these can cause social disruptions and dis-welfare in the community, and worse translating into ethnic tensions and conflicts.

---

[8] Irene Y.H. Ng, "Being poor in a rich 'Nanny State': Developments in Singapore social welfare", in Linda Y.C. Lim (eds.), *Singapore's Economic Development, Retrospection and Reflections* (pp. 279–297) (Singapore: World Scientific Publishing, 2016).
[9] Department of Statistics Singapore, *Yearbook of statistics 2015*.
[10] Nurhidayah Hassan, *Developing an analytical framework on social cohesion in Singapore: Reflections from the framing of social cohesion debates in the OECD and Europe* (Singapore, EU Centre, 2013).
[11] Azad Latif, *Hearts of resilience: Singapore's Community Engagement Programme* (Singapore: Institute of Southeast Asian Studies, 2011).

Social workers and social sector professionals can engage families in the low-income group to participate in early educational start-up programmes which can enable the children to be more numerate and literate. Early start-up programmes targeted at two to four years old at community levels supported by concerted and coordinated efforts of various community self-help groups such as Singapore Indian Development Association (SINDA), Yayasan Mendaki, Chinese Development Assistance Council (CDAC), NTUC My First Skool and PAP Community Foundation (PCF), can help reach out sooner to stimulate their early learning interest. Also, family matched saving projects involving low-income families to become more financially literate and be better motivated to upgrade their skills could be implemented at the local community level as this programme will be more accessible to them. Where needed, group boarding centres in the neighbourhood can be initiated particularly to cater for the young who are prone to parental neglect and care and be made easily accessible to their parents.

Addressing skills training issues

With globalisation, it is envisaged that Singapore like other developed economies, will be confronted with more competition from developing economies with both skilled and unskilled manpower for market share of products and services. This situation will be inevitable and the likelihood is that wages are going to be depressed as the offers by the developing world will be cheaper, efficient and effective. So, to meet such challenging scenario, Singapore has limited options but to take steps to train every young child and person up the higher economic value chain in market products and services such as marine and biological sciences, medicine and pharmacy, chemical and nano-technology, food safety and production, precision and aeronautical engineering, building and housing construction, and environmental and water resource technology. Human service professionals can help organise family life, self-help and community education programmes that will kick start interest among low-income parents to know about community resources and how they can tap them for their betterment. Many more children from low-income households can be helped through such early socio-educational intervention projects to realise their human potential and skills to work in globalised industries and workplaces. A more challenging option will be to start a few boarding schools under enterprise models for children with fractured family life as well as very low-income families. The boarding school environment will be nurturing and supportive for them to learn appropriate social and life skills and families can opt voluntarily to participate in the scheme and have access to their children.

Dealing with the issues of silver tsunami

As anticipated, there will be a beginning of the silver tsunami before 2025, where more families will be afflicted by the burdens in caring for their less mobile elderly parents.[12] This social burden will be more pronounced among dual career and young adult families and more so if they have terminally sick elderly parents. Besides social and economic costs, families may have to find more accessible social and daycare services. Along with this need for supportive care services, families will also face grief and loss of their elderly parents for which social care services to help family members cope with such emotions will be helpful. In response to the social, psychosocial and health consequences facing the greying elderly population,[13] personnel working in health and family service settings can play a role to help promote community care cooperatives and community hospice care services to support families with elderly needing different social care services and support.[14]

The rise in the many elderly needing healthcare and social service support will lead to debates on issues related to end life and the allocation of healthcare resources. Human service professionals will have to face

---

[12] David Chan, John Elliott, Gillian Koh, Lily Kong, Sudha Nair and Ern Ser Tan, et al., "Social capital and development", in Mui Teng Yap and Christopher Gee (eds.), *Population outcomes: Singapore 2050* (Singapore: Institute of Policy Studies, Lee Kuan Yew School of Public Policy, National University of Singapore, 2014).

[13] Lena L. Lim and Ee-Heok Kua, "Living alone, loneliness, and psychological well-being of older persons in Singapore", *Current Gerontology and Geriatrics Research*, 2(1), pp. 33–40, 2011.

[14] Angelique Chan, Chetna Malhotra, Rahul Malhotra and Truls Østbye, "Living arrangements, social networks and depressive symptoms among older men and women in Singapore", *International Journal of Geriatric Psychiatry*, 26(6), pp. 630–639, 2011.

such debates of Singapore society and prepare families with elderly persons to have plans before life ends. This is to ensure that one will have less traumatic troubles in living through the tertiary period of one's life. Therefore, it will be helpful if social agencies involved in elderly care can engage families at appropriate time in making end of life plans for elderly relatives in their frail years. Such preparations are critical as families will be better prepared to deal with issues of death and dying.

Many elderly will have long years to live after their mandatory retirement. In fact, the whole aspect of retirement has to be reviewed as the elderly of tomorrow will have much knowledge and expertise which can still be tapped to contribute socioeconomically to our society and it will be demeaning to let ageism dictate the working shelf life of the seniors. With declining population, retirement issue should deserve a relook and life-long working could be planned.[15] Our society must be graceful in valuing the seniors and find various ways to engage them in productive and meaningful activities.

Issues of out-sourcing to in-sourcing

It is observed that there is an increasing trend by social and community sectors to outsource community activities. Why is the case? In the name of efficiency and the urgency for quick turnover, organisers and providers of services often face time constraints. Therefore most community activities are planned within a short time frame and often tied to the term of office holders. Such an emphasis can make volunteer groups or organisations insular and not development oriented. They then become task- or activity-centred and slowly digress from being people-centred which is aimed at promoting self-help and community ownership of those who are beneficiaries of the community activities and social programmes. As such, many social and community organisations and volunteer groups adopt a less outreaching approach to understand the changing needs of the community. In the longer term, such a move will make them more

---

[15] Mui Teng Yap and Christopher Gee (2015), "Ageing in Singapore: Social issues and policy challenges", in David Chan (ed.), *50 Years of Social Issues in Singapore* (pp. 3–30) (Singapore: World Scientific Publishing, 2015).

detached from keeping in touch with the needs of people who are uninvolved or are vulnerable to social problems.

Encountering issues of centralisation of leadership

The leadership in social and community organisations is greying and more attention should be devoted to encourage and enlist resourceful younger residents to help manage them. Many community organisations have become gerontocratic and can be less responsive to the changing needs of the neighbourhoods. In the making, they can become senior citizen clubs which will only meet one specific group of the resident population, namely the elderly. So far, punctuated attempts have been made to renew the leadership and these are unlikely to rejuvenate community organisations.

It is observed that the rate participation of lower-income households and minorities is not as significant and this could be due to the less tangible benefits offered by the programmes delivered by community groups and organisations. The participation of both minorities and lower-income families are critical in maintaining social cohesion and community bonding. Hence, more concrete services to meet their social and economic needs will address the public goods dilemma as this will reduce their cost for participation. When community organisations do not bear this in mind in their service delivery, both minorities and low-income households will not be motivated to participate in some mainstream community activities.

Another significant development in the older neighbourhoods of Singapore is the hollowing out of the more resourceful and younger residents. When this process accelerates, these neighbourhoods become eventually silver communities. This is also compounded by a higher outflow of the young to the exuberant facilities of other New Towns. It is envisaged that there will be depletion of social and leadership resources and these neighbourhoods are likely to slow down and become less attractive to new residents. Inevitability, social burdens for care will increase unless more community care services and support networks are encouraged through community development efforts.

Enhancing self-help and community ownership

There should be less outsourcing contracts and more in-sourcing activities by mobilising residents to forms not-for-profit organisations or social enterprises. Such attempts will provide more opportunities for residents to participate in decision making so that they can take ownership. Community care groups and support networks can be formed. This will make participants engage in problem solving instead of being passive recipients of services.[16] Community organisations widen the base of participation by residents forming various interest groups or task forces to work on several social issues and projects such as security watch and crime prevention, cooperative care services, improvements to recreational facilities, pollution control, thrift through micro-credit groups, and environmental enhancement causes. It will be useful where possible to encourage residents to take charge in finding more effective ways to deal with local matters and with the support of the Town Councils (TCs) and Community Development Councils (CDCs). This will truly be promoting community development as local residents will learn and find more realistic solutions to solve their specific needs and problems and become accountable for their decisions.

However, with the move towards information technology, people could become impersonal and more homebound, social interactions could be reduced and social bonding could be threatened. Therefore, all the more personalised outreaching efforts have to be complemented with online contacts.

Rejuvenating leadership and organisational renewal

It is also observed that a significant number of grassroots leaders of community organisations in the mature housing estates are about above 50 years old. These organisations face difficulties in recruiting younger residents to take up leadership. With the greying of the organisational

---

[16] Mohamad Maliki Bin Osman, "Social issues in developing a community in Singapore", in David Chan (ed.), *50 years of social issues in Singapore* (pp. 189–203) (Singapore: World Scientific Publishing, 2015).

leadership, there is urgency to rejuvenate the leadership of community organisations by attracting younger professionals to participate them. It is not just sufficient to recruit them but they must be mentored with some committed older leaders. With attachment to specific mentors, they can be anchored to the organisations and this will reduce attrition facing younger persons taking up leadership in organisations dominated by seniors. A rejuvenated leadership will continue to be vibrant and relevant to meet the needs and aspirations of younger generation of residents. We must also attract younger people-centred community leaders who must be given all the support to carry out community problem solving activities. People-centred community leaders are proactive and they should not be piled with so much tasks that they then suffer burnout. More importantly, the young leadership should be given management skills training to understand the needs of residents so that they can help make community organisations responsive to tackling emerging social needs.

Reaching out to lower-income residents and minorities

As Singapore is an increasingly globalised, open economy, it is inevitable the residents with low skills are likely to face depressed wages and this can lead to widening income gap. Singaporeans with better skills are likely to move ahead while those with low skills and less literacy in information technology will fall behind in income. Social stratification based on socioeconomic classes confounded by ethnicity may surface if excessive free market competition is not tempered.[17] As a consequence, social conflicts could emerge and when this is capitalised by political and racial fanatics, our community harmony and cohesion could be fractured. As such, community organisations like CDCs can take preventive measures to deliver community-based self-help programmes such as social and educational assistance, computer training, youth vocational guidance and

---

[17] Paul Cheung, "Income growth and redistribution in Singapore: Issues and challenges", in Soon Hock Kang and Chan-Hoong Leong (eds.), *Singapore perspectives 2012: Singapore inclusive: Bridging divides* (pp. 7–22) (Singapore: World Scientific Publishing, 2012).

counselling programmes, family-life and development activities, and continuing learning programmes to help the socially disadvantaged groups. As a long-term measure for people capability building, it is important to develop more re-skill training schemes.

There appears a re-emergence of ethnic ghettoes in one to two-room neighbourhoods and it must be addressed quickly by providing mixed room housing types (one- to three-room units). These social investment efforts can help to reduce the social frictions between classes and ethnic groups. Fanatics will find less temptation to exploit the race card as the problems facing low-income families appear across all ethnic groups. Hence, the realistic solution is to help level up the capabilities of all disadvantaged families despite their ethnicity.

Singapore is indeed a multiracial society comprising of Chinese (77.7%), Malays (14.1%), Indians (7.9%) and others (1.4%). It is crucial that various efforts both at the social policy and community activity levels, are consciously implemented to generate better racial understanding and where necessary to encourage multiracial involvement of residents and community leaders. To strengthen Singapore's social landscape, it is desirable to encourage multi-ethnic participation in social and recreation activities organised by grassroots organisations, civic and social organisations, TCs and CDCs. In the longer term, social harmony is critical to the socio-economic well-being of Singapore's communities of different ethnic backgrounds.

Renewal and rejuvenation of aging neighbourhoods

It will be evident that in the next two decades, a number of silver neighbourhoods will appear. If attempts by the public housing authority to renew and rejuvenate these neighbourhoods are slower than population aging in these places, then these estates will become listless and socially rundown. Local social and economic activities will slow down and younger people will not be attracted to live in these neighbourhoods as seniors will dominate.[18] Ultimately there will be more families facing the need for care of elderly

---

[18] Im Sik Cho and Blaž Križnik, *Community-based urban development: Evolving urban paradigms in Singapore and Seoul* (New York: Springer, 2017).

parents or relatives. As many of these households have working family members, they will face the burden of care.[19] Social breakdowns are likely without accessible social support and community care services delivered at the local level. Therefore, there will be demands for more community-based programmes to cater to the needs of families who have frail aged family members.[20] The number of such families is expected to increase from the next decade. In light of this situation, more community groups, voluntary welfare organisations together with the involvement of residents as well as hospitals, will have to work as partners to provide community care services such as home-help, meals service, daycare, integrated housing and community nursing.[21] Here, community care cooperatives could be formed to offer services which will be more convenient and accessible to the families with frail elderly needing care and attention. There is potential for this type of social enterprises to be established with participation of families as one of the stakeholders.

Preparing personnel in social service sector

The management curricula for social sector training should not be based on a parochial orientation namely emphasising a remedial management model. The curricula must fire the imagination of the human service professions to equip them the knowledge and skills to examine issues with a new perspective, challenge assumptions of our current management practice, and find new sets of management strategies in social service delivery. Imbibing eclectic management thinking is essential because in the social and economic sectors, competition has intensified as a result of slower growth and resource limitations. It is new ideas and innovations that will

---

[19] Lena L. Lim and Tze Pin Ng, "Living alone, lack of a confidant and psychological well-being of elderly women in Singapore: The mediating role of loneliness", *Asia-Pacific Psychiatry*, 2(1), pp. 33–40, 2010.

[20] Keng Hua Chong, Wei Quin Yow, Debbie Loo and Ferninda Patrycia, "Psychosocial well-being of the elderly and their perception of matured estate in Singapore", *Journal of Housing for the Elderly*, 29(3), pp. 259–297, 2015.

[21] J. Ong, M. Lim and L. Seong, "The Singapore experience: Understanding the older persons who utilize community rehabilitation services", *International Journal of Integrated Care*, 13(8), 2013.

make social service delivery more effective. Therefore, human service professionals should be trained to have a development and outreaching focus and to deal at front end where there is wider client or consumer base rather than just sorting the small tail end of the problem which can be complicated. In short, more focus be directed at social development to prevent human problems rather than just dealing with people when brokered.

Conclusion

Social investment efforts must encourage people to taking ownership of the various social and economic activities which are delivered in the various neighbourhoods in partnership with a number of groups. To be impactful, social service organisations or groups cannot continue to assume that they know what residents want but to outreach to appraise their social needs or requirements. In short, social investments should in the due course promote self-help and the focus should be to encourage mutual help and not dependency and helplessness.

As community needs become more complex and challenging, there will an increase in interest groups which will lobby resource and policy holders to advance their group agenda. Therefore, leaders of social and community organisations will have to be more objective and work for the interest of the majority. For them to continue to be viable and effective, there must be active attempts to recruit, motivate and retain younger leaders who are committed to find ways to meet the interest of the wider good. Unless there are such committed social and community leaders, it will be more trying to fortify the social health of the community.

As Singapore becomes more globalised, social needs and problems are increasingly challenging to solve as they will require the efforts of a number of key players. Therefore, community problem solving will need the partnership of several parties. The partnership model of the government, community organisations and groups, corporate sector and philanthropic individuals can be encouraged as such model emphasises on the belief in sharing the social burdens. All partners involved in community problem solving have shared social responsibilities. Both manpower and matching grants are allocated to various projects to be carried out by community groups, social enterprises, non-profit sector and community organisations. The social consequences for not furthering social investments can cause social barriers and divisions and thereby precipitating the growing number of non-productive citizens who can be a liability to the society. Worse is that they become disruptive to the well-being of the community and more funds will be needed to habilitate them. Hence, social investments at an early stage of a person's life will make the society more vibrant.

Part 7

Social Work Training and Practice

Chapter 31

Some challenges for social work education*

S. Vasoo[†]

Introduction

Social work education is becoming increasingly challenged by the need to reorganise and strengthen its educational curriculum on the management of social services and promotion of human values education. This is because the social and organisational environment of the social services sector also broadly known as human services is becoming less predictable and there is also increasing erosion of human values. This is further compounded by changing expectations, values, and demands of the consumers. Amidst this, there is an increasing pressure to devolve central control of social services, a drive towards privatisation of social services, and a beginning wave of demands from an aging population whose needs for personal and health care will become more acute. In the light of the various social changes and uncertainties, it is indeed interesting to note that

---

*From Vasoo, S. (1993). Some challenges for social work education. *Hong Kong Journal of Social Work*, 27(2), 34–39. Copyright @ 1993 by *Hong Kong Journal of Social Work*. Reprinted with permission.

This write-up sums up some points raised on the need to review and strengthen the social work educational curriculum on the management of social services and promotion of human values education. Much of the points are also covered on subsequent discussions on social work education.

[†]Head, Department of Social Work and Psychology, National University of Singapore.

social work education has not responded as quickly as it should in making curriculum changes in training social workers to be more competent in managing social services and to be promoters of human values education. Besides this, social work education's role in promoting human values education cannot remain docile. It must take an active part in this aspect. A number of reasons can be identified for the dilemmas facing social work education.

Social work education and management

Social work curriculum has over the years mainly concentrated on efforts to enhance interpersonal practice skills which are rather client-centred in perspective. Such a training emphasis though relevant in preparing social workers to acquire good helping skills appears to be inadequate in equipping social workers the competence to deal with the clients' environment, in particular the human service delivery systems. As a consequence social workers are perceived by resource holders to be more suited for front-line and middle management responsibilities in social services. They are assigned to these levels of management because of their interpersonal practice competence. The confinement to these areas of responsibilities does narrow the opportunities of social workers to influence decisions which have impact on policies related to the management of social service delivery. This dilemma has its setbacks which are observed by Gummer and Edwards (1988:15) who both state that:

> Because of the lack of input from human service professionals at the policy formation level, social administrators have to implement policies that, increasingly, run counter to their conceptions of desirable programs. Moreover, being confined for the most part to mid-management positions — positions traditionally associated with considerable responsibilities and limited powers in organisations of all types — social administrators are experiencing a growing sense of frustration, impotence and futility in their job.

The feeling of lack of efficacy in managing the organisational system and environment seems to be associated to middle level management bind faced by social workers (Perlmutter, 1982). However, this situation can also be precipitated by the slow response of social work training institutions to develop further training in the management of social services for middle level management staff.

Social work training also tends to prepare social workers to be good in client management than to be good in people and organisation management. This is because earlier generation of social work educators have had their training based on psychodynamic perspective. Such a training focus does pose a danger of socializing beginning social workers into a state of learned helplessness shared by their clients. This in turn perpetuates the residual approach in the management of social problems which can be effectively addressed by the preventive and developmental approach. In essence, social work training must instill into trainees application of the cardinal principle of promoting self help in various contexts. It must encourage people to become more self-reliant in the social and economic pursuits and be more socially responsible to improve their communities (Vasoo: 1984).

Over the years, social work curriculum has not kept quick pace with the need to equip students with the skills to use information technology in decision making. The growth of information technology has to be taken advantage of by social workers. As new information about consumer profiles and behaviours are generated, it is cogent that such information be tapped quickly to chart organisational plans and strategies to improve the service delivery. Since information on consumer profiles and behaviours is scattered, it will be useful to develop a more co-ordinated system in these aspects for social workers to utilize.

It is also noted that social work management training does not focus much on the skills in the mobilisation, use, and control of external resources. At the same time, workers find themselves ill-prepared to develop strategies in drawing support of other human service professionals and resource holders who can contribute to the development of their organisations and community. The neglect of such a training emphasis does not sharpen the workers' skills to widen the organisational base and strengthen the networks of relationships relevant to the improvement of social service delivery (Shapira, 1971).

It is also pointed out that social workers are generally less skillful in analysing the cost-effectiveness of the services provided by their agencies. With the growing competition for resources and the need to assess the impact of the services provided, social workers in management levels will increasingly be expected to be accountable. The inability to be versatile in analysing and the outcome of the service delivery can prevent social workers to acquire better insight for effective management of resources and services.

Strengthening management training

There is an urgency for the training of social workers to be centred in preparing them for top and middle levels of management as there is a growing demand for such levels of staffing in the social services. However, training institutions must have a realistic and comprehensive picture of the employment markets and trends in the social services sector. This together with the employment patterns of social workers will enable the training institutions to develop and strengthen curricula for management training of social workers (Gummer and Edwards, 1988:21). If haphazard plans are exercised, there is a danger of mismatch between training needs and social work management manpower requirements. It is therefore crucial that social work training institutions review their training objectives to produce sufficient manpower with either interpersonal or management practice skills. There are several practical steps that social work training institutions can take when designing and developing management curricula.

The curricula must equip trainees to be skilful to visualize the dynamics of the social service market. In understanding this aspect they can develop a clearer sense of service direction for their organisations and make in-roads into areas where there are potential needs to be met.

Management training in social work must prepare trainees to acquire skills to utilize some technological knowledge for implementing a management information system. Besides this, their management roles can be further enhanced if they are given training in financial and fiscal management, computerisation of administrative functions, strategic planning, organisational diagnosis and development, policy analysis, public and community relations, project proposal and presentation, and service evaluation (Gummer and Edwards, 1988:21). With greater upward mobility of social workers from direct social work practice to middle and top management positions, training institutions should look into ways in organising professional development programmes in human service management for these professionals so that they can be more effective managers when they are promoted. Such training programmes as Gummer and Edwards (1988:22) advocate must focus on 'hard' management skills.

Social work management curricula should not be based on a parochial orientation namely emphasizing an interpersonal management model. The curricula must be geared to promote a kaleidoscope management thinking which fires the imagination of human service workers and equips them to examine issues with a new perspective, challenge assumptions of our current management practice; and find new sets of management strategies in social service delivery. A birds eye view management thinking is essential because in the social and economic sectors, competition has intensified as a result of slower growth and resource limitations. It is new ideas and innovations that will make social service delivery more effective.

Dealing with erosion of human values[1]

The social health of any progressive society is dependent on the moral fibre of its people and their capacity to find social antigens to counter decadent values which erode the moral and social responsibilities of its people. In recent years, social work education as a whole has been subjected to critical examinations, particularly in its role in preparing its professionals to promote human values education which will help to prepare the young to become socially and morally responsible people. However, social work education like education as a whole, is affected by the socio-political ethos prevalent in the society (Gopinathan, 1980:172). Throughout human civilization, it has been demonstrated time and again that without an open, honest and sincere socio-political ethos, the roles of

---

[1] These are beliefs in and actions to promote positive regard and concern for the well-being of people and the promotion of public good.

social work education and other institutions as a social and moral transmitter are subverted and it hence becomes insidiously erroded.

In many developing countries, tremendous resources both in terms of finance and manpower have been invested on education of people which is more often than not based on the assumption that it will achieve both social and economic development. However, the promise of achieving social and economic betterment is not yet realized (Eng, 1983:214). What is more alarming is that we are witnessing more societies becoming divisive, violent, corruptible and inhumane. All these consequences do affect the roles and functions of social work education today. However, if social work education is not to become a victim of decadent values, it must make frontal attacks on undesirable values which undermine the well being of a society. It is therefore important for social work education to contribute to the development of human service professionals with impeccable character to man social service institutions efficiently and effectively. Unless this is the situation, human betterment cannot be translated into reality. It will be a common rhetoric which we will hear now and then.

It cannot be denied that the foundation of human values is laid by the family and then chronologically through formal educational processes. The social and moral values acquired by the young are accumulative and these are a sum total of the exposure to an educational curriculum influenced by the prevailing socio-political ethos of a given society. It is here where social work education can contribute.

Promoting human values education[2]

For societies to progress and thrive it must have socio-political ethos based on honesty, respect, tolerance, patriotism, non-communalism, non-corruptibility, adherence to law and order, equal opportunity based on meritiocracy and mutual support. This ethos provides the precursors for the nurturing of our young adults to have a built-in social cultural ballast which enables them to choose positive human values and

---

[2] It covers the teaching of ethics, moral codes as well as good citizenship.

discard those that are negative and decadent. In short, social work can contribute in designing values education which covers moral and civics education.

It is therefore important to prepare social work students to have skills to participate in the promotion of human values education through schools. Social workers can contribute to help design school curriculum to facilitate helping behaviour. Human values education can help to prevent people from becoming self-centred selfish and uncaring. A school curriculum with social work inputs can be designed to encourage the young to participate in community based helping activities.

It cannot be denied that clear delineation of human values education policy are basic cornerstones to the wholesome development of the young. Therefore, a conducive educational environment which adheres closely to the philosophy of education and promotes human values education, will help;

> to develop the minds, body and spirit; to foster the intellectual, physical and social and moral growth of each child (Report, 1987:11).

In the light that a large amount of the community's resources will continue to be deployed to support tertiary education to benefit a small group of intellectuals, policy makers must ensure that those who graduate from the institutions of higher learning including social work training institutions are imbued with positive human values. This prepares them to be people with good character who will fill places of responsibilities in the public and private service sectors. When we have successive groups of better qualified people whose character and human values orientation are beyond reproach, then it is possible to continuously regenerate a caring and sharing community.

It is a world view of most social work and other educationalists that human values education if carefully designed, can play an important role in incalcating into students desirable social and moral codes. Formal human values education must start as early as possible, especially when a child begins school. It would be too late by the time he is in tertiary educational institutions to be exposed to human values education. At the best, tertiary educational institutions can play a role in reinforcing the foundations of human values education which should have its early beginnings during the person's formative years in school. Tertiary educational institutions can create the institutional climate to enhance human values education through their academic programmes.

Conclusion

In conclusion, social work training institutions must constantly review their curricula for the management of social services and promotion of human values education. They must respond with flexibility to discharge efficiently and effectively their primary mission to train social work manpower to manage social services competently and at the same time to contribute in inspiring various social institutions to implement human values education. In contributing to human resource development, social work training institutions have to appreciate the needs of the management environment of social services as well as to take educated steps to contribute in innoculating people to strengthen their human values.

References

Eng Soo Peck. Education and Development: Era of Hope and Disillusionment, *Singapore Journal of Education*. Vol. 5(1), 1983, pp. 14–19.

Gopinathan, S. Moral Education in a Plural Society: A Singapore Case Study. *International Review of Education*. Vol. 26, 1980, pp. 171–185.

Gummer, Burton and Edward, Richard L. The Enfeebled Middle: Emerging Issues in Education for Social Administration, *Administration in Social Work*. 1988, 12(3), pp. 13–22.

Perlmutter, F.D. Caught in Between: The Middle Management Bind, *Administration in Social Work*. 1983, 7(3/4), pp. 147–161.

Report to the Minister for Education, *Towards Excellence in Schools*. Ministry of Education, Singapore, 1987.

Shapira, S.F. Politics, Professionalism, and the Changing Federalism. *Social Service Review*. 1981, 55(1), pp. 78–92.6

Vasoo, S. Reviewing the Direction of Community Development in Singapore, *Community Development Journal*. 1984, Vol. 19(1), pp. 7–19.

Chapter 32

The social work profession in response to challeging times: The case of Singapore*

S. Vasoo[†]

The social work profession in Singapore should brace itself in facing challenging times ahead. These challenges are precipitated by changing demographic profiles which to some extent remain unpredictable. At the same time, the expectations and demands of various people are changing. Since independence in 1965, Singapore has undergone significant economic and social transformation. The social and economic landscape of the island city state has changed progressively under the People's Action Party (PAP) government since 1959. Better housing, security, health, education, environment and employment opportunities have been achieved

---

*From Vasoo, S. (2013). The social work profession in response to challenging times: The case of Singapore. *Asia Pacific Journal of Social Work and Development, 23*(4), 315–318. Copyright © Department of Social Work, National University of Singapore, Singapore, reprinted by permission of Taylor & Francis Ltd, http://www.tandfonline.com on behalf of Department of Social Work, National University of Singapore, Singapore.

This paper reviews the challenges of the social work profession in Singapore, which is rather client-centred in their perspective. The importance of social and environmental changes has to be considered. Some of the points raised earlier in having a more robust social work education and training are covered.

[†]Department of Social Work, National University of Singapore, Singapore, swkvasoo@nus.edu.sg.

because of good political leadership with responsible and honest people in government. This has been a precursor to and the backbone of the economic and social progress which Singapore has been able to make. Without this type of forthright and talented leadership in the policy-making machinery, no society — not even Singapore — will be able to move ahead in its social and economic redevelopment.

In the context of such developments, the social work profession has to be aware of the trends in social changes confronting Singapore. In order that social workers can continue to play an effective role, it is important for them to become more aware of internal and external factors which affect the efficiency and effectiveness of the social services and the community organizations in which they are involved. The identification of a number of factors such as manpower, facilities, funding resources, leadership and other related organizational issues, and the manner in which these areas are managed, will determined whether the profession will make meaningful contributions.

The social work curriculum has, over the years, mainly concentrated on efforts to enhance interpersonal practice skills which are rather client-centred in their perspective. Such a training emphasis, though relevant in preparing social workers to acquire good helping skills, appears to be inadequate in equipping social workers with the competence to deal with the clients' environment, in particular the human service delivery systems. As a consequence, social workers are perceived by resource holders to be more suited for front-line and middle-management responsibilities in social services. They are assigned to these levels of management because of their interpersonal practice competence. The confinement to these areas of responsibilities narrows the opportunities of social workers to influence decisions which have an impact on policies related to the management of social services delivery. We must note that responding only to people's specific problems is a narrow approach. We have to pay more attention to the larger consumers of social services who have the resources to contribute.

Information technology is becoming more important to social work. The growth of information technology has to be taken advantage of by social workers. As new information about demographic profiles and behaviours is generated, it is cogent that such information be tapped quickly to chart organizational plans and strategies. Since information on demographic profiles and behaviours is scattered, it will be useful to develop a more coordinated information system on these aspects for social workers and other interested groups to utilize.

The social work profession, like other helping professions, needs to adopt a preventive and developmental perspective. Although addressed to some extent, this area deserves closer attention because, more often than not, human service professionals tend to take a remedial or a disease focus approach in their work with their client populations. Such an orientation does not help to deal with the prevention of human breakdown. It will be cogent for our human service professionals to help individuals and families to be imbibed with good human values and social skills, and to be encouraged to acquire relevant technical skills. It is hoped that future write-ups will deal with this important aspect, as human wellness has to be given more emphasis and attention. Social workers can make more effective contributions if they help to mobilize more helping hands to be involved in community development and community building. We must play an active role in preventing social problems by building better support networks among people.

There are a number of necessary steps which social workers must be ready to take in order to increase competencies in analysing social trends and predicting outcomes of various social interventions. Firstly, social workers must be able to visualize changes in the social and human environment. Having understood the demands within our environment, we can then develop a clearer sense of direction in providing relevant services to strengthen the family. Secondly, we must constantly upgrade our skills. This can be achieved, provided that we have more opportunities to get together for the exchange of views and experience. It is through these forums and exchanges that effective helping techniques are acquired. Thirdly, there is a need to adopt more critical thinking. This process involves the examination of issues from a new perspective, the challenging of assumptions of our intervention plans and finding helping strategies to reach out to people who need to strengthen their support networks. Social workers can encourage more people in our society to extend a helping hand to others and to encourage them to participate in various self help programmes to build a more viable community. The challenge in the next lap is to mobilize more helping hands in community problem solving.

It is also pointed out by the author and other researchers that social workers are generally less skillful in analyzing the cost-effectiveness of the services provided by their agencies. With the growing competition for resources and the need to assess the quality and impact of the services provided, social workers at management level will increasingly be expected to be accountable. The inability to be versatile in analyzing the outcome of the service delivery can prevent social workers from acquiring better insight for effective management of resources and services.

It will be important and timely for the training of social workers to be centred on preparing them for middle-level and top management as there is a growing demand for such key levels of staffing in the social services. However, training institutions must have a realistic and comprehensive picture of the employment markets and trends in the social services sector. This, together with the employment patterns of social workers, will enable the training institutions to develop and strengthen curricula for management training of social workers. In today's changing social service context, it is impossible to overemphasize the need for social workers with top management skills to run large social-sector institutions as strategic outcomes and cost inputs become required by resource providers.

The social work curriculum today must equip trainees to be skilful in visualizing the dynamics of the social service market. Capabilities in anticipating social issues and problems are skills much valued in the social service sector. In understanding this aspect, personnel in the social service sector can develop a clearer sense of service direction for their organizations and make inroads into areas where there are potential needs to be met and ensure that proactive steps are taken to tackle them.

The management curricula for social work should not be based on a parochial orientation — namely, emphasizing an interpersonal management model. The curricula must fire the imagination of social workers and others in the human service professions to equip them with the knowledge and skills to examine issues with a new perspective; to challenge the assumptions of our current management practice; and to find new sets of management strategies in social service delivery. Introducing eclectic management thinking is essential because, in the social and economic sectors, competition has intensified as a result of slower growth and resource limitations. It is new ideas and innovations that will make social service delivery more effective. Therefore, social workers should be trained to have a development focussed approach to deal with frontline problems of clients or consumers so that their problems do not become too complicated at the end.

As anticipated, we shall see a beginning of the 'silver tsunami' before 2025, in which more families will be afflicted by the burdens of caring for their less mobile elderly parents. This social burden will be more pronounced among dual-career and young adult families, and even more so if they have terminally sick elderly parents. Besides the social and economic costs, families may have to find more accessible social and daycare services. Along with this need for supportive care services, families will also face grief at the loss of their elderly parents; thus social care services to help families members cope with grief and loss will be helpful. In response to the social, psychosocial and health consequences facing the greying elderly population, social workers working in health and family service settings can play a role in helping to promote community care co-operatives and community hospice care services to support families with elderly members who need different social care services and support. The rise in the many elderly needing healthcare and social service support will lead to debates on issues related to end of life and the allocation of healthcare resources. Social workers will have to face such debates about Singapore society.

During the last decade, Singapore society has seen a widening income gap and there is now a sector of 'new poor' — those who are trapped in poverty because of depressed wages arising from imported cheap labor and low skills. This sector of the population requires closer attention because the children of these families are likely to be disadvantaged, as they will not acquire the numeracy and literacy levels required to start them off in primary schooling. This is because parents do not have the educational capacity to prepare their children, to be educationally ready in numeracy and literacy to compete with their contemporaries whose parents are more educated or schooled. These 'new poor' families have both family and social difficulties which, unless addressed early, can lead to various kinds of social breakdown. Here, social workers in Family Service Centres (FSCs) can work in concert with various community groups to initiate early social and educational intervention programs such as family mentoring, counselling, family education, educational head start, care networks, income supplement projects and early reading. When more children in low income families are to be reached out to benefit from early supportive education and literacy programmes, they will be better prepared for schooling to develop their potential. The community and policymakers can assist by allocating more resources to mitigate against a lack of opportunities, in order to help many low-income children who otherwise may be ill-equipped to benefit from education and skills training opportunities. In the longer term, the social divide may be further widened when more low-income children fail to acquire the knowledge and skills that can prepare them to earn a livelihood, not only in Singapore, but also globally. When the social gap widens, the consequences will not be good for the Singapore community, as a divided community may be socially unhealthy for Singapore. Social workers can engage families in the low-income group to participate in early head-start programmes which can enable the children to be more numerate and literate. Family-matched saving projects to help low-income families become more financially literate and to better motivate them to upgrade their skills could be implemented at the local community level, as this will be more accessible to them.

With globalization, it is envisaged that Singapore, like other developed economies, will be confronted with more competition from developing economies with both skilled and unskilled manpower for market share for product and services. This situation will be inevitable, and the likelihood is that wages will be depressed as the services offered by the developing world will be cheaper, more efficient and more effective. So, to meet these challenging scenarios, Singapore has little option but to take steps to train every young child and persons with higher skills up in areas such as marine and biological sciences, medicine and pharmacy, chemical and nanotechnology, food safety and production, precision and aeronautical engineering, building and housing construction, and environmental and water resource technology. Social workers can help to organize family life, with self-help and community education programmes that will kick-start an interest among low-income parents in knowing about community resources and how they can tap into them for their betterment. Many more children from low-income families can be helped, through such early socio-educational intervention projects, to realize their human potential and skills and to be able to work in globalized industries and workplaces.

In the coming decade the world will become more globalized; therefore, the social work profession and other human service professionals must begin to acquire more analytical skills in order to gather information that will predict more precisely emerging social problems. In doing so, more effective social solutions and problem-solving strategies can be implemented. More importantly, we must not continue to solve problems in the old ways, but take more proactive steps to challenge the old assumptions and find innovative ways to deal with more complex problems of the future. In short, we must look for good outcomes in dealing with specific issues and mobilize the appropriate manpower to help change things for the better.

Chapter 33

Straddling teaching and field practice: Facing the challenges — Associate Professorial Fellow S Vasoo, 1987–2001*

Academic background

S Vasoo, an Associate Professorial Fellow in the Department of Social Work, National University of Singapore, graduated with a Doctorate, and a Masters in Social Work for which he was awarded the Jean Robertson Book Prize for excellence, from the University of Hong Kong. He also holds a Diploma in Social Studies with Distinction from the University of Singapore.

He has authored a number of monographs and articles on social issues which have been published both locally and internationally. Dr Vasoo was

---

*Reprinted with permission from Department of Social Work, National University of Singapore.

This paper covers the recollections of Dr S Vasoo's experiences in straddling between academic teaching and doing social work and as one of the past Head of the Social Work Department at the National University of Singapore. He also touches on the social service projects which he had pioneered, some challenges of social work education, and social issues facing Singapore in the near future. Some of the views presented are drawn from his earlier writings and working experience in the social work arena.

Associate Professorial Fellow S Vasoo

awarded Honorary Life Membership of the Singapore Association of Social Workers for his outstanding contributions to social work in Singapore. He was a Member Parliament from 1984 to 2001 and he also served as the Chairman of the Government Parliamentary Committee for Community Development.

He was appointed as Executive Director of the Singapore Council of Social Service and the Community Chest of Singapore from 1983–1986. In addition, he has initiated the development of a number of community organisations aimed at promoting the well-being of the family, the welfare of the physically and mentally challenged, the provision of better services for the elderly and educational support for the young.

He now volunteers as an Advisor to various committees in the community including the Singapore Central Community Development Council. In addition to being appointed a Justice of the Peace in 2005, he was awarded the Distinguished Alumnus Award (2007) of the Faculty of Social Sciences, University of Hong Kong and the Outstanding Alumnus of the Department of Social Work and Social Administration, University of Hong Kong in 2010.

Introduction

After working for about 10 years as a social work practitioner in the Singapore Children's Society and the Singapore Council of Social Services (SCSS), I was invited to join the Department of Applied Social Studies which was to see several changes in name later. The first change was to the Department of Social Work and Social Administration in 1966; then to the Department of Social Work and Psychology in 1986 and subsequently reverting to the name, Department of Social Work in 2006. One cannot predict what future events can result in another change of name but should such a situation arise, it would suggest that social work can respond to human development and change within the context of Singapore.

I am particularly honoured to share the recollections of my experiences as one of the past Heads of the Department. Besides this, I would also like to touch on the pioneering of social service projects I have undertaken as an academic, the challenges of social work education and the social work profession, and lastly on social issues. I personally feel that the picture will be incomplete if my effort is just confined to a description of the milestones of what has been laid during my tenure as Head. Such an emphasis will be less interesting and rather dry as the focus will be mainly on curriculum changes, excluding the academic contributions on matters outside the classroom which has relevance to social work training. The making of this tapestry adds colour to the discussion, and demonstrates what social work academics possess and can contribute in building the profile of social work as well as engaging in community problem-solving.

Early induction

It is not difficult to recount my first academic journey beginning as a Senior Tutor in the-then Applied Social Studies Department in 1971. This is because I was least prepared to take on this job other than being offered a promising academic opportunity which I could not turn down.

The reflections at this stage remind me, rather nostalgically, of the things I encountered in the early years of my teaching career for which I was inadequately prepared or trained. In hindsight, I must say I could have been a better teacher had I been equipped with the necessary teaching skills. In those days we learned to sink or swim as there was no Centre for Development of Teaching and Learning to train us. One tried one's best to cope with the teaching demands of the time as academics were highly regarded. I did not let my lack of teaching skills deter me from continuing with my job. That would have been a defeatist outlook and contrary to my belief that things could be better if I learnt not to pontificate over what improvements I should have made in teaching. I must say that my early inroad into teaching was indeed an eye-opener as I had the chance of being challenged by older social work students who had years of working experience in the Social Welfare Department of Malaysia and the Ministry of Social Affairs in Singapore. Coincidently, I had also worked for a few years in the social service sector.

Many of the mature students in their thirties were robust in probing issues based on their strong groundwork exposure and tested me on the applicability of social work theories in the field. However, there were others who did not have the fundamentals in social science and social work. I had learnt much of the practical issues they raised and these reflected the realities of the delivery of social and welfare service in the two countries in the sixties. This enhanced my learning curve besides forging a close fellowship with each of the students which remains to this day. However, in 1974, the Diploma course for Social Studies was discontinued. I must admit that I had a wonderful experience teaching the many mature students in the early seventies during which there were many student strikes in the University. Much of these were a passing phase of one's journey where students registered strong views on social life and situations.

Those early inroads into teaching, of being challenged by older mature students imprinted on me a need for field experience besides merely possessing an academic perspective of social work training. At the same time, I, too, yearned to return to the field and the opportunity arose when I was offered a position as Administrative Officer in the Singapore Council of Social Service. Such an opportunity gave me a chance to understand more fully the problems on the ground and the issues faced by the voluntary social service sector, particularly the non-governmental organizations. This working stint in the national organization opened my mind to real social service issues with an added academic dimension, and this choice, helped me to be better equipped to examine social issues and problems.

Straddling the field and teaching

I spent about forty years straddling between the field and teaching and this is indeed a modest record compared to others who have covered these two arenas for a longer period. In the early seventies, it was not difficult to juggle between the field and teaching because there was limited social work manpower and employers were supportive of any suitable arrangement. I was fortunate to have been exposed to the respective arenas which could only come about with goodwill and the continued pushing of one's frontiers of learning to combine the theory and practice of social work.

Most sceptics in either arena would say that one cannot have the best of both worlds and only one specific area can be mastered at a time. This

Teaching in 2012

viewpoint may be rather narrow and it will not be helpful in a globalizing world to confine the younger professionals to a specific arena as this will not open the window of their minds but may make them insular in their thinking. To recollect, the straddling that I experienced did result in a number of positive outcomes for social work training and the delivery of social services. For the record, it is useful to briefly describe them but a full audio version is available at the Singapore National Archive.

Pioneering projects in the field

There were a number of pioneering projects which were implemented whilst I was straddling between academia and the field. Though some of these projects came ahead of their time, they acted as precursors to the many community services which have been delivered subsequently in the Singapore community. This was because these projects were found to be, indeed, relevant to meeting the emerging social needs of the community.

For posterity, I see the necessity to bring out some of the more significant projects which have contributed to the development of social services to meet the social needs of the elderly, volunteers, disabled and low-income families in Singapore. More importantly, these pioneering projects provide a record of some successful outcomes of the passionate involvement of a group of selfless individuals who volunteered their time in joining me to realize helping activities which transform lives.

One interesting project, namely the Henderson Community Home for Senior Citizens, was formulated and launched in 1974 by a small staff team which I led under the Singapore Council of Social Service. This Community Home was managed by the Chinese Women's Association and the idea was to enable single elderly migrant workers, with no immediate support network or relatives to look after them when they became frail and lonely. The whole objective, then and now was to help these elderly, and others like them, to continue to live in communities and environments they were familiar with. The success of this project prompted many voluntary social organizations with the support of the government to implement this concept in the various public housing neighborhoods. Today, studio apartments have been added with the inclusion of a social service centre run by a social service agency.

Another notable project which made an impact on the family's coping capacity was the establishment of Family Service Centers (FSCs) in the early 70s. Such a model of service delivery was tested out some thirty-four years ago through a pioneering project, Ang Mo Kio Social Service

A student in the 70's involved in community outreach work

Centre, now known as the Ang Mo Kio FSC. The establishment of this FSC model was not smooth sailing as no agency was willing to bring its services to the housing heartland as they were then operating services on a centralized basis and in the urban city area. Hence, they were reluctant to move their services to the housing estates because of poor funding and availability of premises which had to be approved by the Housing and Development Board (HDB). Some policy makers were rather hesitant to endorse and financially support the promotion of FSCs to the Social Service Sector which was viewed as being unproductive. However, it can be argued that social expenditure can help families and, in particular, vulnerable children to become independent, economically productive and valued members of our society, if help can be extended to them early.

When the British forces in Singapore withdrew in the early 70's, there was concurrently a reduction in the number of volunteers attached to the local welfare homes. Consequently, the Singapore Council of Social Service (SCSS) was in urgent need for more volunteers to serve the various local charities and I was entrusted with the task of mobilizing volunteers. The promotion of Volunteer Week, the establishment of the Volunteer's Bureau and, later, the Volunteer Action and Development Centre were initiated under the SCSS and today we see the establishment of a national body, the National Voluntary and Philanthropic Centre in place.

Another unusual development was the pioneering efforts of a few young social work students, namely, Ngiam Tee Liang and the late Lai Long Tiew who were under my tutelage in a youth outreach project in Toa Payoh New Town. This was the first community-based youth outreach work launched in the early 70s, when I was working as a community worker in Singapore Children's Society, Toa Payoh Branch. Initially, there was reluctance from some key board members to venture into this aspect of the work. With a concerted push by some interested persons and I, the outreach work for youths and families became a service delivery model for many children and youth service agencies today. In those days, we were seen as group of do-gooders who were doing unrealistic so-called "early intervention work" with problematic and vulnerable youths and children who were labelled as 'beyond reach'. Looking back, we believed in what we did and this inspired me to further undertake new projects to deal with more challenging and tougher human issues requiring a community education approach.

Community education campaigns were not actively pursued in the late 70s as there were other pressing basic problems such as unemployment, housing, education, healthcare, large families and poverty and these aspects required governmental intervention. Nevertheless, being in the national NGO, was an advantage as I had a group of volunteers and the flexibility to initiate two public education campaigns, namely the Senior Citizen's Week and the Month for the Disabled, which were directed at creating more public awareness of the issues and problems of ageing and the public stigma about the disabled. All these drives proved relevant and useful and today they have become national education campaigns.

In the field of autism, the Department made a major contribution by helping to start a Center for Assessment and Psychological Treatment of Children affected by autism. With my support and encouragement, Associate Professor, Dr. Vera Bemard-Optiz initiated the Behavioral Intervention Center for Children (BICC) in 1992. With much assistance, she managed to successfully develop the Center and promote interest among students in social work and psychology to acquire social and psychological skills to work with children with special needs. The services for children with autism spectrum was poorly developed in the early days and today many others have been inspired to set up voluntary welfare organisations to develop services for children with the autism spectrum.

More recently in 2006, it was observed at the grassroots' level by grassroots' leaders and I, that in older housing estates like Ang Mo Kio, quite a sizeable number of frail elderly persons were living on their own. There were also some elderly parents of families with working children facing difficulties in managing their daily activities. Consequently, some of the elderly faced isolation and were unable to meet their daily needs or routines. Some others faced fatal accidents without being discovered for days, and in some cases the families have no choice but to admit them into nursing homes. With a growing number of elderly persons, it is anticipated that more working families will be stressed even with domestic help as they have to cope with the problems of the care of their elderly. In response to this social trend, Miss Pang Kee Tai who was then working in Ang Mo Kio FSC and I helped to initiate the Community Care Network (CCN) scheme together with the grassroots volunteers of Ang Mo Kio. Such a scheme with part-time paid care persons was found to be a realistic

Dr Vasoo with children from CSDA's matched savings programme

and cost effective means to meet the emerging needs of the elderly when giving community care and support services.

Many elderly persons can be enabled to age in place, and be prevented from premature admission into Homes. Following the successful demonstration of the scheme, many NGOs and the governmental sectors recognized that the scheme could be replicated at the national scale and was worthy of implementation, with the provision of government grants to different community groups and organizations. As I had foreseen and unsurprisingly, there were some doubts raised by policy makers and key social sector agencies of the viability of the scheme. Subsequently, after its success was demonstrated, many groups were eager to launch the scheme after 2010, and today it is indeed gratifying to note that the scheme is taking root in the community.

Managing social work and psychology

After my stint of fieldwork as Executive Director of the Singapore Council of Social Service, I returned to take up the post of Head of Social Work and Psychology in 1986. This was an interesting period of academic development which I was persuaded to accept by both Professor Edwin Thumboo, then Dean of the Faculty of Arts and Social Sciences and Ann Elizabeth Wee, the retiring Head. I was tasked to help develop Psychology which was first offered as a minor subject in the early 1980's until 1986, when it was launched as a full programme hosted together with Social Work, which has a more established academic history. This conjoint academic development was indeed challenging to me, as many social work and a few psychology academic colleagues of the Department, as well professionals of the respective disciplines in the field, were watching closely how things would develop and the academic resources that would be deployed thereon. I was mindful of this delicate situation. Being always an advocate of aiding the small and the less established, I persuaded my social work academic colleagues to be enabling and supportive of the minority psychology colleagues and to help them to grow and to develop a brand name for the psychology programme.

I must record that our social work academic colleagues have been very generous in giving me the leeway to direct much departmental resources, at their expense, to quickly strengthen the psychology program. They demonstrated the true spirit of sharing and caring and I faced no major setbacks in strengthening the position of Psychology as an important course, despite the feelings of uncertainty of some top academic administrators of the added value of this discipline to social sciences in the Faculty. My social work colleagues, in the true spirit of social work professional values and skills, gave their whole-hearted support to the-then fledgling psychology colleagues to put relevant psychology courses on the University map. There were only two psychology colleagues at the start of the programme and in two years, that is in 1988, four more psychology staff joined the Department and this helped to boost student enrolment. The finding of psychology talent began without any rancour among academic colleagues as opposed to the disquiet that has been shown in very recent years in Singapore. This is because there were limited local talents in the field of psychology unlike in other more developed economies and such talents were unnecessary if psychology learning and research is to advance in Singapore.

During my watch, the search for better psychology talents was pursued rigorously amidst some minor discomfort faced by a few colleagues.

Faculty members of the Department of Social Work & Psychology

However the emphasis in this talent selection was for personnel who would give their long term commitment to the Department. This approach impacted on the Department and later resulted in the scouted talent putting psychology research and publications, namely social and industrial psychology, on the international radar. Professor Ramadhar Singh who has since retired and is now Distinguished Professor at Indian Institute of Management, Banglore, contributed to this through his work in social psychology. Another lasting mark made was the identification of six local talents to be groomed for potential future faculty appointments. All of them made it for lectureship after their PhD studies in psychology overseas and I am proud that they now anchor the Psychology Department.

On reflection, I must say that it was not easy to manage both psychology and social work staff but in the case of psychology, each of them had their own academic agenda. Understandably, like all other academics in most tertiary institutions, each one expects the best of resource support and a reasonable teaching load. This aspect was somewhat difficult to juggle especially when student numbers in psychology kept increasing so quickly before staff numbers could catch up. I had to persuade them to share their misery equally but eventually some others had to carry the burden so that teaching could continue. Mediation of problems between staff was the main tool employed. On a few occasions, there were outbursts between psychology staff which I had to hold down. The fact that I was unbiased and impartial gave me credence and resulted in positive outcomes. In all the things that I administered, I was never partial to either the social work or psychology staff then and I hope this will be appreciated in the annals of the local psychology programme development.

As for the social work program, the growth was steadily maintained and efforts were focused on hiring senior tutors to plan for succession of senior staff who would be retiring in the next 8–10 years. The social work staff, as I had sensed, were tolerant and moved on with their work with pride and the hope that they would be academically liberated. This eventually happened in 2006.

When I completed fourteen years of service as Head in 2000, the Psychology programme had grown by leaps and bounds. There were almost 12 times more staff compared to the time when it first began. Psychology, by then, had had a good head start. Social Work remained steady and was also moving ahead. With its top academic staff in the various academic pragrammes, we must bear in mind that to make a mark in the academic ladder we must have not only committed staff but also staff with academic and personal integrity, together with a passion for service are qualities of which will inspire students to give their best in the work world and to the community.

Social work training and the social work profession

As I have spent most of my working life teaching and doing social work, it would be indeed not inappropriate that I share my views about social work training and the social work profession. I have given my opinion and thoughts on a number of occasions over the years in seminars and conferences and recently presented my viewpoints when I was awarded one of the most distinguished alumni of the Department of Social Work and Social Administration, University of Hong Kong in 2010. Some of the points that I will raise may have been articulated before but nevertheless, they are worth repeating because the core issues in social work training and the profession have has not changed. In other words, the substance remains but the forms change with time.

As I review the social work curriculum, it has over the years concentrated on the enhancement of clinical and interpersonal practice skills. Such training concentration which appears to be client-centered is still relevant. It can be expanded to include a wider domain dealing with the clients' environment and the social service delivery system. In remaining in the said domain, social workers are perceived by policy makers and resource holders to be front-line and middle management workers. They are emplaced in these levels of management because of their interpersonal practice competence. To confine social work to just these areas of skills training is to narrow the opportunities for social workers to influence decisions which impact on policies related to the management of social service delivery. We must note that serving just specific problems of people can be narrow if we do not acquire competency to examine in greater depth, the factors in the social environment, which may affect people in need. We have to also pay more attention to engage those with resources, as well as the larger consumers of social services, who all have the ability to contribute to the betterment of the community. Social workers can encourage more people in our society to extend a helping hand to support various self-help and community care programmes which can help build a more livable and viable community. The challenge in the next phase is to mobilize more caring people to participate in community problem-solving.

The Social Work profession in Singapore has played a part through periods of dire poverty to a state of affluence. The profession has responded to the various social life course demands in the context of Singapore. One of its tasks is to prod the conscience of those in control of social and economic resources, to deploy them in ways which are helpful in meeting community needs and reducing human problems. I must reiterate here that social work roles in promoting human well-being and progress are always evolutionary and adaptive as they try to keep to the tempos of change. More can be done when social work collaborates with other professions and community groups to promote community well-being and to assist the vulnerable and the weak. Working and networking with concerned individuals and groups is becoming an important strategy for social work to adopt, as this can play a role in socializing people to participate in helping activities.

I foresee that the social work profession will be subjected to increasing challenges precipitated by changing demographic profiles and declining social and economic resources. At the same time, the expectations and demands of various people are changing. In order that the social work profession can continue to play an effective role, it is desirable for social workers to become more aware of factors affecting the efficiency and effectiveness of the organizations' service delivery. The understanding of these factors such as manpower, facilities, leadership and other related organizational issues and the manner in which these are managed, will determine the profession's credibility and standing.

On some social issues

There are some pertinent challenges facing Singapore in the near future and as Singaporeans we should be aware of them so that proactive steps can be taken to tackle these issues. It is invaluable to encourage good ideas from the ground and implement actions to further improve the lives of people who are disaffected. I have other reflections on social and political issues which I do not propose to highlight as these are already fully covered in Singapore's Oral Archive and the Hansard Proceedings where readers can get access to them.

One major social issue facing Singapore is economic restructuring in the light of the globalization of both labour and capital. The world economy, and in particular the economic situation in the Asian region, is becoming more competitive as the requirements for investments, bigger export markets and labour become acute. As the new economy following the internet revolution is shaping up, old skills will become obsolete very quickly and IT skills and new knowledge in software, electronic and bio-science engineering and life-sciences, have to be acquired. All these changes can affect older workers who have less skills and may suffer retrenchment. They may have to take on other jobs which are less attractive and, where necessary, they have to re-skill themselves if they want to continue to be gainfully employed. Also, the relocation of labour intensive industries to countries with cheaper labour can displace the less skilled workers whose livelihood will have to be attended to. Though efforts to assist them through workfare and work support schemes are implemented, these can be improved by increasing further the cash component payment or by implementing a work bonus scheme for low income, less skilled workers to stay employed. Ultimately it is the widening income divide that policy makers must seek to address and this will prevent social dislocation or strife in our Singapore society.

Another lingering critical issue is the maintenance of racial harmony and social cohesion. Singaporeans cannot take race relations for granted and must learn to appreciate various ethnic and cultural groups whether they are Malays, Indians, Chinese or Eurasian. Racial discrimination and prejudice should not be encouraged as this will lead to conflicts and riots. It is crucial to see that racial tension and troubles do not occur in Singapore. However, it is a fact that racial conflicts have become serious in many countries and their societies have broken up and regressed as a result. Many lives can be lost when a society breaks down and it is difficult to rebuild that society. One does not need to go too far to see the tragedies of race conflicts in many places. So an important measure to minimize racial problems from surfacing is to ensure that rewards and incentives are given to all Singaporeans on the basis of their ability and merit and not on the basis of color and religion. This key principle must be observed in social policies.

Singapore, as predicted by many analysts and policy makers will be confronted by a rapid decline in population. Singapore society is not replacing itself. The current replacement rate of about 1.2 persons is well below the replacement rate of 2 persons. This means that Singapore will have less manpower to run its services and industries and this can slow down its economic growth. It is predicted that people will not be encouraged to retire in future. However, on the other hand, with a greater elderly population, there will be more future discourses on end-of-life issues. It is likely that more pointed debates on pro-life and pro-choice matters will arise. Controversial views on prolonging or terminating life are expected to surface and the community can become divided in the process of finding a solution. It is a dreadful decision to make but in reality an ageing society has to confront this.

In addressing the problem of an ageing population, there will be more appeals, through various sources, to encourage the young to settle down and, where possible, to have a family. At the same time, our society cannot avoid seeing more elderly persons in our population and that more funds will have to be set aside for health care if people do not have healthy life styles. The healthcare burdens will grow and therefore Singapore needs to prepare people to stay healthy and have savings for their retirement.

Conclusion

Lastly, having spent almost 50 years of my life in social work teaching and work in the social service sector, I believe that a good concentration of teaching both in the class room and in the field will help to groom versatile social work graduates. I have also observed that improvements in community and people wellbeing can result when social institutions are able to gamer persons with drive, honesty and integrity into its leadership. Non-profit organizations need such people but more so in other types of social institutions. For our society to continue to be progressive, it is undeniable that we need to have more good and honest people to run our social institutions whether governmental, non-governmental or the private sectors. If we do not have leaders of such high calibre to manage the various institutions, then we will not be able to make things better. Our lives will become worse and we will all end up losers.

Part 8

Conclusion

Chapter 34

The future of community development: Issues and challenges*

S. Vasoo

Some pertinent questions should be raised about the future of community development[1] and the challenges ahead.[2] What is the optimistic or at worst the pessimistic picture facing community development? These are not necessarily binary questions. The responses are not a black or white as community issues are dynamic and changing. Let us examine the pessimistic side first and then the optimistic aspects.

---

*This article covers some of the future as well as the current issues facing community development work in the Singapore context. Given the changing and emerging social issues facing the Singapore community and its housing neighbourhoods, it is urgent that community development intervention and efforts by various community groups and social and community service professionals adopt a proactive approach in reaching out to people. The views and comments of this concluding chapter is a reprint, which is also published, in an edited book by S. Vasoo, Bilveer Singh and Xian Jie Chan titled *Community Development Arenas in Singapore* (Singapore: World Scientific Publishing, 2019).

[1] In this article, community development is defined as efforts either jointly or on their own of Government, corporate sector community organisations, not for profit groups and or voluntary welfare organisations (VWOs) to promote community betterment and community problem-solving by involving people based on mutual help or self-help and planned changes. The outcome is community ownership in promoting community well-being.

[2] Stephen Hawking, *Can We Predict the Future in Brief — Answers to Questions* (UK: John Murray Publishers, 2018), pp. 87–98.

Pessimistic community scenario

The downside will be that communities will be so self-centric and socially divisive that individuals and community groups are at loggerhead over socio-political and resources allocation matters. Conflicts amongst community groups over all social and livelihood matters can become so protracted and eventually be untenable for people to co-operate and work for the interest of the majority living in the community. If the community has to slide down to this state of affair, then people will become more individualistic and less open to extend mutual care and support in community problem-solving. At worst, the neighbourhoods will be hollowed out by the better endowed leaving first then others, to more vibrant and supportive communities. The possibility of a pessimistic scene can carry some negative consequences. This situation can provoke some groups to surface to find some workable solutions in the midst of contending forces in the community, which try to oppress change for community betterment.[3] However, the community efforts will indeed be very trying to improve and put things right.

Optimistic community scenario

With an optimistic picture, the community setting will be lively and vibrant as people will look beyond themselves and see one another as a supportive network and willing to share and care for with all others better or less endowed. Those who are better and resourceful will be prepared to share their surpluses with those who are poorer. Altruistic behaviours are likely to be displayed by people and this is indicative that they have social and community responsibility. Community development efforts must help promote such altruistic behaviours as this will encourage the growth and development of more social support networks and consequently act as precursors for the formation of social and community agencies and even social enterprises. In communities

---

[3] David Chan (ed.), *Public Trust in Singapore* (Singapore: World Scientific Publishing, 2018), pp. 3–18.

with optimism, people normally aspire to be progressive and innovative to find creative ways in community problem-solving. It is envisaged that there will be many types of resources in the community and these can be tapped to support those in need of them. Hence, a social exchange bank with the depository of both human needs and supply services can be established to promote social exchanges at affordable cost to users. In fact, with the development of artificial intelligence based on aggregative technologies, a number of community-based social exchange banks can be formed. Good corporate governance will be required to help such social exchange banks to function effectively and in the interest of the community.[4]

Community development can be efficacious if it enhances the development of social and human capital by enabling social and community groups to develop self-help and mutual aid co-operatives. These social set-ups or enterprises can address social issues such as problems of loneliness, need for care and support, requirements for educational enrichments, acquiring and upgrading vocational skills, delinquency, crime and security issues, childcare and healthcare needs, unemployment and employability matters, and personal and family related difficulties. Notably, some of these social issues are tackled by social and community agencies in their own agency-centric ways. It will be more effective and efficient to pay more attention on the development of better inter-community agency partnership and efforts.[5]

Against this backdrop, it will be appropriate to examine the community development efforts in Singapore. In the last four decades or so, it has focused much on social and recreational activities. Consequently, community organisations or groups have gravitated to become task or programme-centred. The outsourcing of community services to the private sector is becoming a norm and this can affect the quality of services contracted out.

---

[4] Ibid., pp. 61–68.
[5] S. Vasoo, "Investment for the Social Sector to Tackle Key Social Issues in Critical Issues", in S. Vasoo and Bilveer Singh (eds.), *Critical Issues in Asset Building in Singapore's Development* (Singapore: World Scientific Publishing, 2018), pp. 21–36.

Some issues

First, the increasing moves on outsourcing community activities and services can make community organisations insular and they then become task- or activity-centred and slowly digress from being people-centred which is aimed in promoting self-help and community ownership. Hence, many community organisations and groups have adopted a less outreaching approach to understand the changing needs of the community. In the longer term such a move will make them more detached from keeping in touch with the needs of people who are uninvolved or at the margins.

Second, the leadership of community organisations is graying. More attention should be devoted to enlist resourceful younger residents to help manage them. Many community organisations have become gerentocratic and can be less responsive to the changing needs of the neighbourhoods. Consequently, they can become senior citizen clubs, which will only meet the needs of one specific group of the resident population, namely the elderly. So far, punctuated attempts have been made to renew the leadership and as such, it is unlikely to rejuvenate community organisations.

Third, it is observed that the rate of participation of lower-income households and minorities is not as significant and this could be due to the less tangible benefits offered by the programmes delivered by community groups and organisations. The participation of both minorities and lower-income families is critical in maintaining social cohesion and community bonding. Hence, more concrete services are to be provided to meet their social and economic needs. This will address the public goods dilemma, as this will reduce their cost for participation. When community organisations do not bear in mind of this matter in their service delivery, both minorities and low-income households will not be motivated to participate in some mainstream community activities.

Fourth, another significant development in the older neighbourhoods of Singapore is the hollowing out of the more resourceful and younger residents. When this process accelerates, these neighbourhoods become eventually silver communities. A higher outflow of young people who are attracted by exuberant facilities of other New Towns also compounds this. It is anticipated that there will be a depletion of community and leadership resources in these neighbourhoods. This will inevitably slow down and become less attractive to new residents. Inevitability, social burdens for care will increase unless more community care services and support networks are encouraged through community development efforts.

Meeting the challenges

Some challenges confronting community development in Singapore have been identified. It is therefore appropriate to discuss a few ideas to deal with these challenges. Policy makers, community leaders and social workers may consider undertaking to enhance community development efforts in the context of Singapore.

Enhancing self-help and community ownership

There should be less outsourcing contracts and more in-sourcing activities by mobilizing residents to form not for profit organisations or social enterprises. Such attempts will provide more opportunities for residents to participate in decision making so that they can take ownership. More community care groups and support networks can be established. This will make participants not passive recipients of services and be engaged in problem solving. Community organisations widen the base of participation by residents forming various interest groups or task forces to work on various social issues and projects such as security watch and crime prevention, co-operative care services, improvements to recreational facilities, pollution control, thrift through micro-credit groups, and environmental enhancement projects. It will be useful to encourage residents to take charge in finding more effective ways to deal with local matters. In this case, the support of the Town Councils (TCs) and Community Development Councils (CDCs) will be helpful. This is truly be promoting community development as local residents will learn and find more realistic solutions to solve their specific needs and problems and become accountable for their decisions.

However, with the move towards information technology, more people could become impersonal, homebound, social interactions could be reduced, and social bonding could be threatened. Therefore, personalised outreaching efforts can be carried out with on-line contacts.

Leadership rejuvenation and organisational renewal

It is observed that a significant number of grassroots leaders of community organisations in the mature housing estates are above 50 years old. These organisations face difficulties in recruiting younger residents to take up leadership.[6] With the graying of the organisational leadership, there is urgency to rejuvenate the leadership of community organisations by attracting younger professionals to participate them. It is not just sufficient to recruit them. Some committed older leaders must mentor them. With attachment to specific mentors, they can be better affiliated to the organisations and this will reduce attrition facing younger persons taking up leadership in organisations dominated by seniors. A rejuvenated leadership will continue to be vibrant and relevant to meet the needs and aspirations of younger generation of residents. We must also attract younger people-centred individuals to become community leaders and be given all the support to carry out community problem-solving activities. People-centred community leaders are usually proactive. They should not be piled up with so many tasks as this can make them suffer from burnout. More importantly, young leaders should be given management skills training so that they can understand the needs of residents. This can help make community organisations responsive to tackling emerging social needs.[7]

Reaching out to lower income residents and minorities

Singapore is an open economy and becoming more globalised. It is inevitable the residents with low skills are likely to be faced by depressed wages and this can lead to widening income gap.[8] Singaporeans with

---

[6] S. Vasoo, *Neighborhood Leaders Participation in Community Development* (Singapore: Academic Press, 1994); S. Vasoo (2002), *New Directions in Community Development in Extending Frontiers* (Singapore: Eastern University Press, 2002), pp. 20–36.

[7] S. Vasoo, "Community Development in Singapore; Issues and Challenges", in S. Vasoo and Bilveer Singh (eds.), *Community Development Arenas in Singapore* (Singapore: World Scientific Publishing, 2019).

[8] Goh Chok Tong, *Prime Minister's National Day Rally Speech 2000* (Singapore Government: Ministry of Information and the Arts), pp. 22–25.

better skills are likely to move ahead while those with low skills and less literate in information technology will fall behind in income. Social stratification based on social-economic classes confounded by ethnicity may surface if excessive free market competition is not tempered. Consequently, social conflicts could emerge when political and racial fanatics emerge to capitalise the situation. Our community harmony and cohesion could be fractured.[9] As such, community organisations, namely CDCs together with other NGOs can take preventive measures to deliver community-based self-help programmes such as social and educational assistance, computer training, educational head start for children of low-income families, child care services, youth vocational guidance and counseling programmes, family-life and development activities, and continuing learning programmes to help the socially disadvantaged groups. As a long-term measure for people capability building, it is important for us to develop more educational head start projects for low-income children in the nursery age group. The increase of such projects through community partnership of various self-help groups, unions, co-operatives and not for profit organisations will help children from disadvantaged background to level up to acquire productive skills for their future livelihood. Matched savings schemes tied up with such projects can be initiated. These community development efforts can help to reduce the social frictions between classes and ethnic groups. Fanatics and extremists will find it less tempting to exploit the race card as the problems facing low-income families cut across all ethnic groups. Therefore, the realistic solution is to help level up the capabilities of all disadvantaged children despite their color or ethnicity.[10]

Singapore is indeed a multi-racial society comprising of Chinese (74.3%), Malays (13.4%), Indians (9%) and others (3.2%).[11] It is crucial that various efforts both at the social policy and community activities

---

[9] Lee Kuan Yew, *From Third World to First — The Singapore Story 1965–2000* (Singapore: Times Media, 2000), pp. 143–157.

[10] S. Vasoo, "Investment for the Social Sector to Tackle Key Social Issues", in S. Vasoo and Bilveer Singh (eds.), *Critical Issues in Asset Building in Singapore's Development* (Singapore: World Scientific Publishing, 2018), pp. 21–36.

[11] *Statistics on Demographic Characteristics* (Singapore: Department of Statistics, 2018).

levels are consciously implemented to generate better racial understanding. Where necessary steps are to be taken to encourage multi-racial involvement of residents and community leaders.[12] To strengthen Singapore's social landscape, it is desirable to encourage multi-ethnic participation in social and recreation activities organised by grassroots organisations, civic and social organisations, TCs and CDCs. In the longer term, social harmony is critical to the social and economic well-being of Singapore's communities of different ethnic persuasions.

Renewal and rejuvenation of ageing neighbourhoods

It will be evident that in the next two decades or so, we will see a number of 'silver' neighbourhoods emerging. If attempts by public housing authorities to renew and rejuvenate these neighbourhoods are slower than population ageing in these places, then they will become listless and socially run down. Local social and economic activities will slow down and younger people will not be attracted to live in these neighbourhoods as seniors will dominate the localities. Ultimately, there will be more families facing the need for care of elderly parents or relatives.[13] As many of these families have working family members, they will face the burden of care. Social breakdowns are likely without accessible social support and community care services delivered at the local level. Therefore, there will be demands for more community-based programmes to cater to the needs of families who have frail aged family members. The number of such families is expected to increase in the next decade. In light of this situation, more community groups, voluntary welfare organisations together with the involvement of residents as well the hospitals, will have to work as partners to provide community care services such as home-help, meals service, daycare, integrated housing and community nursing. Here, community care co-operatives could be formed to offer services,

---

[12] Raj Vasil (2000), *Governing Singapore* (Leonards NSW: Allen and Unwin, 2000), pp. 84–85; S Vasoo and Bilveer Singh, "Introduction", in S Vasoo and Bilveer Singh (eds.), *Critical Issues in Asset Building in Singapore's Development* (Singapore: World Scientific Publishing, 2018).

[13] *Report by Inter-Ministerial Committee on Ageing* (Singapore: Ministry of Community Development, 1999).

which will be more convenient and accessible to the families with frail elderly needing care and attention. There is potential for this type of social enterprise to be established with participation of families as one of the stakeholders.[14]

Conclusion

Community development efforts must encourage people to take ownership of the various social and economic activities, which are delivered, in the various neighbourhoods in partnership with a number of groups. To have impact, community organisations or groups cannot continue to assume that they know what residents want but to outreach to appraise their social needs or requirements. In short, community development should promote self-help and the focus should be to encourage mutual help and not dependency and helplessness.

As Singapore becomes more globalised, social needs and problems will become more challenging to solve, as it will require the efforts of a number of key players. Therefore, community problem-solving will require the partnership of several parties. The partnership model of the Government, community organisations and groups, corporate sector and philanthropic individuals can be encouraged as such a model, emphasis on the belief in sharing the social burdens. All partners involved in community problem-solving have shared social responsibilities. Both manpower and matching grants are allocated to various projects to be carried out by community groups, social enterprises, non-profit sector and community organisations.

As community needs become more complex and challenging there will be an increase in interest groups which will lobby resource and policyholders to advance their group's agenda. Therefore, leaders of community organisations and community groups will have to be more objective and work for the interest of the majority. To have viable and effective community organisations, there must be active attempts to recruit,

---

[14] S. Vasoo and Kalyani Mehata Mehta, "Organization and Delivery of Long-Term Care in Singapore: Present Issues and Future Challenges", *Journal of Aging & Social Policy*, 13(2/3), 2001, pp. 185–201.

motivate and retain younger leaders to commit to find ways to meet the interest of the wider good. Unless we have such committed community leaders, it will be more trying to fortify the social health of the community.

Community development must include amongst its strategies that social and community workers are to be trained and equipped with social and analytical skills so that they can visualize clearly the current and emerging trends in social issues and problems facing various neighbourhood communities in Singapore. The use of aggregative technologies to pool resources both within and outside the communities to set up a social exchange bank could be implemented for community so that there could be more effective responses to problem solving. As most communities have many types of their own resources in such areas like social, vocational, educational, medical, healthcare, technological, engineering financial, environmental, agricultural and aqua-culture, could be pooled and deployed to those groups that need them. All in all, community development must play a more prominent role in helping individuals and community groups to level up so that social gaps can be narrowed and reduced.[15] This can reduce or prevent serious social conflicts and help to inoculate against social infections in our communities.

---

[15] David Chan, *People Matter* (Singapore: World Scientific Publishing, 2015), pp. 49–54; S. Vasoo, "Investment for the Social Sector to Tackle Key Social Issues", in S. Vasoo and Bilveer Singh (eds), *Critical Issues in Asset Building in Singapore's Development* (Singapore: World Scientific Publishing, 2018), pp. 21–36.